Gender and Politics

Series Editors
Johanna Kantola
University of Tampere
Tampere, Finland

Sarah Childs
Birkbeck, University of London
London, UK

The Gender and Politics series celebrated its 7th anniversary at the 5th European Conference on Politics and Gender (ECPG) in June 2017 in Lausanne, Switzerland having published more than 35 volumes to date. The original idea for the book series was envisioned by the series editors Johanna Kantola and Judith Squires at the first ECPG in Belfast in 2009, and the series was officially launched at the Conference in Budapest in 2011. In 2014, Sarah Childs became the co-editor of the series, together with Johanna Kantola. Gender and Politics showcases the very best international writing. It publishes world class monographs and edited collections from scholars—junior and well established—working in politics, international relations and public policy, with specific reference to questions of gender. The titles that have come out over the past years make key contributions to debates on intersectionality and diversity, gender equality, social movements, Europeanization and institutionalism, governance and norms, policies, and political institutions. Set in European, US and Latin American contexts, these books provide rich new empirical findings and push forward boundaries of feminist and politics conceptual and theoretical research. The editors welcome the highest quality international research on these topics and beyond, and look for proposals on feminist political theory; on recent political transformations such as the economic crisis or the rise of the populist right; as well as proposals on continuing feminist dilemmas around participation and representation, specific gendered policy fields, and policy making mechanisms. The series can also include books published as a Palgrave pivot.

More information about this series at
http://www.palgrave.com/gp/series/14998

Moira Dustin · Nuno Ferreira
Susan Millns
Editors

Gender and Queer Perspectives on Brexit

palgrave
macmillan

Editors
Moira Dustin
School of Law
University of Sussex
Brighton, UK

Susan Millns
School of Law
University of Sussex
Brighton, UK

Nuno Ferreira
School of Law
University of Sussex
Brighton, UK

Gender and Politics
ISBN 978-3-030-03121-3   ISBN 978-3-030-03122-0   (eBook)
https://doi.org/10.1007/978-3-030-03122-0

Library of Congress Control Number: 2018962362

This Palgrave Macmillan imprint is published by the registered company Springer Nature Switzerland AG
The registered company address is: Gewerbestrasse 11, 6330 Cham, Switzerland

This book is dedicated to Hege Skjeie, who made an important contribution to gender equality in Norway and beyond, and was an enthusiastic collaborator on this and many other initiatives.

Preface

We wish to thank all contributors to this book for the effort and energy they have dedicated to their pieces and to the project more generally. Their enthusiasm and commitment throughout were clear proof that the topic was urgent and the project had merit.

We also wish to thank the Sussex European Institute (http://www.sussex.ac.uk/sei/) and the School of Law, Politics and Sociology (LPS) of the University of Sussex (http://www.sussex.ac.uk/lps/) for their financial and logistical support throughout this project. Thanks to this support we were able to hold the workshop 'Feminist and Queer Perspectives on Brexit' on 17 November 2017, at the University of Sussex, and the event 'Looking Forward: Gender and Equality post-Brexit' on 4 July 2018, at the Houses of Parliament, which Seema Malhotra MP was kind enough to host.

Our heartfelt desire is that this collection will not only offer a significant contribution to the growing body of academic literature on Brexit, but also—and perhaps most importantly—raise awareness and help to identify policy avenues in relation to the potential gender and queer impacts of Brexit. Our wish is that the contributions in this collection help academics, policymakers and civil society understand these potential impacts better and address them more effectively.

Brighton, UK
August 2018

Moira Dustin
Nuno Ferreira
Susan Millns

vii

CONTENTS

NOTES ON CONTRIBUTORS

Columba Achilleos-Sarll is a Ph.D. ESRC funded student at the University of Warwick in the Politics and International Studies (PAIS) department. She previously gained an M.Phil. in International Relations from the University of Oxford. Her research lies at the intersection between feminist and postcolonial theory, UK foreign policy and the Women, Peace and Security (WPS) agenda. She recently published in the *Journal of International Women's Studies*: 'Reconceptualising Foreign Policy as Gendered, Sexualised and Racialised: Towards a Postcolonial Feminist Foreign Policy (Analysis)'.

Nazneen Ahmed is a Research Associate on the AHRC Connected Communities research project 'Making Surburban Faith: Design, Material Culture and Popular Creativity in Suburban Faith Communities' and is based in the geography department at UCL. She is also an embroiderer and writes literary fiction, poetry and children's fiction. Her unpublished novel was recently shortlisted for Penguin Random House's Write Now mentorship scheme.

Amy Barrow is a Senior Lecturer at Macquarie Law School (Sydney, Australia). Amy researches on the intersection between gender, international law, peace and security; and law and society in Hong Kong and other Asian contexts. Amy is a member of the WILPF Academic Network, a think tank connecting academics and peace activists working on issues of gender, peace and security. She is a founding member of the Everywoman Everywhere Coalition, which grew out of the Initiative on

Violence against Women at the Harvard Kennedy School's Carr Center for Human Rights Policy. Along with Joy Chia, she co-edited the book *Gender, Violence and the State in Asia* published by Routledge in 2016.

Eugenia Caracciolo di Torella is an Associate Professor at Leicester Law School. Her main research interest is in the area of gender equality at both domestic and EU level. She is particularly interested in the policies and legislation for the reconciliation of work and family life, an area where she has published extensively. On the topic of gender equality, she has co-authored reports for the European Commission and the European Parliament (FEMM committee).

Since 2009, she regularly contributes to the EU Commission founded project PROGRESS aimed at raising awareness of gender equality. She is a member of the AHRC founded Families and Work Network (University of Reading).

Carmelo Danisi is a Research Fellow at the University of Sussex and Adjunct Professor of International Law at the University of Bologna— Forli campus. After a Ph.D. scholarship (University of Genova, Italy— 2009/2012), he has been employed at the University of Bologna as postdoc fellow for three years (2012/2015). In 2015, he was a Endeavour Research Fellow at the Australian National University with the project 'The principle of the best interests of the child in the context of migration'. He is the author of a number of publications in the field of international human rights law, especially in relation to non-discrimination and migration in the framework of the ECHR and the EU. He has been involved in several research projects concerning EU and international law, involving legal analysis for the EU Agency for fundamental rights, the Western Sahara and EU external policy, and gender-based violence. At the University of Sussex, he has joined the SOGICA Project's Research Team (an ERC funded project).

Peter Dunne is a Lecturer in Law at the University of Bristol. His scholarship focuses on the areas of family law, medical law and European Union law. He has a particular interest in the intersections of law, gender and sexuality. Peter regularly publishes in leading peer-reviewed journals, including *Social and Legal Studies* and *Medical Law Review*. His scholarship has been referenced by numerous public bodies, including the Equality Authority of Ireland and the Hong Kong Inter-Departmental Working Group on Gender Recognition. In 2015, Peter was invited to provide expert evidence to the UK Parliament's Transgender Equality Inquiry. With Marjolein van den Brink, Peter is currently undertaking EU-funded research into the equality rights of trans and intersex populations in Europe. Prior to entering academia, Peter worked as a human rights advocate in the USA and Europe.

Moira Dustin is a Research Fellow at the University of Sussex. She is working on the European Research Council project SOGICA—Sexual Orientation and Gender Identity Claims of Asylum: a European human rights challenge (2016–2020), which explores the status and legal experiences of asylum-seekers across Europe claiming international protection on the basis of their sexual orientation or gender identity (SOGI) and will determine how the European asylum systems can treat more fairly asylum claims based on the claimant's SOGI. She has a Ph.D. in Gender Studies from the London School of Economics where she is a Visiting Fellow at the Centre for Analysis of Social Exclusion (CASE). Before joining the University of Sussex, Moira was Director of Research and Communications at the Equality and Diversity Forum, a network of equality and human rights organisations, where she coordinated the Equality and Diversity Research Network. Moira has also worked at the Refugee Council, providing advice and information and developing national services for refugees and asylum-seekers.

Nuno Ferreira is a Professor of Law at the University of Sussex. Previously, he was a Senior Lecturer at the University of Liverpool (2012–2016) and Lecturer at the University of Manchester (2006–2012). He has also been a Visiting Professor at Wuhan University (China) and the School of Law of the University of Lisbon (Portugal). Nuno did his undergraduate law studies at the University of Coimbra (Portugal) and University of Bologna (Italy) and is a member of the Portuguese Bar. He worked as a legal consultant at the Legal Affairs and Litigation Department of the Portuguese Securities Market Commission (CMVM) and as a research fellow at the Centre of European Law and Politics at the University of Bremen (ZERP) (Germany). Nuno's teaching and research focus on human rights, European law, children's rights and asylum and refugee law. Nuno is a Horizon 2020 ERC Starting Grant recipient, leading the project SOGICA—Sexual Orientation and Gender Identity Claims of Asylum (2016–2020), and Co-director of the Sussex Centre for Human Rights Research.

Marzia Fontana is Honorary Research Associate at the Institute of Development Studies, University of Sussex. She has researched and written extensively on gender equality, international trade, labour markets, unpaid work and gender-aware economy-wide modelling. She has worked on collaborative projects with various international organisations such as ILO, FAO, UN Women, UNCTAD, UNDP, UNIDO, the World Bank and IFPRI and has fieldwork experience mostly in South and South-East Asia. Recent publications include a study on gender equality in trade agreements for the FEMM Committee of the European Parliament and a paper on gender equality and inclusive industrial development for UNIDO.

Yvonne Galligan is a Professor of Comparative Politics at Queen's University Belfast. She is also Director of the Queen's Gender Initiative and founding Director of the Centre for the Advancement of Women in Politics. She has authored and/or edited 7 book publications, 6 book-length reports for national and European agencies, 20 authored/co-authored journal articles, as well as over 50 other publications including chapters in peer-reviewed volumes. Professor Galligan presently leads the QUB team in the 2016–2019 Horizon 2020 SAGE project—Systemic Action for Gender Equality (in Higher Education). She is expert in the political, legislative and legal aspects of national and European policy relating to gender equality. She is a member of the Royal Irish Academy's Ethical, Political, Legal and Philosophical Studies Committee, a Fellow of the Academy of Social Sciences and member of the Royal Society of Arts. In 2014, she received an OBE for her services to Higher Education in Northern Ireland. In July 2017, she received an Honorary Doctorate of Social Science from Edinburgh University.

Aisha K. Gill, CBE is a Professor of Criminology at University of Roehampton, UK. Her main areas of interest and research are health and criminal justice responses to violence against black minority ethnic and refugee women in the UK, Iraqi Kurdistan and India. She has been involved in addressing the problem of violence against women and girls/'honour' crimes and forced marriage at the grass-roots level for the past eighteen years. Her recent publications include articles on crimes related to the murder of women, femicide, coercion and forced marriage, child sexual exploitation and sexual abuse in South Asian communities, female genital mutilation and sex-selective abortions. She is a Fellow of the Royal Society of Arts and editorial member of the Feminist Review Collective.

Cathrine Holst is a Professor of Sociology at the University of Oslo. She is also connected to ARENA Centre for European Studies and CORE—Centre for Research on Gender Equality. Holst's research interests are political sociology and democracy research, feminist and political theory, European integration, and gender and family policy. She is currently leader of a large research project on the role of experts in policymaking, 'Expertization of public inquiry commissions' (EUREX). Holst has published in journals such as *Science and Public Policy, Acta Sociologica* and *International Studies in the Philosophy of Science* and is editor of several recent and forthcoming special issues including in *European Politics and Society, Social Epistemology* and *Journal of Public Deliberation.* Her most recent book is *Expertisation and Democracy in Europe* (2018).

Dieuwertje Dyi Huijg is completing her doctoral research in sociology at the University of Manchester. Based on phenomenological conversations with racially privileged feminist activists from São Paulo (Brazil), her thesis concerns a theoretical exploration of intersectional agency at the junction of structural advantage and structural disadvantage. Her perspective as a disabled intra-EU migrant in the UK, reflections on tension in the intersectional impact of the Brexit Project and a resurrected interest in the gendered impact of free trade agreements led to the current study.

Ingi Iusmen is a Lecturer in Governance and Policy at the University of Southampton. Her research tackles key questions about the European policy process, especially as it relates to child care issues and the provision of children's rights at EU and national levels. She has published in leading journals such as the *Journal of Common Market Studies, International Journal of Law, Policy and the Family,* the *Journal of European Public Policy, Wes European Politics,* and the *British Journal of Politics and International Relations.* Her books include *Children's Rights, Eastern Enlargement* and the *EU Human Rights Regime* (2014, sole-authored, Manchester University Press) and *The EU as a Children's Rights Actor: Law, Policy and Structural Dimensions,* co-edited with Helen Stalford (2016, Budrich Academic Publishers).

Benjamin Martill is Dahrendorf postdoctoral fellow in Europe after Brexit at the London School of Economics and Political Science. His research interests lie at the nexus of European studies and International

Relations. He is editor (with Uta Staiger) of *Brexit and Beyond: Rethinking the Futures of Europe* (UCL Press) and his work has been published in *Security Studies, International Politics* and the *Journal of Political Ideologies.*

Susan Millns is a Professor of Law at the University of Sussex. Susan Millns holds postgraduate degrees from the University of Kent (D.Phil.), the University of Paris I (Panthéon-Sorbonne) (Diplôme d'Etudes Approfondies; Droit Public Comparé des Etats Européens) and the European University Institute, Florence (LL.M. International, European and Comparative Law). She taught previously at the University of Liverpool (1991–1997) and the University of Kent (1997–2006) before taking up a Chair in Law at Sussex. She has also held visiting fellowships at the European University Institute (Florence) from 2000 to 2001 as a Jean Monnet Fellow and from 2002 to 2004 as a Marie Curie Fellow in the Robert Schuman Centre for Advanced Studies. She presently holds visiting professorial appointments at the University of Lille 2 and the Université Paris Descartes.

Christel Querton is a Barrister at Lamb Building specialising in asylum, immigration and human rights law. She is currently a doctoral candidate funded by the Arts and Humanities Research Council at Newcastle University Law School researching the international protection in the EU of persons fleeing armed conflict from a gender perspective. She teaches the M.A. in Refugee Protection and Forced Migration Studies at the University of London. Christel is also a Trustee of the Asylum Research Centre Foundation and an Advisory Committee member of the Women's Project at Asylum Aid. She previously worked at Asylum Aid and Wilson Solicitors LLP.

Emma Ritch is the Executive Director of Engender, Scotland's feminist policy and advocacy organisation. Her interests include women and the economy, intersectionality, violence against women, and the relationship between women's equality and women's human rights. She is a member of the First Minister's Advisory Council on Women & Girls, the Scottish National Action Plan for human rights leadership forum, the advisory group of the Scottish Women's Rights Centre and the Scottish Women's Budget Group. She chairs the Rape Crisis Scotland board, is vice-convener of the board of Close the Gap and is a board member of the European Women's Lobby.

Hege Skjeie was Professor of Political Science at the University of Oslo. Her research specialized on Nordic and European equality institutions, human rights law and policy, citizenship, political representation, ideational power and elite politics. Public positions of trust included among others the Committee on Post-Public Employment Restrictions, which decides on interim periods for former cabinet ministers, state secretaries and political advisers when they leave public office for private sector jobs/appointments (2009–) and the first joint Equality Tribunal, which monitors all Norwegian non-discrimination and equality legislation (2006–2009). Skjeie chaired the Gender Equality Commission (2010–2012) which delivered two comprehensive public inquiry reports to the government (NOU 2011:18 and NOU 2012: 15). For her academic and public service, she received the ECPR/ECPG Gender & Politics Career Achievement Award in 2017.

Iyiola Solanke holds the Chair in EU Law and Social Justice at the University of Leeds and an Academic Bencher of Inner Temple. Her recent publications include *Discrimination as Stigma* (Hart, 2017) and *EU Law* (Pearson, 2015).

Mary-Ann Stephenson is the Director of the Women's Budget Group. She has worked for women's equality and human rights for over twenty years as a campaigner, researcher and trainer. She was previously Director of the Fawcett Society and a Commissioner on the Women's National Commission. She is a founder member of Coventry Women's Voices and a board member at Coventry Rape and Sexual Abuse Centre. She has a Ph.D. in Law from the University of Warwick.

Mari Teigen is the Head of CORE—Centre for Research on Gender Equality and NORDICORE—Centre for Research on Gender Equality in Research and Innovation. Her current research specialises on analysis of gender equality policy; social elites, gender quotas in corporate boards, gender segregation in the labour market and in research and innovation. Teigen is member of the National Publication Committee; board member Centre for Gender Research, University of Oslo; member of the programme board of the BALANSE, the Research Council of Norway; co-editor of *Comparative Social Research*, member of the editorial board of *Nordic Journal of Working Life Studies; Sosiologisk Tidsskrift; NORMA International Journal for Masculinity Studies.*

Lara Walker is a Senior Lecturer in Law at the University of Sussex. Her research is in the field of private international law of the family and focuses mainly on child abduction and maintenance.

Michelle Weldon-Johns is a Law Lecturer at Abertay University. Her main research interest is employment and equality law, with a specific focus on the boundaries between work and family life from an employment law perspective. She has a particular interest in work–family conflict from the standpoint of working fathers and alternative family models. Her research has primarily been from a UK and EU perspective, but some of her work has adopted a comparative analysis including Sweden and the USA. She has also done some research on employment law and Scotland.

PART I

Setting the Context to Gender and Queer Perspectives on Brexit

CHAPTER 1

Brexit: Using Gender and Queer Lenses

Moira Dustin, Nuno Ferreira and Susan Millns

1   It's not Only About Trade and Migration

On 23 June 2016 the people of the United Kingdom (UK) voted in a referendum narrowly in favour of leaving the European Union (EU). This historic result, which has led to the UK Government's decision to end the UK's more than four-decade long membership of the EU in 2019, has important consequences that will be felt far into the future. Such consequences may affect people across the EU and beyond, but the greatest impact will be felt by individuals living in the UK.

Some people will meet the challenges that lie ahead with resilience and will take full advantage of the opportunities that regaining some law-making competences and a new form of politics promise. Others may be less fortunate and may see the rights and protections offered by the

M. Dustin · N. Ferreira (✉) · S. Millns
Sussex Law School, School of Law, Politics and Sociology, University of Sussex, Brighton, UK
e-mail: N.Ferreira@sussex.ac.uk

M. Dustin
e-mail: M.Dustin@sussex.ac.uk

S. Millns
e-mail: S.Millns@sussex.ac.uk

© The Author(s) 2019
M. Dustin et al. (eds.), *Gender and Queer Perspectives on Brexit*,
Gender and Politics, https://doi.org/10.1007/978-3-030-03122-0_1

EU starkly withdrawn, leaving them more vulnerable and with diminished horizons and fewer prospects and resources than previously.

Much has been said about Brexit, but the bulk of the debate and commentary has focused broadly on matters such as trade and migration (see Sect. 2). Very little has so far been said about the way Brexit matters from gender and queer perspectives.[1] This collection examines the opportunities and challenges, the rights and wrongs, and the prospects and risks of the Brexit debate from this particular perspective—that of gender and sexuality. Women and gender and sexual minorities have been historically marginalised and their voices have tended to be less audible in political debates—both nationally and at the European level. In essence, this collection explores how Brexit might change the equality, human rights and social justice landscape, but from gender and queer viewpoints. We envisage that Brexit will impact upon women and gender and sexual minorities in a variety of ways and will potentially present particular challenges for these groups.

Our starting point is the breakdown of voting in the referendum which demonstrates that, overall, men and women do have different views of Brexit (as do different generations) (Cain 2016; Clarke et al. 2017). Furthermore, in the political sphere, and in terms of party politics, Brexit has seen opportunities created for female politicians and paved the way for Britain's second female Prime Minister. Additionally, Brexit impacts upon a myriad of policy areas that are highly important to women and gender and sexual minorities—employment law, discrimination law, single market, free movement, migration, citizenship rights, to name but a few.

This collection will examine a number of core themes and poses fundamental research questions around the barely recognised gendered and queer dimensions of Brexit, exploring the risks and opportunities for women and queer communities in the UK and in Europe. These questions include, but are not limited to the following:

---

[1] 'Queer' will be used in this context to refer to all non-heterosexual and non-cisgender dimensions of the Brexit debate. The term 'queer' will be used interchangeably with 'sexual and gender minorities'. We acknowledge that not everyone we wish to refer to may identify with either one or the other, but we will use them as shorthand for practical reasons.

- What does Brexit mean for women and queer people in politics in Britain today?
- How will the human rights of women and of gender and sexual minorities be affected by Brexit?
- How does Brexit impact upon debates in the UK on intersectionality?
- What is the impact of withdrawal from the single market on women and gender and sexual minorities, particularly in relation to free movement rights?
- What is the impact of Brexit trade policy for women and gender and sexual minorities?
- What does Brexit mean for citizenship and national identity from gender and queer perspectives?
- What is the impact of Brexit on children and families and does this have a gender or queer dimension?
- Is there a gender and queer perspective on Brexit and devolution?
- What can be learnt from other countries about the potential impact of Brexit for women and gender and sexual minorities?

This collection will answer these and other questions by offering a multidisciplinary, policy-oriented and intersectional analysis of Brexit from a gendered and queer perspective. The importance of doing this becomes even clearer, if one considers the academic and policy debates about Brexit so far.

2   A MYRIAD OF TAKES ON BREXIT

Academic and policy commentary on Brexit has been extensive and has led to prolific activity in practically all academic disciplines and policy sectors. In the light of the continuous outpouring of Brexit news and developments, the most obvious outlet for such commentary has become blogs, amongst them *The UK in a Changing Europe*,[2] the *LSE's Brexit blog*,[3] the *Monckton Chambers' Brexit blog*,[4] *The Brexit Blog*,[5] and the *CEP Brexit Blogs*.[6]

[2] http://ukandeu.ac.uk.
[3] http://blogs.lse.ac.uk/brexit/.
[4] https://www.monckton.com/brexit-blog/.
[5] http://thebrexitblog.ideasoneurope.eu/.
[6] http://cep.lse.ac.uk/BREXIT/blogs.asp.

These outlets consider a range of relevant aspects, most frequently relating to trade and migration issues. In such blogs, we can also find some short pieces on the gender dimensions of Brexit, such as in relation to residency rights and child care (Shutes 2017), the views of women on Brexit (Guerrina et al. 2016), gender dimensions of Brexit beyond employment rights (Guerrina 2016), the EU's contribution to gender policies in the UK (O'Brien 2016), and women's participation in the Brexit political process (Achilleos-Sarll 2017). On the queer dimensions of Brexit, there are also some blog pieces, although these are rare (Danisi et al. 2017). Equally, as blog pieces, these are necessarily short and present very narrow analyses of particular issues.

More encompassing, complex and nuanced analyses of the gender and queer dimensions of Brexit can be found in a handful of journal articles. Amongst these, it is worth mentioning pieces that have explored the overall gendered dimension of the Brexit process (Guerrina and Masselot 2018), links to political developments across the Atlantic (Hozic and True 2017), family life and migration (Majella 2017), political parties' voting choices (Heppell et al. 2017) and the impact of Brexit on UK's equality law (Wintemute 2016). These and other journal articles demonstrate a developing academic interest in the gender and queer perspectives on Brexit, but are far from exhaustive of this theme.

Several longer pieces, namely monographs and edited collections, have also explored Brexit. Some have adopted encompassing approaches, attempting to consider a broad range of angles (Fabbrini 2017; Alexander et al. 2018), others have concentrated on the causes, negotiation process and future avenues (Armour and Eidenmüller 2017; Armstrong 2017; Clarke et al. 2017), and yet others have focused on particular issues in the post-Brexit era, such as the relationship with the Commonwealth (Clegg 2017), the financial services sector (Alexander et al. 2018), and the international economic position of the UK (Morgan and Patomaki 2017). These books show a growing interest in the academic debate about Brexit, but none of these deals explicitly with the gender and queer dimensions of Brexit.

The dearth of academic and policy analysis of the gender and queer angles on Brexit needs to be addressed, and this edited collection will go a long way in filling this worrying gap in scholarly and policy debate.

3   Setting the Context, Assessing the Impact, Listening to Devolved Voices and Looking Beyond Our Borders

To answer the questions posed above and thoroughly assess the Brexit debate from gender and queer perspectives, in this collection we present a broad range of contributions that help to understand the context for this debate, assess the possible impact of Brexit on the UK, its component nations and the EU, and also what repercussions there may be for relationships between the UK and the rest of the world. The contributions collected here have been authored by academics and activists from the UK, other European countries and beyond, including both internationally established and promising scholars and lobbyists. In this way, the collection reflects a variety of opinion, new thinking and unpublished research on this subject matter, both from academia and NGOs.

The collection is divided into four parts. Part I lays out the foundations for gender and queer analyses of specific policy areas and transversal themes that are provided in the rest of this collection. Part II then gathers several contributions that concentrate on how Brexit will have an impact in the UK on particular areas of legal and policy activity. Part III moves on to focus on the views of devolved jurisdictions in the UK. Finally, Part IV complements all the previous contributions by considering how Brexit may have an impact beyond the UK and EU spaces.

Thus, following on from this first introductory chapter briefly exploring why Brexit matters for women and queer individuals and why it is important to adopt gender and queer lenses to analyse Brexit, Part I of the collection continues in Chapter 2, with Achilleos-Sarll and Martill's contribution which argues that the campaign for Britain to leave the EU and the subsequent Brexit process have been dominated by discourses of toxic masculinity. These discourses, it is argued, have manifested themselves in two distinct ways: firstly, through the deployment of language that was associated with deal-making, and, secondly, through the deployment of language associated with militarism. This has been compounded by a campaign that has been dominated by a coterie of elite, white males—whose values have come to define the discourses surrounding the negotiations, which produced and (re-)produced power relations, prejudices and myths during the Brexit campaign, and now with regards to the content of a Brexit 'deal'. Drawing on a combination of critical feminist theory, documentary analysis and elite, semi-structured interviews with individuals close to the process, Achilleos-Sarll and Martill discuss the extent to which Brexit has been dominated by discourses of militarism, which overinflated Britain's assumed global role in the world emphasising strength, security, global power and deal-making. These discourses have tended to equate the negotiations to a business transaction, positioning Anglo-European discussions in conflictual terms. Achilleos-Sarll and Martill conclude with four potential (gendered) consequences of these discourses: setting the UK on the path towards a 'harder' Brexit; the consolidation of free-market norms and retrenchment of social policies; the diversion of attention from domestic to international distributional consequences; and the persistent under-representation of women and minority groups in politics. In Chapter 3, Gill and Ahmed further help to understand the relevant context for this collection, by examining Brexit's specific impact on the lives of black and minority ethnic (BME) women. In the immediate aftermath of the referendum result, BME women became the focus of an outpouring of racist and Islamophobic attacks and assaults, and Gill and Ahmed examine this impact through two prose–poetic creative pieces written by themselves as British Asian authors. Through these personal pieces, Gill and Ahmed trace the embodied effects of the referendum result upon the everyday lives of BME women. By using creative methods, Gill and Ahmed are able to represent and reflect upon Brexit in all its contradictory multiplicities. Such methods also enable Gill and Ahmed to view Brexit's consequences using an intersectional feminist lens, and thus consider the effect Brexit is having, and will continue to have, on gender, race, religion and class relations.

Part II is opened by Caracciolo di Torella, who, in Chapter 4, explores the potential implications of Brexit on work-life balance. Caracciolo di Torella mantains that, although in this area the EU has not been above criticisms, it has been instrumental in shaping an agenda and creating a policy and normative framework that has enhanced the position of carers and counterbalanced the UK's neoliberal approach. This chapter identifies three possible scenarios that may materialise in terms of how the UK Government will address future legislation: a status quo, a progressive and a regressive scenario. Caracciolo di Torella not only argues that the regressive scenario is the most likely one and that leaving the EU is likely to jeopardise any achievements in this area, but also asserts that the consequences of Brexit will be felt correspondingly by the EU, thus there being no 'winners'. In Chapter 5, Dyi Huijg explores the impact of the UK's departure from the EU on the UK's National Health Service (NHS), specifically on health, healthcare and social care available to people with disabilities and illnesses. Dyi Huijg adopts an intersectional, disability-oriented critical analysis of Brexit to assess health management, care, and social and medical barriers for EU migrants in the UK. This, in turn, highlights another side of the gendered character of Brexit and situates Brexit in a context of hostility against both disabled people and migrants, specifically, and points to the role that health management plays in migration control and the gender dimension of the roles of migrant carer and patients. Walker's contribution in Chapter 6 considers the opportunities and losses arising from Brexit in the context of cross-border family law. Walker concentrates on the main legal provisions that will be affected by Brexit in this context, namely Brussels IIa, the Maintenance Regulation and the Civil Protection Order Regulation. Walker considers from a gender perspective the effect that Brexit will have on the relevant procedural rules, affecting areas such as child abduction, divorce, maintenance, domestic violence and parental responsibility. In family law, the role of caring has gender-based consequences, such as loss of earnings from employment; therefore, the ongoing enforcement of orders in this context is imperative post-Brexit. There are several mechanisms for ensuring this ongoing enforcement, but in some areas there will be gaps in the law. Walker highlights where these gaps might be and explains why there is currently no solution in these areas. In Chapter 7, Solanke argues that an intersectional analysis of Brexit suggests that Black British children are the forgotten victims of the decision to leave the EU. Owing to the nationality of their primary carer—most commonly women—their rights as British and EU citizens have been pushed aside in the Brexit negotiations by both the European Commission and the UK Government. Solanke focuses attention on the '*Zambrano* children' born to third country national parents and incorporates their interests in the process of leaving the EU. Solanke concludes that if these children are to continue to enjoy their full rights as British and Union citizens after Brexit, their parents must enjoy the full rights enjoyed by migrant EU citizens in the Withdrawal Agreement.

In Chapter 8, contributed by Iusmen, the focus shifts to the protection of unaccompanied minors (UAMs). Iusmen discusses the implications of Brexit on UAMs from a gender perspective, by arguing that male UAMs, in particular, will be most affected by it. Without the EU regime (legal and policy) of rights protection, male UAMs in the UK will face reduced children's rights protection, lack of specific safeguards for UAMs, such as guardianship, and, therefore, will be exposed to the risks of child trafficking and exploitation. Remaining within the policy field of asylum, Chapter 9, by Querton, examines the likely impact of Brexit on refugee recognition in the UK from a gender perspective. Querton applies a gender lens to a historical analysis of the impact of the Qualification Directive 2004, part of the Common European Asylum System (CEAS), on asylum practice in the UK. Querton suggests that, considering historic practice and existing international and regional refugee and human rights obligations, leaving the EU is unlikely to immediately and significantly have an impact on decision-making in gender-related asylum claims. Nonetheless, Querton also highlights the risks associated with the loss of an (EU) legal framework underpinned by fundamental rights and effective remedies. Querton concludes that leaving the EU may contribute to a hostile environment, with consequences for asylum law, which in turn will have an impact on the recognition of refugees from a gender perspective.

Complementing the gender analysis of Brexit with a queer perspective, Danisi, Dustin and Ferreira, in Chapter 10, assess the potential impact of Brexit in relation to the situation of lesbian, gay, bisexual, trans, queer, intersex and other (LGBTQI+) individuals. Danisi, Dustin and Ferreira argue that, despite the very limited consideration of sexual orientation and gender identity (SOGI) issues in analyses of Brexit, there is no doubt that Brexit will affect SOGI minorities on a range of levels, including likely serious effects in terms of human rights and equality policy, 'soft law' instruments, socio-cultural environment, economic resources, regional variations within the UK and civil society vibrancy. This conclusion emerges from the authors' examination of UK achievements in this field when compared to the developments occurred at EU level to advance, directly and indirectly, the full enjoyment of LGBTQI+ people's rights, both through hard and soft law tools and the case law of the Court of Justice of the EU. Danisi, Dustin and Ferreira thus conclude that it is necessary to remain alert to legal and policy developments that may detrimentally affect SOGI minorities both in the UK, when the EU will stop working as an external 'standards-setting' actor, and in the EU, when the UK will stop supporting the advancement of the EU's equality agenda. Offering another queer analysis of Brexit, Dunne, in Chapter 11, critically evaluates the likely consequences of Brexit for SOGI rights. He identifies the key EU contributions to LGBTQI+ protections in the UK and considers the status of those guarantees beyond Union membership. While Dunne acknowledges how the

EU—both symbolically and practically—has helped to re-shape queer intersections with law in this jurisdiction, he nonetheless argues that, for many reasons (political and legal), Brexit is unlikely to fundamentally alter existing rights and entitlements.

Part III of the collection concentrates on specific views and concerns from devolved jurisdictions within the UK. In Chapter 12, Weldon-Johns examines the Scottish Government's desire to maintain ties with EU law post-Brexit in the context of employment and equality law, particularly in relation to those laws that have an impact on work-family conflict. Weldon-Johns critically examines whether there is, or could be, a distinctly Scottish perspective in the context of work-family rights post-Brexit, particularly from a gender perspective. Weldon-Johns argues that the rights of working fathers will be most vulnerable post-Brexit, with related consequences for working mothers. Weldon-Johns also argues that although Scotland adopts a potentially distinct approach in the fields of employment and equality law, the current legal frameworks do not enable Scotland to retain continuity with EU law. Weldon-Johns concludes that if Scotland were to gain law-making powers in these fields, there is the potential for a distinctly Scottish approach towards work-family conflict post-Brexit. Ritch contributes with Chapter 13, again focussing on Scotland. Ritch explores the levels of engagement of women and women's organisations in the two referenda over the past five years, first on Scotland's place in the UK and then in the EU. Ritch argues that the level of engagement with these two referenda has differed considerably, with the independence referendum having seen the establishment of new women's organisations and networks to counteract a seeming marginalisation of women's concerns in the official campaigns, whilst the European referendum saw limited national public engagement by women's and other civil society organisations, and lacked a particular gender focus even in feminist spaces. Ritch also discusses how Scottish feminist policy organisations are contemplating further devolution and how they can continue to engage post-Brexit with pan-European feminist structures like the European Women's Lobby, and its joint campaigning for (still) relevant instruments such as the Istanbul Convention.

Chapter 14, by Galligan, offers us a Northern Irish perspective on the Brexit vote, and the possible consequences of Brexit for Northern Ireland, from a gender point of view. Galligan outlines the constitutional and policy challenges of Brexit for Northern Ireland, the Republic of Ireland, and the UK-Ireland relationship. Galligan also considers gender differences in the Brexit vote, before addressing in a substantive manner the perceptions of women as to the likely obstacles and opportunities that Brexit can bring. Galligan concludes that Brexit necessarily destabilises the hard-won gains of the peace process and will have negative consequences for political and diplomatic relationships across and between the two jurisdictions. Significantly, for women on the island of Ireland, and particularly in Northern Ireland, Brexit heralded the prospect of unwanted change in the materiality of their lives.

Part IV considers the impact of Brexit beyond the UK and EU spaces. In Chapter 15, Barrow explores the implications of Brexit on the EU's defence and security policy through the lens of gender. Barrow considers in particular the UN women, peace and security agenda, supported by the EU, namely through the mainstreaming of gender in the EU's Common Security and Defence Policy (CSDP). Barrow asserts that these important policy developments are at risk and concludes that, whether the UK and the EU negotiate a 'hard' or 'soft' Brexit, the integration of a gender perspective in defence and security policymaking may be undermined and have detrimental consequences. Stephenson and Fontana, in Chapter 16, shift the focus to the potential economic and trade impact of Brexit from a gender perspective. Stephenson and Fontana build on the well-established knowledge that trade agreements can have significantly varying impacts on different groups of women and men, as a result of differences in economic position, caring responsibilities and political power. Stephenson and Fontana assess the gendered impacts of the possible trade agreements that the UK will enter into post-Brexit, by focussing on the implications of trade agreements for employment, for consumption and for the provision of public services. By identifying the key gender issues to consider, Stephenson and Fontana offer advice on the best trade agreement avenues to follow. In Chapter 17, Holst, Skjeie and Teigen bring to the fore the Norwegian perspective, often hailed as a possible model the UK might follow. Norway has, since 1994, been a Member State of the European Economic Area (EEA) Agreement. This Agreement made Norway a full participant in the EU's internal market, including in the area of gender equality policy. Holst, Skjeie and Teigen take issue with a 2012 comprehensive public inquiry report on the consequences of Norway's affiliation status that concluded that EEA commitments and other EU agreements had limited impact on the scope and content of actual policy-making in the gender area. Holst, Skjeie and Teigen thus critically examine this claim through a discussion of EU influences on four core gender equality policy themes: anti-discrimination law, work-life balance, gender mainstreaming, and gender quotas for corporate boards. Holst, Skjeie and Teigen conclude that Norway's affiliation status has, in fact, been relevant to policy development in this area. Finally, in Chapter 18, we offer some concluding remarks on the overall theme of gender and queer perspectives on Brexit, drawing from key insights in the contributions to this volume and advancing some future lines of research which hopefully will continue to advance the debate in this area.

We are conscious that this collection does not exhaust all the possible issues that deserve to be unearthed and critiqued from gender and queer perspectives in the context of Brexit. Indeed, at the event *Looking Forward: Gender and Equality post-Brexit*, held at the UK Parliament in July 2018 and co-organised by the University of Sussex and the Equality and Diversity Forum Research Network, discussions brought up yet another plethora of gender-related issues that grass-root groups and practitioners in diverse fields are having to face as a consequence of the EU referendum and the prospect of Brexit.[7] These issues crop up when least expected and have intricate and intersectional implications that require much sophisticated analysis, informed debate and ethical view-points. This will be the task of a life-time, however, we are confident that this collection sets us on the right path to face the challenges ahead.

BIBLIOGRAPHY

Achilleos-Sarll, Columba. 2017. Where are the Women at the Big Boys' Table? *UCL Brexit Blog*, June 26. https://ucl-brexit.blog/2017/06/26/where-are-the-women-at-the-big-boys-table/.

Alexander, Kern, Catherine Barnard, Eilís Ferran, Andrew Lang, and Niamh Moloney. 2018. *Brexit and Financial Services: Law and Policy*. Oxford: Hart Publishing.

Armour, John, and Horst Eidenmüller (eds.). 2017. *Negotiating Brexit*. C. H. Beck, Hart and Nomos: München, Oxford and Baden-Baden.

Armstrong, Kenneth A. 2017. *Brexit Time: Leaving the EU—Why, How and When?*. Cambridge: Cambridge University Press.

Cain, Ruth. 2016. Post-truth and the 'Metropolitan Elite' Feminist: Lessons from Brexit. *Feminists@Law Journal* 6 (1): 1–8.

---

[7] Sussex European Institute, 'What Will Brexit Mean for Gender Equality?' University of Sussex, 12 July 2018, http://www.sussex.ac.uk/sei/newsandevents?id=45378/.

Clarke, Harold D., Matthew Goodwin, and Paul Whiteley. 2017. *Brexit: Why Britain Voted to Leave the European Union*. Cambridge: Cambridge University Press.

Clegg, Peter (ed.). 2017. *Brexit and the Commonwealth: What Next?* Abingdon, Oxon and New York: Routledge.

Danisi, Carmelo, Moira Dustin, and Nuno Ferreira. 2017. Queering Brexit. *The UK in a Changing Europe*, October 26. http://ukandeu.ac.uk/queering-brexit/.

Fabbrini, Federico (ed.). 2017. *The Law & Politics of Brexit*. Oxford: Oxford University Press.

Guerrina, Roberta. 2016. Gender and Brexit: Moving Beyond the EU's Focus on Women's Employment Rights. *LSE's Brexit Blog*, May 23. http://blogs.lse.ac.uk/brexit/2016/05/23/gender-and-brexit-moving-beyond-the-eus-focus-on-womens-employment-rights/.

Guerrina, Roberta, Toni Haastrup, and Katharine Wright. 2016. Stop Relegating Women's Views on Brexit to the Gender Silo. *LSE's Brexit Blog*, May 25. http://blogs.lse.ac.uk/brexit/2016/05/25/stop-relegating-womens-views-on-brexit-to-the-gender-silo/.

Guerrina, Roberta, and Annick Masselot. 2018. Walking into the Footprint of EU Law: Unpacking the Gendered Consequences of Brexit. *Social Policy and Society* 17 (2): 319–330.

Heppell, Timothy, Andrew Crines, and David Jeffery. 2017. The United Kingdom Referendum on European Union Membership: The Voting of Conservative Parliamentarians. *JCMS: Journal of Common Market Studies* 55 (4): 762–777.

Hozic, Aida A., and Jacqui True. 2017. Brexit as a Scandal: Gender and Global Trumpism. *Review of International Political Economy: RIPE* 24 (2): 270–287.

Kilkey, Majella. 2017. Conditioning Family-Life at the Intersection of Migration and Welfare: The Implications for "Brexit Families". *Journal of Social Policy* 46 (4): 797–814.

Morgan, Jamie, and Heikki Patomaki (eds.). 2017. *Brexit and the Political Economy of Fragmentation: Things Fall Apart*. Abingdon, Oxon and New York: Routledge.

O'Brien, Charlotte. 2016. The EU Talks the Talk on Gender Equality—But in a Male Voice. The Conversation, March 8. https://theconversation.com/the-eu-talks-the-talk-on-gender-equality-but-in-a-male-voice-55966.

Shutes, Isabelle. 2017. When Unpaid Childcare Isn't 'Work': EU Residency Rights Have Gendered Consequences. *LSE's Brexit Blog*, July 20. http://blogs.lse.ac.uk/brexit/2017/07/20/when-unpaid-childcare-isnt-work-eu-residency-rights-have-gendered-consequences/.

Wintemute, Robert. 2016. Goodbye EU Anti-Discrimination Law? Hello Repeal of the Equality Act 2010? *King's Law Journal* 27 (3): 387–397.

CHAPTER 2

Toxic Masculinity: Militarism, Deal-Making and the Performance of Brexit

Columba Achilleos-Sarll and Benjamin Martill

1   INTRODUCTION

Existing accounts of the referendum campaign and Brexit have observed differences in voting patterns between men and women, as well as the disproportionate risk that women will be disadvantaged by withdrawal from the European Union (EU), however, little has been said from a gendered perspective about the discourses that surrounded the Brexit campaign. Drawing on a combination of critical feminist theory, documentary analysis and elite semi-structured interviews, this chapter demonstrates the extent to which Brexit has been dominated by discourses surrounding the institutionalization of a dominant masculinity,

C. Achilleos-Sarll
Department of Politics and International Studies,
University of Warwick, Coventry, UK
e-mail: C.Achilleos-Sarll@warwick.ac.uk

B. Martill (✉)
London School of Economics and Political Science,
Clement's Inn, London, UK
e-mail: B.M.Martill@lse.ac.uk

© The Author(s) 2019   15
M. Dustin et al. (eds.), *Gender and Queer Perspectives on Brexit*,
Gender and Politics, https://doi.org/10.1007/978-3-030-03122-0_2

which manifested in two principal ways. Firstly, through the deployment of language that was associated with militarism and, secondly, through language that was associated with business interests and 'deal-making' rhetoric. Discourses of militarism highlighted Britain's assumed global role in the world emphasising strength, security and global power, whilst discourses of 'deal-making' equated the negotiations to a business trans-action and, consequently, represented Anglo-European relations in conflictual terms—as a contest between two sides. We argue that these dominant constructs are problematic in that they preclude the emer-gence of an approach based on dialogue, equality, empathy, care or oth-er-regardingness. Moreover, they inhibit fundamental conversations that address, and call attention to, the gendered social consequences of post-Brexit policies in the United Kingdom (UK).

The decision of the British electorate to leave the EU on 23 June 2016 sent shockwaves through the political establishment, the interna-tional community and, of course, the financial markets. As rapid political changes led, in the weeks thereafter, to the succession of Theresa May as Conservative leader and prime minister, Brexit dominated the domes-tic political agenda—and, indeed, has continued to do so. Much of the existing analyses have only scratched the surface of the gendered dimen-sions of the discourses surrounding Brexit. The kind of questions being asked—which way women voted, for instance, or how many women were represented—echo feminist concerns of the liberal mainstream, but have not conceptualised the complex ways in which the campaign itself was profoundly gendered. Critical feminist accounts, moreover, whilst advancing the appropriate analytical tools to delve deep into the study of gendered discourses, have paid more attention to the gendered *con-sequences* of Brexit than they have to the gendered nature of the cam-paign itself, and the subsequent effects this has had post-referendum. We therefore argue that existing analyses have failed to address the gendered discourses invoked during the campaign which (re-) produced, and (re-) articulated masculinity in old-new ways. Taking our lead from Aida A. Hozić and Jacqui True's work on the role played by masculinist inter-elite competition and the representations of masculinity and femininity which resulted from these struggles, in this chapter we examine how the rhetoric of 'deal-making' and the language of militarism emerged during the campaign and found a foothold in post-referendum British politics.

Revealing the mechanisms by which Brexit discourse is both gendered and gendering is fundamental to understanding how, and in what ways, the Brexit campaign was performed; what led to Brexit; what Brexit embodied; and ultimately attempting a (tentative) prediction of what its consequences might be. Revealing the masculinist, militarist, racialised and heteronormative nature of Brexit discourse can go some way to explaining how this is currently affecting, and how it will continue to affect, the negotiations and their outcome. We therefore argue that discourses around militarism, and subsequently typologies of 'deal-making' utilised by the state, offer fertile terrain for highlighting how such discourses (re-)produced gendered hierarchies. The historical valorisation of traits usually associated with masculinity—strength and resilience—are confirmed and reinforced by this discourse, whereby such traits are believed to be the necessary prerequisites for political office. In these current times of "masculinist political revival" (Mellstrom 2016; 135) the example of Brexit has broader relevance. As such discourses are becoming increasingly deployed across the Western world, a predominantly white electorate is being encouraged to throw their support behind these businessmen-cum-leaders—from Donald Trump to Andrej Babiš—leaders who attach themselves to, and frequently deploy, military metaphors and business language (Politico 2015).

Our argument proceeds as follows. In the next section, we review the literature on gender and Brexit within both public opinion research and critical feminist theory. We note the lacuna existing within this field more broadly when it comes to critical studies of the (gendered) discourses surrounding the referendum campaign. In the subsequent section we outline our theoretical framework, justifying our focus on gendered configurations and practices through an engagement with critical feminist approaches. To follow, we empirically chart the emergence and deployment of gendered discourses before, during, and after the referendum campaign, illustrating how these have served to frame the debates surrounding Brexit. In the concluding section we summarise our argument and reflect on some of the implications that follow from a focus on the gendered nature of these discourses for understanding the Brexit process and how it is likely to unfold in the coming years.

2   Gendered Studies of Brexit

Brexit has invited much scholarly discussion from a range of academic perspectives. While it is not possible to do justice to this burgeoning literature here, it is worth highlighting the emergence of a number of studies aiming to make sense of the causes and consequences of Brexit from an analytical—as opposed to partisan political—standpoint (e.g. Armstrong 2017; Clarke et al. 2017; Evans and Menon 2017; Glencross 2016; Martill and Staiger 2018; Oliver 2018; Outhwaite 2017). In spite of the salience of the male dominated nature of the Brexit campaign and calls to increase female representation in the negotiations (Branigan 2017), it is perhaps surprising that academic accounts of Brexit have had little to say on the question of gender. None of the edited volumes noted above, for instance, contain specific chapters on gender and Brexit, and none of the monographs consider this perspective in any great detail. Rather, gendered discussions of Brexit have taken place predominantly through the 'blogosphere', with a number of prominent feminist contributions emerging in the run-up to—and in the immediate aftermath of—the referendum (e.g. Haastrup et al. 2016; Shutes 2017). Nevertheless, some preliminary work on gender and Brexit may be found in research on British politics and public opinion that have focused on gendered patterns of voting and campaign support, and in the emerging literature on critical feminist International Political Economy (IPE) and Brexit. In this section we briefly discuss both of these approaches. While we find these literatures helpful, we argue that neither is fully equipped or has attempted to explore the nature of the gendered discourses that pre-dated—and to a large part determined—the referendum result.

There has been some analysis of the gender variable in public opinion research on Brexit, which has sought to use gender as a variable to understand differing attitudes towards the EU. Goodwin and Heath (2016), in an early analysis, for instance, argued that Brexit could be best explained by the combination of educational inequality and rapid economic change. They argued that for many individuals this resulted in the 'double whammy' of being "at a significant disadvantage in the modern economy [and] also being further marginalised in society by the lack of opportunities they faced in their low-skilled communities". Whilst they did not find that gender was a significant factor explaining individual decisions, they did suggest that "people in favour of the death penalty and harsher prison sentences in general, and who are against equal opportunities for women and homosexuals [were] much more likely to support leave". Age, and a generational divide, was often invoked as a significant explanatory factor, with three-quarters of 18–24 year olds voting to remain, and 60% of elderly voters supporting the leave campaign

(Wilson 2017, 546). Attitudes towards immigration has been another recurring theme, with scholars noting that support for a leave vote was higher in areas which had seen rapid increases in migration from Central and East European countries and especially where public services had not kept pace with the resulting increase in demand (Goodwin and Milazzo 2017, 452; Wilson 2017, 547). The most sophisticated analyses of the vote address the interactions between these recurring, foregoing variables. Clarke et al. (2017), for example, examine the relative impact of a host of potentially competing and confounding variables, including political affiliation, class, income, age, region, and, of course, gender, eliciting a more comprehensive picture. Interestingly, they find that whilst support for EU membership has traditionally been higher among men (2017, 83), "Leave voting did not vary by gender. Among both men and women, 51% reported that they voted to leave" (2017, 154). Whilst other studies have reported similar findings for the 'null hypothesis' when examining attitudes for men and women, it should also be noted that, among the 18–24 year olds, women were more strongly in favour of remaining than men, with 80% of female 18–24 year olds opposing Brexit, compared with 61% of their male counterparts (Cain 2016, 3). While this does suggest that gender was a significant factor in the vote, even if its effects were not necessarily linear, such analyses obscure how the gendered effects of Brexit run deeper than voting patterns.

Other work on gender and Brexit has emerged from critical feminist writings on the topic and offer important insights relevant to our approach. Hozić and True, for instance, have advanced a critical feminist IPE perspective on Brexit, which they describe as a 'scandal', an event able to animate the public imaginary in seemingly unintended ways since it "unmask[ed] deep political and material fault-lines in society" (Hozić and True 2017, 271). The authors suggest that just because "gender differences between men and women's vote were not observed in the referendum at the aggregate national level", does not mean Brexit was not gendered in other more nuanced and complex ways. We need to acknowledge, they argue, the extent to which gender, intersecting with other identity markers expose 'intersectional inequalities', since it is at the intersection of these identity markers—gender, race, class, etc.—that the complex gendered effects of Brexit become apparent. For instance, the greatest losers from globalisation, they argue, are not the "traditional working classes but poor, migrant women from minority racial, ethnic and religious groups" (Hozić and True 2017, 279). Brexit, they argue, was itself a product of a process of the subjectification of women—and others, including migrants—whose participation in debates was limited by a coterie of elite white males engaged in an inter-elite conflict which they transformed, and escalated, into a public issue (Hozić and True 2017, 276). Guerrina and Masselot (2018) offer another important contribution from a critical feminist perspective. They argue that Brexit "carries a substantial risk to the interests of traditionally marginal groups (including women) who have hitherto been covered by the EU legal framework" (2018, 319). This is, they posit, a consequence of government opposition in the UK to gender equality policies on the grounds they run counter to business interests. The marginality of gender and equality, they argue, reflects the high-low policy binary whereby "the interests of business are likely to trump over other fundamental principles, e.g. equality" (327). They conclude that, ironically, any post-Brexit economic crisis will likely reinforce this tendency, given the gendered impact of austerity and the use of 'crisis' narratives to defend business-centric policies (Guerrina and Masselot 2018, 319).

The literature on Brexit from a gendered perspective has highlighted important, yet unexplored, aspects of the vote and its consequences, as well as the necessity to explore Brexit through a gendered lens and to apply "a feminist curiosity" (Enloe 2004). However, these existing works have not fully accounted for the role played by gendered discourses in the campaign itself, or how these will likely come to affect the outcome of the Brexit process. By discourses we refer here to "system[s] of meanings, of ways of thinking, images and worlds that…shape how we experience, understand and represent ourselves as men and women [and] shape many other aspects of our lives and culture" (Cohn 1993, 228–229). Public opinion research has little to say on gendered discourses since it is stuck in something regarding, in ontological terms, a 'liberal feminist trap'; by using gender as an explanatory variable, these studies do not have the conceptual dexterity to grasp the underlying gendered nature of the campaign they are studying. Rather, the consensus in these approaches is that the role played by gender is minimal, since males and females tended to vote in similar ways in the referendum. The task of understanding gendered discourses is, of course, much better suited to critical feminist approaches, of which we have offered a few examples. And yet, whilst critical feminist works on Brexit remain in their infancy and will no doubt proliferate in the years to come, it is notable that no studies to date have examined specifically the gendered discourses at the heart of the Brexit campaign. By fixation on the (not insignificant) consequences of the Brexit vote, we argue that existing critical feminist accounts of Brexit have paid insufficient attention to how the campaign unfolded, the nature of the ideas that came to prominence, and the subsequent impact of these ideas on the post-Brexit political environment in the UK. Overlooking the gendered discourses of the Brexit campaign is problematic, since these ideas are ascendant, and will go a long way to determining the consequences of Brexit.

We situate our argument within the emerging body of critical feminist scholarship on Brexit, in order to contribute an exploration of the gendered nature of discourses surrounding Brexit, which, we argue, have not received adequate attention in the existing literature. Taking inspiration from, yet moving beyond, Hozić and True who interrogate the agents of Brexit, as well as the intersectional inequalities that made Brexit conceivable, we focus on the production of gendered configurations in the discourse that surrounded the Brexit campaign.

We focus in particular on two prominent discourses associated with the referendum campaign: militarism and deal-making. The language of the campaign, we argue, was problematically steeped in and wedded to gendered signifiers surrounding militarism and business rhetoric, reflective of a history of male domination and the valorisation of certain masculine traits in the political domain. Understanding how these discourses played out, we argue, is fundamental to understanding what Brexit represented and also where the process is likely to lead over the next few years. Moreover, it provides a useful supplement to pre-existing work on the referendum by highlighting the role of gendered discourses in animating the campaign. Whilst much scholarship has discussed the toxicity surrounding representations of immigrants in the campaign (e.g. Clarke et al. 2017, 88; Schimmelfennig 2018) our study shows that toxic representations of femininity and masculinity also played a prominent role in the debate.

The aforementioned lens complicates our understanding of the Brexit campaign, as well as the issues that gained traction during the debates. We argue that the gendered consequences of Brexit cannot be understood outside of these gendered discourses produced in the run-up to the campaign and now ascendant in British public life. By valorising such masculinist traits as national prestige and power (militarism) and the need for tough-talking business attitudes in politics ('deal-making'), these discourses have significant implications with regards to how the gendered consequences of Brexit are likely to unfold. In the next section we outline our theoretical framework, justifying our focus on gendered discourses through an engagement with critical feminist approaches.

3   Toxic Masculinity: Discourses of Militarism and Deal-Making

To explore the gendered dynamics of Brexit, we must move beyond liberal feminist categories of representation (male/female) and the 'gender variable' and instead scrutinise the language, and systems of meanings, deployed in the referendum campaign as well as in the negotiations that followed. In other words, we need to examine the language of Brexit; following Marysia Zalewski's injunction to pay attention to the "power and work" that gender is doing in any given discourse (Zalewski 2010, 5). This calls for a critical feminist perspective: one that is able to comprehend the constitutive role of discourses and identities, since "we rely on gender to make sense of ourselves and our world and the complex ways in which the self and world interact" (Shepherd 2017, 23). The conception of gender we advocate is also broad, since "without understanding that gender is at once a noun, a verb, and a logic it is nearly impossible to understand that gender is a relational and dynamic construct that operates in and through other power relations" (Shepherd 2017, 21).

Gendered norms and institutionalised gender bias construct particular representations which themselves constitute identities that establish certain possibilities whilst excluding others (Doty 1996). The study of discursive practices, and in particular discourses that valorise idealized notions of masculinity fix identities in binary, hierarchal, gendered and thus exclusionary and violent orders. As argued by David Duriesmith the history of certain masculinities has "produced the practice of international politics (through the promotion of white rationalism, militarism, etc.), and at the same time the configuration of international relations produces certain kinds of masculinities as individuals look to conform to the configurations that are sanctioned within the world of 'high' politics" (Duriesmith 2018). These idealized notions are inherently violent as they produce structural intersectional inequalities. We argue that discourses reflecting toxic masculinities emerged during the Brexit campaign in two distinct ways: through the deployment of language that was associated with militarism, and through language that was associated with business interests and 'deal-making' rhetoric. We outline the salience of these discourses below.

Firstly, an analysis of the gendered discourses of Brexit reveals an emphasis on militarist themes, language, values and ideology. Militarism as "an underlying system of institutions, practices, values and cultures" (Sjoberg and Via 2010, 7) is premised, broadly, on "the normalization and legitimation of war" (Stavrianakis 2018, 3). Critical feminists therefore challenge the "artificial construction of boundaries between 'war' (one day) and 'not war' (the next day)" (Sjoberg and Via 2010, 7) in order to draw attention to the continuum of violence and to highlight how gendered identities and hierarchies sustain militarism in everyday civilian life. Militarist values thus become normalized as the everyday architecture of society operates to sustain its value: from toys, fashion and consumer goods to taxation and sporting events. Militarism has historically valorised traits usually associated with both masculinity and heteronormativity, which are perceived as 'positive' qualities: heterosexuality, strength, power, autonomy, resilience, and competence. The logic follows that the deployment of militaristic language, in both overt and covert ways, demonstrates strength and resolve. As an extension of this argument, we highlight that the deployment of militaristic language, and the concomitant conscious and subconscious adoption of militarist values, was evident across the Brexit campaign.

Secondly, in addition to emphasising militarist language, Brexit discourse fixated on the promulgation of market logics and values linked to success in the 'business*man*'s world'. Operating within the public sphere, the spatial domain of the market and the corporate world represents distinctly masculinised spaces, within which "competitive individualism, reason and self-control" are idealised (Hooper 2001). This arena also relies on the reproduction of gendered stereotypes: "Men, operating within a hegemonic normative code, have thought to possess the appropriate skills, knowledge, and temperament to design and maintain the institutions of the state, while most women—assumed to be irrational, fragile, and dependent,—have tended to be relegated to supporting roles as low grade clerks, cleaners, tea ladies, and wives" (Lovenduski 2005, 147). Moreover, given the dominance of the market as a social institution, the resulting masculinity formed within the business arena places men in a "strong position to claim hegemony in the gender order of the societies they dominate" (Connell and Wood 2005). A successful businessman, according to the discourse, equates to a successful leader—someone who "can get the job done" (Lopatka 2017). The rhetorical power of this discourse is evident in contemporary populist claims, from Donald Trump to Andrej Babiš, who claim that their business acumen will secure a good deal for their country (Capehart 2015, 479–480; *The Guardian* 2017).

An emphasis on military might and businessman-like deal-making have, we argue, been particularly prominent in the Brexit debate, both before and after the referendum. The deployment of business rhetoric, in conjunction with the frequent use of military metaphors in adversarial styles of debates during the Brexit campaign, all of which were articulated in public statements made by politicians—"negotiating [and] pursuing a hard Brexit" to get "Britain firing in all areas again" (May 2016)—linguistically favoured, even if at times subtle and hidden from view, presumptions about masculinity and femininity. The motif created by the repetitive use of this deal-making and militarist language revealed a social category, or 'ideal type', through which, we argue, the discourse of a Brexit deal is subsequently being performed. The deployment of business and militarist language—associated with men, masculinity and heteronormativity—not only meant that business priorities would trump gender equality (Guerrina and Masselot 2018) but that ideas associated with masculinity would trump those associated with femininity. The foregoing discourses become evident when unpacking the language that was used across the campaign and in the negotiating forum, revealing a gendering of the elusive 'Brexit deal'. Deploying such language simultaneously frees the presently 'unknown' Brexit deal, its potentially catastrophic consequences and its masculinised 'action heroes' from any association with what may be considered feminine values (nurturing a relationship with the EU based on compassion, listening, intellection and emotional responsiveness, say). This binary opposite or 'other' to masculinity, although not inherently feminine, is always subordinate to the prevailing masculinity, usually located within the domestic sphere, reinforcing the 'high politics'/'low politics' binary.

4   Brexit and the Culture of British Politics

Britain joined the European Economic Community (EEC), the forerunner to today's EU, in 1973 under the Conservative government of Edward Heath. The UK had taken the decision to seek membership of the Common Market in the early 1960s, as its economic performance stagnated and as the economies of the original 'six' in the EEC raced ahead. Fearing an Anglo-American 'Trojan horse' with British accession, French president Charles de Gaulle vetoed applications from Harold

Macmillan in 1963 and Harold Wilson in 1967, and it was only after de Gaulle's replacement by the more moderate Georges Pompidou that the UK was able to join. Attitudes towards European integration in Britain have differed from those on the continent; membership was 'sold' to the British people, instrumentally, to bolster the UK's role in the world and to improve its economic performance (De Burca 2018). The European project was therefore never internalised by much of the population, and support for integration rested upon the EU's ability to deliver for its citizens (Isiksel 2018; Scharpf 1999; Sternberg 2013). Although support for the Common Market crossed party political lines, in the early years opposition came predominantly from Labour, which regarded the EEC as a capitalist project. Harold Wilson, having been elected prime minster in 1974 on a leftist platform, held the first referendum on British membership of the EEC in 1975, in which 67% of the British electorate voted to stay in. This pattern reversed itself somewhat in the 1990s, as pro-European Prime Minister Tony Blair sought to re-orient Labour as the party of the liberal centre, and as the Maastricht Treaty substantially increased the sovereignty cost of EU membership that had so irked right-wing Conservatives in previous decades. From this moment on, the Conservatives remained riven by the Europe question, and efforts by successive leaders, from John Major to David Cameron, to put the matter to rest failed (Martill and Staiger 2018, 6). In doing so, successive leaders were able to capitalise on latent Eurosceptic attitudes among the British population and, more specifically, within the Conservative party itself.

Brexit can therefore be traced back to the elite politics of the political right in the years since the 2008 financial crisis. In consequence, Brexit, as a process, was both instigated, and subsequently led, by a predominantly male and almost exclusively white elite, from a mainly upper-class socio-economic background, whose desires to extend their pre-existing inter-elite conflict led to the creation of the Brexit 'scandal' (Hozić and True 2017). In 2013, Cameron promised a referendum partly to hedge against the rising threat to the Conservative Party's right flank from a rising UKIP and to settle once-and-for all the 'Europe question' that had bedevilled the Tory party since the negotiation of the Maastricht Treaty in 1992. Cameron's decision to hold an in-out referendum reflected a hubristic attitude on his behalf, which was firmly ingrained in his privileged background; he was used to winning and he believed he would be able to pull off another swift victory, thereby cementing his rule over the party (Glencross 2018). Cameron's offer of a referendum was predicated on the Conservatives winning a majority in the 2015 general election, which they subsequently, albeit narrowly, achieved. His announcement that the referendum would be held on 23 June 2016 offered a unique opportunity for Tory challengers to capitalise upon—and reinforce—growing nationalist, Eurosceptic and anti-immigrant sentiment within the grassroots of the party. Thus, whilst some of the individuals supporting the leave campaign were dyed-in-the-wool Eurosceptics, others—including Cameron's Old Etonian rival Boris Johnson—had previously indicated support for remaining in the EU and were surprised by all accounts at the eventual victory of the leave campaign (Soubry 2016). The referendum offered the opportunity for would-be challengers both to bolster their rightist credentials and to precipitate a reshuffling of the political chess board.

The Brexit 'game' was rooted in a deeper political culture, and gender regime, in the UK that is characterised by adversarialism and conflict drawn from the elite, public school debate culture on which the system was originally based. Reinforced by the persistence of the British 'class-system', inequality in the education sector, and even the physical contours of the legislative chamber, this argumentative style of politics was evident throughout debates over Brexit. Support for this interpretation is evident across parties. A Conservative member of the House of Lords noted that British politics "is a system of rivalry [between] two sides. It's different from the other Member States, where you have got more often coalitions, more often consensus approach…There is quite a big element of 'rah-rah' so they are kind of opposing one another with electoral battles in between".[1] Another interviewee—a UKIP MEP—stated, in Britain "the relationship between government and opposition is childish. It's characterised by yah-boo politics. There is often an irresponsible lack of consensus and cooperation … On back and front-benchers, an old saying comes to mind 'the people opposite us are our opponents, and our enemies are behind us'".[2] Moreover, as suggested to us by a former parliamentary representative, "the UK system is designed to have that sort of government-opposition mentality [as] it is even

[1] Interview conducted by Benjamin Martill and Anton Gromoczki, House of Lords, 20 July 2017.

[2] Interview conducted by Oliver Patel and Jose Feio, Brussels, 25 July 2017.

physically designed as a parliament to look like that...in the UK, the system, the politics, the debate can move very quickly, lot of sparring and shouting at each other".[3]

It is therefore no coincidence that the decision to hold a referendum, the nature of the campaign itself, and the subsequent leave victory, were all linked to this entrenched system. As one Labour member of the Lords articulated: "Brexit is to a degree a product of the...confrontational culture and a decrease in political representation [which] provides a backdrop in which the negotiations will develop".[4] These behavioural norms are part of, and intimately connected to, an established gender regime operating in the House of Commons, characterised by "requirements for masculine dress codes, provision for hanging up one's sword but not looking after one's child, admiration for demagoguery and conflict, adversarial styles of debates, a chamber whose acoustics favour loud voices, and the frequent use of military metaphors" (Lovenduski 2005, 147). The public-school debating culture of British politics has had, we argue, important consequences for both the tone, and the nature, of the campaign, especially with regard to the crucial question of who has been empowered to speak. Just as the origins of Brexit lay in the inter-elite politics between privileged white males within the Conservative party, so too did elite white males come to dominate the campaign they had now unleashed onto the British public.

The key protagonists in the Europe debate as it unfolded from 2013 onwards were David Cameron, Nick Clegg, Ed Miliband, and Nigel Farage—all white men who had attended either elite schools, elite universities, or both. In fact, during the campaign, men were afforded 85% of press coverage (Centre for Research in Communication and Culture 2016). Conversely, women were only noticeably present when men wished to discuss 'women's' issues. As Haastrup et al. noted at the time, "the campaign continues to be dominated by male 'experts' and a presumption that women will vote on the basis of emotive issues of special interest to them, such as maternity leave policies" (Haastrup et al. 2016). Moreover, this culture provided fertile ground for the continued use of business rhetoric reinforcing 'deal-making', and the ability of the UK to

---

[3] Interview conducted by Benjamin Martill, Brussels, 19 July 2017.

[4] Interview conducted by Benjamin Martill and Anton Gromoczki, House of Lords, 20 July 2017.

negotiate the best deal for the UK, alongside the frequent deployment of military metaphors. Unsurprisingly, therefore, the discourses used by the two campaigns tapped into traditional 'male' concerns—and masculinised politics—regarding security, the market, strength, and the protection of 'their' families. This discursive element serves to reinforce existing male dominance of politics by associating male traits with those issue-areas and priorities deemed most 'important' for the country. The dominance of male 'experts' in determining the course of the Brexit campaign owed as much to the discourse of 'high politics' as it does to the entrenched positions held by males in British politics. As Haastrup et al. argued in the run-up to the vote, "issues pertaining to 'high politics'—security and defence, and the economy—have remained squarely the prerogative of men. As a result, when women's voices and expertise have been included, it has been to speak about social politics and policies" (Haastrup et al. 2016). For issues that were considered to be not directly applicable to 'women', women were side-lined in the debate and effectively silenced. This was compounded for women from minority groups who were also silenced by their immigration status—despite, according to Hozić and True, the fact that "austerity politics and global chains of migrant labour" are aspects upon which the UK economy depends (Hozić and True 2017, 271).

5   The Campaign Discourse: 'Make Britain Great Again'

The 1975 referendum campaign was overtly gendered, sexist and sexualised. One noteworthy offering from the 1975 campaign, published in the *British European*, featured a page three model in a Union Jack bikini accompanied by the headline 'Europe is Fun', and a secondary headline entitled: "More Work and More Play Too!" (Payne 2017). Another choice offering from the 'in' campaign, this time from the Liberal Party, invited the reader to "say yes to a liberal Europe...For your family's sake", claiming EEC membership offered 'dad' "a bigger say at work with a share in his firm's profit" and 'mum' "a rising standard of living with secure food supplies" (Liberal Party 1975). Similar narratives were also elements of the 'out' campaign. "Housewives", one leaflet from the National Referendum Campaign stated, "are paying more and more hard-earned cash for fewer and fewer goods" because of the EEC (National Referendum Campaign 1975) (Fig. 1).

Fig. 1 Young man and woman holding pro-membership campaign material from the *British European*, the paper of the pro-EEC European Movement, 1971 Image © CN Media Group. Reprinted with permission

This overt sexism was replaced in the 2016 campaign with a more insidious—yet just as problematic—gendered discourse emphasising militarism and 'deal-making'. In a sign of clearly changed times, the literature in the 2016 campaign made no explicit references to "mums" or "housewives", nor did either campaign deem it appropriate to make scantily dressed women part of their message. Rather, the 2016 campaign was gendered, we argue, in a different respect, for the discourse surrounding the referendum—particularly, though not exclusively, that of the leave campaign—made prominent a number of gendered themes linked specifically to militarism and market-oriented discourses. Specifically, discourses cohered around notions of strength, security, global power, and the protection of vulnerable women. These gendered discourses are no less damaging than the 'overt' sexism of the 1975 campaign; insofar as they represent these themes as gender neutral, these

discourses are more insidious, and therefore potentially more dangerous. The two recurring elements, which emerged mainly from the pro-
Brexit campaign, we argue, are a preoccupation with British military
strength and power (militarism) and a belief in the importance of the
application of business skills to the conduct of politics ('deal-making').
Understanding these discourses is critical to understanding Brexit.

To begin with, militarist discourses largely played out against the background of Britain's assumed global role, the product of its power, prestige
and (unsubtly venerated) history of colonial rule. Much of this discourse
harked back to a supposedly 'better time': "What we achieve by voting
LEAVE", one leaflet from the right-wing Bruges Group noted, is "a better
vision for Britain's future, in control of our own global affairs" (Bruges
Group 2016). The 'vision' of Leave.EU, in its campaign material, was to
"leave the European Union. Restore the country's power over its laws.
Save £12bn of taxpayers' money. Build stronger ties with the rest of the
world" (Leave.EU 2016a). The Better Off Out campaign, meanwhile,
emphasised the important of Britain's history: "Stonehenge and medie-
val cathedrals speak of antiquity, while our parliaments demonstrate our
democratic heritage and the great castles remind us of our unconquered
military heritage" (Better off Out 2016). The Conservatives' leave campaign argued for "an optimistic global view of Britain", claiming "we
would both gain influence and prosper outside an unreformed EU"
(Conservatives for Britain 2016a), while Labour's argued it was "time to
leave the EU and join the World" (Labour Leave 2016). Underpinning
much of the pro-free-market discourse of the leave campaign, moreover, was this emphasis on Britain's return to the global order, jettisoning
the parochialism of its decades-long European dalliance. Grassroots Out,
evoking a collective 'we', stated they were in favour of leaving the EU "to
allow us to make our own laws in our own country [and] to allow British
businesses to trade freely across the world" (Grassroots Out 2016). Vote
Leave, for their part, argued a post-Brexit Britain would be "free to trade
with the whole world" (Vote Leave 2016a).

The second prominent gendered theme in the referendum discourse
lies, we argue, in the embrace of a market discourse and the valorisation of business skills and 'deal-making' in the conduct of politics.[5] The
Conservatives for Britain campaign, for example, argued that "Britain

---

[5] It should be noted, perhaps unsurprisingly, that support for the free-market did not
feature in the campaigns. From the Labour ('Labour Leave') and Green ('Green Leave')

needs a better deal from the EU...Britain needs fundamental change so that we can control our borders, trade freely around the world and return power to Parliament to block harmful EU rules" (Conservatives for Britain 2016b). Leave.EU, for its part, argued that "with its right to strike deals restored, the UK will be able to gain better access to those markets that buy most of our goods and services" (Leave.EU 2016b). The Vote Leave campaign noted that "the UK has no trade deals with important countries like China, India and Australia. If we vote to remain in the EU, we won't be able to make our own deals" (Vote Leave 2016a). Another leaflet noted the "UK isn't allowed to negotiate our own trade deals...Instead of making a deal which is best for the UK, we have to wait for 27 other countries to agree it" (Vote Leave 2016b). Tim Martin, the Eurosceptic boss of pub chain J.D. Wetherspoon who campaigned openly for a leave vote, suggested the UK's relations with the EU should mirror the logic of firms, noting "if we [the UK and EU] can't agree on a deal, then we'll find another supplier. It sounds harsh, but that's business and that's trade...It cannot be seriously suggested that the French, Germans and others will wish to cease trading with us or will be able to afford to" (Martin 2016, 3).

6   After the Vote: The Brexiter Worldview Ascendent

The leave campaign emphasised certain recurring themes in its effort to convince voters they would be better off if the UK left the EU. These repeatedly emphasised norms centred on national power and prestige, the benefits of the free market, and the need for good deal-making vis-à-vis the EU and the wider world. Together these elements cohered into a simple message: Without the EU, Britain is free to head out into the wider world and strike deals with whomever 'we' please. Equating state-craft with market oriented, businessman-like values and thus individuality and choice, creates a discourse that reinforces what Cynthia Enloe describes as the "connective tissues" of patriarchy: the "large and small, subtle and blatant forms of racialised sexism, gendered misogyny and masculinised privileged" (Enloe 2017, ix–x). This valorises ideas associated with masculinity at the heart of politics and claims to sovereignty

campaigns, which focused instead upon the EU's treatment of Greece, its support for 'tax-dodging multinationals', and its contribution to insecurity in the East (e.g. Labour Leave 2016; Green Leaves 2016).

which, given the green light, ride roughshod over ideas that either challenge or call an end to this business-as-usual politics. Moreover, the discourse taps into a latent nostalgia for the British Empire and the power and control it afforded the colonisers—both economic and otherwise, subsequently reinforcing the persistent and dogged connections to historical and contemporary racisms, sexisms and classisms. Talk of trade and power, for example, "melancholically recall[s] British imperial and colonial rhetoric…Fantasy-imperialism thus meshes with anti-globalisation sentiment—the macho national dominance that will supposedly quell global feminisation" (Cain 2016, 1).

The leave victory heralded the rise, in many respects, of the Brexiter worldview propounded by the (right-wing) leave campaign over the months preceding the vote. This was reinforced by Theresa May's insistence, upon taking over the Conservative leadership and premiership from David Cameron, that 'Brexit means Brexit'. In confirming that the UK would leave the EU and, moreover, would not accept any solution in which Britain remained in 'through the back door', May indicated that a compromise—or a 'soft Brexit'—was off the table as far as HM Government was concerned. Moreover, May moved to institutionalise the Brexit process, establishing the Department for Exiting the EU (DExEU), appointing leave supporters to lead key departments, including the Foreign & Commonwealth Office (FCO) (Boris Johnson), the Department for International Trade (DIT) (Liam Fox) and DExEU (David Davis), as well as triggering—after a lengthy legal battle—Article 50 itself on 29 March 2017. In her Lancaster House speech of 17 January, in which she responded to growing pressure to make clear her plans for Brexit, May outlined her vision of Britain as "a great global trading nation" (Martill 2017a). By confirming that the UK would not accept the free movement of persons or the supremacy of EU law, and by strongly hinting that contributions into the future EU budget would be problematic, May all but precluded a 'softer' form of Brexit being achieved. By aping the rhetoric of Vote Leave and UKIP—of a strong global Britain—she further contributed to the promulgation of the deal-making discourse. "No deal", she (in)famously declared, "is better than a bad deal" (May 2017). In her keenness to emphasise this stark, and reductive, dichotomy, May used the word 'deal' 16 times in her speech (Jackson-Preece 2017). Such was the extent to which May appropriated the discourse of the 'Brexiteers' that Nigel Farage tweeted in response that he could "hardly believe that the PM is now using the phrases and words that I've been mocked for using for years" (Farage 2017). As the negotiations began, David Davis summed up the purpose of the talks succinctly: "Michel and I are both going for a good deal" (*The Independent* 2017).

The first round of negotiations began on 19 June 2017, with David Davis leading the UK delegation in talks with the EU's Michel Barnier and his team, who had been afforded a strict mandate by the European Council. Controversially, and very visibly, only one woman was appointed to the British negotiating team. Whilst this was, for some, a reflection of "the fact that while most civil servants are female, and 11% are from ethnic minorities" (Branigan 2017), it invited the predictable response that the UK government was side-lining women in the Brexit process, and falling back on antiquated, exclusionary and elitist modes of conducting politics (Achilleos-Sarll 2017; O'Brien 2017). Throughout the negotiations the hostile rhetoric against the EU externally and so-called "remoaners" domestically also continued unabated. Whilst the former has been depicted as a bullying external other, the latter have been portrayed as illegitimate obstructionists. Pro-Brexit Conservative MP Jacob Rees-Mogg depicted Commission president Jean-Claude Juncker as "a pound shop Bismarck, arrogant and bullying but without the charm", noting that "[h]e has nothing to intimidate us with and the British people always stiffen their sinews when threatened" (Politico 2017). Leave Means Leave, a pro-Brexit pressure group, meanwhile, urged "those who supported Remain not to seek to delay, obstruct or dilute the Brexit process—but to accept the verdict of the British people and embrace the huge opportunities on the horizon for a free and independent United Kingdom" (Leave Means Leave 2018).

Militarist themes, moreover, underlay many of these claims, and in some cases was made plainly explicit. Reacting to claims Brexit could challenge the British claim to sole sovereignty of Gibraltar, Defence Secretary Michael Fallon suggested that the UK would be prepared to use military force to defend the territory, while former Conservative leader Michael Howard drew a parallel between Britain's retention of Gibraltar and its defence of the Falkland Islands in the 1982 conflict (Williams 2017). Nostalgia for British military might also saturates the discourse, as attested by the frequent analogies between Brexit and the Dunkirk evacuation of 1940. As Emile Simpson has argued: "If the cultural roots of Brexit are reduced to one sentiment, it is that

Britain did not win two world wars to be run by Germany via Brussels" (Simpson 2017). While Nigel Farage exhorted his followers to watch the Christopher Nolan movie *Dunkirk*, a pro-Brexit commentary in the *Daily Telegraph* argued: "For Brexit to work, we need Dunkirk spirit not 'Naysaying Nellies'" (Pearson 2017).

Time and again this rhetoric valorised strength at the negotiating table and sought to portray concessions and compromise as weak and inferior. Towards the end of 2017, considerable support emerged on the Conservative right to prepare for a 'no deal' scenario, in which the UK would exit the EU without any agreement on the terms of its withdrawal. This was viewed by some on the right as a goal in and of itself—a clean break from Brussels—whilst for others preparing for such a scenario was seen as a means of bolstering the credibility of British claims that they would "walk away from the table" if offered anything less than a comprehensive free trade agreement. Nigel Farage argued, for instance, that a no deal scenario "would hurt Europe far more than it would hurt us (BBC News 2018). Even Cabinet ministers seemed to endorse an open attitude towards 'no deal', with Liam Fox claiming that "[l]eaving without a deal would not be the Armageddon that people project" (*EU Observer* 2018). Even following the conclusion of the first round of negotiations, and the acceptance of the preliminary agreement by the European Council on 15 December, there was still considerable pressure from within the Conservative party for Theresa May to reject any transition deal and 'fight' against demands from Brussels that the UK maintain freedom of movement for EU citizens. The discussion of the 'no deal' scenario highlighted the pernicious link between deal-making and militarism that lies at the heart of the Brexiter ideology: Britain will use its power and prestige to force concessions from the EU, negotiating from a position of strength to obtain a better deal for the British people.

Whilst it may not be surprising that the emphasis on deal-making increased as the Brexit negotiations loomed, it is necessary to bear in mind the specific nature of this discourse, which not only conceptualised the negotiations themselves as an exercise in bargaining and deal-making, but also stressed the need for a strong individual as the best means to achieve this. The assumptions underlying this view, made explicit in other public utterances by Cabinet ministers and in Conservative campaigning material, was that the exercise was a zero-sum affair in which the EU was to be seen as the adversary and in which the distributional gains and losses would fall along national lines. The discourse also promulgated the ideal of strength, portraying this as the most significant attribute Britain needed in order to get its own way (Martill 2017b). The obsession with the projection of strength lay behind May's (much-mocked) depiction of her administration as 'strong and stable'. In other words, the negotiations were treated as a hard-hitting business deal rather than a gentle act of strategic diplomacy aimed at obtaining a mutually amicable (and beneficial) withdrawal. The discourse embraced macho values of strength and portrayed the negotiations as an all-or-nothing scenario.

7 THE CONSEQUENCES OF THE MILITARIST AND DEAL-MAKING DISCOURSES

The discourse underlying the leave campaign and now ascendant in the Brexit process—valorising militarism and deal-making—are likely to have profound consequences for the manner in which Brexit unfolds and, subsequently, in terms of the gendered outcomes of the process. In this final section we outline four distinct consequences of this discourse: the contribution towards a 'harder' Brexit; the consolidation of free-market norms and retrenchment of social policies; the diversion of attention from domestic to the international distributional consequences; and the persistent under-representation of women and minority groups in politics. In each of these respects, the real-world consequences of these masculinist discourses—toxic as they are in themselves—will prove more damaging for women, and minority groups, than for the white male electorate.

Firstly, these masculinist discourses preclude the possibility of achieving an outcome of the Brexit negotiations based on dialogue, equality, empathy, care and other-regardingness, all values which would be needed in order to maintain beneficial political linkages across the continent and prevent the social consequences of a damaging 'hard' Brexit. As we have demonstrated above, discourses of militarism and deal-making both push in the direction of a hard-line negotiating strategy, one that portrays the talks as a zero-sum bargaining game in which losses are to the advantage of the 'adversary' and in which concessions and compromise are viewed as feminine—and, therefore, undesirable—traits. Given the requirement for some form of compromise and the benefits that will accrue to both sides through participation in EU programmes—or perhaps even the EU's internal market—such a hard-line approach is misguided. The brinksmanship justified under such slogans as 'from a position of strength' and 'getting the best deal' is likely to bring about a harder Brexit than a more conciliatory approach to the negotiations, and this will have important implications for UK and EU citizens.

Secondly, the individualist worldview inherent in these discourses—emphasising strength, self-reliance and decisive leadership—delegitimises policies based around the collective defence of common welfare, including social policies designed to support child rearing and other forms of care falling outside traditional definitions of 'work'. This is, moreover, likely to be reinforced by the aforementioned move towards a 'hard Brexit', given the protection afforded to women by EU directives and regulations in recent years, and the UK's consistent opposition to both EU encroachment on member state policies in this area, and to the promotion of 'anti-competitive' welfare policies (Guerrina and Masselot 2018, 9). As evidence of the likely shift, the UK government's damaging austerity policies, implemented from 2010 onwards, have disproportionately affected women—and especially Black, Asian and Minority Ethnic (BAME) women—by cutting public sector employment and depriving lone parents (predominantly women) of welfare and support (O'Brien 2017; Sandhu and Stephenson 2015). Thus, the move towards a hard Brexit and the dominance of masculinist rhetoric together make more likely a ramping up of the business-friendly, neoliberal economic policy of the past three decades, and presage a concomitant reduction in the willingness of the government to provide sufficient support for social welfare programmes and policies.

Thirdly, the emphasis of masculinist discourses on national strength and prestige diverts attention to the international at the expense of the domestic, and in doing so occludes discussion of the distributional consequences of Brexit. Just as GDP figures—beloved by proponents of the free-market—convey only aggregate national growth, and not the distributional imbalances that may be lurking underneath, so too does a focus on *national* success necessarily come at the expense of attention to *domestic* consequences. These are likely to be more damaging for women than they are for men, not least since "the role of the EU as a gender actor is largely undisputed [and] equality policies are now one of the most widely developed areas of European social policy" (Guerrina and Murphy 2016, 874). Masculinist pro-Brexit discourses reinforce spatialised boundaries between the international, national, domestic and local, as well as between 'high' and 'low' politics—the oft-drawn distinction in foreign affairs discourses between important ('high politics') questions of international security on the one hand and mere domestic, social, affairs ('low politics') on the other—whereby gender has effectively been subsumed under discussions about women's employment or maternity rights, thus relegating women to the domain of social policy, thought to be confined to the 'domestic' sphere despite the fact that gendered consequences will be felt across all sectors of British society.

Fourthly, the dominance of discourses valorising strength and deal-making, by reinforcing stereotypes of 'maleness' and 'manliness', undercut efforts to afford women and minority groups greater representation in the corridors of power. By portraying the male archetype as the only means of achieving the 'best deal', perspectives that cut across a spectrum of identities are correspondingly delegitimised. This is evident already in the frequent criticisms of Theresa May as a 'weak individual'—however perilous her parliamentary situation—and in the lack of female representation on the British negotiating team. The story of May's premiership to date belies any narrative of female empowerment; derided by her party as a 'weak' leader and struggling to command the requisite authority to govern, May's ascension is more a reminder that women "reach positions of leadership at precarious or risky times" (Hozić and True 2017, 276) than it is an indication that a corner has been turned. In response, May has sought to associate herself with ostensibly 'male' values, with her aforementioned emphasis on strength and stability an obvious case in point. The lack of representation more generally is a stark reminder that women remain marginalised, excluded and silenced within British politics and, furthermore, that some women—namely those who reside outside the elite, remain more marginalised than others. Underrepresentation is both a metaphor and a reminder of the circulating gendered discourses in European and British politics adversely affecting women and minority groups.

8 Conclusion: Critical Feminism, Toxic Masculinity, and Brexit

A critical feminist lens focuses attention on areas currently excluded, or ignored, by mainstream theories and positivist epistemologies. Postpositivist and feminist critiques challenge such exclusions, androcentric biases, and gendered and racialised hierarchies, both from within the discipline of IR, and within the discourse and practice of global politics. According to Peterson "feminist scholarship offers many resources for rethinking 'givens', redrawing boundaries, and re-visioning our horizons" (Peterson 1992, 191). This being the case, we have argued in this chapter that scholars need to pay particular attention to the discourses surrounding the Brexit campaign in order to fully comprehend the consequences of the vote. And, whilst there is a growing literature on Brexit that takes seriously the need for a gendered perspective, we have argued these have not fully succeeded in accounting for the role played by gendered discourses in the campaign. Works on public opinion, whilst taking seriously the need to analyse the campaign and to include a focus on gender, have remained wedded to liberal feminist ontologies that do not offer a sufficiently deep conception of gender. Critical feminist works, in contrast, whilst offering a more theoretically nuanced account of the relationship between gender, power and neo-liberalism, have had little to say about the dominant discourses in the campaign.

By drawing on critical feminist theory and undertaking analysis of the writings of the pro-Brexit campaign in the UK, we have argued that the campaign and the subsequent negotiations have been dominated by a toxic masculinity that manifested in two particular ways. Firstly, through the deployment of language that was associated with militarism and, secondly, through language associated with deal-making and business rhetoric. Based on a worldview of power, militarism and winner-take-all competiveness, this Brexit discourse views Britain's EU membership as a challenge to its global power and prestige and a restraint on its free-trading ambitions, and equates the Brexit negotiations with high-powered business talks rather than acts of diplomacy, valorising strength in the face of the (European) adversary. These discourses gathered strength in the run-up to the referendum, such that the result was a decision to leave the EU, and they have become highly influential since the vote, with the rhetoric of Theresa May's Conservative administration contributing to the masculinist Brexiteer worldview and its obsession with strength, stability and 'deal making'. We therefore must remain cognizant of these prevailing discourses, which rely on old-new gendered norms and hierarchies.

Looking forward, we have isolated four potential consequences of these discourses: the increasing likelihood of a 'harder' Brexit; the consolidation of free-market and neo-liberal norms and the corresponding retrenchment of welfare and social policies; the diverting of attention away from the distributional consequences of Brexit at the domestic level; and the continued underrepresentation of women, and minority groups, in British and European politics. Drawing attention to these potential consequences, and the gendered discourses upon which they rely, goes someway to challenge current, and mainstream, analyses of Brexit with the intention to offer a counter narrative in order to highlight and to disrupt dominant structures of power.

Acknowledgements We would like to thank Moira Dustin for detailed comments on the manuscript and Daniel Payne at the LSE Archives for his assistance in tracking down material from the referendum campaign(s). We would also like to thank participants of the Feminist and Queer Perspectives on Brexit Workshop at Sussex University for their very helpful comments on an earlier draft.

Bibliography

Achilleos-Sarll, C. 2017. Where Are the Women at the Big Boys' Table? *UCL Brexit Blog*, June 26. Available at: https://ucl-brexit.blog/2017/06/26/where-are-the-women-at-the-big-boys-table/.

Armstrong, K.A. 2017. *Brexit Time: Leaving the EU—Why, How and When?* Cambridge: Cambridge University Press.

BBC News. 2018. Brexit: EU 'Surprised' at UK No-Deal Planning Concerns, January 9. Available at: http://www.bbc.co.uk/news/uk-politics-42625474.

Better off Out. 2016. Are You British...or European? Available at: https://digital.library.lse.ac.uk/objects/lse:kop408mix/read/single#page/1/mode/1up.

Branigan, T. 2017. All White and Just One Woman. Why Is Our Brexit Team like This? *The Guardian*, June 22. Available at: https://www.theguardian.com/commentisfree/2017/jun/22/all-white-one-female-uk-brexit-team-negotiating-eu-diversity.

Bruges Group. 2016. The EU and Your Top Three Concerns. Available at: https://digital.library.lse.ac.uk/objects/lse:lal729hud/read/single#page/4/mode/1up.

Cain, R. 2016. Post-Truth and the 'Metropolitan Elite' Feminist: Lessons from Brexit. *Feminists@Law Journal* 6 (1): 1–8.

Capehart, K.W. 2015. Hyman Minsky's Interpretation of Donald Trump. *Journal of Post Keynesian Economics* 38 (3): 477–492.

Centre for Research in Communication and Culture. 2016. Gender Balance in EU Referendum Coverage. Loughborough University Centre for Research in Communication and Culture. Available at: https://blog.lboro.ac.uk/crcc/eu-referendum/gender-balance-eu-referendum-coverage/.

Clarke, H.D., M. Goodwin, and P. Whiteley. 2017. *Brexit: Why Britain Voted to Leave the European Union*. Cambridge: Cambridge University Press.

Cohn, C. 1993. Wars, Wimps, and Women: Talking Gender and Thinking War. In *Gendering War Talk*, ed. M. Cooke and A. Woollacott, 227–246. Princeton, NJ: Princeton University Press.

Connell, R.W., and J. Wood. 2005. Globalization and Business Masculinities. *Men and Masculinities* 7 (4): 347–364.

Conservatives for Britain. 2016a. About Our Campaign. Available at: https://digital.library.lse.ac.uk/objects/lse:hol558buv/read/single#page/1/mode/1up.

Conservatives for Britain. 2016b. Britain Needs a Better Deal from the EU. Available at: https://digital.library.lse.ac.uk/objects/lse:jur367ber/read/single#page/1/mode/1up.

Doty, R.L. 1996. *Imperial Encounters*. London: University of Minnesota Press.

Duriesmith, C. 2018. Manly States and Feminist Foreign Policy: Revisiting the Liberal State as an Agent of Change. In *Revisiting Gendered States: Feminist Imaginings of the State in International Relations*, ed. S. Parashaw, J.A. Tickner, J. True, and Preface by V. Spike Peterson. New York: Oxford University Press.

De Burca, G. 2018. How British Was the Brexit Vote? In *Brexit and Beyond: Rethinking the Futures of Europe*, ed. B. Martill and U. Staiger. London: UCL Press.

Enloe, C. 2004. *The Curious Feminist: Searching for Women in a New Age of Empire*. London: University of California Press.

Enloe, C. 2017. *The Big Push: Exposing and Challenging the Persistence of Patriarchy*. Oakland, CA: University of California Press.

EU Observer. 2018. May on Mission Impossible in Brussels. *EU Observer*, January 31. Available at: https://euobserver.com/uk-referendum/139551.

Evans, G., and A. Menon. 2017. *Brexit and British Politics*. Oxford: Wiley.

Farage, N. 2017. Tweet. January 17. Available at: https://twitter.com/nigel_farage/status/821336404257017856?lang=en.

Glencross, A. 2016. *Why the UK Voted for Brexit: David Cameron's Great Miscalculation*. Basingstoke: Palgrave Macmillan.

Glencross, A. 2018. Cameron's European Legacy: How Brexit Demonstrates the Flawed Politics of Simple Solutions. In *Brexit and Beyond: Rethinking the Futures of Europe*, ed. B. Martill and U. Staiger, 22–27. London: UCL Press.

Goodwin, M., and O. Heath. 2016. Brexit Vote Explained: Poverty, Low Skills and Lack of Opportunities. *Report for the Joseph Rowntree Foundation*, August 31. Available at: https://www.jrf.org.uk/report/brexit-vote-explained-poverty-low-skills-and-lack-opportunities.

Goodwin, M., and C. Milazzo. 2017. Taking Back Control? Investigating the Role of Immigration in the 2016 Vote for Brexit. *British Journal of Politics and International Relations* 19 (3): 450–464.

Grassroots Out. 2016. We Want to Leave the EU. Do You? Available at: https://digital.library.lse.ac.uk/objects/lse:tax397guv.

Green Leaves. 2016. I'm with the Previous Corbyn. Available at: https://digital.library.lse.ac.uk/objects/lse:zin692viq.

The Guardian. 2017. Anti-establishment Billionaire Andrej Babiš to be Named Czech PM. *The Guardian,* 22 October 2017. Available at: https://www.theguardian.com/world/2017/oct/22/anti-establishment-billionaire-andrej-babis-to-be-named-czech-pm.

Guerrina, R., and A. Masselot. 2018. Walking into the Footprint of EU Law: Unpacking the Gendered Consequences of Brexit. *Social Policy & Society* 17 (2): 319–330.

Guerrina, R., and H. Murphy. 2016. Strategic Silences in the Brexit Debate: Gender, Marginality and Governance. *Journal of Contemporary European Research* 12 (4): 872–880.

Haastrup, T., K. Wright, and R. Guerrina. (2016). Women in the Brexit Debate: Still Largely Confined to 'Low' Politics. *LSE Brexit Blog,* 17 June 2016. Available at: http://blogs.lse.ac.uk/brexit/2016/06/17/women-in-the-brexit-debate-still-largely-confined-to-low-politics/.

Hooper, C. 2001. *Manly States: Masculinities, International Relations, and Gender Politics.* New York: Columbia University Press.

Hozić, A.A., and J. True. 2017. Brexit as a Scandal: Gender and Global Trumpism. *Review of International Political Economy* 24 (2): 270–287.

The Independent. 2017. Brexit: Second Round of Talks Fails to Produce Breakthrough on Key Disputes, Says EU's Chief Negotiator, July 20. Available at: http://www.independent.co.uk/news/uk/politics/brexit-talks-second-round-eu-uk-fails-to-produce-breakthrough-citizens-rights-chief-negotiator-a7850736.html.

Isiksel, T. 2018. Square Peg, Round Hole: Why the EU Can't Fix Identity Politics. In *Brexit and Beyond: Rethinking the Futures of Europe,* ed. B. Martill & U. Staiger. London: UCL Press.

Jackson-Preece, J. 2017. Britain Risks Securitising Its Future Relationship with the EU. *LSE Brexit Blog,* October 3. Available at: http://blogs.lse.ac.uk/brexit/2017/10/03/brexit-risks-securitising-the-future-relationship-with-the-eu/.

Labour Leave. 2016. It's Time to Leave the EU and Join the World. https://digital.library.lse.ac.uk/objects/lse:feb267kop/read/single#page/1/mode/1up.

Leave.EU. 2016a. It's Time to Leave. Available at: https://digital.library.lse.ac.uk/objects/lse:suv872voy/read/single#page/1/mode/1up.

Leave.EU. 2016b. Know the Facts! Available at: https://digital.library.lse.ac.uk/objects/lse:yog899meb/read/single#page/1/mode/1up.

Leave Means Leave. 2018. 'Message from Our Co-chairmen' Leave Means Leave Website. Available at: http://www.leavemeansleave.eu/. Accessed 31 Jan 2018.

Liberal Party. 1975. Don't Slam the Door on Europe. Available at: https://digital.library.lse.ac.uk/objects/lse:did995mod.

Lopatka, J. 2017. Billionaire Businessman Babis Is at Heart of Czech Political Crisis. *Reuters*, May 4. Available at: https://www.reuters.com/article/us-czech-government-babis/billionaire-businessman-babis-is-at-heart-of-czech-political-crisis-idUSKBN1800ZH.

Lovenduski, J. 2005. *Feminizing Politics*. Cambridge: Polity.

Martill, B. 2017a. Britain Has Lost a Role, and Failed to Find an Empire. *UCL European Institute Comment*, January 17. Available at: http://www.ucl.ac.uk/european-institute/analysis/2016-17/martill-may-speech.

Martill, B. 2017b. Brexit and UK Foreign Policy: 'Keeping Britain Great' or 'Putting the Great Back into Great Britain'? Available at: http://www.dahrendorf-forum.eu/brexit-and-uk-foreign-policy-keeping-britain-great-or-putting-the-great-back-into-great-britain/.

Martill, B., & U. Staiger. 2018. Introduction. In *Brexit and Beyond: Rethinking the Futures of Europe*, ed. B. Martill and U. Staiger, 1–18. London: UCL Press.

Martin, T. 2016. I'm Out for Democracy. *Wetherspoon News*, vol. EU Referendum Special, pp. 2–3.

May, T. 2016. The Good That Government Can Do. Speech Delivered at the Conservative Party Conference in Birmingham, 5 October 2016. Available at: http://press.conservatives.com/post/151378268295/prime-minister-the-good-that-government-can-do.

May, T. 2017. Theresa May's Brexit Speech in Full. *The Daily Telegraph*, January 17. Available at: http://www.telegraph.co.uk/news/2017/01/17/theresa-mays-brexit-speech-full/.

Mellstrom, U. 2016. In the Time of Masculinist Political Revival. *International Journal for Masculinity Studies* 11 (3): 135–138.

National Referendum Campaign. 1975. We Must Get Out. Available at: https://digital.library.lse.ac.uk/objects/lse:zuk322nuk?id=lse%3Azuk322nuk#page/1/mode/2up.

O'Brien, C. 2017. There's Only One Women on the UK Brexit Negotiating Team—Here's Why It Matters. *The Conversation*, July 25. Available at: https://theconversation.com/theres-only-one-woman-on-the-uk-brexit-negotiating-team-heres-why-that-matters-81506.

Oliver, T. 2018. *Understanding Brexit: A Concise Introduction*. Bristol: Policy Press.

Outhwaite, W. 2017. *Brexit: Sociological Responses*. London: Anthem Press.

Payne, D. 2017. Britain and Europe. *LSE Archives Division Website*. Available at: http://www.lse.ac.uk/Library/Collections/Collection-highlights/Britain-and-Europe.

Pearson, A. 2017. For Brexit to Work, We Need Dunkirk Spirit Not 'Naysaying Nellies'. *Daily Telegraph*, August 1. Available at: http://www.telegraph.co.uk/women/politics/brexit-work-need-dunkirk-spirit-not-naysaying-nellies/.

Peterson, S. 1992. Transgressing Boundaries: Theories of Knowledge, Gender and International Relations. *Millennium* 21 (2): 183–206.

Politico. 2015. The Czech Donald Trump. *Politico website*, 29 October 2015. Available at: https://www.politico.eu/article/babis-czech-sobotka-politics-trump-berlusconi/.

Politico. 2017. Jacob Rees-Mogg Calls Juncker a 'Pound Shop Bismarck', August 30. Available at: https://www.politico.eu/article/jacob-rees-mogg-calls-juncker-a-pound-shop-bismarck/.

Sandhu, K., and Stephenson, M. 2015. Layers of Inequality—A Human Rights and Equality Impact Assessment of the Public Spending Cuts on Black Asian and Minority Ethnic Women in Coventry. *Feminist Review* 109: 169–179.

Scharpf, F.W. 1999. *Governing in Europe: Effective and Democratic?* Oxford: Oxford University Press.

Schimmelfennig, F. 2018. Brexit: Differentiated Disintegration in the European Union. *Journal of European Public Policy* [online first].

Shepherd, L. J. 2017. *Gender, UN Peacebuilding and the Politics of Space: Locating Legitimacy.* Oxford: Oxford University Press.

Shutes, I. 2017. When Unpaid Childcare Isn't 'Work': EU Residency Rights Have Gendered Consequences. *LSE Brexit Blog*. Available at: http://blogs.lse.ac.uk/brexit/2017/07/20/when-unpaid-childcare-isnt-work-eu-residency-rights-have-gendered-consequences/.

Simpson, E. 2017. Brexit's Dunkirk Fantasyland. *Foreign Policy Voice*, August 7. Available at: http://foreignpolicy.com/2017/08/07/brexits-dunkirk-fantasyland/.

Sjoberg, L., and S. Via. 2010. Introduction. In *Gender, War, and Militarism: Feminist Perspectives*, ed. L. Sjoberg and S. Via. Oxford: Praeger.

Soubry, A. 2016. Interview with Anna Soubry MP, 25 June 2016. Channel 4 News. Available at: https://www.youtube.com/watch?v=ERHfuzyic8M&feature=youtu.be&t=2m1s.

Stavrianakis, A., and M. Ster. 2018. Militarism and Security: Dialogue, Possibilities, and Limits. Introduction: Special Issue on *Militarism and Security: Dialogue, Possibilities, and Limits* 49 (1–2): 3–18.

Sternberg, C.S. 2013. *The Struggle for EU Legitimacy: Public Contestation, 1950–2005.* Basingstoke: Palgrave.

Vote Leave. 2016a. Five Positive Reasons to Vote Leave and Take Back Control. Available at: https://digital.library.lse.ac.uk/objects/lse:sav235yoh/read/single#page/5/mode/1up.

Vote Leave. 2016b. The UK and the European Union: The Facts. Available at: https://digital.library.lse.ac.uk/objects/lse:pen598xoz/read/single#page/2/mode/1up.

Williams, J. 2017. Why Britain Just (Briefly) Threatened to Go to War with Spain. *Vox*, April 3. Available at: https://www.vox.com/world/2017/4/3/15161114/britain-threatens-war-spain-gibraltar-brexit.

Wilson, G.K. 2017. Brexit, Trump and the Special Relationship. *British Journal of Politics and International Relations* 19 (3): 543–557.

Zalewski, M. 2010. I Don't Even Know What Gender Is: A Discussion of the Connections Between Gender, Gender Mainstreaming and Feminist Theory. *Review of International Studies* 36 (1): 3–27.

CHAPTER 3

A New World Order?

Aisha K. Gill and Nazneen Ahmed

1 Introduction

The impending, if still uncertain, British exit from the European Union has had, and will continue to have, a significant effect on gender relations and the lives of women and children in the UK, in particular. Even so, as a range of commentators have observed, the debate prior to, and even following, the referendum result was dominated by male politicians (Lucas 2016; Lewis 2016; Gupta 2017). Yet, especially among feminist legal scholars, the implications of Brexit for women have been a source of discussion, speculation and thoughtful academic analysis since calls for the referendum began (Cain 2016; Guerrina and Murphy 2016; Hozić and True 2017). Susan Millns (2018), for example, considers Brexit's potential effect on employment rights and mobility for women and children, given that much UK law on these areas is directly derived from EU policy:

> Consider what is at stake. Women's rights to equal pay, non-discrimination, maternity and subsequently parental leave, to protection at work as

A. K. Gill (✉)
Department of Social Sciences, University of Roehampton, London, UK
e-mail: a.gill@roehampton.ac.uk

N. Ahmed
UCL Department of Geography, London, UK

© The Author(s) 2019

M. Dustin et al. (eds.), *Gender and Queer Perspectives on Brexit*,
Gender and Politics, https://doi.org/10.1007/978-3-030-03122-0_3

pregnant and breast-feeding mothers and as part-time workers derive from European Union Law. British law such as the Equal Pay Act 1970, the Sex Discrimination Act 1975 and the more recent Equality Act 2010 (which brings together much of the pre-existing anti-discrimination law) were introduced in order to give effect to European Community (as it then was) obligations found in the Treaty of Rome 1957 and various pieces of secondary EU legislation such as the Equal Treatment Directive.[1]

However, alongside these implications for women, which are inherent in the impending changes to legal frameworks and the absence of female voices in the political debate, the referendum result has also had, and will continue to have, an effect on women's everyday lives. We argue that it has already had a particular impact upon the lives of black and minority ethnic (BME) women, who, in the immediate aftermath of the referendum result, became the focus of an outpouring of racist and Islamophobic attacks and assaults due to a toxic combination of misogyny and xenophobia that appeared to find legitimisation in the "Leave" result. In the wake of this hatred, Sweta Rajan-Rankin (2017) argues that considering Brexit from an intersectional feminist analytical perspective can uncover how "the Brexit vote has unearthed and reinvigorated the politics of difference and social inequalities which have for long complicated Britain's diversity project. A Black Feminist analysis makes visible these tensions and explodes popular myths of 'us' and 'them', which have long been nurtured within nationhood narratives" (Rajan-Rankin 2017, 2).

Racist incidents rose by 23% in the eleven months following the referendum result (Bulman 2017). While hate crime statistics do not reveal incidents committed specifically against women, Tell MAMA, the national project that records anti-Muslim hate crimes, noted in its 2016 report that Muslim women were especially vulnerable to racist abuse after the referendum, with a majority of Islamophobic incidents involving a Muslim female victim and a male perpetrator: "In the total number of cases reported to us in 2016, a disproportionately high number of victims (38%, $n=295$) were Muslim women wearing Islamic clothing who were sometimes actively intimidated, and even physically attacked, in public" (Tell MAMA 2017). The disproportionate focus upon women's

---

[1] Millns, S., n.d., What Does Brexit Mean for Women? http://www.sussex.ac.uk/eu/articles/brexit-women, accessed 11 March 2018.

bodies as sites for xenophobic attack during and after the referendum result was also demonstrated in the savage violence that Gina Miller[2] faced as a non-white female campaigner for Remain (Bock 2017).

In the light of these incidents and the ongoing uncertainties that the Brexit process has produced, in this chapter, we investigate a series of questions through presenting and analysing two personal accounts of the referendum result that we have written as British Asian women. How did this toxic post-result atmosphere make BME women feel as they went about their normal lives? What were the embodied effects of the referendum result for BME women?

We explore these questions through two creative, personal pieces of writing that were produced for the POEM journal special issue, "Women On Brexit," published in 2017 (Sampson et al. 2017). This specially commissioned journal issue considered the effect of Brexit through the poetic medium, and resulted in a wide range of direct and indirect meditations from female contributors on the meaning of Brexit. These varied from reflections on imperial nostalgia to discussions of the ways families have been divided by the issue of Brexit and ruminations on migration, Britishness and identity. Our two pieces are drawn together here to consider the particularities and specificities of Brexit for BME women.

The two pieces take different prose–poetic approaches to Brexit, but share some aspects that speak to BME women's broader shared experiences of Brexit, as delineated above. What is striking in the two pieces is how the effect of Brexit and the tide of violence and hostility it produced reminded both authors forcibly of other historical moments, as well as personal experiences of racism, that they had experienced at other points in their lives. In this respect, Brexit was not extraordinary; rather, it was a distillation, perhaps a culmination, of specific kinds of unspoken, intangible, yet physically felt experiences of hostility, unwelcome attitudes and xenophobia. Indeed, the second piece, *1 of Every 2*, translates Brexit into a timeline of events that also questions what it means to be British, thus situating Brexit as both a unique and a historically familiar event.

Both accounts very precisely mark the moment the authors discovered the result, and the feelings of shock, fear and sadness that followed. For both BME authors, Brexit did not simply involve certain legal and

[2] This included daily racist and sexually violent social media communications during the campaign, death threats, and a case of harassment that resulted in the subsequent conviction and jailing of the perpetrator (Rawlinson 2017).

governance issues, but signified something far greater: a of dramatic break with a set of values, a symbol of a certain kind of politics in which difference is no longer welcome. Both authors express feelings of isolation, vulnerability and fear, as if able to foretell the violence that has yet to come. In 'One of every two' *Ahmed* powerfully expresses the profoundly embodied sense of paranoia and vulnerability that accompanied being a visibly 'Other' Muslim British woman in the days after the Leave result, and the attendant sense of isolation and exposure.

There are also differences between the two accounts, suggesting the contradictions and complexities Brexit has provoked in terms of identity and belonging among the British Asian diaspora. Responding to this, *Gill's* piece 'Go Home', considers the relationship between masculinity, diasporic identities and Britishness in its reflections upon the number of British Asians who voted for Leave. It is striking that the pro-Leave quotation in this piece from a British Asian comes from a young man: a man whose life chances, aspirations and legal rights may be affected quite differently from those of women and children in the post-Brexit era.

2   A Personal Response

Much of the challenge of Brexit lies its sheer uncertainty, which makes clear analysis and understanding almost impossible, as expressed here by Ruth Cain (2016):

> For British feminist legal studies, as indeed for all socio-economic scholarship in the UK, these are discomfiting and confusing times. Lack of information on the sheer complexity of the legal and political form and consequences of the vote to leave the European Union has left the nation adrift on meaningless aphorisms, such as Prime Minister Theresa May's 'Brexit means Brexit'—whether Brexit actually means a true 'go-it-alone' for Britain remains mysterious. (Cain 2016, 1)

This uncertainty also has lived consequences. Both pieces end by reflecting on the current state of uncertainty, noting that it is having a profound effect on women's psychological, physical and financial wellbeing— as Gill observes, "we know that any financial insecurity, recession or increase in austerity affects women first and foremost". Both pieces end on a profoundly unsettled and unsettling note, wondering exactly what Brexit will mean and what its lasting legacies will be.

'One of every two'
Four hours

One of every two.

I step onto the bus more warily today. I keep my head down. I feel my heart beating double-time in my chest.

One of every two, one of every two.

I look for an unoccupied pair of seats. Sitting next to someone today seems risky, somehow. I feel exposed, vulnerable. My scarf feels like a too-bold thing, today.

One of every two, one of every two.

I catch myself doing it over and over. If I do not stop, I will go mad. I will not be able to leave the house. I will fold up and inwards and never straighten out. Always counting, counting.

One of two, one of two.

Despite myself, I look at faces and try to work it out. I hear snippets of conversations and my body springs tight in anticipation. I am still counting.

One of two, one of two.

I try a hesitant smile at someone. If they smile back, or if they do not, then I will know. They do not smile back. But I do not know. Today is not a day for smiles.

One of two, one of two.

All day I go about in this kind of paranoid, nightmarish stupor. The victorious side seems to leer with triumph on television, the defeated seem shell-shocked and scared for what the future holds. And everywhere I go in Southampton today, a city that voted 54% for Leave, I keep grouping people into lots of two, trying to work out which of them voted that way.

One of every two.

Four hours earlier

It is Ramadan. I wake up for suhoor at two in the morning and sleepily put on the television as I eat my yoghurt and watermelon. I turn it off almost immediately, heart pounding. I can't get back to sleep; I toss and turn, heartsick, feverish until dawn breaks. But light does not bring light.

In the morning, my body weighted with dread, I turn the news back on. The usual studied neutrality in the presenters' voices has been replaced with a discernible disbelief, as they read out the results of who voted, and how.

One of every two.

24 hours

The day after the result, I help run a stall that celebrates religious diversity and migration in London at something called the Utopia Fair. After what felt like a lurch into dystopia, this experience is more than a little disorientating. In the airy quadrant at Somerset House, there is uplifting music and bright interactive displays showing how academic research can help us imagine a better future, a more connected community. It is surreal, today.

We are showcasing our research project Making Suburban Faith, in which we worked with young people from Brentside School, West London. We asked the students to design a shared faith space for at least two of the area's faith communities to use together. Almost all the models they came up with incorporated separate spaces for prayer and communal places for socialising, demonstrating a fine-tuned awareness of how groups can live together with respect for difference. We hadn't guided them in this. It came from them—from their experiences of living in London and attending a highly diverse, richly multicultural school. Though the students drew on familiar, local religious buildings for inspiration, their models were bold, fantastical, surprising. Spaces of possibility.

A woman walks up to the stall, and while she looks at the photographs of these bright young people, working hard at designing a tolerant, open future, she begins weeping. "What have we done to them?" she asks, pointing to the pictures of the students. I shake my head, and find myself weeping with her.

One of every two.

One week

The weekend after the Brexit referendum, a fascist group from Portsmouth travels to Southampton to celebrate what they perceive as a victory against immigration. Over 400 people opposed to what this group stands for gather peacefully in the city centre to meet them. There is music, and the placards proudly declare, 'Refugees Welcome'. The cheerful atmosphere feels necessary, but also an effort, like Christmas dinner after a bereavement. It is a kind of healing, or the start of it at least. We smile bravely at one another, but dip frequently into sombre, head-shaking reflection as the Saturday shoppers stand and gawp at us. We wait for the fascists to turn up, to let them know that they are the ones not welcome. In the end, they decide not to march. We are too many. They go home.

One of every two.

Two weeks

My son, nearly four, has been best friends with A for two years, almost half their small lives. A is half Spanish, half Colombian. At the park today, A's mother takes a deep breath as she tells me that they will be leaving for Colombia in the next few months. See, she says ruefully, they also had a referendum there, but it had an optimistic result. Her family feels precarious here now, and they cannot live that way.

I have no words that can reassure. My son and his best friend will be separated by continents to scratch out their friendship on Skype and email, not in playgrounds with their trucks. I watch as the two of them hug and giggle and hug again. The sadness that has been building in me in layers and thickens again. I hope they will stay friends. I hope they will defy the borders and shutters and grow together in love and friendship, despite those who wish to separate them.

One of every two.

−/+

On 23 May 1937, 4000 children from the Basque region of Spain arrived at the Southampton docks, seeking refuge from the Spanish Civil War. They were homed temporarily in a camp just outside Southampton, in Stoneleigh. From there, over a period of months, they were moved to accommodation around the country. After the war ended, some of the children returned to Spain; others remained to make their lives in the UK. In Southampton, a plaque hangs on the wall of the Central Library, commemorating the children's arrival and remembering the city's part in offering them refuge.

The dock cities of Southampton and London have always been diverse places, always in flux, always open. Both have long and rich histories of migration. They were crucial in facilitating the British Empire, and have flourished as a result of the migration needed to support that empire. Our students' designs, the Utopia Fair and the counter-demonstration are all, in their own ways, examples of shared urban traditions of tolerance, understanding and openness that have endured throughout periods of uncertainty and intolerance. There have been other events like Brexit: nation-shaking events, such as the 1905 Aliens Act, fascist blackshirts marching upon Cable Street in 1930s London, Enoch Powell's 'Rivers of Blood' speech and its bloody consequences. They have come and gone, and migrants still remain.

This is not much consolation. Things will change, now. Months on, we still do not know how. People who do not feel welcome will leave. Others may not be allowed to enter. Perhaps our children will not have the same opportunities, the same freedoms, that we did. Events that have followed tell us the world's borders are hardening, that hatred is growing like a fattening monster. This is frightening for those of us who are multiple and who are other.

I hold onto this. Only one of two voted for Leave and all it stood for. The other did not. The other, who is now reeling, weeping, gathering, making, protesting.

Alongside the shock and devastation so many still feel in Brexit's wake is an urge to address the implications of the Leave vote, and the complex circumstances that led us to this point. In the following account of the referendum, attempts are made to change or at least question some of the narratives by which we live our daily lives, and to identify possible threats to our respective cultures and communities. Only then can we begin to navigate and combat the deep harm—cultural, social, political and economic—that Brexit represents.

"Go home"

The result of the UK's referendum on EU membership came as a surprise to many. Before heading for New York City, I had already sent off my postal vote—I knew for certain why my vote was so important, and I had vociferously expressed that concern to friends and acquaintances. Having noted too that the debate was being dominated by white men in pinstriped suits, I had added my name to numerous Remain campaigns, urging everyone in our communities to vote on 23 June.

My vote to remain was cast in support of hope and in recognition of all those who have fought for peace across Europe. While acknowledging that the EU system is far from perfect, crucially for those of us working to end violence against women, it must be noted that Europe's politico-economic union has established important frameworks that protect women living in the UK. My vote to remain was, therefore, also cast in the hope that many of those hard-fought legal rights and gains would be protected. The EU has made important laws in the area of employment, such as safeguarding parental leave and helping defend part-time workers (the majority of whom are women) from exploitation, and we know that any financial insecurity, recession or increase in austerity affects women first and foremost.

A few days before the referendum, as part of its 'Out' campaign, the far-right party, UKIP, unveiled a poster showing a queue of refugees with the slogan 'Breaking Point', along with a plea for the UK to leave the EU. Like most of the Leave campaigns, this poster suggested that unrestricted immigration from Europe could lead to greater competition for government services, with the tone of panic and loss of social control creating a lingering implication that uncontrolled immigration could even put British women at greater risk of sexual violence. Boris Johnson's 'Vote Leave' campaign, too, was built on racist, xenophobic rhetoric that blamed an influx of immigrants for overtaxing of schools and the healthcare system. Those of us against this nasty politics of scapegoating were standing up for the next generation, looking outwards rather than inwards and marching forward in the face of this hateful ideology.

When I was flying back from New York on the evening of 23 June, the pilot announced that the Leave campaign had won by a narrow margin. A casual silence followed, as though nothing of much note had happened. I was gutted, but it seemed my feelings were not widely shared. Only one person mirrored my sense of disbelief about the situation I was returning to in Blighty.[3]

Having landed, I phoned my brother, and he informed me that not everyone in our family had voted to remain. He joked that "Some of them have shut the door". *"Forgotten their journey from the Pind"* [village back home in the Punjab]… To top it all off, my 18-year-old niece, who was planning a weekend post-A-level break in Barcelona, seemed to be upset mostly because she wished she had bought her euros before the date of the referendum result.

I felt an overwhelming sense of dread. Why did so many British Asians vote to leave the EU? And why were they exhibiting the same xenophobic attitude as many of the white British Leave voters? Waiting in the early hours of the morning at Heathrow, I read through a Desi family WhatsApp chat group. A group of Sikh Punjabi friends and family had posted 257 messages between 23 and 24 June. Most expressed concerns about immigration, stating them in the same xenophobic 'us versus them' rhetoric used by white racists:

[3] An informal term meaning 'Britain' or 'England'.

Kick them out, it's my country and I am voting out. (Second-generation Asian male)

Fact—why don't you see what percentage of Eastern Europeans have committed crimes in this country since coming here 10–15 years [ago]—then compare [it to] when our fathers came here. And you still want them in?? (Second-generation Asian male)

One of the Punjabi women (who happened to be the sister of the above commenter) responded:

I'm happy in Hackney, all races and dogs! (Second-generation Asian female)

Growing up in an inner-city area of the East Midlands in the 1980s, I was surrounded by racism, poverty, social exclusion and inequality. Racial harassment was the norm and being called a 'Paki' was a daily occurrence—at school, on the street and even at the corner shop. It was vicious, visceral and sometimes deadly. It was also an explicit expression of the racist animosity of the larger society that my family and I inhabited back then.

For this to rear its ugly head again has replanted a seed of vulnerability in me and my fellow Asian friends that, in many ways, has caught us off guard. I have lost count of the number of racist posts my friends have reported on social media feeds since 24 June. Once again, our right to be here is being questioned. "Go home you fucking Paki", people say.

Go home? But this *is* my home. You can't send me and my family back. We don't have another home; we thought this was our home. There is a strong feeling of being pulled backwards. For example, one of my good friends posted the following on her Facebook timeline on 26 June 2016:

So, today, for the first time in a very long time on the streets of London, I have just been called the P*** word by a van driver who refused to stop for me at a zebra crossing and almost mowed me down. What is going on people?

The EU referendum result has provided a legitimate platform for multiple forms of revictimisation and discrimination. These racist attitudes are deeply rooted in our society, and no safetypin campaign is able to gloss over them.

Prepare yourselves for a future of atavistic nationalism. In calling a referendum, our (now former) Prime Minister David Cameron has unleashed a bevy of problems with ramifications that will play out for generations. He should not have called the referendum in the first place. The former Prime Minister of Belgium, Guy Verhofstadt, summed up the crisis: "The Brexiters do not have a clue what needs to be done. Cameron, Johnson and Farage behave like rats fleeing a sinking ship."

In London, the only credible politician to steady the ship has been the Mayor of London, Sadiq Khan. At the annual Pride march, he expressed a defiant message of reassurance to local communities, calling on Londoners to stand together against the tide of increasing reported hate crimes after the Brexit EU referendum vote:

> I want to send a particular message to the almost one million Europeans living in London, who make a huge contribution to our city—working hard, paying taxes and contributing to our civic and cultural life. You are welcome here. We value the enormous contribution you make to our city and that will not change as a result of this referendum. (Khan 2016)[4]

The crisis we are facing in the aftermath of this referendum, however, is deepening, with political meltdown and Machiavellian treachery among politicians unable to curb their egos and deal with the Brexit mess they have created. It is difficult to know what the costs of the referendum result for minorities and women will be. The racist fallout is just the beginning of this calamity. There is no off-the-shelf solution. Much is at stake. What we face now is finding how to live in a new world order in which hard-fought rights could be drastically undermined, in what can only be described as an atmosphere of fear and hatred against a backdrop of economic and social disruption.

3   CONCLUSION

23 June 2016 has inscribed itself into UK history. The advisory referendum has taken place, and we must bear the consequences. At the time of writing, the date we are set to leave the EU is 29 March 2019

---

[4] Sadiq Khan's Brexit EU referendum response in full: 'There Is no Need to Panic', *The Independent*, June 24, 2016 http://www.independent.co.uk/news/uk/sadiq-khans-brexit-eu-referendum-response-in-full-there-is-no-need-to-panic-a7100071.html, accessed 16 March 2018.

at 11 p.m.—although at this moment, no one really knows the conditions under which that will happen. But while the Brexit story cannot have a happy ending, we also cannot forget the 48% who did not get the result that they hoped or voted for. All we can do is offer an intervention based on our own personal experience of the vote. There is no going back—and so, for the sake of the generations who will follow us, we must remain steadfast in continuing to work for a fairer, more just society, and for cooperation and understanding across cultures and borders.

We have chosen to approach this intervention using creative writing methods rather than a conventional academic analysis. There is a growing body of academic writing reflecting on the benefits of using creative methods for academic enquiry (Rinehart 1998; Mannay 2016; Kara 2015). The benefits of such methods include making research accessible to non-academic stakeholders, uncovering areas of research enquiry that may not have been visible using traditional methods and developing trust between researcher and respondent. Rinehart (1998), in reflecting upon the particular value of creative writing for research, argues that these methods can draw out the embodied and lived experiences that lie the heart of social sciences and humanities research: "There is a sense of lyricism and even of magic in lived experience that is outside the ken of quantitative social 'science' discourse: by reducing experience to its component parts, some of this magic—for want of a better word—is lost" (Rinehart 1998: 201).

Here, the use of creative methods has been especially useful because of the complexity and intangibility of our topic. Brexit is a fractured, contradictory, uncertain entity, one we don't entirely know the meaning of. Is it an event? If so, when will it take place? Is it a verb? Then where does one 'Brexit' from? Is it a collective noun? Then who does it include, and who does it, and will it, exclude? Using creative methods has allowed us to represent and reflect upon this entity in all its contradictory multiplicities and include a range of voices and perspectives; it has also enabled us to view Brexit's consequences using an intersectional feminist lens and thus consider the effect Brexit is having, and will have, on gender, race, religion and class relations.

BIBLIOGRAPHY

Atkins, C. 2016. British Far Right Celebrates Brexit Vote, Trump Offers Congratulations. http://www.peoplesworld.org/article/british-far-right-celebrates-brexit-vote-trump-offers-congratulations/. Accessed 8 Jan 2018.

Birch, S. 2016. Our New Voters: Brexit, Political Mobilisation and the Emerging Electoral Cleavage. *Juncture: The Institute for Public Policy Research* 23 (2): 107–110.

Bock, P. 2017. Brexit Activist Gina Miller: I Never Expected This Much Racist Abuse. March 10. https://www.newstatesman.com/politics/staggers/2017/03/brexit-activist-gina-miller-i-never-expected-much-racist-abuse. Accessed 15 Mar 2018.

Bulman, M. 2017. Brexit Vote Sees Highest Spike in Religious and Racial Hate Crimes Ever Recorded. *The Independent*, July 7. http://www.independent.co.uk/news/uk/home-news/racist-hate-crimes-surge-to-record-high-after-brexit-vote-new-figures-reveal-a7829551.html. Accessed 15 Mar 2018.

Cain, R. 2016. Post-truth and the 'Metropolitan Elite' Feminist: Lessons from Brexit. *Feminists@Law* 6 (1): 1–8. http://journals.kent.ac.uk/index.php/feministsatlaw/article/view/259. Accessed 13 Mar 2018.

Casalicchio, E. 2016. Theresa May: Britain Wants a Red, White and Blue Brexit. https://www.politicshome.com/news/uk/political-parties/conservative-party/theresa-may/news/81482/theresa-may-britain-wants-red. Accessed 8 Jan 2018.

Coulter, S., and B. Hancké. 2016. *A Bonfire of the Regulations, or Business as Usual? The UK Labour Market and the Political Economy of Brexit*. http://onlinelibrary.wiley.com/doi/10.1111/1467-923X.12245/full. Accessed 15 Mar 2018.

Duff, A. 2016. Article 50: How to Leave the European Union. https://www.degruyter.com/downloadpdf/j/tfd.2016.29.issue-3/tfd-2016-0034/tfd-2016-0034.xml. Accessed 8 Jan 2018.

Gill, A.A. 2016. AA Gill Argues the Case Against Brexit. *The Times*, June 12. http://www.thetimes.co.uk/article/aa-gill-argues-the-case-against-brexit-kmnp83zrt. Accessed 8 Jan 2018.

Guerrina, R., and H. Murphy. 2016. Strategic Silences in the Brexit Debate: Gender, Marginality and Governance. *Journal of Contemporary European Research* 12 (4): 873–880.

Gupta, R. 2017. Brexit: Where Were Women's Voices? July 2. http://rahilagupta.uk/2017/07/02/brexit-where-were-womens-voices/. Accessed 15 Mar 2018.

Hozić, A., and J. True. 2017. Brexit as a Scandal: Gender and Global Trumpism. *Review of International Political Economy* 24 (2): 270–287.

Hubolt, S. 2016. The Brexit Vote: A Divided Nation, a Divided Continent. *Journal of European Public Policy* 23 (9): 1259–1277.

Inglehart, Ronald F., and Pippa Norris. 2016. Trump, Brexit, and the Rise of Populism: Economic Have-Nots and Cultural Backlash. https://ces.fas.

harvard.edu/uploads/files/events/Inglehart-and-Norris-Populism.pdf. Accessed 8 Jan 2018.

Kara, H. 2015. *Creative Research Methods in the Social Sciences: A Practical Guide*. Bristol: Policy Press.

Kent, A. 2016. Political Cartography: From Bertin to Brexit. *The Cartographic Journal* 53 (3): 199–201.

Lewis, H. 2016. Brexit Is a Feminist Issue. *The Guardian*, March 20. https://www.theguardian.com/politics/2016/mar/20/women-europe-referendum-debate-brexit. Accessed 12 Mar 2018.

Lucas, C. 2016. 'White Men in Grey Suits' Dominating EU Debate, Says Caroline Lucas. *The Guardian*, January 27. https://www.theguardian.com/politics/2016/mar/20/women-europe-referendum-debate-brexit. Accessed 12 Mar 2018.

Mannay, D. 2016. *Visual, Narrative and Creative Research Methods: Application, Reflection and Ethics*. Abingdon: Routledge.

Millns, S. n.d. What Does Brexit Mean for Women? http://www.sussex.ac.uk/eu/articles/brexit-women. Accessed 11 Mar 2018.

Onions, I. 2016. European Referendum Result: Bristol Votes by Large Majority to Remain in European Union. http://www.bristolpost.co.uk/referendum-result-bristol-votes-by-large-majority-to-remain-in-europe/story-29439074-detail/story.html#yOockoblid3Vv8Oz.99. Accessed 15 Mar 2018.

Pettifor, A. 2016. Brexit and Its Consequences. *Globalizations*: 127–132. http://www.tandfonline.com/doi/abs/10.1080/14747731.2016.1229953. Accessed 8 Jan 2018.

Rajan-Rankin, S. 2017. Brexit Logics: Myth and Fact—A Black Feminist Analysis. *Feminists@Law* 7 (2): 1–2. http://journals.kent.ac.uk/index.php/feministsatlaw/article/view/423/1072. Accessed 11 Mar 2018.

Rawlinson, K. 2017. Viscount Jailed for Offering Money for Killing of Gina Miller. *The Guardian*, July 13. https://www.theguardian.com/uk-news/2017/jul/13/viscount-jailed-for-offering-money-for-killing-of-gina-miller. Accessed March 21, 2018.

Rinehart, R. 1998. Fictional Methods in Ethnography: Believability, Specks of Glass, and Chekhov. *Qualitative Inquiry* 4 (2): 200–224.

Rose, A. 2016. Why Estimates of the Trade Effects of the Eurozone Vary so Much. http://faculty.haas.berkeley.edu/arose/VoxWhy.pdf. Accessed 23 Dec 2016.

Sampson, F., A.K. Gill, and M. Arshi. 2017. Women on Brexit. *Poem: International English Language Quarterly* 5 (2–3): 148–160.

Tell MAMA. 2017. *2016 Annual Report: A Constructed Threat: Identity, Intolerance and the Impact of Anti-Muslim Hatred*. London: Faith Matters.

Wallace, H. 2016. Heading for the Exit: the United Kingdom's Troubled Relationship with the European Union. *Journal of Contemporary European Research* 12 (4): 809–815.

PART II

The UK and the EU: What Future Ahead?

CHAPTER 4

The Unintended Consequences of Brexit: The Case of Work-Life Balance

Eugenia Caracciolo di Torella

1   INTRODUCTION

On 23 June 2016, with a narrow majority the UK decided to leave the European Union (EU), a process known as Brexit, thus ending a membership spanning over four decades (Raitio and Raulus 2017).[1] The debate for and against Brexit was run on emotional arguments rather than rational facts and, as a result, it was at best simplistic and at worst

---

[1] The 'Vote Leave, Take Control' campaign won by 51.9–48.1%; England voted for Brexit by 53.4–46.6%, as did Wales, by 52.5–47.5%. Scotland and Northern Ireland both backed the 'Britain Stronger in Europe' campaign. Scotland voted against Brexit by 62–38%, so did Northern Ireland where 55.8% voted to remain and 44.2% to leave.

I am indebted to all the participants to the EFTA High Level Seminar on European Labour Authority and Work-Life Balance, Brussels 13 March 2018 where some of the ideas in this paper were first discussed and to G. James, O. Golynker, A. Masselot and A. Stewart for comments on earlier versions. Any errors are my sole responsibility.

E. Caracciolo di Torella (✉)
Leicester Law School, University of Leicester, University Road, Leicester, UK
e-mail: eugenia.caracciolo@leicester.ac.uk

© The Author(s) 2019   61
M. Dustin et al. (eds.), *Gender and Queer Perspectives on Brexit*,
Gender and Politics, https://doi.org/10.1007/978-3-030-03122-0_4

misleading. It simply did not convey the risks and the complexities of leaving the EU. The main reasons why people voted to leave related to immigration, fisheries, economic considerations and national sovereignty, with 'Brussels' portrayed as a faceless bureaucrat taking national power away (Guerrina and Murphy 2016). However, it soon became clear that the consequences of leaving the EU are more wide-reaching than originally envisaged. This is because of the degree to which EU law and policy have become embedded in and intertwined with the UK legal system: the greater the reliance of a specific national policy on the EU, the greater the impact will be (Guerrina and Masselot 2018). In many cases, Leavers did not anticipate these effects. Indeed, the Vote Leave campaign showed an 'overarching blindness' (Guerrina and Masselot 2018, 1) to such links.

This chapter joins those voices that have expressed their concern for the impact that Brexit is likely to have on employment and social rights and on the consequences on marginalised groups such as women and carers—the majority of whom are women (Fawcett Society 2018; McCrudden 2018). In particular, it focuses on the principle of work-life balance. It maintains that, although the work of the EU in this area has not been above criticism (Crompton and Lyonette 2006; Caracciolo di Torella and Masselot 2010; McGlynn 2001; Busby and James 2011; Busby 2011), it has been instrumental in shaping an agenda and creating a policy and normative framework that has counterbalanced the UK's neoliberal approach.

This chapter is organised as follows. Section 2 explores the development of the concept of work-life balance in EU law and how it has become part of UK employment law and policy. Section 3 proceeds to analyse how the EU and the UK have engaged with specific groups, namely pregnant workers and new mothers, on the one hand, and fathers, working parents and carers, on the other. Section 4 then focuses on the consequences of Brexit for work-life balance. It identifies three scenarios or approaches that might be used by the UK Government to address future EU legislation. There is, however, so much more than 'just legislation' at stake. Domestic policies and legislation will no longer be underpinned by the EU framework and principles, nor will UK workers be able to benefit from the 'safety net' provided by the Court of Justice of the European Union (CJEU).[2] The analysis would not be complete without considering the 'Brexit effect' on the EU, which is examined in Sect. 5. This chapter concludes that leaving the EU is likely to jeopardise and stifle any achievements in this area. Thus it would be important, although unlikely, to have a clear commitment from the Government that the rights involved will not be affected and that the UK Government will keep a constructive dialogue open with the EU in this area. The consequences of Brexit will not be felt only by the UK, however. Although to a different (and much lesser) extent, they will also be felt by the EU. This is truly a situation where there are no winners.

2 THE CONCEPT OF WORK-LIFE BALANCE

Work-life balance is now a well-established feature that has become part of the language of UK employment legislation. Its origins are in the EU and can be traced back to the 1974 Social Action Plan that called for measures to 'ensure that the family responsibilities of all concerned may be reconciled with their job aspiration' (see *Journal of Social Welfare and Family Law* 2015).[3] The principle was devised to allow *mothers* to be able to look after their young family while carrying on working, thus contributing to the economy. Thus work-life balance started its life with a clear economic connotation. Since then, however, thanks to a sophisticated array of primary and secondary legislation, it has developed beyond recognition and it is now accepted that it is a broad and flexible concept covering a variety of situations. Today, it has been extended to fathers and, to a degree, to other carers; it is also no longer restricted to young children but also to other dependants. The CJEU case law, in the main, has been instrumental to this process[4]; for example, it has

---

[2] EU (Withdrawal) Bill 2017–19, Clause 6(1)(a).

[3] Council Resolution of 21 January 1974 Concerning a Social Action Programme, OJ 1974 C 1/13. Prior to 1974, the only document that referred to these issues was the 1961 European Social Charter. However, Article 27 established the right to *maternity* leave and the economic, legal and social protection of *family life, mothers* and *children* (emphasis added) and it was not until the 1996 (R)ESC that Article 27 was amended to cover the Rights of Workers with Family Responsibilities to Equal Opportunities and Equal Treatment.

[4] There have also been some disappointing decisions such as Case C-218/98, *Oumar Dabo Abdoulaye and Others and Régie Nationale des Usines Renault SA*, ECLI:EU:C:1999:424 and Case C-5/12, *Marc Betriu Montull v INSS*, ECLI:EU:C:2013:571.

interpreted work-life balance as a 'natural corollary' of the fundamental right to equality[5] Furthermore, the inclusion in the EU Charter of Fundamental Rights (CFR)[6] of a specific provision stating that '[t]o reconcile family and professional life, everyone shall have the right to protection from dismissal for a reason connected with maternity and the right to paid maternity leave and to parental leave following the birth or adoption of a child' (Article 33(1)) has conferred a constitutional value upon it. The commitment to work-life balance has been more recently confirmed by the European Pillar on Social Rights[7] (Bell 2018; Plomien 2018). Although non-binding, this initiative covers a range of rights connected to social policy and, ultimately, aims to 'stand up for the rights of its citizens in a fast-changing world' (Junker 2017). More specifically it is based on 20 principles one of which specifically provides that '[p]arents and people with caring responsibilities have the right to suitable leave, flexible working arrangements and access to care services. Women and men shall have equal access to special leaves of absence in order to fulfil their caring responsibilities and be encouraged to use them in a balanced way' (Principle 9). This is strengthened by a commitment to affordable childcare (Principle 11a) as well as long term care (Principle 18). The trajectory of the principle of work-life balance from an economic tool to an investment in citizens is thus clear.

In the UK, the concept of work-life balance has come a long way from it modest origins. Although placed on the EU agenda in 1974, it was only over two decades later, when the New Labour Government came to power in 1997, that the UK started to embrace it (Lewis and Campbell 2007; McColgan 2000). In the introduction to the White Paper *Fairness at Work*, the then Prime Minister Tony Blair referred to the need 'to change the culture of relations in and at work (…) to reflect a new relationship between work and family life (…) where to be a good parent is not in conflict with being a good employee' (Blair 1999). *Fairness at Work* introduced an array of family-friendly measures, ranging

---

[5] Case C-243/95, *Hill and Stapleton v The Revenue Commissioners and Department of Finance*, ECLI:EU:C:1998:298, para. 42 (my emphasis); Case C-1/95, *Hellen Gerster v Freistaat Bayern*, ECLI:EU:C:1997:452, para. 38.

[6] 2010/C 83/02.

[7] https://ec.europa.eu/commission/priorities/deeper-and-fairer-economic-and-monetary-union/european-pillar-social-rights_en, accessed 25 July 2018.

from 'keeping-in touch' days to paternity leave (James 2007). If work-life balance was New Labour's child, it was subsequently adopted by the Conservative-Liberal Democrat Coalition Government (Golynker 2015). The Coalition Government indeed took some important steps that furthered its development. Unfortunately, since then the Conservative Government that followed has been less committed to these issues and has dropped the needs of parents and carers from the agenda to focus on productivity (Golynker 2015).

3   THE EU ACQUIS AND THE UK LEGISLATION

In practice, work-life balance entails specific rights aiming to protect parents in the workplace. This section analyses how these rights have developed at EU and UK level, with a view to showing how far EU principles and legislation have shaped UK legislation and policy.

Expectant and New Mothers

Pregnant workers and new mothers in the UK can now rely on 52 weeks of maternity leave: 26 weeks of ordinary maternity leave and 26 weeks of additional maternity leave.[8] Of these, the two weeks after the birth are compulsory. Maternity pay lasts for 39 weeks[9]: for the first six weeks, pay is at 90% of weekly earnings or a flat rate of £145.18 (whichever is lower) and for the remainder of the leave at a flat rate. Prima facie, this might be seen more generous compared with the 14 weeks offered by the Pregnant Workers Directive. Furthermore, the Children and Families Act 2014 for the first time included commissioning mothers in case of surrogacy (s. 122). This can also be seen as an improvement on the EU situation.

Let us not forget, however, that EU provisions and the CJEU case law have triggered and shaped the UK framework of rights for pregnant women and new mothers in the workplace. To start with, before the CJEU's (then European Court of Justice, ECJ) seminal decision

---

[8] The Maternity and Parental Leave Regulations 1999 (SI 1999/3312), as amended by the Maternity and Parental Leave and Paternity and Adoption Leave (Amendment) Regulation 2006.

[9] The Statutory Maternity Pay, Social Security (Maternity Allowance) and Social Security (Overlapping Benefits) (Amendment) Regulations 2006 (SI 2006/2379).

in *Dekker*,[10] the UK had not addressed pregnancy and maternity as an equality issue. On that occasion, the Court established two pivotal principles. First, only women can become pregnant, therefore the refusal to engage a pregnant woman because of pregnancy or maternity amounts to direct discrimination on grounds of sex; second, in the case of pregnancy, the absence of a male comparator is irrelevant. Before this judgment, in England, as only women could become pregnant, simply there was no comparison and therefore no discrimination: 'when she is pregnant a woman is no longer a woman. She is a woman, as the Authorised version [of the Bible] accurately puts it, with child and there is no masculine equivalent'.[11] The principle was tested again in English courts a few years later, when Mrs. Webb, after being employed on a temporary contract to replace another woman on maternity leave, discovered that she was herself pregnant. When her position was terminated, she claimed unlawful dismissal. The domestic tribunals and courts maintained that she had not suffered discrimination, because a man absent in similar circumstances would have been dismissed too. When the case was finally referred to the Court of Justice, it was ruled that, as only women can become pregnant, treating them unfavourably because of pregnancy amounted to direct discrimination contrary to the Equal Treatment Directive.[12]

In the same vein, before the 1992 Pregnant Workers Directive, in the UK individuals had to be employed for two years before claiming maternity pay.[13] This had the effect of excluding thousands of individuals from entitlement to maternity rights. By contrast, in the case of *Danosa,* the CJEU expressly held that *all* pregnant workers are entitled to protection, regardless of how the relationship with an employer is classified.[14] The Pregnant Workers Directive has also led to other rights being introduced

---

[10] Case C-177/88, *Elisabeth Johanna Pacifica Dekker v Stichting Vormingscentrum voor Jong Volwassenen (VJV-Centrum) Plus*, ECLI:EU:C:1990:383.

[11] *Turley* v *Allders Department Stores Ltd* [1980] IRLR 4.

[12] Case C-32/93, *Carole Louise Webb v EMO Air Cargo* (UK) Ltd, ECLI:EU:C:1994:300. Council Directive 76/207/EEC of 10 February 1975 on the implementation of the principle of equal treatment for men and women as regards access to employment, vocational training and promotion, and working conditions OJ [1976] L 39/40 1976, as amended by Directive 2002/73, OJ [2002] L 269/15 2002.

[13] S 35 Employment Protection Act 1975.

[14] Case C-232/88, *Dita Danosa v LKB Līzings SIA*, ECLI:EU:C:2010:674.

into UK legislation, such as the duty to assess the workplace for specific risks to pregnant workers and new mothers and to make adjustments for those employees who are at risk of harm. Prior to that, a woman who could no longer carry out her normal duty because of pregnancy could have been dismissed if no alternative employment was available.[15] Other rights introduced include the right to take time off to attend antenatal appointments, a prohibition on dismissal from the beginning of the pregnancy until the end of maternity leave, as well as the maintenance of terms and conditions of employment during the maternity leave.

The UK Government traditionally perceived the rights discussed above as imposing constraints and 'red tape' on business.[16] Thus, it is not surprising that it strongly opposed the introduction of the Pregnant Workers Directive which in order to be adopted had to change its legal base from an equality measure (at the time, Article 119 of the Treaty establishing the European Community (EC), requiring unanimity in the Council) to a health and safety measure (at the time, Article 118a EC requiring qualified majority). More recently, the UK blocked the revision of the Pregnant Workers Directive proposed in 2008[17] which aimed to substantially strengthen the rights of women. In particular, it objected to the proposed increase in paid maternity leave, as it was considered too burdensome for employers. On that occasion, Nigel Farage, the UK Member of the European Parliament (MEP) and a prominent voice in the Brexit debate, commented '[t]he European Parliament, in their foolishness, have voted for increased maternity pay. I'm off for a drink'.[18]

Provisions for Fathers, Parents and Carers

Even if initially fathers were not part of the work-life balance discourse at EU level, in recent years, their role as caregivers has increasingly been discussed in policy documents (e.g. European Commission 2008; Caracciolo di Torella 2014). Furthermore, the CJEU has taken a very proactive stance. In the case of *Roca Alvarez*, it held that 'the position of

---

[15] S. 60 EPA 1978.

[16] In order to address this the UK Government developed the 'Cutting Red Tape Reviews' aimed at freeing firms from over-regulation and increase productivity, https:// civilservice.blog.gov.uk/2014/10/31/the-red-tape-challenge/, accessed 25 July 2018.

[17] COM (2008) 600/4, as part of the Work-Life Balance Package (COM (2008) 635).

[18] Nigel Farage (@Nigel_Farage) Twitter, 20 October 2010.

a male and female worker, father and mother of a young child, are comparable with regard to their possible need (...) to look after the child'.[19] The same message was then reiterated in the same terms in the case of *Maïstrellis*.[20] Despite this growing awareness, to date, EU law does not grant fathers an *individual right* to leave and pay.[21] The only reference to fathers in the legislation is in the Amended Equal Treatment Directive[22] and in the Recast Directive.[23] Article 2(7) of the Amended Equal Treatment Directive states that the Directive 'is (...) without prejudice to the right of Member States to recognise distinct rights to paternity and/or adoption leave'. Article 16 of the Recast Directive on paternity and adoption leave confirms that '[t]hose Member States which recognise (paternity) rights shall take the necessary measures to protect working men (...) against dismissal due to exercising those rights and ensure that, at the end of such leave, they are entitled to return to their jobs or to equivalent posts on terms and conditions which are no less favourable to them, and to benefit from any improvement in working conditions to which they would have been entitled during their absence.' In other words, the current EU legislation simply requires those Member States that already provide for such rights to take the necessary measures to protect against discrimination individuals who use those rights.

Prima facie, the position of fathers as caregivers might appear more robust at domestic level. In the UK, paternity leave, for those who qualify,[24] was introduced by New Labour in 2002.[25] The Coalition

---

[19] Case C-104/09, *Pedro Manuel Roca Álvarez v Sesa Start España ETT SA*, ECLI:EU:C:2010:561, at para. 24, ECLI:EU:C:2015:473.

[20] Case C-222/14, *Konstantinos Maïstrellis v Ypourgos Dikaiosynis, Diafaneias kai Anthropinon Dikaiomaton*, ECLI:EU:C:2015:473.

[21] See Recital 13 and Article 2(7) of the Council 2002/73/EC, OJ [2002] L269/15.

[22] Council Directive 76/207/EEC of 10 February 1975 on the implementation of the principle of equal treatment for men and women as regards access to employment, vocational training and promotion, and working conditions OJ [1976] L 39/40 1976, as amended by Directive 2002/73, OJ [2002] L 269/15 2002.

[23] Directive 2006/54/EC of the European Parliament and of the Council of 5 July 2006 on the implementation of the principle of equal opportunities and equal treatment of men and women in matters of employment and occupation (recast), OJ [2006] L/204.

[24] An employee must have worked 26 weeks by the 15th week before the baby is due and have given notice 15 weeks before the due date of when the leave is to start.

[25] The Paternity and Adoption Leave Regulation 2002 (SI 278).

Government further strengthened the rights of fathers and introduced the Additional Paternity Leave that has now been substituted by the Shared Parental Leave (SPL)[26] (Mitchell 2015). None of these rights has proven particularly successful, however. A Trade Union Congress (TUC) analysis found that whereas 91% of fathers took some leave after childbirth and 71% took paternity leave of one or two weeks immediately after the birth, only 0.6% took additional paternity leave in 2011 and 2012 (Eurofund 2015, see also Gordon 2017 and Weldon-Johns 2011). SPL allows the birth mother to curtail her maternity leave and share the rest with the father. Moreover, whilst SPL is available to both parents, in reality the father or the mother's partner can only access it if the mother is both eligible and willing to relinquish her maternity leave. In other words, it is *her* decision to elect to take SPL (Horton 2018). Furthermore, the SPL's sheer complexity and poor level of payment mean that, despite the intention to provide parents with choice, it defeats the attempt of involving fathers in childcare (James 2016). In practice, this right challenges neither fathers' traditional positions within the family and paid work, nor their parenting role. Thus, although at the moment EU law does not grant fathers individual rights,[27] it offers a framework to develop them.

EU law is to be credited with triggering the adoption of gender neutral rights at domestic level. Most notably, the Employment Act 1999 granted parents 13 weeks leave per year in order to look after their children up to the age of eight. The right was based on the Parental Leave Directive, from which the UK originally had been excluded when John Major (the then Conservative Prime Minister) successfully negotiated an opt-out from the Social Chapter of the Maastricht Treaty (Hervey 1994). It was only when the New Labour Government came into power that the UK opted into the Social Chapter and the Directive was implemented. The UK, however, has traditionally given this right a restrictive interpretation (Caracciolo di Torella 2007). Essentially, if the employer and the employee cannot reach a mutually convenient agreement, the default option applies, namely the leave can only be taken in blocks of weeks with no more than four weeks in a given year. The Coalition Government sought to expand the scope of the domestic right that is

[26]Shared Parental Leave Regulations 2014.

[27]But see the discussion in section 'The EU Acquis: So Much More Than Just Legislation and Case Law'.

now available to parents of children up to the age of 18.[28] Although far from perfect, the right is potentially an important one. It was the first UK instrument that de facto granted rights to fathers. The TUC has calculated that today some 8.3 million parents are potentially eligible to use that right (TUC 2018/2016, 8).

The Parental Leave Directive also introduced a right to 'reasonable' time off to provide urgent assistance to dependants, which can be used not only by parents but also by people who have other dependants.[29] This could be the case, for example, of a breaking down of childcare arrangements or if a relative or a dependant falls ill, making it an entitlement not only for parents but also for carers.[30] This is truly the first measure that acknowledges that work-life balance is not limited to children. The TUC has recently estimated that this right has been used by 5.3 million employees (TUC 2018/2016, 9).

Another domestic provision triggered by EU law has been the Flexible Working Regulation.[31] Since its introduction, it has been amended on several occasions. Following the Children and Families Act 2014, it applies to any employee who has been continuously working with the same employer for at least 26 weeks. The right can be used by parents and carers to gain more control over their family arrangements. It thus has the potential to stimulate cultural change and make flexible working practice the norm. In practice, however, recent case law has highlighted how this right has been interpreted as instrumental to enhance productivity and prioritising the needs of employers' needs over those of parents and carers. In 2015, the Employment Tribunal (ET) held that the rejection of a request for flexible working arrangements, because it was not in the interest of the business as it would cause 'minor but more than minimal inconvenience', was acceptable.[32] In the same vein, in a further case, despite acknowledging that requiring women to work full time might place them at a disadvantage, as they are more likely to be sole parents, it

---

[28] The Flexible Working Regulations 2014, No. 3221.

[29] S. 57A(1) ERA 1996.

[30] *Darlington v Alders of Croydon Unreported Employment Tribunal*, Case n. 2304217/01 and *Qua v John Ford Morrison Solicitor* [2003] ICR 482 (EAT).

[31] S. 80 ERA 1996.

[32] *Whiteman v CPS Interiors Ltd and Others*, ET/2601103/2015.

prioritised the employer's legitimate aim to have 'efficient secretarial support throughout the week'.[33]

4 THE POST-BREXIT SCENARIO: AN EDUCATED GUESS

After having looked at how the relevant domestic legislation is heavily shaped and influenced by the EU, this chapter will now seek to assess the likely impact of Brexit on this area. There are three possible scenarios: a *status quo*, a progressive and a regressive one.

The Status Quo and the Progressive Scenarios

In the *status quo* scenario, the situation will remain largely unchanged. The domestic legislative framework will remain the same and, as the UK statutory framework in this area is prima facie more comprehensive than the EU one, one might not expect UK workers' rights to be compromised on the UK's departure from the EU. Indeed, Theresa May has promised to guarantee workers' rights after leaving the EU (Mance 2017). In this scenario, the UK might also 'voluntarily' adopt new EU legislation, as it would make business sense. This scenario, however, is, at least politically, unlikely. Furthermore, even if in some form or another current rights may continue to exist, the situation could occur where, in a specific domestic dispute, a national judge might give a restrictive interpretation of EU-derived rights. In this case, a precedent could potentially be set and there would no longer be the 'safety net' provided by the CJEU, which when it comes to social rights in general and work-life balance in particular, has traditionally taken a progressive stance. Indeed, UK courts will not be bound by CJEU decisions made on or after the end of the Brexit transition period.[34] The CJEU jurisprudence will not bind the Supreme Court or the or the High Court of Justiciary; there is merely a commitment that 'in deciding whether to depart from any retained EU case law, the Supreme Court or the High Court of Justiciary must apply the same test as it would apply in deciding whether to depart from its own case law'[35] (Department for Exiting the European Union 2018). Equally the CFR will no longer be binding

---

[33] *Smith v Gleacher Shacklock*, ET/2202747/2015.

[34] European Union (Withdrawal) Act 2018, Clause 6(1)(a).

[35] European Union (Withdrawal) Act 2018, Clause 6(4) and (5).

on the UK (Clause 5(4) The EU (Withdrawal) Act 2018). This is regrettable, as the CFR enhanced the constitutional dimension of work-life balance (or reconciliation between work and family life) and has been relied upon by the CJEU.

A *progressive* scenario would see the UK 'free' to develop its own legislation in this area and to build upon and improve on current EU standards. This argument, however, does not consider that there is nothing in the relevant Directives that would prevent the UK from providing higher standards now.[36] Furthermore, it is an established principle that Directives cannot be used to lower domestic standards that are already higher.[37] Indeed, it can be argued that the UK is already 'progressive' in the sense that its legislation in this area is already more developed than the EU's: the period of maternity leave is considerably longer under domestic law, fathers already have the possibility to take paternity leave and pay, the system of leave under SPL is geared in such way as to offer more choice to parents.[38] Furthermore, recently the Children and Families Act 2014 has provided rights to commissioning mothers in surrogacy agreements.[39] These rights, at the moment, are lacking at EU level (Caracciolo di Torella and Foubert 2015). However, a closer look reveals that these initiatives are mainly cosmetic: mothers might have longer leave and fathers can have a specific entitlement, but it is unlikely that they can afford to enjoy it in its entirety. Equally, the complexity of SPL casts doubts on its effectiveness as an instrument to promote

[36] For example, Article 27(1) of the Recast Directive (Minimum Requirements) states that 'Member States may introduce or maintain provisions which are more favourable to the protection of the principle of equal treatment than those laid down in this Directive'.

[37] Article 27(2) of the Recast Directive (Minimum Requirements) states that '[i]mplementation of this Directive shall under no circumstances be sufficient grounds for a reduction in the level of protection of workers in the areas to which it applies' and in the without prejudice to the Member States' right to respond to changes in the situation by introducing laws, regulations and administrative provisions which differ from those in force on the notification of this Directive, provided that the provisions of this Directive are complied with'; in the same vein Article 1(3) of the Pregnant Workers Directive states that '[t]his Directive may not have the effect of reducing the level of protection afforded to pregnant workers, workers who have recently given birth or who are breastfeeding as compared with the situation which exists in each Member State on the date on which this Directive is adopted'.

[38] See the discussion in section 'Provisions for Fathers, Parents and Carers'.

[39] S. 122 Children and Families Act 2014.

change. In light of this, it is questionable how progressive the UK might prove to be post-Brexit.

The Regressive Scenario

In reality, however, future UK Governments will be free to decide the course of action in areas currently regulated by EU law. Thus, depending on the agreed terms of the relationship with the EU, the UK will not be obliged to implement any EU-level future developments. This scenario is likely to be a regressive one. A discussion on future developments is particularly pertinent in the context of work-life balance because, at the time of writing, the Council of the EU and the European Parliament are discussing the adoption of the proposed Work-Life Balance Directive[40] (Caracciolo di Torella 2017). Although the final outcome of this legislative proposal is still uncertain, it gives a firm sense of the policy discussion in this area and the direction that the EU wants to take.

Under the regressive scenario, it is questionable whether the UK will seek to mirror the potential benefits of the Work-Life Balance Directive. This is regrettable since, in any case, if adopted, the Directive may not automatically apply to the UK (UK Parliament 2017). By building upon existing provisions, the proposed Directive will considerably enhance the work-life balance of parents and carers. It repeals the Parental Leave Directive (Article 19) and broadly strengthens the right to parental leave, introduces individual rights for fathers and carers, and, finally, grants the possibility for working flexibly to parents and carers.

As for parental leave, the main innovations relate to the fact that Member States shall ensure an adequate income, at least at the level of sick pay (Article 8), and that the right to take the leave will be 'on a part-time basis, in blocks separated by periods of work or in other flexible forms' (Article 5(6)). These changes would affect the UK, where domestic provisions on parental leave have traditionally been unpaid and inflexible.[41] These would encourage the uptake, in particular by fathers, which so far has been minimal both across Europe and in the UK (Eurofund 2015). The proposed Directive also introduces an individual right to paternity leave (Article 4), intended as a short period of leave of at least

---

[40] COM (2017) 253 final, 2017/0085 (COD).

[41] *Rodway v South West Trains* [2005] IRLR 583 as noted by Caracciolo di Torella (2007).

ten working days, for fathers around the time of the birth of a child. Furthermore, in this case, leave will be compensated (Article 8). The right is not only for fathers, but also for second parents, and is granted irrespective of marital or family status as defined in national law (Article 4). This would not necessarily improve the existing UK legal framework, but it would add an 'extra layer' of protection. Perhaps more remarkable is the introduction of a specific provision for carers' leave, defined as 'a worker providing personal care or support in case of a serious illness or dependency of a relative' (Article 6). This grants working carers at least five working days of leave per year in the event of serious illness or dependency of a relative. Needless to say, it is a significant improvement: at the time of writing neither EU (Caracciolo di Torella 2016) nor UK (Herring 2013) legislation caters comprehensively for the needs of informal carers. Indeed, in the UK context, Herring has long suggested 'carers get a raw deal' (2007). This is a cause for concern, as it has a clear effect on women's participation in the employment market: at the time of writing, the closest the current legislation comes to granting carer leave is leave for *force majeure*,[42] which provides that workers can take unpaid time off for workers caring for seriously ill or dependent relatives. Although this is the only true *family*—rather than just *child*—friendly provision, it is a right to take time off to (swiftly) address emergencies, rather than a right to care. Article 6 builds on this provision and grants working carers the right to take at least five days per year, compensated at least at sick pay level.

Finally, Article 9 confers upon parents and carers the possibility to request to work flexibly and to adapt their working schedules to their personal needs and preferences, so that they can better balance their work and caring responsibilities. Prima facie this is the least innovative of the measures at both domestic and EU level. Its importance should not be underestimated, however. The proposed measure is important for three main reasons. First, conceptually, this is the first time that flexible forms of employment have been expressly linked to the broader concept of caring responsibilities. Previously, legislation prohibited discrimination on grounds of part-time work, but was not devised with working parents (and certainly not carers) in mind. Secondly, it adds the possibility of working remotely to the traditional flexible working arrangements.

---

[42] Already contemplated in Article 7(1) Directive 2010/18/EU (OJ 2010 L68/13) on Parental Leave and in Article 7 of the proposed Directive.

There is a wealth of evidence that suggests that this is crucial to allow individuals (in particular women) to remain in employment when they have children. Parents and carers will be able, for example, to reduce their commuting time and the expenses involved. Thirdly, Article 9 provides the possibility of returning to full-time work when individual circumstances change. The renewed focus on flexibility is an overdue, welcome and concrete way to address the needs of working parents and carers. Its full potential is reinforced by the European Pillar of Social Rights. Principle 5 expresses a commitment 'to *fair* and equal treatment'[43] regarding working conditions, 'regardless of the type and duration of the employment relationship'. Had it been in place before, cases such as *Coleman*[44] might not have occurred. That specific case, referred to the CJEU by an English court, concerned a request from an employee to work flexibly in order to care for her disabled child. The request was refused and Ms Coleman was branded as 'lazy' and 'not committed' because she had to take time off to care for her disabled son. By contrast, the proposed Directive and principle 5 of European Pillar of Social Rights would lay the foundation to address situations such as this differently, or at least to see them from a different perspective.

The proposed Directive is perhaps only one of the many steps that should be taken to offer those who have on-going caring responsibilities the opportunity to care on a regular basis whilst working. Yet, it is an unprecedented initiative that has the real potential to reconceptualise the area. Under the regressive scenario, these enhancements to existing rights may not be taken up by the UK.

The EU Acquis: *So Much More Than Just Legislation and Case Law*

It is not only the uncertainty concerning the status of the current legislation, as well as the implementation of future laws, that is a cause for concern: there is much more at stake than 'just' legislation. To start with, the principle of work-life balance has also developed through a sophisticated set of non-legislative instruments, such as soft law measures, exposure to benchmarking mechanisms and financial tools (Fagan and Rubery 2017). Soft law includes Opinions, Communcations and policy

---

[43] Emphasis added.

[44] Case C-303/06, *Coleman v Attridge Law and Steve Law*, ECLI:EU:C:2008:415. But see, also, the case C-221/13, *Mascellani v Ministero della Giustizia*, EU:C:2014:2286.

papers (Mosher and Trubek 2003) and it presents a variety of benefits. To start with, because it is not binding, it offers greater flexibility, which fits better with the diverse national legal systems of the Member States. These may indeed lack the necessary political will and the resources to create individual rights. Soft law can also be a more apt instrument than hard law under certain circumstances, because it does not incorporate the inevitable compromises that can water down the substantive content of the measures. In this way, it can provide evidence of the EU and Member States' commitment to specific issues; it can also be used as an interpretative instrument by national courts, and it has paved the way for the adoption of binding measures. The proposed New Start Programme to Support Work-Life Balance for Working Parents and Carers[45] is the most recent example. Ultimately, in the area of work-life balance, soft law has been instrumental in creating a strategy and shaping a culture that is conducive to gender equality.

Exposure to benchmarking mechanisms, such as the Open Method of Coordination (OMC), is also important when it comes to work-life balance. OMC is a process that relies on the regular monitoring of progress to meet specified agreed targets, thus allowing Member States to compare their efforts and learn from the experiences of others (Zeitlin 2005, 2007). In the words of the European Council, it is 'a means of spreading best practice and achieving greater convergence towards the main EU goals' (European Council 2000). OMC is particularly useful in areas such child and eldercare, where differences between Member States are considerable or where the EU has no or few competences (Radulova 2009). In keeping with its aim to enhance standards and foster an environment where Member States co-operate, within this framework Member States have agreed important principles. Without this framework, the UK will inevitably become more insular. Finally, financial tools such as the European Social Funds and the European research and development funding have made possible the creation of several initiatives. A good example is the recent EU commitment in the proposed Directive to make funding available to develop child and long term care facilities in the Member States. The proposed Directive will also provide funding under the Programme for Employment and Social Innovation[46] for

[45]COM (2017) 252 final.
[46]http://ec.europa.eu/social/main.jsp?catId=1081.

new pilot schemes addressed to employers for the development of innovative working arrangements such as family leave and flexible working arrangements.

It is thus very likely that the removal of these mechanisms will have a negative impact on the rights of UK workers that are trying to reconcilie work and family life.

Furthermore, whilst the UK has historically leaned towards approaching this area in terms of individual rights aimed at protecting autonomous choices, productivity and economic considerations, the EU, although not immune to criticisms and economic reasoning (Fagan and Rubery 2017), has sought to balance these considerations with a more social rights based approach. In other words, over the years the EU has striven to develop a 'human face' (Ferreira 2016) and has played a pivotal role in including gender equality in the agenda. The EU approach is rooted in well-established principles (Tridimas 2006; Craig 2012) that underpin its policy and legislation. For example, Article 2 of the Treaty establishing the European Union (TEU) lists the values on which the Union is established as:

> ... [t]he respect for *human dignity*, freedom, democracy, equality, the rule of law and respect for human rights, including the rights of persons belonging to minorities. These values are common to the Member States in a society in which pluralism, non-discrimination, tolerance, justice, *solidarity* and equality between women and men prevail.[47]

In this context, the principles of human dignity and solidarity are particularly relevant. Although complex to define and apply in practice, dignity is not a new concept in EU law. Prior to its inclusion in the Treaty,[48] the CJEU had already described it as one of the general principles of EU law,[49] but it was

---

[47] Emphasis added.

[48] Dignity is further reiterated in provisions of the EU Charter of Fundamentals Rights where the entire first chapter of refers to the concept of dignity. In addition, the concept of dignity is contained in Articles 25 (Rights of the Elderly) and 31 (Fair and Just Working Conditions).

[49] In Case C-168/91, *Christos Konstantinidis v Stadt Altensteig–Standesamt and Landratsamt Calw–Ordnungsamt*, ECLI:EU:C:1993:115, Advocate General Jacobs stated that 'the constitutional traditions of the Member States in general allow for the conclusion that there exists a principle according to which the State must respect not only the individual's physical well-being, but also his dignity, moral integrity and sense of personal identity' (ECLI:EU:C:1992:504 at para. 39). Furthermore, in Case C-13/94, *P v S and Cornwall County Council*, ECLI:EU:C:1996:170, the CJEU held, in relation to the treatment of transsexuals in the

the cases of *Omega*[50] and *Coleman* (C-303/06)[51] that gave prominence to the concept. In the first case, for the first time the CJEU clearly defined the 'respect for human dignity as a general principle of law' (para. 34). In the second case, Advocate General Maduro, in his Opinion, indicated that dignity entails 'the recognition of equal worth of every individual'[52] (para. 9, but see also para. 8–10, 12–13, 15 and 22), which arguably must be protected regardless of the economic contribution that an individual can make. Thus, human dignity represents a crucial principle that can highlight and protect the needs of vulnerable individuals engaged in caring relationships, be those cared for and/or carers (Moon and Allen 2006). The reference to solidarity is also important. Solidarity refers to the sharing of both advantages, such as prosperity, and burdens equally and justly among society's members. Indeed the EU CFR expressly places Article 33 on the Right to Reconcile Work and Family Life under the heading of 'Solidarity'. Solidarity is also mentioned in Article 3 TEU, which states that the Union 'shall promote … *solidarity between generations* and protection of the rights of the child'. This is an expression of the principle that 'providing care for people over the life cycle is a social responsibility, an obligation that reflects our ties to one another as a human community' (Brenner 2009, 189). Article 3 further refers to a commitment to promote 'the well-being of its peoples'. An expression of these principles can be found in some provisions of the EU CFR, namely the rights of children (Article 24), elderly people (Article 25), and of persons with disabilities (Article 26). This ethical dimension has been recently reiterated in the Pillar of Social Rights (Bell 2018).

Taken together, these provisions lay the foundation for an emerging EU ethic of care that underpins the relevant legislation (Caracciolo di Torella 2016). The ethic of care, originally introduced by Gilligan's seminal work (1982), challenged traditional gendered assumptions about care and in particular moral development and reasoning in young boys (thus men) and girls (thus women). Gilligan developed her moral theory

---

workplace, that 'to tolerate such discrimination would be tantamount, as regards such a person, to a failure to respect the dignity and freedom to which he or she is entitled, and which the Court has a duty to safeguard' (at para. 22).

[50] Case C-36/02, *Omega Spielhallen- und Automatenaufstellungs-GmbH v Oberbürgermeisterin der Bundesstadt Bonn*, ECLI:EU:C:2004:614.

[51] Case C-303/06, *Coleman v Attridge Law and Steve Law*, ECLI:EU:C:2008:415.

[52] ECLI:EU:C:2008:61.

in contrast to that of Kohlberg (1981, 1984), whose model had established that boys were found to be more morally mature than girls. Whilst boys tend to be more comfortable with an ethic of justice that emphasises 'questions of fairness, equality, individual rights, abstract principles, and the consistent application of them' (Held 2006, 15), girls tend to use an ethic of care that focuses 'on attentiveness, trust, responsiveness to need, narrative nuance, and cultivating caring relations. Whereas an ethic of justice seeks a fair solution between competing individual interests and rights, an ethic of care sees the interest of carers and cared for as importantly intertwined rather than as simply competing' (Held 2006, 15). Gilligan argued that it was not the case that boys (thus men) are more mature than girls (women), but simply that they speak 'in a different voice'. Over the years Gilligan's work has been further developed and critiqued (e.g. Tronto 1993; Held 2006; Feder Kittay 1999; Ruddick 1980). In particular, its valorisation of a female voice has been portrayed as problematic (Munro 2007). Not all females are innately caring, self-sacrificing and nurturing or any more capable of these traits than men (Rhode 1991, 309) and certainly women should not be constructed as such. Nevertheless, the ethic of care remains attractive as it provides a useful starting point: it is a tool that emphasises the importance of *responsibilities* and *relationships*—rather than *rights*—and is based on the idea that life is a series of mutual and interdependent relationships without which we would not exist (Meyers 2004). The ethic of care approach is also attractive because it considers both the needs of carers and of the cared for: in this sense, it offers an important tool to re-evaluate the legal framework of the work-life balance discourse. The primary focus should be: what is my proper obligation within the context of this relationship?; rather than: is it my right to do X? (Held 2006). This chapter maintains that the EU underlying principles of dignity, solidarity and equality are an expression of an emerging EU ethic of care.

A further useful theoretical approach that is emerging from some EU instruments, in particular case law, is that proposed by Fineman (1995). Fineman theorises the family as a bundle of caring relationships, rather than traditional stereotypical roles where one person assumes the 'mothering' role and the other that of the 'dependent child' (1995, 235 et seq). It is not crucial to this model that the mothering role is assumed by the mother, as it can equally be undertaken by the father. Thus this model de-genders the caring relationship and acknowledges the rights and obligations that both mothers and fathers have towards their family.

Many advocate that this model should become the norm (James 2009b; Ciccia and Bleijenbergh 2014) and it is encouraging to see that it underpins the proposed Work-Life Balance Directive.

A greater promotion of an ethic of care and of Fineman's theorisation of the family, already implicit in EU law, could radically transform institutions and legal rights in this context. If we are willing to accept that caregiving is an evolving concept and one that does not need to be gendered (James 2009b; Sevenhuijsen 2003), then an ethic of care provides the tool to challenge individualistic approaches to law and policy. To introduce an ethic of care approach in the legislation would mean to acknowledge the moral value of relationships and to give a legal foundation to the principle (Clough 2014; Herring 2013).

This should be contrasted with the rhetoric of business and productivity that underpins these work-life balance measures in the UK.[53] Its historical and ongoing failure to include the ethic of care when drafting policies on work life balance, has meant that whilst a superficially attractive framework of rights has been developed, this continues to reflect a dominant neoliberal approach that promotes, prioritises and rewards autonomy, individualism and market-making above informal, unpaid care-giving (Bridgeman 2007). The UK approach was clearly expressed by the UKIP leader, Nigel Farage, speaking to an audience in the City: '[i]n many cases women make different choices in life to the ones men make, simply for biological reasons. A woman who has a client base, has a child and takes two or three years off—she is worth far less to her employer when she comes back than when she went away because that client base won't be stuck as rigidly to her portfolio' (reported in BBC News 2014; Mason 2015).

This is not to say that these principles do not exist in the UK legal structure. Dignity, for example, is a well known concept in medical law.[54] Nonetheless, they are not part of an overarching set of principles with constitutional standing. True, they belong to a set of international provisions that, when the EU framework will no longer apply, will still be part of the UK legal background. Amongst these provisions, to mention a few examples, are the Universal Declaration of Human Rights (UDHR),

---

[53] See, in particular, the discussion on flexible working arrangements, supra at section 'Provisions for Fathers, Parents and Carers'.

[54] See, for example, the recent case of *Alder Hey Children's NHS Foundation Trust v Evans* [2018], EWHC 308 (Fam).

whose Preamble refers to 'the inherent dignity and the equal and inalinable rights of all members of the human family', and the European Convention on Human Rights (ECHR), in particular Article 8 on respect for family life and Article 14 on the prohibition of discrimination.[55] The European Court of Human Rights (ECtHR) has held that, even if Article 8 does not expressly mention care, family life does indeed depend on close, continuing and practical ties.[56] Its case law not only seems to acknowledge the rights of carers, but it also suggests that parents and children have a right to bond, regardless of the way in which a family is created (Foubert and Imamović 2015).[57]

Other relevant international documents are the International Labour Organisation (ILO) Convention on Workers with Family Responsibilities (n. 156) and the accompanying Recommendation (n. 165). The ILO instruments have been pivotal in shaping both the EU legislation and domestic legislation (Adams 2013).

Theoretically, these instruments might continue supporting in the UK the emerging 'ethic of care framework' that is now provided by EU law. Yet, these instruments contain international obligations; as such, they do not confer any direct entitlements to individuals under UK law (Wyatt 1982). Thus, their impact will be more limited than the impact of EU instruments that can be invoked directly by individuals. Furthermore, specifically concerning the ECHR, in the UK there has for sometime now been talk of replacing it with an British 'Bill of Rights' (Choudhry and Herring 2010). To date, it is unclear what will be covered in such Bill of Rights. Recently, it has been argued that withdrawal from the EU will contribute even more to removing the political obligation for the UK to continue as a party to the ECHR (McCrudden 2018).

---

[55] The relevance of the ECHR is also evident in other Articles, such as Article 3 on the protection from torture or inhuman or degrading treatment.

[56] As summarised in *Al-Nashif v Bulgaria* (Application No. 50963/99) (2002) 36 EHRR 655.

[57] *Petrovic v Austria* (Application No. 20458/92) (1998) 33 EHRR 307 and more recently, *Markin v Russia* (Application No. 30078/06) (2012) EqLR 489 and *Topčić-Rosenberg v Croatia* (Application No. 19391/11) (2013) 58 EHRR 1113.

A Brexit Effect for the EU?

It would be simplistic to assume that the effects of the Brexit vote will be experienced only in the UK: the EU will also feel the impact. On the one hand, Brexit might be beneficial to the overall progress in the EU of gender equality in general and work-life balance in particular. It is no secret that historically the UK has opposed developments in social legislation in favour of deregulation. Without the UK 'dragging its heels' (Fagan and Rubery 2017, 17), the progress of social policy will have a better chance of going ahead. Of course, the UK was not alone in challenging social legislation, but it was a 'significant barrier to progress' (McCrudden 2018, 32). For example, the Council has recently agreed its negotiating position on the Work-Life Balance Directive for parents and carers (EU Council 2018). On the basis of this mandate, the Council Presidency will now be able to start negotiations with the European Parliament once the latter has adopted its position. This bodes well for this specific Directive and indicates that, in the future, it will be easier to legislate in this area.

On the other hand, over the years the UK has made a tangible contribution to the development of EU law and has acted as a 'critical friend' both in the legislative process and in the Court. In relation to the latter, the UK has both submitted preliminary references that have helped to define key concepts and contributed through its judges and advocates general who have produced a significant body of opinions and judgments (Suk 2017).

For example, in the case of *Commission v France*,[58] it was Advocate General Slynn who, already in the mid 1980s, laid the foundations to the philosophy that still underpins the reasoning of the CJEU. In the case, he argued against keeping certain special rights for women introduced by the French Government aimed to protect them and ensure equality with men. Somewhat ahead of its time, he argued that:

> [a] father, in modern social conditions, may just as much be responsible for looking after sick children or need to pay childminders; he may no less for health reasons need to retire early or to have time off from certain stressful jobs. France's insistence on the traditional role of the mother,

---

[58] Case 312/86, *Commission of the European Communities v French Republic*, ECLI:EU:C:1988:485.

as I see it, ignores developments in society whereby some men in 'single parents families' have the sole responsibility for children or whereby parents living together decide that the father will look after the children, in what would traditionally have been the mother's role, because of the nature of the mother's employment.[59]

The role that UK judges have played was recently acknowledged by Eleanor Sharpston, the current UK Advocate General, who said that 'the UK has made a very strong contribution to this court and the evolution of EU law since it joined in terms of injecting a degree of pragmatism (...) Some very good [UK] people have served the court—Lord Gordon Slynn, Sir Konrad Shiemann and Sir Francis Jacobs—and they have made a difference ... it would be a pity to lose their contribution' (Bowcott 2016).

The loss of expertise will not only be felt at the level of law making or of the judiciary. As highlighted above, the UK will no longer be able to use the research funding and network available to the other Member States. This will mean that UK academics, who are experts in this area will not, at least for an initial phase, be included in comparative research projects and that UK experts will potentially no longer be included in networks such as Equinet and the various experts networks established by the European Commission. The loss of expertise will affect the EU as much as the the UK.

5   Conclusions

Brexit is a fact (Hendrickx 2016). Even if many of those who supported the Vote Leave campaign wish for a chance to reconsider their opinion, it is clear that there is no way back: the United Kingdom will leave the EU in March 2019. The multiple effects of this decision are still unfolding before our eyes. At the moment, it is difficult to predict with precision its ramifications. This chapter has attempted to engage with the potential, and perhaps unexpected, effects of Brexit in the discrete area of work-life balance. Indeed, although not many would have thought it likely that Brexit could have an impact on this field, there is little doubt that this will be the case.

---

[59] Opinion of AG Slynn, ECLI:EU:C:1988:428 at 6328.

Although not above criticism, in this area the EU has been the driving force for progress in the UK and has counterbalanced the UK's neoliberal approach. By creating new rights for women to balance work with care, encouraging men to play a greater role in family life, and increasingly recognizing the role of carers, the EU has firmly placed work-life balance on the agenda and has strengthened the protection of parents and carers in the workplace. It has been the catalyst for the adoption of relevant domestic legislation: thanks to the input of EU law, UK parents and carers have gained real and substantive rights. So, what will the position be once the UK is no longer part of the EU?

This chapter has identified three possible scenarios. The first one is the status quo scenario. In this case the UK will keep the existing provisions: employment and social rights in this area would remain the same. On the one hand, it could be argued that it will simply be politically unlikely that the UK will accept current EU provisions. On the other hand, however, it could be the case that the UK will decide to continue complying with current EU requirements anyway, because it makes sense from a business perspective. This view can be supported by the consideration that it is unlikely that any government would be keen to scale back such rights in any meaningful or immediate way—or that larger employers would want to abandon their existing family-friendly policies, given their significance as a recruitment and retention tool. It is possible, however, that exemptions around family leave rights could be introduced for small employers.

Another possibility, the progressive scenario, sees the UK 'free' to develop its own legislation in this area in a more progressive and forward thinking fashion than the current EU standards. Yet, the UK has already shown that it could be more progressive than the EU and has not always chosen to do so. Furthermore, any truly progressive developments in this area will depend from the type of domestic government (i.e. a Labour rather than a Conservative led government), rather than from EU standards.

In reality, a more regressive scenario is likely to emerge. Simply put, to improve or merely maintain the EU legacy in this area of law will simply not be a priority in the next few years. Any decision is very likely to be influenced by the economic climate. Just as the 2008 financial crisis was seen as a reason to cut back on social services (Guerrina 2015, 2017), it is likely that the post-Brexit climate will justify a similar approach to work-life balance policies. This appears clear from the discussion in the UK Parliament, where it was held that, despite 'the Government's commitment to facilitating the balance of work with family and other commitments', the Work-Life Balance Directive should 'not disrupt existing national systems unfavourably' (UK Parliament 2017). In addition, the UK is not yet convinced that legislation at EU level is the best way of achieving work-life balance (UK Parliament 2017). As such, it will seek to 'retain as much flexibility as possible for Member States to maintain or develop their own systems of leave and pay for workers with caring responsibilities' (Griffiths 2018). Thus, without the underpinning provided by the EU principles, domestic legislation in this area might continue to exist, but as a tool to regulate the needs of the employment market, rather than an instrument to invest in citizens.

Taken overall, the vote for Brexit poses serious and concrete risks that hard-fought achievements will be slowed down, if not reversed. Ultimately, this will impact on potentially vulnerable individuals, such as carers. Paradoxically, the very concept of work-life balance has never been more important. Work-life balance measures are an essential tool to allow individuals to work. Furthermore, at a time where it is still uncertain what the criteria will be for allowing non-UK citizens currently living in the UK to remain or to ensure that others will have the possibility to enter, it is of utmost importance to make sure that these individuals will have the possibility to be in paid employment and contribute to the economy (Shutes and Walker 2018).

This is why there is the need for a clear and express commitment from the Government that the EU legacy in this field will be upheld and, ideally, that the UK will continue to keep pace with EU developments.

In conclusion, it is reasonable to assert that the post-Brexit future of work-life balance policies and legislation that have helped many families to provide financially for their dependants whilst caring for them, is at best uncertain, at worse worrying. Worrying also is the broader impact that a post-Brexit scenario on work-life balance will have on gender equality, as the majority of carers remain women. And even more worrying is the fact that gender continues to be 'the most significant and pervasive silence' (Guerrina and Masselot 2018, 2) in current debates on the Brexit negotiations. One thing is certain, however: if UK workers will ultimately be losers, nobody will be a winner.

BIBLIOGRAPHY

Adams, Lee. 2013. The Family Responsibilities Convention Reconsidered: The Work-Family Intersection in International Law Thirty Years On. *Cardozo Journal of International and Comparative Law* 22: 201.

BBC News. 2014. Farage: Women Must Sacrifice Family Life to Succeed in City, January 20. https://www.bbc.co.uk/news/uk-politics-25813230. Accessed 22 July 2018.

Bell, Mark. 2018. The European Pillar on Social Rights and EU Employment Law. Lecture Delivered for the LLM/Diploma Employment Law, University of Leicester, March 3.

Blair, Toni. 1999. Forward to *Fairness at Work, Department of Trade and Industry*, Cm 3969. The Stationery Office.

Bowcott, Owen. 2016. We Don't Decide National Cases: ECJ Veteran Wipes Away Eurosceptics Barbs. *The Guardian*, April 19. https://www.theguardian.com/law/2016/apr/19/we-dont-decide-national-cases-ecj-veteran-swipes-away-eurosceptic-barbs. Accessed 2 May 2018.

Brenner, Johanna. 2009. Democratizing Care. In *Gender Equality, Transforming Family Divisions of Labor*, ed. J. Gornick and M. Meyers. New York: Verso.

Bridgeman, Jo. 2007. Accountability, Support or Relationship? Conceptions of Parental Responsibility. *Northern Ireland Legal Quarterly* 58: 307–324.

Busby, Nicole. 2011. *A Right to Care?* Oxford: Oxford University Press.

Busby, Nicole, and Grace James. 2011. *Families, Care-Giving and Paid Work—Challenging Labour Law in the 21st Century*. Cheltenham and Northampton, MA: Edward Elgar.

Caracciolo di Torella, Eugenia. 2007. New Labour, New Dads—The Impact of Family Friendly Legislation on Fathers. *Industrial Law Journal* 36 (3): 318–328.

Caracciolo di Torella, Eugenia. 2014. Brave New Fathers for a Brave New World? Fathers as Caregivers in an Evolving European Union. *European Law Journal* 20 (1): 88–106.

Caracciolo di Torella, Eugenia. 2016. Shaping and Re-shaping the Caring Relationship in European Law: A Catalogue of Rights for Informal Carers? *Child and Family Law Quarterly* 28 (3): 261–279.

Caracciolo di Torella, Eugenia. 2017. An Emerging Right to Care in the EU: A "New Start" to Support Work-Life Balance for Parents and Carers. *ERA Forum* 18 (2): 187–198.

Caracciolo di Torella, Eugenia, and Annick Masselot. 2010. *Reconciliation of Work and Family Life in EU Law and Policy*. Basingstoke: Palgrave Macmillan.

Caracciolo di Torella, Eugenia, and Foubert Petra. 2015. Surrogacy, Pregnancy and Maternity Rights: A Missed Opportunity for a More Coherent Regime of Parental Rights in the EU? *European Law Review* 40 (1): 52–69.

Choudhry, Shazia, and Herring Jonathan. 2010. *European Human Rights and Family Law*. Oxford Hart.

Ciccia, Rossella, and Bleijenbergh Inge. 2014. After the Male Breadwinner Model? Childcare Services and the Division of Labor in European Countries. *Social Politics* 21 (1): 50–79.

Clough, Beverly. 2014. What About Us? A Case for Legal Recognition of Interdependence in Informal Care Relationships. *Journal of Social Welfare and Family Law* 36 (2): 129–148.

Council of the EU. 2018. Leave and Flexible Work for Parents and Carers: Council Agrees General Approach on the Draft Directive on Work-Life Balance, PRESS RELEASE 372/18 21/06/2018.

Craig, Paul. 2012. *EU Administrative Law*. Oxford: Oxford University Press.

Crompton, Rosemary, and Clare Lyonette. 2006. Work-Life Balance in Europe. *Acta Sociologica* 49: 379–393.

Department for Exiting the European Union 2018. European Union (Withdrawal) Bill: Explanatory Notes. https://publications.parliament.uk/pa/bills/cbill/2017-2019/0005/en/18005en.pdf. Accessed 28 July 2018.

Eurofund. 2015. Promoting Uptake of Parental and Paternity Leave Among Fathers in the European Union. https://www.eurofound.europa.eu/sites/default/files/ef_publication/field_ef_document/ef1508en.pdf. Accessed 10 May 2018.

European Commission. 2008. Employment, Social Affairs and Equal Opportunities, Opinion on New Forms of Leave (Paternity Leave, Adoption Leave and Filial Leave).

European Council. 2000. *Lisbon European Council: Presidency Conclusions*. 23–24 March. http://www.europarl.europa.eu/summits/lis1_en.htm. Accessed 22 October 2015.

Fagan, Colette, and Jill Rubery. 2017. Advancing Gender Equality Through European Employment Policy: The Impact of the UK's EU Membership and the Risks of Brexit. *Social Policy & Society* 17 (2): 10–21.

Fawcett Society. 2018. *Sex Discrimination Law Review*. https://www.fawcettsociety.org.uk/sex-discrimination-law-review-final-report. Accessed 25 July 2018.

Feder Kittay, Eva. 1999. *Love's Labour Essays on Women, Equality and Dependency*. New York: Routledge.

Ferreira, Nuno. 2016. The Human Face of the European Union: Are EU Law and Policy Humane Enough? An Introduction. In *The Human Face of the European Union: Are EU Law and Policy Humane Enough?* ed. N. Ferreira and D. Kostakopoulou, 1–14. Cambridge: Cambridge University Press.

Ferreira, Nuno, and Dora Kostakopoulou (eds.). 2016. *The Human Face of the European Union: Are EU Law and Policy Humane Enough?* Cambridge: Cambridge University Press.

Fineman, Martha. 1995. *The Neutered Mother, the Sexual Family and Other Twentieth Century Tragedies*. London and New York: Routledge.

Foubert, Petra, and Šejla Imamović. 2015. The Pregnant Workers Directive: Must Do Better. Lessons to Be Learned from Strasbourg? *Journal of Social Welfare and Family Law* 37 (3): 309–320.

Gilligan, Carol. 1982. *In a Different Voice*. Cambridge and London: Harvard University Press.

Golynker, Oxana. 2015. Family Friendly Reform of Employment Law in the UK: An Overstretched Flexibility. *Journal of Social Welfare and Family Law* 37 (3): 378–392.

Gordon, Sarah. 2017. Few Families Opt for Shared Parental Leave. *Financial Times*, 18 September. https://www.ft.com/content/2c4e539c-9a0d-11e7-a652-cde3f882dd7b. Accessed 25 July 2018.

Griffiths, Andrew. 2018. Letter to Sir William Cash, January 17.

Guerrina, Roberta. 2015. Socio-Economic Challenges to Work-Life Balance at Times of Crisis. *Journal of Social Welfare and Family Law* 37 (3): 368–377.

Guerrina, Roberta. 2017. Gendering European Economic Narratives: Assessing the Costs of the Crisis to Gender Equality. In *Gender and the Economic Crisis in Europe*, ed. J. Kantola and E. Lombardo, 95–115. Cham: Springer.

Guerrina, Roberta, and Annick Masselot. 2018. Walking in the Footprint of EU Law: Unpacking the Gendered Consequences of Brexit. *Social Policy & Society* 17 (2): 319–330.

Guerrina, Roberta, and Hailey Murphy. 2016. Strategic Silences in the Brexit Debate: Gender, Marginality and Governance. *Journal of Contemporary European Research* 12 (4): 872–880.

Hantrais, Linda. 2018. Assessing the Past and Future Development of EU and UK Social Policy. *Social Policy & Society* 17 (2): 265–279.

Held, Virginia. 2006. *The Ethic of Care*. Oxford: Oxford University Press.

Hendrickx, Frank. 2016. The UK After the Brexit: Handle with Care (Editorial). *European Labour Law Journal* 7 (2): 166–167.

Herring, Jonathan. 2007. Caring. *Law and Justice Christian Law Review* 159: 89–102.

Herring, Jonathan. 2013. *Caring and the Law*. Oxford: Hart Publishing.

Hervey, Tamara. 1994. Social Policy: A Happy Ending or a Reworking of the Fairy Tale? In *Legal Issues of the Maastricht Treaty*, ed. O'Keeffe and P. Twomey. London: Wiley Chancery.

Horton, Rachel. 2018. Employment/Labour Law. In *Great Debates on Gender and Law*, ed. R. Auchmuty. London: Palgrave Macmillan.

James, Grace. 2007. Enjoy Your Leave, but "Keep in Touch": Help to Maintain Parent/Workplace Relationships. *Industrial Law Journal* 36 (3): 313–316.

James, Grace. 2009a. *The Legal Regulation of Pregnancy and Parenting in the Labour Market*. London and New York: Routledge-Cavendish.

James, Grace. 2009b. Mothers and Fathers as Parents and Workers: Family-Friendly Employment Policies in an Era of Shifting Identities. *Journal of Social Welfare and Family Law* 31 (3): 271–283.

James, Grace. 2016. Family-Friendly Employment Laws (Re)assessed: The Potential of Care Ethics. *Industrial Law Journal* 45 (4): 477–502.

Jenkin, I., 2017. Is Brexit Bad for Women? *The Financial Times*, July 7. https://www.ft.com/content/a1ec120c-6307-11e7-91a7-502f7ee26895. Accessed 25 July 2018.

Junker, J.C., 2017. Proclamation of the European Pillar of Social Rights. https://ec.europa.eu/commission/priorities/deeper-and-fairer-economic-and-monetary-union/european-pillar-social-rights_en. Accessed 2 May 2018.

Kohlberg, Lawrence. 1981. *Essays in Moral Development Volume 1: The Philosophy of Moral Development.* New York: Harper and Row.

Kohlberg, Lawrence. 1984. *Essays in Moral Development Volume 2: The Psychology of Moral Development.* New York: Harper and Row.

Lewis, Jane, and Mary Campbell. 2007. UK Work/Family Balance Policies and Gender Equality, 1997–2005. *Social Politics* 14 (4): 4–30.

Mance, Henry. 2017. Theresa May Vows to Expand Workers' Rights. *Financial Times*, May 15. https://www.ft.com/content/c13ee5d0-38c3-11e7-821a-6027b8a20f23. Accessed 25 July 2018.

Mason, Rowena. 2015. Nigel Farage: It's a 'Fact of Life' That Mothers Will Earn Less in Some Jobs. *The Guardian*, 5 March. https://www.theguardian.com/politics/2015/mar/05/nigel-farage-its-a-fact-of-life-that-mothers-will-earn-less-in-some-jobs. Accessed 14 May 2018.

McColgan, Aileen. 2000. Family-Friendly Frolics? The Maternity and Parental Leave Etc. Regulations 1999. *Industrial Law Journal* 29 (2): 125–143.

McCrudden, Christopher. 2018. EU Equality Law in the Age of Brexit. *European Equality Law Review* 1: 30–38.

McGlynn, Clare. 2001. Reclaiming a Feminist Vision: The Reconciliation of Paid Work and Family Life in European Union Law and Policy. *Columbia Journal of European Law* 7 (2): 241–272.

Meyers, Christopher. 2004. Cruel Choices: Autonomy and Critical Care Decision-Making. *Bioethics* 18 (2): 104–119.

Mitchell, Gemma. 2015. Encouraging Fathers to Care: The Children and Families Act 2014 and Shared Parental Leave. *Industrial Law Journal* 44 (1): 123–133.

Moon, Gay, and Robin Allen. 2006. Dignity Discourse in Discrimination Law: A Better Route to Equality? *European Human Rights Law Review* 6: 695.

Mosher, James, and David Trubek. 2003. Alternative Approaches to Governance in the EU: EU Social Policy and the European Employment Strategy. *Journal of Common Market Studies* 41 (1): 63–88.

Munro, Vanessa. 2007. *Law and Politics and the Perimeter: Re-evaluating Key Debates in Feminist Theory*. Oxford: Hart Publishing.

Plomien, Ania. 2018. EU Social and Gender Policy Beyond Brexit: Towards the European Pillar of Social Rights Social. *Policy & Society* 17 (1): 281–296.

Radulova, Elissaveta. 2009. The Construction of EU's Childcare Policy Through the Open Method of Coordination. *European Integration Online Papers* 13 (1), Art. 13. http://eiop.or.at/eiop/texte/2009-013a.htm. Accessed 25 July 2018.

Raitio, Juha, and Helena Raulus. 2017. The UK EU Referendum and the Move Towards Brexit. *The Maastricht Journal of European and Comparative Law* 24 (1): 25–42.

Rhode, Deborah. 1991. *Justice and Gender*. Cambridge: Harvard University Press.

Ruddick, Sara. 1980. Maternal Thinking. *Feminist Studies* 6 (2): 342–367.

Sevenhuijsen, Selma. 2003. The Place of Care: The Relevance of the Feminist Ethic of Care for Social Policy. *Feminist Theory* 4: 179–197.

Shutes, Isabelle. 2018. When Unpaid Childcare Isn't 'Work': EU Residency Rights Have Gendered Consequences. http://blogs.lse.ac.uk/brexit/2017/07/20/when-unpaid-childcare-isnt-work-eu-residency-rights-have-gendered-consequences/. Accessed 11 May 2018.

Shutes, Isabelle, and Sara Walker. 2018. Gender and Free Movement: EU Migrant Women's Access to Residence and Social Rights in the UK. *Journal of Ethnic and Migration Studies* 44 (1): 137–153.

Suk, Julie. 2017. Equality After Brexit: Evaluating British Contributions to EU Anti Discrimination Law. *Fordham International Law Journal* 40: 1536–1552.

Tridimas, Takis. 2006. *The General Principles of EU Law*. Oxford: Oxford University Press.

Tronto, Joan. 1993. *Moral Boundaries: A Political Argument for an Ethic of Care*. London: Routledge.

TUC. 2018/2016. Women Workers' Rights and the Risks of Brexit. https://www.tuc.org.uk/sites/default/files/Women_workers_and_the_EU.pdf. Accessed 10 May 2018.

UK Parliament. 2017. Parental and Carers' Leave Directive. https://publications.parliament.uk/pa/cm201719/cmselect/cmeuleg/301-xii/30107.htm. Accessed 25 November 2018.

Ungerson, Clare. 2000. Cash in Care. In *Care Work: Gender, Class and the Welfare State*, ed. M. Herrington Meyer, 69–88. New York: Routledge.

Weldon-Johns, Michelle. 2011. The Additional Paternity Leave Regulations 2010: A New Dawn or More "Sound-Bite" Legislation? *Journal of Social Welfare and Family Law* 33 (1): 25–38.

Wyatt, D. 1982. New Legal Order or Old. *European Law Review* 7 (3): 147–166.

Zeitlin, Jonathan. 2007. Strengthening the Social Dimension of the Lisbon Strategy. *The Belgian Review of Social Security* 2: 459–473.

Zeitlin, Jonathan, Philippe Pochet, with Lars Magnusson. 2005. *The Open Method of Coordination in Action: The European Employment and Social Inclusion Strategies*. Brussels: P.I.E. – Peter Lang.

CHAPTER 5

The Vulnerable, the Dependant and the Scrounger: Intersectional Reflections on Disability, Care, Health and Migration in the Brexit Project

Dieuwertje Dyi Huijg

1 Introduction

Most likely, you will have seen buses drive through the UK in 2016 for the Vote Leave campaign warning you about the greedy character of the European Union (EU).[1] 'We send the EU £350 million a week,' read the buses, 'let''s fund our NHS instead. Let's take back control.' Priti Patel (then Employment Minister, Conservatives) argued that the 'leave vote is vital if we are to protect the NHS for future generations' (Mason 2016). The NHS is suffering, seems to be the message, because the EU and its citizens come to the UK to abuse the system. '[H]ealth tourism from the EU,' emphasises Gisela Stuart MP (chair of Vote

---

[1] Some of the studies refer to EEA migrants, others to EU migrants; for the sake of simplicity, I use the term EU migrants.

D. D. Huijg (✉)
Department of Sociology, The University of Manchester, Manchester, UK
e-mail: Dieuwertje.Huijg@manchester.ac.uk

© The Author(s) 2019
M. Dustin et al. (eds.), *Gender and Queer Perspectives on Brexit*,
Gender and Politics, https://doi.org/10.1007/978-3-030-03122-0_5

Leave campaign, Labour), 'has cost [the UK] billions' (ibid.). Patients seeking medical treatment come in such large numbers from the EU, Dalgleish (cancer specialist, UKIP) argues, that it endangers the NHS into a 'complete collapse' (Hervey 2016). The choice of the referendum, concludes Louise Bours MEP (health affairs spokesperson, UKIP), is between the NHS and the EU (ibid.).

While the specificity of the "£350million a week" claim is new, the claims, mentioned above, are neither party specific nor specific to Brexit. In 2013, the then Home Secretary Theresa May (currently Prime Minister, Conservatives) claimed that intra-EU migrants abused their access to healthcare and benefits (Travis 2013). In contrast, Hanefeld et al. (2013) argued that most 'medical tourism' finds its way to predominantly private 'high-end specialist expensive procedures [that may actually] generate substantial revenue'. Healthcare costs of British migrant pensioners living in the EU will double in the case of post-Brexit reliance on the NHS (Hervey et al. 2017, 11). And 'EU citizens from other Member States,' the European Commission (EC) states,

> use welfare benefits no more intensively than the host country's nationals. Mobile EU citizens are less likely to receive disability and unemployment benefits in most countries studied. […] economically non-active EU mobile citizens account for a very small share of beneficiaries and […] the budgetary impact of such claims on national welfare budgets is very low. (EC 2013; see also Milieu Ltd and ICF GHK 2013)

The accuracy of the claims regarding medical tourism and disproportionate (ab)use of benefits by EU citizens has been challenged since 2013 (Harris 2016; Migration Observatory 2016; UKICE, n.d.). While the "£350 million a week" claim had already been debunked before the referendum (James 2016; UK Statistics Authority 2016), the Vote Leave campaign only took it out from their website post-referendum (Griffin 2016) and, near the time of the referendum, the false claim was believed by approximately 47% of the people (cf. Ipsos MORI survey in James 2016).

The UK currently moves through the "post-referendum pre-Brexit era".[2] Herein, concerns about EU citizens' "medical tourism" and "benefits abuse" have moved to the periphery, UK tourists' use of EU healthcare gained priority, and the (collapsing state of the) NHS continues

---

[2] The collection of information for this chapter closed on 24 July 2018.

to play a prominent role. At the same time, worried about post-Brexit disability rights and the position of disabled people, Disability Rights UK (DRUK) was unsuccessful in their request for a full disability-specific equality assessment of the impact of the UK's exit,[3] specifically on: 'a) disabled EU citizens living in the UK, b) carers, c) disabled British citizens living in other EU countries',[4] as well as on d) 'disabled people's independence through reducing the PA [personal assistant, DDH] workforce' (Mackley and Jarret 2017, 3).

If not ignored (e.g. Outhwaite 2017) or deemed abusers, disabled people seem to fall in the category "vulnerable" in the Brexit Project (e.g. Home Office 2018c). Disability and disabled people's own views, then, are marginalised. Taking my own intersectional perspective as a disabled EU citizen as a point of departure, I explore in this chapter the Brexit Project in terms of its (anticipated) impact on migration, health, healthcare and social care, on disability rights, and on carers' and disabled and ill people's lives. I argue that these need to be situated in the increasing hostility, precarity and vulnerabilisation that disabled and ill people have been facing in the UK in the last decade.

2   As a Disabled EU Citizen...

From the perspective of an EU citizen who is both disabled and chronically dependent on the NHS, putting disability, health and care at the centre of the Brexit Project requires critical assessments of its impact on (e.g. legal, social, economic, medical, political) borders and barriers in disability rights and regulations, as well as of its impact on these borders and barriers in access to, for instance, health management, the trade in and development of medication and medical devices, benefits, independent living and social care.

Chronically ill since 2003, I have relied on regular visits to medical specialists, medical treatment and expensive medication; facing the rarity of resistant uveitis,[5] I am awaiting the development of new drugs to calm my oedematous retinas. I am an EU citizen and disabled—with a disabled freedom pass and an NHS medical exemption certificate to evidence

---

[3] Note the Briefing for the House of Lords (Haves 2018).

[4] Unfortunately, a discussion of disabled UK citizens' challenges in the EU falls beyond the scope of this chapter.

[5] Uveitis is a type of eye inflammation.

the blessing of the state with post-Brexit validity. According to the Leave campaign, I contribute to the collapse of the NHS and, while not a medical tourist, I am an expensive patient—a 'disabled body deemed a health and financial risk to the citizenry and burden to the State' (Soldatic and Meekosha 2013, 195). In 2015–2016, I faced unfamiliar health issues, including fear of a potential death sentence. Aware of the "scrounger", "cheaters" and "burden" discourse in everyday and institutional ableism (Campbell 2012, 214; EHRC 2017b, 30–32; Ryan 2018a, b; Yeo 2015, 525), I do everything I can to avoid applying for benefits out of fear of the (infamous) "disabling" social security system and its eligibility assessments (e.g. see Barr et al. 2016). Unsurprisingly, I am oblivious to buses promising more money for the NHS or otherwise anti-EU geopolitical preoccupations. The sentence is lifted the month before the referendum; life is reinstated and I try to ignore my vulnerability and to look forward. When the outcome of the referendum is (marginally) in favour of the Leave campaign, I join others in their challenge of the geopolitical, class and race privilege that EU citizens demonstrate in newspapers and too many places on the internet. Then, the insecurity of my position post-Brexit hits me.

The Home Office sends numerous emails to EU citizens to 'provide certainty about our rights' (e.g. Home Office 2017a, 2018b; Home Secretary 2017; Prime Minister 2017). The Home Office publishes a Technical Note (2017b), later confirmed by the Draft Withdrawal Agreement (DWA) (EC 2018), clarifying that post-Brexit citizens' rights are based on pre-Brexit EU Treaty Rights. This is exactly, however, what I and others feared; 'only those EU citizens who can evidence "five years of continuous and lawful residence as a worker, self-employed person, student, self-sufficient person, or family member thereof",' hence as "qualified persons" exercising EU Treaty Rights, 'can acquire settled status.' Various groups do not meet these requirements (or cannot evidence that they do) and, not qualified persons are arguably not lawfully in the UK. Disabled EU citizens who rely on benefits and EU carers—who care for disabled, ill and elderly relatives (predominantly women and disproportionately disabled themselves)—who receive Carer's Allowance (CA, also a type of benefit), do not qualify for the "economic self-sufficiency" clause.[6] These groups of, what I call, "disqualified persons" cannot acquire 'settled

---

[6] This includes those who are self-sufficient but without Comprehensive Sickness Insurance (CSI). However, in their Statement of Intent, the Home Office (2018c, para. 2.3) intends to abolish the CSI requirement for "those applying under the EU Settlement Scheme."

status under the [DWA] [...] per the conditions set out in Article 16 of Directive 2004/38 (paragraph 10, Technical Notes)' (Huijg 2017).

This institutional ableism pre-dates Brexit and, not particular to the UK, is grounded in EU citizenship and "economic self-sufficiency" requirements. As Waddington discusses (2017, 196), there are exceptions in EU law to the exercise of freedom of movement (FoM) rights by disabled intra-EU migrants due to situations where the right to reside (discussed below) can be denied by Member States. In comparison to the UK population in general, unsurprisingly there is a higher employment rate among intra-EU migrants (Bruzelius et al. 2015; Rienzo 2016), therefore, the percentage of *disabled* "inactive" intra-EU citizens is likely lower.[7] Nonetheless, as the stories collected by Disire illustrate (2018a), we exist; Jana (Slovakia), Bettina (Germany), Rudy (Belgium) and Anita (Portugal) have been working as full-time carers for their disabled relatives and discover that they might not be "qualified persons"; Yragael (France) came to the UK as a child and saw his benefits stopped (until his MP intervened) under EU migration restrictions.

Stories that discuss anxiety about Brexit present EU citizens in privileged positions in terms of class, race and nationality, and, although unnamed, abledness. Lewis (2013, 873) addresses how intersectionality welcomed 'experiences at the margins as ground of theory making'. One's individual experience is never isolated; rather, an intersectional interpretation urges, it is contextually situated in often tensional collective lived experiences and knowledge thereof (see Huijg, forthcoming). Recognising the geopolitical privilege of EU citizenship, my fear to be discovered as "disqualified" or "unlawful" is grounded in (differentially) shared concerns of disabled EU citizens and carers, and their experiences with and knowledge of increasing disability precarity in the UK.

3   TRADE, REGULATIONS AND FUNDING

The UK's budgeting, deregulatory and privatising policies in the realm of the NHS and health precede both Brexit and austerity (see Pollock 2000; Pollock et al. 1999). Already in 2007, the UK successfully challenged the EC with regards to 'workplace health and safety

---

[7] I have not found (approximate) numbers (e.g. see Sumption and Kone 2018, 3).

regulation as a trade-off between safety and cost' (Rothstein 2016, 26).[8] The impact of the neoliberalisation of the NHS, however, is not limited to health concerns *in stricto* sensu; let us think of the commercial selling off (or "transfer") of NHS buildings, land and leaseholds to private owners and investors for lucrative purposes (Naylor and Chand 2017). Unsurprisingly, there are concerns that the UK's withdrawal from the EU will enable a deepening and widening of disability, care and health-specific neoliberal trends. Unable to provide a comprehensive analysis thereof, I will briefly turn here to the areas of trade, regulations and funding where the UK's withdrawal might leave a footprint.

Trade

'Patients could find', the Association of the British Pharmaceutical Industry (ABPI 2018b) warns, 'that supplies of their medicines will be disrupted when the UK leaves the EU'. In terms of trade related post-Brexit health effects, then, people in the UK should not limit their worry about their access to, for example, (affordable) fruit and vegetables (DEFRA 2017; Schoen and Lang 2016)[9]; disruption in trade regulations and custom checks and rates can also have a knock-on effect on the supply chain, import and the access to "consumption" of, for instance, medical devices (e.g. needles); on the access to accident and emergency trauma packs that are flown in from the EU due to custom checks; on the intra-European transport of human tissue (e.g. blood, organs); and, particularly, on the transport of expensive and innovative pharmaceutical drugs. The European Medicines Agency (EMA) has already made the decision to relocate from London to Amsterdam in 2019, and future membership is uncertain (e.g. House of Commons 2018a, 9–10, 14–15). Moreover, pharmaceutical companies, the Brexit Health Alliance (2018) cautions, are considering moving to continental Europe and, with them, their quality test control and manufacturing processes. Disruption in harmonised EU regulations and ethics can have further post-Brexit effects where the UK depends on the EU, such as with regards to the surveillance of the safety of products already on the

[8]Arguing that 'on health and safety, the UK has one of the strongest records in Europe' (House of Commons 2018b, para. 122), the Government, ironically, 'proposes that the UK and the EU commit to the non-regression of labour standards' (para. 123).

[9]Affordable access is already a concern for many people in the UK.

market; drug licensing processes; and the development of and access to (new) medication, medical devices and treatments, and the testing and (clinical) trials thereof. This might particularly impact smaller patient groups and those with "rare diseases" (ABPI 2018a; AoMRC, n.d.; Barber 2017; Brexit Health Alliance 2018; House of Commons 2018a; Simpkin and Mossialos 2017; Yuille 2018; Zanon 2016). Since none of this has been negotiated, recent documents are either little informative and/or explicitly concerning (DExEU 2018; EC 2018; HM Government 2017; House of Commons 2018a),[10] including where it comes to 'maximising trade and investment opportunities', rather than citizens' well-being, under WTO regulations (HM Government 2018b).

Regulations

Despite the aforementioned deregulation in the UK in the realm of, for instance, working conditions, regulations at the level of the EU have greatly benefitted disabled people and disability rights in the UK, Lawson and Sayce highlight (2017, 11); to exemplify, Lawson and Sayce (2017, 11) bring attention to the prohibition of disability discrimination on the work floor (Employment Equality Directive 2000/78); the requirement of Braille labels on packaging of medication (EU Medicinal Products for Human Use Directive 2004/27); and the accessibility standards for websites and mobile apps (Public Sector Websites and Mobile Applications Directive 2016/2102). There are, then, 'thousands of regulations and rules that [originate in the EU] governing the design, functionality and usability of almost every product and object in the home and general environment, indoors and outdoors, which contain elements of disability related consideration' (Lawson and Sayce 2017, 7). Even if the Prime Minister Theresa May keeps her word that the Government will 'convert existing EU regulations into UK law when we leave' (Mackley and Jarret 2017, 4), and all concerns have been addressed (e.g. Haves 2018, 14–16), disabled people will not benefit

---

[10]For instance, Ben Bradshaw MP (House of Commons 2018b) points out that the Future Relationship document addresses infectious diseases—and health threats and health security (e.g. HM Government 2018a, para. 2.2.f)—but does not address issues of health with regards to 'patients' lives and safety [which] will be in danger if there is any interruption at all to the supply of vital medicines and medical equipment into this country'.

from EU-based regulations, such as the European Accessibility Act,[11] that will likely be formalised *after* the UK's exit (EHRC 2017b, 42; House of Common 2017).

While UK residents have to miss out on EU regulations beneficial to disabled people post-Brexit, leaving the EU *does* create the possibility for the UK to align its disability policies with the Convention on the Rights of People with Disabilities (CRPD) and the concluding observations of the UN Committee on the Rights of People with Disabilities (ComRPD), to deepen its commitment to disability equality rather than relying on EU policy and law (e.g. EHRC 2017b; Lawson and Sayce 2017; Pring 2018b). This hypothetical scenario is very promising. Yet, the UK's commitment to 'greater liberalisation of services, markets and trade' (DExEU 2018, 26) is certainly not promising. With the UK Government's track record of (re)producing disability injustice (as discussed below), there is fear on the ground that Brexit could intersectionally worsen disability, gender and race inequality even more, particularly since the implementation and reinforcement of austerity, budget cuts and the hostility against disabled and ill people, migrants and people seeking asylum. Despite the Prime Minister's aforementioned discursive commitment, she already clarified that she does not support the incorporation of the EU Charter of Fundamental Rights (cf. DExEU, n.d.; Mackley and Jarret 2017, 4), signalling further concerns with regards to the Government's commitment to human rights and, specifically, disability rights in the UK (EHRC 2018a).

Funding

Because of budget cuts and a consequential decrease in funding available from local governments (VODG 2017, 8), UK voluntary and community organisations that work in the area of disability rights and for disabled people have become increasingly dependent on EU funding (Williams et al. 2018). For instance, 19% of social care is funded by the voluntary sector (VODG 2017, 3). Considering the decrease in local funding that organisations have received nationally, the potential impact of Brexit is worrisome and will particularly affect marginalised groups, such as disabled people, women groups, Black, Asian, Minority Ethnic

---

[11] This will benefit disabled people's access to, for instance, smartphones, banking services, computers, and transport.

and Refugee (BAMER) communities, young people not in education, and post-incarcerated groups. Specifically intersectionally disadvantaged groups are at risk; let us think of disabled women underrepresented in women groups or (post-)incarcerated populations that disproportionately consist of people with Attention Deficit Hyperactivity Disorder (ADHD). The Government does intend to continue existing EU funding. However, its objective is to receive 'value for money [...] in line with our domestic priorities' to 'best serve the UK's national interests', rather than aiming at (intersectionally) prioritising and benefiting disabled people (Haves 2018, 19).

4   BREXIT, CARE, DISABILITY AND GENDER

Social care and healthcare are intrinsically marked by disability, as well as by race, migration and gender. The people who provide care—e.g. social care workers, PAs, nurses, midwives and medical care professionals—are, as a group, predominantly women and disproportionately, first, black and brown women and, second, migrant women from inside and outside the EU.[12] The people who disproportionately depend on (their) care are disabled people.

Aligned with the aforementioned concerns about deregulation, there are fears in the social care sector, the VODG cautions (2017, 5), that worsening working conditions due to 'the removal of aspects of employment legislation which have their origins in EU law' will have a further knock-on effect on recruitment. Yet, the national vacancy rate of the care sector as a whole is, with 6.6% in 2017, already substantially higher than the average rate (VODG, 6). Next to obstacles in the realm of non-EU migration control, the (gendered) shortage of care staff has increased for various reasons. There has been a decrease in qualified nursing, midwifery and health visiting staff, particularly in "disability fields" (RCN 2017, 13).[13] There are insufficient training bursaries for nurses (UKICE 2018, 4). There is insufficient training of nurses and doctors (Hervey and McCloskey 2018). Finally, in line with the "Brexit effect" that

---

[12]Approximately 80–87% of the nurses, auxiliaries and assistants are female. In the NHS and privately, 19–28% of the nursing and midwifery workforce were not born in the UK; around 5–6% is born in another EU country (RCN 2017, 9–10).

[13]There is an 18.4% drop in learning disabilities/difficulties and 6.2% in mental health nursing.

healthcare and social care professional and research organisations warned about (Fahy et al. 2017; HitEU 2018; James 2016; Moore 2016; Zanon 2016), there has been a 96% post-referendum drop in 'applications for nursing vacancies in the NHS by EU nationals' (HitEU 2018), a 87% drop in new EU members,[14] and 29% more left the Nursing and Midwifery Council in 2017/2018 (NMC 2018, 4).

'[T]he current social care [staff] crisis,' Baroness Campbell warns the Government (House of Lords 2017a), 'will worsen and disabled people will lose the right to independent living, as set out in Article 19 of the UN convention [i.e. CRPD]' (see further below). Disabled people have already insufficient access to PAs "from" the UK, she highlights, and, as such, depend on migrant workers coming from the EU. This care and support is necessary for many disabled people to live independently, else they risk, Lawson (in Bulman 2017) cautions, '[sliding] back into institutions.' Considering (re)institutionalisation in times of austerity (e.g. see Bulman 2017; EHRC 2017b, 17–18; EHRC 2018b; Pring 2017, 2018a), this warning is timely. The UK's 'independence', then, risks contributing to disabled people's dependency.

5   Intra-EU Migration, Disability and Benefits

While the social security system and NHS are being dismantled by the Government, discourse and policy that posit EU citizens as their abusers are not recent. Already in 1994, the Habitual Residence Test (HRT) was introduced in response to EU benefit tourism concerns. The HRT was intensified in 2010–2015, under the Coalition Government, in order to 'protect the integrity of the UK benefits system and discourage benefit tourism' (Department for Work and Pensions in Harris 2016, 130). The HRT assesses length and continuity of residence in the UK, future intentions and interests and, most relevant for disabled citizens, employment prospects. People failing the HRT are ineligible for means-tested benefits, such as Housing Benefit, Job Seeker Allowance (JSA) and Employment and Support Allowance (ESA) (Kennedy 2011b, 1–4 and 7, n22). Grounded in EU law and based on FoM regulations (Harris 2016, 144–145), hence with consequences for "disqualified persons", the "right to reside" (RtR) requirement was added to the HRT in 2004

---

[14]There continues to be an increase in non-EU workers (NMC 2018, 12).

to 'prevent abuse of the benefit system by people who came to the UK' (Harris 2016, 141).

In 2013, May (then Home Secretary) writes a letter with other EU Member States to the EC accusing new intra-EU migrants of abusing healthcare and benefits (Travis 2013). While these claims were already debunked, this ideological ableism nevertheless finds its way into policy. In the same year, the Home Office and Department of Health (2013, 1) proposed restrictions to non-EU migrants' access to free NHS healthcare. From 2014 onwards, restrictions were gradually introduced to affect both newly arriving EU citizens and unemployed EU citizens already residing in the UK; for instance, unless "permanently incapacitated" or with "compelling evidence" to work again in the near future, for former workers who were unemployed JSA would also end after six months (Harris 2016, 148; Rutledge 2016, 2). Post-referendum, May (now Prime Minister) unsurprisingly aims to further restrict EU nationals' access to benefits (Fenton 2017). These restrictions are also, then, disability specific.

"Broadly speaking, a person who moves from one EEA country to another," the Government formulates, "has a right to reside if they are economically active, or are able to support themselves" (Kennedy 2011a, 4). Only those who are "socially and economically established" are being enabled by the Government "to make a legitimate claim on [the country's] public resources" (Harris 2016, 131). In turn, this right is at risk when "genuine and effective" economic self-sufficiency—be that through work or otherwise—is at risk and, with that, the benefits attached to it (Kennedy 2015). The RtR and the "economic activity" and self-sufficiency clause impact various groups differently. Ackers (2004) highlights the gendered and intergenerational aspects of (transnational) care and intra-EU migration in the way that EU citizenship privileges people in paid work. Women are disproportionately affected, both when they take on fulltime *unpaid* caring responsibilities, such as for their (non-disabled) children (Shutes and Walker 2018, 139), and when they do fulltime *paid* care work for their disabled relatives, since CA is not considered ground for economic self-sufficiency under the UK application of EU law. In turn, those who are not (sufficiently) economically active due to disability and/or ableism are the ones who need benefits the most; their access to many benefits, however, relies on access to work.

Since the Government has worked for years towards limiting migrants' and disabled people's access to benefits, it is perhaps surprising that they recognise that their measures 'could have an impact on "vulnerable groups"' (Kennedy 2015, 24), specifically in terms of 'disability and carers' benefits' (Kennedy 2015, 8). Disability *specific* benefits—such as Personal Independence Payment (PIP), Disability Living Allowance (DLA) and CA—are meant to 'meet the day-to-day living costs of those who are unemployed or unable to work because they are sick' and to 'alleviate the extra costs associated with disability and housing costs'; they are also tested against the RtR requirement (Rutledge 2016, 3). While lacking access to benefits is problematic for most groups of people, as touched upon, these restrictions disproportionately impact disabled people. Benefits do not only fund material living needs, such as a place to live and food to eat, but also access to, for instance, disability specific forms of care, independent living and, ironically, work. Restricting access to benefits, then, is not a disability-neutral tool for intra-EU migration control. Moreover, as the Windrush scandal reporting exemplifies (e.g. see Eno 2018; Gentleman 2018; O'Carroll 2018), the control over access to healthcare and disability-related benefits operates as a geopolitical and raced tool for non-EU/UK migration and citizenship control. This includes the sharing of non-clinical data of "immigration offenders" between NHS Digital and the Government for the purpose of enforcing immigration law (EHRC 2018c, 64; HM Government 2018c).[15] As an (intersectionally) ableist mechanism, rather, the control of access to benefits privileges the FoM and access to permanent residency of EU citizens (and migrants in general) who are either not disabled or whose disability does not affect their economic self-sufficiency, hence RtR. In addition, it is still unclear whether "settled status" includes non-UK residents' *equal* access to benefits and services post-Brexit. This is relevant, to reiterate, as disabled people disproportionately depend on access to benefits, healthcare and social care. Therefore, this control has not only been designed to limit those undesirable EU migrants who are 'a burden on the social assistance system of the host State during their period of residence' (EC 2018, 14; Waddington 2017, 201), but, rather, is intended to limit the access of disabled intra-EU migrants who are or, within five years of continuous residence, become "too disabled to be economically self-sufficient" for permanent residency.

---

[15]While the Memorandum of Understanding has supposedly been suspended since May 2018 (EHRC 2018c), this is not reflected in official information (DoH and HO 2017; HM Government 2018c).

6 THE INTERSECTIONAL PRECARITY OF DISABILITY

At the start of 2017, a White Paper was published presenting '12 principles [guiding] the Government in fulfilling the democratic will of the people of the UK' (HM Government 2017, 2).[16] 'I read the White Paper carefully', Baroness Sherlock cautions, 'and I could not find the words "disabled", "disabled people" or "disability" anywhere in it' (House of Lords 2017a). While Baroness Sherlock's remarks concern disability in light of Brexit, the general track-record of the Government's policies and actions with regards to disabled and ill people has not been promising. In response to 'a formal request [in 2013] from a number of organizations of persons with disabilities' in the UK, the ComRPD initiated an investigation and concluded 'that there is reliable evidence that the threshold of grave or systematic violations of the rights of persons with disabilities has been met in the State party' (2016, 3 and 21–22). The UK Government published the ComRPD's report, with the relevant explanation, but its 'response to the report [is to reject] all the recommendations made'; 'the Government does not intend to take any action' (Kennedy et al. 2017).[17]

Substantially, and obviously, more disabled than non-disabled people are economically inactive (Shaw Trust 2016, para. 3.5). Dependency on the social security system is intrinsic to the reality of disability; dependency on others and the State, however, should not be the same as vulnerability or fragility. Social security should be the safety net for disabled and ill people, enabling them to live as 'active citizens'; while dependent, to live independently and with dignity, exercise autonomy, define their own needs and choices, and contribute to policies—e.g. regarding Brexit—that concern them, but also to provide sufficient means for autonomy and to be protected against major risks and contingencies (cf. Halvorsen et al. 2017, 2).

'[N]eoliberal state measures not only individualize,' Soldatic and Meekosha assert (2013, 198), 'but also directly blame those who are suffering from structural disadvantage.' Let us think of the ESA claimants who are sanctioned, but cannot challenge their sanction due to a 95% decline in legal aid granted to 'welfare cases involving disability benefits' (UK Parliament 2018a). Having structurally underpaid disabled people with

---

[16] "Democratic will of the people" is a reference to the (marginally favourable) outcome of the referendum.

[17] See also Haves (2018).

mental health conditions, the Department of Work and Pension (DWP) has been ordered by court, for instance, to review approximately 1.6 million of their PIP claims (UK Parliament 2018b; see also WPC 2018a, b). Considering the (increasingly) gendered character of mental health inequality (MHF 2016, 14 and 15; Patalay and Fitzsimons 2017; Thorley 2017), it is likely that disabled women are disproportionately impacted by these unjust PIP assessments. The Government has been strongly criticised for their welfare-to-work programmes (e.g. Hudson-Sharp et al. 2018). Perhaps unsurprisingly, pre-Brexit poverty among disabled people has been severe (EHRC 2017b, 16 and 46–47; Fitzpatrick et al. 2018, 27–28 and 36; Tinson et al. 2016, 4 and 12).[18]

Reacting to the numerous CRPD's recommendations, recently the Government stated, however, that they want to help 'more disabled people find and stay in employment' (Haves 2018, 9). Ironically, by reinforcing austerity, the Government has aimed at precisely the opposite by increasing barriers to work (e.g. Hale and StopChanges2AtW 2017). While little intersectionally disaggregated data is available (EHRC 2017b, 10 and 35; Sandhu and Stephenson 2015, 172), disparities point to the relation between gender and disability injustice, such as regarding gender inequality among disabled people in fulltime work, or a disability pay gap marked by gender inequality,[19] as well as among non/disabled women (EHRC 2017b, 21; 2018c, 89; Longhi and Platt 2008, 11).[20] With the lower median hourly rate that disabled people receive (EHRC 2017a, 8), less disabled women in fulltime work, as well as disablism at the employment door (e.g. see Stephenson and Harrison 2011, 13, fn. 19), "economic self-sufficiency" is difficult to achieve for disabled women, and particularly for disabled black and brown women.

7   Disability and Settled Status After Brexit

Late 2017, the Home Office shared their intention to distinguish between EU citizens who fall and those who do not fall 'within the scope of the Withdrawal Agreement' (Home Office 2017b). Differentially impacting

---

[18]For a contrasting governmental perspective, see Haves (2018, 13).

[19]11% of disabled men and twice the amount (22%) of disabled women experience a pay gap (Longhi and Platt 2008, 11).

[20]Depending on the type of impairment, difference in pay between non-disabled and disabled women ranges between 4.3 and 18.9% (EHRC 2018c, 89).

non-disabled and disabled EU citizens, the latter group might be 'refused status', 'be in the UK unlawfully', 'not be entitled to access work or other services' and, as if that was not enough, they 'may be asked to leave' (Home Office 2017b, para. 18). As I have discussed above (see also Huijg 2017), if disabled people cannot access, 'for instance, medication, medical treatment, general access to healthcare, non-medical care, housing and benefits,' it is dubious how they (or we), lawfully or unlawfully, can practically live in a post-Brexit UK. At the same time, also 'returning' to one's country of birth is generally not an option; if not because of the lack of family ties, finances, and (native) language skills, then because of initial (very) long waiting times to access care, services and benefits (see also Benson 2018; Disire 2018b; Lawson and Sayce 2017).

Migration control through care and benefits dependency is by no means particular to (white Northern and Western) European disabled citizens' and carers' situation, whose hegemonic whiteness and Europeanness provides them with relative "protection".[21] In contrast, the control of dependency on care and benefits is gravely multiplied by the State through intersectional race, faith and migration specific management, policing and institutionalisation, such as in the Windrush scandal (see also Aspinall and Watters 2010, vi; CRPD 2017, 6; EHRC 2017a, 107; 2018c, 92; Haves 2018, 10; Heath-Kelly and Strausz 2018; Roberts and Harris 2002). While fear is real on the basis of disability precarity, due to racial and geopolitical "protection", it is unlikely that dis/abled EU migrants will be (similarly) treated as foreign national offenders (FNOs) and, as such, detained (cf. Home Office 2018a; see also the3million 2018, 2).[22]

In line with the Joint Report and the Draft Withdrawal Agreement (EC 2017, 2018) and grounded in the ideological requirements of lawful residency, economic self-sufficiency and "not being a benefit burden", the Home Office expresses their intention in their regular email updates to provide "settled status" to EU migrants 'who paid into the system' and, consequentially, can be assured about their access to 'residence, healthcare and benefits' (e.g. Home Office 2017a; Home Secretary 2017;

---

[21] Further research is required on the geopolitical, racial and ethnic-national differences in the impact of Brexit on the position of, on the one hand, white Northern and Western Europeans and, on the other hand, Eastern and Central European migrants, Roma populations and intra-European migrants of colour in the UK.

[22] See previous comment.

Prime Minister 2017).[23] On 23 March, EU citizens received another email, this time with the message that the recently formalised agreement on citizens' rights meant that:

> if you are an EU citizen living in the UK before the UK leaves the EU on 29 March 2019 you will be able to continue to live and work in the UK. Your rights to healthcare, work arrangements and access to benefits will continue. (Home Office 2018b)

Some EU citizens' campaigning groups feel that these announcements by the Home Office regarding post-Brexit "settled status" for EU migrants are promising and possess positive implications for disabled people (e.g. see UKCEN 2018), even though the Government did not seem to depart from the requirements as set out in EU Treaty Rights. Having the Government's disability track record in mind, I stay cautious about disabled EU citizens' pre-Brexit and, as such, post-Brexit un/lawful residency status.

Although a "No Deal Brexit" is increasingly becoming a realistic option, just before completing this chapter (July 2018) the Government published two documents: the Statement of Intent (SoI) (Home Office 2018c) and the Legislating for the Withdrawal Agreement (LWA) White Paper (DExEU 2018). The SoI presents the EU Settlement Scheme (EUSS) through which EU citizens and family members can apply for "settled status"—a legal position similar, but not equal, to Indefinite Leave to Remain.[24] The LWA sets out expectations for the EU (Withdrawal Agreement) Bill. Although the LWA covers a wider range of issues, both SoI and LWA discuss citizens' rights. Seemingly diverting from DWA and EU Law, the EUSS SoI presents an application process with only 'three simple stages' that EU citizens have to go through in the EUSS[25]; they have to 'prove their identity, be checked they are not a serious criminal, and evidence their residence in the UK'

---

[23] All the emails originate from the service of the Home Office to keep EU citizens in the UK informed.

[24] As secondary legislation, EUSS will fall under section 3(2) of the Immigration Act 1971 (see Home Office 2018c, 37).

[25] Various groups, such as victims of domestic violence (unpaid) carers, and disabled people, and those receiving benefits, are expected to face difficulties in this process and, in case of a rejection, without clarity about the appeal procedure (see Schiek 2018; Sumption and Kone 2018).

(Home Office 2018c, 2).[26] This seems promising. While "lawful (residency)" does not appear in the SoI, access to public services, healthcare, pensions, and other benefits in the UK under settled status will remain subject to 'to the same rules as now' (Home Office 2018c, 6 and para. 7.1). Again, this suggests that the inequality pre-Brexit will continue post-Brexit. The SoI adds that the EUSS *reflects* 'current EU law rights' in accordance with FoM (Home Office 2018c, 37). Different from the SoI, in turn, the LWA is aligned with the DWA and, as such, with the already discussed disability specific limitations of the application of EU Law. The LWA states that 'EU citizens *lawfully* residing in the UK [...] will be able to stay' (DExEU 2018, para. 24, emphasis added), of which the details will be provided in the SoI (para. 25). Lawful residency is offered as the groundwork for SoI and, as such, the EUSS; in contrast to the SoI, only those EU citizens who have continuously *and lawfully* lived in the UK 'for at least five years will be able to apply to stay indefinitely by getting "settled status"'; they are 'free to live [in the UK], have access to public funds and services and go on to apply for British citizenship' (DExEU 2018, para. 25a). This question of 'lawfulness', acquisition of post-Brexit equal access under settled status, and (other) EU Law based contradictions between the SoI and LWA (Home Office 2018c, 37) require clarification.

8 Final Considerations

Brexit is presented as a moment of departure from the EU; a departure that is suggested to symbolise and materialise geopolitical, economic and legal "independence". While this departure has not yet happened—and assuming it will actually happen on 29 March 2019—Brexit as a project has been in the making for years, if not decades or centuries. Various race critical, migration and postcolonial scholars, for instance, have situated Brexit in (nostalgia for) Empire, rather than legal, political and economic independence in and of itself (e.g. Bhambra 2017; El-Enany 2016, 2017; Emejulu 2016). On a more limited scale, the Brexit Project consists of both the moment of the UK's departure and the process leading up to and following the exit date. I discussed that it is both connected to and goes beyond trade negotiations, care, migration and benefits

---

[26] The CSI requirement seems to be off the table.

control, and citizens' rights; for instance, post-Brexit loss of EU funding, trade barriers and deregulation can affect the availability of medication and medical devices, healthcare workers and social care provision.

In this chapter, I have started with my own lived experience as someone facing and fearing the consequences of Brexit, while also aware of the geopolitical and race privilege this brings (including the loud silence thereabout and (re)production thereof) among hegemonic voices—and I urge more research that intersectionally problematises privilege and hegemony in the Brexit Project. While returning from potential terminality is likely not a collective experience, neither my fear nor my vulnerability are unique. '[T]he vulnerability of such a [disabled] body', Titchkosky reminds me, 'is not located in the body itself, but in the social construction of the environment' (2003, 244, fn. 1). Unrestricted to legal citizenship questions, disabled people are not intrinsically vulnerable; rather, disabled people—as cheaters, scroungers, dependant, expensive, frauds, a burden, undesirable—are *vulnerabilised* by the State affecting their capacity for active citizenship. As such, I have addressed that the fear of disability in the Brexit Project is grounded in disability-specific restrictions to FoM, to subsequent restrictions to access to benefits (and healthcare) in the EU (e.g. see Harris 2016, 146; Waddington 2017), and their UK particular application, as well as in intersectionally increasing disability precarity in the UK. In short, this fear is grounded in 'grave or systematic' disability inequality. Acquiring the right to have "the same access as now," then, would not be sufficient for disabled people.

The Brexit debate, Lawson and Sayce caution, is not addressing the question of what 'kind of society we want to live in', but, instead, focusses, on citizens as workers (2017, 5). Making sense of society, migration and citizenship merely in terms of labour, socio-economic productivity and "independence" is grounded in neoliberal (non-dis) abled and gendered ideas of citizenship. Also trade, funding and regulations are, however, intersectionally marked by disability, gender, health and care. It is ironic, but arguably not coincidental, that the move towards geopolitical independence and self-sufficiency is situated in a (rather hostile) environment that punishes disabled and ill people for lacking independence and economic self-sufficiency, while simultaneously restricting their equal access thereto. The question that Lawson and Sayce offer us, in contrast, invites a different approach to citizenship; one that does not centre, what one could call, a "burden model of disability", wherein disability is made sense of in terms of health and financial risk management and wherein disabled lives are framed and blamed as the State's burden (cf. Soldatic and Meekosha 2013). Rather, this different approach should see disability in terms of active citizenship (cf. Halvorsen et al. 2017). Not grounded in nostalgic aspirations for (imperial) independence, the centring and learning from, rather than marginalising, "disabled life" can enable a society built on *inter*dependence, in the interpersonal as well as the institutional and geopolitical sphere (cf. Mingus 2017).

Considering the track record of the Government's categorical 'grave or systematic violations' of disability equality and rights, reassurances that the Government takes their obligations in the area of Brexit very seriously and disabled citizens need not fear (cf. Lord Callanan in House of Lords 2017b) are hardly reassuring. Continued access to, for instance, disability rights, medication, medical devices and care has not yet been guaranteed. And although the SoI seems promising at first, the relation between the SoI and LWA leaves various questions unanswered regarding lawfulness, settled status and equal access to benefits that will impact disabled and other "vulnerable" groups. The Government will need to guarantee, then, that EU citizens with post-Brexit settled status will have equal rights to UK citizens. Further, Brexit would be a good opportunity to implement the CRPD and the Committee's recommendations (2016, 2017) and vastly increase and improve disabled people's access to disability affirmative active citizenship. Unfortunately, the UK's exit from the EU will most likely increase current disability vulnerabilisation and precarity; it is unlikely that a discontinuation of Brexit would initiate a process (adequately) addressing change and otherwise "heal" the current Government's disablist actions, policies and their impact and, instead, prioritise intersectional disability justice. It is not unsurprising at all, then, that the (anticipated) impact of the UK's exit on health, care and disability has received so little attention and disabled people fear Brexit.

BIBLIOGRAPHY

ABPI. 2018a. Industry Backs Findings of New Health and Social Care Committee Report into Brexit. Association of the British Pharmaceutical Industry (ABPI), March 21. https://www.abpi.org.uk/media-centre/news/2018/march/industry-backs-findings-of-new-health-and-social-care-committee-report-into-brexit/. Accessed 28 Apr 2018.

ABPI. 2018b. Patients Must Get the Medicine They Need After Brexit. Association of the British Pharmaceutical Industry (ABPI), January 28. https://www.abpi. org.uk/media-centre/news/2018/january/patients-must-get-the-medicine-they-need-after-brexit/. Accessed 28 April 2018.

Ackers, Louise. 2004. Citizenship, Migration and the Valuation of Care in the European Union. *Journal of Ethnic and Migration Studies* 30 (2): 373–396.

AoMRC. n.d. House of Commons Health Select Committee: Brexit and Medicines, Medical Devices and Substances of Human Origin Inquiry. AoMRC Submission with Contributions from FPM/RCP/RCR. Academy of Medical Royal Colleges (AoRMC). https://www.aomrc.org.uk/wp-content/uploads/2017/11/HoC-Health-Select-Comm-Brexit-medicines-medical-devices-and-substances...pdf.

Aspinall, P., C. Watters. 2010. *Refugees and Asylum Seekers. A Review from an Equality and Human Rights Perspective.* Research Report 52. Equality and Human Rights Commission (EHRC) and University of Kent. https://www.equalityhumanrights.com/en/publication-download/research-report-52-refugees-and-asylum-seekers-review-equality-and-human-rights.

Barber, S. 2017. Brexit and Medicines Regulation. Number 8148, Briefing Paper, House of Commons Library, November 20. https://researchbriefings.parliament.uk/ResearchBriefing/Summary/CBP-8148#fullreport.

Barr, B., D. Taylor-Robinson, D. Stuckler, R. Loopstra, A. Reeves, and M. Whitehead. 2016. 'First, Do No Harm': Are Disability Assessments Associated with Adverse Trends in Mental Health? A Longitudinal Ecological Study. *Journal of Epidemiology and Community Health* 70 (4): 339–345.

Benson, M. 2018. What Does Brexit Mean for Disabled Migrants and Carers from the European Economic Area? A Conversation with Dieuwertje Dyi Huijg, Yragael Alexis and Christiane Link [Podcast]. *The Sociological Review Website*, February 16. https://www.thesociologicalreview.com/blog/what-does-brexit-mean-for-disabled-migrants-and-carers-from-the-european-economic-area.html. Accessed 1 March 2018.

Bhambra, G.K. 2017. Locating Brexit in the Pragmatics of Race, Citizenship and Empire. In *Brexit: Sociological Responses*, ed. William Outhwaite, 91–99. London and New York: Anthem Press.

Brexit Health Alliance. 2018. Brexit and the Impact on Patient Access to Medicines and Medical Technologies. Briefing, Brexit Health Alliance (BHA), January 29. http://www.nhsconfed.org/resources/2018/01/brexit-impact-patient-medecines-medical-technologies.

Bruzelius, C., R. Ehata, M. Seeleib-Kaiser. 2015. Key Characteristics of EU Migrant Citizens in the UK. *The UK in a Changing Europe*, December 11. http://ukandeu.ac.uk/explainers/key-characteristics-of-eu-migrant-citizens-in-the-uk-and-northwest-england/. Accessed 26 May 2018.

Bulman, M. 2017. Brexit: Losing Care Staff from EU Could Force Disabled People from Their Homes, Report Warns. *The Independent*, June 24.

https://www.independent.co.uk/news/uk/home-news/brexit-disability-rights-care-staff-leave-home-eu-a7805566.html. Accessed 27 Apr 2018.

Campbell, F.K. 2012. Stalking Ableism: Using Disability to Expose 'Abled' Narcissism. In *Disability and Social Theory: New Developments and Directions*, ed. Dan Goodley, Bill Hughes, and Lennard J. Davis, 212–229. Houndmills: Palgrave Macmillan.

CRPD. 2016. Inquiry Concerning the United Kingdom of Great Britain and Northern Ireland Carried out by the Committee Under Article 6 of the Optional Protocol to the Convention. Report of the Committee (CRPD/C/15/R.2/Rev.1). United Nations Committee on the Rights of Persons with Disabilities (CRPD), October 6. http://tbinternet.ohchr.org/_layouts/treatybodyexternal/Download.aspx?symbolno=CRPD%2fC%2f15%2fR.2%2fRev.1&Lang=en.

CRPD. 2017. Concluding Observations on the Initial Report of the United Kingdom of Great Britain and Northern Ireland (CRPD/C/GBR/CO/1). United Nations Committee on the Rights of Persons with Disabilities (CRPD), October 3. http://tbinternet.ohchr.org/_layouts/treatybodyexternal/Download.aspx?symbolno=CRPD/C/GBR/CO/1&Lang=En.

DEFRA. 2017. 3.1 Origins of Food Consumed in the UK 2016 [National Statistics]. Food Statistics in Your Pocket 2017—Global and UK Supply, November 14. https://www.gov.uk/government/publications/food-statistics-pocketbook-2017/food-statistics-in-your-pocket-2017-global-and-uk-supply. Accessed 29 April 2018.

DExEU. 2018. *Legislating for the Withdrawal Agreement Between the United Kingdom and the European Union* (Cm 9674). White Paper, Department for Exiting the European Union (DExEU), July 24. https://www.gov.uk/government/publications/legislating-for-the-withdrawal-agreement-between-the-united-kingdom-and-the-european-union.

DExEU. n.d. *The Withdrawal Bill. Factsheet 6: Charter of Fundamental Rights* [Factsheet]. Department for Exiting the European Union (DExEU). https://assets.publishing.service.gov.uk/government/uploads/system/uploads/attachment_data/file/678333/Factsheet_6_-_Charter_of_fundamental_rights.pdf.

Disire. 2018a, n.d. Case studies. *Disire*. http://disire.org/case-studies/. Accessed 1 May 2018.

Disire. 2018b, n.d. Disabled People and Brexit. *Disire*. http://disire.org/disabled-people-and-brexit/. Accessed 15 March 2018.

DoH, and HO. 2017. *Memorandum of Understanding Between Health and Social Care Information Centre and the Home Office and the Department of Health* [Memorandum]. Department of Health and Social Care (DoH) and Home Office, December 20. https://www.gov.uk/government/publications/information-requests-from-the-home-office-to-nhs-digital.

EC. 2013. Impact of Mobile EU Citizens on National Social Security Systems. *European Commission (EC). Employment, Social Affairs and Inclusion,* October 14. http://ec.europa.eu/social/main.jsp?langId=en&catId=89& newsId=1980. Accessed 07 May 2018.

EC. 2017. Questions and Answers—The Rights of EU27 and UK Citizens Post-Brexit, as Outlined in the Joint Report from the Negotiators of the European Union and the United Kingdom [Memo]. European Commission (EC) Representation in United Kingdom, December 12. https://ec.europa.eu/ unitedkingdom/services/your-rights/Brexit_en. Accessed 22 Apr 2018.

EC. 2018. *Draft Agreement on the Withdrawal of the United Kingdom of Great Britain and Northern Ireland from the European Union and the European Atomic Energy Community.* European Commission (EC): Task Force for the Preparation and Conduct of the Negotiations with the United Kingdom under Article 50 TEU, March 19. https://ec.europa.eu/commission/publications/ draft-agreement-withdrawal-united-kingdom-great-britain-and-northern-ireland-european-union-and-european-atomic-energy-community-0_en.

EHRC. 2017a. *Being Disabled in Britain: A Journey Less Equal.* Report. Equality and Human Rights Commission (EHRC), April 3. https:// www.equalityhumanrights.com/en/publication-download/ being-disabled-britain-journey-less-equal.

EHRC. 2017b. Disability Rights in the UK. Independent Mechanism. Updated Submission to the UN Committee on the Rights of Persons with Disabilities in Advance of the Public Examination of the UK's Implementation of the UN CRPD. Equality and Human Rights Commission (EHRC). https://www.equalityhumanrights.com/en/publication-download/ disability-rights-uk-updated-submission-un-committee-rights-persons.

EHRC. 2018a. Brexit and the EU Charter of Fundamental Rights: Our Concerns. Equality and Human Rights Commission (EHRC), January 18. https://www.equalityhumanrights.com/en/what-are-human-rights/how-are-your-rights-protected/what-charter-fundamental-rights-european-union-0. Accessed 13 May 18.

EHRC. 2018b. NHS U-turns on Discriminatory Policies. Equality and Human Rights Commission (EHRC), May 31. https://www.equalityhumanrights.com/ en/our-work/news/nhs-u-turns-discriminatory-policies. Accessed 3 June 2018.

EHRC. 2018c. *Pressing for Progress: Women's Rights and Gender Equality in 2018. Full Report and Recommendations.* Report. Equality and Human Rights Commission (EHRC), July 23. https://www.equalityhumanrights. com/en/publication-download/pressing-progress-womens-rights-and-gender-equality-2018.

El-Enany, N. 2016. Brexit as Nostalgia for Empire. Critical Legal Thinking, June 19. http://criticallegalthinking.com/2016/06/19/brexit-nostalgia-empire/. Accessed 1 Mar 2018.

El-Enany, N. 2017. Brexit Is Not only an Expression of Nostalgia for Empire, It Is also the Fruit of Empire. *LSE Blog*, November 5. http://blogs.lse.ac.uk/brexit/2017/05/11/brexit-is-not-only-an-expression-of-nostalgia-for-empire-it-is-also-the-fruit-of-empire/. Accessed 1 Mar 2018.

Emejulu, A. 2016. On the Hideous Whiteness Of Brexit: 'Let Us Be Honest About Our Past and Our Present if We Truly Seek to Dismantle White Supremacy', June 28. https://www.versobooks.com/blogs/2733-on-the-hideous-whiteness-of-brexit-let-us-be-honest-about-our-past-and-our-present-if-we-truly-seek-to-dismantle-white-supremacy. Accessed 3 Dec 2017.

Eno, I. 2018. The Case of Albert Thompson is Abhorrent, But Not Exceptional. *The BMJ Opinion*, March 15. Retrieved from: http://blogs.bmj.com/bmj/2018/03/15/irial-eno-the-case-of-albert-thompson-is-abhorrent-but-not-exceptional/. Accessed 2 Apr 2018.

Fahy, N., T. Hervey, S. Greer, H. Jarman, D. Stuckler, M. Galsworthy, et al. 2017. How Will Brexit Affect Health and Health Services in the UK? Evaluating Three Possible Scenarios. *The Lancet* 390 (10107): 2110–2118.

Fenton, S. 2017. Theresa May Plans to Stop EU Migrants Claiming Benefits as Part of Brexit Negotiations. *The Independent*, 2 January. http://www.independent.co.uk/news/uk/politics/brexit-theresa-may-stop-eu-migrants-uk-benefits-claim-latest-european-union-a7505311.html. Accessed 3 June 2018.

Fitzpatrick, S., G. Bramley, F. Sosenko, and J. Blenkinsopp. 2018, 6. Destitution in the UK 2018. Heriot-Watt University. Commissioned by: Joseph Rowntree Foundation (JRF). https://www.jrf.org.uk/report/destitution-uk-2018.

Gentleman, A. 2018. 'The Stress Is Making Me Ill': Woman's Immigration Battle After 51 Years in UK. *The Guardian*, March 26. http://www.theguardian.com/uk-news/2018/mar/26/the-stress-is-making-me-ill-womans-immigration-battle-after-51-years-in-uk. Accessed 26 Mar 2018.

Griffin, A. 2016. Brexit: Vote Leave Wipes NHS £350m Claim and Rest of Its Website After EU Referendum. *Independent*, June 27. https://www.independent.co.uk/news/uk/home-news/brexit-vote-leave-wipes-nhs-350m-claim-and-rest-of-its-website-after-eu-referendum-a7105546.html. Accessed 2 Mar 2018.

Hale, C., and StopChanges2AtW. 2017, 10. Barriers to Work: A Survey of Deaf and Disabled People's Experiences of the Access to Work Programme in 2015/2016. Commissioned by: Inclusion London. https://www.inclusionlondon.org.uk/campaigns-and-policy/act-now/barriers-work-deaf-disabled-employees-losing-due-changes-governments-access-work-programme/.

Halvorsen, R., B. Hvinden, J. Bickenbach, D. Ferri, and A.M. Guillén Rodriguez. 2017. Introduction Is Public Policy in Europe Promoting the Active Citizenship of Persons with Disabilities? In *The Changing Disability Policy System: Active Citizenship and Disability in Europe*, ed. H. Rune, H. Bjørn, B. Jerome, F. Delia, and A.M. Guillén Rodriguez, 1–11. London: Routledge.

Hanefeld, J., D. Horsfall, N. Lunt, and R. Smith. 2013. Medical Tourism: A Cost or Benefit to the NHS? *PLOS ONE* 8 (10): e70406.

Harris, N. 2016. Demagnetisation of Social Security and Health Care for Migrants to the UK. *European Journal of Social Security* 18 (2): 130–163.

Haves, E. 2018. Disability in the UK: Rights and Policy Debate on 28 June 2018 (LLN-2018-0071). Library Briefing, House of Lords, June 21. https://researchbriefings.parliament.uk/ResearchBriefing/Summary/LLN-2018-0071.

Heath-Kelly, C., and E. Strausz. 2018. Counter-Terrorism in the NHS. Evaluating Prevent Duty Safeguarding in the NHS. University of Warwick Department of Politics and International Studies. https://warwick.ac.uk/fac/soc/pais/research/researchcentres/irs/counterterrorisminthenhs/.

Hervey, T. 2016. Healthier After Brexit? *The UK in a Changing* Europe, March 22. http://ukandeu.ac.uk/healthier-after-brexit/. Accessed 9 Mar 2018.

Hervey, T., and S. McCloskey. 2018. Article 50 One year On: Brexit, Health and the NHS. *The UK in a Changing Europe*, April 6. http://ukandeu.ac.uk/brexit-health-and-the-nhs/. Accessed 23 Apr 2018.

Hervey, T., S. McCloskey, and M. Flear. 2017. Patients. In *Brexit and the NHS*, ed. The UK in a Changing Europe (UKICE), 10–11. Retrieved from: http://ukandeu.ac.uk/wp-content/uploads/2018/03/Brexit-and-the-NHS-.pdf.

HitEU. 2018. *Factsheet. 2018 Edition.* Healthier IN the EU (HitEU). https://www.healthierin.eu/factsheet.

HM Government. 2017, February. *The United Kingdom's Exit from and New Partnership with the European Union.* White Paper, February. www.gov.uk/government/uploads/system/uploads/attachment_data/file/589189/The_United_Kingdoms_exit_from_and_partnership_with_the_EU_Print.pdf.

HM Government. 2018a. The Future Relationship Between the United Kingdom and the EU (Cm 9593). Policy Paper, July 12. https://www.gov.uk/government/publications/the-future-relationship-between-the-united-kingdom-and-the-european-union.

HM Government. 2018b. *The Impact of Brexit on the Pharmaceutical Sector: Government Response to the Committee's Ninth Report.* Eleventh Special Report.. Department for Business, Energy and Industrial Strategy, July 9. https://publications.parliament.uk/pa/cm201719/cmselect/cmbeis/1426/142602.htm.

HM Government. 2018c. NHS Entitlements: Migrant Health Guide, January 8. https://www.gov.uk/guidance/nhs-entitlements-migrant-health-guide. Accessed 23 July 2018.

HO and DoH. 2013. *Regulating Migrant Access to Health Services in the UK* (IA No: HO 0095) [Impact Assessment]. Home Office (HO) and Department of Health (DoH). https://www.parliament.uk/documents/impact-assessments/IA13-24F.pdf.

Home Office. 2017a. Subject Email: *Citizens' Rights Agreement* [Mailing list]. Email Recipient: Dieuwertje Huijg, December 8.

Home Office. 2017b. Technical Note: Citizens' Rights, Administrative Procedures in the UK. Policy Paper, November 8. https://www.gov.uk/government/publications/citizens-rights-administrative-procedures-in-the-uk/technical-note-citizens-rights-administrative-procedures-in-the-uk.

Home Office. 2018a. Adults at Risk in Immigration Detention (Version 3.0) [Statutory Guidance]. Home Office (HO), July 2. https://www.gov.uk/government/publications/adults-at-risk-in-immigration-detention.

Home Office. 2018b. Subject Email: *Brexit Negotiation Update for EU Citizens* [Mailing list]. Email recipient: Dieuwertje Huijg, March 23.

Home Office. 2018c. EU Settlement Scheme: Statement of Intent, June 21. https://www.gov.uk/government/publications/eu-settlement-scheme-statement-of-intent.

Home Secretary. 2017. Subject Email: *Agreement Reached with EU Providing Certainty of Your Rights* [Mailing list]. Email recipient: Dieuwertje Huijg, December 19.

House of Common. 2017. *Leaving the EU: Disabled People's Services* [Transcript: Debate (Vol. 627)]. House of Commons, July 11. https://hansard.parliament.uk/Commons/2017-07-11/debates/39B4240B-C528-44A2-89E8-5A72D087F622/LeavingTheEUDisabledPeople%E2%80%99SServices.

House of Commons. 2018a. *Brexit: Medicines, Medical Devices and Substances of Human Origin*. House of Commons, March 21. https://publications.parliament.uk/pa/cm201719/cmselect/cmhealth/392/39202.htm.

House of Commons. 2018b. EU: Future Relationship White Paper [Statement]. House of Commons, July 12. https://hansard.parliament.uk/commons/2018-07-12/debates/5C45D798-0286-4298-BBDE-44C860396ECD/EUFutureRelationshipWhitePaper.

House of Lords. 2017a. *Brexit: Disabled People* [Transcript: Question for Short Debate (Vol. 778)]. House of Lords, February 2. https://hansard.parliament.uk/lords/2017-02-02/debates/BF5C6387-2D05-403D-A0E8-ABB6BA4E4DF6/BrexitDisabledPeople.

House of Lords. 2017b. *Brexit: Equalities Impact Assessment* (Nr. 787) [Transcript: Debate], December 21. https://hansard.parliament.uk/Lords/2017-12-21/debates/25B2A992-5960-4534-B701-642266550481/BrexitEqualitiesImpactAssessment.

Hudson-Sharp, N., N. Munro-Lott, H. Rolfe, and J. Runge. 2018. *The Impact of Welfare Reform and Welfare-to-Work Programmes: An Evidence Review*. Research report 111. National Institute of Economic and Social Research (NIESR). Commissioned by: Equality and Human Rights Commission (EHRC), March 2018. https://www.equalityhumanrights.com/en/publication-download/cumulative-impact-tax-and-welfare-reforms.

Huijg, D.D. 2017. Brexit and Its Impact on Disabled EU Citizens and Carers in the UK. Migrant Rights' Network, December 18. Available at: https://www.academia.edu/35476382/Brexit_and_its_impact_on_disabled_EU_citizens_and_carers_in_the_UK_Blog_post_. Accessed 1 Mar 18.

Huijg, D.D. Forthcoming. Intersectional Agency. A Theoretical Exploration of Agency at the Junction of Social Categories and Power Based on Conversations with Racially Privileged Feminist Activists from São Paulo, Brazil. PhD thesis, University of Manchester, Manchester.

James, A. 2016. Editorial. Exposing the Brexit Campaign's NHS Lies. *Nurse Prescribing* 14 (7): 317.

Kennedy, S. 2011a. *EEA Nationals: The 'Right to Reside' Requirement for Benefits* (SN/SP/5972) [Standard Note]. House of Commons Library, December 5. https://researchbriefings.parliament.uk/ResearchBriefing/Summary/SN05972#fullreport.

Kennedy, S. 2011b. *The Habitual Residence Test* (SN/SP/416) [Standard Note]. House of Commons Library, May 18. https://researchbriefings.parliament.uk/ResearchBriefing/Summary/SN00416#fullreport.

Kennedy, S. 2015. Measures to Limit Migrants' Access to Benefits. Briefing Paper No. 06889. House of Commons Library, June 17. https://researchbriefings.parliament.uk/ResearchBriefing/Summary/SN06889#fullreport.

Kennedy, S., A. Jones, W. Wilson, T. Jarett, and A. Powel, A. 2017. The UN Inquiry into the Rights of Persons with Disabilities in the UK. Briefing Paper No. 07367. House of Commons Library, March 27. https://researchbriefings.parliament.uk/ResearchBriefing/Summary/CBP-7367#fullreport.

Lawson, A., and L. Sayce. 2017. *The Implications of Brexit for Disability Rights. Influencing Future Debate and Policy.* Report. Commissioned by: Disability Rights UK, June.

Lewis, G. 2013. Unsafe Travel: Experiencing Intersectionality and Feminist Displacements. *Signs* 38 (4): 869–892.

Longhi, S., and L. Platt. 2008. Research Report 9: Pay Gaps Across Equalities Areas. University of Essex Institute for Social and Economic Research. Commissioned by: Equality and Human Rights Commission (EHRC). https://www.equalityhumanrights.com/en/publication-download/research-report-9-pay-gaps-across-equalities-areas.

Mackley, A, and T. Jarret. 2017. *Consultation with Disabled People on the Effect on Their Services of the UK Leaving the EU* (Number CDP-2017-0136) [Debate Pack]. House of Commons Library, July 10. https://researchbriefings.parliament.uk/ResearchBriefing/Summary/CDP-2017-0136.

Mason, R. 2016. NHS Loses £700m a Year on Treating EU Citizens, Brexit Campaign Claims. *The Guardian*, April 4. http://www.theguardian.com/politics/2016/apr/05/nhs-loses-700m-a-year-treating-eu-citizens-brexit-campaign-claims. Accessed 8 Apr 2018.

MHF. 2016. *Fundamental Facts About Mental Health 2016*. Report. Mental Health Foundation (MHF). London. https://www.mentalhealth.org.uk/publications/fundamental-facts-about-mental-health-2016.

Migration Observatory. 2016. EU Migration, Welfare Benefits and EU Membership (Pre-referendum). Migration Observatory—University of Oxford, May 2. http://www.migrationobservatory.ox.ac.uk/resources/reports/eu-migration-welfare-benefits-and-eu-membership/. Accessed 9 Mar 2018.

Milieu Ltd., and ICF GHK. 2013. *A Fact Finding Analysis on the Impact on the Member States' Social Security Systems of the Entitlements of Non-active Intra-EU Migrants to Special Non-contributory Cash Benefits and Healthcare Granted on the Basis of Residence*. Directorate-General for Employment, Social Affairs and Inclusion (European Commission) https://publications.europa.eu/en/publication-detail/-/publication/c6de1d0a-2a5b-4e03-9efb-ed522e6a27f5.

Mingus, M. 2017. Access Intimacy, Interdependence and Disability Justice [Lecture]. Leaving Evidence, April 12. https://leavingevidence.wordpress.com/2017/04/12/access-intimacy-interdependence-and-disability-justice/. Accessed 9 Mar 2018.

Moore, A. 2016. Brexit: What Now for Nurses? *Nursing Standard (2014+)* 30 (46): 18.

Naylor, R., and K. Chand. 2017. Should we Welcome Plans to Sell off NHS land? *BMJ*, 358. https://www.bmj.com/content/358/bmj.j4290.

NMC. 2018. *The NMC Register*. Report. Nursing and Midwifery Council (NMC), March 31. https://www.nmc.org.uk/globalassets/sitedocuments/other-publications/the-nmc-register-2018.pdf.

O'Carroll, L. 2018. DWP Sent Windrush Pensioner £33,000 Bill for Disability Benefits. *The Guardian*, April 20. http://www.theguardian.com/uk-news/2018/apr/20/dwp-sent-windrush-pensioner-33000-bill-for-disability-benefits. Accessed 22 Apr 2018.

Outhwaite, W. (ed.). 2017. *Brexit: Sociological Responses*. London and New York: Anthem Press.

Patalay, P., and E. Fitzsimons. 2017, 9. Mental Ill-health Among Children of the New Century: Trends Across Childhood with a Focus on Age 14. Briefing Paper, Centre for Longitudinal Studies, London. http://www.cls.ioe.ac.uk/news.aspx?itemid=4646&itemTitle=One+in+four+girls+is+depressed+at+age+14%2C+new+study+reveals&sitesectionid=27&sitesectiontitle=News.

Pollock, A.M. 2000. Will Intermediate Care Be the Undoing of the NHS? Here's Another Bit of Covert Privatisation. *BMJ* 321 (7258): 393–394.

Pollock, A.M, M.G Dunnigan, D. Gaffney, D. Price, and J. Shaoul. 1999. Planning the "New" NHS: Downsizing for the 21st Century. *BMJ* 319 (7203): 179–184.

Prime Minister. 2017. Subject Email: *Message to EU Citizens Living in the UK* [Mailing list]. Email recipient: Dieuwertje Huijg, October 19.

Pring, J. 2017. 'Hard Brexit' Could See Disabled People Lose Right to Independent Living, Say Peers. Disability News Service (DSN), February 9. https://www.disabilitynewsservice.com/hard-brexit-could-see-disabled-people-lose-right-to-independent-living-say-peers/. Accessed 30 Apr 2018.

Pring, J. 2018a. NHS Bodies Face Legal Action by Human Rights Watchdog Over Care Home Threat. Disability News Service (DSN), March 22. https://www.disabilitynewsservice.com/nhs-bodies-face-legal-action-by-human-rights-watchdog-over-care-home-threat/. Accessed 12 Apr 2018.

Pring, J. 2018b. TUC Disabled Workers' Conference: UN Convention 'Must Become Part of UK Law'. Disability News Service (DSN), May 31. https://www.disabilitynewsservice.com/tuc-disabled-workers-conference-un-convention-must-become-part-of-uk-law/. Accessed 3 June 2018.

RCN. 2017. *The UK Nursing Labour Market Review 2017* [Review]. Royal College of Nursing (RCN), December 2017. https://www.rcn.org.uk/professional-development/publications/pub-006625.

Rienzo, C. 2016. Characteristics and Outcomes of Migrants in the UK Labour Market [5th revision]. Briefing. Migration Observatory Briefing. COMPAS Migration Observatory, University of Oxford, January 2016.

Roberts, K., and J. Harris. 2002. *Disabled Refugees and Asylum Seekers in Britain: Numbers and Social Characteristics* (NLCB 1816 05.01 KR/JHa). Report. Social Policy and Research Unit. University of York.

Rothstein, H. 2016. Did We Do Enough to Understand EU Conflicts Over Risk and Regulation Before Brexit? In *Regulation Scholarship in Crisis? Discussion Paper Nr. 84*, ed. Martin Lodge, 26–31. Centre for Analysis of Risk and Regulation (CARR), LSE.

Rutledge, D. 2016. EU Citizens' Access to Welfare Benefits: Past, Present and Future. EU Referendum Position Papers No. 5, Commissioned by: Immigration Law Practitioners' Association (ILPA), May 13. http://www.ilpa.org.uk/resource/32133/eu-referendum-position-paper-5-welfare-benefits.

Ryan, F. 2018a. If You've Not Been Hit by Tory Cuts Yet, Your Time May Soon Be Up. *The Guardian*, April 12. http://www.theguardian.com/commentisfree/2018/apr/12/austerity-cuts-marginalised-services-public. Accessed 12 Apr 2018.

Ryan, F. 2018b. Is This Truly Britain—A Land That Spies on Sick and Poor People? *The Guardian*, February 1. http://www.theguardian.com/commentisfree/2018/feb/01/spy-on-your-neighbour-britain-demonisation-benefit-claimants-disabled-people. Accessed 17 Mar 2018.

Sandhu, K., and M.-A. Stephenson. 2015. Layers of Inequality—A Human Rights and Equality Impact Assessment of the Public Spending Cuts on Black Asian and Minority Ethnic Women in Coventry. *Feminist Review* 109 (1): 169–179.

Schiek, D. 2018. Home Office 'Statement of Intent' for EU Citizens' Settled Status in the UK. QPol, Queen's University Belfast, June 26. http://qpol.qub. ac.uk/home-office-statement-intent-settled-status/. Accessed 7 July 2018.

Schoen, V., and T. Lang. 2016. Horticulture in the UK: Potential for Meeting Dietary Guideline Demands. Policy Brief, Commissioned by: Food Research Collaboration, March 24.

Shaw Trust. 2016, May. Shaw Trust Written Submission to: 'Work and Pensions Select Committee Inquiry: Disability Employment Gap', May 2016. https:// www.shaw-trust.org.uk/Media-policy/News/May-2016/Our-Response-to-the-Disability-Employment-Select-C.

Shutes, I., and S. Walker. 2018. Gender and free Movement: EU Migrant Women's Access to Residence and Social Rights in the U.K. *Journal of Ethnic and Migration Studies* 44 (1): 137–153.

Simpkin, V.L., and E. Mossialos. 2017. Brexit and the NHS: Challenges, Uncertainties and Opportunities. *Health Policy* 121 (5): 477–480.

Soldatic, K., and H. Meekosha. 2013. Disability and Neoliberal State Formations. In *Routledge Handbook of Disability Studies*, ed. Nick Watson, Alan Roulstone, and Carol Thomas, 195–210. London: Routledge.

Stephenson, M.-A., and J. Harrison. 2011. Unravelling Equality: The Impact of the United Kingdom's Spending Cuts on Women. *The Political Quarterly* 82(4): 645–650.

Sumption, M., and Z. Kone. 2018. Unsettled Status? Which EU Citizens Are at Risk of Failing to Secure Their Rights After Brexit? Migration Observatory, COMPAS University of Oxford, April 12. www.migrationobservatory.ox.ac. uk/resources/reports/unsettled-status-which-eu-citizens-are-at-risk-of-failing-to-secure-their-rights-after-brexit.

the3million. 2018. EU Settlement Scheme: Statement of Intent. An Analysis by the3million, July 11. https://www.the3million.org.uk/publications.

Thorley, C. 2017. Not by Degrees: Improving Student Mental Health in the UK's Universities. Institute for Public Policy Research (IPPR), September. https://www.ippr.org/research/publications/not-by-degrees.

Tinson, A., H. Aldridge, T.B. Born, and C. Hughes. 2016. Disability and Poverty. Why Disability Must Be at the Centre of Poverty Reduction. New Policy Institute. Commissioned by: Joseph Rowntree Foundation, August. https://www.npi.org.uk/files/3414/7087/2429/Disability_and_poverty_MAIN_REPORT_FINAL.pdf.

Titchkosky, T. 2003. *Disability, Self, and Society*. London: University of Toronto Press.

Travis, A. 2013. Benefit Tourism Warnings by Theresa May Get Short Shrift from Europe [Newspaper Article]. *The Guardian*, April 29. http://www. theguardian.com/world/2013/apr/29/benefit-tourism-theresa-may-europe. Accessed 3 June 2018.

UK Parliament. 2018a. Legal Aid Scheme: Social Security Benefits [Written Question (130690): Asked by Gloria De Piero, Answered by: Rory Stewart]. UK Parliament, March 1. https://www.parliament.uk/business/publications/written-questions-answers-statements/written-question/Commons/2018-03-01/130690/. Accessed 7 July 2018.

UK Parliament. 2018b. Personal Independence Payment: Mental Illness [Written Question (124308): Asked by Debbie Abrahams, Answered by: Sarah Newton]. UK Parliament, June 23. https://www.parliament.uk/business/publications/written-questions-answers-statements/written-question/Commons/2018-01-23/124308/. Accessed 10 July 2018.

UK Statistics Authority. 2016. UK Statistics Authority Statement on the Use of Official Statistics on Contributions to the European Union. UK Statistics Authority, May 27. https://www.statisticsauthority.gov.uk/news/uk-statistics-authority-statement-on-the-use-of-official-statistics-on-contributions-to-the-european-union/. Accessed 22 Apr 2018.

UKCEN. 2018. Settled Status and Citizens' Rights—What Has Been Agreed? UK Citizenship for European Nationals (UKCEN), March 27. http://www.ukcen.co.uk/settled-status-and-citizens-rights-what-has-been-agreed/. Accessed 30 Mar 2018.

UKICE. 2018. *Brexit and the NHS*. Report. The UK in a Changing Europe (UKICE), March 14. http://ukandeu.ac.uk/wp-content/uploads/2018/03/Brexit-and-the-NHS-.pdf.

UKICE. n.d. How Many EU Migrants Claim Benefits in the UK? *The UK in a Changing Europe (UKICE)*. http://ukandeu.ac.uk/fact-figures/how-many-eu-migrants-claim-benefits-in-the-uk/. Accessed 9 Mar 2018.

VODG. 2017. *BREXIT. Risks and Rights: How Social Care Can Survive Brexit*. Report. Voluntary Organisations Disability Group (VODG). https://www.vodg.org.uk/news/government-must-focus-on-how-brexit-affects-the-voluntary-social-care-sector/.

Waddington, L. 2017. The Potential for, and Barriers to, the Exercise of Active EU Citizenship by People with Disabilities: The Right to Free Movement. In *The Changing Disability Policy System: Active Citizenship and Disability in Europe*, ed. Rune Halvorsen, Bjørn Hvinden, Jerome Bickenbach, Delia Ferri, and Ana Marta Guillén Rodriguez, 196–214. London: Routledge.

Williams, S.I., S. Rogers, and S. Prosser. 2018. *Shared Prosperity, Shared Rights: Replacing EU Funding for Equality and Human Rights After Brexit*. Report. Commissioned by: The Equality and Diversity Forum (EDF), February 2018. http://www.edf.org.uk/edf-report-shared-prosperity-shared-rights-replacing-eu-funding-for-equality-and-human-rights-after-brexit/.

WPC. 2018a. *PIP and ESA Assessments (HC 829)*. Seventh Report of Session 2017–19. House of Commons Work and Pensions Committee (WPC), February 14. https://www.parliament.uk/business/committees/committees-

a-z/commons-select/work-and-pensions-committee/news-parliament-2017/
pip-esa-full-report-17-19/.
WPC. 2018b. *PIP and ESA Assessments: Claimant Experiences (HC 335)*.
Fourth Report of Session 2017–19.. House of Commons Work and Pensions
Committee (WPC), February 9. https://publications.parliament.uk/pa/
cm201719/cmselect/cmworpen/355/35502.htm.
Yeo, R. 2015. 'Disabled Asylum Seekers?... They Don't Really Exist': The
Marginalisation of Disabled Asylum Seekers in the UK and Why It Matters.
Disability and the Global South 2 (1): 523–550.
Yuille, M. 2018. Brexiters' Clinical Trials Conundrum. Scientists for EU, April 20.
http://www.scientistsforeu.uk/brexiters_clinical_trials_conundrum. Accessed
28 Apr 2018.
Zanon, E. 2016. What Implications Could Brexit Have for NHS Patients? NHS
European Office (NHS Confederation), July 15. http://www.nhsconfed.
org/confed18. Accessed 29 Apr 2018.

CHAPTER 6

The Potential Effects of Brexit on the Cross-Border Circulation of Private Family Law Judgments; with a Particular Focus on Questions Relating to Gender

Lara Walker

1 INTRODUCTION

The family and family law, traditionally involve gender-based questions relating to the social construct of the family and social issues more broadly, which are related to gender, such as caring and motherhood. The demands and responsibilities of these roles are not necessarily compatible with paid work and can limit a mother's access to full-time work. EU law includes Regulations that focus on family law, but these mainly relate to procedural elements rather than substantive family law which still varies widely between Member States. The main purpose of the EU law in this area is to resolve disputes on jurisdiction and allow the free circulation of judgments, between Member States, on issues such as divorce, parental responsibility and maintenance. This free circulation of

L. Walker (✉)
Sussex Law School, School of Law, Politics and Sociology,
University of Sussex, Brighton, UK
e-mail: lw264@sussex.ac.uk

© The Author(s) 2019
M. Dustin et al. (eds.), *Gender and Queer Perspectives on Brexit*,
Gender and Politics, https://doi.org/10.1007/978-3-030-03122-0_6

judgments is built upon the principle of mutual trust. The interpretation of concepts and provisions in the Regulations is supported by case law from the Court of Justice of the European Union (CJEU). This paper examines the potential impact of Brexit in the area of family law, and analyses whether this has any effect on gender.

The Regulations which this contribution focuses on are Brussels IIa,[1] the Maintenance Regulation,[2] and the Civil Protection Regulation.[3] Brussels IIa applies in relation to matters such as divorce, parental responsibility, custody, access and foster care. A full list of the scope of application can be found in Article 1 of Brussels IIa. Brussels IIa is currently being Recast,[4] and the UK has opted to participate in the recast procedure. It is likely that the Recast Regulation will enter into force prior to the date of Brexit. The Maintenance Regulation applies to maintenance between spouses, child support and other forms of family maintenance (as permitted under national laws [Article 1]). Maintenance for the purpose of the Regulation covers both periodical and lump sum payments, as long as that lump sum payment is designed to allow one spouse to provide for himself or herself, or to meet the needs of the party.[5] The Civil Protection Regulation enables the enforcement of protection measures in other Member States. It can apply to civil orders in areas such as domestic violence and forced marriage. In England and Wales relevant orders are occupation orders, non-molestation orders and forced marriage protection orders. This contribution will focus on

[1] Council Regulation (EC) No. 2201/2003 of 27 November 2003 concerning jurisdiction and the recognition and enforcement of judgments in matrimonial matters and the matters of parental responsibility, repealing Regulation (EC) No. 1347/2000 [2003] OJ L338.

[2] Council Regulation (EC) No. 4/2009 of 18 December 2008 on jurisdiction, applicable law, recognition and enforcement of decisions and cooperation in matters relating to maintenance obligations [2009] OJ L7/1.

[3] Regulation (EU) No. 606/2013 of the European Parliament and of the Council of 12 June 2013 on mutual recognition of protection measures in civil matters [2013] OJ L181.

[4] European Commission, Proposal for a Council Regulation on jurisdiction, the recognition and enforcement of decisions in matrimonial matters and the matters of parental responsibility, and on international child abduction (recast) COM (2016) 411 final. For further information on the Recast process see http://www.europarl.europa.eu/legislative-train/theme-area-of-justice-and-fundamental-rights/file-matrimonial-matters-matters-of-parental-responsibility-%E2%80%93-brussels-iia-revision.

[5] Judgment of 27 February 1997, *Van den Boogaard v Laumen*, C-220/95, EU:C:1997:91.

private family disputes that fall within these Regulations and will exclude public family law matters such as foster care.[6]

This contribution argues that the incomplete application of these EU Regulations following Brexit will create both opportunities and losses for UK families post Brexit, in the context of gender. The contribution will start by explaining the rules in the Regulations in more detail and highlighting the problems with the approach of the EU (Withdrawal) Bill (EU(W)B) in this context. The contribution will then highlight opportunities arising from Brexit for women, before outlining the losses. The loss of the reciprocal application of the EU Regulations following Brexit will affect families throughout the UK, but there will be some regional variances because the national law in England and Wales differs from the laws in Scotland and Northern Ireland. Where a comment relates specifically to a particular legal system this will be stated in the contribution.

2   BRUSSELS IIA, THE MAINTENANCE REGULATION AND RECIPROCITY

Brussels IIa and the Maintenance Regulation contain rules on jurisdiction, recognition and enforcement and central authorities. Brussels IIa also includes special rules on child abduction which build on the 1980 Abduction Convention.[7] This contribution will discuss the basis of these rules to explain how these rules operate within Member States.

In the context of divorce, Article 3 Brussels IIa provides a number of jurisdictional bases. The rules apply as alternatives, there is no hierarchy. On relationship breakdown one party might want to sue in the country of the families' habitual residence (e.g., Belgium), and the other party might want to sue in the country of the spouses joint nationality (e.g., France). Article 19 Brussels IIa aims to resolve these conflicts of

---

[6] It is useful to note that there are other Regulations in this area, which deal with matrimonial property and applicable law on divorce, but the UK does not participate in these. Council Regulation (EU) No. 1259/2010 of 20 December 2010 implementing enhanced cooperation in the area of the law applicable to divorce and legal separation [2010] OJ L343/10 (Rome III); Council Regulation (EU) No. 2016/1103 of 24 June 2016 implementing enhanced cooperation in the area of jurisdiction, applicable law and the recognition and enforcement of decisions in matters of matrimonial property regimes (Matrimonial Property Regulation).

[7] The Hague Convention of 25 October 1980 on the Civil Aspects of International Child Abduction.

jurisdiction by giving priority to the court first seised. This is known as lis pendens. Although this promotes legal certainty, the rule has been criticised because it can be restrictive and it does not necessarily mean that the court with the closest connection to the dispute hears the case (Ní Shúilleabháin 2010). The approach directly contradicts the traditional English common law approach of *forum conveniens*,[8] which aims to find the most appropriate forum but does not provide legal certainty. The same system operates under the Maintenance Regulation, whereby proceedings can be held in the creditor or the defendant's habitual residence, or in a court where connected proceedings are being heard, such as the divorce court.[9]

Regulations are directly applicable (meaning that no implementing legislation is actually required), but most Member States enact implementing legislation in this area nevertheless (Hess and Spancken 2014). In England and Wales the jurisdictional provisions in Brussels IIa have been implemented directly into national law, through section 5 of the Matrimonial Causes Act 1973 (as amended) and are included on all divorce forms. Even when the divorce does not have an EU element, every divorce in England and Wales must comply with the jurisdictional provisions in the EU Regulation. Recent statistics on divorce in England and Wales suggest that more women apply for divorce than men, and that 78% of same-sex divorces involved female couples (Office of National Statistics 2017). It is unclear why this is but, even though more women apply for divorce than men, divorce as a matter of status is not in itself gendered. However, the consequences of divorce are gendered because women are usually maintenance creditors following divorce. This is linked to societal constructs such as caretaking, women traditionally being lower earners and the effects of career breaks on career progress. As Fineman argues, '[f]athering as a social activity is understood more as the assumption of economic, rather than caretaking responsibility... It is motherhood as a social and cultural practice that is burdened by our

---

[8] See *Villiers v Villiers* [2018] EWCA Civ 1120, where one party was trying to argue that *forum conveniens* could still be applied in maintenance jurisdiction disputes between Scotland and England. The court held that the 2011 Maintenance Regulations (which implement the EU Maintenance Regulation) remove the ability to rely on *forum conveniens* in intra UK maintenance disputes.

[9] Maintenance Regulation Articles 3–5. Article 4 provides for jurisdiction based on a choice of court agreement, but this provision does not apply to child maintenance.

policies' (2005). Consequently, jurisdiction for divorce matters because jurisdiction for disputes relating to the consequences of divorce can be linked to jurisdiction for divorce.

The other key element of the relevant instruments are the provisions on recognition and enforcement. This is rather complex, because the instruments contain a number of different procedures for recognition and enforcement. In some areas a declaration of enforceability is required prior to enforcement and in other circumstances individuals can proceed directly with enforcement. Where a declaration of enforceability is required, the grounds for refusing to grant this are extremely narrow. In either situation, the rules under the Regulation are simplified in order to secure enforcement in as many cases as possible, so that decisions can freely circulate within the EU. The ease of enforcement of maintenance orders is particularly important for women.

Reciprocity and the EU Withdrawal Bill

In accordance with the House of Commons EU Withdrawal Bill,[10] these Regulations will be adopted into national law and will continue to apply in the UK until they have been replaced with other legislation. The key problem with this is that these instruments are based on reciprocity. The UK can continue to apply these rules following the date of Brexit, but they will not be useful without the support of other Member States. The EU(W)B recognises reciprocal arrangements are an area of deficiency, but it leaves it open for these laws to be amended in due course.[11] It does not provide an alternative solution to these rules which is significantly different, because the rules in the Regulations will still be retained on Brexit. In the context of Brussels IIa and the Maintenance Regulation, the rules on lis pendens and recognition and enforcement only apply between Member States. Therefore, when the UK leaves the EU, the other Member States will no longer have to enforce maintenance, child support or parental responsibility decisions arising from one of the three UK jurisdictions (England and Wales, Scotland and Northern Ireland). In contrast, the courts across the UK will still have to enforce child support decisions originating in France. The effect of the

---

[10]European Union (Withdrawal) Bill (HC Bill 147) 21/12/2017 provisions 2 and 3.
[11]European Union (Withdrawal) Bill (HL Bill 102) 08/05/2018.

EU(W)B is to create a one-way system. This is entirely unhelpful in relation to a system based on reciprocity, which is designed to allow the circulation of judgments within the internal market. It should be glaringly obvious to the Government that 'orders that are not enforceable are not worth the paper they are written on' (Lowe 2017).

Before withdrawing from the EU, the Government needs to ensure that a mechanism is included so that family law judgments can still be enforced in other Member States. This is imperative because the EU rules on free movement of people have resulted in increased migration. Migration patterns create additional problems for bi-national families, and changes in these patterns are often interconnected with divorce, separation and cohabitation (Morano-Foadi 2007, 17). These problems will most likely continue following Brexit. Changes in relation to access to employment will also encourage families, or family members, to migrate to other EU Member States. Therefore, the continued enforcement of family law judgments from the three UK jurisdictions, in the remaining Member States, is imperative.

The EU(W)B, in its current format, does not assist with this therefore it is insufficient and another solution is required from the date of exit. Members of the Brexit Family Law Group have argued for a special agreement, so that the EU Family Law Regulations will continue to apply post-Brexit. Although there are undoubtedly some merits to this solution it also raises a number of obstacles. The obvious one is that this would require the continued jurisdiction of the CJEU in this area. It is highly unlikely that the Government will agree to this, although Members of the House of Lords are more sympathetic (Sherlock 2017). Another obstacle is that these Regulations will continue to be recast. After the UK has left the EU, representatives will no longer be able to participate in the negotiating process when the instruments are being recast. This may mean that the future Regulations contain some provisions which are unacceptable to UK officials. Currently, if the UK has an issue with one of the Regulations in this area, then it does not need to opt-in. If a special agreement is reached in this area, it is unlikely that this will continue to include an opt-in provision. Any solution along these lines, although better for individuals, will put the UK in a worse position than in the pre-Brexit context.

The alternative solution is for these Regulations not to be included in the EU(W)B and the UK to ensure that the relevant Hague Conventions apply from the date of withdrawal from the EU. These Conventions are:

the 1980 Abduction Convention, the 1996 Children's Convention,[12] and the 2007 Maintenance Convention.[13] However, there are some problems with this. Steps will have to be taken to ensure that the 1996 Children's Convention and the 2007 Maintenance Convention continue to apply after Brexit (Lowe 2017; Beaumont 2017). It should also be noted that the provisions contained in these Conventions are not equivalent to the provisions in the Regulations, and these differences may leave some gaps in the law. This contribution will now look at these issues in more detail and argue that in some areas the differences between the Hague Conventions and the EU instruments will result in opportunities in the context of gender, and in other areas this will result in losses.

3   OPPORTUNITIES ARISING FROM BREXIT

An important area where Brexit will have an effect is the civil aspects of child abduction. The main rules on child abduction are still contained in the 1980 Abduction Convention, which every Member State is party to.[14] The aim of the Convention is to return children to the country of their habitual residence, immediately prior to the wrongful removal or retention, so that any further decisions on where the child should live can be made by the court with the closest connection to the child. There are three exceptions in Article 13 of the 1980 Abduction Convention to the main rule which favours return. These exceptions apply when the left behind parent has either consented to or otherwise acquiesced to the removal (13(1)(a)), where the return would put the child at grave risk of physical or psychological harm (13(1)(b)), or where the child otherwise objects to the return (13(2)). However, these exceptions are not widely used and in most cases that require a judicial decision a return is ordered (Lowe 2011). The courts in England and Wales are particularly cautious of issuing non-return orders, and in 2008 did so in only 8% of cases,

---

[12]The Hague Convention of 19 October 1996 on Jurisdiction, Applicable Law, Recognition, Enforcement and Co-operation in Respect of Parental Responsibility and Measures for the Protection of Children.

[13]The Hague Convention of 23 November 2007 on the International Recovery of Child Support and Other Forms of Family Maintenance.

[14]https://www.hcch.net/en/instruments/conventions/status-table/?cid=24, accessed 20 December 2017. Most Member States have ratified the Convention, but Bulgaria for example is party to the Convention via accession.

compared to a global average of around 15% during that year (Lowe 2011).[15] The strict approach taken in some countries does not always appear justified (Bruch 2004, 535), with the result that return orders are made in cases where the parties cannot be adequately protected on return.[16] Another point to note is that it is predominantly mothers who are the abducting parents; three studies put this figure at around 70% (Lowe 2011; Kruger 2011; Trimmings 2013).[17]

Child abduction cases often involve women, who have married or partnered spouses abroad, returning to their home country with their children (Silberman 2000; section 'Detailed Analysis of Three European Cases Involving the Second-Chance Procedure' below).[18] The decision to return can be related to gendered issues, such as motherhood and caring. Fineman terms caring as derivative dependency, because those who take responsibility to care for a dependant person such as their child are dependent on resources to allow them to undertake that care (2005). If these mothers return to their homeland, they can receive support with childcare from their wider family, which has become more important since they have become a single parent and formed a single-income household. Other women may be escaping domestic violence (Lamont 2011; Weiner 2000). In most cases the mother's attempt to relocate will be unsuccessful, because she will be required to return to the country of origin in accordance with the 1980 Abduction Convention. Lady Hale has commented that when working in the High Court she often felt that her role was to oppress women, specifically mothers, because of the high volume of cases on child abduction (Hale 2017, 1).

Child Abduction and Brussels IIa

Brussels IIa builds on the 1980 Abduction Convention by including additional rules in the context of child abduction. In particular, Article

[15] In 2015 the global refusal rate dropped to 12% (Lowe 2018).

[16] Courts often issue undertakings to try and secure the safety of the child and the mother on return, but these orders are not necessarily enforceable and the undertakings are regularly broken (Freeman 2014, 11–12).

[17] A study carried out on abduction applications from 2015 suggests this figure is now higher at 73% (Lowe 2018).

[18] In 2008 60% of taking parents were going home, compared to 58% in 2015 (Lowe 2018).

11 of the Regulation includes an additional procedure that allows the court in the state of the child's habitual residence to make a further order, subsequently to an Article 13 1980 Abduction Convention non-return order, which might trump the non-return order (second-chance procedure). If the left-behind parent is successful, when making an application under the second-chance procedure, then the order requiring the child to return is automatically enforceable in the state of refuge. It is extremely difficult for women to relocate with children following relationship breakdown, but Brussels IIa creates an additional hurdle in the small number of cases where a 1980 Article 13 Hague non-return order has been issued. This second-chance procedure was implemented due to a belief that Article 13(1)(b) was not being applied properly in practice, but the EU did not consider who abducts and why, nor the influence of domestic violence on child abduction when these rules were developed (Lamont 2011). Perhaps unsurprisingly, the gender of the abducting parent was female in 83% of cases involving the second-chance procedure. (Beaumont et al. 2016a). This is higher than the percentage of women abductors in 1980 Abduction Convention cases. Therefore the additional procedure imposed by Brussels IIa oppresses women further in this context.

The second-chance procedure in Brussels IIa has been largely unsuccessful and the case law is unhelpful and controversial. In the cases where there was an order requiring the return of the child, the order was only legally enforced within the EU in 18% of cases (Beaumont et al. 2016a), and in one case the child only returned for 6 months[19] (Beaumont et al. 2016a, b). In *Bradbrooke*, where the mother returned to her native Poland following relationship breakdown,[20] and *Rinau* the fathers re-abducted their child on the basis of the legal order.[21] The father in *Bradbrooke* did this whilst the mother had allowed a period of contact between the child and the father. She was unaware of the Belgian order when she allowed the child to spend time with his father. In *LA* the Lithuanian authorities had failed to enforce an order which required the child to return to England.[22] The father eventually took the child

---

[19] *Re A (Custody Decision after Maltese non-return Order)* [2006] EWHC 3397 (Fam).

[20] *Bradbrooke c Aleksandrowicz*, R.G. N°: 2014/JR/73 et N°: 2014/FA/113.

[21] Judgment of 11 July 2008, *Rinau*, C-195/08 PPU, EU:C:2008:406.

[22] *LA v SA* unreported.

to the USA, partially to avoid a European arrest warrant (EAW). The authorities in the USA managed to get the child to return to England, however this was not required by the rules under Brussels IIa, which do not apply in America, nor did the principle of mutual trust apply. These cases indicate that the authorities in European States have been unable to enforce the orders (showing little sign of the enhanced cooperation underpinned by mutual trust) and parents have taken the law into their own hands. This causes disruption and uncertainty for the children involved. The concern for children can also be seen in a case where the state of refuge was France and the French authorities were very apprehensive about enforcing the order. In this case the French authorities kept ordering further psychological assessments of the child, because they were concerned for her welfare. During this time the child turned 16 and the French authorities no longer had to enforce the order as the regime no longer applied (Beaumont et al. 2016b).[23] These cases highlight the problems with this procedure more generally, to show that the problems run further than the oppression of women but also negatively affect children and other family members involved in the second-chance procedure. The ongoing proceedings are also costly and create a feeling of distrust in the legal system.

Detailed Analysis of Three European Cases Involving the Second-Chance Procedure

The cases that have been heard by the CJEU and the EU Commission have also been particularly severe and the CJEU has taken a very restrictive interpretation of the Regulation. In *Aguirre Zarraga*,[24] the mother had taken her daughter (Andrea) from Spain to Germany, the country of her nationality. The German courts issued a non-return order under Article 13(2) of the Abduction Convention, because Andrea had demonstrated that she objected to returning to Spain. In the second-chance proceedings the Spanish courts refused to hear the mother and Andrea via video-link, insisting that they had to return to Spain for the trial. This obviously created some difficulties, because if they returned to Spain they

---

[23]For further information on national case law under this additional procedure see Beaumont et al. (2016a, b).

[24]Judgment of 22 December 2010, *Aguirre Zarraga v Simone Pelz*, C-491/10 PPU, EU:C:2010:828.

might have their documents seised and be unable to return to Germany again. They did not return for the proceedings, and the decision issued by the Spanish court required that Andrea returned to Spain and lived with her father. The German authorities queried whether they had to enforce the order, which they argued did not comply with fundamental rights such as Article 24 of the Charter on Fundamental Rights (CFR).[25] The CJEU held that there were no circumstances in which the enforcing court could refuse enforcement; the only remedy was to appeal the decision in Spain. The approach of the CJEU has been criticised from a children's rights perspective (Kuipers 2012; Schulz 2013). There are also difficulties with this from a gender perspective. The mother was not heard in these proceedings, which also directly affected her and her relationship with her daughter. Travelling to Spain was risky, because if her documents were removed, or if she had been subject to criminal proceedings, this could affect her ability to return to Germany and her employment there. However, the decision of the Spanish courts was never enforced by the German authorities, and Andrea remained in Germany with her mother.

Povse was heard by the CJEU,[26] and then twice before the European Court of Human Rights (ECtHR), where both the mother and the father brought proceedings against Austria.[27] The mother (Doris) took the daughter (Sofia) to Austria, the country of her nationality, in February 2008. The initial 1980 Abduction Convention non-return order was given by Austria, under Article 13(1)(b), because it was believed that both Sofia and Doris were at risk of harm on return to Italy, because of alleged abuse towards Sofia and domestic violence towards Doris. In 2009, during the second-chance proceedings, the Italian authorities issued an order requiring that Doris returned to Italy with Sofia and lived with her there. In this case social services were to provide housing for the mother and the child.[28] If the mother refused to return Sofia was to live in Italy with her father. The CJEU held that the order must either be enforced in Austria, or appealed in Italy on the basis that there had been a change of circumstances. Enforcement in Austria

---

[25] Charter of Fundamental Rights of the European Union, OJ 2010 C83/02.

[26] Judgment of 1 July 2010, *Povse v Alpago*, C-211/10 PPU, EU:C:2010:400.

[27] Application No. 3890/11; *M.A v Austria* Application No. 4097/13.

[28] Application No. 3890/11, para. 21.

could not be refused on this basis. The Austrian authorities attempted to take enforcement action but the order was not enforced.[29]

In November 2011, almost 4 years after the initial removal, the Italian courts issued an order which required that Sofia return to Italy immediately and live with her father. By the time this order was made, Sofia had no contact with her father and she no longer spoke Italian. Sofia and Doris brought proceedings against Austria before the ECtHR, because the Astrain courts ordered the enforcement of the Italian order, and argued that the enforcement of the order violated their right to private and family life under Article 8 of the ECHR. The ECtHR simply applied the *Bosphorus* presumption[30] (Costello 2006; Glas and Krommendijk 2017) and did not look at the rights of the individuals in any detail, despite the fact that Sofia was being forced to leave her mother, her primary carer, and go to live with her other parent with whom she did not even share a common language. The inference made by the ECtHR was that the mother should have brought proceedings against Italy rather than Austria, however Doris argued that she did not have the resources to bring more proceedings in Italy and she did not qualify for legal aid there. Both the CJEU and the ECtHR adopted a strict technical approach to the decision, but neither took account of the actual difficulties faced by Sofia and Doris. The ECtHR could have taken a different approach, which was more consistent with the realities of that family's life (Walker 2017a). Despite the endless litigation, Sofia never returned to Italy and she remained in Austria with her mother, the mother's new partner and her new brother.

In *Šneersone*, the court of origin was also Italy.[31] One of the reasons the mother (Jeļizaveta) took the child (Marko) to Latvia was because she was not receiving child support payments from the father, even though child support had been ordered by the Italian court. The child's grandmother had been sending money from Latvia, which Jeļizaveta was using to support herself, but when the grandmother could not send this

---

[29]These cases create problems for national authorities because they are private family law disputes, rather than public family law disputes, so the child is not at risk of harm. In general, for private disputes, national authorities will not use force to remove a child from their primary carer if the child does not want to leave. Some countries may take measures against the parent frustrating contact, such as fines, but they should not punish the child.

[30]*Bosphorus Hava Yollari Turizm v Ireland* (2006) 42 EHRR 1.

[31]*Šneersone and Kampanella v Italy* (2011) Application No. 14737/09.

money anymore, she decided to return to Latvia. The allegations in the case report suggest Jeḷizaveta was having financial difficulties in Italy. These problems are likely to be linked to her caring obligations and her ability to find employment in Italy. The Gender Equality Report indicates that the employment rate of women in Italy is only 52%, whereas in Latvia it is 72% (European Commission 2017, 10).[32]

The Latvian court refused to return the child on the basis of Article 13(1)(b). There was concern that if Marko was separated from his mother, this would negatively affect his development and could even create neurotic problems and illnesses. Marko was only four at the time of the Latvian proceedings and it was believed that he should remain with his mother, who had been his primary carer in Italy. During the 1980 Abduction Convention proceedings the Latvian court considered that Jeḷizaveta would not be able to return to Italy with the child because of her financial situation there, so Marko should remain in Latvia with his mother. However, in the second-chance proceedings the Italian court then ruled that Marko should return to Italy and live primarily with his father. He was to see his mother for one month a year during the summer, in Italy. The Latvian authorities ordered further psychological reports, arguing that this would not be in Marko's best interests. Latvia brought an action against Italy before the European Commission, but this was unsuccessful.[33] The Commission held that Italy had violated neither the Regulation nor the general principles of EU law. Jeḷizaveta also brought proceedings before the ECtHR against Italy the state of the court that issued the judgment, rather than before the enforcing state. The ECtHR held that the order of the Italian authorities, which required the return of the child to Italy, violated Jeḷizaveta's and Marko's right to family life. Marko remained with his mother and was not returned to Italy.

The CJEU has taken a strict textual approach to interpreting the Regulation in these cases on enforcement. Although this might be legitimate to some extent, this has not necessarily been the approach of the CJEU in other areas. In the context of Brussels IIa, the CJEU and the Commission have been very reluctant to take account of general principles of EU law such as fundamental rights and gender equality. This

---

[32] The employment rate of men in Italy is 72%, compared to 75% in Latvia.

[33] *Šneersone and Kampanella v Italy* (2011) Application No. 14737/09, paras. 39–45.

creates problems due to issues related to structure and access to the two supra-national courts. The ability to sue the correct court in the ECtHR is difficult structurally, because of the requirement to exhaust domestic measures. This is particularly problematic in cases relating to Article 11(8) of Brussels IIa, where there are often proceedings going on in two Member States at the same time. One state is ruling on the substantive issues, and the other state is making a decision on enforcement (or non-enforcement). Because of the often extreme effects of the substantive judgment in these cases, it is difficult to argue that the solutions in this area are purely procedural. The Courts consider that the case can be resolved by application to the court with jurisdiction, but the courts fail to appreciate problems with accessing that court and the restrictions on the right to a fair hearing if the court refuses to hear the parties via video-link. The effect of procedural processes, and the practical and financial difficulties of petitioning an alternative court to address the point of change in circumstances, are not considered (Lamont 2017a).

The CJEU also fails to address the issues surrounding the return of a terrified mother who has fled domestic violence. The expectation that a woman who has managed to escape a perpetrator should return for a court hearing regardless of whether there are effective protective measures in place seems misplaced. Further the presumption that the child can return without the mother is impractical in cases where the child is very young, and in other cases it is unlikely that the mother will be happy to send the child back alone. The reality of caring and dependency means that this outcome would be very unusual. One benefit of the proposed Recast in this area is that it clarifies that the judgment requiring the return should be a final judgment that includes a full assessment of the merits of the case (Beaumont et al. 2016c). This was skewed in the current version by an unhelpful decision by the CJEU in *Povse*. The notion that one summary order can be trumped by another summary order given in a different Member State clearly undermines mutual trust and the system does not support families (Beaumont et al. 2016a). The Recast Regulation maintains the second-chance procedure but clarifies that the order under the second-chance procedure will have to be a full merits decision taking account of all the facts of the case.[34] In the

---

[34] European Commission, Proposal for a Council Regulation on jurisdiction, the recognition and enforcement of decisions in matrimonial matters and the matters of parental responsibility, and on international child abduction (recast) COM (2016) 411 final.

future, the CJEU might be more willing to review orders that do not appear appropriate. However, in *Šneersone* there was clearly a final order and the Commission was not at all sympathetic to the negative effects of the order on the mother and the child. To date the CJEU has not been sensitive to the structural and procedural factors, and the second-chance procedure in itself further restricts the free movement of parents, in particular mothers who might have moved for good reasons.

In relation to the gender equality scheme more broadly, a lack of access to resources can impede free movement of the mother. The desire to move might be based on a desire to find employment. The Gender Equality Report shows that in some countries there is a greater discrepancy between the employment rate of men and woman than others. Italy and Spain have a wide discrepancy, and low rates of employment for women compared to Austria, Germany and Latvia (European Commission 2017). In addition, the Report encourages certain countries to improve their provision of affordable childcare. The list of countries includes Italy and Spain (European Commission 2017, 13). Finally, many households are still dependent on male income. This factor increases the risk of that household falling into poverty in the case of relationship breakdown (European Commission 2017, 26). According to the report, 70% of couples with children would fall into poverty if a father were to lose his job. The same risks are prevalent if the relationship breaks down and the father does not make child support or maintenance contributions. When taking these factors into account, it is clear why women may want to return to the country of their nationality following a relationship breakdown. They will be able to secure assistance from their wider family, and they might have a better chance of gaining access to the employment market and affordable childcare. Families in these situations have reported that 'it is more problematic for women than for men to live outside their own culture when the family splits up and children are involved' (Morano-Foadi 2007, 9). There can also be problems in relation to cases where there has been domestic violence. In such cases the return of the child and the mother to the first State for the hearing increases the risk to the mother. These mothers will be particularly concerned about the loss of their passport and their inability to flee again. They might also have problems accessing domestic violence refuges in this state, even though a judge may presume this option will be available (Bruch 2004, 537).

Despite the work done by the EU on gender equality in other areas, 'the gender dynamics affecting both men and women are ignored in the shaping of the European remedy for child abduction.' (Lamont 2011, 376–377). These factors have not been addressed in the Recast, which retains the second-chance procedure.[35] Therefore, the loss of the second-chance procedure and the case law of the CJEU in this area represents an opportunity in regards to gender and the specific characteristics of societal consequences for women. While the 1980 Abduction Convention could also be considered to create problems in the context of gender, and is unlikely to be updated, the EU position is significantly worse despite the regular revisions of Brussels IIa.

4   LOSSES ARISING FROM BREXIT

This contribution will now assess the areas where Brexit could result in a loss for those involved in cross-border family disputes. The areas for potential loss following Brexit relate to: (1) the ongoing enforcement of decisions on parental responsibility, (2) the enforcement of civil protection orders for adults, (3) the ongoing recognition of British divorces throughout Europe and the cross-border recovery of maintenance and child support due to the likely loss of the Maintenance Regulation, and (4) the loss of mutual trust and the influence of the CJEU.

Parental Responsibility

In relation to private law proceedings, the 1996 Children's Convention is good enough to fill any perceived gaps in relation to parental responsibility. The main difference between the rules on parental responsibility in Brussels IIa and the 1996 Children's Convention, in the context of gender, relates to the recognition and enforcement procedure. The key difference between the two recognition and enforcement procedures is that under the 1996 Children's Convention the enforcing court can review jurisdiction at the recognition and enforcement stage if one of the parties argues that this is necessary (Article 23(2)(a)). A check on jurisdiction at this point could fundamentally delay proceedings, and if a declaration of

---

[35] European Commission, Proposal for a Council Regulation on jurisdiction, the recognition and enforcement of decisions in matrimonial matters and the matters of parental responsibility, and on international child abduction (recast) COM (2016) 411 final.

enforceability is refused this could mean that the applicant (potentially the mother) would have to seek a new order in an alternative state. This will increase costs for both the applicant and the respondent.

The other difference, after the Brussels IIa Recast enters into force, is that there will no longer need to be a declaration of enforceability for custody decisions circulating under the Regulation (access decisions are already automatically enforceable). However, most of the current grounds for refusal of a declaration of enforceability will remain; they will just be applied at the enforcement stage instead (Beaumont et al. 2016c). The only notable change to the grounds in the recast will be the removal of the exception relating to the views of the child,[36] which arguably has some importance (Beaumont 2017). Under the current version of the Regulation a court can refuse to grant a declaration of enforceability for a decision on parental responsibility if the child was not heard by the court that issued the order.[37] However, both instruments contain an exception that can be applied when one of the holders of parental responsibility was not heard during the proceedings.[38] The ability to review jurisdiction and the need for a declaration of enforceability could create a delay at the enforcement stage. However, the EU Fams Project Report suggests that, despite the abolition of the declaration of enforceability,[39] enforcement remains complex (MPI Luxembourg 2017). Therefore the removal of the need for a declaration of enforceability has not necessarily reduced costs nor streamlined enforcement.

Another difference relates to jurisdiction for access following a court-sanctioned relocation. Under the 1996 Children's Convention, following the relocation, the new state immediately has jurisdiction for any further disputes concerning the child. Under Brussels IIa the state of the child's former habitual residence retains jurisdiction for 3 months following the relocation. From a gender perspective, in most cases, it is likely to be the mother that relocates with the child. Following relocation it would be simpler if she could then bring proceedings in the new state rather than having to return to the old state if she wishes to vary

[36] Ibid, proposed Article 38, deleting Article 23(b).

[37] *Re D (A Child) (Recognition of Foreign Order) (Reunite Child Abduction Centre intervening)* [2016] EWCA Civ 12.

[38] Brussels IIa, Article 23(d) (retained in Article 38 recast); 1996 Children's Convention, Article 23(2)(c).

[39] This is commonly referred to as the *exequatur* procedure.

the order. Although there are some small technical differences which could be seen as negative, the differences are not insurmountable and decisions on parental responsibility in private law proceedings should still be able to circulate under the 1996 Children's Convention.[40] Unfortunately, there are likely to be problems during the transition period if Brussels IIa is retained, as outgoing orders will no longer be recognised and enforced under this instrument, but incoming orders will need to be. Without reciprocity, the incorporation of the rules into UK law through the EU(W)B is meaningless and the UK should move straight to the application of the 1996 Convention unless there is support for an alternative special agreement.

Civil Protection Orders

The Civil Protection Orders Regulation allows orders made in one Member State to be automatically enforceable in all EU Member States.[41] The Regulation does not contain rules on jurisdiction (see Dutta 2016 for further details), so any civil protection order made by an EU Member State can be enforceable under this Regulation. The Regulation is designed to apply to measures to protect against gender-based violence or violence in close relationships, such as physical violence, harassment, sexual aggression, stalking, intimidation or other forms of indirect coercion (Recital 6). Therefore, the Regulation can provide assistance in domestic abuse cases, including coercive control, provide protection against forced marriage and provide assistance in abduction cases where protection measures are necessary to ensure the child and the mother can return safely to the state of origin. These types of abuse are usually (but not always) gender based.

The Civil Protection Orders Regulation is an important mechanism to protect women in the EU, who have family in different Member States. This Regulation was referred to in *RB v DB*,[42] in relation to the return of a child to the country of origin following a child abduction. However, because the measures were mainly designed to protect the child, the judge relied on the 1996 Children's Convention rather than

---

[40]For a detailed analysis of these differences see Beaumont (2017).

[41]See Articles 1, 2(1), 3(4) and 4.

[42][2015] EWHC 1817 (Fam).

the Regulation. Unfortunately, however, the 1996 Convention cannot protect women in circumstances of domestic abuse or forced marriage, as it is designed to protect children predominantly. Practitioners have indicated that the Civil Protection Orders Regulation is used often in abduction cases, however, it has not been regularly referred to in reported cases. For example, in *Re X, Y and Z (children)*,[43] the judge commented that protective orders can be considered in the future as may become appropriate. Following Brexit, civil protection orders made in the UK will no longer be enforceable in the remaining Member States. Instead women will have to seek a new order in the relevant Member State. The loss of the Civil Protection Order Regulation will be a loss for the protection of women from gender-based abuse within the EU, as there is no equivalent document at The Hague level.

Divorce and Finance

There are also problems with divorce and finance. There is no widely ratified international Convention on divorce that is equivalent to Brussels IIa.[44] Therefore, divorces may go unrecognised which can be problematic if one party wants to get married again or make claims relating to the consequences of divorce. In England and Wales the traditional jurisdiction rules have been completely replaced by the rules in Brussels IIa, so it might also be the case that domestic law will be changed again following Brexit.

In regard to maintenance, the 2007 Maintenance Convention can provide some solutions but overall it is not as comprehensive as the Maintenance Regulation. The 2007 Maintenance Convention covers both child support and adult maintenance. The provisions on child support are likely to be effective enough going forward (Beaumont 2017). For example, both the Maintenance Regulation and the 2007 Maintenance Convention allow child support decisions to be taken in the state of the creditor's habitual residence.[45] The Convention does have

---

[43] *(Retrospective Leave to Remove from the Jurisdiction)* [2016] EWHC 2439 (Fam) [48].

[44] The Convention of 1 June 1970 on the Recognition of Divorces and Legal Separations only has 20 Contracting States in total (12 of these are EU Member States), and it does not contain any rules on jurisdiction.

[45] For example, in a case where the mother lives in England with the child, and the father lives in Poland, the English courts will almost always have jurisdiction for child support and parental responsibility because this is the habitual residence of the child and maintenance

additional hurdles at the recognition and enforcement stage, however, it is difficult to envisage how this would reduce the circulation of child support decisions with other Member States in Europe where the decision was made in the state of the creditor's habitual residence. If this is a simple child support decision, the rules should apply in the same way, unless there are exceptional circumstances. The Convention also includes provisions on central authorities and legal aid for child support applications, which applicants can choose to use (Walker 2017b).

In the context of spousal maintenance and maintenance on divorce, the situation can be more complicated. There is likely to be more scope for competing alternative jurisdictions. However, the Convention does not contain any direct rules on jurisdiction, so this means that there are no lis pendens provisions to organise which court should have jurisdiction where more than one court could potentially have jurisdiction. Where one of the courts seised is in an EU Member State, then that jurisdiction will benefit from the direct rules in the Maintenance Regulation; this will no longer be the case in the UK. This is likely to create problems for maintenance creditors living in the UK going forward, as this could lead to irreconcilable judgments which run the risk of not being recognised and enforced in another state. The loss of direct rules on jurisdiction has the potential to negatively impact on maintenance creditors in the UK, particularly where maintenance is being decided at the time of divorce. Where maintenance proceedings are being heard post-divorce, the risk of competing jurisdictions is lowered.

The provision of adult maintenance (including lump sum payments) and child support, and the inability to enforce these orders, following divorce or the breakdown of a relationship, can create negative consequences for women. This is linked to social constructs such as caring, part-time work, delayed promotions because of time out from employment and as a consequence lower wages. These problems are not decreasing at a great rate, if at all, and have consequences for women achieving economic independence whilst in a relationship and following relationship breakdown. The European Commission estimate that it will

---

creditor. The child support decision can still be enforced in Poland because the indirect rules of jurisdiction in the Convention allow for jurisdiction based on the habitual residence of the creditor (Article 20(1)(c)) or the habitual residence of the child (Article 20(1)(d)).

take more than a century to close the overall gender gap in earnings and state that 'the disproportionate weight of care responsibilities on women will continue to shrink their economic independence and have a lifelong effect on their career, earnings and pensions.' (European Commission 2017, 53). The difficulty in achieving economic independence highlights the importance of the ongoing enforcement of maintenance obligations across borders, whether as a one-off payment (designed to promote independence through a clean break) or through periodical payments for adult maintenance or child support.

The CJEU and Mutual Trust

Another disadvantage of Brexit is the loss of the contribution of the CJEU more broadly. Although the CJEU has had some negative impact in this area, there are also positive elements to the CJEU role in this context. The Court can provide important decisions on aspects of law to ensure the "autonomous" interpretation of that matter in all Member States.[46] The definition of maintenance for the purpose of EU law was a very important development. National laws vary extensively on what they consider to be maintenance and where the distinction between maintenance and matrimonial property lies. The law of England and Wales makes little distinction between maintenance and property on the relationship breakdown of married couples and instead applies a broad set of principles on a discretionary basis. This was one of the reasons why the UK did not choose to participate in the Matrimonial Property Regulations. This is very different to the Member States with a community of property regime, which make a clear distinction between property and maintenance. This creates some difficulties within the UK, as the Scottish legal system is mixed and contains some civil law traditions in this area. In *Van den Boogaard*[47] the CJEU took a broad approach to maintenance, allowing it to cover payments relating to need, including lump sum payments (which in some regimes would traditionally be regarded as property). The requirement for all Member States to consider maintenance in the same way for the purposes of the Regulation

---

[46] In this area the CJEU uses the term "autonomous" interpretation in its judgments, to mean that a term should be interpreted consistently in all Member States.

[47] Judgment of 27 February 1997, *Van den Boogaard v Laumen*, C-220/95, EU:C:1997:91.

means that it is easier for decisions to circulate in this area, because national definitions should not be considered. This improves life for maintenance creditors, predominantly women.

Article 2 of the 2007 Maintenance Convention does not include a definition of maintenance. The Explanatory Report suggests that "maintenance" should be interpreted broadly and include lump sum payments and other mechanisms that are used to support the needs of the parties, and refers to the case law of the CJEU (Borrás and Degeling Explanatory Report, 2013, para. 65). This gives the impression that the definition of maintenance used in the 2007 Maintenance Convention should be the same as that in the EU Maintenance Regulation. However, unlike the decisions of the CJEU, the Explanatory Report is not legally binding. Only decisions considered to be a decision on "maintenance" can circulate under the 2007 Maintenance Convention (Article 19). Since there is no definition of maintenance and no supra-national court to oversee this and create a definition of maintenance in the future, this may impede the circulation of judgments if the enforcing court considers a decision is not a maintenance decision and therefore not enforceable under this Convention.[48] This may be particularly problematic for decisions originating in England and Wales due to the broad approach taken to maintenance in this jurisdiction. The CJEU has also given important decisions on habitual residence.[49] These principles have now been imported directly into national law in relation to the habitual residence of children and apply to all decisions, whether they are intra EU or not.[50]

The EU principle of mutual trust is also a matter for debate. Lamont argues that this will be a notable loss following Brexit (2017b). However, others have criticised the extent to which mutual trust is actually an effective principle (Weller 2015; Walker 2015; Beaumont et al. 2016a). The nature of the second-chance procedure (see Sect. 3 above) sheds doubt in relation to the effectiveness of mutual trust within the EU, and the extent

[48]There is not a Convention on matrimonial property which the decision could be enforced under. Instead national law would apply to enforcement. The only Convention on matrimonial property relates to applicable law.

[49]Judgment of 2 April 2009, *A*, C-523/07 EU:C:2009:225; Judgment of 22 December 2010, *Mercredi v Chaffe*, C-497/10 PPU, EU:C:2010:8; Judgment of 8 June 2017, *OL v QP*, C-111/17 PPU, EU:2017:436.

[50]*In the Matter of A (Children)* [2013] UKSC 40; *In the Matter of B (A Child)* [2016] UKSC 4.

to which the principle supports the enforcement of intra-EU orders in practice. Lamont argues that it assists with co-operation between authorities in Member States (2017b). However, Central Authorities also operate under The Hague Conventions, and it is usually the same Central Authorities that operate under both systems. Some Central Authorities are undoubtedly more efficient than others (Walker 2015), but this is true of EU and non-EU Central Authorities. Where a Central Authority is under-resourced and struggling to fulfil their work load, this remains the case regardless of whether there is any increased cooperation due to mutual trust. In addition to Central Authority cooperation, there is also The Hague Judicial Network, which is designed to encourage cooperation and coordination between judges in Hague cases.

5   Conclusion

The consequences of Brexit in relation to private family law disputes provides some opportunities and losses in relation to gender. In many areas, The Hague Conventions can fill the gaps left by the EU Regulations, and the loss of the second-chance procedure for child abduction is a benefit in the context of gender. The cross-border circulation of judgments concerning parental responsibility, protection measures in relation to children and judgments on child support should for the most part be largely unaffected. However, in order for these Conventions to fill the gap, steps need to be taken to ensure they remain applicable on the date of exit, such as through the ratification of the 2007 Maintenance Convention.

The areas where The Hague Conventions will not adequately be able to fill the gaps are the enforcement of civil protection measures for adults in the context of domestic violence and forced marriage, divorce jurisdiction, the recognition of divorce, and the organisation of jurisdiction and enforcement for maintenance disputes on divorce. In order to fill these gaps the UK will need to reach a special agreement with the EU so that the Regulations continue to apply. Without a special agreement, the adoption of these Regulations into national law through the EU(W) B is meaningless, because these Regulations rely on reciprocity. An area of ongoing dispute is the role of the CJEU. If these Regulations continue to apply, the UK would need to accept the ongoing jurisdiction of the CJEU. The role of the CJEU in this area has been mixed, with some of the decisions having a negative effect on gender-based roles. This is primarily related to the positioning of the CJEU as a supra-national court. It is clear that the ongoing enforcement of family law judgments is necessary to ensure that women continue to receive maintenance to help reduce the negative impact of caring; and so that protection measures can still be enforced to help to reduce the ongoing risks of domestic violence and abuse. It remains unclear how this will be achieved post-Brexit.

BIBLIOGRAPHY

Beaumont, P. 2017. Private International Law Concerning Children in the UK After Brexit: Comparing Hague Treaty Law with EU Regulations. *Child and Family Law Quarterly* 29 (3): 213–232.

Beaumont, P., L. Walker, and J. Holliday. 2016a. Conflicts of EU Courts on Child Abduction: The Reality of Article 11(6)-(8) Brussels IIa Proceedings Across the EU. *Journal of Private International Law* 12 (2): 211–260.

Beaumont, P., L. Walker, and J. Holliday. 2016b. Conflicts of EU Courts on Child Abduction: Country Reports. Project Report. University of Aberdeen, Aberdeen, Scotland.

Beaumont, P., L. Walker, and J. Holliday. 2016c. Parental Responsibility and International Child Abduction in the Proposed Recast of Brussels IIa Regulation and the Effect of Brexit on Future Child Abduction Proceedings. *International Family Law Journal* 4: 1369–5762.

Borrás, A., and B. Degeling. 2013. Explanatory Report to the 2007 Hague Convention. The Hague: Permanent Bureau.

Bruch, C.S. 2004. The Unmet Needs of Domestic Violence Victims and Their Children in Hague Child Abduction Cases. *Family Law Quarterly* 38 (3): 529–545.

Costello, C. 2006. The *Bosphorus* Ruling of the European Court of Human Rights: Fundamental Rights and Blurred Boundaries in Europe. *Human Rights Law Review* 6 (1): 87–130.

Dutta, A. 2016. Cross-Border Protection Measures in Europe. *Journal of Private International Law* 12 (1): 169–184.

European Commission. 2017. 2017 Report on Equality Between Women and Men in the EU. http://ec.europa.eu/justice/gender-equality/files/annual_reports/2017_report_annual_gender-equality.pdf. Accessed 24 Nov 2017.

Fineman, M. 2005. *The Autonomy Myth: A Theory of Dependency*. New York: The New Press.

Freeman, M. 2014. Parental Child Abduction: The Long-term Effects. International Centre for Family Law, Policy and Practice. Available at: http://www.childabduction.org.uk/images/longtermeffects.pdf.

Glas, L., and J. Krommendijk. 2017. From *Opinion 2/13* to *Avotiņš*: Recent Developments in the Relationship Between the Luxembourg and the Strasbourg Courts. *Human Rights Law Review* 17 (3): 567–587.

Hale, B. 2017. Taking Flight—Domestic Violence and Child Abduction. *Current Legal Problems* 70 (1): 1–14.

Hess, B., and S. Spancken. 2014. The Effective Operation of the EU Maintenance Regulation in Member States. In *The Recovery of Maintenance in the EU and Worldwide*, ed. P. Beaumont et al. Oxford: Hart Publishing.

Kuipers, J.J. 2012. The (Non) Application of the Charter of Fundamental Rights to a Certificate for the Return of the Child. *European Human Rights Law Review* 4: 397–412.

Kruger, T. 2011. *International Child Abduction: The Inadequacies of the Law*. Oxford: Hart Publishing.

Lamont, R. 2017a. Commentary on App. No. 3890/11 *Povse v Austria*. In *Rewriting Children's Rights Judgments*, ed. H. Stalford, K. Hollingsworth, and S. Gilmore, 513–528. London: Bloomsbury Publishing.

Lamont, R. 2017b. Not a European Family: Implications of Brexit for International Family Law. *Child and Family Law Quarterly* 29 (3): 267–280.

Lamont, R. 2011. Mainstreaming Gender into International Family Law? The Case of International Child Abduction and Brussels II Revised. *European Law Journal* 17 (3): 366–384.

Lowe, N. 2011. A Statistical Analysis of Applications Made in 2008 Under the Hague Convention of 25 October 1980 on the Civil Aspects of Child Abduction, Part III National Reports (HCCH). Available at: https://www.hcch.net/en/publications-and-studies/details4/?pid=5421&dtid=32.

Lowe, N. 2017. What Are the Implications of the Brexit Vote for the Law on International Child Abduction? *Child and Family Law Quarterly* 29 (3): 253–266.

Lowe, N. 2018. Prel. Doc. No. 11 A—Part I A Statistical Analysis of the Applications made in 2015 Under the Hague Convention of 25 October 1980 on the Civil Aspects of Child Abduction. Available at: https://www.hcch.net/en/instruments/conventions/publications1/?dtid=32&cid=24.

Morano-Foadi, S. 2007. Problems and Challenges in Researching Bi-national Migrant Families Within the EU. *International Journal of Law, Policy and the Family* 21 (1): 1–20.

MPI Luxembourg. 2017. Planning the Future of Cross-Border Families: A Path Through Co-ordination. http://www.eufams.unimi.it/wp-content/uploads/2017/06/Report-on-Internationally-Shared-Good-Practices-v2.pdf. Accessed 1 February 2018.

Ní Shúilleabháin, M. 2010. Ten Years of European Family Law: Retrospective Reflections From a Common Law Perspective. *International and Comparative Law Quarterly* 59 (4): 1021–1053.

Office of National Statistics. 2017. Divorces in England and Wales: 2016. Available at: https://www.ons.gov.uk/peoplepopulationandcommunity/birthsdeathsand-marriages/divorce/bulletins/divorcesinenglandandwales/2016. Accessed 17 Jan 2018.

Schulz, A. 2013. The Abolition of Exequatur and State Liability for Human Rights Violations Through the Enforcement of Judgments in European Family Law. In *A Commitment to Private International Law—Essays in Honour of Hans van Loon*, ed. Permanent Bureau, 515. Cambridge: Intersentia.

Sherlock. 2017. European Union (Withdrawal Bill)—Second Reading (Day 2). Wednesday 31 January 2018. http://www.parliamentlive.tv/Event/Index/2e325b35-2337-41cd-a992-b92f3ef4a8aa. Accessed 1 Feb 2018.

Silberman, L. 2000. The Hague Child Abduction Convention Turns Twenty: Gender Politics and Other Issues. *New York University Journal of International Law and Politics* 33 (1): 221–250.

Trimmings, K. 2013. *Child Abduction Within the European Union*. Oxford: Hart Publishing.

Walker, L. 2015. *Maintenance and Child Support in Private International Law*. Oxford: Hart Publishing.

Walker, L. 2017a. *Povse v Austria*. In *Rewriting Children's Rights Judgments*, ed. H Stalford, K. Hollingsworth, and S Gilmore, 519. Oxford: Hart Publishing.

Walker, L. 2017b. New (and Old) Problems for Maintenance Creditors Under the EU Maintenance Regulation. In *Cross-Border Litigation in Europe*, ed. P. Beaumont, M. Danov, K. Trimmings, and B. Yuskel, 771–786. Oxford: Hart Publishing.

Weiner, M.H. 2000. International Child Abduction and the Escape from Domestic Violence. *Fordham Law Review* 69 (2): 593–706.

Weller, M. 2015. Mutual Trust: In Search of the Future of European Union Private International Law. *Journal of Private International Law* 11 (1): 64–102.

CHAPTER 7

Who Speaks for the Zambrano Families? Multi-level Abandonment in the UK and EU

Iyiola Solanke

1 INTRODUCTION

Intersectionality (Crenshaw 1989; Solanke 2017) is a theory developed by critical race feminists (Wing 2013) to identify the eclipse of black women from the protection offered by traditional frameworks of anti-discrimination law. First adopted in the USA to highlight the legal lacuna into which black women employees at General Motors fell,[1] it has developed into a general analytical approach now used in a wide variety of disciplines (Hill Collins and Bilge 2016). In relation to anti-discrimination law, it encourages analyses that 'disrupt' traditional ways of seeing and talking about discrimination in order to identify those groups that disappear due to a synergy (Solanke 2011) of stigmatised statuses (Scales-Trent 1989; Solanke 2017). This contribution adopts an intersectional analysis to highlight the

---

[1] *Degraffenreid v General Motors* 413 F Supp 142 (E.D. Mo 1976).

I. Solanke (✉)
School of Law, The Liberty Building, University of Leeds, Leeds, UK
e-mail: i.solanke@leeds.ac.uk

© The Author(s) 2019
M. Dustin et al. (eds.), *Gender and Queer Perspectives on Brexit*,
Gender and Politics, https://doi.org/10.1007/978-3-030-03122-0_7

predicament of a vulnerable and stigmatised group that has been forgotten and abandoned by civil society, in politics and law during the ongoing drama of Brexit: black families, in particular those headed by women raising their children alone. It should be noted that 'black' is used in this contribution as a political term that prioritises oppressed African, Asian, Arab and Caribbean peoples as global majorities rather than 'ethnic minorities'.

The abandonement of black women and children is well illustrated in the debates on enjoyment of EU citizenship rights. Thus far the focus is on just two groups enjoying free movement and residence rights under EU law—UK citizens living in other parts of the EU (predominantly Spain)[2] and EU citizens from other parts of the EU (predominantly Poland) living in the UK.[3] Excluded are stationary EU citizens (many of whom are infants) and their parents from beyond the EU (many of whom are female) who also derive residence rights from EU law—the so-called 'Zambrano Carers' whose rights were established under Article 20 TFEU in a case of the same name before the Court of Justice of the European Union (CJEU).[4]

Since the *Zambrano* case, it has become apparent that the majority of those benefitting from Zambrano citizenship rights under EU law are families headed by black women. According to data from the Department of Work and Pensions (DWP), 57% of Zambrano carers have Nigerian, Jamaican or Ghanaian nationality. In their gender equality analysis, the DWP also noted that 94% of Zambrano carers are lone parents and of these only 21% are men—79% are women.[5] One can safely conclude from this data that the majority of Zambrano families comprise black mothers from beyond the EU bringing up black British children alone. The link with EU citizenship is crucial for these infants because it provides residency rights under EU law for their parents from beyond the EU. EU law is essential for these families because without its protection the parents face deportation. A key question is therefore what will happen to these parents and their children—who are British citizens—after Brexit? How will these British children continue to

[2] http://ukandeu.ac.uk/fact-figures/how-many-british-citizens-live-in-the-eu/.

[3] http://ukandeu.ac.uk/fact-figures/how-many-eu-citizens-live-in-the-uk/.

[4] C-34/09, *Gerardo Ruiz Zambrano v Office national de l'emploi (ONEm)*, ECR 2011 I-01177.

[5] DWP 'Access to benefits for those who will have a "Zambrano" Right to Reside and Work—Equality Analysis for The Social Security (Habitual Residence) (Amendment) Regulations 2012'. Available online at: https://assets.publishing.service.gov.uk/government/uploads/system/uploads/attachment_data/file/220217/eia-zambrano-right-to-reside-and-work.pdf.

enjoy the most fundamental necessity of childhood—parenting? Parenting has been described as the "single largest variable implicated in childhood illnesses and accidents; teenage pregnancy and substance misuse; truancy, school disruption, and underachievement; child abuse; unemployability; juvenile crime; and mental illness" (Kolvin et al. 1990).

At present, this question is not on the agenda of any of the negotiators and activists in Brussels and London, even though it concerns a status straddling national immigration law and EU law. The main Brexit campaign groups represent white, able-bodied women, men and their families who have the skills, qualifications and resources to cross borders repeatedly—at the 2017 European Parliament hearing[6] on citizens' rights after Brexit the key groups represented were 'the 3million' who campaign on behalf of the 3 million EU citizens living in the UK and 'British in Europe', who lobby for the millions of British citizens living throughout the EU. The Zambrano families are also absent from the Brexit campaigns for women's rights—women's groups, such as the Fawcett Society, do not prioritise the Zambrano families.[7] Some family lawyers and scholars have highlighted the rights of the child on the Brexit agenda but the work done to date focuses on *migrant* child citizens whose parent hold the nationality of a Member State.[8] There is thus no Brexit campaign, legal practitioner or academic activity to defend the interests of non-migrant black British child citizens and their migrant non-EU mothers.

Most worryingly, the Zambrano families have been excluded from the Brexit negotiations themselves—they are invisible to the Department for Exiting the European Union (DExEU). When asked about the *Zambrano* case by MP Stephen Gethins,[9] the Brexit Minister at that time, David Davis, admitted a total lack of knowledge[10]:

[6]LIBE-EMPL-PETI Joint Hearing on 'Citizens Rights after Brexit', Brussesl, 1 Feb 2018, Brussels, http://www.europarl.europa.eu/committees/en/libe/events-hearings.html?id=20171004CHE02641.

[7]Upon enquiry to the Fawcett Society, I was directed to its #FaceHerFuture campaign, a coalition set up to safeguard women's rights and set a positive agenda for change post-Brexit: https://www.fawcettsociety.org.uk/faceherfuture.

[8]https://www.liverpool.ac.uk/law/research/european-childrens-rights-unit/brexit/.

[9]Scottish Nationalist Party MP representing Glasgow.

[10]https://hansard.parliament.uk/Commons/2017-03-09/debates/0ABAE361-C45F-4E12-B753-33392BA30DC3/ScottishDevolution?highlight=zambrano#contribution-083A7EFE-9706-4925-8B66-C8B51DB1A3FA. See also private communication with the Home Office and the Brexit Commission.

I am not familiar with the individual case the hon. Gentleman raises. I will look at it in detail and come back to him, as is my normal approach. I say this, however: the European Court of Justice will not rule over the United Kingdom after the date of Brexit. That does not mean that we will not have a very humane, sensible and straightforward policy with respect to things such as family relationships, which the hon. Gentleman talks about.

This contribution will examine the extent to which both the UK government and the EU are adopting a 'humane, sensible and straightforward policy' towards these black women and their children. The December 2017 Joint Report[11] on progress during phase 1 of negotiations under Article 50 TEU on the United Kingdom's orderly withdrawal from the European Union (the Joint Report),[12] agreed by the UK and the EU as concluding Phase 1 of the withdrawal from the EU, suggests the policy misses this aspiration by a long distance—the Zambrano infant citizens and their mothers are effectively disenfranchised by exclusion from all of the rights set out in that document. This may be expected of the British government, given its official commitment to create a hostile environment towards immigrants[13] regardless of their relationship to British

---

[11] Henceforth 'Joint Report'. Fully entitled 'Joint Report from the Negotiators of the European Union and the United Kingdom Government on Progress During Phase 1 of Negotiations Under Article 50 TEU on the United Kingdom's Orderly Withdrawal from the European Union', available online at: https://www.gov.uk/government/publications/joint-report-on-progress-during-phase-1-of-negotiations-under-article-50-teu-on-the-uks-orderly-withdrawal-from-the-eu.

[12] https://ec.europa.eu/commission/sites/beta-political/files/joint_report.pdf; https://ec.europa.eu/commission/publications/joint-report-negotiators-european-union-and-united-kingdom-government-progress-during-phase-1-negotiations-under-article-50-teu-united-kingdoms-orderly-withdrawal-european-union_en or https://www.gov.uk/government/publications/joint-report-on-progress-during-phase-1-of-negotiations-under-article-50-teu-on-the-uks-orderly-withdrawal-from-the-eu.

[13] In 2012, Home Secretary Theresa May declared the aim to create in Britain 'a really hostile environment for illegal migration,' https://www.telegraph.co.uk/news/uknews/immigration/9291483/Theresa-May-interview-Were-going-to-give-illegal-migrants-a-really-hostile-reception.html, however this policy has also affected the lives of many British citizens who arrived in the UK after World War 2. See http://www.bbc.com/news/av/uk-politics-43831563/windrush-what-is-the-hostile-environment-immigration-policy and https://ukhumanrightsblog.com/2018/05/29/could-the-windrush-scheme-be-open-to-legal-challenge/.

citizens and Britain, but it is disappointing to see that the EU leaders in the Commission and the Council have accepted and acquiesced to this national abandonment of citizens.

This contribution begins with an explanation of the Zambrano case and in Sect. 2 sets out the national responses to it. Section 3 then provides a brief summary of the agreement on citizens' rights set out in the Joint Report to signal the close of Phase 1 of the Brexit negotiations. Following this, in Sect. 4, I explore the hostile policy adopted in the UK to engineer destitution for Zambrano carers and the case law arising from the Zambrano Amendments. Assessment of these cases also does not inspire confidence in the promise of a future humane, sensible and straightforward policy for these families. In Sect. 5, I chart the judicial abandonment of the legal principle of 'best interests' of the child and the disenfranchisement of black British citizens. Finally, in Sect. 6, I consider action to safeguard the future of the Zambrano families within the context of the EU agenda to prioritise citizens and protect the rights of the child.

2 Zambrano Infants and Their Carers

In 1999, Mr. Zambrano arrived in Belgium with his wife and child on a visa. The family immediately applied for asylum as victims of political persecution in Colombia. His application was rejected, but due to the genuine danger of torture in Colombia, the family was not removed from Belgium. Mr. Zambrano appealed against the rejection and during the 12 years over which the appeal progressed, he found stable employment: despite not having a work permit, he secured a job with a company called Plastoria, which for 5 years made regular social security and employment insurance contributions on his behalf.

Most importantly, however, during this time he had two more children, who by virtue of Belgian law against statelessness became Belgian citizens and, as a corollary, EU citizens. Thus, when the Belgian authorities came to consider the refusal to grant him unemployment benefit as a result of his irregular status, the issue had to be looked at both under national social security law and through the prism of rights granted to EU citizens under Articles 20 and 21 TFEU.[14] Article 20 TFEU automatically bestows EU citizenship upon all those holding the

---

[14] Treaty on the Functioning of the European Union.

nationality of one of the member states—this is a status that cannot be applied for or denied. Article 21 TFEU gives all EU citizens the 'right to move and reside freely within the territory of the Member States', subject to conditions. Previous case law from the CJEU[15] has held that parents may derive a right of residence from their child EU citizen. The key question was whether Mr. Zambrano could likewise rely on the citizenship rights of his children to enjoy a derived right of residence—in contrast to these previous cases, his children had remained in the member state of which they were nationals. The situation revolved around Belgian citizens—the two children Jessica and Diego—who had never left Belgium. Would the absence of a cross-border element make this a 'wholly internal' situation and thus irrelevant for EU law?

The Employment Tribunal in Brussels used the preliminary reference procedure in Article 267 TFEU to send three questions to the CJEU. First, focusing on the Treaties, it asked whether Articles 18, 20 and 21 TFEU taken together or separately could 'confer a right of residence upon a citizen of the Union in the territory of the Member State of which that citizen is a national, irrespective of whether he has previously exercised his right to move within the territory of the Member States?' Secondly, turning to the EU Charter of Fundamental Rights (CFR), it asked whether these three articles of the TFEU, when put together with Articles 21, 24 and 34 CFR, meant that such rights must be protected in relation to an infant-citizen, even where the infant-citizen has not exercised free movement rights and is dependent for their enjoyment upon a third country national (TCN) parent. Finally, the Belgian Tribunal asked whether, given this constellation of rights in EU law and the circumstances of a non-migratory infant-citizen, where the TCN parent 'fulfils the condition of sufficient resources and the possession of sickness insurance by virtue of paid employment making him subject to the social security system of that State', national law must grant the TCN parent an exemption from the requirement to hold a work permit.

The European Commission and all eight intervening member states—including the UK—agreed unanimously that this was a 'wholly internal' situation and, as such, beyond the scope of EU law. However, Advocate

---

[15] Case C-200/02, *Catherine Zhu and Man Lavette Chen v Secretary of State for the Home Department* [2004], ECR I-9925; Case C-413/99, *Baumbast and R v Secretary of State for the Home Department*, ECR 2002 I-07091.

General Sharpston argued that persons should not be treated in the same way as goods and services: in Zambrano she argued that people-focused citizenship rights differ conceptually from the free movement rights of economic objects. Taking *Rottman*[16] and *Chen*[17] as a new starting point, she argued that once nationality is granted to persons:

> ...the children [Jessica and Diego] became citizens of the Union and entitled to exercise the rights conferred on them as citizens, concurrently with their rights as Belgian nationals. They have not yet moved outside their own Member State. Nor, following his naturalisation, had Dr Rottmann. If the parents do not have a derivative right of residence and are required to leave Belgium, the children will, in all probability, have to leave with them. That would, in practical terms, place Diego and Jessica in a position capable of causing them to lose the status conferred [by their citizenship of the Union] and the rights attaching thereto.

For AG Sharpston, the question of deportation of a parent thus fell within the ambit of EU law, because children cannot exercise their rights as European Union citizens (specifically, their rights to move and to reside in any Member State) fully and effectively if they have to leave the EU, and they can only remain in the EU with the presence and support of their parents.

The Grand Chamber of the CJEU summarized the three questions posed into one:

> whether the provisions of the TFEU on European Union citizenship are to be interpreted as meaning that they confer on a relative in the ascending line who is a third country national, upon whom his minor children, who are European Union citizens, are dependent, a right of residence in the Member State of which they are nationals and in which they reside, and also exempt him from having to obtain a work permit in that Member State.[18]

It answered this question in the affirmative, finding in favour of Mr. Zambrano directly under Article 20 TFEU. Importantly, the CJEU held that the Citizenship Directive was irrelevant—the Zambrano family

---

[16] C-135/08, *Janko Rottmann v Freistaat Bayern*, ECR 2010 I-01449.

[17] C-200/02, *Chen*.

[18] Zambrano.

were not 'beneficiaries' envisaged in its Article 3(1) because the children
were not 'Union citizens who move to or reside in a Member State other
than that of which they are a national…'[19] After just three short paragraphs of reasoning, the CJEU gave its decision. Recalling the division
of responsibilities between the Union and the Member States, the Grand
Chamber repeated the bold mantra declared in *Grzelczyk* that "citizenship of the Union is intended to be the fundamental status of nationals
of the Member States."[20] This declaration forms the crux of reasoning,
for immediately thereafter the Chamber decides:

> In those circumstances, Article 20 TFEU precludes national measures
> which have the effect of depriving citizens of the Union of the genuine
> enjoyment of the substance of the rights conferred by virtue of their status
> as citizens of the Union. A refusal to grant a right of residence to a third
> country national with dependent minor children in the Member State
> where those children are nationals and reside, and also a refusal to grant
> such a person a work permit, has such an effect.[21]

This effect was assumed because, as argued by AG Sharpston, refusal of
a right of residence to Mr. Zambrano would result in a situation where
the infant Union citizen would be compelled to leave the EU with their
parents. Refusal of a work permit would have the same impact: "if a work
permit were not granted to such a person, he would risk not having sufficient resources to provide for himself and his family, which would also
result in the children, citizens of the Union, having to leave the territory
of the Union." Such circumstances would deny the infants any enjoyment of the "substance of the rights conferred on them by virtue of their
status as citizens of the Union." The Grand Chamber thus concluded
that Article 20 TFEU:

> precludes a Member State from refusing a third country national upon
> whom his minor children, who are European Union citizens, are depend-
> ent, a right of residence in the Member State of residence and nationality
> of those children, and from refusing to grant a work permit to that third
> country national, in so far as such decisions deprive those children of the

---

[19] Zambrano.

[20] Case C-184/99, *Rudy Grzelczyk v Centre public d'aide sociale d'Ottignies-Louvain-la-Neuve*, ECR 2001 I-06193.

[21] Zambrano.

genuine enjoyment of the substance of the rights attaching to the status of European Union citizen.[22]

It is ironic that although this ruling is premised upon the traditional model of a male breadwinner family (Crompton 1999; Blome 2017), the majority of Zambrano families in the UK are headed by single black women.[23]

3   The National Response to the Zambrano Ruling

The response to the Zambrano ruling varied from sympathetic and tempered to hostile and alarmist. In Ireland, the response was the former: the Minister of Justice made a statement on the implications of the ruling and how it would be implemented and requested an 'urgent examination' of 120 cases currently before the Irish courts involving dependent Irish children who had non-national third country parents. In addition, the Minister requested a review of cases where infant Irish citizens had left Ireland due to refusal to allow their parents to remain and those cases where removal of such families was pending. According to the Justice Minister, parents of Irish children who had been deported could apply to return to Ireland: 'They are in a position where they can communicate with the Department of Justice and their situation will be reviewed. Unless there are exceptional circumstances that entitle the State to refuse them they should be able to come back' (Solanke 2012).

Denmark, likewise, called for those rejected for family reunification to reapply. The then Immigration Minister, Søren Pind, pledged to follow the ruling and review its impact on immigration policy for the 10,000 Danes who had had their applications for family reunification rejected since 2002. Yet, concern was also raised that the less restrictive immigration control would undermine the stability of welfare provision. Former immigration minister, Birthe Rønn Hornbech, described the ruling as 'a bomb under the welfare system' and suggested the introduction of a protective measure—a minimum length of residency requirement (an 'accumulation principle')—whereby immigrants would have to reside in Denmark for a minimum number of years in order to qualify for welfare services. This was supported by Danish Socialists and Conservatives.

---

[22] Zambrano.
[23] DWP 2012.

The comment by Morten Messerschmidt, Danish People's Party (DF) representative in the European Parliament, is indicative of the misunderstanding of the ruling: 'If we allow more people to come in and take money out of the till while being under no obligation to pay anything back, we'll soon be on the verge of bankruptcy.'

German media reflected this hostile and alarmist response. *The Spiegel* declared that the Zambrano ruling now means that 'illegal immigrants living in the Union may stay if their child is an EU citizen.'

Some of these fears were allayed by two later cases, *Dereci*[24] and *McCarthy*.[25] These cases clarified that compulsion to leave the EU relates solely to practical or factual consequences. The rupture of strong emotional and psychological ties within the family would not demonstrate compulsion—diminution of the enjoyment of family life does not engage Zambrano rights. However, the CJEU did not clarify the scope of 'practical consequences': would the removal of the rights to basic welfare benefits compel departure from the EU?

This question arose following action by the UK government, informed by the official policy of hostility towards immigrants.[26] Even though the Zambrano infants are British citizens, the Government decided that their parents should be in the same position as any other non-national lacking a lawful right to reside in UK law. Law was used to create an *unequal* right of residence for Zambrano parents and carers, by blocking an automatic consequence of the case, namely access to mainstream welfare support.

Three Regulations[27] were designed to specifically exclude anybody residing on the basis of *Zambrano* from rights to social assistance that

[24] Case C-256/11, *Dereci and Others*, ECR 2011 I-11315.

[25] Case C-434/09, *Shirley McCarthy v Secretary of State for the Home Department*, ECR 2011 I-03375.

[26] http://www.telegraph.co.uk/news/uknews/immigration/9291483/Theresa-May-interview-Were-going-to-give-illegal-migrants-a-really-hostile-reception.html; https://www.theguardian.com/uk-news/2017/sep/18/fighting-the-home-office-womans-traumatic-two-year-battle-to-stay-in-uk.

[27] The Social Security (Habitual Residence) (Amendment) Regulations 2012 (SI 2012/2587), amending the Income Support (General) Regulations 1987 (SI 1987/1967); The Child Benefit and Child Tax Credit (Miscellaneous Amendments) Regulations 2012 (SI 2012/2612), amending the Child Benefit (General) Regulations 2006 (SI 2006/223); The Allocation of Housing and Homelessness (Eligibility) (England) (Amendment) Regulations 2012 (SI 2012/2588), amending the Allocation of Housing and Homelessness (Eligibility) (England) Regulations 2006 (SI 2006/1294).

they would otherwise have as lawfully resident persons. In 2012, at the same time that the EEA Regulations 2006 implementing Citizenship Directive 2004/38 were amended to give effect to the *Zambrano* decision, the Conservative/Liberal Democratic Coalition government introduced the Immigration (European Economic Area) (Amendment) (No. 2) Regulations 2012 (the 'Zambrano Amendments'). Since then, Zambrano carers—those in work and those out of work—have been banned from key mainstream housing and welfare benefits under national law. The 'Zambrano Amendments' exclude these families from income-related benefits, including income support, jobseekers allowance, employment allowance, pension credit, housing benefit, council tax benefit, child benefit and child tax credit. The DWP data above suggests that the majority of those who bear the brunt of this are black British children and their female lone parents.

4   EU CITIZENSHIP AND THE JOINT REPORT OF DECEMBER 2017: THE EXCLUSION OF THE ZAMBRANO FAMILIES

Given the centrality of immigration in the EU Referendum, campaigns immediately sprang up to protect the rights of those who have exercised their citizenship privileges under EU law. These campaigns for citizen's rights after Brexit have focused on two migrant groups who enjoy residency rights under EU law: citizens from other parts of the EU who are now resident in the UK and UK citizens who are resident in other parts of the EU. These tend to be persons who have moved as adults either to study, work or join their families. Yet, as discussed above, EU law also provides as an exception residency rights for citizens who have not moved to another member state. Those benefitting from Zambrano citizenship rights under EU law tend to be children and non-EU nationals, two groups not represented by either of these mainstream campaigns. As a consequence of their invisibility in campaigns and negotiations, the Zambrano families are explicitly excluded from the protection set out in the December 2017 Joint Report.[28]

---

[28]See also the answer given by President Juncker to the question on this from MEP Julie Ward at: http://www.europarl.europa.eu/sides/getAllAnswers.do?reference=E-2018-001369&language=EN.

On 15 December 2017, the Brexit Negotiator for the Commission Michel Barnier confirmed that the British government had done enough to complete the first phase of negotiations in its withdrawal from the EU. The Joint Report sets out the core areas where the EU and UK have reached agreement in principle. As well as setting out a framework on the 'divorce bill' and the complex question of Northern Ireland, the final core area is the approach to protecting the rights of Union citizens in the UK and UK citizens in the Union.

Although the words 'in principle' are peppered throughout the document, para. 36 of the Joint Report requires the UK government to adopt a 'Withdrawal Agreement & Implementation Bill' (WAIB) to implement the Joint Report and fully incorporate the citizens' rights set out in it into UK law. This Bill, once adopted, would thus be binding upon both sides—the UK and the institutions of the Union as well as its 27 Member States (pursuant to Article 216(2) TFEU). According to the Joint Report, in the UK this new piece of legislation would act as the primary source of citizens' rights—having effect on primary legislation and prevailing over inconsistent or incompatible legislation, until expressly repealed by Parliament. As things stand at present, therefore, there are no plans on either side to extend the significant protections set out in the Joint Report to the Zambrano families.

Extensive arrangements are set out in the Joint Report for enforcing EU citizenship rights post-Brexit. The rights established in the Report are to be interpreted consistently by both the UK and the EU. Contrary to the 'red lines' set out by the Conservative government, the role of the CJEU remains strong—Union law citizenship concepts are to be interpreted in line with the case law of the CJEU. However, UK courts will oversee these rights in dialogue with the EU: provision is made for a mechanism to be established that mirrors the current reference procedure under Article 267 TFEU (para. 37, Joint Report). In addition, an independent national monitoring agency is to be set up by the UK to ensure conformity with EU law and respond to citizens' complaints (para. 39, Joint Report). Finally, the Report envisages a mutual right to intervene, whereby the UK Government can participate in 'relevant'[29] cases before the CJEU and the European Commission can do the same in relevant cases before UK courts and tribunals.

[29] 'Relevant' is not defined in the Report.

The Report sets out that EU citizenship rights will be enjoyed by:

Union citizens who in accordance with Union law legally reside in the UK, and UK nationals who in accordance with Union law legally reside in an EU27 Member State by the specified date, as well as their family members as defined by Directive 2004/38/EC who are legally resident in the host State by the specified date, fall within the scope of the Withdrawal Agreement (for personal scope related to frontier workers, see paragraph 15, and for social security, see paragraph 28) (...). (para. 9)

Paragraph 10 continues to secure rights to equal treatment for these groups of Union citizens: '...any discrimination on grounds of nationality will be prohibited in the host State and the State of work in respect of Union citizens and UK nationals, and their respective family members covered by the Withdrawal Agreement.'

The Report mandates that specific family members—irrespective of their nationality—not yet residing in the UK or EU will 'be entitled to join a Union citizen or UK national right holder after the specified date for the life time of the right holder, on the same conditions as under current Union law' (para. 11).

This may not immediately appear to exclude the Zambrano families, but these guarantees are all premised upon the Citizenship Directive, the same legal instrument declared not relevant to the Zambrano case by the CJEU: 'family members' are defined as per Articles 2 and 3(2)(b) of Directive 2004/38/EC[30] (Citizenship Directive) to include spouses and registered partners, co-habitees and children (paras. 12 and 13). Frontier workers and their families are also given the same protection in para. 15. Furthermore, paras. 20 and 21 establish that the conditions for acquiring the right of residence under the Withdrawal Agreement (WA) are those set out in Articles 6 and 7 of the Citizenship Directive. Those in these protected categories will also be able to acquire the right to permanent residence under the WA as per the conditions set out in Articles 16, 17 and 18 of the Citizenship Directive.

---

[30] Directive 2004/38/EC of the European Parliament and of the Council of 29 April 2004 on the right of citizens of the Union and their family members to move and reside freely within the territory of the Member States amending Regulation (EEC) No. 1612/68 and repealing Directives 64/221/EEC, 68/360/EEC, 72/194/EEC, 73/148/EEC, 75/34/EEC, 75/35/EEC, 90/364/EEC, 90/365/EEC and 93/96/EEC (Text with EEA relevance).

Under para. 28 of the Joint Report, rules on the co-ordination of social security set out in Regulation 883/2004[31] and 987/2009[32] also apply. In addition to the European Health Insurance Card (EHIC) Scheme and rules on healthcare, the principle of equal treatment as enjoyed under Articles 18, 45 and 49 TFEU shall be enjoyed. This includes the right to be treated equally to nationals for workers, the self-employed, students and economically inactive citizens in respect to social security, social assistance, health care, employment, self-employment and setting up and managing an undertaking, education (including higher education) and training, social and tax advantages. Privileges in relation to the recognition of qualifications are also extended. In para. 33, 'paramount importance' is attached to both Parties providing as much certainty as possible to UK citizens living in the EU and Union citizens living in the UK about their future rights.

Any observer of the twists and turns in the Brexit negotiations will note that, in stark contrast to the government's EU Withdrawal Bill, the Joint Report substantially retains pre-Brexit rights for EU migrant citizens after Brexit. However, those who do not fall within these categories—non-EU nationals, non-migrant EU and UK citizens—have no access to such rights. This applies to the Zambrano infants and their carers, who enjoy residence rights protected by EU law but are not migrants. As these infants are UK citizens residing in the UK, and therefore not migrant EU citizens, they do not fall under the Citizenship Directive.

Neither the UK nor the EU have as yet specified what rights these children and their parents will have. As concluded by the House of Commons, this group has 'been ignored during the first phase of negotiations.'[33] The Joint Report explicitly states in para. 14 that: "The right

---

[31] Regulation (EC) No. 883/2004 of the European Parliament and of the Council of 29 April 2004 on the coordination of social security systems (Text with relevance for the EEA and for Switzerland) (OJ L 166, 30.4.2004, p. 1).

[32] Regulation (EC) No. 987/2009 of the European Parliament and of the Council of 16 September 2009 laying down the procedure for implementing Regulation (EC) No. 883/2004 on the coordination of social security systems (Text with relevance for the EEA and for Switzerland) (OJ L 284, 30.10.2009, pp. 1–42).

[33] Para. 21, House of Commons Home Affairs Committee 'Home Office Delivery of Brexit; Immigration,' 3rd Report of Session 2017–19, https://publications.parliament.uk/pa/cm201719/cmselect/cmhaff/421/421.pdf.

to be joined by family members not covered by paragraphs 12 and 13 after the specified date will be subject to national law." This short sentence promises long term destitution for the Zambrano families: the treatment of these families to date by the Conservative government does not reflect humanity or sensitivity[34] and sadly, the Joint Report entrenches at the EU level the disenfranchisement of black British children and their non-European mothers practiced at the national level.

5   ENGINEERING DESTITUTION FOR BLACK WOMEN HEADS OF ZAMBRANO FAMILIES

The Zambrano Amendments were specifically designed to preclude Zambrano carers, predominantly black women heads of households, from accessing mainstream benefits. As a result of the Zambrano Amendments, the child British citizens in their care will not receive entitlements such as free school meals, school uniforms or travel passes, regardless of whether their parents work or not. Black British children and their parents are dependent for survival upon funding provided by local authorities using limited emergency powers in Section 17 of the Children Act 1989.[35] This raises questions not only about race, citizenship and the ethics of excluding (mostly female) working migrants from income-related benefits, but also about the likely childhood experiences and integration of a new generation of black British citizens raised under such exclusionary conditions. The Zambrano Amendments effectively disenfranchise a social group already characterised by marginalization.[36] If the (mostly female) parents are unequal residents, the children will as a corollary be unequal citizens, not only in childhood but also into adolescence and potentially throughout

---

[34] This is illustrated by many of the contributions in Ferreira and Kostakopoulou (2016).

[35] Section 17 is designed to prevent childhood destitution on a residual, temporary, short-term emergency basis by providing minimal support. It does not create a 'specific or mandatory duty owed to an individual child.' Ryder LJ described it as a 'target duty' creating a discretion for a local authority to decide how to meet an individual child's need. Consideration need not be limited to the individual child's welfare, but can include the resources of the local authority, existing provision for the child or the needs of other children. See *R (C) v London Borough of Southwark* [2016] EWCA Civ 707; [2016] HLR 36 [12].

[36] See in general, EHRC 'Is Britain Fair'? Online at: https://www.equalityhumanrights.com/en/britain-fairer.

adulthood. It is clear that no consideration was given to the impact of the Amendments upon these children during the consultation phase.[37] The government decided not to 'goldplate'[38] the protection set out for them in EU law but on the contrary took action to deprive it of any value.

Although the legality of the Zambrano Amendments has been challenged in a series of cases, they have ultimately been upheld in the decision of the Supreme Court in *HC*.[39] In one of the first legal challenges, *Harrison*,[40] LJ Elias introduced the standard *dicta* for understanding the Zambrano principle. Dismissing a broad approach to the CJEU ruling, he stated:

> … The right of residence is a right to reside in the territory of the EU. It is not a right to any particular quality or [sic] life or to any particular standard of living. Accordingly, there is no impediment to exercising the right to reside if residence remains possible as a matter of substance, albeit that the quality of life is diminished.[41]

This interpretation, that the substance of the Zambrano right to reside remains intact even if the Zambrano carer is left destitute and without adequate resources to care for the British citizen child, has been entrenched in subsequent cases. It is hard not to conclude that judges have decided that Zambrano carers—predominantly black women—have no right to expect support to provide safe and secure lives for their British children, but should rather expect to be seen and treated as de facto 'benefit tourists.' For their children who are British citizens, and differ from other British citizens only because their mothers come from beyond the EU, this means they have no right to the quality of life guaranteed to their fellow citizens.

---

[37] Hale, UKSC [41].

[38] Goldplating is defined by the European Commission as "exceeding the requirements of EU legislation when transposing Directives into national law." See Commission Communication: Review of the "Small Business Act" for Europe, COM (2011) 78 final, 23 February 2011 and Vaughne Miller, EU Legislation: Government action on 'goldplating' (Standard Note SN/IA/5943).

[39] *R (on the application of HC) (Appellant) v Secretary of State for Work and Pensions and others (Respondents)* [2017] UKSC 73.

[40] *Harrison v Secretary of State for the Home Department* [2013] CMLR 580.

[41] Harrison.

It is worth looking at the details of these cases to understand how women become Zambrano carers and the conditions they must survive with this status. Two good examples are *HC* and *Sanneh*,[42] two African women who became financially stricken mothers of black British & EU citizens. HC arrived in the UK from Algeria in 2008 on a six-month visitors' visa. In 2010 she married Mr. H, a British national and they had two children. In October 2012, before the birth of her second child, she left the marital home due to domestic violence. Jamil Sanneh arrived in the UK from Gambia in 2006 on a student visa that did not permit her to work or to have recourse to benefits or other public funds. In September 2009 she had a child with a Gambian divorcee who had gained British nationality by his first marriage. The two did not marry but the daughter, Awa, became a British citizen through her father. Her visa expired in December 2009 and was not extended due to withdrawal of family financial support. Awa's father had no interest in his new family and shortly after her birth, Sanneh became Awa's sole carer.

HC was financially dependent upon her husband and had no resources of her own. She sought refuge with her sister in Oldham, but could not stay there in the long-term. She approached Oldham Council for assistance in November 2012. This was initially refused, but limited emergency and temporary housing, and financial assistance were eventually provided under s.17 of the Children Act 1989. From August 2013, she and her children were placed in interim housing in a two-bedroom accommodation and given £55 per week for food and £25.50 for bills. Sanneh also struggled financially: when she finally received the benefits wrongly paid to Awa's father, she had a monthly income of £477 made up of child benefit, child tax credit and child support. She supplemented her income with short term loans and irregular payments from Awa's father but could not cover all of her monthly payments including £250 a month rent, £55 council tax, £25 water rates and £50 for gas and electricity. She and Awa lived on food parcels. In June 2011, as she was prohibited from working, she applied for income support, which was refused. In July 2011, she applied for interim payments and these were also refused. Her situation deteriorated in 2012: in January she was evicted and had to be rescued by provision of emergency housing; in April her child tax credit was withdrawn; in August her child benefit was

---

[42] HC v Secretary State for Work and Pensions [2013] EWHC 3874 (Admin); R (on the application of Sanneh) v Secretary of State [2013] EWHC 793 (Admin).

withdrawn. She was then granted income support from 14 September 2012. However, as she was granted permission to work on 1 September 2012, income support was withdrawn on 8 November 2012.[43]

HC and Sanneh claimed residence rights as Zambrano carers—this was not challenged. Their difficulties arose when they sought access to mainstream social security benefits—including income support, child tax credit and child benefit—as Zambrano carers. They challenged the legality of the Amendments but judges decided that the blanket refusal of welfare benefits was legal—it did not compel a Zambrano carer to leave the EU. Sanneh argued that a parent who was prevented from working and accessing to benefits would be compelled to leave: the denial of access to child benefits created a situation where she would be forced to leave the UK due to lack of means, and in the absence of an alternative carer she would have to take her daughter with her. She also argued that the CJEU raised an irrebuttable assumption that withholding a right of residence and the ability to work from a non-EU carer upon whom an EU child is dependent would compel the parent and hence the child to leave EU territory. Thus "where a parent cannot work (for either legal or practical reasons), it must be assumed that without a right of residence and an entitlement to mainstream non-contributory benefits, such a result will equally follow."[44] HC did not argue compulsion to leave, but simply that as the TCN parent of two black British children resident in the UK, she should have EU law rights to reside and work in the UK, derived from her children's rights as British and EU citizens.

It was also argued that the Zambrano Amendments discriminated against *Zambrano* carers and their EU national children on the basis of nationality and sex. In relation to nationality, the preclusion of recourse to public funds[45] was designed to target TCN and, therefore, inevitably also directly discriminated against their children of British nationality, contrary to the prohibition on discrimination on grounds of nationality in Article 18 of the TFEU. Furthermore, the blanket exclusion from any social welfare assistance or entitlements from the State was discrimination in relation to enjoyment of rights as EU citizens under Article

---

[43] In January 2013, the original decision was set aside and remade due to an error on a point of law made by the First Tier Tribunal.

[44] Sanneh [79].

[45] See the No Recourse to Public Funds Network at: http://www.nrpfnetwork.org.uk/Pages/Home.aspx.

20 of the Treaty. In relation to sex, the Zambrano amendments were indirectly discriminatory: HC was discriminated against in relation to her standard of living on the basis of her membership of a group which is overwhelmingly female. Her automatic and absolute exclusion from in-work and out-of-work benefits and from social advantages which would make it easier for her as a single mother to join the workforce was presented as unjustifiable indirect sex discrimination. Given that the majority of children and adults are black, it could also have been argued that the Amendments discriminated on the basis of race, however the data to support this argument may not have been available at the time.

The question for the national judges was how to interpret the blanket ban on access to mainstream welfare, regardless of work, introduced by the Zambrano Amendments: does 'genuine enjoyment' require more than just skeleton support that may leave both the carer and a British infant citizen on the brink of poverty and destitution? In other words, does a borderline and unstable existence equate to *compulsion* to leave?

In *Sanneh*, Hickinbottom J rebutted all arguments, essentially because Sanneh coped too well—her case was lost because she was able to survive the destitution into which she was thrown. Following Elias J, Hickinbottom J stated that Zambrano carer cases rest upon evidence of *absolute compulsion* to leave in the absence of the claimed rights, in this case child benefits. He decided that her continued presence showed clearly she had been able to cope without them—in spite of desperate and precarious conditions, she had managed without benefits for four years and thus she failed the *Zambrano* test of compulsion. Under Section 17 of the Childrens Act, she would be provided with housing and basic income; she also now had the right to work. The judge noted her 'management and human resources skills' and concluded that "...all of the evidence points to the Claimant being absolutely determined to stay in the United Kingdom, and there being no realistic possibility of her leaving because of financial circumstances..." Thus, he ruled that 'there was no realistic prospect of Sanneh being compelled to leave the United Kingdom' and the right of Awa:

> ...as an EU citizen to reside in the territory of the EU is not in jeopardy, and will not be in jeopardy in the period during which the Claimant's entitlement to the benefits will be determined. In those circumstances, EU law

is simply not engaged at all: there is no EU law right that requires the protection of this court, now.[46]

Supperstone J referred regularly to *Sanneh* in *HC*, citing in particular Hickinbottom's literal approach to compulsion to leave. Compulsion would practically only arise through deportation or by "force of economic necessity (e.g. by having insufficient resources to provide for his EU children because the state refuses him a work permit)." Compulsion did not arise from a ban on access to welfare benefits. Supperstone opined that the Zambrano right to residence did not confer a right to receive social benefits and that the refusal of such a right did not amount to direct nationality discrimination, associative discrimination, or reverse discrimination. He did acknowledge that there could be indirect nationality discrimination but found that this was justifiable; the Amending Regulations were deemed a proportionate means of furthering the legitimate aim of protecting scarce public resources, "including from individuals who move to, or remain in, the UK in order to take advantage of its welfare system."[47] HC was therefore put in the same category as a 'benefit tourist', rather than treated as the mother of a British citizen.

The centrality of 'compulsion' was confirmed in *Ayinde* and *Thinjom*,[48] where the Court held that residence rights exist under *Zambrano* only if established *beyond any doubt* that the EU citizen would leave the Union if the carer left. Demonstration of an assumption that the citizen will leave is insufficient—it must be a matter of fact that the UK citizen will be forced to leave the EU. In this case, where an elderly British citizen relied upon his non-EU national wife to care for him, the fact of his incapacity was used as evidence of the lack of compulsion to leave: Mr. Stephens was simply unable to leave, compulsion or not.[49] *Ayinde* confirms the guidance in *Hines* that 'genuine enjoyment' is limited to practical safeguarding of British citizen's EU rights under Article 20 TFEU and nothing more. This case illustrates that no consideration is given to whether it would be reasonable for the female carer to leave and the impact upon the citizen's life, even the best interests of the child.

---

[46] Sanneh [103].
[47] Sanneh [59].
[48] Ayinde and Thinjom [2015] UKUT 560 (IAC).
[49] Ayinde and Thinjom [53].

6 ABANDONEMENT OF 'BEST INTERESTS' AND THE DISENFRANCHISEMENT OF BLACK BRITISH CHILDREN

The CJEU gives the 'best interest test' a central role in its assessment of infant citizens rights under Article 20 TFEU. In *Chavez Vilchez*, it stated explicitly that the assessment of the compulsion to leave the EU:

> 72 '...must take into account, in the best interests of the child concerned, all the specific circumstances, including the age of the child, the child's physical and emotional development, the extent of his emotional ties both to the Union citizen parent and to the third-country national parent, and the risks which separation from the latter might entail for the child's equilibrium.'[50]

In *Hines*[51] which explicitly required consideration of the rights of the child, the national court replaced this test with a lower standard. Maureen Hines, a Jamaican woman without permission to remain in the UK, was refused housing assistance despite being mother to a five-year old black British boy, Brandon. Lambeth local authority decided that even if the refusal caused Hines to leave the UK, Brandon's father, who had a right to permanent residence in the UK, could look after him: Brandon already spent two days and nights a week with his father. Hines unsuccessfully appealed Lambeth's decision in June 2013 but was given permission to further appeal two specific questions to the Court of Appeal (CA): first whether the judge should have applied a higher level of review given the engagement of Article 20 TFEU and, secondly, whether the judge used the correct test when considering whether the removal of the mother jeopardized the continued residence of Brandon in the EU—should the judge have considered the CFR based 'best interests' of the child instead of the statutory test of practicality laid out in Regulation 15A (4A)(C) of the Immigration Regulations 2006?

The argument for Hines was that as Regulation 15A (4A)(C) was introduced to implement EU law (the Zambrano principle), Lambeth's decision had to take into consideration EU human rights law, in

---

[50] C-133/15 H.C. Chavez-Vilchez and Others v Raad van bestuur van de Sociale verzekeringsbank and Others.

[51] Hines v Lambeth London Borough Council: [2014] EWCA Civ 660; [2014] WLR (D) 238.

particular Articles 7 (respect for private and family life) and 24 (rights of the child) CFR. Hines argued that the correct question was therefore not the statutory practicality test, but the best interests test that considered the fundamental rights of the child to have regular contact with her parents and enjoy family life. Vos disagreed—in his judgment of May 2014 he negated both questions. First, Article 20 TFEU did not affect the intensity of the review—the correct standard had been applied—and secondly, the engagement of Article 20 TFEU via Regulation 15A (4A) (C) of Regulation 2006 did not call for a different test.

LJ Vos agreed that the removal of a parent would normally be against the best interests of the child and therefore clearly contrary to Article 24(3) CFR. However, he accepted the *Harrison* test, which essentially meant that Brandon's welfare 'cannot be the paramount consideration because that would be flatly inconsistent with the statutory test'[52] of whether he would be unable to reside in the UK if his mother left. At no point was it considered that the statutory test might be faulty. It is worth reading the paragraph in full to appreciate the ease with which the usual best interests test is decentred to secure a decision in line with the government anti-immigrant policy:

> In my judgment, however, the welfare of the child cannot be the paramount consideration because that would be flatly inconsistent with the statutory test which is whether the child would be unable to reside in the UK if the mother left. It will, in normal circumstances, be contrary to the interests of a child for one of its parent carers, whether the primary carer or not, to be taken away from him or her. It would certainly be contrary to article 24(3) of the Charter.

Hines would only be entitled to housing assistance if refusal compelled Brandon to depart the UK. As Brandon's father was deemed to be 'responsible and caring' [29], this would not be so—the boy could live with him. Thus, the substance of Brandon's EU right to residence was not impaired: he could in theory be cared for by his father, even if in practice this was not in his best interests due to his father's 12-hour shifts at work. His father was subsequently made redundant—putting his ability to *provide* for Brandon in question. However, bizarrely the judge found the fathers unemployment status an advantage, describing the job

---

[52] Hines [22].

as an 'impediment'[53] the removal of which freed the father to care for Brandon.

Judges have continued to reject arguments calling for consideration of the best interests of the child. The decision in *Hines* kept 'best interests' out of the *Zambrano* principle. In *HC*, in response to the argument that Article 24 CFR called for the best interests of the child to be considered, Supperstone J stated:

> 70... there is no general requirement under EU law for Member States to provide parents with a particular level of support, regardless of their right to reside. The Defendants are, in my view, entitled to make legislation which properly reflects the rights of Zambrano carers and their children as a matter of EU law.[54]

HC confirmed that in law there is no guarantee to a particular quality of parenting as a Zambrano citizen, only a recognition of its existence. The consequences of this retreat from the 'best interests' principle can be seen in *Kapopole*,[55] where the judge neglected to confirm the existence of alternative care for the British child but rejected the appeal based on an assumption that the two sisters of the applicant would care for him.[56] Children of Zambrano carers, who are British citizens, should therefore not expect judges to defend their full enjoyment of the Marshallian trilogy of social, political and civil citizenship (Marshall 1950). It is questionable whether partial enjoyment of citizenship is *genuine* enjoyment.

The idea of partial enjoyment of citizenship was crystallised by the CA in 2015 when it considered an appeal by Sanneh.[57] LJ Arden affirmed *Hines* and created what she called the 'effective citizenship principle'. This principle was designed to focus on the child but keep the idea of best interests at the margins—at the core was instead the obligation upon member

---

[53] Hines [29].

[54] *The Queen (on the application of HC) v Secretary of State for Work and Pensions Secretary of State for Communities and Local Government Hm Revenue & Customs Oldham Metropolitan Borough Council* [2013] EWHC 3874 (Admin) [70].

[55] *Kapopole v Secretary of State*, Appeal Upper Tribunal (Immigration and Asylum Chamber) Number: IA/05877/2014.

[56] This decision was over-ruled on appeal.

[57] Sanneh et al. v Home Secretary [2015] EWCA Civ 49.

states to avoid decisions that make 'the rights of EU citizenship ineffective.' This meant, as per LJ Arden that "member states may not indirectly remove the benefits of a person's status as an EU citizen"—an idea that is some distance from protecting the best interests of the child citizen.

The CA set the principle in CJEU jurisprudence arising from case law on the EU cross-border social benefits legislative ('EU CBSBL') scheme set out in the Citizenship Directive, the Long Term Residence Directive[58] and the Family Reunion Directive.[59] According to LJ Arden this included cases such as *Baumbast* and *Chen* but not *Zambrano*, *HC* or *Sanneh*—in the latter cases, rights were derived directly under Article 20 TFEU placing them outside EU citizenship, the 'EU CBSBL scheme' and the right to non-discrimination in EU Law (Article 18 TFEU and Article 21 CFR). This approach allowed the CA to conclude, following CJEU in *Patmalniece*,[60] that Zambrano carers do not enjoy a right to non-discrimination on the ground of nationality under Article 18 TFEU. It was then further determined that rights derived from an EU citizen are not EU rights [95] thus even if "their status is derived from the EU citizenship rights of the child as interpreted by the CJEU", "EU law has no competence in the level of social assistance to be paid to the carer". As this is 'exclusively governed by national law', Article 21 CFR could not be relied upon—the CFR only applies to acts of the member states when they are implementing EU law.[61]

The CA did not defer to the CJEU but to the legislative policy of the Home Office. The Court accepted the Home Office explanation to justify the Zambrano policy as manifestly well-founded. The reasons given included: reduction of costs by allocating benefits to those with the greatest connection with the country, encouragement of regularization for undocumented immigrants, encouraging TCNs wishing to have children here to ensure that they had sufficient resources to support themselves and their children, and reduction of "benefits tourism".

---

[58] Council Directive 2003/109/EC of 25 November 2003 concerning the status of third-country nationals who are long-term residents, OJ L 16, 23.1.2004, pp. 44–53.

[59] Council Directive 2003/86/EC of 22 September 2003 on the right to family reunification, OJ L 251, 3.10.2003, pp. 12–18.

[60] *Patmalniece v Secretary of State for Work and Pensions* [2011] 1 WLR 783, para. 83.

[61] Article 51 Charter. See also *Dano v Jobcenter Leipzig* (Case C-333/13) [2015] 1 WLR 2519 [91], although in this case the Court was only considering non-contributory benefits under Regulation No. 883/2004.

No evidence was presented or requested to allow an independent assessment of these reasons by the CA.

As in previous decisions, the CA ruled that the idea of 'genuine enjoyment' does not 'require the State to guarantee any particular quality of life' to a 'Zambrano carer'—protection from compulsion to leave does not provide as a corollary a right for parent and child to live free from want and poverty. Member States may determine autonomously access to benefits where individual situations fall outside of the scope of EU Directives.

This decision was largely upheld by the Supreme Court in November 2017, which deliberated for 5 months before delivering its decision on the appeal in *HC*. The Supreme Court relied upon the post-Zambrano caselaw[62] and the dicta of Elias LJ in *Harrison* to support the conclusion that, while the principle of residence was a narrow one based in EU law, entitlement to and levels of benefit were a matter for national law. The CJEU decision in *Ymeraga* was relied upon to confirm that the exercise of derived rights are not an implementation of EU law for the purposes of Article 51 CFR.[63]

Despite the continued absence of any strong evidence, the Supreme Court supported the government's justifications for the Zambrano Amendments, and agreed with the CA that they fell within the wide margin of discretion allowed to national governments under both EU and ECHR law. No link was made between the treatment of the mother and the life experience of the British child. The UKSC decision focused on the immigration status of HC rather than her parental (mother) status or the status of her child. Sadly, British nationality did not improve the situation of the non-EU mother; rather non-EU nationality worsened the situation of the British child—the child was disenfranchised, becoming in effect a TCN like its mother.

Of the judges involved with this case, only Supreme Court President Lady Brenda Hale focused on the rights of the child. Her additional comments at the end of the judgment placed the infants front and centre:

---

[62] C-256/11, *Murat Dereci and Others v Bundesministerium für Inneres*, ECR 2011 -00000; *Rendón Marín v Administración del Estado (Judgment: Citizenship of the Union)* [2016] EUECJ C- 165/14; [2017] QB 495; *S v Secretary of State for the Home Department* (Case C-304/14) [2017] QB 558; [2017] 2 WLR 180.

[63] *Ymeraga v Ministre du Travail, de l'Emploi et de l'Immigration* (Case C-87/12) [2013] 3 CMLR 33, paras. 41–43.

39. I have found this a very troubling case. It is not a case about adults' rights. It is a case about children's rights – specifically the right of these two very young British children to remain living in their own country and to have the support which they need in order to enable them to do so. Self-evidently they need the support of their mother in the shape of the care which she is able to give them. But they also need support in the shape of a place to live and enough to live on.

She stressed the distinction between Zambrano carers and other non-EU citizens, stating 'Yet *Zambrano* carers are not like any other TNSs. They have British (or other EU citizen) children dependent upon them.'[64] She was also the only judge to raise the fundamental issue overlooked by the government—'how these children would be supported if the parent looking after them was unable to work, whether because of the demands of child care or for any other good reason' [41].

Although she ultimately agreed with the majority that the situation of *Zambrano* carers and their children falls beyond EU social security law, Lady Hale nonetheless saw a route through which EU law was engaged: as the introduction of the Zambrano Amendments is undeniably an implementation of the principle set out in the Zambrano ruling, they fall within the scope of EU law (as per Article 51 CFR). The government may have breached EU law with them as Article 21 CFR states:

Any discrimination based on *any ground such as* sex, race, colour, ethnic or social origin, genetic features, language, religion or belief, political or any other opinion, membership of a national minority, property, birth, disability, age or sexual orientation shall be prohibited.

Lady Hale suggested discrimination arose due to the arbitrary creation of two types of infant British citizen: one child who is cared for by a Zambrano—status parent who is a TCN with no recourse to public funding, and another child cared for by a non-Zambrano status parent with full entitlement to mainstream benefits and social assistance. The stigmatization of the former child due to the accident of birth to a non-EU national parent would constitute discrimination.

Unlike her colleagues, she dismissed the justifications given on behalf of the government:

[64] [41].

51. ...I am not impressed by the justifications given by the respondents' witnesses...They were addressed to the parents, viewed as third country nationals rather than *Zambrano* carers, and not to the children. A child-focussed approach would have been quite different. Thus the first aim, allocating benefits to those with the greatest connection with this country, would obviously include allocating benefits to British children who were born here and have lived here all their lives. The second aim, of strengthening immigration control, is irrelevant to children who are not subject to it. Their *Zambrano* carers are only here to support them and for a long as they need that support. A third aim, of saving money, is less than compelling, given that what has in fact happened is a transfer of responsibility from one arm of government to another.

It is often argued that judicial independence is crucial because courts represent the last refuge of the citizen against the state. The Courts have not only failed the Zambrano infants, but their sanction of the legislative disenfranchisement through policy may have emboldened the government in their abandonment of these families during Brexit.

7   Zambrano Families and Brexit

The idea of effective citizenship has been developed by the courts against the backdrop of hostility to immigrants, and it is against this background that Brexit is taking place. It is therefore not surprising that the Zambrano infants have been abandoned by the UK in the Brexit negotiations. An examination of the Zambrano case law does not lead to the conclusion that UK policy for those households and families headed by single black women will be 'humane, sensitive and reasonable'. Post-Brexit, on the contrary, it suggests that these families will be denied continuation of any rights currently provided under EU law. The likelihood of deportation of black women who head Zambrano families should not be doubted—the government has already shown its intentions in the case of *Ayinde* and *Thinjom*. The government position can also be seen in reports that Lilya Breha, a Ukrainian woman, faces expulsion after her five-year old British child—on whom her stay was dependent—was murdered by her partner.[65]

We should expect no less from Prime Minister Theresa May, who during her tenure as Home Secretary argued for a restrictive approach

---

[65] https://www.mirror.co.uk/news/uk-news/mum-boy-five-beaten-death-11794657.

to these families: in *Yekini*, she pushed for the courts to incorporate the need for a *compelling* reason to explain why the father of an infant British citizen could not assume full parental responsibility for his care.[66] The stance of her government to effectively deprive these children of full citizenship, because their primary carer holds the 'wrong' (i.e. a non-EU) nationality is in keeping with the anti-immigrant policies instituted during her time at the Home Office.

However, if the goal of Brexit is to 'make Britain great' then that should not be at the expense of a group of its most vulnerable citizens: black children. These children should not be treated like migrants simply because their parents come from beyond the EU. The vision for them is simple—to enjoy their full birthrights as British citizens. This requires the state to do less rather than more—the Zambrano amendments should be repealed so that their mothers can escape a hand-to-mouth existence, at the mercy of ever-dwindling local authority budgets, and can raise their children in an environment free of punitive action by the government.

What should the EU do? It is surprising that the European Commission negotiators have also abandoned its infant EU citizens. The UK policy of hostility to immigrants is not only inconsistent with the EU fundamental freedoms but also with goals set out in the Europe 2020 Strategy[67] and the Stockholm Programme[68] to protect citizens 'wherever they are in the world,'[69] "fully recognise the potential of migration for building a competitive and sustainable economy" and "achieve the effective integration of legal migrants, underpinned by the respect and promotion of human rights." Indeed, the main goal of the Union action in relation to freedom, security and justice is:

> Advancing people's Europe, ensuring that citizens can exercise their rights and fully benefit from European integration. It is in the areas of freedom, security and justice that citizens expect most from policy-makers as this is

---

[66] *Yekini v Southwark* [2014] EWHC 2096 (Admin).

[67] Commission Communication 'EUROPE 2020 A strategy for smart, sustainable and inclusive growth' COM (2010) 2020.

[68] Council of the European Union, 'The Stockholm Programme—An open and secure Europe serving and protecting the citizens' Brussels, 2 December 2009 (17024/09) and Commission Communication 'Delivering an area of freedom, security and justice for Europe's citizens—Action Plan Implementing the Stockholm Programme' COM (2010) 171.

[69] COM (2010) 171, 4.

affecting their daily life. Women and men in Europe rightly expect to live in a peaceful and prosperous Union confident that their rights are fully respected and their security provided.[70]

Furthermore, the Action Plan specifically states that the European area of freedom, security and justice "must be an area where all people, *including third country nationals*, benefit from the effective respect of the fundamental rights enshrined in the Charter of Fundamental Rights of the European Union."[71] This goal may no longer be a priority for the UK government, but it should remain so for the EU Brexit negotiators both during negotiations and any transition phase.

In addition, in 2011, the Commission adopted a policy specifically focused on children.[72] It highlighted the emphasis in the Lisbon Treaty on the promotion and protection of the rights of the child: Article 3(3) TEU explicitly requires the EU to promote the protection of the rights of the child and Article 24 of the CFR recognises children as independent and autonomous holders of rights. International obligations, including the United Nations Convention on the Rights of the Child (UNCRC), are also cited as the source of the standards and principles that should guide EU policies and actions in all matters that have an impact on the rights of the child. The Commission stated that:

> In view of the strong and reinforced commitment to the rights of the child in the Treaty of Lisbon and in the Charter of Fundamental Rights, the Commission believes it is now the time to move up a gear on the rights of the child and to transform policy objectives into action. The Europe 2020 Strategy sets out a vision for the 21st century of a Europe where the children of today will have a better education, access to the services and to the resources they need to grow up and, one day, lead Europe into the 22nd century.

Thus, the Commission proposed 'An EU Agenda for the Rights of the Child' which will 'reaffirm the strong commitment' of all EU institutions

---

[70]COM (2010) 71, 2.

[71]COM (2010) 71, 2.

[72]Communication setting out an EU Agenda for the Rights of the Child (COM [2011] 60). See also Stalford (2012).

and Member States to the promotion, protection and fulfilment of the rights of the child in all relevant EU policies and achieve concrete results. The future goal is for any EU policy that directly or indirectly affects children to be designed, implemented, and monitored taking into account the principle of the 'best interests of the child enshrined in the EU Charter of Fundamental Rights and in the UNCRC.' Why, then, is the Commission allowing child citizens to be abandoned during Brexit? As shown above, the commitment is especially needed now for the Zambrano children who are being disenfranched in Britain through law.

What should the CJEU do? As a first step, the Zambrano principle should be strengthened by inclusion of an explicit mention of the 'best interests' concept. The CJEU has continued to develop citizenship rights for stationary EU citizens under Article 20 TFEU—for example in *K.A and Others*,[73] it held that a member state refusal to examine a request for family reunification between an EU and TCN, solely because of an active entry ban against the TCN, can be a breach of Article 20 TFEU if the refusal compels the EU citizen to leave the EU and thereby deprives EU citizens of the genuine enjoyment of citizenship rights.[74] These rights should then be anchored in the Joint Report and WA before the UK leaves the EU.

8   CONCLUSION

This contribution sought to focus attention specifically on the *Zambrano* families and citizens who at present have no recourse to public funding and after Brexit may lose their right to residence. An intersectional analysis of Brexit highlights that black women and black British children living under the Zambrano principle are forgotten casualities of the decision to leave the EU. I have attempted to show that because of Brexit there is a group of infant black British citizens who are not only living in poverty but will almost definitely be deprived of all citizenship rights if their carers—predominantly black women—lose their right to reside in the UK under EU law.

Due to the non-EU status of their primary carer, the rights of these infants as British and EU citizens have been pushed aside in the Brexit

---

[73] C-82/16, *K.A and Others v Belgium*, nyr.

[74] For commentary see *Sarah Progin-Theuerkauf*, http://europeanlawblog.eu/2018/05/22/k-a-and-others-the-zambrano-story-continues/.

negotiations by the European Commission and the UK government as well as national judges. In addition, their precarious position has been over-looked in the binary campaigns focusing on Union citizens in the UK and UK citizens in the EU. However, as put by Lady Hale, *Zambrano* carers are not like any other TCN—they have British children dependent upon them. Thus, if these infants are to continue to enjoy their full rights as British and Union citizens after Brexit, their parents must enjoy the full rights enjoyed by migrant EU citizens in the WA. For this to happen, campaigns on the retention of migration rights should lobby on behalf of these non-migrant Union citizens as well as those who migrate.

The Statement of Intent published by the British Government on June 21 does not improve the situation—it confirms that the WA does apply to the Chen parents as well as the Ibrahim and Texeira children but not to the Zambrano carers. It states only that further provision will be made in the 'immigration rules' for this group but there is no indication of when the further details on the new status to be created for them will be available or what it will incorporate.[75] Contrary to the claims of David Davis, there is no humane policy being developed for the Zambrano families after Brexit and there does seem to be a race to the bottom in UK citizenship law and policy,[76] most punitive upon those with strong rights, who will lose them if associated with the 'wrong' persons, such as those lacking rights. British citizenship is no longer the guarantor of equal treatment imagined by Marshall. The Zambrano amendments and UK case law manifest and entrench the government policy of hostility, which is now not only directed towards immigrants, but also those related to and dependent upon them. It is questionable whether *Dereci* went this far in focusing on 'practical consequences': would the CJEU condone a life of want and poverty for EU citizens? It seems that the spirit of *Zambrano* is being unwritten in Britain—*Hines, Harrison, HC* and *Sanneh* illustrate that according to the British judicial interpretation, the best interests of the child and quality of life hold no over-riding relevance in the application of

[75] EU Settlement Scheme, Statement of Intent, S 6.12 (21 June 2018). Available at: https://assets.publishing.service.gov.uk/government/uploads/system/uploads/attachment_data/file/718237/EU_Settlement_Scheme_SOI_June_2018.pdf.

[76] Speech by David Davis M.P., Minister for Exiting the European Union on 20.2.2018 at: https://www.gov.uk/government/news/david-davis-foundations-of-the-future-economic-partnership-speech.

the *Zambrano* principle. The ease with which this divisive administrative policy has dislodged an internationally valued legal concept is alarming.

As Lady Hale suggests, it must be asked whether Article 15A(4A)(c) of Regulation 2006 and the *Harrison/Hines* tests are compatible with EU law. It is unlikely given Brexit that the CJEU will receive a reference on this question from a British court—the UKSC agreed with LJ Vos[77] that there was no question to be referred to the CJEU. However, there are hundreds of courts in the other 27 Member States who could refer a question on this—any CJEU decision taken before Exit Day will remain part of UK law.

There is however a faster alternative to intervention of the CJEU: campaigners, politicians, academics and lawyers in the UK and the EU should replace the multi-level abandonement with multi-level advocacy and demand that decision makers bring Zambrano families within the scope of the Joint Report and WA so that policies and principles, in particular non-discrimination and the 'bests interests of the child', apply in the same way to all infant UK and EU citizens regardless of whether they are migrants or the nationality of their parents. Brexit was presented to the British public as a pathway back to a national democracy; action must be taken to ensure that this promise is kept for all citizens, including black British children and their parents, wherever they are from.

BIBLIOGRAPHY

Blome, A. (ed.). 2017. *The Politics of Work-Family Policy Reforms in Germany and Italy.* Abingdon, Oxon; New York, NY: Routledge.

Crenshaw, K. 1989. Demarginalising the Intersection of Race and Sex: A Black Feminist Critique of Antidiscrimination Doctrine, Feminist Theory and Antiracial Politics. *University of Chicago Legal Forum* 139.

Crompton, R. (ed.). 1999. *Restructuring Gender Relations and Employment: The Decline of the Male Breadwinner.* Oxford: Oxford University Press.

EHRC 'Is Britain Fair'? Online at https://www.equalityhumanrights.com/en/britain-fairer.

Ferreira, N., and D. Kostakopoulou (eds.). 2016. *The Human Face of The European Union.* Cambridge: Cambridge University Press.

Hill Collins, P., and S. Bilge. 2016. *Intersectionality—Key Concepts.* Cambridge, UK: Polity Press.

---

[77] LJ Vos stated in Hines '...is clear from *Zambrano* and *Dereci* as applied in *Harrison* and there is therefore no need for the point to be referred to the CJEU for a preliminary ruling...' [25].

House of Commons Home Affairs Committee 'Home Office Delivery of Brexit; Immigration' 3rd Report of Session 2017–19. https://publications.parliament.uk/pa/cm201719/cmselect/cmhaff/421/421.pdf.

Kolvin, I., F.J. Muller, D. Scott, S.R.M. Gatzanis, and M. Fleeting. 1990. *Continuities of Deprivation: The Newcastle 1000 Family Study.* Avebury: Alderson.

Marshall, T.H. 1950. *Citizenship and Social Class: And Other Essays.* Cambridge: Cambridge University Press.

Scales-Trent, J. 1989. Black Women and the Constitution: Finding Our Place, Asserting Our Rights. *Harvard Civil Rights-Civil Liberties Law Review* 24 (1): 9–44.

Solanke, I. 2009. Putting Race and Gender Together: A New Approach to Intersectionality. *Modern Law Review* 72 (5): 723.

Solanke, I. 2011. Infusing the Silos in the Equality Act 2010 with Synergy. *Industrial Law Journal* 40 (4), 336.

Solanke, I. 2012. Using the Citizen to Bring the Refugee in: Gerardo Ruiz Zambrano v Office national de l'emploi (ONEM). *Modern Law Review* 75 (1) MLR 78–121, 108ff.

Solanke, I. 2017. *Discrimination as Stigma.* London: Hart.

Stalford, H. 2012. *Children and the European Union.* London: Hart.

Vaughne Miller. EU Legislation: Government Action on 'goldplating' (Standard Note SN/IA/5943).

Wing, A. 2013. *Critical Race Feminism: A Reader (Critical America).* New York: New York University Press.

CHAPTER 8

Unaccompanied Migrant Children and the Implications of Brexit

Ingi Iusmen

1 Introduction

The year 2015 saw an unprecedented number of refugees arriving to the EU. For instance, in 2015 and 2016 nearly one in four asylum applicants in the EU was a child (European Commission 2016a). Despite this influx of child refugees, the effectiveness and impact of European and national responses to address the plight of vulnerable refugee children has been limited and not fit for purpose, particularly as reflected by a widening gap between the EU's asylum laws and the actual asylum practices of the Member States (Trauner 2016). More generally, the influx of refugees, along with the tight budgetary constraints of some of the Member States, have exposed the deficiencies of the common EU asylum policy, the so-called Common European Asylum System (CEAS), and, in particular, have unearthed the fragmented and disjointed interventions to uphold the rights of refugee children.

I. Iusmen (✉)
Politics & International Relations, Social Sciences, University of Southampton, Southampton, UK
e-mail: I.Iusmen@soton.ac.uk

© The Author(s) 2019   185
M. Dustin et al. (eds.), *Gender and Queer Perspectives on Brexit*,
Gender and Politics, https://doi.org/10.1007/978-3-030-03122-0_8

It is widely contended that EU asylum laws only provide minimum standards of protection, and despite EU-led harmonisation efforts, national governments still enjoy flexibility in how they meet those standards (Chetail et al. 2016). At the same time, the European refugee crisis (Niemann and Zaun 2018) has further exposed the failure of EU institutions and political leaders to Europeanize asylum and refugee policies in time (Bauböck 2018), as well as the gaps in the protection of human rights of refugees arriving to Europe. Not only did the current refugee crisis test the effectiveness of the CEAS in coping with an unprecedented influx of migrants, but it also revealed the existing legal and policy loopholes in human rights protection, particularly in relation to vulnerable groups, such as child refugees.

Moreover, the refugee crisis has further revealed the existing protection deficiencies and failures to uphold the rights of refugee children. The legal provisions in the CEAS generated limited opportunities both for the protection of children's rights in line with the UN Convention on the Rights of the Child (CRC) principles and for their effective enforcement during the asylum procedures. Within migrant children, the category of unaccompanied minors (UAMs)[1] is in a particularly vulnerable situation, given that their rights and protection can easily fall through the cracks of the asylum, migration and child protection systems. Indeed, UAMs face an exceptionally grim situation due to ineffective protection policies (Smith 2003), as well as being exposed to a broader attitude of 'victimisation and criminalisation' (Ayotte 2000) towards them across Europe.

This chapter will assess the effects and implications of Brexit on the protection of UAMs in the UK from a gender perspective. It is argued that male UAMs, in particular, will be the UAM category most affected by Brexit. Without the EU legal and policy regime of protection afforded by the recent proposals to reform the CEAS, male UAMs in the UK will face reduced children's rights protection, lack of specific safeguards for UAMs, such as guardianship, and, therefore, will be exposed to the risks of child trafficking and exploitation. This will particularly be

---

[1] 'Unaccompanied children' refers to the category of children—as defined by the UN Convention on the Rights of the Child—who are outside their country of origin and who have been separated from both parents and other relatives and are not being cared for by an adult, who, by law is responsible for doing so. It includes a child who is left unaccompanied after they have entered the territory of an EU Member State (Art.2(1) of the Directive 2011/95/EU Recast Qualification, OJ L 337, 20.12.2011).

the upshot of the British authorities' decision not to endorse the most recent EU legal proposals concerning child safeguarding in reception, determination of the best interests of the child, as well as the EU legal requirements on effective guardianship. This will mean that UAMs arriving in the UK will be exposed to circumstances and provisions that fail to uphold their rights as children. The first section examines both the legal and policy dimension of child refugees at international and European levels, by showing that, indeed, UAMs are the most vulnerable child refugee group. The first section will further explore the failure of the EU and national policies to protect UAMs in Europe, as exposed by the refugee crisis. The second section examines the policy approach to UAMs in the UK and how the UK has dealt with those UAMs that arrived during the refugee crisis. The final section examines the implications of Brexit on the situation of UAMs in the UK: it is argued that male UAMs will be most affected, given that they constitute the largest group of UAMs. This is compounded by the fact that the UK has refused to join the new proposed reforms of the CEAS, which will enhance the legal protection of children's rights of UAMs in Europe.

2   Unaccompanied Migrant Children in Europe

International Refugee Law and Children's Rights

The protection of refugee children or children seeking asylum is not well defined and addressed by the international instruments relevant to this category of children. The status of asylum-seeking children, and particularly the unaccompanied ones, is to a certain extent vague and uncertain, as non-citizens or aliens (Benhabib 2004) and as children, generally regarded as 'apolitical' (Nakata 2015) and with rights not fully enforced at the domestic level. The primary international instrument governing the rights and status of refugees under international law, namely the 1951 Convention Relating to the Status of Refugees or the so-called Geneva Refugee Convention,[2] makes no reference to refugee children. Indeed, article 1A(2) of the Refugee Convention on the definition of refugee makes no specific reference to children and, therefore,

---

[2] UN General Assembly, *Convention Relating to the Status of Refugees*, 28 July 1951, United Nations, Treaty Series, vol. 189, p. 137, available at: http://www.refworld.org/docid/3be01b964.html.

it has been claimed that the Refugee Convention has been interpreted and applied via an 'adult-focused lens' (Crock 2006, 244). As Bhabha (2003, 266) rightly puts it, children seeking asylum or refugee protection rarely benefit from it directly due to the fact that children 'have simply not been thought of as appropriate subjects of asylum applications or refugee status grants'. According to some scholars, refugee children predominantly face two types of challenges when attempting to access international refugee protection (Pobjoy 2017, 3). First, it is the challenge of invisibility, namely the failure to recognise the child's status as a refugee. Second, there is the challenge of incorrect assessment, namely 'in cases where a child's claim is assessed independently, a failure to interpret the Convention [Refugee Convention] in a manner that takes into account the fact that the applicant is in fact a child' (Pobjoy 2017, 3).

The key tensions between the international protection of children's rights in line with the standards and principles enshrined in the CRC, on the one hand, and the enforced immigration control, on the other hand, have been widely debated by scholars (Watters 2007; Vitus and Lidén 2010; Bhabha 2009, 2014). Despite these intrinsic tensions, the CRC has been globally and nationally accepted as the main children's rights instrument contributing to 'standard setting, implementation and monitoring' (Hanson 2014; Vandenhole 2015) in relation to children's policies and matters. Therefore, in an asylum and refugee context, the CRC could provide the most substantive framework of minimum standards and obligations that national authorities owe to a child. Indeed, it has been argued that the CRC could inform the Refugee Convention in two significant ways (Pobjoy 2017, 6–7). First, the CRC could be used as a procedural guarantee informing the refugee determination process, while, second, it could also provide an interpretative aid informing the interpretation of the Refugee Convention definition of 'refugees' by taking into account the broader international human rights instruments. However, despite this evident need of employing the provisions in the two Conventions to bolster the protection of the rights of refugee children, national authorities have refrained from applying the CRC and its jurisprudence when assessing the legal status of refugee children (Pobjoy 2017).

The category of UAMs has further challenged the legal and policy approaches to addressing the plight of refugee children. In the absence of parents or guardians, the focus shifted to the status of unaccompanied children as 'children', which, consequently, triggered the need to address the legal status and rights of children in international refugee and asylum law. This meant that, in practical terms, it did become necessary for states to address a child's claim for international protection when the child arrived unaccompanied in that respective country (Tuitt 2000; Bhabha 2014). In other words, the arrival of UAMs has led to a legal paradigm shift in terms of how refugee children are treated by national and supranational legal provisions: in practice, this meant that UAMs acquired the right to apply for refugee status and, therefore, their rights as children could be protected as part of this process. Despite this, there have been limited and fragmented provisions in EU asylum and migration law focusing on the rights and entitlements of UAMs in the Union. As shown below, the CEAS includes important provisions that address the situation of refugee and asylum-seeking children, however, it fails to target the specificities and complexity of the UAMs' situation.

EU Asylum Policy and Children's Rights

The emergence of a CEAS since the late 1990s has been hailed as a concerted European effort whereby the Member States would gradually harmonise their asylum procedures and policies. It has been shown that there is a certain degree of Europeanisation of national asylum systems (e.g. Guild 2006; Toshkov and de Haan 2013) and of the 'securitisation' focus of the EU migration and asylum policies (Guild 2006). Despite EU-led efforts towards harmonising asylum standards and procedures, there is still no comparable and uniform system, apart from a set of minimum standards that all national governments have to follow when dealing with asylum seekers at the domestic level. Nonetheless, due to the refugee crisis which reached a peak in 2015, the pressure on the EU to reform its asylum policy has reached a tipping point (Trauner 2016). Indeed, as shown below, the Commission has taken important steps towards reforming the CEAS to protect refugee children's rights, and the human rights of refugees more generally.

The advance of the 'fortress Europe' (Bendel 2005) and the subsequent focus on migration control and security at the expense of the human rights protection of refugees and asylum seekers constitutes one of the main features of the CEAS. Indeed, migration and asylum concerns have increasingly been perceived as a law-and-order matter and have become 'securitized' (Guild 2006). This is also reflected by how various EU Member States first and foremost suspect asylum seekers of being 'bogus' and of seeking to take advantage of the national welfare systems.

The prioritisation of security and migration control at the expense of the human rights protection of asylum seekers was also evidenced by the limited provisions protecting the rights of the child in the CEAS. To this end, since 2009 the EU has adopted a set of revised or recast laws that make up the core of the CEAS. These include the recast versions of the Asylum Procedures,[3] Reception Conditions[4] and Qualification[5] Directives, as well as the Dublin III-Regulation,[6] which were aimed at strengthening the legal protection of rights of child refugees. Indeed, these recast laws include some child-specific provisions, such as child participation. Furthermore, the EU has addressed the protection of migrant children, including UAMs, from trafficking in human beings by adopting a new Anti-Trafficking Directive in 2011.[7]

Despite the EU's recast CEAS laws, which include legal guarantees such as the child's right to be heard, right to legal representation and right to family reunification, there are still significant gaps in the EU asylum *acquis* with respect to UAMs. For instance, there are limited child-specific provisions with respect to the conditions of entry of UAMs (European Migration Network 2015) and the 'best interests of the child' principle is not applied in a comprehensive manner or even at all. Furthermore, while there are EU asylum rules applicable to those UAMs applying for asylum, there are only a few specific provisions in EU legislation that apply to UAMs who arrive to the EU, yet do not apply for international protection. It should be noted that, in compliance with the EU *acquis*, national governments have to meet the specific minimum safeguards they have in place for those UAMs applying for asylum in the EU. Generally, these safeguard measures vary significantly across the Member States. At the same time, the non-asylum seeking UAMs face more challenges, given that some of the Member States do not have legislation that distinguishes between this category of UAMs and those who seek asylum, and therefore treat the former as third country nationals (TCNs). What transpires from the above is that UAMs are an

---

[3] Procedures Directive 2005/85/EC (recast 2013/32/EU).

[4] Reception Conditions Directive 2003/9/EC (recast 2013/33/EU).

[5] Qualification Directive 2004/83/EC (recast 2011/95/EU).

[6] Dublin II Regulation 343/2003 (recast 604/2013).

[7] Directive 2011/36/EU on prevention and combating trafficking in human beings and protecting its victims in the Official Journal of the European Union (OJ L 101, 1 15.4.2011).

intrinsically vulnerable category of child migrants and, as a consequence of that, the Committee on the Rights of the Child called for the Convention State Parties 'to take into account the special vulnerability of unaccompanied and separated children' and to consider child-sensitive assessment procedures of their protection needs (UN Committee on the Rights of the Child 2005).

The UAMs in Europe thus face an extremely vulnerable situation due to the lack of clarity regarding the responsibility for migrant children at the national level in general, and UAMs in particular. For instance, UAMs are often confronted with limited protection and insufficient access to services, as well as slow family reunification, relocation and asylum procedures: all these challenges render them vulnerable and at high risk of abuse and trafficking (UNICEF 2017). The current evidence has shown that the lengthy uncertainty about these children's legal circumstances has left them 'living in limbo' (House of Lords 2016, 3). Furthermore, the vast majority of UAMs face a 'culture of disbelief and suspicion' vis-à-vis both their status as 'refugees' and their age category as 'children' (House of Lords 2016, 3). Additionally, the poor implementation of the existing EU asylum law and national measures relevant to this category of child refugees has further augmented the vulnerability and victimization suffered by UAMs across Europe.

The refugee crisis that hit Europe since 2015 further exposed the shortcomings and failures of the CEAS and national policies to assist and protect vulnerable refugee groups, such as UAMs. For instance, the situation of UAMs in the EU is well-documented: in countries such as Greece, they were placed in detention centres, and due to bad reception conditions and treatment, a significant number of UAMs went missing (Digidiki and Bhabha 2018). Furthermore, the EU faced the recent crisis neither having a common position, nor being united in its approach. According to a Human Rights Watch report, the EU and the Member States 'struggled to develop an effective and principled response to the hundreds of thousands of asylum seekers and migrants who reached Europe. Narrow government interests too often displaced sound policy responses, delaying protection and shelter for vulnerable people and raising questions about the Union's purpose and limits' (Human Rights Watch 2016). Indeed, due to financial pressures and a culture of disbelief across Europe regarding the UAMs' status, most often national authorities chose to overestimate the age of UAMs who lacked documentation in order to avoid having to take responsibility for a minor, thus limiting financial expenses for the public budget (House of Lords 2016). According to leading children's rights charities, the 'overstretching of resources had created incentives for national authorities not to treat minors as children' (Save the Children cited in House of Lords 2016, 9).

All in all, this section showed that the plight of UAMs at an international level in general, and at a European level in particular, is complex and most often their protection falls between the cracks of asylum, migration and child protection systems. As shown in section four below, the EU institutions are currently attempting to address some of these legal and policy shortcomings. Nevertheless, the situation of UAMs in the UK is slightly different to the one in Europe, primarily due to UK's reluctance to opt into the EU's asylum and migration legislation.

3   Unaccompanied Migrant Children in the UK

Between 2015 and 2016, the figures of UAMs claiming asylum in the EU was 160,000.[8] During the same period, over 6000 UAMs claimed asylum in the UK, approximately 4% of the total claims in the EU.[9] At the end of March 2017, the number of UAMs seeking asylum children increased by 6% compared to 2016: up to 4560 from 4300 children (Home Office 2017). Against this backdrop, the UK has adopted a more distinctive approach—compared to other EU Member States—to child refugees in general, and UAMs in particular, due to its selective compliance with EU asylum law and policy. This selective compliance with CEAS rules, as discussed below, has implications for the situation of UAMs in the UK after Brexit, as this will mean that the new CEAS proposals aimed at addressing the rights violation experienced by UAMs in Europe, including the UK, will not be applicable in a British context.

The UK joined only the first phase of CEAS rules, namely the Temporary Protection Directive, and those on Asylum Procedures, Qualification and Reception Conditions adopted between 2000 and 2005. The EU Member States have further agreed—from 2009 to 2013—the second phase of the CEAS legislation. The UK government chose not to participate fully in this reform process, with the Home Office stating: '[W]e do not judge that adopting a common EU asylum

---

[8]https://fullfact.org/immigration/asylum-seekers-uk-and-europe/.

[9]http://ec.europa.eu/eurostat/statistics-explained/index.php/Asylum_quarterly_report.

policy is right for Britain' (Secretary of State for the Home Department 2011, 2). It has been argued that the second phase of the CEAS legislation further strengthens the human rights protection of refugees and asylum seekers arriving to Europe by imposing extra obligations on the Member States to respect human rights matters during asylum procedures. While some of the problems faced by UAMs in the UK are similar to the ones encountered by child migrants in the EU, others are more specific to the UK context. For instance, the 'culture of suspicion' vis-à-vis their age category as children, and their consequent limited access to relevant services, is a particular obstacle faced by unaccompanied child migrants in the UK (House of Lords 2016).

The current policy governing the situation of UAMs arriving to the UK is based on the Immigration Act 2009 and its amended version of 2016.[10] The Immigration Act 2009 imposes a statutory duty on the Secretary of State, and those acting on his/her behalf, to ensure that all decisions relating to the 'immigration, asylum or nationality' of children are discharged having regard to their welfare.[11] This legal duty is linked to specific guidance on how to conduct a "best interests" assessment, which amounts to a welfare checklist for immigration.[12] UAMs can enjoy international protection if they are considered as refugees by applying for asylum on the basis of the Refugee Convention (or Article 3 of the European Convention on Human Rights[13]).

---

[10] https://www.gov.uk/government/collections/immigration-bill-2015-16.

[11] *Borders, Citizenship and Immigration Act* (2009), section 55, available at: http://www.legislation.gov.uk/ukpga/2009/11/section/55.

[12] UK Visas & Immigration, *Section 55 Guidance*, 12 October 2011, available at: https://www.gov.uk/government/uploads/system/uploads/attachment_data/file/431346/Section_55_v12.pdf.

[13] According to the *UNHCR Manual on Refugee Protection and the ECHR*: 'the Court considers that Article 3 of the ECHR can be used by those in need of international refugee protection. While the ECHR is not an international instrument concerned with the protection of refugees per se, Article 3 has been interpreted by the Court as providing an effective means of protection against all forms of return to places where there is a risk that an individual would be subjected to torture, or to inhuman or degrading treatment or punishment. In many respects, the scope of protection provided by Article 3 is wider than that provided by the 1951 Convention, though in others it is more limited'. Available at: http://www.unhcr.org/3ead2d262.pdf.

Refugees should apply for asylum when they arrive in the UK on the basis that it would be unsafe for them to return to their country of origin because of fear of persecution. For adult applicants, the procedure involves a meeting with an immigration officer (known as a 'screening') and then an asylum interview with a caseworker. However, the procedures and processes that apply to UAMs are different, primarily due to their status as *children*, and second, due to their arriving without their family, hence *unaccompanied*. Therefore, refugee children who arrive in the UK without their parents or carers are usually placed into the care of their nearest public authority and will often live with approved foster carers if there are no suitable family members or guardians to care for them. However, the type of care and processes involved in its provision constitute a devolved matter, which is the outcome of the division of responsibility between national and devolved authorities with regard to immigration and child protection matters. Indeed, whilst immigration and asylum constitute a reserved matter for the UK Government, child protection and children's social care are mainly devolved. For instance, in the case of England, policy strategies relevant to the broader category of vulnerable children, including UAMs, can be found in *Putting Children First* (2016), and the provisions contained in the *Children and Social Work Act* (2017).

UAMs arriving to the UK are generally placed in the child protection system if they are identified as needing child care. A young person under 18, without an adult to care for them, is entitled to the same rights as other looked-after children and young people, including accommodation, some finance, education, statutory health assessments, support and reviews. They can be provided, on humanitarian grounds, with discretionary leave to remain until 17 ½ years old, which means that the detailed processing of an asylum application is postponed for when they are older. They are entitled to legal aid. To this end, as much information as possible should be gathered using an appropriate interpreter at an early stage, as this will be relevant to their application. Any parentless child has to be placed in the child care system: this applies to UAMs, if they are identified as children and without a family. However, the establishment of their status as children can only occur after lengthy procedures, as discussed below.

The UAMs who arrived to the UK during the refugee crisis pursued two channels: the first one was the Dublin Regulation, which allowed UAMs to arrive to the UK on family reunification grounds, and the second option was the Dubs scheme,[14] which brought UAMs from Calais. The Dublin System establishes criteria for allocating responsibility for processing asylum claims: it does so by allocating responsibility to the state responsible for the asylum seeker's entry to the EU, and it includes provisions on family reunification. The Dubs scheme was supported by Lord Alfred Dubs, who himself was a child refugee who came to the UK during the Second World War. The Dubs scheme, known as Section 67, came into force in April 2016 via an amendment to the Immigration Act 2016 and it required the Home Secretary to bring a specified number of unaccompanied refugee children to the UK after local authorities approved it, via the so-called National Transfer Scheme. While the scheme did not include a target number, Lord Dubs and his supporters had suggested that the UK could help 3000 of the most vulnerable UAMs. The UAMs who arrived under the Dubs scheme were distributed across the UK as part of the National Transfer Scheme, where they came under the care of local authorities. Because of their vulnerable circumstances, the majority were placed in foster care. All under-16s and girls were provided with emergency foster care before being transferred, while older children were placed into temporary accommodation.

The arrival of UAMs to the UK via these two channels was the outcome of the UK's decision not to participate in the intra-EU relocation of refugees,[15] including child refugees. The UK government has, however, recently indicated, in response to amendments tabled to the Immigration Act 2016, a change in its stance towards relocation regarding unaccompanied children specifically. So far, only 480 children of the expected 3000 UAMs arrived to the UK, which was highly criticised by refugee campaigners, particularly as it seems that the Government decided to cap the numbers of UAMs that would be transferred to the UK via the Dubs scheme (*The Guardian* 2017b). A further 700 unaccompanied children had arrived in the UK under separate EU-wide rules, including rules in the Dublin Regulation, which contains provisions that can help to reunite families.

---

[14] The UK adopted a scheme to enable a number of unaccompanied children to come to live safely in the UK—even if they did not have family links here. This was called the Dubs Amendment. It was named after a man who led the scheme being introduced, called Lord Alf Dubs. See http://www.bbc.co.uk/newsround/38932500.

[15] http://www.bbc.co.uk/newsround/38932500.

Furthermore, there have also been concerns about children who came under EU Dublin regulations, which allow for family members to be reunited. National authorities responsible for these UAMs said some were placed with family members they barely knew or whom they had not seen for years (*The Guardian* 2017a). Additionally, some of the families—who were not given any government support to help pay for the child's needs—struggled to look after them (*The Guardian* 2017a). What transpires from the above is that the implementation of both the Dubs scheme and the Dublin Regulation provisions regarding family reunification failed the UAMs who arrived in the UK.

The UK opted out from the Family Reunification Directive[16] namely the Council Directive 2003/86/EC of 22 September 2003 on the right to family reunification (OJ L251, 3 October 2003). The UK government's decision to opt out from this Directive was justified by its preventive approach, whereby children with refugee status in the UK should be prevented from sponsoring their parents and families to join them. The UK opt-out position was intended to curtail the perverse incentives for children to be encouraged to leave their country and undertake a hazardous journey to the UK. In light of this, it can be argued that UAMs in the UK face a disadvantageous situation compared to those UAMs in the EU. The UK's decision to opt out from some of the key EU legal instruments aimed at protecting the rights of refugees, including refugee children and UAMs, means that the minimum standards of protection, including the protection of children's rights, which are met across Europe, are, therefore, not enforced in the UK.

The structural shortcomings of UK asylum policy, such as the lengthy asylum process, further contributed to the deterioration of UAMs' plight after their arrival to the UK. No wonder, therefore, that it has rightly been claimed that the UK is shirking its responsibility to care for thousands of unaccompanied migrant children, dismissing them as 'someone else's problem' (House of Lords 2016). The failure to protect their rights as children and refugees manifested via the reception conditions and the bureaucratic limbo that the UAMs had to face, which is part of the asylum application process. Given that most of these UAMs were treated with suspicion by national authorities, they often became

---

[16]Among the EU Member States, only Britain and Denmark have opted out from the Family Reunification Directive.

the victims of traffickers and people smugglers (House of Lords 2016). According to the House of Lords EU Home Affairs Subcommittee Report 'the EU and its member states, including the UK, may have lost sight of the plight of unaccompanied migrant children. [The children] face a culture of disbelief and suspicion. Authorities try to avoid taking responsibility for their care and protection' (House of Lords 2016, 4). In brief, British national authorities prioritised immigration control over the protection of refugees' rights, which is an approach that was also widely pursued by some of the European governments.

The UK's selective involvement with the CEAS legislation, especially the second phase, which the UK decided to ignore altogether, can partly explain the failure to protect the rights of UAMs at the domestic level. This protection deficiency is further augmented, as discussed below, by a crucial Brexit consequence: the decision of the UK government not to abide by the proposed reforms to the CEAS, which are intended to boost the protection of rights of vulnerable groups, such as UAMs. As is discussed below, the EU institutions, particularly the Commission, have recently proposed a set of legal instruments aimed at addressing the violations of rights faced by refugees more generally: given that the UK is leaving the Union, then these legal provisions will not apply to the UAMs arriving in the UK. Furthermore, these new EU legal proposals could address some of the key shortcomings and failures that the British policy on UAMs currently faces, particularly on the ground. As discussed below, the differences between the protection of UAMs in the UK and those in other EU countries will be further augmented due to Brexit and the UK's decision not to opt into the new legal proposals to amend some of the CEAS rules.

4   Effects of Brexit on Unaccompanied Migrant Children in the UK

All UAMs and separated children share two key characteristics. First, they are *children* and, therefore, they should be treated, first and foremost, as children and their rights enshrined in the CRC should be upheld. Second, these categories of children are entitled to *special protection*—compared to other categories of children—particularly due to their being temporarily or permanently deprived of their family environment. In light of this, the UK's decision to leave the EU, or Brexit, will have implications for the broader category of UAMs in general, and the male UAMs in particular. It is argued that the gendered dimension is particularly salient in relation to male UAMs, as boys make up just under 90% of those UAMs accessing child care services, with girls just over 10%, the majority of which—both boys and girls, are aged between 14 and 17 years.[17] As of 31 March 2017, 4560 UAMs had applied for asylum in the UK (Home Office 2017). The gendered impact of Brexit in relation to male UMAs is assessed here, particularly in the light of the failure of the UK government to embrace and implement—in the future—the new Commission-led CEAS proposals to enhance the rights of UAMs in Europe, as is discussed below.

It is widely contended that exiting the EU would affect negatively the traditionally marginal groups (Guerrina and Masselot 2018). Furthermore, matters linked to gender and equality did not constitute the focus of the public debate during the EU referendum campaign, which raises significant questions about the implications of these issues for the post-Brexit settlement (Guerrina and Murphy 2016; Hozić and True 2017). It has been shown that the EU played a leading role in the development of gender equality principle in the UK (Guerrina 2005; Kantola 2010). In light of this, it is expected that in the post-EU membership environment, gender equality in the UK will be affected, as UK women will not benefit from the EU-level advocacy for gender equality (Guerrina and Masselot 2018, 9). In the same vein, by choosing not to adopt and implement the latest EU legal proposals aimed at upholding the rights of UAMs and therefore, at addressing the failings of the current national and EU approaches to asylum, the UK further exposes male UAMs to contexts where their rights and needs can be overridden by migration-control objectives, rather than human rights protection goals.

The refugee crisis unearthed the failures in all EU Member States, including the UK, to protect UAMs. One of the key shortcomings vis-à-vis UAMs across Europe includes the absence of integrated child protection systems, which should be focused on the best interests of the child and, therefore, should treat UAMs first and foremost as children, whatever their immigration status (House of Lords 2016). It is widely contended that the UK government's selective participation in the CEAS, and particularly its decision to opt out from the second phase of CEAS, has undermined 'the EU's ability to develop a coherent or adequate

---

[17] https://www.refugeecouncil.org.uk/what_we_do/childrens_services/about_the_childrens_section.

approach to this humanitarian crisis' (European Union Committee 2015). It has been shown that there was a persistent unwillingness of EU governments, including the UK government, to treat the humanitarian crisis brought about by the influx of refugees with the seriousness that it deserved (House of Lords 2016, 10).

Paving the way for the reforms of the CEAS was the publication of the Commission Communication '*Towards a Reform of the Common European Asylum System (CEAS) and enhancing legal avenues to Europe*' of 6 April 2016, where the Commission acknowledged the intrinsic weaknesses of the current EU asylum system in times of migratory and refugee crisis, and highlighted five priority areas where the CEAS should be structurally overhauled. Some of the key priorities outlined in the Commission Communication are the further harmonisation of the CEAS rules to provide for more equal treatment across the EU, reducing the pull factors to come to the EU, as well as achieving overall greater convergence (European Commission 2016b). The Commission proposes to replace the Asylum Procedures Directive[18] with a Regulation aimed at establishing a fully harmonised common EU procedure for international protection to reduce differences in recognition rates from one Member State to the next, discourage secondary movements and ensure common effective procedural guarantees for asylum seekers (European Commission 2016b, c). In the same vein, a new Qualification Regulation will replace the Qualification Directive,[19] and targeted modifications are envisaged for the Reception Conditions Directive.[20]

In July 2016, the Commission put forward legislative proposals for the reform of the CEAS. The main aim behind these proposals is the completion of the CEAS reform by making it more efficient, fair and humane, and which could work effectively both in times of normal and in times

[18] Directive 2013/32/EU of the European Parliament and of the Council of 26 June 2013 on common procedures for granting and withdrawing international protection, OJ L 180, 29.6.2013, pp. 60–95.

[19] Directive 2011/95/EU of the European Parliament and of the Council of 13 December 2011 on standards for the qualification of third-country nationals or stateless persons as beneficiaries of international protection, for a uniform status for refugees or for persons eligible for subsidiary protection, and for the content of the protection granted, OJ L 337, 20.12.2011, pp. 9–26.

[20] Directive 2013/33/EU of the European Parliament and of the Council of 26 June 2013 laying down standards for the reception of applicants for international protection, OJ L 180, 29.6.2013, pp. 96–116.

of high migratory pressure. The proposals focus on the establishment of a common procedure for international protection, uniform standards for protection and rights granted to beneficiaries of international protection and the further harmonisation of reception conditions in the EU (European Commission 2016b, c). The proposals further include reinforced safeguards for asylum seekers with special needs and for UAMs: with respect to these two vulnerable categories, a guardian should be assigned at the latest five days after an application has been made.

In July 2017, the Member States, as part of the Council of the EU, agreed to start negotiations on the proposed Qualification Regulation and Procedures Regulation (European Commission 2016b, c). This new regulation is relevant to UAMs, as it aims to ensure that Member States will apply common criteria for the identification of persons genuinely in need of international protection. The main provisions in this proposed Regulation which are relevant for the protection of UAMs include the guarantees for more effective guardianship and care (the Procedures Regulation and the Reception Conditions Regulation), upgrading of the principle of the best interests of the child to apply to the full EU asylum law, rather than limiting it to a child-specific article, as well as child safeguarding in reception and training of staff working directly with children (European Commission 2016a, 6). In the same vein, the Dublin Regulation will be reformed to cater better for the needs and rights of child migrants, and UAMs in particular. The proposed Dublin Regulation, which will form the basis of the Dublin system, aims to make the 'best interests of the child' a primary consideration for all Member States (European Commission 2016d). According to the Commission, under the new system 'the rights of unaccompanied minors will be strengthened and the assessment of the best interests of the child reinforced. The proposal clarifies that the Member State where the minor first lodged his or her application for international protection will be responsible, unless it is demonstrated that this is not in the best interests of the minor'[21] (European Commission 2016d). The new Dublin Regulation proposal ensures that, prior to transferring an UAM to another Member State, the transferring Member State will have to make

[21] For instance, under Art. 3.5 of the Commission proposal it is stated that 'the rights of unaccompanied minors have also been strengthened through better defining the principle of the best interests of the child and by setting out a mechanism for making a best interests of the child-determination in all circumstances implying the transfer of a minor' (European Commission 2016d, 14).

sure that the receiving Member State will take the necessary measures to safeguard their rights without delay.

In the UK, one of the main violations of the rights of the child in relation to UAMs is the age assessment procedure. Given the absence of a EU-wide accepted and non-invasive procedure for assessing UAMs' age medically, there is substantial evidence showing the use of non-medical age assessments primarily in the UK (House of Lords 2016). The tendency to deploy intrusive and non-child friendly procedures to assess UAMs' age is rooted in the 'culture of disbelief and suspicion' (House of Lords 2016, 3) that British authorities display with respect to UAMs. In other words, there is strong reluctance to treat UAMs as children by believing their stories and narratives: this practice opposes the CRC recommendation[22] which requires that in cases of uncertainty regarding children's age, they should be treated first and foremost as children until the contrary is proven.[23] This treatment of UAMs can have serious consequences on the welfare and well-being of UAMs: if they are considered adults rather than children, then in practice this means that they are denied access to welfare services and support, being placed in detention centres with adults, not being provided with a legal guardian and not receiving public funding for legal representation during the asylum process. Furthermore, until the age assessment procedure is completed, UAMs, being treated as adults, are exposed to the risk of deportation procedures under the Dublin Regulation, through a reversal of the 'benefit of the doubt' principle in practice (AIDA 2015). Yet, the proposed reforms to the CEAS, particularly regarding the reception conditions, which require the Member States to ensure that individual gender and age sensitive vulnerability and needs assessment of children are carried out upon arrival in line with the 'best interests of the child' principle (European Commission 2016b) can further address the shortcomings in the age assessment procedures employed in the UK. In light of the Brexit outcome, the male UAMs would benefit in particular from this

[22] According to the CRC General Comment No. 6: 'The assessment must be conducted in a scientific, safe, child and gender-sensitive and fair manner; avoiding any risk of violation of the physical integrity of the child; giving due respect to human dignity; and in the event of remaining uncertainty, should accord the individual the benefit of the doubt such that if there is a possibility that the individual is a child, s/he should be treated as such' (UN Committee on the Rights of the Child 2005, 10).

[23] UN Committee on the Rights of the Child, General Comment No. 6 (2005).

EU proposed legislation, given that they constitute the vast majority of the UAM population arriving to the UK.

Another shortcoming of the UK's approach to UAMs is their insufficient access to services, particularly mental health services (House of Lords 2016). One explanation for this is the cost of providing this type of services by local authorities. For instance, councils currently receive a daily rate of £114 (£798 per week) for UAMs younger than 16 years and £91 for 16–17 year olds (£637 per week). However, the average weekly cost for one UAM arriving in the local council is much higher: in practice this means that providing UAMs with access to mental health services constitutes a financial challenge to local authorities. There is limited knowledge within local authorities about the specific health and wellbeing needs of UAMs (House of Lords 2016) and it is widely known that the assessment of emotional health and well-being and mental health is a complex process (Chase et al. 2008). The circumstances of UAMs are extremely stressful, particularly from a mental health perspective. Their situation constitutes the outcome of a combination of the circumstances in the country of origin, the journey to and arrival in the UK, and the possibility of a refusal and return to the country of origin. All these distinctive processes are prone to generate trauma of various types, including separation and loss, dislocation, rupture and uncertainty (Simmonds and Merredew, NA). No wonder, therefore, that the vast majority of UAMs in Europe, including the UK, struggle with mental health problems, such as post-traumatic stress disorder, depression and very high levels of anxiety (AIDA 2017). In light of these, there is a crucial need for the services provided by local authorities to fully understand the plight and circumstances of UAMs. As a recent report published by the House of Lords put it, 'there is no access to services, despite massive research, carried out by some very influential academics in the UK, showing that if a young person has come from a conflict zone they are likely to have suffered some form of trauma… There is no access to services for mental health support. It is lacking hugely' (House of Lords 2016, 47).

One of the reasons why the UAMs' situation is mishandled by further increasing the trauma they have already suffered and failing to uphold their rights as children, is strongly linked to how the 'best interests of the child' principle is applied in practice by the relevant professionals in touch with UAMs. In the UK, the 'best interests of the child' principle was enshrined in national law by means of the Immigration Act 2009. However, the principle is often not observed in practice (Coram

Children's Legal Centre evidence cited in the House of Lords 2016). In the same vein, the investigation conducted by the Joint Committee on Human Rights (JCHR) in 2013 into the human rights of UAMs in the UK found that immigration concerns were generally prioritised over children's rights, while no attention was paid to the best interests of such children during the asylum and immigration processes which they experienced (House of Lords 2016, 32). Given the deficiencies in determining and applying the 'best interests' principle to UAMs, the UK government was urged to 'develop, apply and routinely monitor national guidance on how to conduct 'best interests' assessments with regard to unaccompanied minors' (House of Lords 2016, 69), by particularly establishing a Best Interests Determination process. The lack of operationalization of the 'best interests' principle in practice, along with the culture of disbelief and suspicion UAMs face after arriving in the UK, were conducive to the detention of UAMs in adult detention centres for a significant amount of time (*The Guardian* 2017c).[24] Furthermore, recently the Independent Chief Inspector of Borders and Immigration (2018) published a study that documented the 'failure to demonstrate that the child's 'best interests' were a primary concern' (Independent Chief Inspector of Borders and Immigration 2018, 6) by those professionals and services dealing with UAMs. The key finding of the report is that the 'best interests' of the child were not properly considered throughout the asylum process, including how those interests were met for those UAMs transferred from one Local Authority area to another under the National Transfer Scheme (Independent Chief Inspector of Borders and Immigration 2018).

These specific shortcomings could be addressed if the UK were to adopt and enforce the proposed reform to the CEAS. The new proposed reforms, particularly of the Dublin III Regulation and the Qualification Regulation, intend to upgrade the 'best interests of the child' principle to apply to the full EU asylum law, rather than only to the child specific provisions. In light of Brexit, these proposed changes to CEAS could have further boosted the compliance with CRC principles in the UK, such as the 'best interests of the child', which, as shown above, fails to be operationalised in practice. For instance, the proposed reform of the Dublin III Regulation provides for the enhancement of rights protection by 'better defining the principle

---

[24] For instance, in March 2017, a Court of Appeal's ruling criticised Home Office policy and claimed that immigration officers could not simply disbelieve the age given by child refugees (*The Guardian* 2017c).

of the best interests of the child and by setting out a mechanism for making a best interests of the child-determination in all circumstances implying the transfer of a minor' (European Commission 2016d). In the same vein, the Qualification Regulation stipulates that provisions such as 'the availability of appropriate care and custodial arrangements, which are in the best interests of the unaccompanied minor, should form part of the assessment as to whether that protection is effectively available' (European Commission 2016b). In essence, the main implication here of Brexit on male UAMs is a missed opportunity—by UK's decision not to be part of the reformed CEAS—of providing legal safeguards and obligations aimed of ensuring that key CRC principles, such as the 'best interests of the child'—are operationalised and applied effectively in practice in matters concerning UAMs during asylum and immigration processes.

The new CEAS proposals aimed to enhance the human rights protection dimension of the EU asylum law should, indeed, have a positive impact on the situation of UAMs in Europe. As discussed above, the new changes proposed by the Commission should enhance the protection of children's rights during asylum and migration procedures, which is currently fragmented and often lacking in practice both in the EU Member States and in the UK. More specifically, the reinforcement of the need to apply the 'best interests of the child' principle to the majority of the asylum law and procedures, as well as the inclusion of safeguards for a more effective provision of guardianship and care, are expected to address some of the deficiencies that the EU and UK asylum systems currently face vis-à-vis child refugees, including UAMs. Brexit entails that the UK will not be endorsing these legal proposals, so the treatment of UAMs in the UK, particularly male UAMs will continue to be defective and insufficient from a children's rights perspective. In other words, the male UAMs in particular—given that they constitute the largest number of UAMs arriving in the UK—will not benefit from these measures, which could address shortcomings faced in the UK, such as the assessment of the best interests, implementation of more effective guardianship, provisions on age assessment procedures, as well as more comprehensive guardianship safeguards.

5   Conclusion

This chapter discussed the protection of UAMs in the EU and the UK from legal and policy perspectives. It was shown that the refugee crisis exposed the weakness and the gaps in rights protection of both the

CEAS and UK policy. What transpires from the analysis is that there are crucial deficiencies and loopholes, both in terms of the design and implementation of legal and policy measures. To this end, the EU institutions proposed courses of action to address some of these shortcomings. Leaving the EU means that the UK will not be taking part in the coordinated and common efforts taken by national governments at EU level to tackle shared problems and challenges. Indeed, the UK will be aiming to solve transnational problems—such as influx of refugees—by appealing only to national means and instruments, which is detrimental to effective solutions, given the cross-border character of most of these issues. As the UNICEF chief rightly put it, there is 'a lot of added value in a common European response. These are transnational challenges. These are challenges that relate to data-sharing and closer co-operation among child protection authorities, migration authorities and other services in different countries. This is best done in a common, co-ordinated way because if we try to do it piecemeal, as we see at the moment, we leave a lot of protection gaps open' (Verena Knaus cited in House of Lords 2016, 12).

BIBLIOGRAPHY

AIDA (Asylum Information Database). 2015. *Detriment of the Doubt: Age Assessment of Unaccompanied Asylum-Seeking Children.* AIDA Legal Briefing No. 5, December.

AIDA. 2017. *The Concept of Vulnerability in European Asylum Procedures.* Report, August 31.

Ayotte, W. 2000. *Separated Children Coming to Western Europe: Why They Travel and How They Arrive.* London: Save the Children.

Bauböck, R. 2018. Refugee Protection and Burden-Sharing in the European Union. *Journal of Common Market Studies* 56 (1): 141–156.

Bendel, P. 2005. Immigration Policy in the European Union: Still Bringing Up the Walls for Fortress Europe? *Migration Letters* 2 (1): 20–31.

Benhabib, S. 2004. *The Rights of Others: Aliens, Residents, and Citizens*, vol. 5. Cambridge: Cambridge University Press.

Bhabha, J. 2003. More Than Their Share of Sorrows: International Migration Law and the Rights of Children. *Saint Louis University Public Law Review* 22: 253–293.

Bhabha, J. 2009. Arendt's Children: Do Today's Migrant Children Have a Right to Have Rights? *Human Rights Quarterly* 31 (2): 410–451.

Bhabha, J. 2014. *Child Migration and Human Rights in a Global Age.* Princeton: Princeton University Press.

Chase, E., A. Knight, and J. Statham. 2008. *Promoting the Emotional Wellbeing and Mental Health of Unaccompanied Young People Seeking Asylum in the UK.* London: Thomas Coram.

Chetail, V., P. De Bruycker, and F. Maiani (eds.). 2016. *Reforming the Common European Asylum System: The New European Refugee Law.* Leiden: Brill.

Crock, M. 2006. *Seeking Asylum Alone: A Study of Australian Law, Policy and Practice Regarding Unaccompanied and Separated Children.* Sydney: Federation Press.

Digidiki, V., and J. Bhabha. 2018. Sexual Abuse and Exploitation of Unaccompanied Migrant Children in Greece: Identifying Risk Factors and Gaps in Services During the European Migration Crisis. *Children and Youth Services Review.* https://doi.org/10.1016/j.childyouth.2018.02.040.

European Commission. 2016a. 10th European Forum on the Rights of the Child. The Protection of Children in Migration, November 24, updated 29 March 2017.

European Commission. 2016b. Proposal for a Regulation of the European Parliament and of the Council on the Standards for the Qualification of Third-Country Nationals or Stateless Persons as Beneficiaries of International Protection, for a Uniform Status for Refugees or for Persons Eligible for Subsidiary Protection and for the Content of the Protection Granted and Amending Council Directive 2003/109/EC of 25 November 2003 Concerning the Status of Third-Country Nationals Who Are Long-Term Residents, COM(2016) 466 final, Brussels, July 13.

European Commission. 2016c. Towards a Sustainable and Fair Common European Asylum System. Press Release, May 4.

European Commission. 2016d. Proposal for a Regulation of the European Parliament of the Council Establishing the Criteria and Mechanisms for Determining the Member State Responsible for Examining an Application for International Protection Lodged in One of the Member States by a Third-Country National or a Stateless Person (Recast), COM(2016) 270 final, Brussels, May 4.

European Migration Network. 2015. *Policies, Practices and Data on Unaccompanied Minors in the EU Member States and Norway.* Available at: http://ec.europa.eu/anti-trafficking/sites/antitrafficking/files/emn_study_2014_uams.pdf.

European Union Committee. 2015. *The United Kingdom Opt-into the Proposed Council Decision on the Relocation of Migrants Within the EU*, 2nd Report, Session 2015–16, HL Paper 22.

Guerrina, R. 2005. *Mothering the Union: Gender Equality Politics in the EU.* Manchester: Manchester University Pres.

Guerrina, R., and A. Masselot. 2018. Walking into the Footprint of EU Law: Unpacking the Gendered Consequences of Brexit. *Social Policy and Society* 17 (2): 1–12.

Guerrina, R., and H. Murphy. 2016. Strategic Silences in the Brexit Debate: Gender, Marginality and Governance. *Journal of Contemporary European Research* 12 (4): 872–880.

Guild, E. 2006. The Europeanisation of Europe's Asylum Policy. *International Journal of Refugee Law* 18 (3–4): 630–651.

Hanson, K. 2014. 'Killed by Charity'—Towards Interdisciplinary Children's Rights Studies. *Childhood* 21 (4): 441–446.

Home Office. 2017. Safeguarding Strategy Unaccompanied Asylum Seeking and Refugee Children. November. Available at: https://www.gov.uk/government/uploads/system/uploads/attachment_data/file/656425/UASC_Safeguarding_Strategy_2017.pdf.

House of Lords. 2016. Children in Crisis: Unaccompanied Migrant Children in Europe. Available at: https://publications.parliament.uk/pa/ld201617/ldselect/ldeucom/34/34.pdf.

Hozić, A., and J. True. 2017. Brexit as a Scandal: Gender and Global Trumpism. *Review of International Political Economy* 24 (2): 270–287.

Human Rights Watch. 2016. Human Rights Watch World Report, 2016: European Union Events of 2015. Available at: https://www.hrw.org/world-report/2016/country-chapters/european-union-0.

Independent Chief Inspector of Borders and Immigration. 2018. *An Inspection of How the Home Office Considers the 'Best Interests' of Unaccompanied Asylum Seeking Children.* August–December 2017. Available at: https://assets.publishing.service.gov.uk/government/uploads/system/uploads/attachment_data/file/695310/An_inspection_of_the_best_interests_of_unaccompanied_asylum_seeking_children_March_2018.pdf.

Kantola, J. 2010. *Gender and the European Union.* Basingstoke: Palgrave.

Nakata, S. 2015. *Childhood Citizenship, Governance and Policy: The Politics of Becoming Adult.* New York, NY: Routledge.

Niemann, A., and N. Zaun. 2018. EU Refugee Policies and Politics in Times of Crisis: Theoretical and Empirical Perspectives. *Journal of Common Market Studies* 56 (1): 3–22.

Pobjoy, J. M. 2017. *The Child in International Refugee Law.* Cambridge: Cambridge University Press.

Secretary of State for the Home Department. 2011. Report to Parliament on the Application of Protocols 19 and 21 to the Treaty on European Union and the Treaty on the Functioning of the European Union (TFEU) in Relation to EU Justice and Home Affairs (JHA) Matters (1 December 2009–30 November 2010). Presentation to Parliament, London, January.

Simmonds, J., and F. Merredew. (NA). The Health Needs of Unaccompanied Asylum Seeking Children and Young People. Available at: https://www.nice.org.uk/guidance/ph28/evidence/looked-after-children-ep23-unaccompanied-asylum-seeking-children-john-simmonds-and-florence-merredew2.

Smith, T. 2003. *Separated Children in Europe: Policies and Practices in European Union Member States* [Online]. Save the Children. Available at: http://www. separated-children-europe-programme.org/separated_children/publications/ reports/index.html#comparative_analysis.

The Guardian. 2017a. Revealed: Rescued Refugee Children Facing Limbo—And Worse—In UK, October 19.

The Guardian. 2017b. Legal Challenge to Cap on Dubs Child Refugee Scheme Fails, November 2.

The Guardian. 2017c. Child Asylum Seekers May Have Been Illegally Detained, Rules Court, March 9.

Toshkov, D., and L. de Haan. 2013. The Europeanization of Asylum Policy: An Assessment of the EU Impact on Asylum Applications and Recognitions Rates. *Journal of European Public Policy* 20 (5): 661–683.

Trauner, F. 2016. Asylum Policy: The EU's 'Crises' and the Looming Policy Regime Failure. *Journal of European Integration* 38 (3): 311–325.

Tuitt, P. 2000. The State, the Family and the Child Refugee. In *Revisiting Children's Rights: 10 Years of the UN Convention on the Rights of the Child*, ed. D. Fottrell. The Netherlands: Brill.

UN Committee on the Rights of the Child. 2005. General Comment No. 6: Treatment of Unaccompanied and Separated Children Outside Their Country of Origin, 1 September 2005, CRC/GC/2005/6. Available at: http://www2.ohchr.org/english/bodies/crc/docs/GC6.pdf.

UNICEF. 2017. Refugee and Migrant Crisis in Europe. Humanitarian Situation Report #24. Available at: https://data2.unhcr.org/en/documents/download/ 58578.

Vandenhole, W. 2015. Children's Rights from a Legal Perspective. In *Routledge International Handbook of Children's Rights Studies*, 27. Abingdon: Routledge.

Vitus, K., and H. Lidén. 2010. The Status of the Asylum-Seeking Child in Norway and Denmark: Comparing Discourses, Politics and Practices. *Journal of Refugee Studies* 23 (1): 62–81.

Watters, C. 2007. *Refugee Children: Towards the Next Horizon*. Abingdon: Routledge.

CHAPTER 9

The Impact of Brexit on Gender and Asylum Law in the UK

Christel Querton

1   INTRODUCTION

On 23 June 2016, 51.9% of more than 30 million people in the United Kingdom (UK) voted in a referendum to leave the European Union (EU). Despite the subject of migration featuring prominently in the period leading up to the referendum, the UK Government has been virtually silent on the envisaged post-exit asylum landscape (European Parliament 2017b, 9). A leaked Home Office document noted the UK intended to remain a "safe haven for those fleeing persecution" and the UK would continue to adhere to the Refugee Convention (*The Guardian* 2017, para. 7). It appears that the UK Government has not and does not intend to make any impact assessment of leaving the EU on refugee protection, let alone a gender impact assessment in this area (House of Commons 2017c, para. 17.15).

This work was supported by the Arts and Humanities Research Council and the Northern Bridge Doctoral Training Partnership.

C. Querton (✉)
Law School, Newcastle University, Newcastle upon Tyne, UK
e-mail: C.Querton2@newcastle.ac.uk

© The Author(s) 2019
M. Dustin et al. (eds.), *Gender and Queer Perspectives on Brexit*,
Gender and Politics, https://doi.org/10.1007/978-3-030-03122-0_9

209

Moreover, there was little to no recognition of gender and equality issues in the campaign leading up to the referendum, nor have these important issues been considered in the subsequent negotiations (Guerrina and Masselot 2018, 2). Whereas existing literature on the impact of leaving the EU from a gender perspective has focused on economic, social and political rights (Jenkins 2017; Kilkey 2017; Shutes and Walker 2018), this chapter contributes to the discussion by specifically addressing the likely impact of Brexit on asylum law through a gender lens. There is a multitude of political, economic and legal interests at play in the negotiations to leave the EU, alongside the ongoing debates around the EU (Withdrawal) Bill 2017–19.[1] As a result, it would be extremely difficult to predict with certainty what the impact will be on asylum law in the UK (European Parliament 2017b, 11). Consequently, this chapter attempts to answer this question by looking at the specific issue of refugee recognition from a gender perspective.

To assess the likely impact of leaving the EU, this chapter will firstly undertake a historical analysis of UK practice prior to and after the adoption of the Common European Asylum System (CEAS) by focusing on specific provisions of particular relevance to persons fleeing gender-related persecution. This legal analysis suggests that the absence of EU obligations in the field of asylum law is unlikely to have an immediate and substantive impact on the recognition of refugees from a gender perspective in the UK. However, this section highlights the importance of preserving the ability of refugees to enforce their rights and access effective remedies. Secondly, this chapter will examine the scope and nature of the UK's international and regional refugee and human rights obligations which exist independently of its obligations under EU law. This section notes the increasing relevance of human rights norms in ensuring a gender-sensitive interpretation of the refugee definition, but again raises concerns regarding the enforcement of rights outside of the EU legal framework and the significance of ensuring continued supra-national oversight. Adopting a gender lens, this chapter evaluates the prospects and risks or opportunities resulting from changes in the legal framework governing the recognition of refugees in the UK.

---

[1] European Union (Withdrawal) Bill 2017–19 (HL Bill 79) (18 January 2018), https://publications.parliament.uk/pa/bills/lbill/2017-2019/0079/18079.pdf, accessed 2 February 2018. At the time of writing, the Bill is being debated in Parliament.

2   INTERNATIONAL REFUGEE LAW AND THE COMMON EUROPEAN ASYLUM SYSTEM

All EU Member States, including the UK, are parties to the UN Convention Relating to the Status of Refugees 1951 and its Protocol Relating to the Status of Refugees 1967.[2] In 2016, there were approximately 40,000 asylum applicants in the UK, 31% of whom were women (Eurostat 2017). Interpreting the refugee definition in a gender-sensitive manner is essential to accurately determine asylum claims and understand the reasons why persons flee their countries of origin due to existing power relations (UNHCR 2002a, para. 2). Such a perspective assumes that men and women have different experiences due to socially constructed notions of gender and their respective relationship to the State (Charlesworth et al. 1991, 616). The United Nations High Commissioner for Refugees (UNHCR) in its *Guidelines on Gender-Related Persecution*, defined gender as follows:

> Gender refers to the relationship between women and men based on socially or culturally constructed and defined identities, status, roles and responsibilities that are assigned to one sex or another, while sex is a biological determination. Gender is not static or innate but acquires socially and culturally constructed meaning over time. (2002a, para. 3)

The UK's international refugee law obligations are complemented in the EU by a set of instruments aiming to harmonise legislation and practice between Member States under a framework known as the CEAS established under the Treaty on the Functioning of the European Union (TFEU).[3] Although pre-CEAS instruments tended to focus mostly on process rather than protection, it was generally agreed within refugee law scholarship that those measures instigated further deterrence against refugees in the UK (Harvey 2000, 330–331; Stevens 2004, 367–368). The TFEU sets out that the aim of CEAS is to establish a common policy "with a view to offering appropriate status to any third-country

---

[2] Convention Relating to the Status of Refugees (adopted 28 July 1951, entered into force 22 April 1954) 189 UNTS 137; Protocol Relating to the Status of Refugees (adopted 31 January 1967, entered into force 4 October 1967) 606 UNTS 267.

[3] Treaty on the Functioning of the European Union (consolidated version) [2012] OJ C326/47.

national requiring international protection and ensuring compliance with the principle of *non-refoulement*" (Article 78). However, it is the objective of limiting the secondary movement of asylum seekers between EU Member States as a result of disparities in their practices and legislation which led to the adoption of a series of measures establishing minimum standards and later common standards in relation to the qualification of third country nationals as refugees or persons who otherwise need international protection, asylum procedures, reception conditions, and determining the State responsible for examining applicants' claims for international protection (European Commission 2001). The four main CEAS instruments comprised the Qualification Directive 2004,[4] the Asylum Procedures Directive 2005,[5] the Reception Conditions Directive 2003[6] and the Dublin Regulation.[7]

As a result of continued divergence in EU Member States' refugee recognition rates and asylum procedures, those instruments underwent a process of reform starting in 2010 which recast the first phase instruments of the CEAS (Recast Qualification Directive 2011[8]; Recast Asylum Procedures Directive 2013[9]; Recast Reception Conditions

---

[4] Council Directive 2004/83/EC of 29 April 2004 on minimum standards for the qualification and status of third country nationals or stateless persons as refugees or as persons who otherwise need international protection and the content of the protection granted [2004] OJ L304/12.

[5] Council Directive 2005/85/EC of 1 December 2005 on minimum standards on procedures in Member States for granting and withdrawing refugee status [2005] OJ L326/13.

[6] Council Directive 2003/9/EC of 27 January 2003 laying down minimum standards for the reception of asylum seekers [2003] OJ L31/18.

[7] Council Regulation (EC) No 343/2003 of 18 February 2003 establishing the criteria and mechanisms for determining the Member State responsible for examining an asylum application lodged in one of the Member States by a third-country national [2003] OJ L50/1.

[8] Directive 2011/95/EU of the European Parliament and of the Council of 13 December 2011 on standards for the qualification of third-country nationals or stateless persons as beneficiaries of international protection, for a uniform status for refugees or for persons eligible for subsidiary protection, and for the content of the protection granted [2011] OJ L337/9.

[9] Directive 2013/32/EU of the European Parliament and of the Council of 26 June 2013 on common procedures for granting and withdrawing international protection [2013] OJ L180/60.

Directive 2013[10]; Dublin III Regulation).[11] The UK decided not to opt-into the three recast Directives due to concerns over limits they would place on the national system, but remains bound by their earlier versions (Protocol 21 TFEU; House of Commons 2017a, para. 10.12). Thus, for many years already, the UK has not been bound by the same standards as most other EU Member States and its involvement with EU asylum policies became more marginal (European Parliament 2017b, 23). Although it did not opt-into the second phase CEAS Directives, the UK has continued to take part in the Dublin Regulation, which determines the State responsible for examining an asylum claim.

Despite two rounds of CEAS instruments aiming to achieve EU harmonisation, the "continued fragmentation of the asylum system" and the continued disparity in refugee recognition rates in the EU led the European Commission to propose replacing the Directives with Regulations (European Commission 2015, para. III.3). Such Regulations would limit Member States' margin of appreciation in implementing the standards that currently apply under the Directives, because Regulations are binding in their entirety and directly applicable in all Member States (Article 288 TFEU). The UK decided not to opt-into the new Regulations, because they "would further limit the Government's ability to take decisions on the UK asylum system at national level and in the UK national interest" (House of Commons 2017a, para. 10.5).

The draft EU (Withdrawal) Bill provides for EU law and domestic legislation transposing EU law to be 'retained' in UK law. Once the UK has left the EU, decisions will be made regarding whether to keep, amend or repeal that legislation (Department for Exiting the European Union 2018, para. 23). A new Immigration Bill has been promised to bring in any legislative changes to take effect upon the UK exiting the EU and it may be that the Government takes this opportunity to revise

---

[10]Directive 2013/33/EU of the European Parliament and of the Council of 26 June 2013 laying down standards for the reception of applicants for international protection [2013] OJ L180/96.

[11]Regulation (EU) No 604/2013 of the European Parliament and of the Council of 26 June 2013 establishing the criteria and mechanisms for determining the Member State responsible for examining an application for international protection lodged in one of the Member States by a third-country national or a stateless person (recast) [2013] OJ L180/31.

the laws pertaining to those seeking international protection in the UK (*The Guardian* 2017, para. 1.8).

3   GENDER AND THE QUALIFICATION DIRECTIVE 2004

The Qualification Directive 2004 is the most important instrument of the CEAS, as it "goes to the heart" of the Refugee Convention in providing more detailed definitions determining who qualifies as a refugee (Lambert 2006, 161). A refugee is defined under international law and EU law as a person who "owing to a well-founded fear of being persecuted for reasons of race, religion, nationality, political opinion or membership of a particular social group, is outside the country of nationality and is unable or, owing to such fear, is unwilling to avail himself or herself of the protection of that country" (Article 1A(2) Convention Relating to the Status of Refugees 1951; Article 2(c) Qualification Directive 2004). The UK has transposed this exact definition into domestic legislation (Regulation 2 Qualification Regulations 2006[12]; para. 334(ii) Immigration Rules (HC395)). The Qualification Directive 2004 was ground-breaking in international refugee law, however, because it elaborated significantly on several elements of the "minimalist definition" of the Refugee Convention (Storey 2008, 8).

As reflected in the definition of gender provided above, gender may be relevant to qualification as a refugee in terms of understanding whether particular treatment amounts to persecution but also in terms of the reasons for that ill-treatment and, thus, whether persecution is for reasons of one of the five Refugee Convention grounds. The UNHCR *Guidelines on Gender-Related Persecution* state that "it is widely accepted that [gender] can influence, or dictate, the type of persecution or harm suffered and the reasons for this treatment" (UNHCR 2002a, para. 6). Moreover, gender dynamics, understood as the "socially constructed roles, behaviours, activities and attributes that a given society considers appropriate for women and men" (Article 3(c) Istanbul Convention 2011),[13] determine and influence the power of certain actors of persecution or protection and therefore represent an essential consideration in

---

[12]The Refugee or Person in Need of International Protection (Qualification) Regulations 2006.

[13]Convention on Preventing and Combatting Violence Against Women and Domestic Violence (adopted 11 May 2011, entered into force 1 August 2014) CETS 210.

asylum decision-making. Thus, particular provisions of the Qualification Directive 2004 with specific relevance from a gender perspective are evaluated in this section to assess their historical impact on UK asylum practice.

The only references to gender in the Qualification Directive 2004 are found in the provisions relating to the assessment of facts and circumstances, the notion of 'acts of persecution' and the Refugee Convention ground of 'Particular Social Group' (PSG). Article 4(3)(c) of the Qualification Directive 2004 requires asylum decision-makers to take into consideration "the individual position and personal circumstances of the applicant, including factors such as background, gender and age, so as to assess whether, on the basis of the applicant's personal circumstances, the acts to which the applicant has been or could be exposed would amount to persecution or serious harm". This was transposed into para. 339 J(iii) of the Immigration Rules (HC395). Article 9(2)(f) of the Qualification Directive 2004 provides that acts of persecution, as defined in the Directive, can take the form of "acts of a gender-specific or child-specific nature". This provision was not transposed into domestic legislation, but the UK Border Agency (now the Home Office) set out in its Asylum Policy Instruction on *Gender Issues in the Asylum Claim* that "acts of a gender-specific nature, other than sexual violence, may also constitute persecution. Whether a particular action amounts to persecution requires the decision-maker to reach a judgement in each case" (2010, 4). Any reference to gender was eventually excluded from the Regulations transposing the Directive (Qualification Regulations 2006).

Despite the UK's agreement with the EU to select which CEAS measures it wished to opt-into, the UK was an important actor in the negotiations of the first phase measures, including the Qualification Directive 2004, and was "quite successful in influencing their content" (Lambert 2006, 163; European Parliament 2017b, 23). Prior to its adoption, the UK Government considered that the impact of the Directive on the number of persons recognised as refugees would be limited (House of Lords 2002, para. 14, 62). When the Qualification Directive 2004 was transposed into domestic law, the Home Office set out its view that UK practice was already equivalent to that provided in the Qualification Directive through a mixture of statutory and policy provisions and that implementation would not have a significant impact (Home Office 2006, para. 7.1). Thus, it is suggested that as the development of asylum law and policy in the UK relied only marginally on EU asylum legislation, the adoption of the Qualification Directive 2004 has had little impact in the UK compared to other EU Member States. Consequently, the absence of those obligations is unlikely to significantly change existing law and practice. This claim is illustrated below by discussing different elements of the refugee definition of particular relevance to gender, namely the status and role of non-state actors, the concept of 'internal relocation' and the Convention ground of PSG.

Non-state Actors

The question of whether non-state actors may be considered agents of persecution or agents of protection in international refugee law is highly relevant from a gender perspective, because it has been claimed that many gender-related asylum claims involve persecution by non-state actors, including domestic violence, forced marriage, female genital mutilation, rape and sexual violence (Anker 2001, 392). Prior to the development of the CEAS, the practice of EU Member States regarding the conceptualisation of non-state actors as agents of persecution differed widely (Wilsher 2003). Although the Council of the EU recognised non-state actors as agents of persecution, it also required the encouragement, permission or a deliberate failure to act by the authorities (Joint Position 1996, para. 5.2).[14] As a result, persons fearing gender-based violence within the family or the community were refused refugee status due to the absence of State involvement (Phuong 2002, 530). Whereas Germany and France did not recognise non-state actors of persecution prior to the adoption of the Qualification Directive 2004, the UK had recognised non-state actors of persecution since at least 1998, when the House of Lords considered the risk of persecution from opposing clans in Somalia under the Refugee Convention (ECRE 2000; House of Lords 2002, para. 158–163).[15] The concept was one of the most controversial

---

[14]Council of the European Union. Joint Position of 4 March 1996 defined by the Council on the basis of Article K.3 of the Treaty on European Union on the harmonized application of the definition of the term 'refugee' in Article 1 of the Geneva Convention of 28 July 1951 relating to the status of refugees (96/196/JHA) [1996] OJ L63/2.

[15]*Secretary of State for the Home Department, Ex parte Adan, R v.* [1999] 1 AC 293 (2 April 1998); see also *Secretary of State for the Home Department, Ex Parte Adan R v. Secretary of State for the Home Department Ex Parte Aitseguer, R v.* [2001] 2 AC 477 (19 December 2000).

aspects of the negotiations of the Qualification Directive 2004 due to inconsistent State practice (Phuong 2002, 531). The eventual adoption of the concept within the Directive (Article 6 Qualification Directive 2004) has been hailed as an achievement by civil society and academics (Mullally 2011, 460).

The question of whether "protection" of "the country of nationality" in the refugee definition is in accordance with international law if it encompasses protection by non-state actors has been the subject of extensive debate, not least due to non-state actors' lack of accountability under international law, the temporary nature of their exercise of authority and their limited ability to enforce the rule of law (House of Lords 2002, para. 72–78; UNHCR 2005, 18; ECRE 2008, 16–17). However, the concept was codified in Article 7 of the Qualification Directive 2004, which set out that protection against persecution could be provided by the State or "parties or organisations, including international organisations, controlling the State or a substantial part of the territory of the State", and "protection is generally provided when [those actors] take reasonable steps to prevent the persecution or suffering of serious harm, inter alia, by operating an effective legal system for the detection, prosecution and punishment of acts constituting persecution or serious harm, and the applicant has access to such protection". The explicit endorsement of the concept in the Qualification Directive has had a detrimental impact on international protection jurisprudence, since this made the debate of whether *de facto* State entities could be actors of protection under international law redundant (Lambert 2006, 174).

Although Article 7 of the Qualification Directive 2004 was transposed into UK law by removing the words "*inter alia*", the issue had already been considered by the courts in the UK (Regulation 4 Qualification Regulations 2006). Moreover, the provision of the Qualification Directive 2004 "virtually mirrored" existing jurisprudence (Storey 2008, 38). In 2000, the Immigration and Asylum Tribunal (the Tribunal) had determined that the proper interpretation of the notion of protection by the country of nationality in the refugee definition was not limited to that country's State authorities.[16] The position was later endorsed when the courts established "a pragmatic or functional approach according to which the issue of whether a de facto entity could

[16] *STARRED FD (Protection, UNMIK, Arif, IFA, Art1D) (Kosovo) CG* [2000] UKIAT 00001, para. 2, 12, 14.

afford Refugee Convention protection is essentially a question of fact".[17] Thus, pre-existing jurisprudence in the UK, as illustrated by the example of non-state actors of protection, suggests that the adoption of the Qualification Directive 2004 did not have a significant impact on practice and jurisprudence in the UK.

The Recast Qualification Directive 2011 incorporated additional safeguards in relation to the application of the principle by providing that the entities had to be "willing and able to offer protection" which "must be effective and of a non-temporary nature" (Article 7). Although jurisprudence from the Tribunal had already established that the nature of protection had to be "effective",[18] the Home Office expressed concerns that the amended provision in the Recast Qualification Directive 2011 would "place the burden on Member States to show that non-State agents who might protect the applicant are "willing and able to enforce the rule of law" (House of Lords 2009, para. 16). If the operation of a formal legal system was a requirement for the existence of protection from persecution by non-state actors, this went too far according to the Home Office (House of Lords 2009, para. 16). Thus, by deciding not to opt-into the Recast Qualification Directive 2011 and in the resulting absence of more rigorous safeguards introduced in the second phase of the CEAS, UK practice continued to adopt the wider pragmatic approach to the concept of non-state actors of protection, which could result in the rejection of asylum claims based on protection from family members or clans (Hathaway and Storey 2016, 489). Such an approach may have significant gendered consequences. As women often fear persecution by non-state actors, there is a need to ensure that protection by non-state actors is effective and that this protection does not lead to risks of other forms of harm or becomes contingent on living in circumstances contrary to fundamental human rights (Querton 2017).

If the UK Government repeals the Qualification Regulations 2006 after exiting the EU, it will remove the express provision of the concept of non-state actors of protection from domestic legislation. In theory, this would enable advocates to challenge the lawfulness of the concept. However, as this approach pre-dated the Qualification Directive 2004, the legal changes arising from Brexit may not have a substantial impact

---

[17] *SF (Sufficiency of Protection-KAA-Michigan Guidelines) Iraq CG* [2002] UKIAT 07376, para. 13.

[18] *DM (Majority Clan Entities Can Protect) Somalia* [2005] UKAIT 00150, para. 22.

on practice regarding non-state actors of protection in the UK, although it may nonetheless create an opportunity to challenge the practice.

Internal Relocation

Another concept which is not expressly provided for in the Refugee Convention, but which developed in international jurisprudence, is the concept of 'internal flight alternative' or 'internal relocation'. The principle is that if a person does not have a well-founded fear of persecution throughout the territory of origin, the refugee definition is not met. UNHCR recommends that where there is a risk of State persecution, it is generally presumed that internal relocation is not a viable alternative to international protection (UNHCR 2003, para. 14). However, gender-based violence is mostly, although not exclusively, undertaken by non-state actors (Farrior 2009). Thus, the concept is of particular relevance for persons fleeing gender-based violence and women, because many fear being persecuted by non-state actors (Anker 2001, 392; Wallace 2013). As a result, persons fearing persecution from non-state actors are more likely to be refused asylum through reliance on this concept, as it is regularly considered that the risk of persecution is localised (Bennett 2008). Consequently, where consideration is given to whether it is reasonable to expect asylum applicants to relocate internally in the country of origin, UNHCR has recommended that the personal circumstances of applicants, including sex, be taken into consideration (UNHCR 2003, para. 25). UNHCR provided early guidance in the application of the principle, highlighting that the proposed relocation had to be reasonable under all the circumstances before a person could be excluded from refugee protection (UNHCR 1979, para. 91).

The application of the concept in UK jurisprudence has been traced back to 1985, albeit with little consideration to any "clear or settled framework for analysis" (Storey 1998, 101–105). Notwithstanding the absence of express reference to the principle in the Refugee Convention, it was eventually established as an essential and inherent element flowing from the Refugee Convention's reference to refugees' ability and willingness to avail themselves of their country's protection (Symes and Jorro 2003, 208).[19] The Court of Appeal considered that protection in the

---

[19] *Karanakaran v Secretary of State for the Home Department* [2000] 3 All ER 449 (25 January 2000).

proposed area of relocation had to be effective and whether applicants could reasonably be expected to move depended on whether it would be "unduly harsh" for them to do so.[20] The 'unduly harsh' test required consideration of practical access to the proposed area of relocation, safety and any undue hardship *en route* and in the area of proposed relocation, and the quality of protection determined by basic norms of human rights protection.[21] Pre-CEAS, the notion had been incorporated into para. 343 of the Immigration Rules (now para. 339O (HC395)), which provided that "if there is a part of the country from which the applicant claims to be a refugee in which he would not have a well-founded fear of persecution, and to which it would be reasonable to expect him to go, the application may be refused." The presumption that internal relocation did not apply in cases of State persecution was also already set out in a decision from the Tribunal from 1998.[22] The principle, articulated in an almost identical manner, was then adopted in the Qualification Directive 2004 and provided that international protection may be refused "if in a part of the country of origin there is no well-founded fear of being persecuted or no real risk of suffering serious harm and the applicant can reasonably be expected to stay in that part of the country" (Article 8(1)).

Contrary to the UK, some EU Member States had not applied the internal relocation concept, whether in legislation or case law, prior to the Qualification Directive 2004. France, for example, first introduced the concept in its legislation in December 2003, pre-empting the adoption of the Directive (Article 1 Loi No 2003-1176).[23] In practice, the *Office Français de Protection des Réfugiés et Apatrides*, the authority making first instance asylum decisions in France, did not apply the principle of internal relocation until at least 2014 (ECRE 2014). However, the European Commission has proposed that the discretionary application of the principle be replaced with a mandatory provision (Article 8 European Commission 2016a). An amendment to the proposal tabled by the

---

[20] *Robinson, R (on the application of) v Secretary of State for the Home Department & Anor* [1998] QB 929 (11 July 1997), para. 29.

[21] *Robinson, R (on the application of) v Secretary of State for the Home Department & Anor* [1998] QB 929 (11 July 1997), para. 18.

[22] *Acevedo* 18334, cited in Symes and Jorro (2003, 224).

[23] Loi n° 2003-1176 du 10 décembre 2003 modifiant la loi n° 52-893 du 25 juillet 1952 relative au droit d'asile, NOR: MAEX0300032L.

European Parliament seeks to retain its discretionary character, whereas EU Member States appear to have settled for a draft provision mandating authorities to 'examine' rather than 'determine' any internal relocation alternative (Amendment 75 European Parliament 2017a; Article 8 Council of the EU 2017a, b). Thus, as EU negotiations on a future Qualification Regulation may create a lack of clarity as to the discretionary nature of the principle, the UK's absence of future legal obligations in this respect may provide an opportunity to challenge the practice. However, as UK practice of relying on the principle of internal relocation pre-dated the adoption of the Qualification Directive 2004 and its application of the principle mirrored the provision adopted in the first phase CEAS instrument, it is suggested that Brexit would not significantly impact on UK practice in relation to the interpretation and application of the internal relocation concept.

Particular Social Group

Literature in the field of international refugee law suggests that asylum decision-makers disproportionately rely on the Convention ground of PSG in gender-related cases, resulting in rigorous scrutiny and frequent appeals (Cheikh Ali et al. 2012, 45; Foster 2014). Despite those drawbacks, the application of the concept by the higher courts in the UK has been at the forefront of international jurisprudence and has recognised a wide array of groups defined by their sex and gender (Cheikh Ali et al. 2012, 55; Querton 2012a).

The Qualification Directive 2004 was the first regional legislative instrument seeking to define when a group shall be considered to form a PSG, "in particular" where:

> Members of that group share an innate characteristic, or a common background that cannot be changed, or share a characteristic or belief that is so fundamental to identity or conscience that a person should not be forced to renounce it, and that group has a distinct identity in the relevant country, because it is perceived as being different by the surrounding society. (Article 10(1)(d))

This provision was one out of only three provisions which referred expressly to gender, although it went no further than to state that "gender related aspects might be considered, without by themselves alone creating a presumption for the applicability of this Article". Just before the deadline for transposition of the Qualification Directive 2004, the House of Lords concluded that women in a given society do not need to meet both criteria of the definition to constitute a PSG.[24] Lord Bingham specifically stated that if the PSG definition found in the Qualification Directive 2004 was interpreted as requiring both criteria to be satisfied, it would propound "a test more stringent than is warranted by international authority" (para. 16). Nonetheless, the Upper Tribunal later failed to apply the judgment that the two limbs of the definition are not cumulative on the basis that "the observations of their Lordships were obiter, although very persuasive, because it is clear that their Lordships did not decide the cases" under the domestic Qualification Regulations 2006 or the Qualification Directive 2004[25] (Querton 2012a).

These developments indicate that the Qualification Directive 2004 enabled the UK lower courts to impede earlier progress in the interpretation of the Refugee Convention from a gender perspective. Thus, the adoption of the Qualification Directive 2004 appears to have acted as a means of restricting the definition of PSG, rather than improving practice in the UK from a gender perspective. In relation to this particular provision, Brexit and the potential repeal of the Qualification Regulations 2006 may provide an opportunity for redressing recent practice in the Tribunal.

Enforcement of Rights

Despite some of the drawbacks regarding the provisions of the Qualification Directive 2004 from a gender perspective discussed above, the future absence of legal obligations under EU law may have an impact on asylum seekers and refugees' ability to effectively enforce their rights through the courts. After leaving the EU, the UK Government will no longer have an obligation to transpose the Directive and thus may repeal the Qualification Regulations 2006 and amend the asylum provisions of the Immigration Rules. The significance of enforceable legislative measures in asylum law is epitomised by the fact that despite extensive

---

[24] *Secretary of State for the Home Department v. K, Fornah v Secretary of State for the Home Department* [2007] 1 AC 412 (18 October 2006).

[25] *SB (PSG—Protection Regulations—Reg 6) Moldova CG* [2008] UKAIT 00002, para. 69.

advocacy work in the UK, research continues to demonstrate serious problems of implementation of Home Office gender policies in asylum decision-making (Ceneda and Palmer 2006; Muggeridge and Maman 2011; Querton 2012b). As policy guidance has a different legal status than legislation, the issue of rights enforcement is essential in a post-Brexit legal framework.

The EU (Withdrawal) Bill currently provides that the Qualification Regulations 2006 will become 'preserved legislation', in the sense that they will continue to apply in the UK as purely domestic legislation rather than legislation implementing obligations under EU law (Clause 2). As a result, on the day the UK leaves the EU, those provisions will remain in force. Thus, the immediate impact of Brexit on the criteria for refugee recognition in the UK may be very limited. However, the Bill also proposes powers to make secondary legislation "to enable corrections to be made to the laws that would otherwise no longer operate appropriately once the UK has left the EU" (Department for Exiting the European Union 2018). Although these powers should normally only apply if retained legislation is unable to operate because the UK is no longer a member of the EU, it will cease to operate as intended or will be redundant once the UK leaves the EU, this could potentially create legal uncertainty for persons seeking international protection. Furthermore, amendments to existing provisions determining who qualifies as refugee may occur at a later date, without the need to comply with any obligations under EU law and without oversight by the Court of Justice of the European Union (CJEU).

One of the exceptions to the general approach in the EU (Withdrawal) Bill of retaining EU law is the Charter of Fundamental Rights of the European Union (the EU Charter) (Clause 5(4)). The UK Government has justified this exception on the basis that the rights enshrined in the EU Charter are equivalent to fundamental EU rights which will also be retained (Department for Exiting the European Union 2018). However, the Charter includes additional safeguards such as the free-standing right to non-discrimination and the right to equality and human dignity. Moreover, scholars have claimed that the Charter has ensured that the CJEU interprets CEAS legislation more progressively than merely through international refugee law and guarantees the right to be granted asylum (Ippolito 2015; Gil-Bazo 2008). As failing to retain the Charter cannot guarantee that its substantive rights are not weakened, it is suggested that preserving the EU Charter in domestic legislation would ensure higher standards of international protection (Coppel 2018).

Another major shift in the legal landscape following Brexit will be that decisions of the CJEU made on or after exit will not be binding on UK courts (Clause 6(1)(a) EU (Withdrawal) Bill). Retained CJEU jurisprudence will not bind the UK Supreme Court, although it may only depart from that jurisprudence "where it appears right to do so" (Department for Exiting the European Union 2018, para. 107). Moreover, when interpreting retained EU law, domestic courts will be able to consider CJEU decisions made after the UK has left the EU if considered appropriate to do so (Clause 6(2) EU (Withdrawal) Bill). However, UK courts will no longer be able to request a preliminary ruling from the CJEU (Article 267 TFEU; Clause 6(1)(b) EU (Withdrawal) Bill). Even if the CJEU does not have jurisdiction to interpret the Refugee Convention, it in practice does so through its judgments regarding the CEAS (Garlick 2015). This has the potential to significantly influence the development of international refugee law. So far, many CJEU asylum decisions have focused on procedural issues and few judgments were explicitly gender-related (Yeo 2017; Garlick 2015). Some cases before the CJEU are relevant to gender issues but were concerned with asylum claims based on sexuality and considered the definition of PSG,[26] appropriate safeguards during the asylum procedure such as the prohibition of detailed questioning regarding sexual practice based on stereotypes[27] and the prohibition of relying on psychologist expert reports during the assessment of applicants' credibility to determine their sexual orientation.[28] The right to human dignity and privacy enshrined in the EU Charter have played an important role in the assessment of those issues and the CJEU may be requested to provide preliminary rulings on further questions concerning the substantive interpretation of the refugee

[26] Judgment of 7 November 2013, *X, Y and Z v Minister voor Immigratie, Integratie en Asiel*, Joined Cases C-199/12 to 201/12, ECLI:EU:C:2013:720.

[27] Judgment of 2 December 2014, *A v Staatssecretaris van Veiligheid en Justitie*, Joined Cases C-148/13 to C-150/13, ECLI:EU:C:2014:2406.

[28] Judgment of 25 January 2018, *F (area of freedom, security and justice—Judgment)*, C-473/16, ECLI:EU:C:2018:36.

definition from a gender perspective in the future. Thus, the loss of both the CJEU jurisdiction and individual rights under the EU Charter may lead to a lowering of international protection standards in the UK.

4   THE POST-BREXIT REFUGEE PROTECTION LANDSCAPE: INTERNATIONAL AND REGIONAL REFUGEE AND HUMAN RIGHTS NORMS AND ENFORCEMENT

After examining individual provisions from the Qualification Directive 2004 which offer interpretative guidance for the recognition of refugees from a gender perspective, this section now turns to consider the wider international and regional legal frameworks which will continue to bind the UK after it leaves the EU. It is suggested here that the impact of Brexit on the recognition of refugees may not be significant, at least at the outset, because the substantive determination of who qualifies as a refugee is grounded in and shaped by international and regional legal regimes which operate independently of the EU and the CEAS. The Refugee Convention remains the cornerstone of refugee protection, and international and regional obligations will continue to apply in the UK, notwithstanding its exit from the EU and the subsequent lack of CJEU jurisdiction. The UK's international and regional refugee and human rights obligations are relevant in several respects, including protection from *refoulement*, the interpretation of the Refugee Convention, and the rights of asylum seekers and refugees. If the Qualification Directive 2004 is restricted to offering interpretive guidance to the Refugee Convention and the recognition rates across EU Member States remain markedly different despite the recasting process, exiting the EU may not necessarily lead to a significant change in the recognition of refugees from a gender perspective in the UK (Storey 2008; European Commission 2016a). Thus, refugee and human rights legal norms and obligations guiding the interpretation of the refugee definition may ensure that the UK exiting the EU will not lead to a lowering of international protection standards (European Parliament 2017b, 24).

Importantly, the CEAS did not displace the Refugee Convention as the cornerstone of international refugee protection in EU Member States. In 1999, the European Council special meeting in Tampere, which set the foundation for establishing the CEAS, highlighted that such a system should be "based on the full and inclusive application" of the Refugee Convention and its Protocol in order to maintain the norm of *non-refoulement*.[29] The legal basis for the adoption of a common asylum policy in the EU requires it to be in accordance with the Refugee Convention (Article 78 TFEU). This approach has also been re-iterated in the recital to the Qualification Directive 2004 (Recital 3) and endorsed by the higher courts in the UK.[30] Thus, the universal principle of protection against return to a country where a person has reason to fear persecution was central from the outset to the process of adopting European asylum legislation.

Moreover, the UK retains its duty to cooperate with the UNHCR (Article 35 Refugee Convention). The UNHCR plays a crucial role in the development of international refugee law through interpretative guidance, including from a gender perspective (UNHCR 2002a). UK jurisprudence has accepted that UNHCR materials may provide guidance of considerable weight, although they are not determinative.[31] In the case of *Fornah*, the House of Lords expressly adopted the definition of PSG set out in the UNHCR *Guidelines on International Protection: Membership of a Particular Social Group* (UNHCR 2002b).[32]

Significantly, the UK must interpret and apply the Refugee Convention in accordance with the general rule of treaty interpretation in international law. Thus, the UK must interpret the Refugee Convention "in good faith in accordance with the ordinary meaning to be given to the terms of the treaty in their context and in the light of its object and purpose" (Article 31(1) 1969 Vienna Convention on the Law of Treaties [VCLT]).[33] These principles aim to limit State parties' discretion in their compliance with their obligations and thereby ensure a consistent interpretation of the Refugee Convention across jurisdictions. Furthermore, the Refugee Convention has potential for dynamic interpretation due to its status as a living instrument to be interpreted in light of modern-day situations and developments in international law

---

[29] European Council (15–16 October 1999). Tampere Presidency Conclusions, http://www.europarl.europa.eu/summits/tam_en.htm, accessed 2 February 2018, para. 13.

[30] *MI & Anor v Secretary of State for the Home Department* [2014] EWCA Civ 826, para. 46.

[31] *HD (Trafficked women) Nigeria (CG)* [2016] UKUT 454 (IAC), para. 21–22.

[32] *Secretary of State for the Home Department v. K, Fornah v Secretary of State for the Home Department* [2007] 1 AC 412 (18 October 2006).

[33] Vienna Convention on the Law of Treaties (adopted on 22 May 1969, entered into force on 27 January 1980) 1155 UNTS 331.

(Article 31(3)(c) VCLT). Despite some more recent criticism, there is broad consensus within international refugee law that a human rights approach to interpreting the Refugee Convention is justified (para. 51 UNHCR 1979; Hathaway and Foster 2014). The Qualification Directive 2004 codified the human rights paradigm for the interpretation of acts of persecution requiring them to "be sufficiently serious by their nature or repetition as to constitute a severe violation of basic human rights [or] be an accumulation of various measures, including violations of human rights which is sufficiently severe" (Article 9). The human rights approach had previously found authority in UK jurisprudence. The House of Lords considered and endorsed this approach by reference to Hathaway's suggested definition of persecution as "the sustained or systematic failure of state protection in relation to one of the core entitlements which has been recognised by the international community".[34] The concept of 'internal relocation' in UK jurisprudence discussed above has also historically been influenced by decisions from international human rights bodies such as the European Court of Human Rights and the Committee against Torture (Storey 1998, 130).

Hence, international human rights law which operates independently of the CEAS framework provides near-universal standards guiding the interpretation of the refugee definition. The UK is a party to various international and regional human rights law instruments of relevance to refugee protection from a gender perspective, including the International Covenant for Civil and Political Rights, the Convention against Torture, the Convention on the Elimination of all Forms of Discrimination against Women, the European Convention on Human Rights and the Convention on the Rights of the Child. The human rights approach in international refugee law looks at these internationally accepted norms for aid in the interpretation of key elements of the refugee definition. Although significant gaps remain, it is particularly in relation to gender that reliance on international human rights norms has ensured a more inclusive and consistent interpretation of the refugee definition to include domestic violence, forced marriage, female genital mutilation and trafficking asylum claims (Mullally 2011). The most recent Council of Europe human rights treaty, the Convention on Preventing and Combating Violence against Women and Domestic Violence

---

[34] *Horvath v. Secretary of State for the Home Department* [2001] 1 AC 489 (6 July 2000).

(the Istanbul Convention), creates new obligations on State parties. State parties must ensure that "gender-based violence against women may be recognised as a form of persecution" in the context of the Refugee Convention and that a "gender-sensitive interpretation is given to each of the Convention grounds". Furthermore, it requires State parties to develop "gender-sensitive reception procedures and support services for asylum-seekers as well as gender guidelines and gender-sensitive asylum procedures" (Article 60). Although it does not provide for an individual complaints mechanism, the group of experts who monitor its implementation may play an important role in standard-setting (Articles 66–67). Moreover, the European Court of Human Rights increasingly relies on human rights norms developed by other international and regional human rights instruments, including the Istanbul Convention, in cases of gender-based violence (Querton 2017). Thus, the increasing cross-reference of norms and principles between human rights instruments further promotes the consistent application of international law in domestic settings. Consequently, it is conceivable that a human rights approach to the determination of asylum claims from a gender perspective may be preserved by judges relying on international and regional human rights instruments as aids to interpretation of the Refugee Convention. However, although the Home Office considers that the UK currently complies with the provisions relevant to gender-related persecution and asylum, and steps are being taken to ratify the Convention, this has not yet been done (Home Office 2017, 23–24, 41).[35]

In addition to reliance on human rights instruments as aids to the interpretation of the refugee definition, human rights monitoring bodies may in the future serve as a means to enforce the protection of refugees in the absence of obligations and enforcement of rights under the EU legal framework in the UK (Gil-Bazo 2015; Mariño Menéndes 2015). The enforcement of rights outside the EU legal framework has been identified in this chapter as an essential issue in the post-Brexit landscape. Some insights may be drawn from considering the practice in other States that are not bound by the CEAS or the jurisdiction of the CJEU in asylum matters. In Denmark, for example, individual complaints

---

[35] Preventing and Combating Violence Against Women and Domestic Violence (Ratification of Convention) Act 2017.

are regularly made to international human rights monitoring bodies.[36] Although the trend in Denmark may be due to the limited rights of appeal at the national level, it may serve as an indication of future remedies in the UK. Nevertheless, those mechanisms have many shortcomings and are less effective than the EU legal framework due to issues of consistency, compliance, enforcement and timescale (Takahashi 2002). In this respect the absence of CJEU jurisdiction and the risk of the UK withdrawing from the ECHR in the future may become particularly detrimental to refugees in the UK.

Accordingly, whereas existing legal frameworks, independent from the CEAS, are likely to preserve the UK's core gender-related international protection obligations, this remains contingent on the UK's continued commitment to and compliance with international and regional human rights instruments. Furthermore, issues of effectiveness in enforcing rights through those mechanisms highlight the significance of the loss of CJEU jurisdiction.

5   CONCLUSION

Owing to space constraints, this chapter has focused on one area of the asylum system in the UK, namely refugee recognition from a gender perspective. However, there are other areas of the asylum system with important gendered dimensions which warrant further examination in light of Brexit. These include asylum procedures, reception conditions and the set of rights guaranteed to those granted refugee status or humanitarian protection status.

An examination of specific provisions of the Qualification Directive 2004 reveals that asylum decision-making in the UK was not substantially transformed by the UK's transposition of this instrument into domestic legislation. Although the Qualification Directive 2004 was ground-breaking in providing a detailed interpretation of the refugee definition, it appears that it initially had little impact on UK practice, but certain provisions (such as the notions of PSG and non-state actors of protection) have over time shown to be problematic from a gender perspective. By applying a gender lens, it is suggested that the UK's opt-into

---

[36] See for example Committee on the Rights of the Child, *I.A.M. v. Denmark*, CRC/C/77/D/3/2016 (25 January 2018); Human Rights Committee, *F. and G. v. Denmark*, CCPR/C/119/D/2530/2015 (28 June 2017).

the Qualification Directive 2004 did not bring about a more inclusive and gender-sensitive interpretation of the refugee definition in the UK. Consequently, the absence of legal obligations under the Qualification Directive 2004 is not likely to have a detrimental impact on the adjudication of gender-related claims in the UK. On the contrary, this may allow the UK to improve current practice and achieve a more gender sensitive interpretation of the Refugee Convention, whilst circumventing future mandatory application of refugee law concepts that have important gendered dimensions, such as the notion of 'internal relocation'.

Moreover, the Qualification Directive 2004 was unsuccessful in harmonising practice across the EU. Gender-sensitive asylum practice, in particular, varies widely in the EU (Cheikh Ali et al. 2012, 130). Overall, this suggests that the first phase of the CEAS failed to ensure that EU Member States adopted common standards and practices from a gender perspective. Thus, considering UK law, case law and practice and the limited gender-specific provisions in the first phase of the CEAS instruments, it is suggested that the existing level of gender-sensitivity in the UK asylum system does not derive from its current obligations under the CEAS.

Therefore, it appears that protection from *refoulement* in the UK is unlikely to be significantly affected by Brexit, due to the legal frameworks that will continue to exist after the UK's withdrawal from the EU. Developments in international and regional refugee and human rights law have increasingly played a significant role in the interpretation of the refugee definition for persons fleeing gender-related persecution. In this regard, however, the ratification of the Istanbul Convention is essential in ensuring a gender-sensitive asylum system in the UK.

Consequently, the existence of effective remedies in a post-Brexit landscape is essential and the ability to enforce rights through legislative provisions and judicial oversight needs to be preserved. Although to date most of the CJEU's decisions may have had limited impact on UK asylum law and practice from a gender perspective, the jurisdiction of the Court would guarantee oversight over future developments. Missing out on the CJEU's potential for purposive interpretation of the CEAS instruments (and by extension the Refugee Convention) through the EU Charter may result in reducing refugee protection in the UK. Moreover, the enforcement of rights under international human rights mechanisms is likely to be less effective than under EU law. Therefore, the role of national courts in ensuring that existing standards on gender and asylum do not decrease has become even more prominent.

Moreover, it is pertinent to reflect on whether Brexit will spur further isolation from regional or international legal instruments and the impact this may have on the protection of refugees in the UK (Yeo 2017). The Conservative Party promised in its 2017 Manifesto to remain a signatory party to the ECHR only until the next general election in 2022 and "while the process of Brexit is under way" (The Conservative and Unionist Party, 37). The UK's human rights legal framework will be reconsidered once the Brexit process has concluded (p. 41). Generally, there appears to be a lack of positive engagement with human rights issues across the UK Government. The chair of the Equality and Human Rights Commission described the UK's response to the last UN Universal Periodic Review as showing "scant regard for its international commitments" (Doward 2017). The failure to ratify the Istanbul Convention to date is a case in point. This suggests that the UK will potentially further isolate itself from the range of regional and international instruments that ensure the protection of refugees, including from a gender perspective. This prospect is supported by claims that UK asylum policy has always been based on self-interest and the UK's approach to refugee protection pre-CEAS was based on deterrence and exclusion, rather than any humanitarian principles (Harvey 2000).

Although the absence of obligations under the Qualification Directive 2004 is unlikely to have an immediate significant impact on refugee recognition from a gender perspective in the UK and existing international and regional refugee and human rights norms and mechanisms may ensure a gender-sensitive asylum system, exiting the EU may have gendered effects with indirect consequences on asylum law (Guerrina and Masselot 2018; Jenkins 2017). Generally, the gender-related impacts of Brexit have been marginalised in debates and the UK Government has failed to conduct any asylum impact assessments, let alone consider that impact from a gender perspective. The loss of fundamental rights, including the right to equality, non-discrimination and human dignity, enshrined in the EU Charter, may contribute to a hostile environment against refugees and gender equality. This, in turn, may eventually have an impact on the recognition of refugees from a gender perspective.

Bibliography

Anker, D. 2001. Refugee Status and Violence Against Women in the Domestic Sphere: The Non-state Actor Question. *Georgetown Immigration Law Journal* 15: 391–402.

Bennett, C. 2008. Relocation, Relocation: The Impact of Internal Relocation on Women Asylum Seekers. Report. Asylum Aid. https://www.asylumaid.org.uk/wp-content/uploads/2013/02/Relocation_Relocation_research_report.pdf. Accessed 2 Feb 2018.

Ceneda, S., and C. Palmer. 2006. 'Lip Service' or Implementation? The Home Office Gender Guidance and Women's Asylum Claims in the UK. Report. Asylum Aid. https://www.asylumaid.org.uk/wp-content/uploads/2013/02/Lip_Service_or_Implementation.pdf. Accessed 2 Feb 2018.

Charlesworth, H., C. Chinkin, and S. Wright. 1991. Feminist Approaches to International Law. *American Journal of International Law* 85 (4): 613–645.

Cheikh Ali, H., C. Querton, and E. Soulard. 2012. Gender Related Asylum Claims in Europe: A Comparative Analysis of Law, Policies and Practice Focusing on Women in Nine EU Member States. http://www.europarl.europa.eu/RegData/etudes/etudes/join/2012/462481/IPOL-FEMM_ET(2012)462481_EN.pdf. Accessed 2 Feb 2018.

Coppel QC, J. 2018. Equality and Human Rights Commission. Opinion: European Union (Withdrawal) Bill—E.U. Charter of Fundamental Rights. https://www.equalityhumanrights.com/sites/default/files/eu-withdrawal-bill-legal-advice-jason-coppel-qc.pdf. Accessed 2 Feb 2018.

Council of the European Union. 2017a. Proposal for a Regulation of the European Parliament and of the Council on Standards for the Qualification of Third-Country Nationals or Stateless Persons as Beneficiaries of International Protection, for a Uniform Status for Refugees or for Persons Eligible for Subsidiary Protection and for the Content of the Protection Granted and Amending Council Directive 2003/109/EC of 25 November 2003 Concerning the Status of Third-Country Nationals Who Are Long-Term Residents (7827/17). http://www.statewatch.org/news/2017/apr/eu-council-qualifications-7827-17.pdf. Accessed 2 Feb 2018.

Council of the European Union. 2017b. Proposal for a Regulation of the European Parliament and of the Council on Standards for the Qualification of Third-Country Nationals or Stateless Persons as Beneficiaries of International Protection, for a Uniform Status for Refugees or for Persons Eligible for Subsidiary Protection and for the Content of the Protection Granted and Amending Council Directive 2003/109/EC of 25 November 2003 Concerning the Status of Third-Country Nationals Who Are Long-Term Residents—Mandate for Negotiations with the European Parliament (10475/17). http://www.statewatch.org/news/2017/jul/eu-council-qualifications-mandate-to-negotiate-10475-17.pdf. Accessed 2 Feb 2018.

Department for Exiting the European Union. 2017. The United Kingdom's Exit from and New Partnership with the European Union White Paper, Cm9417. https://www.gov.uk/government/uploads/system/uploads/attachment_data/file/589189/The_United_Kingdoms_exit_from_and_partnership_with_the_EU_Print.pdf. Accessed 2 Feb 2018.

Department for Exiting the European Union. 2018. European Union (Withdrawal) Bill: Explanatory Notes. https://publications.parliament.uk/pa/bills/cbill/2017-2019/0005/en/18005en.pdf. Accessed 2 Feb 2018.

Doward, J. 2017. Britain Faces Rebuke Over Refusal to Back More Than 100 UN Human Rights Targets. *The Observer*, September 16. https://www.the-guardian.com/law/2017/sep/16/britain-un-human-rights-brexit. Accessed 2 Feb 2018.

European Commission. 2001. Proposal for a Council Directive on Minimum Standards for the Qualification and Status of Third Country Nationals and Stateless Persons as Refugees or as Persons Who Otherwise Need International Protection (COM(2001) 510 Final).

European Commission. 2015. Communication from the Commission to the European Parliament, the Council, the European Economic and Social Committee and the Committee of the Regions: A European Agenda on Migration (COM(2015) 240 Final, 13 May 2015). https://ec.europa.eu/anti-trafficking/sites/antitrafficking/files/communication_on_the_european_agenda_on_migration_en.pdf. Accessed 2 Feb 2018.

European Commission. 2016a. Proposal for a Regulation of the European Parliament and of the Council on Standards for the Qualification of Third-Country Nationals or Stateless Persons as Beneficiaries of International Protection, for a Uniform Status for Refugees or for Persons Eligible for Subsidiary Protection and for the Content of the Protection Granted and Amending Council Directive 2003/109/EC of 25 November 2003 Concerning the Status of Third-Country Nationals Who Are Long-Term Residents (COM(2016) 466 Final).

European Commission. 2016b. Proposal for a Regulation of the European Parliament and of the Council Establishing the Criteria and Mechanisms for Determining the Member Stare Responsible for Examining an Application for International Protection Lodged in One of the Member States by a Third-Country National or a Stateless Person (Recast) (COM(2016) 0270 Final).

European Council. 1999. Tampere Presidency Conclusions, October 15–16. http://www.europarl.europa.eu/summits/tam_en.htm. Accessed 2 Feb 2018.

European Council for Refugees and Exiles ('ECRE'). 2000. Non-state Agents of Persecution and the Inability of the State to Protect. http://www.refworld.org/pdfid/3ae6b3430.pdf. Accessed 2 Feb 2018.

European Council for Refugees and Exiles ('ECRE'). 2008. The Impact of the EU Qualification Directive on International Protection. https://www.ecre.org/wp-content/uploads/2016/07/ECRE-The-Impact-of-the-EU-Qualification-Directive-on-International-Protection_October-2008.pdf. Accessed 2 Feb 2018.

European Council for Refugees and Exiles ('ECRE'). 2014. Actors of Protection and the Application of the Internal Protection Alternative: National Report—France.   http://www.refworld.org/publisher,ECRE,,,543bbdb60,0.html. Accessed 2 Feb 2018.

European Parliament—Committee on Civil Liberties, Justice and Home Affairs. 2017a. Report on the Proposal for a Regulation of the European Parliament and of the Council on Standards for the Qualification of Third-Country Nationals or Stateless Persons as Beneficiaries of International Protection, for a Uniform Status for Refugees or for Persons Eligible for Subsidiary Protection and for the Content of the Protection Granted and Amending Council Directive 2003/109/EC of 25 November 2003 Concerning the Status of Third-Country Nationals Who Are Long-Term Residents (COM(2016) 466 final).

European Parliament—Committee on Civil Liberties, Justice and Home Affairs. 2017b. The Implications of the United Kingdom's Withdrawal from the European Union for the Area of Freedom, Security and Justice. http://www.europarl.europa.eu/RegData/etudes/STUD/2017/596824/IPOL_STU(2017)596824_EN.pdf. Accessed 2 Jan 2018.

European Union (Withdrawal) Bill 2017–19 (HL Bill 79). 2018, January 18. https://publications.parliament.uk/pa/bills/lbill/2017-2019/0079/18079.pdf. Accessed 2 Feb 2018.

Eurostat. 2017. Asylum and First Time Asylum Applicants by Citizenship, Age and Sex Annual Aggregated Data (Rounded), last updated 4 October 2017. http://ec.europa.eu/eurostat/web/asylum-and-managed-migration/data/database. Accessed 2 Feb 2018.

Farrior, S. 2009. Human Rights Advocacy on Gender Issues: Challenges and Opportunities. *Journal of Human Rights Practice* 1 (1): 83–100.

Foster, M. 2014. Why We Are Not There Yet: The Particular Challenge of 'Particular Social Group'. In *Gender in Refugee Law: From the Margins to the Centre*, ed. E. Arbel, C. Dauvergne, and J. Millbank, 17–45. London: Routledge.

Garlick, M. 2015. International Protection in Court: The Asylum Jurisprudence of the Court of Justice of the EU and UNHCR. *Refugee Survey Quarterly* 34 (1): 107–130.

Gil-Bazo, M.-T. 2008. The Charter of Fundamental Rights of the European Union and the Right to Be Granted Asylum in the Union's Law. *Refugee Survey Quarterly* 27 (3): 33–52.

Gil-Bazo, M.-T. 2015. Refugee Protection Under International Human Rights Law: From Non-refoulement to Residence and Citizenship. *Refugee Survey Quarterly* 34 (1): 11–42.

Guerrina, R., and A. Masselot. 2018. Walking into the Footprint of EU Law: Unpacking the Gendered Consequences of Brexit. *Social Policy and Society* 17 (2): 1–12.

Harvey, C. 2000. *Seeking Asylum in the UK: Problems and Prospects.* London: Butterworths.

Hathaway, J., and M. Foster. 2014. *The Law of Refugee Status*, 2nd ed. Cambridge: Cambridge University Press.

Hathaway, J., and H. Storey. 2016. What Is the Meaning of State Protection in Refugee Law? A Debate. *International Journal of Refugee Law* 28 (3): 480–492.

Home Office. 2006. Explanatory Memorandum to the Refugee or Person in Need of International Protection (Qualification) Regulations 2006 No. 2525. http://www.legislation.gov.uk/uksi/2006/2525/pdfs/uksiem_20062525_en.pdf. Accessed 2 Feb 2018.

Home Office. 2017. Ratification of the Council of Europe Convention on Combating Violence Against Women and Domestic Violence (Istanbul Convention)—Report on Progress. https://www.gov.uk/government/uploads/system/uploads/attachment_data/file/656565/CCS207_CCS1017309396-1_HO_Istanbul_Convention_report__PRINT_READY.PDF. Accessed 2 Feb 2018.

House of Commons European Scrutiny Committee. 2017a. EU Asylum Reform, January 11. https://publications.parliament.uk/pa/cm201617/cmselect/cmeuleg/71-xxiii/7113.htm#_idTextAnchor015. Accessed 2 Feb 2018.

House of Commons European Scrutiny Committee. 2017b. EU Asylum Reform: Revision of the Dublin Rules and the Establishment of an EU Agency for Asylum, April 19. https://publications.parliament.uk/pa/cm201617/cmselect/cmeuleg/71-xxxvi/7105.htm. Accessed 2 Feb 2018.

House of Commons European Scrutiny Committee. 2017c. EU Asylum Reform, November 29. https://publications.parliament.uk/pa/cm201719/cmselect/cmeuleg/301-iii/30119.htm. Accessed 2 Feb 2018.

House of Lords European Union Committee. 2009. Asylum Directives: Scrutiny of the Opt-In Decisions, Appendix 4: Qualification Directive—Explanatory Memorandum. https://publications.parliament.uk/pa/ld200910/ldselect/ldeucom/6/607.htm. Accessed 2 Feb 2018.

House of Lords Select Committee on the European Union. 2002. Defining Refugee Status and Those in Need of International Protection. https://publications.parliament.uk/pa/ld200102/ldselect/ldeucom/156/156.pdf. Accessed 2 Feb 2018.

Ippolito, F. 2015. Migration and Asylum Cases Before the Court of Justice of the European Union: Putting the EU Charter of Fundamental Rights to Test? *European Journal of Migration and Law* 17 (1): 1–38.

Jenkins, I. 2017. Is Brexit Bad for Women? *The Financial Times*, July 7. https://www.ft.com/content/a1ec120c-6307-11e7-91a7-502f7ee26895. Accessed 2 Feb 2018.

Kilkey, M. 2017. Conditioning Family-Life at the Intersection of Migration and Welfare: The Implications for 'Brexit Families'. *Journal of Social Policy* 46 (4): 797–814.

Lambert, H. 2006. The EU Asylum Qualification Directive, Its Impact on the Jurisprudence of the United Kingdom and International Law. *International and Comparative Law Quarterly* 55: 161–192.

Mariño Menéndez, F.M. 2015. Recent Jurisprudence of the United Nations Committee Against Torture and the International Protection of Refugees. *Refugee Survey Quarterly* 34 (1): 61–78.

Muggeridge, H., and C. Maman. 2011. Unsustainable: The Quality of Initial Decision-Making in Women's Asylum Claims. Report. Asylum Aid. https://www.asylumaid.org.uk/wp-content/uploads/2013/02/unsustainableweb.pdf. Accessed 2 Feb 2018.

Mullally, S. 2011. Domestic Violence Asylum Claims and Recent Developments in International Human Rights Law: A Progress Narrative? *International and Comparative Law Quarterly* 60 (2): 459–484.

Phuong, C. 2002. Persecution by Non-state Agents: Comparative Judicial Interpretations of the 1951 Refugee Convention. *European Journal of Migration and Law* 4 (4): 521–532.

Querton, C. 2012a. The Interpretation of the Convention Ground of 'Membership of a Particular Social Group' in the Context of Gender-Related Claims for Asylum: A Critical Analysis of the Tribunal's Approach in the UK. Refugee Law Initiative Working Paper No. 3. http://sas-space.sas.ac.uk/4690/5/RLI_Working_Paper_No.3.pdf. Accessed 2 Feb 2018.

Querton, C. 2012b. 'I Feel Like as a Woman, I'm Not Welcome': A Gender Analysis of UK Asylum Law, Policy and Practice. Report. Asylum Aid. https://www.asylumaid.org.uk/wp-content/uploads/2013/02/ifeelasa-woman_report_web_.pdf. Accessed 2 Feb 2018.

Querton, C. 2017. The Role of the European Court of Human Rights in the Protection of Women Fleeing Gender-Based Violence in Their Home Countries. *Feminists @ Law* 7: Multimedia.

Shutes, I., and S. Walker. 2018. Gender and Free Movement: EU Migrant Women's Access to Residence and Social Rights in the UK. *Journal of Ethnic and Migration Studies* 44 (1): 137–153.

Stevens, D. 2004. *UK Asylum Law and Policy: Historical and Contemporary Perspectives*. London: Sweet & Maxwell.

Storey, H. 1998. The "Internal Flight Alternative" (IFA) Test and the Concept of Protection. In *Current Issues of UK Asylum Law and Policy*, ed. F. Nicholson and P. Twomey, 100–132. Aldershot: Ashgate.

Storey, H. 2008. EU Refugee Qualification Directive: A Brave New World? *International Journal of Refugee Law* 20 (1): 1–49.

Symes, M., and P. Jorro. 2003. *Asylum Law and Practice*. London: Reed Elsevier (UK) Ltd.

Takahashi, S. 2002. Recourse to Human Rights Treaty Bodies for Monitoring of the Refugee Convention. *Netherlands Quarterly of Human Rights* 20 (1): 53–74.

The Conservative and Unionist Party. 2017. Manifesto: Forward, Together: Our Plan for a Stronger Britain and a Prosperous Future. https://www.conservatives.com/manifesto. Accessed 2 Feb 2018.

The Guardian. 2017. The Draft Home Office Post-Brexit Immigration Policy Document in Full. https://www.theguardian.com/uk-news/2017/sep/05/the-draft-home-office-post-brexit-immigration-policy-document-in-full. Accessed 2 Feb 2018.

United Kingdom Border Agency ('UKBA'). 2010. Asylum Policy Instruction on Gender Issues in the Asylum Claim. https://www.gov.uk/government/uploads/system/uploads/attachment_data/file/257386/gender-issue-in-the-asylum.pdf. Accessed 2 Feb 2018.

United Nations High Commissioner for Refugees ('UNHCR'). 1979, Re-issued 2011. Handbook and Guidelines on Procedures and Criteria for Determining Refugee Status Under the 1951 Convention and the 1967 Protocol Relating to the Status of Refugees.

United Nations High Commissioner for Refugees ('UNHCR'). 2002a. Guidelines on International Protection No. 1: Gender-Related Persecution within the Context of Article 1A(2) of the 1951 Convention and/or Its 1967 Protocol Relating to the Status of Refugees (HCR/GIP/02/01).

United Nations High Commissioner for Refugees ('UNHCR'). 2002b. Guidelines on International Protection No. 2: "Membership of a Particular Social Group" Within the Context of Article 1A(2) of the 1951 Convention and/or Its 1967 Protocol Relating to the Status of Refugees (HCR/GIP/02/02).

United Nations High Commissioner for Refugees ('UNHCR'). 2003. Guidelines on International Protection "Internal Flight or Relocation Alternative" Within the Context of Article 1A(2) of the 1951 Convention and/or 1967 Protocol Relating to the Status of Refugees.

United Nations High Commissioner for Refugees ('UNHCR'). 2005. Annotated Comments on the EC Council Directive 2004/83/EC on Minimum Standards for the Qualification and Status of Third Country

Nationals or Stateless Persons as Refugees or as Persons who otherwise need International Protection and the Content of the Protection granted (OJ L 304/12 of 30.9.2004).

Wallace, R. 2013. Internal Relocation Alternative in Refugee Status Determination: Is the Risk/Protection Dichotomy Reality or Myth? A Gendered Analysis. In *Contemporary Issues in Refugee Law*, ed. S.S. Juss and C. Harvey, 289–310. Cheltenham: Edward Elgar.

Wilsher, D. 2003. Non-state Actors and the Definition of a Refugee in the United Kingdom: Protection, Accountability or Culpability? *International Journal of Refugee Law* 15 (1): 68–112.

Yeo, C. 2017. The Impact of Brexit on UK Asylum Law. Refugee Law Initiative's 8th International Refugee Law Seminar Series. https://soundcloud.com/refugeelawinitiative/the-impact-of-brexit-on-uk-asylum-law. Accessed 2 Feb 2018.

CHAPTER 10

Queering Brexit: What's in Brexit for Sexual and Gender Minorities?

Carmelo Danisi, Moira Dustin and Nuno Ferreira

1 UK SEXUAL AND GENDER MINORITIES IN TROUBLED WATERS?

Have you ever had the feeling that you have gone to sleep in one place and woken up in another? On 24 June 2016, many people in the UK had that feeling: as if they had gone to bed in a cosmopolitan and global European Union (EU) Member State and woke up in a country prone

This contribution builds on a shorter piece published by the authors as a blog entry (Danisi et al. 2017). The authors are members of SOGICA (www.sogica.org), a four-year (2016–2020) research project funded by the European Research Council (ERC) that explores the social and legal experiences of individuals across Europe claiming internal

C. Danisi · M. Dustin · N. Ferreira (✉)
Sussex Law School, School of Law, Politics and Sociology, Freeman Building, University of Sussex, Brighton, UK
e-mail: N.Ferreira@sussex.ac.uk

C. Danisi
e-mail: C.Danisi@sussex.ac.uk

M. Dustin
e-mail: M.Dustin@sussex.ac.uk

© The Author(s) 2019
M. Dustin et al. (eds.), *Gender and Queer Perspectives on Brexit*,
Gender and Politics, https://doi.org/10.1007/978-3-030-03122-0_10

to isolationism and protectionism, risking its economic and social development because of imperial nostalgia and moral panic about 'loss of sovereignty' and 'mass migration'. That feeling of fear and nostalgia—translated into the referendum result favouring the UK leaving the EU—inevitably affected many individuals who identify or are identified as members of minorities based on their sexual orientation or gender identity (SOGI).[1] Considering statistics indicate that more than one million people aged 16 and over in the UK identify as lesbian, gay or bisexual (Office for National Statistics 2017a), and that to this figure we can add those who identify as transsexuals, non-binary, intersex, queer, etc., it is clear that there are sizeable SOGI minorities in the UK. Yet, although the possible impact of Brexit has been scrutinised from many angles, there has been very limited analysis of how it may affect these minorities.[2]

Many analyses post-referendum have attempted to precisely determine the demographics of referendum voting preferences. Voters' age, urban/rural setting, region, social class, ethnicity, income, education levels, political party preference, media and social media preferences, financial situation, place of birth, national identity, and marriage status have all been linked to certain voting tendencies (Barr 2016; BBC News 2016b; Busquets Guàrdia 2016; Goodwin and Heath 2016; Lambert 2016; McGill 2016). None of these analyses, however, have inquired into a

protection on the basis of their sexual orientation or gender identity (SOGI) (grant agreement No. 677693). The authors wish to thank the pertinent and useful suggestions offered by Bal Sokhi-Bulley, Philip Bremner, and the participants at the workshop 'Europe, Brexit and Human Rights' held on 22 November 2017 and organised by the Sussex Rights and Justice Research Centre, and the workshop 'Feminist and Queer Perspectives on Brexit' held on 17 November 2017 and organised by the Sussex European Institute, both at the University of Sussex.

[1]We recognise that 'SOGI minorities' is not an ideal expression, to the extent that not everyone we wish to refer to may identify with it, but for practical reasons we will use it as shorthand to refer to everyone who does not identify as heterosexual or cis-gender; we ask readers to interpret this expression in this broad sense throughout this contribution.

[2]The only relevant analyses of which the authors are aware other than the one they have produced (Danisi et al. 2017) have been published by Wintemute (2016), Cooper (2018), Cooper et al. (2018) and the Trade Union Congress (2018).

possible link between self-identification as a member of SOGI minorities and Brexit voting preference. The closest that such analyses have come to SOGI issues can be found in a report concluding that those in favour of the UK remaining in the EU (generally referred to as 'Remainers') are more likely to accept same-sex marriage, in particular those 'Remainers' who support the Labour Party (Ipsos MORI 2017). Despite this very limited consideration of SOGI issues in analyses of Brexit, there is no doubt that Brexit will affect SOGI minorities on a range of levels. These include likely serious effects in terms of human rights and equality policy, 'soft law' instruments, socio-cultural environment, economic resources, regional variations within the UK and civil society vibrancy, as will be seen.

This contribution offers what is, to our knowledge, the first comprehensive academic assessment of the Brexit process in relation to the situation of SOGI minorities and submits that SOGI minorities should prepare for very significant challenges from all quarters as a consequence of Brexit. This is particularly timely in light of the 2017 UK Supreme Court decision in *Walker v Innospec Limited*,[3] where the Court relied on EU law to hold a provision of the Equality Act 2010 unlawful for violating pension rights of same-sex couples.[4] In Sect. 2, we start by identifying the role of the EU in developing a legal and policy framework that protects the rights of SOGI minorities. We will argue that, although the EU has played an important role in this field, its actions have often fallen short of desired aims, mostly owing to lack of law-making powers. In Sect. 3 our attention moves to the UK legal and policy framework in relation to SOGI minorities and the extent to which that framework has been a product—or not—of EU influence. We show that, while there may be no immediate threat to the current framework protecting SOGI minorities, there are reasons for concern in relation to several matters not of a strictly legal nature. In Sect. 4, we then note that SOGI minorities elsewhere in the EU might also be affected by Brexit. Finally, in Sect. 5, we conclude with a reminder of the need to remain alert to legal and policy developments that may detrimentally affect SOGI minorities.

---

[3] [2017] UKSC 47.
[4] This judgment will be further discussed below (Sect. 3).

2   What Has the EU Done for SOGI Minorities?

The EU has often been viewed as *the* SOGI minorities' champion, as well as a 'gender actor' (Ayoub 2016, 47; European Commission 2015a; Guerrina and Masselot 2018). In order to verify this statement, in this section we explore the legislative and policy actions adopted so far at EU level, as well as the approach of the Court of Justice of the European Union (CJEU) in this field. Based on the competences granted to the EU by the Treaties, the analysis shows the EU's attempt to pursue a sort of 'SOGI mainstreaming', thus moving from a sector-specific intervention based on a non-discrimination model towards the full integration of a SOGI perspective in an increasing range of areas, such as migration, asylum, and external relations. This does not, in itself, amount to saying that the EU has always been successful or that this process is complete, especially if we look at the brakes imposed by EU Treaties or at specific countries that might grant higher standards of protection—such as the UK. Rather, the EU's attempt means that its institutions are increasingly willing to act in accordance with its own values which include the respect for human dignity and human rights (see Article 2 of the Treaty on European Union, TEU),[5] at least to the extent that its internal (political) dynamics permit.

Equality First: The EU's Trojan Horse

It is recognised that the 'European project' was born with a strong 'equaliser' soul (Favilli 2008; Rossi and Casolari 2017; Tridimas 2006). Although its original scope was preventing discrimination based on nationality for economic reasons, the (now) Union was eventually able to identify 'equality' as one of its fundamental values and aims (in addition to Article 2 TEU, see also Article 3 of the same Treaty, where the fight against social exclusion and discrimination is stressed) (Bell 2002). At the same time, the Charter of Fundamental Rights of the EU (the Charter) introduced a general prohibition of discrimination based on sexual orientation at Article 21 (gender identity is still not mentioned),[6]

---

[5] Treaty on European Union (consolidated version), OJ C 326, 26 October 2012.

[6] *Charter of Fundamental Rights of the European Union*, OJ C 326, 26 October 2012. Article 21(1) reads as follows: 'Any discrimination based on any ground such as sex, race, colour, ethnic or social origin, genetic features, language, religion or belief, political or any other opinion, membership of a national minority, property, birth, disability, age or sexual orientation shall be prohibited.'

while framing traditional human rights in a non-heteronormative way (see, for example, Article 9 on the right to marriage). Although it does not provide new competences to EU institutions (see Article 51 of the Charter; Spaventa 2016), since 2009 the Charter has served as a 'constitutional' parameter for EU actions, as well as those of Member States when implementing EU law. Consequently, every piece of EU law and policy should be read in a way that may facilitate SOGI minorities' enjoyment of human rights in light of the prohibition of discrimination.[7] It could even be argued that today Article 21 sometimes plays the role of a Trojan horse, potentially maximising the protection of SOGI minorities under EU law in areas where equality secondary law does not apply (Danisi 2015; De Schutter 2011). To put it briefly, as a result of this long process, the prohibition of discrimination based on sexual orientation has developed into an 'unobjectionable' norm within the EU (Elgstrom 2005).

This does not mean that EU institutions have been given full licence to combat SOGI discrimination widely through binding instruments. If we exclude the new Directives on gender equality,[8] which also had clear implications for gender reassignment (Mos 2014), after the entry into force of the Treaty of Amsterdam in 1999,[9] only Directive 2000/78 (the Equality Framework Directive) was enacted.[10] It specifically prohibits direct and indirect discrimination, as well as harassment and victimisation, on the grounds of age, religion or belief, disability and sexual orientation in the field of employment. As a result, Member States are

---

[7] In light of the CJEU's position in *Mangold* (C-144/04), however, the general prohibition based on sexual orientation might have already existed as a general principle of EU law before the entry into force of the Charter (Schiek 2006).

[8] Directive 2006/54/EC of 5 July 2006 on the implementation of the principle of equal opportunities and equal treatment of men and women in matters of employment and occupation (recast), OJ L 204/23, 26 July 2006; and Council Directive 2004/113/EC of 13 December 2004 implementing the principle of equal treatment between men and women in the access to and supply of goods and services, OJ L373, 21 December 2004.

[9] Treaty of Amsterdam amending the Treaty on European Union, the Treaties establishing the European Communities and certain related acts, OJ C 340, 10 November 1997.

[10] Council Directive 2000/78/EC of 27 November 2000 establishing a general framework for equal treatment in employment and occupation, OJ L 303, 2 December 2000. The Directive is based on Article 19 of the Treaty on the Functioning of the EU, TFEU (Treaty on the Functioning of the European Union (consolidated version), OJ C 326, 26 October 2012).

now obliged to prevent, detect and condemn any distinctions based on sexual orientation in relation to conditions for access to employment, including selection criteria and recruitment conditions, and all types and levels of vocational guidance and training; working conditions, including promotion, dismissals and pay; and membership of, and involvement in, an organisation of workers or employers. The continued lack of an agreement between Member States has prevented the adoption of a new equality directive—the so-called 'horizontal' directive—prohibiting sexual orientation discrimination more widely, i.e., in areas beyond employment.[11] Worse, gender identity is largely invisible in the EU legal framework beyond the scope of gender reassignment.

Despite the limited tools available to the EU to empower SOGI minorities, the implementation of the Equality Framework Directive has gone well beyond its authors' imagination, thanks to the interpretation of this instrument provided by the CJEU. Through the adoption of an 'anti-stereotyping approach', based on the Charter and the European Convention on Human Rights (ECHR), EU law proved influential in improving certain aspects of SOGI minorities' lives even in those EU Member States with an already strong equality legislation. Three examples may be useful to prove this. Firstly, the obligations contained in the Directive have been read in light of the social experience of sexual minorities in European society, which signalled persistent and hidden forms of discrimination against SOGI minorities (FRA 2015). Without the CJEU's watchful eye, it would have been impossible to identify public statements reproducing clichés about gay people (e.g. 'there are no gay footballers')[12] as direct discrimination based on sexual orientation prohibited by the Directive. Indeed, homophobic statements have the effect of hampering the employment of (actual or presumed) gay people and, as such, should be fought by Member States. Secondly, thanks to the judgments in *Maruko*,[13] *Römer*,[14] and *Hay*[15] regarding the national treatment of same-sex couples, the CJEU made entirely clear that every

---

[11] Proposal for a directive of 2 July 2008 against discrimination based on age, disability, sexual orientation and religion or belief beyond the workplace, COM/2008/0426 final.

[12] The example is taken from the CJEU's Judgment of 25 April 2013, *Asociaţia Accept*, C-81/12, ECLI:EU:C:2013:275.

[13] Judgment of 1 April 2008, *Maruko*, C-267/06, ECLI:EU:C:2008:179.

[14] Judgment of 10 May 2011, *Römer*, C-147/08, ECLI:EU:C:2011:286.

[15] Judgment of 12 December 2013, *Hay*, C-267/12, ECLI:EU:C:2013:823.

employment benefit should be given to all employees without distinctions based on their civil status when these distinctions mask discrimination based on one's sexual orientation. Since employment benefits are aimed at supporting employees' families, and given that the concept of family is not limited by sexual orientation, measures such as special leaves and pensions (under some conditions) cannot be denied (only) to homosexual employees. Thirdly, in *Hay*,[16] EU judges skilfully qualified marriage as a 'heteronormative notion', itself embedding stigma and discrimination against sexual minorities when it is not granted irrespective of sexual orientation. If EU anti-discrimination law applies, this creates an obligation to treat equally employees who are married and those who have entered into a civil partnership *when* same-sex couples are still excluded from marriage.

These developments make it more striking that, apart from soft law instruments (European Parliament 2012b), gender identity as a general and comprehensive concept is absent in EU law (Bell 2012). Yet, the CJEU has been revolutionary in obliging Member States to protect people whose gender is reassigned from any discriminatory treatment through legislation aimed at prohibiting 'sex' discrimination.[17] Indeed, any distinction based on gender reassignment, including the dismissal or the denial of a state or a survivor's pension, has been identified as discrimination based on sex in *P v S*,[18] *KB*[19] and *Richards*.[20] More recently, in *MB*,[21] the CJEU has set the

---

[16] Ibid. The importance of this approach is even more evident if compared with the more restrictive attitude adopted by the European Court of Human Rights (ECtHR).

[17] While this approach excludes everyone who has not undergone reassignment, people who have undergone gender reassignment enjoy a wider protection under EU law than sexual orientation minorities. In fact, if compared to the Equality Framework Directive, gender Directives also cover access to goods and services and occupational social security schemes. See Millns' chapter in this book for all references on EU gender equality framework.

[18] Judgment of 30 April 1996, *P v S and Cornwall County Council*, C-13/94, ECLI:EU:C:1996:170.

[19] Judgment of 7 January 2004, *K.B. v National Health Service Pensions Agency and Secretary of State for Health*, C-117/01, ECLI:EU:C:2004:7.

[20] Judgment of 27 April 2006, *Sarah Margaret Richards v Secretary of State for Work and Pensions*, C-423/04, ECLI:EU:C:2006:256.

[21] Judgment of 26 June 2018, *MB v Secretary of State for Work and Pensions*, Case C-451/16, ECLI:EU:C:2018:492. The CJEU has tried nonetheless to restrict the scope of the judgment, in light of the Member States' competence in matters of civil status and legal recognition of the change of a person's gender: see points 27–29 and 47.

path for a more radical recognition of transgender people's rights. Relying again on the prohibition of discrimination based on sex, it established that a Member State cannot require a person whose gender was reassigned to satisfy the condition of not being married to a person of the gender that they have acquired in order to be eligible for a state retirement pension at the same age as people with the acquired gender. Interestingly, in this way the CJEU has indirectly embraced an intersectional approach by ensuring that people such as MB should not have to undergo divorce against their religious beliefs in order to avoid discrimination because of their gender reassignment, thus recognising both faith and gender as important identities for an individual.

This range of achievements shows a degree of internal inconsistency within the Union: on one hand, jurisprudential activism in relation to SOGI minorities' quest for equality; on the other, a more hesitant legislative and policy agenda. This is even more palpable if we look beyond the anti-discrimination framework, where the SOGI perspective has not always been integrated.

Mainstreaming a SOGI Perspective… and Its Limits

Looking beyond equality law, SOGI minorities' needs were not usually addressed in the discussions leading to the adoption of most current EU legislation. While the EU has tried to fill this gap through the most recent reforms trying to amend legal provisions that prevented SOGI minorities from enjoying human rights, again it is the CJEU that has played a key role in mainstreaming a SOGI perspective. Developments in two areas that are open to EU intervention, asylum law and freedom of movement, provide a good example of this state of affairs.

To begin with the Common European Asylum System (CEAS), the EU has been able to elaborate a few solutions aimed at improving the experiences of asylum seekers and refugees claiming international protection on SOGI grounds (Balboni 2012; Ferreira 2018). For example, it has at least clarified that SOGI may be used to define a particular social group for the recognition of refugee status under the 1951 Geneva Convention (Article 10(1)(d) of Directive 2011/95/EU).[22]

---

[22] Directive 2011/95/EU of 13 December 2011 on standards for the qualification of third-country nationals or stateless persons as beneficiaries of international protection, for a uniform status for refugees or for persons eligible for subsidiary protection, and for the content of the protection granted, OJ L 337, 20 December 2011.

While the current reform process might strengthen such protection in terms of procedures and reception and by defining individuals claiming asylum on SOGI-related grounds as people with specific needs (Ferreira et al. 2018),[23] the CJEU has already read the relevant provisions in a way that largely complies with the standards set out in the dedicated UNHCR SOGI Guidelines (UNHCR—UN High Commissioner for Refugees 2012). Hence, in *X, Y and Z*[24] the Court rejected the idea that SOGI asylum seekers should be asked to be discreet in order to avoid persecution in their home countries. By the same token, in *A, B, and C*[25] and in *F*,[26] the Court rejected methods that may violate Charter rights when national authorities seek to assess the credibility of an individual seeking asylum who claims to be persecuted on the basis of sexual orientation (Ferreira and Venturi 2017). So, it is recognised that relying exclusively on stereotyped questions or on personality projective tests to confirm one's sexual orientation is not only detrimental to the right to dignity of SOGI asylum claimants (Article 1 of the Charter), but could also amount to a disproportionate interference with the right to respect for private and family life (Article 7 of the Charter).

Moreover, in relation to freedom of movement *within* EU Member States,[27] the EU is bolstering the protection of SOGI minorities while safeguarding Member States' sovereignty (Belavusau and Kochenov 2016; Bell and Selanec 2016; van den Brink 2016). Other than by including non-heteronormative provisions, this result is possible thanks to an interpretation of the EU law in force that grants SOGI minorities equal social recognition. That is why in the *Coman* case, regarding the notion of 'spouse' included in Directive 2004/38/EC on the right of citizens

[23] See EU Commission, *Towards a Reform of the Common European Asylum System and Enhancing Legal Avenues to Europe*, 6 April 2016, COM(2016) 197 final.

[24] Judgment of 7 November 2013, *Minister voor Immigratie en Asiel v X and Y and Z v Minister voor Immigratie en Asiel*, C-199-201/12, ECLI:EU:C:2013:720.

[25] Judgment of 2 December 2014, *A and Others v Staatssecretaris van Veiligheid en Justitie*, C-148-150/13, ECLI:EU:C:2014:2406.

[26] Judgment of 25 January 2018, *F v Bevándorlási és Állampolgársági Hivatal*, C-473/16, ECLI:EU:C:2018:36.

[27] Directive 2004/38/EC of 29 April 2004 on the Right of Citizens of the Union and their Family Members to Move and Reside Freely within the Territory of the Member States amending Regulation (EEC) No. 1612/68 and Repealing Directives 64/221/EEC, 68/360/EEC, 72/194/EEC, 73/148/EEC, 75/34/EEC, 75/35/EEC, 90/364/EEC, 90/365/EEC and 93/96/EEC, OJ L 158, 30 April 2004.

of the Union and their family members to move and reside freely within the territory of the Member States, the CJEU found that, at EU level, this concept is gender-neutral and covers the same-sex spouse of a Union citizen.[28] In fact, even if Member States are not obliged under EU law to legally recognise same-sex marriage, they cannot make their internal legislation a condition for the recognition of the right of such same-sex married couples to move and reside within the Union, as heterosexual married couples in a comparable situation have enjoyed to date. Even more strikingly, although the CJEU seems to restrict this powerful gender-neutral reading of EU law for the sole purpose of granting a derived right of residence to a third-country national for ensuring the effective enjoyment of the status of Union citizen, it strongly asserted that the recognition of 'such marriages [...] does not undermine the national identity or pose a threat to the public policy of the Member State concerned'.[29] Instead, the lack of such a recognition may additionally prevent the enjoyment of the right to family life as protected by Article 7 of the Charter, read in light of Article 8 ECHR (Danisi 2017),[30] thus amounting to an unnecessary restriction prohibited under the Charter.

To be clear, no EU institution has been completely successful in their efforts to advance a normative and cultural change within the Union in favour of SOGI minorities' rights. However, if analysed from a post-Brexit perspective, the emerging link between EU citizenship and the enjoyment of a more comprehensive catalogue of human rights in EU Member States where marriage is solely a 'heteronormative' institution leaves SOGI minorities in the UK in a vulnerable condition. Same-sex couples married in the UK and whose members will be deprived of the Union's citizenship because of Brexit, will experience serious difficulties in having their right to stay as a recognised family unit in those EU Member States that have not legally recognised same-sex marriage.

---

[28] Judgment of 5 June 2018, *Coman*, C-673/16, ECLI:EU:C:2018:385. See also the Opinion of Advocate General Wathelet concerning the same case, delivered on 11 January 2018, which was based more on the principle of non-discrimination (Article 21 of the Charter).

[29] Ibid., point 46 (in contrast to arguments advanced by many Member States that still have not entitled same-sex couples to marry).

[30] See Article 52 of the Charter and, for instance, ECtHR, 21 July 2017, *Oliari and Others v. Italy*, Applications nos. 18766/11 and 36030/11.

The same lack of protection will arise from the impossibility of relying on the CJEU's ability to detect practices harmful to SOGI minorities, as well as from the non-application of new EU Parliament's proposals aimed at mainstreaming SOGI considerations in international relations. Two examples may be useful to clarify this point. First, when the CJEU was asked to specify how to implement Directive 2004/33/EC[31] in relation to blood donors, it was able to identify a homophobic attitude in the imposition of a total ban on blood donations from 'men having sex with other men', in sharp contrast with the right to equality under the Charter (see decision in *Léger*).[32] More importantly, this sort of clarification may nudge the Commission to adopt a more active role in the enforcement of EU law, using all the available powers provided by the Treaties to make sure that Member States mainstream equality for SOGI minorities (e.g. by using infringement procedures). Second, in light of the important role of the EU Parliament in denouncing SOGI-related human rights violations in and outside the EU (e.g. European Parliament 2011, 2012a, 2017), we may recall its attempt to develop an interconnected and comprehensive set of measures in all spheres of action of the EU through a dedicated SOGI *Roadmap* (European Parliament 2012b, 2014). Here, for the first time, intersex people appeared on the EU agenda, and the need to expand the EU's role in promoting and protecting the enjoyment of human rights by SOGI minorities worldwide was stressed in light of the EU's broader obligation to promote human rights through its external policy (Article 3(5) TEU; Smith 2015). In this respect, if we exclude the Commission's attempts to improve the situation of SOGI minorities in accession countries (European Commission 2016) and the adoption of specific *Guidelines to promote and protect the enjoyment of all human rights by LGBTI persons* to be applied in the relationship with non-EU Member States (Council of the European Union 2013), a more radical change may come in the context of international agreements signed by the EU. The EU Parliament is promoting the inclusion of a specific reference to the prohibition of discrimination on SOGI grounds in future economic agreements with third countries, starting from the revision of the Cotonou Agreement

[31] Commission Directive 2004/33/EC of 22 March 2004 implementing Directive 2002/98/EC of the European Parliament and of the Council as regards certain technical requirements for blood and blood components, OJ L 91, 30 March 2004.

[32] Judgment of 29 April 2015, *Léger*, C-528/13, ECLI:EU:C:2015:288.

in 2020.[33] While the positive effects may be noteworthy (Bartels 2017), even from a cultural point of view, the fact that such a move will not bind the UK is not only worrying in itself, but is also compounded by the UK's emerging policy 'towards a common future' with the Commonwealth countries to be pursued in the post-Brexit era, which may omit completely any SOGI considerations (Kirby 2009; Robertson 2018).

3   GOD SAVE THE... QUEERS?

How Did We Get Where We Are and Who Do We Have to Thank?

As the previous section highlights, EU membership is a concern for SOGI minorities living in the UK because of the many different levels on which the EU operates: as a legislator, a regulator, and enforcer, an educator, a campaigner, a mediator, a funder and a bridge builder or facilitator. In this section, we highlight some of these roles, but we start from a different perspective: identifying and assessing the potential benefits for SOGI minorities in the UK of leaving the EU.

Although the majority who voted in favour of Brexit was small, inevitably it will include some or many members of SOGI minorities, although that remains unknown and would be difficult to quantify (it is only with the next Census in 2021 that the UK population will have the option of answering a question about their SOGI: Office for National Statistics 2017b). While many openly SOGI minority parliamentarians were firmly in the Remain camp (*Gay Times* 2016), there was also an organised SOGI lobby arguing in favour of Brexit. The organisation Out & Proud campaigned on the basis that parliamentary sovereignty—not the EU—is the basis of gay rights in the UK, that the UK is at the forefront of SOGI equality and will continue to be so post-Brexit, and—critically—that the EU is no longer a champion for SOGI rights:

---

[33] See Council Decision (EU) 2017/435 of 28 February 2017 on the conclusion of the Agreement amending for the second time the Partnership Agreement between the members of the African, Caribbean and Pacific Group of States, of the one part, and the European Community and its Member States, of the other part, signed in Cotonou on 23 June 2000, as first amended in Luxembourg on 25 June 2005, OJ L 67, 14 March 2017; European Parliament resolution of 11 February 2015 on the work of the ACP-EU Joint Parliamentary Assembly (2014/2154(INI)), para. K1.

'With the addition of socially conservative Eastern European countries in 2004, and countries such as Turkey, Serbia, Macedonia, Albania and Montenegro looking to join, LGBT rights look set to be held back further as those with a less tolerant views [sic] veto legislation, as we have recently seen from Hungary' (Out & Proud, n.d.).

There are two slightly contradictory claims here to be unpicked: the first claim is that the EU was not responsible for SOGI rights advancement in the UK, because the UK was at the forefront of the gay rights agenda; the second assumption is that if the EU was once a champion of gay rights, it no longer is, based on the xenophobic assumption that opening up membership to countries in Eastern Europe and beyond has opened the doors to homophobia and bigotry. Here we have an inversion of homonationalism (Puar 2007), in which the EU no longer defines itself by its progressive position on sexual minorities because Western liberal values have been sacrificed to the 'less tolerant views' of outsiders. The UK needs to withdraw from the EU to maintain its position as a haven from homophobia.

Supporters of this position might point out that, at the time of the referendum, the country was led by a Conservative Prime Minister who introduced gay marriage into the UK.[34] They might draw attention to the parliamentary transgender equality inquiry (Women and Equalities Committee 2016) or to the Government announcement of plans to reform and demedicalise the process for changing one's gender (Government Equalities Office 2017). All of the above could be used to argue that, whether or not the UK's SOGI minorities ever needed the EU to secure equality, that time is past.

To assess the validity of such claims, we look back at the way improvements to SOGI minority rights came about in the UK. It will surprise no one to read that for much of the twentieth century, UK law was a source of persecution rather than protection for SOGI minorities (Moran 1996). Lesbian, bisexual and trans people were not covered or recognised as existing—which was of course both a blessing (if it meant they were shielded from persecution) and a curse (if it meant they needed protection). And even the positive measures that were introduced did not provide anything close to full equality. So, although the 1957 Wolfenden

---

[34] At the Conservative Party Conference in 2011, Prime Minister David Cameron said 'I don't support gay marriage in spite of being a Conservative. I support gay marriage because I am a Conservative' (BBC News 2011, http://www.bbc.co.uk/news/uk-politics-15189614).

Committee published a report recommending that 'homosexual behaviour between consenting adults in private should no longer be a criminal offence', up until 1967, gay and bisexual men could face a maximum sentence of life in prison (Home Office 1957). The 1967 Sexual Offences Act provided only a limited decriminalisation of homosexual acts between men over 21 and in private. The age of consent was lowered to 18 in 1994 (still not equal to the age for heterosexuals).[35] It was not until the Sexual Offences (Amendment) Act of 2000 that the UK had an equal age of consent, for the first time including lesbian relationships.

Moreover, legal changes were not always positive: as late as 1988, under the Thatcher Government, Section 28 of the Local Government Act 1988 stated that a local authority 'shall not intentionally promote homosexuality or publish material with the intention of promoting homosexuality' or 'promote the teaching in any maintained school of the acceptability of homosexuality as a pretended family relationship'. This measure remained on the statute books until it was repealed through the Local Government Act 2003.

From the early 2000s the law started delivering some positive outcomes for SOGI minorities, with the 2002 Adoption and Children Act bringing rights for same-sex couples adopting in England and Wales. Civil partnership for same-sex couples was recognised through the Civil Partnership Act 2004 in 2005. Same-sex marriage was introduced in 2013 (though it is still not recognised in Northern Ireland, despite a vote in favour by the Northern Ireland Assembly in 2015).[36] Legislation on hate speech and hate crime based on SOGI was passed in 2008 and 2012, as part of a series of measures to address these phenomena.[37]

Employment law was an important site of change and is where the critical role of the EU begins to be visible. Responding to a CJEU decision, the Sex Discrimination Act 1975 was amended in 1999 to include gender reassignment (Wintemute 2016).[38] Moreover, the above analysed

---

[35] Criminal Justice and Public Order Act 1994.

[36] Marriage (Same Sex Couples) Act 2013; Northern Ireland Assembly. 2015. "Official Report (Hansard), Monday 2 November 2015 Volume 109, No 1." http://data.niassembly. gov.uk/HansardXml/plenary-02-11-2015.pdf.

[37] Criminal Justice and Immigration Act 2008 and Legal Aid, Sentencing and Punishment of Offenders Act 2012.

[38] Judgment of 30 April 1996, *P v S and Cornwall County Council*, C-13/94, ECLI:EU:C:1996:170.

Equality Framework Directive was the spark for a change of direction in UK discrimination law that directly and indirectly benefitted SOGI minorities (Fredman 2001). One of the earliest achievements was the Employment Equality (Sexual Orientation) Regulations 2003: for the first time, and as a direct result of the implementation of the Equality Framework Directive, lesbians, gays and bisexuals were protected from direct and indirect discrimination, and also harassment and victimisation in the workplace. Yet, this was only part of a broader equality agenda that began to develop after 2000. Prior to this, the UK's equality law and statutory bodies had developed in an ad hoc way over the latter half of the twentieth century to protect individuals only on the grounds of race, gender and disability. The EU Directives set in motion a series of developments culminating in the Equality Acts of 2006 and 2010 and the creation of a statutory Equality and Human Rights Commission (EHRC), as well as the production of government white papers, legislative reviews and stakeholder engagement (Spencer 2008). Civil society organisations came together often for the first time to identify shared concerns and areas of disparity and hierarchies of discrimination (Spencer 2008, 9). Over a number of years, SOGI minority rights organisations—including Stonewall, GIRES and the LGBT Foundation—worked with NGOs covering other areas of discrimination to lobby the Government for a levelling up of the equality law and an independent body to enforce that law—both achieved at least in part through the afore-mentioned Equality Acts. Crucially, these Acts harmonised the UK's hitherto piecemeal equality law, providing some degree of parity of protection for all victims of discrimination (Davis et al. 2016; Hepple 2014).

While causality is always hard to demonstrate with legislation and policy, the EU was *a*—if not *the*—catalyst for a broader equality agenda than had previously existed, one that not only recognised sexual and now gender identity as protected characteristics, but also had the potential for recognising the way these characteristics overlapped and intersected with others—race, gender, disability, etc. Before the Equality Framework Directive, UK equality law had only recognised race, gender and disability as the bases for discrimination and provided protection through different silos of legislation and institutional protection—the Race Relations Acts and the Commission for Racial Equality; the Sex Discrimination Act 1975 and the Equal Opportunities Commission; and the Disability Discrimination Act 1995 and the Disability Rights Commission. The chain of events set in motion by the EU led to the creation of the

EHRC—an independent body that has developed a measurement framework for equality and human rights that recognises intersectionality in a way that the earlier gender, race and disability commissions did not (EHRC 2017).

It is also fair to say that in some areas the UK has gone further than required by the EU. While EU law allows NGOs and other organisations to act on behalf of individual complainants, it largely follows an individual complaint-based model that often fails to recognise the systemic and structural nature of most inequality and turns societal problems into individual ones.[39] Through the Public Sector Equality Duty (section 149 of the Equality Act 2010), UK equality law has an additional positive approach to equality, aimed at securing the rights of individuals without forcing them to seek legal redress in response to a specific case of discrimination (Fredman 2011). The duty could be hugely beneficial for SOGI minorities, for example, as the trigger for schools developing programmes to prevent bullying of SOGI minority children where this is the cause of under-achievement, or in targeted health care to meet the specific needs of lesbian women. Yet, there has been little enthusiasm for fulfilling the duty, which is often portrayed by governments as a bureaucratic burden, for example, when the coalition Government launched the Red Tape Challenge to cut 'unnecessary red tape' and included the Equality Duty as one of the themes of the Challenge (Home Office 2012; Race Equality Coalition 2013).

The UK has also developed a proactive agenda around trans equality—both within and outside Government. The Gender Recognition Act in 2004 gave people the legal right to change their gender and, in July 2017, the Government announced plans to demedicalise the process for changing gender, launch a national SOGI minorities survey, and consult on the reform of the Gender Recognition Act (Government Equalities Office 2017). The parliamentary select committee on women and equality has kept trans rights on the legislative agenda, with a trans equality inquiry reporting in 2016, including many policy and legislative recommendations to the Government (Women and Equalities Committee 2016). Here, as with the Public Sector Equality Duty, the UK's agenda apparently owes little to the EU and has taken initiatives outside the areas of EU competence.

---

[39] Article 9(2) of the Equality Framework Directive.

In the next section we explain why the above narrative does not show that the UK SOGI rights agenda can rely on its own momentum, independent of EU carrots or sticks. Before doing so, it is important to note that the equality agenda has not taken the same path or timeline across the UK's four nations. While the Equality Act 2010 harmonised equality law across England, Scotland and Wales, and equality provisions apply equally across Great Britain in the main, these matters are devolved to Northern Ireland, whose equality law derives largely from Section 75 of the Northern Ireland Act 1998. While some SOGI-related protections are replicated on both sides of the Irish Sea—for example, the provisions on employment protection[40]—there remain disparities in rights unconnected to either the Equality Act 2010 or the Northern Ireland Act 1998. Most notable among these, while civil partnership is available throughout the UK, same-sex marriage does not exist in Northern Ireland. There are particular concerns about the equality and human rights implications of Brexit for people living in Northern Ireland, and these include issues relating to sexual orientation and gender identity, as we consider in the next section. After Brexit, existing areas of EU competence will be repatriated to the UK, but there is considerable uncertainty as to which of these competences will be allocated to Westminster/ Whitehall, and which to the devolved governments across the UK.

In conclusion, it follows that the EU has been an important driver for SOGI rights in the UK, including, on the one hand, discrete rights that benefit individuals on the basis of their SOGI, and, on the other hand, broader pan-equality and human rights protections that recognise SOGI minorities have many other characteristics that interact with each other, potentially making some individuals more vulnerable to discrimination and abuse than others. Looking forward, one might argue that what we have seen is a historical account of why EU membership *was* beneficial for UK SOGI minorities, but that full legal equality has now been achieved. The UK no longer needs EU membership as a stick to make us comply with equality standards. One could argue further that the UK is in the forefront of the SOGI minority rights agenda and has nothing to

---

[40] Measures now in the Equality Act 2010 correspond to those in Employment Equality (Sexual Orientation) Regulations (NI) 2003, Equality Act (Sexual Orientation) Regulations (NI) 2006, Equality Act (Sexual Orientation) (Amendment) Regulations (NI) 2006, Equality Act (Sexual Orientation) (Amendment No. 2) Regulations (NI) 2007.

gain from EU membership on this front. We find such arguments uncon-vincing for several reasons, as we explore in the following section.

No Way of Knowing

In this section, we identity some of the ways in which SOGI minorities would benefit from the UK's continuing membership of the EU. Firstly, most members of SOGI minorities would reject the idea that full equal-ity has been achieved. It is even arguable that there has been regression in some areas, in all likelihood connected to the EU referendum and the political and media climate surrounding it. The rise in hate crime post-referendum was well-observed (Home Affairs Committee 2016) and it was not only ethnic and national minorities who were targeted. Figures released by the charity Galop show that hate crimes against SOGI minorities rose by 147% between July and September 2016 (Galop 2016) and research by Stonewall published in September 2017 claimed a 78% increase in such crimes over a four-year period (Stonewall 2017). So, it seems that the toxic culture created by or related to Brexit has impacted on SOGI minorities, as well as individuals minoritised on the basis of race or ethnicity. The UK has many initiatives—academic, official and within civil society—analysing and addressing this phenom-enon (Home Office 2016; University of Sussex, n.d.). However, hate crime also features strongly in the list of European Commission actions to advance SOGI equality, with a Commission-led group coordinat-ing work including dialogue with IT companies to combat online hate, ongoing data collection by the EU Fundamental Rights Agency (FRA) to monitor the problem, and specific funding allocated to Member States for work tackling hate crime (European Commission 2015b). These ini-tiatives currently include the UK along with other EU Member States, but will not fall within the scope of the EU (Withdrawal) Act 2018, which means the UK will most likely no longer benefit from them. Nor have there been government assurances that the funding currently avail-able through the EU to UK bodies combatting homophobia and trans-phobia will be replaced by the UK Government.[41] Consequently, work

---

[41]For example, Galop, the UK's LGBT anti-violence organisation, is a partner in the project Come Forward: Empowering and Supporting Victims of Anti-LGBT Hate Crimes, funded by the Rights, Equality and Citizenship Programme (2014–2020) of the European Union, http://www.lgbthatecrime.eu/partners.

on hate crime will continue in the UK, but in all likelihood without some of the existing sources of financial support, with fewer connections with European partners and without the cross-country mapping and data collection that provides the potential for comparisons and sharing of good practice between different countries.

Turning to potential improvements in the law, the EU is committed to extending to sexual orientation and gender identity (amongst other grounds) legal protection against discrimination in social protection, social advantages, education and access to and supply of goods and services which are available to the public, to take place sometime in the future through the above mentioned proposed 'horizontal' directive (section "Equality First: The EU's Trojan Horse"). The directive has had a troubled past, with opposition from a number of Member States (including Germany), which means it is unlikely to come into effect before the UK leaves the EU (Equinet 2015). Moreover, it is unclear if the directive will provide any protection on grounds of SOGI over and above what already exists in the UK. However, while the benefits of future EU directives are unknowable, SOGI minorities in the UK are clearly using EU law to secure their rights both in UK and EU courts. A case in point is the UK Supreme Court decision in *Walker v Innospec Limited* (mentioned in Sect. 1), where the Court relied on EU law to hold a provision of the Equality Act 2010 unlawful for violating pension rights of same-sex couples. Similarly, a decision in 2018 supporting the pension entitlements of a trans woman in the UK relies on Council Directive 79/7/EEC on the Progressive Implementation of the Principle of Equal Treatment for Men and Women in Matters of Social Security.[42]

Furthermore, equality is a work in progress. Prior to the turn of this century, few would have anticipated the momentum that currently exists in the trans equality agenda around the world. No one knows what future initiatives there will be at EU level for promoting minority rights, but if the UK is not at the table, it will not be a part of their design or implementation. Similarly, the UK may have a broadly liberal approach to SOGI minorities at present, but its equality framework is an unstable one: the EHRC has experienced a series of reductions in its capacity over the years (Department for Digital, Culture, Media and Sport 2013) and

---

[42]Judgment of 26 June 2018, *MB v Secretary of State for Work and Pensions*, Case C-451/16, ECLI:EU:C:2018:492.

the government department responsible for equality—the Government Equalities Office—is at best a movable feast, tagged on to whichever department contains its minister at any given time. Rights need to be embedded within the permanent structure of institutions and instruments, not dependent on the whims of politicians at any point in time. Here, the EU plays an important stabilising role in setting standards and promoting common values.

Related to the previous point, SOGI minority rights should not be seen in isolation and SOGI minorities are not only affected by policies and laws relating to sexual orientation and gender identity. The UK Government has implemented a programme of austerity measures, including cuts to services and access to justice (House of Commons Justice Committee 2015). These may hit members of the SOGI minorities hard in areas such as recourse to domestic violence services and access to legal aid. While the EU is not a remedy for victims of austerity measures, the Charter includes the right to an effective remedy and to a fair trial, including legal aid to those who lack sufficient resources (Article 47), which can be of assistance to claimants when the matter falls within the scope of EU law (Article 51).

Moreover, equality has not been achieved consistently throughout the UK. As mentioned above, in Northern Ireland, same sex marriage is not recognised. As a consequence of the *Coman* case (section "Mainstreaming a SOGI Perspective… and Its Limits"), EU same-sex spouses who move to Northern Ireland (including couples where one spouse is from Northern Ireland) have the same rights as opposite-sex spouses while the UK remains within the EU. Given that UK citizens in Northern Ireland voted clearly against leaving the EU in contrast to some other parts of the UK, any resultant reduction in rights for SOGI minorities in that country will be a source of frustration (BBC News 2016a).

This exists alongside strong concerns about equality protection in Northern Ireland post-Brexit. While equality law is devolved to Northern Ireland, this does not mean that the Northern Ireland Assembly and Executive can legislate as they wish in this area. Both bodies are constrained by the EU compliance provisions of the Northern Ireland Act 1998. The need to comply with EU standards has provided a basis for challenging SOGI discrimination, for example, resulting in the lifting of the lifetime ban on blood donation by men who have sex with men (Human Rights Consortium 2018, 83; McCrudden 2017). Yet, while there has been much discussion about trade, citizenship and immigration controls, and the prospect of a hard border between the north and south of Ireland, there has been little consideration of the implications of Brexit for equality protection, including the protection of SOGI minorities in Northern Ireland (Curtis et al. 2017). If, after March 2019, equality continues to be devolved to Northern Ireland but the EU no longer provides the floor of minimum standards, then there is a potential for widening disparities of protection between Northern Ireland and Great Britain, in the absence of the EU as a force for harmonisation on issues such as equal marriage for example.

Turning from equality law to human rights more broadly, we have already seen that the Charter contains many principles that are highly relevant to SOGI rights, such as Articles 1, 3 and 7 relating to human dignity, physical and mental integrity and respect for family and private life. The Charter will not be applied in the UK after leaving the EU, but one could argue that the rights it bestows are secured for UK citizens through the ECHR and given further effect at a domestic level by the Human Rights Act 1998 (HRA 1998) (Human Rights Consortium 2018, 83). However, the future of the UK's membership to the ECHR and of the HRA 1998 are doubtful—in fact, it is probably only because of the hugely time-consuming nature of Brexit that there has not been more progress in the Conservative Government's commitment to replace the HRA 1998 with a British 'Bill of Rights' and withdraw from the ECHR. The Conservative Party manifesto makes clear that the HRA 1998 and UK status as a party to the ECHR are only safe during this Parliament and while the Brexit process is underway (The Conservative Party 2017, 37). European courts—both the Court of Justice and the ECtHR—are an important way of holding the UK Government accountable for its treatment of SOGI minorities and the UK's membership of both is under threat (Fenwick and Masterman 2017). Finally, there is also the loss of standardisation or consistency, if not always enhanced protection for people seeking asylum fleeing homophobia and transphobia that is provided by the EU CEAS (section "Mainstreaming a SOGI Perspective... and Its Limits").

Important though legal measures are, equality is not achieved only through law and legal measures in isolation. The EU, through bodies like FRA and programmes such as PROGRESS and the European Refugee Fund, is involved in a host of non-legal and non-regulatory activities that contribute to progress by informing public opinion, educating people, monitoring progress, and commissioning research on gaps in protection.[43] Alongside the formal EU bodies, many NGOs, networks and initiatives related to SOGI minorities bolster solidarity and are the basis for awareness raising and campaigning. Examples include ILGA-Europe and the Hungarian Helsinki Committee, which in 2013 published, with EU support, a training manual on credibility assessment in asylum with chapters on asylum claims lodged by women and SOGI minorities written by UK lawyers and practitioners (Hungarian Helsinki Committee 2013). There is no reason why these links should not survive Brexit, but it seems likely that they will diminish over time, as UK NGOs will have less and less reason and resources to collaborate with NGOs in other EU Member States.

To conclude, while there is no immediate threat to SOGI equality through withdrawal from the EU, that statement must be hedged with the caveats identified in this section. We argue that while the EU has not delivered full-fledged equality for SOGI minorities in the UK, it has certainly been the catalyst for cultural change and a shift in approach with the potential (still unrealised) of moving beyond a silo approach to inequality. While there has not been the progress that many hoped would come from an integrated anti-discrimination and human rights agenda, once outside EU membership, the UK will not be nudged by new legal norms, case law and other initiatives to the same extent as it is now into tackling discrimination beyond formal civil and political rights for SOGI minorities.

---

[43] Past programmes such as PROGRESS, which ran between 2007–2013, provided financial support to civil society organisations to help them embed EU equality law, such as through the Employment Equality (Sexual Orientation) Regulations 2003, raise awareness and train employers and employees (http://ec.europa.eu/justice/discrimination/files/sexual_orientation_en.pdf). The European Refugee Fund (ERF, EUR 630 million over the period 2008–2013) supported EU countries' efforts in receiving refugees and displaced persons and in guaranteeing access to consistent, fair and effective asylum procedures (https://ec.europa.eu/home-affairs/financing/fundings/migration-asylum-borders/refugee-fund_en). In 2017, the EU FRA published a review of the 'Current migration situation in the EU: Lesbian, gay, bisexual, transgender and intersex asylum seekers' (FRA 2017).

4 A European Union Without the UK: A Lose–Lose Situation

The implications of Brexit are not limited to the treatment of SOGI minorities in the UK. The EU–UK divorce may also have consequences for the EU's momentum in forging ahead with SOGI mainstreaming post-Brexit. In the new scenario, the potential negative effects for the protection of the rights of SOGI minorities in all Member States cannot be underestimated. This section tries to answer this final question: what might be the consequences of Brexit for SOGI minorities outside the UK but still within the Union after Brexit?

This is not a rhetorical question: it recognises that the Union retains some of the characteristics of an inter-governmental organisation (for instance, its Member States gather in the Council of the EU, which has a high level of control over the legislative and political agenda in several key areas).[44] Consequently, there is a need for a strong consensus among Member States, as well as among Members of the EU Parliament, in order to pursue SOGI mainstreaming at EU level. A cohesive Council and Parliament are needed to use all powers available to the EU to secure parity of protection for SOGI minorities through new law and policy. Indeed, political dynamics within EU Member States suggest that opponents of SOGI minority rights or, simply, of strengthening the EU equality agenda may gain influence after Brexit. This is where UK membership of the Union could make a difference, building on the UK's legislation, despite the caveats identified above. Given that the UK has been identified as one of EU's most SOGI-friendly countries (ILGA—International Lesbian, Gay, Bisexual, Trans and Intersex Association, Carroll, and Ramón Mendos 2017), the Council of the EU will lose a Member State that did not oppose the adoption of the Equality Framework Directive, is not hampering the adoption of the proposed 'horizontal' equality directive (section "Equality First: The EU's Trojan Horse") and, more generally, has not been against the integration

[44] See Treaties' provisions still requiring special procedures for adopting EU legislation, which are relevant also for SOGI minorities, including Article 19 TFUE on equality related powers or those related to foreign affairs, in light of the conclusions of international agreements with countries with high records of human rights violations towards sexual minorities.

of SOGI perspectives at EU level (Privot and Pall 2014).[45] For its part, the European Parliament will be deprived of a significant number of Members pressing for the implementation of the SOGI *Roadmap* and potentially challenging heteronormativity in the EU framework (or, at least, not holding back such measures).

The Union, as a whole, will also be deprived of one of the few Member States that have introduced same-sex marriage and legally protect the recognition of gender identity.[46] If a restriction to EU nationals' freedom of movement to the UK is a consequence of Brexit, SOGI minorities may also lose the access that freedom of movement provides to greater rights in the UK than exist in some other Member States (see also Cooper et al. 2018). Freedom of movement as a right has encouraged many SOGI minorities to move between Member States without feeling the need to define themselves as permanent residents of any one state. This will inevitably be restricted with the UK's departure from the EU, with particular implications for SOGI minority parents and would-be parents (FRA 2015).

While the UK is not the ideal haven for SOGI minorities for the reasons explored above, for many members of SOGI minorities living outside the UK it is a country where it is possible to express one's identity. This is especially true until greater respect for SOGI rights materialises in their home countries, something that may eventually happen, in part through the influence of EU law, policy and wider cultural harmonisation. It may be argued that, after leaving the EU, the UK will continue to offer a wider protection to SOGI minorities coming from some EU countries because these standards are an integral part of the UK domestic legislation and will continue to be influenced indirectly by the CJEU's case law in those instances where the ECtHR uses CJEU's principles. Nonetheless, if it is true that belonging to the ECHR system currently provides a safety net in most cases and the ECtHR is gradually aligning its interpretative activity

---

[45] For further information, see the EU's Legislative Train Schedule web page (http://www.europarl.europa.eu/legislative-train/theme-area-of-justice-and-fundamental-rights/file-anti-discrimination-directive), the EUR-Lex web page with all relevant documents (https://eur-lex.europa.eu/legal-content/en/HIS/?uri=CELEX:52008PC0426), and Council of the EU, Dossier interinstitutionnel, 2008/0140 (CNS), 8 December 2014, p. 2, http://register.consilium.europa.eu/doc/srv?l=FR&f=ST%2015705%202014%20ADD%201%20REV%202.

[46] See Marriage (Same Sex Couples) Act 2013 and Gender Recognition Act 2004.

to the CJEU's more inclusive reasoning outlined above,[47] the different positions occupied by EU law and the ECHR in the UK legal order currently give greater weight to EU human rights when compared to the ECHR.

Moreover, as mentioned above, SOGI protection standards will no longer follow possible developments in the EU in light of the SOGI mainstreaming process (section "Mainstreaming a SOGI Perspective... and Its Limits"), and the withdrawal from the ECHR and the repeal of the HRA 1998 are still a possibility (even if *legally* dubious).[48] As a consequence, one cannot completely exclude the risk of exposing SOGI minorities already in the UK, as well as those wishing to move to the UK in the post-Brexit era, to levels of protection inferior to EU standards.

All in all, what is certain is that, once outside the EU, the UK will lose any possibility of influencing progress towards greater enjoyment of SOGI minority rights in the EU. Imperfect as its internal legal framework and social structures may be, until today the UK has been instrumental in strengthening within the EU the position of the group of Member States with solid equality agendas vis-à-vis those without. That is why Brexit seems to put both the EU and the UK in a lose-lose situation as far as SOGI minorities are concerned.

5   Hard, Soft or No Fall?

We have argued that Brexit will most likely entail a range of risks, if not consequences, for SOGI minorities in the UK, namely regarding human rights and equality policy, 'soft law' instruments, socio-cultural environment, economic resources, regional variations within the UK and civil society vibrancy. Yet, what will actually happen to SOGI rights if and when the UK formally leaves the EU is obviously an exercise in

---

[47] See Article 52 of the Charter. We are aware that, in areas such as free movement and asylum, the EU seems to provide a higher protection in relation to SOGI minorities than the ECHR. Yet, this protection is in any case limited to EU law's scope of application and may also be offered by the ECtHR's reading of the ECHR as a 'living instrument' in light of the wider range of situations falling within the scope of the ECHR. See Article 1 ECHR on the scope of the Convention, which does not entail the same limitations imposed on the Charter.

[48] In this respect, from an international law perspective, the hypothesis of withdrawal from the ECHR must take into account the fact that, once rights are recognised to people, they cannot be simply removed at will by a State (UN Human Rights Committee 1997; Conforti 2013).

futurology. One thing is clear: there is a likelihood that the fall will be hard for SOGI minorities and anyone else relying on discrimination law to protect them. Although there is discussion about UK citizens being able to retain their 'acquired rights' under EU law in the light of customary international law, for the sake of legal certainty and protection of legitimate expectations, it is very unclear what 'acquired rights' would be protected and whether a certain degree of 'crystallisation' of those rights would be required (Waibel 2017).

In light of the EU (Withdrawal) Act 2018 and Theresa May's well-known wish to withdraw from the ECHR, not only might a future government erode EU-derived norms that currently protect SOGI minorities, but where this results in a human rights violation, it might also try to deprive SOGI minorities of the possibility of resorting to the ECtHR. While the legality of such a withdrawal may be questioned under international human rights law, the possibility of a British 'Bill of Rights' replacing the HRA 1998 serves as little reassurance, knowing that such Bill would most likely narrow down the rights (and their interpretation) currently enjoyed by people in the UK, much in the light of EU and ECHR law.[49] There is, justifiably, a clear sense of fear and emergency that extends to SOGI minorities (Cooper 2018).

Although it is theoretically possible that the UK will not regress from the advances and achievements identified above, SOGI minorities, organisations and communities should be well aware of one thing: over time, they are likely to be deprived of a number of pathways to justice and of more progressive policies (Belavusau and Kochenov 2016). For all its failings and flaws, in many people's eyes the EU symbolises a re-imagination of citizenship across borders, embracing diversity and welcoming SOGI minorities (Belavusau 2015). The reality of policy and law may not entirely live up to this vision, but there has been steady progress that Brexit threatens to slow down or bring to a halt. To compensate for the loss of this legal and policy arsenal, SOGI minorities will need to step up the domestic fight and build new forums for international cooperation. Red alert it is.

---

[49] House of Lords and House of Commons Joint Committee on Human Rights, *A Bill of Rights for the UK? Government Response to the Committee's Twenty-ninth Report of Session 2007–08*, Third Report of Session 2008–09, HL Paper 15/HC 145, 2009.

BIBLIOGRAPHY

Adams, Abi, and Jeremias Prassl. 2017. Vexatious Claims: Challenging the Case for Employment Tribunal Fees. *The Modern Law Review* 80 (3): 412–442.

Ayoub, Philippe M. 2016. *When States Come Out. Europe's Sexual Minorities and the Politics of Visibility*. Cambridge: Cambridge University Press.

Balboni, Marco. 2012. *La protezione internazionale in ragione del genere, dell'orientamento sessuale e dell'identità di genere*. Torino: Giappichelli.

Barr, Caelainn. 2016. The Areas and Demographics Where the Brexit Vote Was Won. *The Guardian*, June 24, 2016, sec. News. http://www.theguardian.com/news/datablog/2016/jun/24/the-areas-and-demographics-where-the-brexit-vote-was-won.

Bartels, Laurent. 2017. *Human Rights Provisions in Economic Partnership Agreements in Light of the Expiry of the Cotonou Agreement in 2020*. Brussels: European Parliament.

BBC News. 2016a. NI Votes Remain in EU Referendum, June 24, 2016, sec. Northern Ireland. http://www.bbc.co.uk/news/uk-northern-ireland-36614443.

BBC News. 2016b. Brexit Vote: The Breakdown, December 7, 2016, sec. UK Politics. http://www.bbc.co.uk/news/uk-politics-38227674.

Belavusau, Uladzislau. 2015. EU Sexual Citizenship: Sex Beyond the Internal Market. *EUI Department of Law Research Paper No. 2015/06*. SSRN: https://ssrn.com/abstract=2575122.

Belavusau, Uladzislau, and Dimitry Kochenov. 2016. On the 'Entry Options' for the 'Right to Love': Federalizing Legal Opportunities for LGBT Movements in the EU. 2016/9. EUI Working Paper Law. San Domenico di Fiesole: European University Institute. http://cadmus.eui.eu//handle/1814/40368.

Bell, Chloe, and Nika Selanec. 2016. Who Is a "Spouse" Under the Citizens' Rights Directive? The Prospect of Mutual Recognition of Same-Sex Marriages in the EU. *European Law Review* 5: 655–686.

Bell, Mark. 2002. *Anti-discrimination Law and the European Union*. Oxford: Oxford University Press.

Bell, Mark. 2012. Gender Identity and Sexual Orientation: Alternative Pathways in EU Equality Law. *The American Journal of Comparative Law* 60 (1): 127–146.

Busquets Guàrdia, Arnau. 2016. How Brexit Vote Broke Down. *Politico*, June 24, 2016. https://www.politico.eu/article/graphics-how-the-uk-voted-eu-referendum-brexit-demographics-age-education-party-london-final-results/.

Conforti, Benedetto. 2013. The Specificity of Human Rights and International Law. In *From Bilateralism to Community Interest: Essays in Honour of Bruno Simma*, ed. Ulrich Fastenrath, Rudolf Geiger, Daniel-Erasmus Khan, Andreas Paulus, Sabine von Schorlemer, and Christoph Vedder, 433–442. Oxford: Oxford University Press.

Cooper, Jonathan. 2018. Why Is No One Talking About the Brexit Threat to LGBT Rights? Jonathan Cooper. *The Guardian*, January 22, 2018. http://www.theguardian.com/commentisfree/2018/jan/22/eu-protection-lgbt-people-persecution-withdrawal-bill-lgbt-gay-rights.

Cooper, Jonathan, Peter Dunne, Anya Palmer, and Keina Yoshida. 2018. *Brexit: The LGBT Impact Assessment*. London: Gay Star News. https://www.gay-starnews.com/wp-content/uploads/2018/04/LGBT-RIGHTS-AND-LEAVING-THE-EUROPEAN-UNION-REPORT.pdf.

Council of the European Union. 2013. Guidelines to Promote and Protect the Enjoyment of All Human Rights by Lesbian, Gay, Bisexual, Transgender and Intersex (LGBTI) Persons, Foreign Affairs Council Meeting 24 June 2013. Luxembourg.

Curtis, John, Paul Bowers, Terry McGuinness, and Dominic Webb. 2017. Brexit Negotiations: The Irish Border Question. House of Commons Library Briefing Paper. Number 8042. UK Parliament. http://researchbriefings.parliament.uk/ResearchBriefing/Summary/CBP-8042#fullreport.

Danisi, Carmelo. 2015. *Tutela Dei Diritti Umani, Non Discriminazione e Orientamento Sessuale*. Napoli: Editoriale Scientifica.

Danisi, Carmelo. 2017. Contextualising Non-discrimation: Towards a New Approach for Sexual Minorities Under the ECHR? In *The European Convention on Human Rights and the Principle of Non-Discrimination*, ed. Marco Balboni, 197–232. Napoli: Editoriale Scientifica.

Danisi, Carmelo, Moira Dustin, and Nuno Ferreira. 2017. Queering Brexit. *The UK in a Changing Europe* (blog). October 26, 2017. http://ukandeu.ac.uk/queering-brexit/.

Davis, Chantal, Nuno Ferreira, Debra Morris, and Anne Morris. 2016. The Equality Act 2010: Five Years On. *International Journal of Discrimination and the Law* 16 (2–3): 61–65.

De Schutter, Oliver. 2011. *Exploring the Lisbon Treaty: New Opportunities for Equality and Human Rights Applied to Sexual Orientation and Gender Identity*. Brussels: ILGA-Europe. https://www.ilga-europe.org/sites/default/files/exploring_the_lisbon_treaty.pdf.

Department for Digital, Culture, Media and Sport. 2013. Comprehensive Review of the Equality and Human Rights Commission's (EHRC's) Budget. https://www.gov.uk/government/publications/comprehensive-review-of-the-equality-and-human-rights-commission-s-ehrcs-budget.

Department for Exiting the European Union. 2017. The Repeal Bill. Factsheet 6: Charter of Fundamental Rights. https://www.gov.uk/government/uploads/

system/uploads/attachment_data/file/642866/Factsheets_-_Charter_of_Fundamental_Rights.pdf.

EHRC—Equality and Human Rights Commission. 2017. Measurement Framework for Equality and Human Rights. https://www.equalityhuman-rights.com/sites/default/files/measurement-framework-interactive_1.pdf.

Elgstrom, Ole. 2005. Consolidating 'Unobjectionable' Norms: Negotiating Norm Spread in the EU. In *European Union Negotiations: Process, Networks and Institutions*, ed. Ole Elgstrom and Christer Jonsson, 29–44. London: Routledge.

Equinet. 2015. Joint Appeal to the German Federal Government. Towards a Consistent Level of Protection Against Discrimination in Europe Overcoming Germany's Blocking of the Proposed Equal Treatment Directive. http://www.equineteurope.org/IMG/pdf/20150723_joint_statement_en.pdf.

European Commission. 2015a. *Combating Sexual Orientation Discrimination in the European Union.* Luxembourg: Publications Office of the European Union.

European Commission. 2015b. List of Actions by the Commission to Advance LGBTI Equality. http://ec.europa.eu/justice/discrimination/files/lgbti_actionlist_en.pdf.

European Commission. 2016. Communication from the Commission to the European Parliament and the Council—2016 Communication on EU Enlargement Policy, 9 November 2016, COM(2016) 715 Final. https://eur-lex.europa.eu/legal-content/en/ALL/?uri=CELEX:52016DC0715.

European Parliament. 2011. Sexual Orientation and Gender Identity at the UN Human Rights Council: European Parliament Resolution of 28 September 2011 on Human Rights, Sexual Orientation and Gender Identity at the United Nations (P7_TA(2011)0427). http://www.europarl.europa.eu/sides/getDoc.do?pubRef=-//EP//NONSGML+TA+P7-TA-2011-0427+0+DOC+PDF+V0//EN.

European Parliament. 2012a. Annual Report on Human Rights in the World and the European Union's Policy on the Matter, Including Implications for the EU's Strategic Human Rights Policy: European Parliament Resolution of 18 April 2012 on the Annual Report on Human Rights in the World and the European Union's Policy on the Matter, Including Implications for the EU's Strategic Human Rights Policy (P7_TA(2012)0126). http://www.europarl.europa.eu/sides/getDoc.do?type=TA&reference=P7-TA-2012-0126&language=EN.

European Parliament. 2012b. *Towards an EU Roadmap for Equality on Grounds of Sexual Orientation and Gender Identity—Study.* Directorate General for Internal Policies, Policy Department C: Citizens' Rights and Constitutional Affairs. Civil Liberties, Justice and Home Affairs. Brussels: European Parliament. http://www.europarl.europa.eu/RegData/etudes/etudes/join/2012/462482/IPOL-LIBE_ET%282012%29462482_EN.pdf.

European Parliament. 2014. Report on the EU Roadmap Against Homophobia and Discrimination on Grounds of Sexual Orientation and Gender Identity:

European Parliament Resolution of 4 February 2014 on the EU Roadmap Against Homophobia and Discrimination on Grounds of Sexual Orientation and Gender Identity (P7_TA(2014)0062). http://www.europarl.europa.eu/sides/getDoc.do?type=TA&reference=P7-TA-2014-0062&language=EN.

European Parliament. 2017. Annual Report on Human Rights and Democracy in the World 2016 and the European Union's Policy on the Matter—European Parliament Resolution of 13 December 2017 on the Annual Report on Human Rights and Democracy in the World 2016 and the European Union's Policy on the Matter (P8_TA(2017)0494). http://www.europarl.europa.eu/sides/getDoc.do?type=TA&reference=P8-TA-2017-0494&language=EN.

Favilli, Chiara. 2008. *La Non Discriminazione Nell'Unione Europea*. Bologna: Il Mulino.

Fawcett Society. 2018. Sex Discrimination Law Review. https://www.fawcettsociety.org.uk/Handlers/Download.ashx?IDMF=e473a103-28c1-4a6c-aa43-5099d34c0116.

Fenwick, Helen, and Roger Masterman. 2017. The Conservative Project to 'Break the Link Between British Courts and Strasbourg': Rhetoric or Reality? *The Modern Law Review* 80 (6): 1111–1136.

Ferreira, Nuno. 2018. Sexuality and Citizenship in Europe: Sociolegal and Human Rights Perspectives. *Social & Legal Studies* 27 (2): 253–265.

Ferreira, Nuno, and Denise Venturi. 2017. Tell Me What You See and I'll Tell You If You're Gay: Analysing the Advocate General's Opinion in Case C-473/16, F v Bevándorlási És Állampolgársági Hivatal. *EU Immigration and Asylum Law and Policy* (blog). November 24, 2017. http://eumigrationlawblog.eu/tell-me-what-you-see-and-ill-tell-you-if-youre-gay-analysing-the-advocate-generals-opinion-in-case-c-47316-f-v-bevandorlasi-es-allampolgarsagi-hivatal/.

Ferreira, Nuno, Carmelo Danisi, Moira Dustin, and Nina Held. 2018. *The Reform of the Common European Asylum System: Fifteen Recommendations from a Sexual Orientation and Gender Identity Perspective*. Brighton: SOGICA/University of Sussex.

FRA—European Union Agency for Fundamental Rights. 2015. *Protection Against Discrimination on Grounds of Sexual Orientation, Gender Identity and Sex Characteristics in the EU—Comparative Legal Analysis*. Luxembourg: Publications Office of the European Union. http://fra.europa.eu/en/publication/2015/lgbti-comparative-legal-update-2015.

FRA—European Union Agency for Fundamental Rights. 2017. Current Migration Situation in the EU: Lesbian, Gay, Bisexual, Transgender and Intersex Asylum Seekers. FRA—European Union Agency for Fundamental Rights. http://fra.europa.eu/en/publication/2017/march-monthly-migration-focus-lgbti.

Fredman, Sandra. 2001. Equality: A New Generation? *Industrial Law Journal* 30 (2): 145–168.

Fredman, Sandra. 2011. The Public Sector Equality Duty. *Industrial Law Journal* 40 (4): 405–427.

Galop. 2016. Written Evidence Submitted by Galop, the LGBT Anti-Violence Charity. Hate Crime and Its Violent Consequences Inquiry—Home Affairs Committee. http://data.parliament.uk/writtenevidence/committeeevidence. svc/evidencedocument/home-affairs-committee/hate-crime-and-its-violent-consequences/written/36588.pdf.

Gay Times. 2016. 30 LGBTI MPs and Peers Call for Britain to Stay in the EU. May 17, 2016. http://www.gaytimes.co.uk/news/36673/ 30-lgbti-mps-peers-call-britain-stay-eu/.

Goodwin, Matthew, and Oliver Heath. 2016. Brexit Vote Explained: Poverty, Low Skills and Lack of Opportunities. JRF. August 26, 2016. https://www.jrf.org.uk/report/brexit-vote-explained-poverty-low-skills-and-lack-opportunities.

Government Equalities Office. 2017. New Action to Promote LGBT Equality. July 23, 2017. https://www.gov.uk/government/news/new-action-to-promote-lgbt-equality.

Guerrina, Roberta, and Annick Masselot. 2018. Walking into the Footprint of EU Law: Unpacking the Gendered Consequences of Brexit. *Social Policy & Society* 17 (2): 319–330.

Hepple, Bob. 2014. *Equality: The Legal Framework.* 2nd Rev. ed. Oxford, UK: Hart Publishing. https://www.amazon.co.uk/Equality-Legal-Framework-Bob-Hepple/dp/1849466394.

Home Affairs Committee. 2016. Inquiry into Hate Crime and Its Violent Consequences Launched—News from Parliament. UK Parliament. July 4, 2016. https://www.parliament.uk/business/committees/committees-a-z/ commons-select/home-affairs-committee/news-parliament-2015/ 160704-new-inquiry-hate-crime/.

Home Office. 1957. Report of the Committee on Homosexual Offences and Prostitution (The Wolfenden Report). https://www.parliament.uk/about/ living-heritage/transformingsociety/private-lives/relationships/collections1/ sexual-offences-act-1967/wolfenden-report-/.

Home Office. 2012. Written Statement to Parliament. Equalities Red Tape Challenge and Reform of the Equality and Human Rights Commission: Outcome. https:// www.gov.uk/government/speeches/equalities-red-tape-challenge-and-reform-of-the-equality-and-human-rights-commission-outcome.

Home Office. 2016. Action Against Hate. The UK Government's Plan for Tackling Hate Crime. https://www.gov.uk/government/uploads/system/ uploads/attachment_data/file/543679/Action_Against_Hate_-_UK_ Government_s_Plan_to_Tackle_Hate_Crime_2016.pdf.

House of Commons Justice Committee. 2015. Impact of Changes to Civil Legal
    Aid under Part 1 of the Legal Aid, Sentencing and Punishment of Offenders Act
    2012, Eighth Report of Session 2014–15, Report, Together with Formal Minutes,
    Ordered by the House of Commons to Be Printed 4 March 2015. https://publi-
    cations.parliament.uk/pa/cm201415/cmselect/cmjust/311/311.pdf.
Human Rights Consortium. 2018. Rights at Risk. Brexit, Human Rights and
    Northern Ireland. http://www.humanrightsconsortium.org/wp-content/
    uploads/2018/01/RIGHTS-AT-RISK-Final.pdf.
Hungarian Helsinki Committee. 2013. *Credibility Assessment in Asylum
    Procedures–A Multidisciplinary Training Manual*, vol. 1. http://www.ref-
    world.org/docid/5253bd9a4.html.
ILGA—International Lesbian, Gay, Bisexual, Trans and Intersex Association,
    Aengus Carroll, and Lucas Ramón Mendos. 2017. *State-Sponsored
    Homophobia—A World Survey of Sexual Orientation Laws: Criminalisation,
    Protection and Recognition*. Geneva: ILGA. http://ilga.org/downloads/
    2017/ILGA_State_Sponsored_Homophobia_2017_WEB.pdf.
Ipsos MORI. 2017. Shifting Ground: Attitudes Towards Immigration and
    Brexit. https://www.ipsos.com/ipsos-mori/en-uk/shifting-ground-attitudes-
    towards-immigration-and-brexit.
Kirby, Michael. 2009. Legal Discrimination Against Homosexuals—A Blind Spot
    of the Commonwealth of Nations? *European Human Rights Law Review* 1:
    21–36.
Lambert, Harry. 2016. EU Referendum Result: 7 Graphs That Explain How
    Brexit Won. *The Independent*, June 24, 2016. http://www.independent.
    co.uk/news/uk/politics/eu-referendum-result-7-graphs-that-explain-how-
    brexit-won-eu-explained-a7101676.html.
McCrudden, Christopher. 2017. The Belfast-Good Friday Agreement,
    Brexit, and Rights. *SSRN Electronic Journal*. https://doi.org/10.2139/
    ssrn.3075206.
McGill, Andrew. 2016. Who Voted for the Brexit? *The Atlantic*, June 25,
    2016. https://www.theatlantic.com/international/archive/2016/06/
    brexit-vote-statistics-united-kingdom-european-union/488780/.
Moran, Leslie. 1996. *The Homosexual(Ity) of Law*. 1st ed. London; New York:
    Routledge.
Mos, Martijn. 2014. Of Gay Rights and Christmas Ornaments: The Political
    History of Sexual Orientation Non-discrimination in the Treaty of
    Amsterdam. *Journal of Common Market Studies* 52 (3): 632–649.
Office for National Statistics. 2017a. Sexual Identity, UK: 2016. https://www.
    ons.gov.uk/peoplepopulationandcommunity/culturalidentity/sexuality/
    bulletins/sexualidentityuk/2016.

Office for National Statistics. 2017b. 2021 Census Topic Research: December 2017—Office for National Statistics. December 2017. https://www.ons.gov.uk/census/censustransformationprogramme/questiondevelopment/2021censustopicresearchdecember2017.

Out & Proud. n.d. Out & Proud. http://out-andproud.squarespace.com/news/.

Privot, Michael, and Allan Pall. 2014. Three Ways to Unlock the EU Anti-discrimination Bill. EU Observer. https://euobserver.com/opinion/127033.

Puar, Jasbir K. 2007. *Terrorist Assemblages: Homonationalism in Queer Times.* Durham; London: Duke University Press.

Race Equality Coalition. 2013. The Race Equality Coalition: PSED Review Submission. http://www.raceequalityfoundation.org.uk/sites/default/files/editor/Race%20Equality%20Coalition%20Submission%20to%20the%20PSED%20review.pdf.

Robertson, Douglas. 2018. Homophobia Is Alive across the Commonwealth—But Our Colonialist Past Makes It Difficult to Solve. *The Independent,* 17 April 2018 edition.

Rossi, Lucia Serena, and Federico Casolari (eds.). 2017. *The Principle of Equality in EU Law.* Basel: Springer International Publishing.

Schiek, Dagmar. 2006. The ECJ Decision in Mangold: A Further Twist on Effects of Directives and Constitutional Relevance of Community Equality Legislation. *Industrial Law Journal* 35 (3): 329–341.

Smith, Karen E. 2015. The EU as a Diplomatic Actor in the Field of Human Rights. In *The European Union as a Diplomatic Actor,* ed. Joachim Koops and Gjovalin Macaj, 155–177. London: Palgrave Macmillan.

Spaventa, Eleanor. 2016. *The Interpretation of Article 51 of the EU Charter of Fundamental Rights: The Dilemma of Stricter or Broader Application of the Charter to National Measures.* Brussels: European Parliament.

Spencer, Sarah. 2008. Equality and Human Rights Commission: A Decade in the Making. *The Political Quarterly* 79 (1): 6–16.

Stonewall. 2017. Hate Crime against LGBT People in Britain Increases by 78 Per Cent Since 2013. Stonewall. September 7, 2017. http://www.stonewall.org.uk/news/hate-crime-against-lgbt-people-britain-increases-78-cent-2013.

The Conservative Party. 2017. The Conservative Party Manifesto 2017. https://www.conservatives.com/manifesto.

Tridimas, Takis. 2006. *The General Principles of EU Law.* Oxford: Oxford University Press.

TUC—Trade Union Congress. 2018. LGBT + Equality: Risks of Brexit. TUC—Trade Union Congress. http://www.edf.org.uk/trade-union-congress-report-brexit-and-lgbt-rights/.

UN Human Rights Committee. 1997. General Comment No. 26: Continuity of Obligations. CCPR/C/21/Rev.1/Add.8/Rev.1.

UNHCR—UN High Commissioner for Refugees. 2012. Guidelines on International Protection No. 9: Claims to Refugee Status Based on Sexual

Orientation and/or Gender Identity Within the Context of Article 1A(2) of the 1951 Convention and/or Its 1967 Protocol Relating to the Status of Refugees (HCR/GIP/12/09). http://www.unhcr.org/509136ca9.pdf.

University of Sussex. n.d. Sussex Hate Crime Project: University of Sussex. http://www.sussex.ac.uk/psychology/sussexhatecrimeproject/.

van den Brink, Martin. 2016. What's in a Name Case? Some Lessons for the Debate Over the Free Movement of Same-Sex Couples Within the EU. *German Law Journal* 17 (3): 421–450.

Waibel, Michael. 2017. Brexit and Acquired Rights. *AJIL Unbound* 111: 440–444.

Wintemute, Robert. 2016. Goodbye EU Anti-discrimination Law? Hello Repeal of the Equality Act 2010? *King's Law Journal* 27 (3): 387–397.

Women and Equalities Committee. 2016. Transgender Equality Inquiry. https://www.parliament.uk/business/committees/committees-a-z/commons-select/women-and-equalities-committee/inquiries/parliament-2015/transgender-equality/.

CHAPTER 11

Brexit: The Likely Impact on Sexual Orientation and Gender Identity Rights in the United Kingdom

Peter Dunne

1 Introduction

This chapter explores the potential impact of Brexit—the process by which the United Kingdom will leave (in early 2019) the European Union—on lesbian, gay, bisexual, transgender (trans), queer and intersex (hereinafter referred to as 'LGBTQI' or 'queer') populations. The chapter identifies key questions of legal and policy importance for queer lives in Britain, and considers how renouncing EU membership may hinder (or help) UK policymakers in finding appropriate resolutions.

Over the past 25 years, the European Union has revealed itself as a (perhaps unlikely) LGBTQI advocate (Boele-Woelki 2008; Barrie 2013; Tryfonidou 2017; O'Cinneide 2015). Queer rights protections are visible at every level of EU law—primary legislation, secondary legislation and in the jurisprudence of the Court of Justice of the European Union (CJEU).

P. Dunne (✉)
University of Bristol Law School, Bristol, UK
e-mail: pd17563@bristol.ac.uk

© The Author(s) 2019
M. Dustin et al. (eds.), *Gender and Queer Perspectives on Brexit*,
Gender and Politics, https://doi.org/10.1007/978-3-030-03122-0_11

Article 10 of the Treaty on the Functioning of the European Union (TFEU) expressly acknowledges that, '[i]n defining and implementing its policies and activities, the Union shall aim to combat discrimination based on... sexual orientation.' Article 10 TFEU is reinforced through a subsequent provision (Article 19(1) TFEU) which empowers EU legislators to 'take appropriate action to combat discrimination based on... sexual orientation.' Read in conjunction with the non-discrimination guarantee in Article 21(1) of the EU Charter of Fundamental Rights, these protections are—in the legal foundations of the Union—a strong affirmation of sexual orientation rights, and recognition of the equal dignity of lesbian, gay and bisexual citizens.

Treaty (and Charter) references to LGB lives have now been buttressed through secondary legislative interventions and case law. Not only have these latter sources of protection further enhanced the entitlements of gay, lesbian and bisexual persons, they have also explicitly embraced and acknowledged the status of trans populations (or, at the very least, those who have the protected characteristic of 'gender reassignment'). Within EU law, particularly important queer-inclusive legislation includes Directive 78/2000 (which extends employment protections to lesbian, gay and bisexual individuals), Directives 2004/83[1] and 2011/95 (which bring sexual and gender minorities within the scope of 'particular social group' for asylum law) and Directive 2006/54 (paragraph 3 of the recitals to which recognises trans experiences within the principle of equal treatment between men and women).

There is also extensive case law in areas, such as employment protections (*P v S and Cornwall County Council*,[2] *KB v NHS Pensions*,[3] *Richards v Secretary of State for Work and Pensions*[4] and *Asociatia ACCEPT v Consiliul National pentru Combaterea Discriminarii*[5]), employment-based partnership rights (*Maruko v VDB*,[6] *Jürgen Römer v Freie und Hansestadt*

---

[1] Article 10(1)(d).

[2] Judgment of the 30 April 1996, Case C-13/94, EU:C:1996:170.

[3] Judgment of the 7 January 2004, Case C-117/01, EU:C:2004:7.

[4] Judgment of the 27 April 2006, Case C-423/04, EU:C:2006:256.

[5] Judgment of the 25 April 2013, Case C-81/12, EU:C:2013:275.

[6] Judgment of the 1 April 2008, Case C-267/06, EU:C:2008:179.

Hamburg[7] and *Hay v Credit Agricole*[8]), immigration practices (*X, Y and Z*[9]; *A, B and C*[10]; *F v Bevándorlási és Állampolgársági Hivatal*[11]) and gay male blood donations (Leger[12]). This body of law and judgments represents substantial (and often ground-breaking [Lardy and Campbell 1996; Tobler and Waaldijk 2009; Chelvan 2014]) queer rights reforms and, at least within certain spheres, has transformed the position and entitlements of LGBTQI populations.

The European Union's queer-focused legal reforms have had tangible impacts upon LGBTQI entitlements in the United Kingdom (this is in spite of claims, during the Brexit referendum campaign, from actors, such as Boris Johnson, that Union law has little relevance for queer populations (Morris 2016)). Core guarantees, such as employment non-discrimination rights, initially secured for UK LGBTQI persons by the EU, are now enshrined in domestic equality legislation (Equality Act 2010, ss. 7 and 12). In 2017, the continuing benefits of Union membership were once again evident when, in *Walker v Innospec*, the UK Supreme Court drew upon the general principle of non-discrimination, as enshrined in Directive 2000/78, to set aside paragraph 9 of Schedule 18 to the 2010 Act, which had created unequal spousal pension rights between opposite-sex and same-sex married couples.[13]

Given the European Union's prioritisation of LGBTQI rights, and the impact which EU law has had upon UK queer communities, there has been—in the wake of Brexit—significant concern that leaving the EU will create a deficit in sexual and gender minority rights (Cooper 2018; Wintemute 2016). These fears were heightened when, in the immediate aftermath of the 2016 vote, there was a sharp upswing in reported incidents of abuse targeted against queer persons across the UK (Townsend 2016; Stone 2016). Observers have expressed fears that, without the over-arching supervision of Europe, LGBTIQ communities will face growing acts of private (and state-approved) discrimination (Cooper 2018).

---

[7] Judgment of the 10 May 2011, Case C-147/08, EU:C:2011:286.

[8] Judgment of the 12 December 2013, Case C-267/12, EU:C:2013:823.

[9] Judgment of 7 November 2013, Cast C-199/12, EU:C:2013:720.

[10] Judgment of 2 December 2014, Joined Cases C-148/13—C-150/13, EU:C:2013:2406.

[11] Judgment of 25 January 2018, Case C-473/16, EU:C:2018:36.

[12] Judgment of 29 April 2015, Case C-528/13, EU:C:2015:288.

[13] [2018] 1 CMLR 26.

This chapter interrogates the potential impact of Brexit on sexual orientation and gender identity rights in the United Kingdom. The chapter is divided into two substantive sections—the first of which identifies the limited *legal* consequences of exiting the Union, while the second acknowledges the legitimacy of soft law and foreign policy concerns. The aim of the chapter is not to downplay the likely negative consequences of Brexit—which, given the comparative precarity of many LGBTQI individuals, are likely to fall particularly hard on queer populations (Uhrig 2013; Scottish Government 2013). Rather, the chapter seeks to understand the actual relationship between UK LGBTQI rights and the European Union, and asks how those rights will be affected when the relationship dissolves in 2019.

2   Interrogating the Negative Consequences of Brexit for UK Queer Populations

It is clear from the introductory section that both: (a) European Union law has enhanced queer rights throughout the 28 Member States; and (b) that law has, in particular, touched the lives of queer persons in the UK. However, to acknowledge the beneficial role of EU legislation and case law—generally and in a UK-specific context—is not to automatically concede that Brexit will have inevitably negative 'queer consequences'. To argue the potentially detrimental queer impact of leaving the European Union, it is not sufficient merely to prove that EU institutions and jurisprudence have been a positive influence. Rather, one must be able to go a step further, illustrating how Brexit will result in the roll-back of LGBTQI protections. In Sect. 2, this chapter suggests that there is (at least an arguable) case that, although separating from the EU may deprive UK queers of future rights developments, Brexit is unlikely to substantially diminish the status and entitlements of LGBTQI populations.

Lack of Political Will to Repeal LGBTQI Rights

Perhaps the strongest indicator against a post-Brexit (mass) repeal of current LGBTQI rights is the apparent lack of political appetite for reform. While, over the past decade, different actors—both political and judicial—have criticised (what they perceive to be) the imposition of queer rights on the UK's legal system (although, most critiques have been directed towards the European Convention on Human Rights (Sumption 2013; Worley 2016)), there are few (if any) movements to reduce or withdraw existing protections based on sexual orientation and gender identity. In a very real sense, queer rights have become enshrined as a core touchstone of contemporary UK politics, and one which seemingly transcends party-political and ideological divides.

In 2018, LGBTQI concerns are now integrated into the policy frameworks of (nearly) all UK-wide (e.g. Conservative Party, Labour Party, etc.) and region-specific (e.g. Scottish National Party, Sinn Fèin, Democratic Unionist Party, etc.) political groups. Most parties have an LGBTQI-affiliation wing, and often play visible roles in LGBTQI Pride celebrations. Supportive events for queer populations regularly take place in government buildings (UK Government 2017a), and the current speaker of the House of Commons, John Bercow MP, has been noted for promoting the equality of sexual and gender minorities (de Peyer 2014).

From a situation where, only half a century ago, the (partial and limited) decriminalisation of same-sex sexual intercourse was a source of immense political division (Dockray and Sutton 2017), the current reality is one in which even ambiguous attitudes towards LGBTQI rights are likely to hinder most UK politicians (the recent example of Tim Farron MP, the former leader of the Liberal Democrat Party, who was roundly criticized for acknowledging conflicts between homosexuality and his Christian faith, is a cautionary tale (Khomami 2017)). It is important to remember that when, in the mid-1990s, EU Member States and institutions were debating the inclusion of 'sexual orientation' in the Treaty of Amsterdam, John Major's government was a staunch opponent of increasing EU powers to legislate for gay equality (at the time, the infamous s. 28 of the Local Government Act was still in force) (Mos 2014, 643–644). Twenty years later, current UK equality legislation, the Equality Act 2010, extends substantially beyond what existing EU law requires in terms of protecting gay, lesbian and bisexual persons who access goods and services. In 2015, when the newly-formed House of Commons Select Committee on Women and Equalities launched its first inquiry, it explored lived experiences of gender recognition—a right which did not exist in the United Kingdom until 2004 (House of Commons Select Committee on Women and Equalities 2016, 11–22). While this sea change in social and political attitudes is undoubtedly attributable (at least in part) to the open, diverse culture which membership of the European Union has fostered, leaving the EU does not appear to signify any move towards queer rights reform.

Even if—as part of the Brexit process—clearer homophobic or transphobic intentions were evident, queer civil society in the United Kingdom is now (as compared with when the UK entered the EU) better-placed to defend against anti-LGBTQI initiatives. As noted, in 1973, same-sex sexual relations (between men) had only been (partially) lawful in England and Wales for six years. Such conduct remained contrary to the law in Scotland and Northern Ireland. While, at the time, well-known, vocal organisations were campaigning for queer rights equality (Cook 2007; Kollman and Waites 2011), they operated in an environment which, at best, encouraged and facilitated their marginalisation and which, at worst, expressed open hostility. In such a climate, there was (as the landmark litigation in *Dudgeon v United Kingdom*[14] proves) a significant need for supra-national oversight—the European Union and the Council of Europe reviewing the UK's treatment of queer communities to ensure basic rights and freedoms.

In 2018, however, the status and political voice of LGBTQI civil society is noticeably enhanced. Queer rights organisations, both UK-wide and regional, are well-funded, well-staffed and politically experienced. Groups such as Stonewall (which admittedly has had a troubled history vis-à-vis the trans community (Gani 2015)), routinely collaborate with policy-makers, seeking to ensure no legislation or policy *about* LGBTQI persons is made *without* those persons. High-profile advocates are frequently invited to contribute expert testimony to Parliament and they can express their views through mainstream print (Jones 2017; Staples 2018) and onscreen media (BBC Newsnight 2018; Channel 4 News 2016).

Overall, when considering the almost five decades of UK membership in the European Union, one can identify the gradual emergence of a confident, well-organised queer civil society. Indeed, perhaps one of the significant legacies of the EU's impact on UK society will be the emergence—both in the area of queer rights and on other human rights questions—of a strong advocacy voice which, even in the absence of EU regulatory frameworks and without EU rights protections, is capable of holding Parliament to account and ensuring that law-makers respect core values.

---

[14][1981] 3 EHRR 40.

Political Will: Two Caveats

The foregoing 'political will' arguments are, however, subject to two important caveats—one practical, one more politically speculative.

The first caveat is an acknowledgment that the above claims are based upon a perceived lack of legislative desire for major LGBTQI reforms. In short: looking at the current make-up of the House of Commons (even with the minority Government's reliance upon Democratic Unionist Party support), there is no evident appetite for statutory withdrawal of key LGBTQI entitlements (e.g. marriage rights, gender recognition, non-discrimination). It is unlikely that, even within a comparatively more flexible law-making framework post-Brexit, homophobic or transphobic bills will command majority support. However, such arguments must recognise the many ways in which, after 2019, Parliament (but more particularly the Government) could more subtly recalibrate existing sexual orientation and gender identity rights. As noted, in *Walker v Innospec*, the UK Supreme Court refused to apply paragraph 18 of Schedule 9 to the Equality Act 2010 to the extent that it violates the general principle of non-discrimination, as given expression in Directive 2000/78.[15] Post-Brexit, will Parliament reapply the 'paragraph 18' rule (Wintemute 2016, 392; Tayleur 2017)? It is not inconceivable that such action could be taken—not as a policy of overt homophobia, but under a more vague principle of restoring parliamentary sovereignty over activist European courts and law-makers. Similarly, there are additional questions about what small, yet significant, changes ministers might seek to introduce if the final 'Great Repeal Bill' includes extensive Henry VIII Clauses (as the Government is currently arguing for (Kouroutakis 2018)).

The second caveat is an acknowledgment that 'political will' arguments may also take an overly benign view of current government intentions towards queer populations. Such arguments are (evidently) grounded in a belief (perhaps naïve) that, despite its troubled past, the modern Tory party has now reached a position where, while it might not be a full-throated LGBTQI advocate, it has accepted certain, core entitlements to which queer communities must have access (this appeared to be the position under the Cameron-Osbourne leadership, 2005–2016).

[15][2018] 1 CMLR 26.

There are, however, other indicators which press against such optimism (Wintemute 2016, 396–397). Brexit is being spear-headed by a Tory party leader, and Prime Minister, who has a chequered voting history for sexual orientation and gender identity rights. Theresa May voted against an equal age of consent and against the introduction of gay adoption (Saeed 2017; Mortimer 2017). Despite her recent commitment to more accessible gender recognition processes, the Prime Minister actually abstained from the parliamentary vote when the Gender Recognition Act 2004 passed the House of Commons (Duffy 2017; Meyjes 2017). In addition, Theresa May has appointed a cabinet, where the main Brexit players (i.e. those with responsibility for shaping the contours of Brexit), including David Davis MP and Liam Fox MP, voted against the recent introduction of marriage equality. Indeed, although the Tory party was the majority partner in the 2010–2015 coalition government (and, therefore, same-sex marriage was their own initiative), a majority of Conservative Members of Parliament actually rejected the Marriage (Same-Sex Couples) Act 2013 (Rogers 2013; BBC 2013). Thus, while the political and social landscape for UK queers—both in terms of Westminster engagement and increasing civil society power—has undoubtedly improved, this chapter does not deny the potential for anti-LGBTQI opportunism in the post-Brexit era.

Sources of LGBTQI Rights Reform in the United Kingdom

In the introductory section, this chapter identified the existing corpus of queer-focused laws in the European Union, and their direct (and indirect) impact on the UK's LGBTQI frameworks. Against that backdrop, it is hard to deny that the EU has improved the rights and lived experiences of queer communities across the United Kingdom, particularly in the sphere of employment rights.

At the same time, one must avoid overstating how much the Union has improved or enhanced queer legal entitlements. Looking to major sexual orientation and gender identity reforms over the past four decades, these movements are striking for their weak links with EU jurisprudence (beyond the broad culture of legal diversity which that jurisprudence has inevitably encouraged). Instead, the catalyst for such reforms can be found in a multiplicity of additional national and supra-national sources. This is important because, if EU law has not required specific policies for LGBTQI rights, there is (at least in principle) no reason why those rights should be threatened post-Brexit.

Since the turn of the twenty-first century, the most contentious and high-profile legal development (but perhaps not the most important development in terms of queer realities) has been the introduction of marriage equality (Barker and Monk 2015; Gilbert 2014, 485–486). Less than ten years after the landmark Civil Partnership Act 2004, opening up marital unions to opposite-sex couples was considered a watershed moment for the equal worth and value of non-heterosexual relationships.

Yet, although marriage equality had already been enacted by a number of EU Member States by 2013, Union law was not a particularly influential consideration in debates on the Marriage (Same-Sex Couples) Act 2013 (and marriage equality certainly did not arise from any EU law requirement (Bell and Selanec 2016, 656)). Paragraph 22 of Directive 2000/78 expressly provides that the directive is 'without prejudice to national laws on marital status and the benefits dependent thereon.' While Article 9 of the EU Charter on Fundamental Rights does not exclude same-sex marriage possibilities, the accompanying 'Explanations' make clear that Article 9 'neither prohibits nor imposes the granting of the status of marriage to unions between people of the same sex' (Explanations 2007, C 303/21).

The decision to extend the definition of marital unions was the result of a political settlement—a decision taken by the 2010–2015 Tory-Lib Dem coalition government that (for a multitude of reasons—some altruistic, others no doubt political) permitting 'gay marriages' was a preferable course to maintaining the status quo. As such, it is difficult to foresee what immediate impact withdrawing from the European Union will have on existing marriage entitlements. The same is also true for other highly visible queer rights reforms, including gay adoption rights,[16] the incorporation of sexual orientation and gender identity into hate crimes law,[17] and extending non-discrimination protections to gay, lesbian and bisexual persons who access goods and services. While it is conceivable that Brexit will facilitate a political culture in which the beneficiaries of such reforms increasingly experience their rights under attack, the simple act of leaving the European Union will not result in (or require) immediate repeal.

In addition to political decision-making, another international actor—the European Court of Human Rights (ECtHR)—has had a

[16] Adoption and Children Act 2002, ss. 49 and 144(4).
[17] Criminal Justice Act 2003, s. 146.

substantial impact on queer rights in this jurisdiction, and certainly one which, in terms of scope and competence, has been broader than that of the EU (Johnson 2016). It was the Strasbourg judges who, in 1981, declared that Northern Ireland's continued criminalisation of consensual homosexual intercourse was a violation of Article 8 of the European Convention on Human Rights (ECHR).[18] In the following years, the ECtHR called upon the UK state to formally acknowledge the preferred gender of trans persons (*Goodwin v United Kingdom*[19]), apply an equal age of consent to homosexual and heterosexual sexual activities (*BB v United Kingdom*[20]), permit gay men to serve openly in the UK armed forces (*Smith and Grady v United Kingdom*[21]), and refrain from imposing increased child maintenance obligations on an ex-wife who formed a relationship with another woman (*JM v United Kingdom*[22]). Much in the same way that, irrespective of whether Brexit takes place, marriage equality rights will continue until the relevant political settlement falters, so too all the rights mentioned in this paragraph should remain until the United Kingdom renounces the European Convention on Human Rights: even if the current government repealed the Human Rights Act 1998, the UK would still be bound to respect these rights under public international law (House of Lords European Union Committee 2016, 8–10). Membership of the European Union has not required gender recognition or an equal age of consent, so leaving the EU should not (at least in theory) undermine those and other entitlements.

Resolution of Future LGBTQI Rights Disputes

A powerful queer-rights critique of Brexit is the loss of existing EU law instruments as a tool for resolving current and future LGBTQI disputes. While, as noted, the United Kingdom has experienced a (comparative) queer rights revolution while (but not always as a consequence of being) a member of the EU (Cretney 2006), many concerns relating to sexual orientation and gender identity remain. Post-Brexit, neither advocates nor judges (nor sympathetic politicians) will be able to rely upon current

---

[18] *Dudgeon v United Kingdom* [1981] 3 EHRR 40.

[19] [2002] 35 EHRR 18.

[20] [2004] 39 EHRR 30.

[21] [2000] 29 EHRR 493.

[22] [2011] 53 EHRR 6.

EU law standards to promote progressive LGBTQI reforms. However, surveying the many pressing issues that currently confront queer communities in the UK, it is not immediately obvious how Union law could affect their resolution. In this final part of Sect. 2, the chapter explores a number of outstanding LGBTQI questions (as well as the current corpus of EU law), and reflects upon how they will be influenced by Brexit.

The following discussion does not address—and is subject to—the caveat that EU law may (in new and transformative ways) develop in the future. Although existing Union rules may have little impact on outstanding LGBTQI concerns, future reforms and initiatives may develop novel EU solutions. This is a powerful observation, with particular relevance for the United Kingdom. The recent opinion of Advocate General Bobek in *MB v Secretary of State for Work and Pensions*,[23] suggesting that Britain's imposition of a divorce requirement prior to acknowledging a trans individual's preferred gender for the purposes of a retirement pension violates Directive 79/7, illustrates how European Union standards can evolve to embrace modern (and future) disputes. The analysis below does not deny this potential relevance of future EU law reforms. Instead, the analysis focuses on whether existing Union frameworks can influence contemporary UK LGBTQI debates.

Gender Recognition Reforms

In 2018, a particularly (politically) sensitive question for queer populations is reform proposals for the Gender Recognition Act 2004 (Dunne 2015; Stonewall 2017; Lewis 2017). Following recommendations from the House of Commons Select Committee on Women and Equalities (House of Commons Select Committee on Women and Equalities 2016, 14), the Government announced, in July 2017, that it would open a consultation on amending the 2004 Act—with the intention of moving towards a model of self-declaration (at present, under s. 2(1) of the statute, applicants for a Gender Recognition Certificate have to prove: (a) a diagnosis of gender dysphoria; and (b) that they have lived in their preferred gender for at least two years prior to their application) (UK Government 2017b). In November 2017, the Scottish Government confirmed that it too would consult on gender recognition reforms and, indeed, it subsequently carried out an on-line public survey, which closed on 1 March 2018 (Scottish Government 2017).

[23]Opinion of the 5 December 2017, Case C-451/16, EU:C:937.

While trans-focused equality was the first 'queer issue' which the European Court of Justice substantively addressed in its case law (*P v S and Cornwall*[24]), it is unclear what role EU law can play in contemporary UK debates on gender recognition. Judgments such as *KB v NHS Pension Service*[25] illustrate how, in certain defined situations, EU Member States—irrespective of whether they formally acknowledge one's preferred gender—must treat trans individuals (or at least those persons who have undertaken a process of 'gender reassignment') as having their lived identity status. However, the European Union (in its legislation or case law) does not, outside the scope of EU law, require the general (legal) affirmation of preferred gender. A Member State can fulfil its extensive Union obligations without providing an over-arching right to gender recognition—indeed, the Irish state withheld formal acknowledgment of preferred gender until 2015 without violating EU law (Sloan 2015).

In such circumstances, where the European Union does not create even a baseline, general 'recognition' entitlement, it is difficult to see what relevance EU law can have for the complex recognition debates that are taking place in the United Kingdom. If Union law does not require legal gender recognition, it cannot be determinative of whether such recognition should extend to children (House of Commons Select Committee on Women and Equalities 2016, 17–19) or be obtained through processes of self-determination (Valentine 2016).

In the context of trans rights, there is even (an arguable) potential in moving away from the shadow of European Union law. Within the domestic UK framework, the substantial body of EU trans non-discrimination jurisprudence is given effect through s. 7 of the Equality Act 2010. Section 7 sets out the protected characteristics of 'gender reassignment'—drawing specifically from EU case law and legislation, such as the Recitals to Directive 2006/54 (although it is important to acknowledge that 'gender reassignment' is a standalone characteristic in the 2010 Act, while, under EU law, 'gender reassignment' forms part of the wider concept of 'sex').

During the recent Transgender Equality Inquiry, a number of contributors voiced concerns with the terminology of 'reassignment' (see generally, House of Commons Select Committee on Women and Equalities

---

[24] Judgment of the 30 April 1996, Case C-13/94, EU:C:1996:170.

[25] Judgment of the 7 January 2004, Case C-117/01, EU:C:2004:7.

2016, 24–27). Their critiques focused on two distinct issues. First, despite the broad definition of 'gender reassignment' in s. 7, embracing those who undertake both physical and non-physical transition pathways, there is still a perception among trans populations that the Equality Act 2010 only covers those who have submitted to surgical intervention. While, on a basic reading of s. 7, this is incorrect, it is understandable that using the language of 'reassignment'—which has historically been linked to trans-focused surgery—might encourage this misperception. Second, there is also an additional, perhaps legitimate, fear that requiring 'reassignment'—whether viewed through the lens of EU jurisprudence or in the specific circumstances of s. 7—excludes persons with fluid or non-static experiences of gender. On its face, the notion of 'reassignment' does appear to suggest movement from one, rigid gender identity to another. If that is the case, however, do EU notions of trans equality leave behind non-binary populations (i.e. those who experience neither a male nor female gender)?

One potential benefit of Brexit could be pulling existing trans-equality protections from underneath the European ('reassignment'-focused) standard and embracing wider, more inclusive ideas of 'gender identity', 'gender expression' and 'sex characteristics' (this latter terminology would include intersex variance, and has been adopted by the Maltese Parliament in its landmark Gender Identity, Gender Expression and Sex Characteristics Act 2015, s. 19). Of course, it must be acknowledged, however, that even without leaving the European Union, Parliament could make such amendments to the structures of s. 7 of the Equality Act 2010. Having failed to engage in this reform up until now, there is nothing to suggest that law-makers (particularly within the context of a Conservative-DUP 'supply and demand' arrangement) are likely to expand s. 7 after Brexit.

Civil Partnership Reform

Another high-profile concern—grounded in considerations of sexual orientation, but impacting the lives of queer and non-queer populations alike—is the current exclusion of opposite-sex couples from civil partnerships (Draghici 2017; Ferguson 2016). This is a question which, in recent years, has gained increasing political visibility, and has now become a source of intense media debate (Burden and Gibb 2018; Thatchell 2018).

When, in 2004, Parliament enacted the institution of 'civil partnership' through the Civil Partnership Act 2004, it limited access to persons who had the same legal gender. The purpose of civil partnership (or at least a perceived purpose) was to create a comprehensive relationship recognition structure, while maintaining a public policy against same-sex marriages (Harding 2006). As noted, in 2013, Parliament opened up marital unions to same-sex couples. However, it maintained the current rules for contracting a civil union. Therefore, the law in England, Wales and Scotland now has a notable peculiarity whereby although, for much of history, queer populations have suffered from overt legal 'othering' and marginalisation, queer individuals (and queer couples) have enhanced formalisation options (Gaffney-Rhys 2014, 173–174). The UK government has justified the (facially discriminatory) disparity between same-sex and opposite-sex relationships on the basis of a 'wait and see'[26] policy: policy-makers should review the operation of queer marriages, and determine how best to proceed with civil partnership institutions (either abolition or expansion to heterosexual relationships).

For the purposes of this chapter, it is interesting to ask: what can European Union law offer to this (somewhat UK-specific) policy debate? The answer appears to be that EU law, even if the UK were to reject Brexit, has little if any role to play. Family law, including formalised relationship status, is one of the most significant areas of legal policy where there is little European-level harmonisation. Given the strong links between, on the one hand, conceptions of family and appropriate child-rearing and, on the other hand, national traditions and culture, the European Union (or at least the Member States of the European Union) has been reluctant to regulate private family relationships. While cases, such as *Maruko* and *Hay*, specify that, within the sphere of employment, employers cannot discriminate against persons who are in formalised same-sex relationships, which have the equivalent status of marriage, European Union law does not require that Member States introduce a queer-inclusive marriage or civil union regime. In such circumstances, it is difficult to see what benefit advocates for opposite-sex civil partnerships can draw from Union law (or what potential benefits they will lose in the post-Brexit era).

Instead, and in spite of the recent ECtHR judgment in *Ratzenbock and Seydl v Austria*,[27] such advocates would be better-served focusing

---

[26] *Steinfeld and Keidan v Secretary of State for Education* [2017] EWCA Civ 81, [3].

[27] App. No. 28745/12 (ECtHR, 26 October 2017).

their efforts on Article 14 ECHR, read in conjunction with Article 8 ECHR. This was the strategy adopted by the appellants in the recent appeal, *Steinfeld and Keidan v Secretary of State for Education*.[28] In that judgment (currently on appeal to the UK Supreme Court), a majority of the Court of Appeal (Lady Justice Arden in dissent[29]) held that, while the disparity between same-sex and opposite-sex couples potentially violates the European Convention, that violation is *currently* proportionate, having regard to the UK government's stated policy of 'wait and see.'[30]

The Intersection of LGBTQI Rights and Religious Freedom

Unlike in the United States (NeJaime and Siegel 2015), the incremental growth of LGBTQI rights across the United Kingdom over the past two decades has not resulted in a substantial religion-focused backlash. While the status of queer individuals within the Church of England—an established faith—has created tension (both among Anglicans and across the wider episcopal ministry) (Clucas 2012), the systematic extension of greater entitlements to queer individuals has not created a deep socio-religious divide in Britain.

It would, however, be misleading to suggest that expanding LGBTQI rights has been without *any* disagreement or legal controversy. In the area of service provision and the performance of public duties, some individuals have complained that queer equality rights require the compromise of faith-based living (Vickers 2010; Cooper and Herman 2013). Following enactment of the Equality Act (Sexual Orientation Regulations) 2007, which are ironically not required by European Union law, a number of religious-centred adoption agencies decided to withdraw their services rather than facilitate same-sex couples (Beckford 2010). Similarly, the ongoing litigation, *Lee v McArthur*,[31] in which a Christian-run bakery refused to produce a pro-marriage equality cake, has ignited public interest on the question of religious accommodations, and led certain politicians to advocate recalibrating legal relations between queer and faith-orientated communities (Williamson 2014).

---

[28] [2017] EWCA Civ 81.

[29] Ibid., [132].

[30] Ibid., [164] and [175].

[31] [2016] NICA 55.

The case is currently on appeal to the Supreme Court, after both the High Court and the Northern Ireland Court of Appeal concluded that there had been unlawful discrimination.

McArthur (and all similar disputes which pit LGBTQI individuals against persons who hold deep, genuine religious convictions) undoubtedly raises complex, politically important questions. The case relates to broad considerations which are not unknown to the CJEU—the Court has recently considered the permissibility of restrictions on wearing the Islamic veil.[32] However, reflecting upon the specific controversies and issues which arise in *McArthur* (and similar cases), what added value (on top of the extensive non-discrimination framework operating in Northern Ireland and generally mirrored in England and Wales) can EU law offer?

First, one must acknowledge that Northern Ireland (like the rest of the United Kingdom) already has a robust equality framework, which recognises both sexual orientation and religious equality rights.[33] In principle, therefore, any rights which Union law provides (and which may guide towards a resolution in *McArthur*) should already be incorporated into the existing national framework.

Second, and perhaps more importantly, it appears that the *McArthur* litigation actually falls outside the scope of EU law (UK non-discrimination law, including the specific laws in Northern Ireland, go beyond EU discrimination guarantees on the question of sexual orientation). While Directive 2000/78 provides robust protections for sexual minorities in employment, and while Directive 2004/113 extends sex equality guarantees to the provision of goods and services, there are currently no EU rules which extend non-discrimination standards in relation to persons who cannot obtain a good or service because of sexual orientation.

Finally, rather than looking to the European Union, a more productive strategy might be to consider the existing case law of the ECtHR. Indeed, both this latter court (*Ladele v United Kingdom, MacFarlane v United*

---

[32] Judgment of the 14 March 2017, *Achbita v G4S Secure Solutions NV*, Case C-157/15, EU:C:2017:203; Judgment of the 14 March 2017, *Bougnaoui v Micropole SA*, Case C-188/15, EU:C:2017:204.

[33] Equality Act (Sexual Orientation) Regulations (Northern Ireland) 2006 (S.R. No. 439 of 2006).

Kingdom[34]) and the UK Supreme Court (*Bull v Hall*[35]) have clarified the obligations on public servants and service providers who confront non-heterosexual sexual orientations (Wintemute 2014) (considering the existence of this substantial case law, it is unclear why disputes, such as *McArthur*, continue to create legal uncertainty in the United Kingdom).

Conclusions on the Resolution of Future LGBTQI Rights Disputes

The forgoing discussions illustrate how, although queer rights in the United Kingdom have substantially advanced over recent decades, outstanding concerns persist. To the specific examples noted above, one can add numerous other controversies, including the continued practice of genital normalizing surgeries on infants who experience intersex variance (Newbould 2016; Danisi 2017, 344–345) and the fraud-focused prosecution of trans individuals who do not reveal their gender history prior to engaging in sexual intercourse (Sharpe 2014). These issues (along with gender recognition reforms, civil partnership status and queer-religious disputes) have immediate and present impact upon the lived experiences of queer communities in the modern United Kingdom.

Yet, for each of the subjects mentioned, it is not fully apparent how, beyond promoting a general culture of queer-inclusiveness throughout its 28 Member States, the European Union (and its legal frameworks) provide a pathway towards resolution. In raising this point, this chapter does not seek to downplay the historic influence of Union law in facilitating important LGBTQI reforms. Indeed, the introductory section specifically recognises the multiple ways in which the European Union has tangibly enhanced queer rights in this jurisdiction. Nor does the chapter seek to reproduce or endorse the nationalistic 'British solutions to British problems' narrative which was a familiar feature of pro-Brexit campaigning. Instead, the above discussion has sought to highlight that, if one is arguing that Brexit will have *negative* consequences for certain queer rights in Britain, there must first (at least) be base-line evidence that EU law has *any* consequences for those rights. However, while the European Union has enhanced (and continues to enhance) gender and sexuality rights in defined sectors, it is unclear whether Union law has relevant answers for the UK's unresolved queer rights questions.

[34] [2013] 57 EHRR 8.
[35] [2013] UKSC 73.

3   Acknowledging Potential Disadvantage: Queer Lives and Queer Loss Post-Brexit

In Sect. 2, this chapter interrogated claims that Brexit and the United Kingdom renouncing membership of the European Union will have numerous, significant (negative) consequences for LGBTQI populations. Exploring existing political trends, the actual sources of queer rights in the UK, and the outstanding legal/social questions which require resolution, Sect. 2 proposed that (at least arguably) Brexit will have a less visible or appreciable impact than many commentators have suggested.

As has already been stressed, however, the aim of this chapter is not to minimise the general threats which Brexit poses to contemporary UK society, including the rights and lived experiences of queer-identified persons. Existing evidence indicates that, on many levels, leaving the European Union *will* tangibly harm the UK—its economy, global status and population. Where the wider United Kingdom suffers as a consequence of isolation from Union law and policies, queer communities will not be exempt from the accompanying detriment.

In Sect. 3, the chapter looks beyond the immediate, *legal* impact of leaving the European Union. Addressing soft law sources and external relations, Sect. 3 identifies ways in which queers (and queer equality) will be disadvantaged through severing ties with Union institutions and the other 27 Member States.

Soft Law and Soft Power

It is often too easy, when reflecting upon how the European Union has impacted sexual and gender minorities, to focus (almost exclusive) on 'law'. The idea of the Union as a queer rights actor—promoting and advancing LGBTQI concerns—is frequently reduced to three elements (already canvassed throughout this chapter): primary legislation (e.g. Article 10 TFEU); secondary legislation (e.g. Directive 2000/78); and case law (*P v S and Cornwall, Maruko, Hay,* etc.). However, such an emphasis on 'hard law' sources undermines (and fails to adequately appreciate) the considerable role which soft law initiatives, and the calculated exercise of soft power, have historically played in achieving queer rights reform throughout the Union (O'Cinneide 2015). In this section, the chapter explores various means by which three institutional bodies (the European Parliament, the European Agency for Fundamental

Rights, and the European Commission) have pursued a progressive queer rights agenda, without creating or requiring new legal protections. The European Parliament has made particularly effective use of soft law instruments to: (a) increase the visibility of queer lives and queer rights across the (expanding) Member States; and (b) shape political debates, with the aim of incorporating LGBTQI concerns into the Union's legislative agenda (Kollman 2009, 42). In the 1980s and 1990s, while numerous Member States (including the United Kingdom) continued to withhold legal gender recognition and certain jurisdictions (including Ireland[36]) still criminalised consensual same-sex intercourse (between men), the European Parliament approved a number of reports and resolutions expressly promoting the non-discrimination rights (including the family rights) of LGBTQI persons (Mos 2014, 637–641). These resolutions/reports were not only important in legitimising what, in many parts of the European Union, remained minority campaigns, but also ensured that, by the mid-1990s, sexual orientation could not be ignored as a valid legislative concern in debates leading to the Treaty of Amsterdam (Mos 2014, 641).

In 2018, the European Parliament (led by an active LGBTQI rights group, Intergroup)—in addition to its enhanced role as co-legislator with the Council of the European Union ('ordinary legislative procedure'), remains a potent soft law actor in the sphere of sexual orientation and gender identity rights. It continues to issue important resolutions,[37] interrogating the reality of queer lives in the European Union, and plays a vital role (often through individual questions and statements in the chamber) in shining a light on contemporary LGBTQI concerns, such as crackdowns on queer identities in Chechnya[38] and the availability of new medical treatments to counteract HIV.[39] Post-Brexit, the United

---

[36] *Norris v Ireland* [1991] 13 EHRR 186.

[37] 'European Parliament resolution on protection and non-discrimination with regard to minorities in the EU Member States' (2017/2937(RSP)); 'European Parliament resolution on the current human rights situation in Turkey' (2018/2527(RSP)).

[38] 'European Parliament resolution on implementation of the Council's LGBTI Guidelines, particularly in relation to the persecution of (perceived) homosexual men in Chechnya' (2017/2688(RSP)).

[39] 'European Parliament resolution of 5 July 2017 on the EU's response to HIV/AIDS, Tuberculosis and Hepatitis C' (2017/2576(RSP)).

Kingdom, and particularly queer populations, will lose the benefit of this highly-influential forum, which has been a driving force behind European queer rights advancement.

The European Union Agency for Fundamental Rights (FRA) is another actor which has made effective use of soft law instruments to advance knowledge about, and respect for, queer communities (Sokhi-Bulley 2011, 293–294). FRA facilitates minimum standards of rights protections across the Member States. Since its establishment, FRA has offered a consistent defence of LGBTQI populations. The first thematic report, which the agency published (in 2008), explored experiences of homophobic discrimination throughout the Union (FRA 2008).

In 2012, FRA undertook a large scale survey of queer populations in the 28 Member States (FRA 2014a). The project attracted more than 90,000 respondents, and offers an invaluable insight into the reality of queer lives. Of particular interest are the facts that: (a) at certain junctures, FRA breaks down the data by reference to country of origin, so that UK readers can obtain an important snapshot of queer experiences in their jurisdiction (see e.g. FRA 2014a, 30, 38 and 43); and (b) the project particularly explores trans realities (FRA 2014b), which helps draw out gender identity from the shadow of LGB concerns. Leaving the EU, and moving forward, queer populations in the United Kingdom will no longer benefit from the work of FRA. In consequence, they will lose a key ally in promoting LGBTQI rights initiatives, lose a reliable source of data on queer experiences, and lose the opportunity to contextualise UK queer rights movements within the framework of a 28 Member State-wide analysis.

A third (and perhaps most important) soft law actor in the sphere of LGBTQI rights is the European Commission (the Commission). The largest EU institution—often characterised as the civil service of the Union—the Commission has broad-ranging executive, quasi-judicial and law-initiating powers. In recent decades, the Commission—through various policies, programmes and campaigns—has been a potent advocate for queer rights advancement.

The European Commission actively supports and funds research into the lived experiences of LGBTQI communities (European Commission 2016). Studies, such as the landmark 2012 report, 'Trans and Intersex People: Discrimination on Grounds of Sex, Gender Identity and Gender Expression (funded by the Commission's Directorate General for Justice) (Agius and Tobler 2012) are primary mechanisms through which European policy-makers (both national and supra-national), as well as Member State civil society organisations (including groups in the United Kingdom), can understand and respond to core concerns facing European queer populations. In addition, the Commission, through various channels, including the European Research Council, facilitates academic research into queer lives, harnessing (and enabling) Europe's vast educational resources to enhance sexual orientation/gender identity protections.[40] The recent multi-institution and multi-country 'Rights on the Move – Rainbow Families in Europe'[41] project illustrates the Commission's commitment to queer-centred research, as does the on-going 'SOGICA – Sexual Orientation and Gender Identity Claims of Asylum: A European Human Rights Challenge' project based at the University of Sussex.[42]

Outside of research, the European Commission also provides practical support and encouragement for LGBTQI advocacy. This not only involves inter-country knowledge exchange programmes, but also includes financial assistance for grassroots advocacy and queer-focused events (European Commission 2016, 13–14). The Commission has a particular concern for young people, and actively facilitates civil society work which pursues youth equality. In recent years, the Commission has provided funding for a number of youth-centred programmes (European Commission 2016, 14), including the International Gay, Lesbian, Bisexual, Transgender, Queer and Intersex Youth and Student Organisation (IGLYO).[43] Such engagement, along with the Commission's numerous other LGBTQI-centred policies, has had a concrete, tangible impact. It creates stronger, more robust queer civil societies (a point already touched upon in Sect. 2), and fosters among the general European public greater awareness and increased tolerance. Leaving the European Union, and removing queer communities from the Commission's jurisdiction, Brexit will deprive the UK's LGBTQI populations of symbolically and practically important existing and future policies.

---

[40]Transrights (2014). https://transrightseurope.com/about-transrights-2/about-transrights/, accessed 13 February 2018.

[41]Rights on the Move—Rainbow Families in Europe (2013). http://www.mirovni-institut.si/data/tinymce/Projekti/ROTM_Neza/Project%20leaflet.pdf, accessed 13 February 2018.

[42]SOGICA—Sexual Orientation and Gender Identity Claims of Asylum: A European Human Rights Challenge. http://www.sogica.org/en/the-project//, accessed 11 April 2018.

[43]'Who We Are', International Gay, Lesbian, Bisexual, Transgender, Queer and Intersex Youth and Student Organisation (2018). http://www.iglyo.com/about/, accessed 13 February 2018.

External Relations

An important, yet perhaps under-explored, aspect of Brexit (and its potential impact on queer populations) is whether leaving the European Union will negatively affect the place of LGBTQI-affirmation in UK foreign policy (i.e. how the UK treats and interacts with LGBTQI communities *outside* the United Kingdom).

A central argument that was observed throughout the Brexit referendum campaign in favour of withdrawing from the European Union was the idea that, free from rigid EU trade frameworks, the United Kingdom would be able to 'strike out on its own', forming new bilateral trade deals (Mason and Asthana 2017; O'Brien 2016). Since assuming the office of Prime Minister, Theresa May has been undertaking a foreign policy charm-offensive, travelling around the world in a bid to encourage inward UK investment and boost UK business prospects abroad (BBC 2018; Merrick 2017).

Yet, from a queer perspective, the Government's new emphasis on third-country trade relations raises important challenges, particularly in terms of the UK's future relationship with queer communities abroad. Many of the countries with which Theresa May is seeking to forge the closest links—Saudi Arabia, Turkey, China—are also jurisdictions with highly questionable (or overtly negative) records on LGBTQI rights (Carroll and Ramon Mendos 2017). In the rush to shore-up the UK's trading opportunities, is there a possibility that the government will compromise (or simply abandon) existing policies which promote queer rights affirmation?

The situation is further complicated by the fact that, within the existing framework of European Union external relations, advocacy for sexual and gender minorities is (at least nominally) a visible priority (Langenkamp 2003; Slootmaeckers et al. 2016). Through generalised foreign policy initiatives, and specific requirements placed upon candidates for accession (Kristoffersson 2013), the EU has consistently identified minimum standards to which all global actors should adhere. There is a risk that—in addition to the consequences for queer persons living inside this jurisdiction—Brexit may also impact official UK policy (and interactions with) LGBTQI populations abroad.

The intersection of Brexit, queerness and external relations raises considerable complexities. Observing the UK government's embrace of jurisdictions with troubling human rights records, there is undoubted cause for alarm. Yet, one must also be careful to avoid overstating either:

(a) the extent to which the EU currently prioritises queer considerations in foreign policy; and (b) the extent to which UK officials are likely to abandon queer equality as an aspect of international diplomacy.

There are at least three possible critiques of EU attitudes towards LGBTQI rights (in the sphere of external relations). First, Union actors adopt an overly narrow approach towards queer equality (Danisi 2017, 353). While the European Union has consistently condemned overt acts of violence and discrimination, they have engaged (noticeably) less with more nuanced topics, such as family relations. This situation raises the fear that EU foreign policy may promote a myopic view of queer realities (in which LGBTQI persons are reduced to objects of violence, without proper discussion of the practical frameworks which regulate queer lives) (Danisi 2017, 356). Second, there is a potentially 'à la carte' incorporation of queer experiences into Union external relations. While the European Union does nominally specify queer freedoms as a baseline requirement, it is unclear to what extent Union actors actually forgo trade opportunities or closer diplomatic ties (including accession) where those requirements are not met. Finally, one might identify a certain hypocrisy in an EU foreign policy of queer affirmation, where LGBTQI persons continue to confront significant legal and social hostilities throughout the 28 Member States (ILGA-Europe 2017; Annicchino 2013, 630).

Against such a contextual background, it is possible to interrogate whether Brexit will have an impact (particularly in the sphere of trade) on how the UK addresses issues of sexual orientation and gender identity in external relations. In practice, it appears (highly) unlikely that LGBTQI persons will wholly disappear from UK foreign policy. Instead, there is a possibility that UK policy-makers and diplomats will pursue pragmatic affirmation. Although favouring general promotions of queer equality, in forums such as the United Nations General Assembly, officials will not withdraw from lucrative trade negotiations merely because questions about LGBTQI equality remain outstanding. While, from a queer perspective, such a situation is non-optimal (and confirms that LGBTQI rights are politically contingent), it is unclear how this post-Brexit reality would differ substantially from current EU attitudes towards queer populations (one might question, given the UK's past history of colonisation, whether UK policy-makers would find it easier to promote queer rights, particularly across the Commonwealth, through EU foreign policy, rather than opening themselves up to charges of (cultural) imperialism and the re-imposition of British values on Global South societies (Dunne 2012)).

4   CONCLUSION

The process of Brexit will have profound consequences for all persons across the UK. This chapter has explored the particular impact which exiting the Union will have for sexual orientation and gender identity rights. The chapter has interrogated fears that Brexit will substantially transform existing LGBTQI frameworks. Having regard to the current political consensus, sources of queer rights in the UK, and contemporary queer disputes, the chapter suggests that the *de jure* outcome of Brexit may be limited for LGBTQI communities.

The chapter is not, however, blind to the potential consequences of removing UK queer communities from the scope of EU protections. It acknowledges that queer individuals, no less than any community or grouping in the United Kingdom (and perhaps more so), will share in the predicted social and economic disadvantages associated with Brexit. In addition, the chapter also recognises the key role which EU soft law and external relations have played in promoting sexual and gender minority rights, both across the 28 Member States and outside the Union. Cut off from existing opportunities for research funding and capacity-building, UK queer communities may indeed (de facto) experience a tangible reduction in quality of life and lived experiences.

BIBLIOGRAPHY

Agius, S., and C. Tobler. 2012. *Trans and Intersex People: Discrimination on Grounds of Sex, Gender Identity and Gender Expression.* Luxembourg: European Commission.

Annicchino, P. 2013. The New Guidelines on Freedom of Religion and LGBTQI Rights in the External Action of the Union. *European Human Rights Law Review* 6: 624–630.

Barker, N., and D. Monk (eds.). 2015. *From Civil Partnership to Same-Sex Marriage—Interdisciplinary Reflections.* London: Routledge.

Barrie, J.H. 2013. European Union Law and Gay Rights: Assessing the Equal Treatment in Employment and Occupation Directive and Case Law on Employment Benefits for Registered Same-Sex Partnerships. *Journal of Civil Law Studies* 6: 617–652.

BBC. 2013. MP-by-MP: Gay Marriage Vote, February 5. http://www.bbc.co.uk/news/uk-politics-21346694. Accessed 13 Feb 2018.

BBC Newsnight. 2018. The UK's Culture War on Social Media and Beyond, January 9. https://www.youtube.com/watch?v=OeMDtx7mBLc. Accessed 13 Feb 2018.

Beckford, M. 2010. Last Catholic Adoption Agency Faces Closure After Charity Commission Ruling. *The Guardian*, August 19. https://www.telegraph. co.uk/news/religion/7952526/Last-Catholic-adoption-agency-faces-closure-after-Charity-Commission-ruling.html. Accessed 11 Apr 2018.

Bell, C., and N. Bačić Selanec. 2016. Who Is a "Spouse" Under the Citizens' Rights Directive? The Prospect of Mutual Recognition of Same-Sex Marriages in the EU. *European Law Review* 41 (5): 655–686.

Boele-Woelki, K. 2008. The Legal Recognition of Same-Sex Relationships Within the European Union. *Tulane Law Review* 80: 1949–1982.

Burden, E., and F. Gibb. 2018. Heterosexuals Close to Getting Right to Civil Partnerships. *The Times*, February 3. https://www.thetimes.co.uk/article/heterosexuals-close-to-getting-right-to-have-civil-partnerships-0nk68v5bf. Accessed 14 Feb 2018.

Campbell, A., and H. Lardy. 1996. Discrimination Against Transsexuals in Employment. *European Law Review* 21 (5): 412–418.

Carroll, A., and L.R. Mendos. 2017. *State-Sponsored Homophobia*. http://ilga. org/downloads/2017/ILGA_State_Sponsored_Homophobia_2017_WEB. pdf. Accessed 13 Feb 2018.

Channel 4 News. 2016. When Feminists Clash; Jack Monroe Debates Transphobic Julia Long (Full Channel 4 News Segment), January 14. https://www.youtube. com/watch?v=93IBkzlXPEs. Accessed 13 Feb 2018.

Chelvan, S. 2014. Y and Z v Minister voor Immigratie en Asiel: A Missed Opportunity or a New Dawn? *European Human Rights Law Review* 1: 49–58.

Clucas, R. 2012. Religion, Sexual Orientation and the Equality Act 2010: Gay Bishops in the Church of England Negotiating Rights Against Discrimination. *Sociology* 56 (5): 936–950.

Cook, M. 2007. From Gay Reform to Gaydar. In *A Gay History of Britain: Love and Sex Between Men Since the Middle Ages*, ed. H.G. Cocks, R. Mills, and R. Trumbach, 178–214. Oxford and Westport: Greenwood World Publishing.

Cooper, J. 2018. Why Is No One Talking About the Brexit Threat to LGBT Rights? *The Guardian*, January 22. https://www.theguardian.com/commentisfree/2018/jan/22/eu-protection-lgbt-people-persecution-withdrawal-bill-lgbt-gay-rights. Accessed 11 Apr 2018.

Cooper, D., and D. Herman. 2013. Up Against the Property Logic of Equality Law: Conservative Christian Accommodation Claims and Gay Rights. *Feminist Legal Studies* 21 (1): 61–80.

Cretney, S. 2006. *Same Sex Relationships: From "Odious Crime" to "Gay Marriage"*. Oxford: Oxford University Press.

Danisi, C. 2017. Promoting Human Rights Through the EU External Action: An Empty "Vessel" for Sexual Minorities? *European Foreign Affairs Review* 22 (3): 341–356.

de Peyer, R. 2014. Speaker John Bercow "Surprised and Delighted" at "Gay Oscar" Nomination. *Evening Standard*, January 9. https://www.standard.

co.uk/news/politics/speaker-john-bercow-surprised-and-delighted-at-gay-oscar-nomination-9050073.html. Accessed 13 Feb 2018.

Dockray, K., and A. Sutton. 2017. *Politics, Society and Homosexuality in Post-war Britain. The Sexual Offences Act of 197 and Its Significance.* London: Fonthill.

Draghici, C. 2017. Equal Marriage, Unequal Civil Partnership: A Bizarre Case of Discrimination in Europe. *Child and Family Law Quarterly* 29 (4): 313–334.

Duffy, N. 2017. Fact Check: What Actually Is Theresa May's Record on LGBT Rights? *Pink News*, May 2. http://www.pinknews.co.uk/2017/05/02/fact-check-what-actually-is-theresa-mays-record-on-lgbt-rights/. Accessed 13 Feb 2018.

Dunne, P. 2012. LGBTI Rights and the Wrong Way to Give Aid. *Kennedy School Review* 12.

Dunne, P. 2015. Ten Years of Gender Recognition in the United Kingdom. Still a "Model for Reform"? *Public Law*, 530–539.

European Commission. 2016. *List of Actions by the Commission to Advance LGBTI Equality.* Brussels: European Commission.

European Union Agency for Fundamental Rights. 2009. *Homophobia and Discrimination on Grounds of Sexual Orientation in the EU Member States: Part I—Legal Analysis.* Luxembourg: FRA EU.

European Union Agency for Fundamental Rights. 2013. *EU LGBT Survey—European Union Lesbian, Gay, Bisexual and Transgender Survey—Main Results.* Luxembourg: FRA EU.

European Union Agency for Fundamental Rights. 2015. *Being Trans in the European Union—Comparative Analysis of EU LGBT Survey Data.* Luxembourg: FRA EU.

Explanations of the Charter of Fundamental Rights of the European Union. 2007. http://eur-lex.europa.eu/LexUriServ/LexUriServ.do?uri=OJ:C:2007:303:0017:0035:EN:PDF. Accessed 13 February 2018.

Ferguson, L. 2016. The Curious Case of Civil Partnership: The Extension of Marriage to Same-Sex Couples and the Status-Altering Consequences of a Wait-and-See Approach. *Child and Family Law Quarterly* 28 (4): 347–364.

Gaffney-Rhys, R. 2014. Same-Sex Marriage but Not Mixed-Sex Partnerships: Should the Civil Partnership Act 2004 Be Extended to Opposite-Sex Couples. *Child and Family Law Quarterly* 26 (2): 173–195.

Gani, A. 2015. Stonewall to Start Campaigning for Trans Equality. *The Guardian*, February 16. https://www.theguardian.com/uk-news/2015/feb/16/stonewall-start-campaigning-trans-equality. Accessed 13 Feb 2018.

Gilbert, A. 2014. From "Pretended Family Relationship" to "Ultimate Affirmation": British Conservatism and the Legal Recognition of Same-Sex Relationships. *Child and Family Law Quarterly* 26 (4): 463–488.

Harding, R. 2006. "Dogs Are 'Registered', People Shouldn't Be": Legal Consciousness and Lesbian and Gay Rights. *Social and Legal Studies* 15 (4): 511–533.

House of Commons Select Committee on Women and Equalities. 2016. *Transgender Equality*. London: Stationary Office.

House of Lords European Union Committee. 2016. *The UK, The EU and a British Bill of Rights*. London: House of Lords.

ILGA-Europe. 2017. *Annual Review of the Human Rights Situation of Lesbian, Gay, Bisexual Trans and Intersex People in Europe*. Brussels: ILGA-Europe.

Jones, O. 2017. Hatred of LGBTQ People Still Infects Society. It's No Time to Celebrate. *The Guardian*, July 27. https://www.theguardian.com/comment-isfree/2017/jul/27/lgbtq-partial-decriminalisation-homosexuality-gay-trans. Accessed 13 Feb 2018.

Johnson, P. 2016. *An Oral History of Sexual Orientation Discrimination and the European Convention on Human Rights*. Oxford: Oxford University Press.

Khomami, N. 2017. Tim Farron Refuses Again to Say Whether Homosexuality Is a Sin. *The Guardian*, June 2. https://www.theguardian.com/politics/2017/jun/02/tim-farron-again-refuses-to-say-whether-homosexuality-is-a-sin-lgbt-rights. Accessed 13 Feb 2018.

Kollman, K. 2009. European Institutions, Transnational Networks and National Same-Sex Unions Policy: When Soft Law Hits Harder. *Contemporary Politics* 15 (1): 37–53.

Kollman, K., and M. Waites. 2011. United Kingdom: Changing Political Opportunity Structures, Policy Success and Continuing Challenges for Lesbian, Gay and Bisexual Movements. In *The Lesbian and Gay Movement and the State: Comparative Insights into a Transformed Relationship*, ed. M. Tremblay, D. Paternotte, and C. Johnson, 181–196. Farnham: Ashgate.

Kouroutakis, A. 2018. The Henry VIII Powers in the EU (Withdrawal) Bill: Political and Legal Safeguards. *UK Human Rights Blog*, February 7. https://ukhumanrightsblog.com/2018/02/07/the-henry-vi-ii-powers-in-the-eu-withdrawal-bill-political-and-legal-safeguards-antoni-os-kouroutakis/. Accessed 13 Feb 2018.

Kristoffersson, M. 2013. *LGBT Rights in the EU Accession Process*. https://lup.lub.lu.se/student-papers/search/publication/3803439. Accessed 14 Feb 2018.

Langenkamp, T.J. 2003. Finding Fundamental Fairness: Protecting the Rights of Homosexuals Under European Union Accession Law. *San Diego International Law Journal* 4: 437–466.

Lardy, H., and A. Campbell. 1996. Discrimination Against Transsexuals in Employment. *European Law Review* 21: 412–418.

Lewis, H. 2017. Is Jeremy Corbyn Right That Trans People Should Be Allowed to Self-Identify Their Gender? July 19. https://www.newstatesman.com/politics/uk/2017/07/jeremy-corbyn-right-trans-people-should-be-allowed-self-identify-their-gender. Accessed 13 Feb 2018.

Mason, R., and A. Asthana. 2017. Boris Johnson: Brexit Will Ussher in New Era of Free Trade Deals. *The Guardian*, April 26. https://www.theguardian.

com/politics/2017/apr/26/boris-johnson-brexit-will-usher-in-new-era-of-free-trade-deals. Accessed 13 Feb 2018.

Merrick, R. 2017. Theresa May Arrives in Middle East to Strengthen Post-Brexit Links with Other Trading Partners. *The Independent*, November 28. www.independent.co.uk/news/uk/politics/theresa-may-middle-east-post-brexit-links-trade-saudi-arabia-jordan-yemen-un-uk-a8080796.html. Accessed 13 Feb 2018.

Meyjes, T. 2017. How MPs Have Voted on Gay Rights Issues, May 1. http://metro.co.uk/2017/05/01/how-mps-have-voted-on-gay-rights-issues-6608750/. Accessed 13 Feb 2018.

Morris, N. 2016. Boris Johnson Urges Gay People to Vote for Brexit. *The Independent*, March 24. http://www.independent.co.uk/news/uk/politics/eu-referendum-boris-johnson-urges-gay-people-to-vote-for-brexit-lgbt-rights-a6950941.html. Accessed 13 Feb 2018.

Mortimer, M. 2017. All the Anti-Gay and Lesbian Stances Theresa May Has Taken in Her Political Career. *The Independent*, April 25. http://www.independent.co.uk/news/uk/politics/theresa-may-lgbt-rights-gay-commons-vote-same-sex-marriage-gay-adoption-tim-farron-a7702326.html. Accessed 13 Feb 2018.

Mos, M. 2014. Of Gay Rights and Christmas Ornaments: The Political History of Sexual Orientation Non-discrimination in the Treaty of Amsterdam. *Journal of Cutaneous Medicine and Surgery: Incorporating Medical and Surgical Dermatology* 52 (3): 632–649.

NeJaime, D., and R. Siegel. 2015. Conscience Wars: Complicity-Based Conscience Claims in Religion and Politics. *Yale Law Journal* 124 (7): 2516–2591.

Newbould, M. 2016. When Parents Chose Gender: Intersex, Children and the Law. *Medical Law Review* 24 (2): 474–496.

O'Brien, Z. 2016. Nigel Farage: Get Behind Brexit as Countries Are RACING to Trade with the UK. *The Express*, June 29. https://www.express.co.uk/news/uk/684235/Nigel-Farage-says-get-behind-Brexit-countries-QUEUE-to-trade-with-UK. Accessed 13 Feb 2018.

O'Cinneide, C. 2015. The Constitutionalisation of Equality with the EU Legal Order: Sexual Orientation as a Testing Ground. *Maastricht Journal of European and Comparative Law* 22 (3): 370–395.

Rogers, S. 2013. Gay Marriage Bill. How Did Your MP Vote? February 6. https://www.theguardian.com/news/datablog/interactive/2013/feb/06/gay-marriage-vote-map-mp. Accessed 13 Feb 2018.

Saeed, S. 2017. Theresa May: Tories and I Were 'Wrong' on Gay Rights in the Past. *Politico*, July 27. https://www.politico.eu/article/theresa-may-tories-gay-rights/. Accessed 13 Feb 2018.

Scottish Government. 2013. Transgender. http://www.gov.scot/Publications/2013/04/7520/4. Accessed 14 Feb 2018.

Scottish Government. 2017. *Review of the Gender Recognition Act 2004—A Consultation.* https://consult.gov.scot/family-law/review-of-the-gender-recognition-act-2004/user_uploads/sct1017251758-1_gender_p4-3-. pdf. Accessed 13 Feb 2018.

Sharpe, A. 2014. Criminalising Sexual Intimacy: Transgender Defendants and the Legal Construction of Non-Consent. *Criminal Law Review* 3: 207–223.

Sloan, B. 2015. The Legal Status of Transsexual and Transgender Persons in Ireland. In *The Legal Status of Transsexual and Transgender Persons*, ed. J.M. Scherpe. Cambridge: Intersentia.

Slootmaeckers, K., Heleen Touquet, and P. Vermeersch (eds.). 2016. *The EU Enlargement and Gay Politics: The Impact of Eastern Enlargement on Rights, Activism and Prejudice*. London: Palgrave Macmillan.

Sokhi-Bulley, B. 2011. The Fundamental Rights Agency of the European Union. A New Panopticism. *Human Rights Law Review* 11: 683–706.

Staples, L. 2018. In Celebrating LGBT + History, We Can't Ignore Britain's Role in Exporting Homophobia. *The Independent*, February 8. https://www. newstatesman.com/2018/02/celebrating-lgbt-history-we-can-t-ignore-britain-s-role-exporting-homophobia. Accessed 13 Feb 2018.

Stone, J. 2016. Brexit Vote Driving Anti-LGBT Hate Crime as Victims Told: "You're Next". *The Independent*, November 5. http://www.independent. co.uk/news/uk/politics/brexit-lgbt-hate-crime-rise-galop-home-affairs-youre-next-a7419111.html. Accessed 13 Feb 2018.

Stonewall. 2017. *A Vision for Change*. http://www.stonewall.org.uk/sites/ default/files/stw-vision-for-change-2017.pdf. Accessed 13 Feb 2018.

Sumption, J. 2013. The Limits of Law, November 20. https://www.supreme-court.uk/docs/speech-131120.pdf. Accessed 13 Feb 2018.

Tayleur, T. 2017. Retention of EU Law: How Much? *New Law Journal* 167 (7758): 15–16.

Thatchell, P. 2018. Marriage? No Thanks. Here's a Better Idea. *The Guardian*, February 7. https://www.theguardian.com/commentisfree/2018/feb/07/ marriage-better-idea-legal-civil-commitment. Accessed 14 Feb 2018.

Tobler, C., and K. Waaldijk. 2009. Case C-267/06, Tadao Maruko v Versorgungsanstalt der Deutschen Buhnen, Judgment of the Grand Chamber of the Court of Justice of 1 April 2008. *Common Market Law Review* 46 (2): 723–746.

Townsend, M. 2016. Homophobic Attacks in the UK Rose 147% in Three Months After Brexit Vote. *The Guardian*, October 8. https://www.theguard-ian.com/society/2016/oct/08/homophobic-attacks-double-after-brexit-vote. Accessed 13 Feb 2018.

Tryfonidou, A. 2017. Discrimination on the Grounds of Sexual Orientation and Gender Identity. In *General Principles of Law: European and Comparative Perspectives*, ed. S. Vogenauer and S. Weatherill, 365–394. Oxford: Hart Publishing.

Uhrig, S.C. Noah. 2013. *An Examination of Poverty and Sexual Orientation in the UK*. United Kingdom: University of Essex.

UK Government. 2017a. Pride Reception 2017: Theresa May's Speech, July 19. https://www.gov.uk/government/speeches/pride-reception-2017-theresa-mays-speech. Accessed 13 Feb 2018.

UK Government. 2017b. New Action to Promote LGBT Equality, July 23. https://www.gov.uk/government/news/new-action-to-promote-lgbt-equality. Accessed 13 Feb 2018.

Valentine, V. 2016. *Non-Binary People's Experiences in the UK*. Scottish Transgender Alliance.

Vickers, L. 2010. Religious Discrimination in the Workplace: An Emerging Hierarchy? *Ecclesiastical Law Journal* 12 (3): 280–303.

Williamson, C. 2014. Gay Cake: DUP MPs Launch Petition in Support of Ashers Bakery in Newtownabbey. *Belfast Telegraph*, November 13. https://www.belfasttelegraph.co.uk/news/northern-ireland/gay-cake-dup-mps-launch-petition-in-support-of-ashers-bakery-in-newtownabbey-30742585.html. Accessed 14 Feb 2018.

Wintemute, R. 2014. Accommodating Religious Beliefs: Harm, Clothing or Symbols, and Refusals to Serve Others. *Modern Law Review* 77 (2): 223–253.

Wintemute, R. 2016. Goodbye EU Anti-Discrimination Law? Hello Repeal of the Equality Act 2010? *Kings Law Journal* 27 (3): 387–397.

Worley, W. 2016. Theresa May Will Campaign to Leave the European Convention on Human Rights in 2020 Election. *The Independent*, December 29. http://www.independent.co.uk/news/uk/politics/theresa-may-campaign-leave-european-convention-on-human-rights-2020-general-election-brexit-a7499951.html. Accessed 13 Feb 2018.

PART III

Voices from UK Countries

CHAPTER 12

Brexit and the Work–Family Conflict: A Scottish Perspective

Michelle Weldon-Johns

1 INTRODUCTION

The Scottish Government's desire to maintain the EU employment and equality law framework and further strengthen employment rights underpins its recently renewed commitment to seek devolution in these areas as a result of Brexit. This reflects wider concerns about the potential impact of Brexit on employment and equality law, which are equally mirrored in the work-family context.[1] Given the Scottish Government's position, this paper will critically examine whether there is, or could be, a distinctly Scottish perspective in the context of work-family rights post-Brexit. In order to do so, the paper will begin by framing the analysis by critically considering gender and work-family conflict.

[1] The term work-family draws from Fineman's (1995) understanding of family care and is used to denote the tension between paid work and family care responsibilities, which can extend beyond the mother-child relationship to encompass other relationships of care (Weldon-Johns 2011). Despite its broader application in general, this paper focuses on traditional parent-child relationships.

M. Weldon-Johns (✉)
Dundee Business School, Abertay University, Dundee, UK
e-mail: m.weldon-johns@abertay.ac.uk

© The Author(s) 2019   305
M. Dustin et al. (eds.), *Gender and Queer Perspectives on Brexit*,
Gender and Politics, https://doi.org/10.1007/978-3-030-03122-0_12

In doing so, it will acknowledge that this concerns gender equality for both men and women as workers and carers. It will then note the potentially gendered implications of Brexit for work-family conflict for both working parents. The paper will then turn to critically examining the Scottish Governments' position on EU employment and equality law in the post-Brexit context. In doing so it will consider in particular: whether Scotland has, in principle, a potentially distinct approach towards employment and equality law; whether there is anything within the current legal framework that would enable Scotland to retain any degree of continuity with EU law; and if Scotland were to gain powers over employment and equality law, is there the potential for a distinctly Scottish approach towards work-family conflict post-Brexit.

The paper will examine the potentially gendered implications of Brexit from the perspective of traditional dual-partnered heterosexual working parents given the challenges within the current package of rights for working fathers, and the difficulties in challenging entrenched gender roles. While the experiences of alternative family models are equally deserving of further consideration (Weldon-Johns 2016), the UK has at times extended rights for atypical family models beyond those guaranteed at an EU level. For instance, the UK has gone further than the Court of Justice of the EU (CJEU) in recognising the rights of intended parents in surrogacy (Judgment of 18 March 2014, *CD v ST*, C-167/12, EU:C:2014:169 and Judgment of 18 March 2014, *Z v A Government Department*, C-363/12, EU:C:2014:159; Children and Families Act 2014 c.6 [CFA 2014]). In contrast, while the CJEU has begun to recognise the role of the working father, and thus gender-neutral parenting (Judgment of 30 September 2010, *Roca Alvarez v Sesa Start Espana ETT SA*, C-104/09, EU:C:2010:561 and Judgment of 16 July 2015, *Maistrellis v Ypourgos Dikaiosynis, Diafaneias kai Anthropinon Dikaiomaton*, C-222/14, EU:C:2015:473), this compares notably with the highly gendered package of rights in the UK. In addition, Article 7 of the Charter of Fundamental Rights of the EU (2012/C 326/02) (CFR) replicates Article 8 ECHR, which has also been used successfully by fathers seeking access to parental leave, again promoting gender-neutral parenting (*Markin v Russia* [2013] 56 EHRR 8). The loss of the CFR and its future development in this area will also have potentially greater implications for working fathers. Consequently, the position of working fathers is arguably the most vulnerable post-Brexit. This has implications not only for working fathers, but also working mothers and possibly alternative family models reflecting the traditional dual-partnered working family model.

2   GENDER AND THE WORK–FAMILY CONFLICT

The reconciliation of work and family life is often primarily viewed through the lens of enabling women to enter into, or remain within, the paid labour market. Recognising the role of, and facilitating gender equality for, working fathers is not often explicitly addressed. This was evident when the reconciliation of work and family life was first addressed, both within the UK and the EU. At this time the underpinning legal framework for work-family rights was primarily maternal in focus, and reinforced stereotypical views of the division between work and private life. This was particularly evident in the jurisprudence of the CJEU in Judgment of 26 October 1983, *Commission v Italy*, Case 163/82, EU:C:1983:295 and Judgment of 12 July 1984, *Hofmann v Barmer Ersatzkasse*, Case 184/83, EU:C:1984:273. In these cases, the rights of working fathers were afforded a secondary status to those of working mothers. The primacy of the mother-child relationship was afforded a special status in both cases, even though there was no biological imperative to do so since the requested leave was only for childcare. The subsequent jurisprudence of the CJEU reinforced the 'special relationship between a woman and her child' (first noted in *Hofmann*, para. 25) and conflated the concepts of maternity and motherhood (McGlynn 2000, 36; Ellis 1991, 170). In doing so, it entrenched the notion of the 'dominant ideology of motherhood' (McGlynn 2000, 41). While the focus on pregnancy and maternity arguably offered some protection for pregnant workers and working mothers, its reach to motherhood undermined the position of working fathers and presupposed that women were primary caregivers (McGlynn 2000; More 1996; Caracciolo di Torella and Masselot 2001; Fredman 2014). This led to a significantly gendered approach towards addressing work-family conflict, which arguably undermined rather than supported the position of working mothers.

Despite this, over the years there has been a growing discussion around the concept of 'new fatherhood' (Lupton and Barclay 1997; Warin et al. 1999). This has, in part, attempted to redefine what it means to be a father, in particular redefining the boundaries of fatherhood identity. In doing so, it has tried to challenge the perception of working fathers solely as primary breadwinners and instead recognise and value their caring role (Lupton and Barclay 1997). One of the key considerations here has been the erosion of the male breadwinner working family model that has positioned fathers as breadwinners and limited their identity as 'worker-carers' (Lewis 2001). There has been academic support for the recognition of all working parents (and carers) as workers and carers (Crompton 1999; Gornick and Meyers 2003; James 2009), and there is merit, particularly from a gender equality perspective, in recognising that both parents do, and should, have equal responsibility for the care of their children.

However, debates around 'new fatherhood' have at times 'problematised fatherhood' (Collier 1999, 2001; Collier and Sheldon 2008). Thus, instead of creating a positive fatherhood identity, they have largely focused on identifying men's behaviour as 'problematic' and in need of change. This has related to what are identified as negative behaviours more generally (Lewis 2001), and in relation to childcare (Collier 1999). Even notions of 'good fatherhood' are potentially problematic because not only can they create expectations of what it means to be a 'good' and 'involved' father, which may be in contrast with their lived experiences, they have also, at times, continued to recognise fathers' breadwinning role as a key aspect of that identity (Collier 2010, 148). Consequently, fathers have found it difficult to relate to the different identities of fatherhood presented to them, which have often remained in contrast with their lived experiences of working and family life (Collier 2001, 2010; Collier and Sheldon 2008). In addition, both Collier (1999) and Miller (2011a, b) have argued that it is problematic to assume that fathers actually want to challenge traditional roles and undertake greater responsibility for childcare. While this may be the case, a key consideration when trying to recognise fathers' caring role should not be to try to force social change on all working fathers, but to facilitate those who want to undertake a more equal role in childcare to do so, thus, recognising the diversity and fluidity of the fatherhood identity (Dermott 2001, 2005; Collier and Sheldon 2008). There are also wider underpinning justifications for engaging fathers in childcare including: recognising the interests of the child and the benefits of developing relationships with both parents (James 2012; Foubert 2017); increasing female participation in the workplace; and challenging gender inequality that can result from women's entrenched role as primary caregiver (Caracciolo di Torella 2015). The main problem that has endured in this context thus far has been the disconnect between the 'new fatherhood' rhetoric and the reality that working fathers have not undertaken a significantly greater role in childcare, which is in part reinforced by the underpinning work-family legislation.

This has been reflected in the rhetoric of successive Westminster Governments about recognising the role of working fathers (Department of Trade and Industry 2003, 2005; HM Government 2011). However, little more than lip-service has been paid to this in practice (for an overview of some critiques of former and current rights see: McColgan 2000; James 2006; Caracciolo di Torella 2007; Weldon-Johns 2011; Mitchell 2015). This is particularly evident in the introduction of UK work-family rights, where there has been no direct EU influence. These have either been gender-specific rights for working fathers, such as the right to paternity leave (Paternity and Adoption Leave Regulations 2002/2788 [PALR 2000]), or gender-neutral rights, such as shared parental leave (Shared Parental Leave Regulations 2014/3050 [SPLR 2014]). Despite being presented as rights enabling both parents to be involved in childcare, the way that they operate in practice reinforces traditional gender roles. For example, the right to paternity leave is short, it is not earnings-related, and it requires fathers to have established continuity of employment with the employer before being able to access it (James 2006; Caracciolo di Torella 2007; Weldon-Johns 2011). The right to shared parental leave is similarly problematic because it does not confer individual rights on working fathers, it is also not earnings-related, and it requires both parents to have established continuity of employment with their employers (Mitchell 2015; Aitkenson 2017). Alongside extensive maternity rights (Employment Rights Act 1996 c.18 [ERA 1996]; Maternity and Parental Leave etc. Regulations 1999/3312 [MPLR 1999]), both rights reinforce the role of mothers as primary caregivers, with fathers relegated to a secondary role (James 2006; Caracciolo di Torella 2007; Weldon-Johns 2011).

Despite the rhetoric of 'new fatherhood', fathers remain relegated to this secondary role. This reinforces the challenges they face when trying to reconcile their identities as fathers with the reality of working life and opportunities to engage in care. Furthermore, within the debates on fatherhood, Collier has previously been critical of the efforts of former governments which, he argued, have tried to effect, as opposed to reflect, societal change (1999, 2001). This may also explain why there has not been the radical change to parenting roles and the division of work and care that the discourse on 'new' and 'engaged' fatherhood might suggest because fathers are struggling to fit into the identities that are being given to them, not ones that they themselves have necessarily sought or defined (Collier 1999, 178; 2001, 537–539 and 542–543). This was particularly evident in the Westminster Government's Impact Assessment on Flexible Parental Leave, enacted as Shared Parental Leave, which estimated that only between 2–8% of fathers would use the right in practice (HM Government 2012, 5 and 25–27), despite the right being aimed at encouraging shared parenting (HM Government 2011, 5–7).

Despite various efforts to redefine the worker-carer model to recognise and encompass working fathers (Crompton 1999; Lewis 2001; Gornick and Meyers 2003), the current UK package of work-family rights continues to reinforce traditional gender roles. This remains the case despite greater recognition of the role of working fathers at an EU level. In particular, the CJEU has begun to recognise the role of the working father, and thus gender-neutral parenting (Caracciolo di Torella 2014), resulting in a move towards the 'levelling up' of substantive equality in this context (Fredman 2014). As Fredman argues, '[s]ubstantive equality … can only be genuinely furthered if pregnancy and parenthood are appropriately distinguished' (2014, 442). This was a significant issue in the earlier jurisprudence involving working fathers which conflated the two. Fredman argues that, in this context, equality should have a substantive value and that should be the social value of parenting. Such an approach would move the debate from the original focus on sameness or difference, wherein likes are treated alike and those who are not alike may be justifiably treated differently. In this context, equality as 'sameness' has been problematic because it produces inappropriate comparisons, as seen in previous discussions on ill man comparators in pregnancy discrimination (Fredman 2014, 445–446; Wintemute 1998). However, the equality as 'difference' approach has also been problematic because it reinforces traditional gender roles (Fredman 2014, 446–450). Thus, Fredman (2014) argues that each approach in practice has continued to undermine genuine gender equality. Instead, she argues, guaranteeing fathers equal access to, and incentives to engage with, work-family rights have the potential to facilitate a move towards substantive equality in the future. In both *Roca Alvarez* and *Maistrellis* there was a change in the reasoning of the CJEU, which appeared to adopt this approach. In both cases, working fathers claimed access to gender-neutral childcare-related rights. However, in both instances this was refused on the basis of their partners' employment status.

Notably in both cases, had the mother been trying to access the same rights she would have been able to do so irrespective of the employment status of her partner. The CJEU ultimately recognised that working fathers were entitled to equal treatment in relation to access to work-family rights. In *Roca Alvarez* the CJEU acknowledged that '[t]he positions of a male and a female worker, father and mother of a young child, were comparable with regard to their possible need to reduce their daily working time in order to look after their child' (para. 24). Thus, drawing a clear distinction between pregnancy and maternity related leave, and leave for the purpose of childcare. The CJEU further noted that,

> to refuse entitlement to the leave at issue in the main proceedings to fathers whose status is that of an employed person, on the sole ground that the child's mother does not have that status, could have as its effect that a woman … would have to limit her self-employed activity and bear the burden resulting from the birth of her child alone, without the child's father being able to ease that burden. (para. 37)

This approach was further endorsed by the CJEU in *Maistrellis*:

> a provision such as the one at issue in the main proceedings, far from ensuring full equality in practice between men and women in working life, is liable to perpetuate a traditional distribution of the roles of men and women by keeping men in a role subsidiary to that of women in relation to the exercise of their parental duties. (para. 50)

In both instances, the CJEU was mindful of both the potential role of working fathers in relation to childcare and the implications for the mother who would otherwise bear the sole burden of childcare responsibility. Despite this, the UK right to Shared Parental Leave, discussed below, retains similar employment status qualifications for both parents.

In the work-family context there remains a tension between recognising and protecting the rights of both working parents as worker-carers, and the underpinning identities of motherhood and fatherhood (James 2009). Failing to acknowledge the implications for working fathers, as has arguably been the case in the UK context, not only continues to exclude them from this discourse, but also further undermines the position of working mothers. Consequently, the future of work-family rights, whatever the relationship with the EU, must be to continue to recognise and support the role of the working father. However, this is one of the key areas of vulnerability post-Brexit in the work-family context.

3   BREXIT–GENDERED IMPLICATIONS FOR WORK-FAMILY RIGHTS

There has been an emerging discussion of the gendered implications of Brexit, particularly for women, and notably in the employment and equality context (Guerrina and Masselot 2018; Fawcett Society 2018; Millns 2016; McColgan 2016). The work-family context has been specifically identified as one where the UK could potentially lose out on EU developments post-Brexit (McColgan 2016; Ford 2016). While this is likely to have disproportionate consequences for women who are largely still primary caregivers (ONS 2016, Figure 2), there are also significant implications for working fathers. As noted above, despite discussions around the emergence of 'new fatherhood', and the greater acknowledgement of fathers' rights by the CJEU, the UK package of work-family rights continues to reinforce traditional gender roles. It will be important to ensure that their work-family rights are also developed and protected post-Brexit.

There are a number of potential areas of vulnerability in the context of the work-family conflict post-Brexit, and each of them has potentially gendered implications. In particular, while it has been argued that the UK has at times been a leader in relation to equality legislation (HC Women and Equalities Committee 2017, 4), this is not equally true in the context of work-family conflict. For instance, it was EU law that guaranteed protections for pregnant workers by recognising that pregnancy discrimination is inherently sex discrimination (Judgment of 8 November 1990, *Dekker v Stichting Vormingscentrum voor Jong Volwassenen (VJV-Centrum) Plus*, C-177/88, EU:C:1990:383), ultimately forcing UK courts to revisit their approach in this context (e.g. in Judgment of 14 July 1994, *Webb v EMO Cargo Ltd*, C-32/93, EU:C:1994:300; [1996] 2 CMLR 990 [HL]). Nevertheless, the position of working mothers and pregnant workers under the current legislative regime, underpinned by EU law, has still not provided women with sufficient safeguards against discriminatory and/or detrimental treatment (Fawcett Society 2018, 37–40; Taylor 2017, 96–97). Consequently, the position of working mothers and pregnant workers is arguably even more vulnerable post-Brexit without the guaranteed floor of EU rights.

This may particularly be the case for protections which impose significant burdens on business (like the situation in *Webb*). It is in this context that the particular gendered implications of Brexit are going to be felt most keenly, with consequences particularly for working mothers.

The wider UK package of work-family rights can be divided into: those that directly derive from EU legislation, namely unpaid parental leave (Parental Leave Directive 2010/18/EU [PLD 2010]; MPLR 1999); those which were in place prior to similar EU legislation, such as maternity leave (ERA 1996; MPLR 1999), dependent care leave (ERA 1996), and the right to request flexible working (ERA 1996; Flexible Working Regulations 2014/1398); and rights which have been introduced and developed solely at a UK level, such as shared parental leave (SPLR 2014), and paternity leave (PALR 2000). In addition to specific work-family rights, working parents are also protected by employment equality law (Equality Act 2010 c.15 [EA 2010]), largely under the protected characteristic of sex, but also pregnancy and maternity, and in some cases disability (Judgment of 17 July 2008, *Coleman v Attridge Law*, C-303/06, EU:C:2008:415). Of these rights, EU-derived work-family rights are most likely to be vulnerable to repeal post-Brexit. However, UK-derived work-family rights, which are largely gender specific rights for working fathers, are also likely to be vulnerable to stagnation and deterioration post-Brexit.

The right to unpaid parental leave is the only solely EU-derived work-family right within the UK package of rights. This entitles working parents with one years' continuous employment to a total of 18 weeks unpaid leave per child, which can be used until the child's 18th birthday. The vulnerability of this right is particularly likely given the limited uptake of the right in practice (Tipping et al. 2012), which may make it easier to withdraw from the statute books. While it is not the most extensive work-family right and has been criticised for reinforcing gender roles (McColgan 2000; Weldon-Johns 2013; Caracciolo di Torella 2014), it is the only one which provides both parents with an individual, non-transferable right to care for their child. In addition, it necessarily focuses on childcare rights since it extends far beyond the post-birth period. Removal of this right would signify a step back in relation to gender equality and the work-family conflict, particularly while the EU is taking significant steps forward in this area.

Arguably the greatest consequence of Brexit is the potential loss of development of domestic law in line with that at a European level

(Barnard 2016; McColgan 2016). The recent jurisprudence of the CJEU is one example of this. Another is the European Parliament and Council proposal for a new directive to replace the current PLD 2010. The new directive has the dual aims of addressing women's under-representation at work and encouraging better sharing of childcare responsibilities between men and women (Proposal for a Directive by the European Parliament and of the Council on Work-life Balance for Parents and Carers and repealing Council Directive 2010/18/EU COM/2017/0253 final). While the proposals are not introducing any significant rights not currently within the UK package of work-family rights, it is the potential for further development in this field that is lost. In particular, it is the change in attitude towards the work-family conflict and gender equality that the proposals embody that could mark a notable step-change between the UK and the EU post-Brexit (see Caracciolo di Torella 2017 for a discussion of the proposals).

There is also the potential future development and impact of the CFR in the interpretation of work-family rights. The Westminster Government have already stated their intention to withdraw from the CFR following Brexit (EU (Withdrawal) Act c.16 ((EU(W)A)), s.5(4)), with much criticism (McCorkindale 2018; Busby 2017; Lock 2017; Yong 2017). While the CFR can only be used to interpret EU law and does not provide free-standing rights, its interpretative potential remains to be seen. In the work-family context Article 7 of the CFR mirrors Article 8 ECHR. Article 8 was relied upon by a father in *Markin v Russia* (2013) 56 EHRR 8 to successfully secure equal access to parental leave, acknowledging that 'insofar as parental leave and parental leave allowances are concerned, men are in an analogous situation to women' (para. 132). The ECtHR upheld the serviceman's complaint that the Russian government had breached his Article 8 right by not affording him access to parental leave on the same terms as servicewomen. In doing so, the ECtHR noted that

[i]t is true that art.8 does not include a right to parental leave or impose any positive obligation on states to provide parental leave allowances. At the same time, by enabling one of the parents to stay at home to look after the children, parental leave and related allowances promote family life and necessarily affect the way in which it is organised. Parental leave and parental allowances therefore come within the scope of art.8 of the Convention. (para. 130)

In Article 53(3) of the CFR it notes that the scope of the rights that correspond with those in the ECHR should be the same. Consequently, a similar interpretation of the scope of Article 7 is likely to be adopted here. This could have significant future implications for the interpretation and development of work-family rights, particularly as the approach of both the CJEU and the ECtHR endorses a more gender-neutral approach to childcare responsibilities.

Furthermore, Article 33 of the CFR refers to 'Family and professional life' and Article 33(1) states that 'The family shall enjoy legal, economic and social protection'. This could be open to a potentially wide interpretation in the work-family context. For instance, it could pave the way for increases in the protections available to working parents, and enhancement of economic rights to paid/earnings-related leave. This would arguably provide families with economic protection when exercising work-family rights. Article 33(2) goes on to state that in order '[t]o reconcile family and professional life, everyone shall have the right to protection from dismissal for a reason connected with maternity and the right to paid maternity leave and to parental leave following the birth or adoption of a child.' While the protections for pregnancy and maternity are greater, the inclusion of an individual right to parental leave is notable here, in particular, given the more recent jurisprudence of the CJEU in this context reinforce fathers' rights.

Within the work-family context there is an underlying tension between reinforcing traditional gender roles and providing opportunities to enhance gender equality. Often initiatives to redress the balance have focused solely on one gender. Brexit has the potential to further entrench traditional gender roles and push fathers even further to the side-lines. This paper will now turn to consider whether there is a potentially differentiated response to this in Scotland.

4 Employment and Equality Law: The Scottish Government's Perspective

Employment and equality law (with limited exceptions) are currently reserved matters under the Scotland Act 1998 c.46 (SA 1998), schedule 5. However, since the results of the Scottish independence referendum, the Scottish Government has unsuccessfully sought devolution of employment and equality law (Scottish Government 2014b, 31–32; Smith Commission 2014). In the period between the referenda the main justification advanced for devolution of employment and equality law was to enable the Scottish Government to achieve 'full fiscal autonomy' (Scottish Government 2015, para. 6, 22–30 and 53–57). The focus and reasoning at that time was to have control over 'key economic levers' to enable the Scottish Government to 'create jobs', 'tackle inequality' (The Scottish Government 2014b, iii), and 'boost competitiveness' (Scottish Government 2015, para. 5, see also para. 21–30). It was also argued that the devolution of equality law would help overcome the '[b]arriers which prevent women from getting into work, participating in society and from earning the same as men...' and '[p]rotection against discrimination could be strengthened' (Scottish Government 2015, para. 54). While the focus was on economic considerations, gender equality was also a key underpinning justification for devolution of these powers. In the period following the referendum on EU membership the narrative has changed slightly to focus more fully on ensuring social justice and the protection of employment and equality rights post-Brexit (Scottish Government 2016a).

Despite the original focus on economic considerations, particularly in the context of employment policy, it was nevertheless clear that the Scottish Government preferred a social partnership model (Scottish Government 2014a, para. 5.25), akin to that at a European level. This indicated a commitment to the European approach towards employment relations (Murphie and Weldon-Johns 2016), which continues to endure following the results of the UK referendum on EU membership. This was further strengthened by Scots clearly voting to remain within the EU as compared with the vote in other parts of the UK (62% voted remain in Scotland as compared with only 46.6% in England (Electoral Commission 2016). Politically this has provided the Scottish Government with some leverage to argue in favour of a differentiated outcome for Scotland (Sturgeon 2016; Scottish Government 2016a, 2018a), or alternatively devolution of key areas to enable Scotland to maintain the legal position post-Brexit (Scottish Government 2016b, Chapter 4). However, the reality, thus far, has been that this has had little impact on intra-UK Brexit negotiations (May 2016). Despite this, the Scottish Government has set out its own proposals regarding its potential future relationship with the EU (Scottish Government 2016b, 2018a).

The Scottish Government's desire to maintain a relationship with the EU, and particularly to guarantee employment and equality rights, is somewhat in contrast to the position of the Westminster Government. The desired future relationship between the UK and the EU still remains unclear and the commitment to maintaining and developing employment and equality rights is less robust. The Westminster Government have stated that employment rights will be maintained in the period post-Brexit (HM Government 2017a, 31–33), leading some to argue that employment and equality laws will not change significantly in the immediate post-Brexit period (Ford 2016; Russell and MacLean 2016). The Westminster Government have also appeared to acknowledge the recommendations of the House of Commons Women and Equalities Committee (2017) and have noted their commitment 'to ensure the continued protection of people's rights not to be discriminated against, harassed or victimised in the provision of goods, services and public functions, housing, transport and education' (HM Government 2017b, 1). However, despite having the opportunity to do so, the Westminster Government has not taken any positive steps to ensure this, for instance by including a constitutional guarantee of equality as proposed by the House of Commons Women and Equalities Committee (2017, 26). The EU(W)A does note that 'due regard' must be had to the EA 2010 when enacting statutory instruments relating to withdrawal (Schedule 7, para. 28(5)), however this is far short of the kind of guarantee proposed here, which would have been more comparable with that in the Human Rights Act 1998 c.42 (HRA 1998). Notably there is also no reference to the employment context here in the commitment to preventing discrimination.

The more pressing concern is the loss of the floor of rights and the future development of these areas of law which are vulnerable to stagnation or deterioration (Barnard 2016; McColgan 2016; Ford 2016; Busby 2017), and not enhancement as the government claims (HM Government 2017a, 31). This is of particular concern given the deregulatory approach that has been adopted in recent years to UK employment rights (Hepple 2013; Ford 2016). Indeed, as Dickens has noted: '[w]orker protection as the objective of labour legislation, addressing the imbalance of power inherent in the employment relationship, has been displaced by regulation in the interest of a free market economy …' (2014, 238). There are some instances of 'gold plating' of EU employment law rights (Russell and Maclean 2016; Beecroft 2011), including some work-family rights, particularly the right to maternity leave, which is likely to be retained post-Brexit. There have also been instances where there has been further extension of rights to atypical family models, particularly in the context of extending maternity leave to intended parents in surrogacy. While the CJEU was unable to extend equivalent maternity rights to intended parents under the Pregnant Workers Directive 92/85/EEC, the UK CFA 2014 redefined adoption leave to include parents in this situation (EEC Directive 92/85 on the Protection of Pregnant Women at Work [PWD 1992]), (*CD v ST* and *Z v A Government Department;* For a discussion of these cases see Caracciolo di Torella and Foubert 2015). This is one area where the UK has the potential to develop the law further than that at an EU level post-Brexit due to the difficulties in achieving consensus, particularly around controversial topics such as alternative reproduction and family care.

Where there has been this enhancement at a UK level, it has often been around maternal rights and/or operates in such a way as to reinforce gender roles rather than challenge them. The desire to maintain and further develop these standards will also undoubtedly wane over time. Such an approach was evident in the recommendations of the previous Beecroft Report on Employment Law (2011), which would appear to strengthen this concern. Some of the key recommendations related, directly or indirectly, to work-family rights and could come to fruition post-Brexit. These include: exempting small businesses from the rights to request flexible working and shared parental leave; removing third party harassment provisions from the EA 2010; and introducing a financial cap for discrimination claims (Beecroft 2011, 5–6 and 8). It is at this point that employment and equality law become vulnerable, especially to 'the interests of the free market economy', as noted above. It is unsurprising that the Scottish Government, along with many others (Guerrina and Masselot 2018; Fawcett Society 2018; Busby 2017; Barnard 2016; Millns 2016; McColgan 2016; Ford 2016), perceive Brexit as a genuine threat to employment and equality rights.

Could Scotland Retain EU Employment and Equality Law Post-Brexit?

The Scottish Government is committed to attempting to either remaining within the EU or maintaining some kind of relationship that will enable the continuation of EU law post-Brexit. It is beyond the scope of this paper to discuss in detail the constitutional implications and likelihood of success of the Scottish Government proposals, but broadly speaking in 2016 these were: independence; to remain within the EEA, either alongside the UK or on their own; or, further devolution of repatriated powers from the EU, such as employment law

(Scottish Government 2016b). The commitment to the devolution of employment law was reiterated in the Scottish Government's programme for government in 2017–18 (Scottish Government 2017a, 27). In January 2018 the Scottish Government (2018a) presented updated proposals, which focused on Scotland remaining within the Single Market. In the context of work-family conflict the key feature of each of these proposals is that the Scottish Government would have the ability to maintain and follow the development of employment and equality law in line with changes at a European level. However, without remaining within the EU they would lose their ability to shape the future development of such legislation at the EU level.

As noted above, employment and equality law are outwith the current devolved competencies of the Scottish Parliament and without some kind of new constitutional arrangement, Scotland will be unable to automatically assume power of these areas post-Brexit (Zahn 2018). One way in which EU employment and equality law could remain applicable in Scotland could be under s.29 of the SA 1998. Under ss.29(1) and (2)(d) acts of the Scottish Parliament are not considered to have the force of law if, among other things, they are 'incompatible with any of the Convention rights or with EU law'. The EU(W)A maintains this position for retained EU law (s.12). This would ensure that retained EU law is protected post-Brexit, and insofar as this relates to EU employment and equality law this will ensure some continuation of that in the immediate period following Brexit. There are a number of caveats to this. Firstly, s.29 only applies to acts of the Scottish Parliament and not acts of the Westminster Parliament. Since all work-family rights are created by either acts or statutory instruments of the Westminster Parliament, this does not guarantee that they will remain in force post-Brexit. Secondly, since it only applies to legislation it has no impact on the continuing application or interpretation of EU law by the Scottish courts. Thirdly, as it refers to retained EU, it is subject to revision by the Westminster Parliament. While it requires the Scottish Parliament to act compatibly with retained EU law, it will not confer any additional guarantees about the implementation or retention of any areas of EU law post-Brexit.

In an attempt to retain control over those areas of EU law that will be repatriated post-Brexit and that are already devolved to the Scottish Parliament, the Scottish Government passed the UK Withdrawal from the European Union (Legal Continuity) (Scotland) Bill (UKEU(LC)(S)B) on the 22 March 2018. The UKEU(LC)(S)B contains various provisions which either retain or incorporate EU law into Scots law post-Brexit. This includes: retaining devolved EU-derived domestic legislation (s.2); incorporating devolved direct EU legislation into Scots law (s.3); retaining the application of s.2(1) of the European Communities Act 1972 c.68 for devolved competencies (s.4); retaining the general principles of EU law and the CFR, including their application by courts and tribunals, in so far as they relate to devolved competencies (s.5); retaining the supremacy of EU law with respect to those laws applying on and after exit day (s.6); allowing the courts and tribunals, where it is considered relevant, to have regard to the principles or judgments of the CJEU when interpreting retained devolved laws (s.10); and enabling Scottish Minister to make provisions corresponding to EU law post-Brexit (s.13), although this explicitly excludes the EA 2010 (s.13(5)(h)). The UKEU(LC)(S)B also makes provision enabling departure from EU law in devolved areas in order to address deficiencies arising from EU withdrawal (s.11).

While the UKEU(LC)(S)B would ensure that there is continuity for those areas already specifically devolved to the Scottish Parliament, it does not go as far as fully embedding EU law beyond the current effects of s.29 of the SA 1998. In order for the UKEU(LC)(S)B to have been effective in this context, the Scottish Parliament would have had to consider the possibility of adopting a similar provision to that in s.3 of the HRA 1998, which would require the Scottish courts to continue to interpret legislation, and common law principles, consistently with relevant principles of EU law. One possible way of achieving this would have been to attempt to retain the CFR more generally, rather than just in relation to devolved areas. This is necessary to ensure that the key principles of EU law continued to permeate all aspects of the application and interpretation of the relevant law in the Scottish context.

However, the UKEU(LC)(S)B has still to receive Royal Assent (SA 1998, s.32) as it is currently subject to legal challenge on the basis that it is outwith the legislative competence of the Scottish Parliament. The case was heard by the Supreme Court on 24–25 July 2018 and the decision was still outstanding at the time of publication. Despite this, leading Scottish experts believe that the UKEU(LC)(S)B is within the Parliament's legislative competence. It focuses on devolved competencies (s.1(4)(a)), and provisions aimed at responding to the status of EU law in this context following Brexit should similarly be within the Parliament's legislative competence (McCorkindale and McHarg 2018). In addition, since the legislation will not come into effect until after EU withdrawal (s.1(3)), the argument that provisions enabling departure from EU law are incompatible with s.29(2)(d) SA 1998 is also considered to be invalid (McCorkindale and McHarg 2018).

Given the current challenges facing the UKEU(LC)(S)B had the Scottish Parliament adopted a broader approach which attempted to retain EU law more fully this would certainly have been subject to a similar challenge. Consequently, while the UKEU(LC)(S)B underscores the clear commitment of the Scottish Government to preserve EU law in a meaningful way post-Brexit, it may be unable to deliver it in practice, and certainly not in its entirety.

Current, and potential, legal frameworks appear unable to accommodate the Scottish Government's ambitions to retain and/or acquire powers over employment and equality law. However, there may be alternative legal frameworks which could enable work-family rights to be protected and developed post-Brexit. Two possibilities are to consider the work-family conflict through the lens of current human rights obligations, or through commitments to international obligations.

5 HUMAN RIGHTS AND WORK-FAMILY CONFLICT

Human rights are currently within the devolved competency of the Scottish Parliament. In addition, s.29(1) and (2)(d) of the SA 1998 requires the Scottish Parliament to act compatibly with Convention rights in addition to their EU obligations. The ECHR was adopted by the Council of Europe and is not part of EU law, thus it will not be directly affected by Brexit. As noted previously, the ECtHR has previously held that Article 8 ECHR can be engaged when seeking equal access to the right to parental leave (*Markin*). This offers the potential, for working fathers in particular, to argue that Article 8 rights have been breached if the state does not afford working parents equal access to work-family rights. This could ensure that the gender-neutral approach towards working parents and care that is emerging at an EU level would not be entirely lost. However, it is important to remember that ECHR places obligations on the state and does not apply as between individuals. Nevertheless, the interpretative obligations under s.3 HRA 1998 do ensure that legislation must be interpreted consistently and so could be used in the application of such legislation as between private individuals (as noted in *X v Y (Employment: Sex Offender) aka X v Y (Unfair Dismissal)* [2004] ICR 1634, para. 57).

While the application of human rights post-Brexit extends across the UK, the SA 1998 contains those additional obligations in s.29 to act consistently with Convention rights. This could be notable because if Scotland were to gain powers over employment and equality law then they would also be required to ensure that they were compatible with Convention rights, including Article 8 and its interpretation in *Markin*. Should the Scottish Parliament subsequently wish to enact work-family legislation then it would arguably be required to ensure that it enacts such rights on a gender-neutral basis, recognising the right to care of both working parents. This could ensure greater recognition of fathers' rights in the future.

6   International Obligations and the Work-Family Conflict

In 2013 the Scottish Human Rights Commission and the Scottish Government launched Scotland's National Action Plan for Human Rights (SNAP) (Scottish Human Rights Commission 2013), which was underpinned with the aim of enabling everyone to live with human dignity. A part of this plan was for Scotland to give effect to its international obligations at home (Scottish Human Rights Commission 2013, Outcome 3). While this related specifically to human rights, it indicated a willingness to comply with international obligations to enhance domestic law. Nevertheless, it is important to note that international obligations are entered into by the UK as the contracting state in the first instance, and so Scotland would be unable to adopt any on their own. In addition, international obligations often lack specificity and enforceable rights. Finally, even if the Scottish government were to try to adhere to international obligations to address the gap left by EU law, this would not be of specific benefit in the work-family context.

While the UK is a State Party to the UN Convention on the Elimination of All Forms of Discrimination against Women 1979 (CEDAW) which includes sex discrimination and maternity leave (Articles 1, 2 and 11), it contains no enforceable rights to either. In addition, as its focus is on women, it does not specifically address the position of working fathers. Although Article 5 notes that 'States Parties shall take all appropriate measures ... (b) To ensure that family education includes ... recognition of the common responsibility of men and women in the upbringing and development of their children,' this appears to be focused on education and culture change rather than work-family rights. Ensuring that protections for women are maintained in domestic law is necessary, but without the commitment to ensuring that the double burden of work and care is not placed solely on women it does more to reinforce traditional gender roles than challenge them.

While Scotland could also look to the International Labour Organisation (ILO) to try to ensure that relevant labour standards are embedded into national law, this is unlikely to be of much benefit in practice. There are two ILO Conventions that are of potential relevance here: the ILO Discrimination (Employment and Occupation) Convention 1958 (No. 111) (ILO D(EO)C 1958), and the ILO Workers with Family Responsibilities Convention 1981 (No. 156) (ILO WFRC 1981). The UK ratified the former in 1999 and this is currently in force, however they have never ratified the latter. However, the ILO D(EO)C 1958 does not offer any specific protections for working parents and could perhaps continue to reinforce gender roles. In Article 5 it recognises that special measures could be adopted to 'meet the requirements of persons who, for reasons such as … family responsibilities … are generally recognised to require special protection … shall not be deemed to be discrimination.' While this would cover maternity leave, it is not as clear whether it would apply more broadly to gender-neutral family or parental leave. In contrast, the ILO WFRC 1981 much more explicitly refers to both parents (Article 1) and extends the discrimination principles in the ILO D(EO)C 1958 to this group (Article 3). However, while the Convention encourages protection against discrimination and dismissal on the grounds of family responsibilities, there is no specific encouragement of the development of gender-neutral work-family rights. Consequently, even if international obligations offered a possible opportunity to maintain standards, the current frameworks do not contain any specific benefits to the work-family conflict.

7   Engaging Men—Could There Be a Distinctly Scottish Approach Towards the Work–Family Conflict?

The likelihood of the various approaches noted above suggests that without significant constitutional changes Scotland will be unable to either retain EU law post-Brexit or gain control of employment and or equality law. However, were Scotland able to secure such powers, the question is then whether the Government would adopt a distinctly Scottish approach towards work-family conflict. As noted above, one of the key issues within the work-family context is the highly gendered nature of such rights, particularly in the UK. Engaging fathers and facilitating a more meaningful role in childcare is necessary to enable those fathers who want to, to care.

The approach of various UK governments to the issue of fathers' childcare role has been consistently weak, as is evident from the House of Commons Women and Equalities Committee Fathers in the Workplace Inquiry (HC Women and Equalities Committee 2016a, 2017). This inquiry found that very few fathers were likely to use the right to Shared Parental Leave (SPL) (only 2–8%), largely because of the low levels of remuneration (HC Women and Equalities Committee 2016b). It also acknowledged that this is contributing to the gender pay gap since it places barriers before fathers, impacting negatively on their ability to take SPL and reinforcing mothers as primary caregivers. This is problematic in general, and reinforces traditional gender roles, despite the 'new fatherhood' rhetoric discussed above. Perhaps even more concerning is that this largely represents the UK's approach towards gender equality and the work-family conflict. The potential consequences of this for the work-family conflict and related rights post-Brexit are troubling. At best, this could mean a continued reinforcement of traditional gender roles by failing to challenge the primacy of maternal rights, as is the case at present. At worst, it could indicate a 'levelling down' and/ or dismantling of the current package of rights, with similar gendered consequences.

This appears in contrast with the work of the Scottish Government to engage men in its gender equality agenda (Scottish Government 2018b). From the initiatives that the Scottish Government have currently pursued, in areas where they do have devolved competencies, it is evident that they have adopted an active role in recognising and valuing the role of fathers in caring for their children. This stems from their commitment in the National Parenting Strategy (2012) to better represent fathers, funding Families Need Fathers to provide advice and support follow separation, and supporting the Fathers Network Scotland deliver the Year of the Dad campaign in 2016. The Scottish Government (2018b) have also taken steps to facilitate recruitment of men in early years childcare, indicating a commitment to valuing male role models both within families and the wider childcare context.

This compares notably with the findings of the Working Families report on The Modern Families Index (2017) and the Women and Equalities inquiry, noted above, which indicates that fathers are now facing a 'fatherhood penalty' when wanting to balance work and family commitments. This, in part, is attributed to current UK legislation which reinforces traditional gender roles and is failing working fathers who want to combine work and care responsibilities. This is arguably reinforced in the Conservatives' Strengthening Families Manifesto (Bruce and Lord Farmer 2017). While the Manifesto aims to 'promote the importance of active fatherhood' (Point C), Policy 8 refers solely to ante-natal care and preparation for fatherhood and Policy 9 on the requirement to name fathers on the birth certificate. While it is undoubtedly important to engage fathers during the ante-natal period, this does not go far enough to recognise and value their childcare role. This is particularly the case given the findings discussed above.

Here it is worth noting that the Scottish Government launched the Nordic-Baltic Policy Statement in 2014, and updated it in 2017, with the aim of strengthening relationships between Scotland and its Nordic and Baltic neighbours, as well as enhancing Scotland's international attractiveness and global outlook, and protecting Scotland's place in Europe (Scottish Government 2017b, 6). Since the policy statement was first adopted, the Scottish Government has adopted a number of initiatives which have been influenced by this experience (see 2017b, 3–5 for more details). The Baby Box initiative is one such example, which entitles every new baby in Scotland to receive a box filled with some essential items that a new baby will need. This adopts a similar Finnish policy (2017b, 3), and shows engagement with policies on children and families. This alignment with its European counterparts is particularly notable from a work-family perspective given the work-family reputation of countries within the Nordic region in particular (for an overview of legislation in this area see Blum et al. 2017).

If Scotland were to achieve control over employment and/or equality law, this alignment of policy could indicate that a like-minded future Scottish Government would be open to adopting a more Nordic approach towards the work-family conflict. This is reinforced in the Scottish Government's current plans, which include learning from the Swedish experience of shared parenting (Scottish Government 2017b, 7). The Swedish model of parental leave is often presented as an 'ideal type' in the work-family context (although this does not necessarily result in equal use in practice, see further Caracciolo di Torella 2000; Weldon-Johns 2011), given its length (480 days), flexibility (it can be used in hourly blocks), and gender-neutral underpinning (Parental Leave Act SFS 1995:584, as amended by SFS 2015:760). While mothers still use the majority of the leave, working fathers are more engaged in care (Statistics Sweden 2016, 39). Greater alignment with this policy approach would offer the opportunity for greater commitment to gender equality and fathers' rights in the future.

While it is not clear that the Scottish Government will be able to achieve devolution of employment and/or equality law or achieve a differentiated outcome post-Brexit, what appears evident is that the current Scottish Government would prefer a different approach to the rest of the UK. This approach appears to be closer to its European, particularly Nordic, counterparts, which could indicate a potentially more 'father' friendly and gender-neutral approach towards the work-family conflict in future.

8   Conclusions: The Implications of Brexit on Work–Family Conflict— A Scottish Perspective

The gendered implications of Brexit are particularly notable in the work-family context. While the UK has few solely EU-derived work-family rights, many others are heavily influenced by the EU position, and those which are solely UK-derived are notably gendered in practice. The position of working fathers is particularly vulnerable given their already secondary status within UK law. This vulnerability at a UK level appears to be challenged when looking at these issues from a Scottish perspective. While the legislative and constitutional mechanisms for adopting a distinctly Scottish perspective are not currently in place, this paper has argued that there could be a distinctly Scottish approach if they were. The current Scottish Government's approach is far more committed to retaining continuity with EU law post-Brexit. In addition, the Scottish Government has been more supportive of fathers in the areas where they have competence, and appear to be much closer to their European, particularly Nordic, counterparts here. This suggests that Scotland could adopt a distinct approach towards the work-family conflict should they ever have the legal mechanisms to do so, and one that would potentially adopt a more gender-neutral approach.

BIBLIOGRAPHY

Aitkenson, J. 2017. Shared Parental Leave in the UK: Can It Advance Gender Equality By Changing Fathers Into Co-Parents? *International Journal of Law in Context* 13 (3): 356–368.

Barnard, C. 2016. Oral Evidence to the Women and Equalities Committee. *Impact of Brexit on Gender*, HC 657 14, September.

Beecroft, A. 2011. Report on Employment Law. URN 12/825.

Blum, S., Koslowski, A., and Moss, P. 2017. International Review of Leave Policies and Research 2017. http://www.leavenetwork.org/lp_and_r_reports/.

Busby, N. 2017. Equality Law, Brexit and Devolution. *Employment Law Bulletin* 142: 4–7.

Bruce, F., and Lord Farmer. 2017. Strengthening Families Manifesto: Policies for a Conservative Government to Strengthen Families.

Caracciolo di Torella, E. 2000. A Critical Assessment of the EC Legislation Aimed at Reconciling Work and Family Life: Lessons from the Scandinavian Model? In *Legal Regulation of the Employment Relation*, ed. H. Collins, P. Davies, and R. Rideout. London: Kluwer Law International.

Caracciolo di Torella, E. 2007. New Labour, New Dads—The Impact of Family Friendly Legislation on Fathers. *Industrial Law Journal* 36 (3): 318–328.

Caracciolo di Torella, E. 2014. Brave New Fathers for a Brave New World? Fathers as Caregivers in an Evolving European Union. *European Law Journal* 20 (1): 88–106.

Caracciolo di Torella, E. 2015. Men in the Work/Family Reconciliation Discourse: The Swallows That Did Not Make a Summer? *Journal of Social Welfare and Family Law* 37 (3): 334–344.

Caracciolo di Torella, E. 2017. An Emerging Right to Care in the EU: A "New Start to Support Work-Life Balance for Parents and Carers". *ERA Forum* 18: 187–198.

Caracciolo di Torella, E., and P. Foubert. 2015. Surrogacy, Pregnancy and Maternity Rights: A Missed Opportunity for a More Coherent Regime of Parental Rights in the EU. *European Law Review* 40: 52–69.

Caracciolo di Torella, E., and A. Masselot. 2001. Pregnancy, Maternity and the Organisation of Family Life: An Attempt to Classify the Case Law of the Court of Justice. *European Law Review* 26 (3): 239–260.

Collier, R. 1995. *Masculinity, Law and the Family*. London and New York: Routledge.

Collier, R. 1999. 'Feminising' the Workplace? Law, the 'Good Parent' and the 'Problem of Men.' In *Feminist Perspective on Employment Law*, ed. Anne Morris and Thérèse O'Donnell. London: Cavendish.

Collier, R. 2001. A Hard Time to Be a Father? Reassessing the Relationship Between Law, Policy, and Family (Practices). *Journal of Law and Society* 28 (4): 520–545.

Collier, R. 2010. *Men, Law and Gender: Essays on the 'Man' of Law*. Oxon: Routledge.

Collier, R., and S. Sheldon. 2008. *Fragmenting Fatherhood: A Socio-Legal Study*. Oxford: Hart Publishing.

Crompton, R. 1999. *Restructuring Gender Relations and Employment: The Decline of the Male Breadwinner*. Oxford: Oxford University Press.

Dermott, E. 2001. New Fatherhood in Practice?—Parental Leave in the UK. *The International Journal of Sociology and Social Policy* 21 (4–6): 145–164.

Dermott, E. 2005. Time and Labour: Fathers' Perceptions of Employment and Childcare. *Sociological Review*, 53: 89–103.

Dickens, L. 2014. The Coalition Government's Reforms to Employment Tribunals and Statutory Employment Rights—Echoes of the Past. *Industrial Relations Journal* 45 (3): 234–249.

Department of Trade and Industry. 2003. *Balancing Work and Family: Enhancing Choice and Support for Parents*. London: Department of Trade and Industry.

Department of Trade and Industry. 2005. *Work and Families: Choice and Flexibility, A Consultation Document*. London: Department of Trade and Industry.

Electoral Commission. 2016. EU Referendum Results. https://www.electoral-commission.org.uk/find-information-by-subject/elections-and-referendums/past-elections-and-referendums/eu-referendum/electorate-and-count-information. Accessed 18 May 2018.

Ellis, E. 1991. *European Community Sex Equality Law*. Oxford: Oxford University Press.

Fawcett Society. 2018. *Sex Discrimination Law Review*. London: Fawcett Society.

Ford, M. 2016. Legal Advice to the TUC: Workers' Rights from Europe: The Impact of Brexit.

Foubert, P. 2017. Child Care Leave 2.0—Suggestions for the Improvement of the EU Maternity and Parental Leave Directives from a Rights Perspective. *Maastricht Journal of European and Comparative Law* 24 (2): 245–263.

Fineman, M. 1995. *The Neutered Mother, the Sexual Family and Other Twentieth Century Tragedies*. New York: Routledge Press.

Fredman, S. 2014. Reversing Roles: Bringing Men into the Frame. *International Journal of Law in Context* 10 (4): 442–459.

Gornick, J.C., and M.K. Meyers. 2003. *Families That Work: Policies for Reconciling Parenthood and Employment*. New York: Russell Sage Foundation.

Guerrina, R., and A. Masselot. 2018. Walking into the Footprint of EU Law: Unpacking the Gendered Consequences of Brexit. *Social Policy and Society*: 1–12. https://doi.org/10.1017/s1474746417000501.

Hepple, B. 2013. Back to the Future: Employment Law Under the Coalition Government. *Industrial Law Journal* 42 (3): 203–223.

HC Women and Equalities Committee. 2016a. Fathers in the Workplace Inquiry. https://www.parliament.uk/business/committees/committees-a-z/commons-select/women-and-equalities-committee/inquiries/parliament-2015/fathers-and-the-workplace-16–17/. Accessed 18 May 2018.

HC Women and Equalities Committee. 2016b. Gender Pay Gap Report. https://publications.parliament.uk/pa/cm201516/cmselect/cmwomeq/584/58402.htm. Accessed 18 May 2018.

HC Women and Equalities Committee. 2017. Ensuring Strong Equalities Legislation After the EU Exit, Seventh Report of Session 2016–17. HC 799.

HM Government. 2011. *Consultation on Modern Workplaces, Flexible Parental Leave*. London: BIS.

HM Government. 2012. *Consultation on Modern Workplaces. Modern Workplaces—Government Response on Flexible Parental Leave—Impact Assessment*. London: BIS.

HM Government. 2017a. *The United Kingdom's Exit from and New Partnership with the European Union*. Cm 9417. London: H.M. Stationery Office.

HM Government. 2017b. Ensuring Strong Equalities Legislation After the EU Exit: Government's Response to the Committee's Seventh Report of Session 2016–17. HC 385.

James, G. 2006. The Work and Families Act 2006: Legislation to Improve Choice and Flexibility? *Industrial Law Journal* 35 (3): 272–278.

James, G. 2009. Mothers and Fathers as Parents and Workers; Family Friendly Employment Policies in an Era of Shifting Identities. *Journal of Social Welfare and Family Law* 31 (3): 271–283.

James, G. 2012. Forgotten Children: Work–Family Reconciliation in the EU. *Journal of Social Welfare and Family Law* 34 (3): 363–379.

Lewis, J. 2001. The Decline of the Male Breadwinner Model: Implications for Work and Care. *Social Politics* 8 (2): 152–169.

Lock, T. 2017. Human Rights Law in the UK After Brexit. Brexit Special Extra Issue, *Public Law* (Nov Supp): 117–134.

Lupton, D., and L. Barclay. 1997. *Constructing Fatherhood: Discourses and Experiences*. London: Sage.

May, T. 2016. Full Speech: Theresa May on 'Britain After Brexit'. *The Spectator*, October 2. https://blogs.spectator.co.uk/2016/10/full-speech-theresa-mays-britain-brexit-speech/. Accessed 18 May 2018.

McColgan, A. 2000. Family Friendly Frolics? The Maternity and Parental Leave Etc. Regulations 1999. *Industrial Law Journal* 29 (2): 125–144.

McColgan, A. 2016. Oral Evidence to the Women and Equalities Committee. *Impact of Brexit on Gender*. HC 657.

McCorkindale, C. 2018. Brexit and Human Rights. *Edinburgh Law Review* 22 (1): 126–132.

McCorkindale, C., and A. McHarg. 2018. Continuity and Confusion: Legislating for Brexit in Scotland and Wales (Part II). UK Constitutional Law Blog, March 7. https://ukconstitutionallaw.org/2018/03/07/christopher-mccorkindale-and-aileen-mcharg-continuity-and-confusion-legislating-for-brexit-in-scotland-and-wales-part-ii/. Accessed 18 May 2018.

McGlynn, C. 2000. Ideologies of Motherhood in European Community Sex Equality Law. *European Law Journal* 6 (1): 29–44.

Miller, T. 2011a. Falling Back Into Gender? Men's Narratives and Practices Around First-Time Fatherhood. *Sociology* 45 (6): 1094–1109.

Miller, T. 2011b. *Making Sense of Fatherhood: Gender, Caring and Work.* Cambridge: Cambridge University Press.

Millns, S. 2016. What Does Brexit Mean for Women? http://www.sussex.ac.uk/eu/articles/brexit-women. Accessed 18 May 2018.

Mitchell, G. 2015. Encouraging Fathers to Care: The Children and Families Act 2014 and Shared Parental Leave. *Industrial Law Journal* 44 (1): 123–133.

More, G. 1996. Equal Treatment in European Community Law: The Limits of Market Equality. In *Feminist Perspectives on the Foundational Subjects of Law,* ed. A. Bottomley. London: Cavendish Publishing.

Morris, A., and T. O'Donnell (eds.). 1999. *Feminist Perspectives on Employment Law.* London: Cavendish Publishing.

Murphie, J., and M. Weldon-Johns. 2016. The Future of Scottish Labour Law: Reconceptualisation and Modernisation. *Juridical Review* 3: 227–254.

ONS. 2016. Changes in the Value and Division of Unpaid Care Work in the UK: 2000 to 2015. London: ONS.

Russell, K., and N. MacLean. 2016. Brexit Analysis Bulletin Employment, Immigration & Human Rights. Shepherd and Wedderburn. http://www.shepwedd.co.uk/sites/default/files/Employment_PostRef_Brexit.pdf.

Scottish Government. 2012. *National Parenting Strategy.* Edinburgh: Scottish Government.

Scottish Government. 2014a. *Working Together Review: Progressive Workplace Policies in Scotland.* Edinburgh: Scottish Government.

Scottish Government. 2014b. *More Powers for the Scottish Parliament.* Edinburgh: Scottish Government.

Scottish Government. 2015. *Beyond Smith—Scottish Government Proposals for More Powers for the Scottish Parliament.* Edinburgh: Scottish Government.

Scottish Government. 2016a. *Scotland: A European Nation.* Edinburgh: Scottish Government.

Scottish Government. 2016b. *Scotland's Place in Europe.* Edinburgh: Scottish Government.

Scottish Government. 2017a. *A Nation with Ambition: The Government's Programme for Scotland 2017–18.* Edinburgh: Scottish Government.

Scottish Government. 2017b. *All Points North: The Scottish Government's Nordic Baltic Policy Statement.* Edinburgh: Scottish Government.

Scottish Government. 2018a. *Scotland's Place in Europe: People, Jobs and Investment.* Edinburgh: Scottish Government.

Scottish Government. 2018b. Engaging with Men. https://beta.gov.scot/policies/gender-equality/engaging-with-men/. Accessed 18 May 2018.

Scottish Human Rights Commission. 2013. *Scotland's National Action Plan for Human Rights.* Edinburgh: Scottish Human Rights Commission.

Smith Commission. 2014. *Report of the Smith Commission for Further Devolution of Powers to the Scottish Parliament.* Edinburgh: The Smith Commission.

Statistics Sweden. 2016. *Women and Men in Sweden: Facts and Figures 2016.* Örebro: Statistics Sweden.

Sturgeon, N. 2016. Full Speech: Nicola Sturgeon on 'The EU Referendum Result'. https://stv.tv/news/politics/1358534-nicola-sturgeon-speech-in-full-after-eu-referendum-result/. Accessed 18 May 2018.

Taylor, M. 2017. *Good Work: The Taylor Review of Modern Working Practices.* London: Royal Society of the Arts.

Tipping, S., J. Chanfreau, J. Perry, and C. Tait. 2012. *The Fourth Work-Life Balance Employees Survey.* Employment Relations Research Series No.122. London: BIS.

Warin, J., Y. Solomon, C. Lewis, and W. Langford. 1999. *Fathers, Work and Family Life.* London: Family Policy Studies Centre for the Joseph Rowntree Foundation.

Weldon-Johns, M. 2011. The Additional Paternity Leave Regulations 2010: A New Dawn or More 'Sound-Bite' Legislation? *Journal of Social Welfare & Family Law* 33 (1): 25–38.

Weldon-Johns, M. 2013. EU Work–Family Policies—Challenging Parental Roles or Reinforcing Gendered Stereotypes? *European Law Journal* 19 (2): 1–20.

Weldon-Johns, M. 2016. From Modern Workplaces to Modern Families—Re-envisioning the Work-Family Concept. *Journal of Social Welfare and Family Law* 37 (4): 1–21.

Wintemute, R. 1998. When Is pregnancy discrimination indirect sex discrimination? *Industrial Law Journal* 27 (1): 23–36.

Working Families. 2017. *The Modern Family Index 2017.* London: Working Families.

Yong, A. 2017. Forgetting Human Rights—The Brexit Debate. *European Human Rights Law Review* 5: 469–479.

Zahn, R. 2018. The Impact of Brexit on Employment Law in Scotland. *Edinburgh Law Review* 22 (1): 160–165.

CHAPTER 13

Foreboding Newness: Brexit and Feminist Civil Society in Scotland

Emma Ritch

1 Introduction

Constitutional politics has inflected Scottish politics over the past five years, as the electorate has voted twice in referenda that have sought its views on Scotland's place in the unions of Europe and the United Kingdom. The level and content of engagement of women and women's organisations in the two referenda stands in stark contrast: feminists carved out space to participate in the Scottish independence referendum but did not find a toe-hold in the debate about Brexit.

The independence referendum campaign that culminated in the vote of September 2014 saw the establishment of new women's organisations and networks to counterbalance a marginalisation of women's concerns in the official campaigns. It also saw a galvanising of the existing women's sector and feminist academics and practitioners to think about the constitutional future of Scotland. The Scotland-specificity of the institutional women's sector became freshly salient as it pivoted to focus on the consequences for women of the likely answers to a particularly Scottish set

E. Ritch (✉)
Engender, Edinburgh, UK
e-mail: emma.ritch@engender.org.uk

© The Author(s) 2019
M. Dustin et al. (eds.), *Gender and Queer Perspectives on Brexit*,
Gender and Politics, https://doi.org/10.1007/978-3-030-03122-0_13

of constitutional questions. There were significant differences of opinion between pro-union and pro-independence women that cut across groups of feminists that had self-organised around other, gendered objectives. However, there was collaboration by women's organisations and networks around the broad purpose of informing and engaging women, enabling women to participate in the national conversation, and in considering the gender dimensions of Scotland's future. Set against this, the much briefer European Union referendum pre-election period of spring 2016, which overlapped with the local government election campaign in Scotland, saw limited national public engagement and lacked much rigorous gender analysis, even in feminist spaces. This referendum failed to see the bridging of some of the fissures created by funding, context, and purpose that lie between the women's sectors in each of the four nations. Consequently, there was no coherent UK women's sector response to the EU referendum. The abbreviated campaign and its location on the terrain of business and trade meant that no feminist Scotland-specific networks or groups were established, and a widespread sense of confusion about the possible outcomes for women prevailed.

Post-referendum, feminist and gender advocates are still largely working in national silos to identify a possible response to the Brexit negotiations. Following the post-independence referendum Smith Commission and the consequent Scotland Act 2016, Scottish feminist policy organisations are contemplating the opportunities and threats of further devolution, and considering the impact on women's equality of new powers coming to Holyrood. Women and women's organisations are also considering how they can continue to engage post-Brexit with pan-European feminist structures like the European Women's Lobby (EWL), and its joint campaigning for (still) relevant instruments such as the Istanbul Convention.

2   CONSTITUTIONAL POLITICS

Feminists and women's organisations in Scotland have long been involved in discussions about constitutional questions, and particularly those that have related to the division of power and responsibility between the UK and Scotland. Before the independence vote, there was sustained activity in the years preceding the referendum on devolution in 1997, and the subsequent re-establishment of the Scottish Parliament in 1999. A coalition of activist women 'mobilised around their feminist and gender identities—sometimes across other significant social and political divisions and identity claims—in order to insert gendered claims into the constitutional reform process' (Mackay 2006) co-ordinated by the Scottish Trades Union Congress (STUC) Women's Committee, formed a 50/50 campaign to push for equal representation within Holyrood. During the eight years that the Scottish Constitutional Convention worked on a blueprint for the Scottish Parliament, this claim of the right to 50/50 equal representation for women 'captured the imagination of women across the spectrum' (Planning Group 2010). Thousands of women in political parties, trade unions, churches, and civic communities worked together in its advocacy, and the Labour Party and Liberal Democrat party ultimately signed an agreement committing themselves to the principle of equal representation and to fielding a gender balance of candidates. When the new Parliament met in April of 1999, 37% of its members were women (Brown 1999).

The work of national feminist policy and advocacy organisations such as Engender, Close the Gap, Rape Crisis Scotland, and Scottish Women's Aid, has intermittently been shaded by constitutional questions since their founding. The pre-2016 Scottish devolution settlement, whereby Scotland had a distinct education system, health service, and legal system, and the Scottish Parliament had competence across health, education, environment, law, economic development, childcare, and housing, has not always been well-understood either by policymakers in Whitehall or by civil society organisations in other parts of the UK. There are differences in the experiences of women and women's equality in Scotland that range across data, law, policy specificities, gender architecture, and political will (Wood 2014a). This has meant that gender equality work within UK networks, such as the End Violence Against Women coalition, or work using international instruments, such as the Convention on the Elimination of All Forms of Discrimination Against Women, has necessitated a great deal of translation and negotiation as to how to present the experiences of women in Scotland and how to call for specific, relevant changes to policy, programmes, and law. As an example of an instance where this advocacy for differentiation was not wholly successful, the United Nations Convention on the Elimination of all forms of Discrimination Against Women Committee's concluding observations in 2013 included a call for the UK Government to develop a UK-wide violence against women strategy (UN CEDAW Committee 2013). As violence against women is a policy area that is entirely devolved to

Scotland, this concluding observation was seen as at best pointless and at worst unhelpfully confusing by gender advocates in Scotland. This was not how the call was read in Northern Ireland, however: women from the Northern Ireland Women's European Platform (NIWEP) expressed a preference for a strategy developed by the UK Government's Government Equalities Office (GEO) over no strategy at all. They were of the view that GEO could be a driver of gender-sensitive practice in their nation in a way that civil society had not been able to achieve. Civil society organisations across the four nations do not have similar, or even equivalent, relationships with the UK Government.

The constitutional awkwardness that colours Scottish women's organisations engagement in UN processes has parallels with the ways in which women's organisations in Scotland and the UK relate to European feminist networks and umbrella organisations, and thereby participate in advocacy at the European level. The EWL is the largest feminist umbrella organisation working across Europe, with a membership of national co-ordinations in each of the member states as well as pan-European organisations. As there is not a UK-wide umbrella organisation in the women's sector, a synthetic co-ordination was created some thirty years ago from organisations working in each of the four nations. The UK Joint Committee on Women is composed of two representatives each from Engender (Scotland), NIWEP, National Alliance of Women's Organisations (England), and Women's Equality Network Wales (WEN Wales). It rotates the roles of chair or convener, Lobby board member, Lobby board alternate, and secretariat around the four organisations. As if a metaphor for the various practical challenges of this solution, the timings that ensure a reasonable rotation do not readily align with those of the Lobby's own term-limits and processes for filling its structures.

3   Newness

An instrumentalist approach to constitutional questions was much in evidence in the first decade of devolution. Feminists and women's networks had worked within a loose coalition of trade unionists, religious bodies, and civil society organisations under the banner of 'Civic Scotland' to shape a Parliament and government that was relatively open and accessible. Symbolic of the openness and gender-sensitivity that women's advocates sought to engender was the establishment of the crèche in the Scottish Parliament (Scottish Parliament 2018) able to be used by members of the public and individuals from organisations who have business at the Parliament and bring their young children with them. Both symbolic and substantive were some of the gender mainstreaming mechanisms within the freshly-minted Parliament: the statutory Equal Opportunities Committee (now the Equality and Human Rights Committee) and the fact that equal opportunities was one of the four principles of the Parliament itself (Brown et al. 1998). Eager to translate the promise of this new way of working into gains for women, gender advocates busied themselves in lobbying the female parliamentarians who had either come from the women's sector in Scotland or who had been most responsive to the calls of the Women 50/50 campaign. Of the flurry of bills that passed the Scottish Parliament in its opening session, the first from a Committee was the Protection from Abuse (Scotland) Bill (SPICe 2003) which sought to increase safety for victim-survivors of domestic abuse.

The burst of activity around the reinstituted Scottish Parliament was animated by the possibility of newness. The building or redesign of institutions compelled by constitutional change offered the possibility of either avoiding or doubling-down on some of the gendered inequalities of the past. Women's organisations pushed forward with ambitions of descriptive and substantive equality in representation, and of gender mainstreaming within Parliamentary business, and began to organise around the idea of a Scottish budget process that incorporated gender budget analysis (O'Hagan 2015).

It was this sense of the possibilities of newness that caught the imagination of gender advocates in Scotland during the independence referendum. The sweep of institutions and powers that would be newly constituted and conferred on an independent Scotland encouraged a bold period of imagining those powers and institutions as shaped, directed, and delivering to meet the needs of women and girls, as well as boys and men. Conversely, the inchoate sense of what was on the table with regards to newness during the brief Brexit referendum kept women's organisations at arm's length. Gender advocates instinctively grasped what Fiona Mackay describes as 'nested newness' (Mackay 2014): that institutions are created with at least a flavour of their context. Whereas Scottish independence, for those enthused by the idea, seemed to be contextualised by a commitment to human rights, equality, and a partly shared sense of the common weal, Brexit appeared to be characterised by exceptionalism, conservatism, scepticism about human rights and broadly progressive values, and insularity.

The Enabling 'Newness': The Independence Referendum

Before the independence referendum, there were high-profile successes for those working around equality. Scotland's marriage equality bill developed out of a painstaking process that brought civil society and political parties together to hash out the detail. Consequently, Scotland's law is considered one of the most progressive in the world, with pro-tections for trans rights, no spousal veto, and the possibility of marriage using gender-neutral forms and religious marriage (Equality Network 2014). Decades of work by violence against women organisations such as Rape Crisis Scotland and Scottish Women's Aid had yielded progressively better gendered strategies to tackle men's violence, and were critical in influencing the development of the pre-referendum Scottish strategy, *Equally Safe* (Scottish Government 2014). This was unheralded in global terms in including primary prevention activity based on the analysis that it is women's economic and political inequality that creates the condu-cive context for men's violence. It made real the slogan that women's inequality is both cause and consequence of violence against women. This relative success in advocating for equalities outcomes in Scotland encouraged organisations to view the prospect of increased devolution, or indeed independence, as presenting a hospitable environment for their work, their calls for action, and ultimately the realisation of equality and rights for their constituency protected groups.

Although women's equality is theoretically possible under almost any constitutional arrangement, the scope for creating institutions afresh appears to offer an opportunity to build gender in with the bricks. Examples of this in Scotland at the time of writing include the creation of a Scottish National Investment Bank (SNIB) to support Scotland's economic objectives and to drive inclusive growth (Scottish Government 2017). Engender, working with gender and labour market experts Close the Gap, the Scottish Women's Budget Group, Women's Enterprise Scotland, the Women in Scotland's Economy research centre (WiSE) and women in STEM specialists Equate Scotland, produced a set of seven principles for a gender-competent SNIB. These spanned calls for a prin-ciple of equality and non-discrimination at the core of the bank; invest-ment in childcare and care as infrastructure; care to be designated as a 'key sector' in Scotland's economic strategy; equal benefit for men and women and boys and girls from the creation of jobs and technologies; wellbeing indicators alongside GVA and GDP; increased capitalisation of women's businesses; and a gender-balanced, gender-competent leadership team (Ritch 2017). With the Scottish Government's response to their consultation on SNIB awaited, it is not possible to see whether women's equality will be integrated into plans for its development. What seems certain, though, is that the creation of the bank represents a moment of possibility for organisations that have been working around women's economic equality, in ways that seems vastly diminished in existing institutions with concretised ways of working, power centres, and priorities.

Similarly, those tentative additional devolutionary steps that were taken after the independence referendum are also presenting opportunities in Scotland for gendering what is inadequately gendered within current UK policy. Engender has created a coalition of women's organisations in Scotland that has charted the extent to which austerity-compelled cuts to social security, described as 'welfare reform', have unequally and harshly fallen on women (Wood 2015). Work by the Women's Budget Group has estimated that the decade of austerity stretching between 2010 and 2020 will see 85 pence in every pound of cuts to pensions, wages, social security, and services come from women's purses. Engender's own work describes the impact on different groups of women, as disabled women, Black and minority ethnic women, and single mothers find themselves coerced into paid work, denied adequate support for independent living, and see dedicated service delivery decrease. We have used this analysis of women's lived experience across domains of care, domestic abuse, employability, labour market participation, and identity to make specific calls for a gendered social security system (Wood 2016a). At the time of writing, a social security bill is making its way through the Scottish Parliament, including commitments to equality and human rights. There are substantial areas of disagreement over the detail, much of which will be set out in statutory instruments, but the tenor of discussion is substantially and substantively different from the policy space from which emerged Universal Credit and the 'rape clause'.[1]

During the period immediately following the independence referendum, when the hastily-established Smith Commission was convened to consider the additional powers that should be devolved to the Scottish

---

[1] The 'rape clause' is an exception to the two-child cap on the child element of Universal Credit, in which women who have conceived a child as a result of rape are able to claim this entitlement for third or subsequent children.

Parliament, Engender opened a survey to inform our response. Although the intensely pressing timescales for participation meant that it was only open for a few days, over a thousand women and men used it to say that they wanted to see equality, social security, and employment law devolved to Scotland (Wood 2014b).

The Foreboding 'Newness': Brexit

In contrast, the 'newness' offered by Brexit—properly, the exiting of Britain from the European Union—appeared to offer limited possibilities for advancing women's equality and rights.

There was a lack of certainty in the prospectus being offered by the Leave campaign, including seemingly vital details around the border bisecting the island of Ireland, the free movement of people, and the extent to which the UK would retain its existing trade relationships and membership of the customs union. This vagueness seemed less promising than an equivalent lack of specificity in some key areas of the independence debate, and the context less conducive to imaginative thought about how any new institutions, laws, programmes, and processes might be gendered.

Successive UK Governments, including the Conservative Government that was in place at the Brexit vote, as well as the previous Coalition Government, have been antipathetic towards women's equality and rights. The prospect of replacing the Human Rights Act with a 'British Bill of Rights' has stuttered in implementation but remains a commitment. The Equality Act 2010, which included all of the anti-discrimination law underpinned by EU law and regulation, had been included in the 2014 UK Government 'Red Tape Challenge' to bin 'unnecessary' and 'excessive' regulation (*Red Tape Challenge* 2011). Persistent failures to gender policy adequately means that unintended consequences are rife: should the UK Government's proposed changes to housing benefit go ahead, 39% of the domestic abuse refuges in England will have to close their doors, with further services reducing the number of beds (Grierson 2017).

Gender Mainstreaming

Women's equality and rights are enabled by having the right gender architecture. Simply put, this architecture consists of laws, processes, institutions, and ways of doing things that create responsibility and accountability for making women's rights a reality (Wood 2014a, 11).

Every day thousands of decisions are made by Scottish Government, public authorities, and private companies that tip the scales towards or away from women's equality. For the past few decades, gender advocates have promoted gender mainstreaming as the only path to ensuring continuing movement in the right direction (Cavaghan 2017). This orients the resources of the state behind the pursuit of gender justice, and builds gender equality considerations into all policy development, spending, and service delivery, rather than restricting it to a few specialist initiatives and interventions.

Gender mainstreaming has matured as a theory, but is not flourishing in practice in Scotland. There are non-trivial challenges to making it work, not least answering the question of how a policy developed outside the mainstream, in feminist spaces, and based on abstract concepts like the 'social construction of gender' becomes part of mainstream policymaking, budgeting, and service delivery. Rosalind Cavaghan's recent book on mainstreaming in the context of the EU notes that 'gender mainstreaming's rise to prominence as a well-accepted policy tool has coincided with a confusing socio-political context where increased acceptance of gender equality as a legitimate, though vaguely-defined, goal co-exists with a common disinterest in, or hostility to, "feminism"' (ibid.).

Engender and other women's organisations see a clear necessity for political commitment and policy focus at every level to make substantive progress against intractable gender gaps. The creative institutional, programme, policy, and legislative bonanza of 'newness' seems to offer a way to cut through some of the inertia around gender mainstreaming. The outcomes of our work to influence the shape of the SNIB and new social security agency may provide some indicator as to whether constitutional change offers much of a short-cut to where we want to be.

4   A Tale of Two Referenda: Women's Experiences of Indyref and EUref

Independence Referendum

The political story of the Scottish independence referendum is well-rehearsed. The UK Government, having watched polls stagnate, thought they could shoot a totemic SNP fox by seeming to capitulate on the demand for a referendum at a time of the Scottish Government's choosing. The Edinburgh Agreement between the UK Government and Scottish Government was duly signed in October 2012, and powers transferred to the Scottish Parliament so that it could legislate for a single-question referendum to be held before the end of 2014. Plans were made for the question 'Should Scotland be an independent country?' to be put to the nation in September 2014.

The two official, designated campaigns were YES Scotland and Better Together. YES Scotland was established by the Scottish National Party, Scottish Green Party, and Scottish Socialist Party. Over time it served as both launch-pad and foil to a loose network of campaigning groups that emerged during the period in the run up to the referendum. Better Together was the more sedate product of an agreement between the Scottish Conservative, Scottish Labour, and Scottish Liberal Democrats to campaign together around a pro-union position. The two official campaigns launched in Spring 2012.

Staff members of both campaigns included women who are publicly and notably committed to gender equality advocacy, including Susan Stewart at YES Scotland (Khaleeli 2014) and Victoria Jamieson at Better Together (Pike 2015). Nevertheless, women were not obviously considered as a constituency by either organisation in the early months of their work. By Autumn 2012, there was sufficient exasperation among many women involved in politics, caused by the male-dominated independence conversation centred around mineral rights and the technical details of referendum implementation, that a number of these women had joined forces to launch Women for Independence (WfI). Press reporting (Barnes 2012) at the time lists founding members of the campaign as 'former SNP candidate and left-wing campaigner Isobel Lindsay, and the ex-Scottish Socialist MSP Carolyn Leckie', noting that 'other backers are Jeanne Freeman, formerly a special adviser to then-First Minister Jack McConnell, Susan Stewart, the first "Ambassador" for the Scottish Government in Washington, DC and Kate Higgins, a leading blogger.' Perhaps indicative of the way that WfI seized imaginations is the fact that the 'former [Labour] special advisor' is now the Scottish Government's Minister for Social Security and the 'leading blogger' is now a special advisor to the same government.

Its purpose was incorporated within the mirroring of its name: "Women for Independence | Independence for Women". It wanted to advocate for a broad range of issues around women's equality or liberation at the same time as campaigning for an independent Scotland. Over the following months and years, it was to galvanise women's participation through a network of local groups, and meet some of the demand for a conversation about how a newly-independent Scotland might satisfy women's thirst for equality and human rights. Although its relationship with institutional feminism was flexible—some of its members were committed feminists while others would shudder to apply that label to themselves—the content of its meetings and events certainly overlapped with well-worn feminist demands. WfI members were concerned with childcare delivery, with the gender pay gap, with developing a healthy care economy, and with ending violence against women. As the group constituted as a collective, members' own specific expertise around campaigning priorities heavily influenced the policy domains with which WfI engaged post-referendum.

WfI emerged as a solution to a problem that is very familiar to gender equality advocates: how to gender a male-dominated political discourse that includes neither women as active participants nor as an area of focus. In doing so, they were part of two broader movements. Invoking the idea of newness, Cat Boyd and Jenny Morrison, who were both involved in the Radical Independence Campaign (RIC), wrote that

> the question we want to answer is not whether Scotland should be an independent country, but how a Yes vote can change the lives of Scottish women. This is a case for radical change, which seeks to expose the current system and explain what "better" would look like. We don't want to see a post-Yes Scottish society that's simply more of the same. (Boyd and Morrison 2014)

Morrison's work later critiqued the impact of the 50/50 gender balancing measures embraced by RIC (Morrison 2015) and its network of local and regional groups, but the question of who got to speak in the public square was given fresh impetus by the independence debate. One of the features of public discussion in the run up to the vote was its very ubiquity. On public transport, in local halls, and in the very streets of Scotland a great public teach-in on the institutions and powers of the nation began. Although this was experienced very differently by those that were pro-independence and those who were pro-union, it is incontrovertible that this uptick in the number of public meetings presented a huge increase in demand for commentators and advocates. This presented a gendered challenge: as in other nations, the paid and volunteer political commentariat in Scotland is overwhelmingly male. With the partial exception of RIC, other pro-independence campaigning groups and discussion spaces that emerged during the referendum campaign—apart from WfI—were also male-dominated and androcentric in their focus and concerns. Women began to notice the relative infrequency that other women were appearing on platforms in halls and platforms online, and as askers of questions and makers of points in these same contexts. They also noticed that the knowledge the Scottish citizenry was beginning to acquire and exchange about the complexities of the devolution settlement did not cover all of the issues that were particularly pertinent to feminists and gender advocates.

WfI developed some tools to make some of this representational bias in commentators visible, including a '#MediaWatch' initiative to count the numbers of male and female participants on Scottish news programmes (Strickland 2017). This provided an evidence-base for pressure—often applied through social media—for more women to be included. The same broad approach was taken to challenging the composition of the panel discussions that were happening in communities all over Scotland. This call for gender-balance was not always well-received during the campaign itself, and has proven contentious in the years since as pro-independence campaigners have sought to regroup and refine their pitch to the electorate. As in so many other contexts, calls for gender justice have been reframed as a bourgeois and trivial impediment to a unified pursuit of a political goal.

The length of the independence campaigning period meant that there was a flourishing of grassroots organisations and networks, including the arts-based National Collective (2011) and Third Sector Yes (Pudelek 2013). A number of pro-independence media organisations came into being, including The National newspaper (Sweeney 2014) and new media CommonSpace, Wings over Scotland, and Bella Caledonia (Gani 2014) along with a wide range of blogs. In addition, the 'think and do' tank Common Weal emerged and began to wrestle explicitly with some of the policy considerations around an independent Scotland. Reports began to trickle back from feminist women that many—if not all—of these endeavours were gender-blind, and that encouraging gender mainstreaming within them was freighted with the same challenge that some of those same women had faced in getting gender on the devolution agenda.

After some pressure from feminists both outwith and within its own advisory structures, Common Weal finally commissioned Dr. Angela O'Hagan to write *Women of Independent Mind: Women's Equality in a Future Scotland* (O'Hagan 2014) with contributions from feminist women from organisations concerned with the labour market, violence against women, trade unions, and the academy. Although this paper was wide-ranging and imaginative, its thesis about the importance of gendering policy did not seem to resonate within the rest of the group's outputs. Common Weal's offerings on many subjects, exemplified by a 2017 paper on social security in Scotland that mentioned neither women nor gender (Dalzell 2017) appeared frustratingly resistant to considering women's different lived experience. The point that women's and men's lives were still so different that this required some consideration was failing to land.

And what of Better Together and the pro-union movement? Did it have its own networks of activists that were organising across different identities and concerns? In short, the answer is no. Although there was a Better Together Women page on the campaign's website, its activity was exceptionally restricted—to little more than a single letter writing campaign—and it had a limited public face. The challenge for Better Together was the asymmetry of the newness of the two offers being put to the public. While the prospect of independence positively thirsted for broadly drawn plans, creative thinking, and wild imaginings, the task for Better Together was essentially to pitch the status quo. The 'single question' of the referendum had closed the door to a vote for a maximalist devolution settlement or 'devo max'. The structure of the referendum meant that the pro-union campaign could not and did not allow for extended meditations on a future constitution for Scotland, or a drastic redrawing of the fundamentals of a social security system. Although campaign grandees were reportedly furious that its nickname escaped, Better Together camped out on the territory of Project Fear; poking at the weak spots in the plans for an independent Scotland and raising an awkward series of questions about currency, pensions, and (ironically) retaining European Union membership (Pike 2015).

Against this backdrop of popular politicisation and the emergence of new networks of activists, organising across constitutional perspectives, what of established feminist civil society organisations? Institutional feminism at the national level in Scotland is primarily contained within the third sector, with the notable exception of the STUC Women's Committee, which is located firmly in the labour movement. Engender, Close the Gap, Scottish Women's Convention, Rape Crisis Scotland, Scottish Women's Aid, and Zero Tolerance are all charities, which is relevant to a reflection on the independence referendum because of the extent to which engaging in political—and especially election activity— is heavily circumscribed by charity law and regulation. In essence, picking a side and saying so publicly is ruled out unless it meets the stiff test of advancing a charity's objects (Mair 2013). In any case, choosing a public position within the independence discussion presented risks to women's organisations, which all had women with pro-union and pro-independence perspectives in their membership, governance structures, and—probably—staff teams. Although these organisations' policy advocacy work was coloured by the constitutional awkwardness of having devolution consistently misunderstood by Whitehall, it is fair to say that the years since devolution had largely displaced constitutional concerns with a focus on domain-specific policy and campaigning work. Day to day and week to week, organisations were focused on making devolution work for women, rather than on thinking about how the devolution settlement might be expanded or transformed into independence.

This is not to say that established women's organisations did not respond to the exploding interest in the independence debate, and use it to think about the possibilities for realising gender justice that newness presented. Engender used its International Women's Day event in 2014 to launch a briefing paper that analysed where power and responsibility for addressing gendered inequalities sat under Scotland's constitutional arrangements, and discussed the implications for women's equality of pursuing the different constitutional options made possible by the referendum (Wood 2014a). This was the culmination of two years' of member and stakeholder discussion under the banner of 'Feminists talk Scotland's futures', and sought to inform decision-makers, civil servants, third sector stakeholders and interested individuals. One of the key information deficits it tried to address was around the devolution settlement itself. Even those who work professionally in policy advocacy have only a partial map of the jagged border between those issues that are reserved to Westminster and those that are devolved to the Scottish Parliament. As an example of the complexity that state and civil society actors are dealing with, the statutory Equality and Human Rights Commission was obliged to tell the Scottish Parliament's Equal Opportunities Committee (now the Equality and Human Rights Committee) in 2008 that 'There is no authoritative source that provides a clear and accessible explanation of the Scottish Parliament's equal opportunity powers and what they mean in practice' (MacKay 2009). The lack of certainty for specialists is underpinned for the individual women in the street by a London-based media that speaks, for example, of Secretaries of State for Education as though their ministries set the direction for education in Wales, Scotland, and Northern Ireland. Engender's paper attempted to provide some clarity on how power is distributed between Holyrood and Westminster within key domains for women's equality and rights.

To counterbalance the androcentric discussion spaces that proliferated in the run up to the referendum, Engender worked with the Centre on Constitutional Change at University of Edinburgh, as well as other stakeholders and partners, to create world café style events where women (and some men) could speak at tables to representatives from WfI and Better Together, and chaired some women-only hustings and town hall meetings. The design of these events acknowledged both the gender disparity in those asking questions in the 'mainstream' town halls, and reoriented the conversation away from well-worn contests around currency, the 'real' economy, and mineral rights, towards care, the gender pay gap, creating an economy for women, and ending violence against women. Other women's organisations did similar thinking in various ways: Close the Gap published a working paper on independence and women's labour market participation (Close the Gap 2014) and other national organisations discussed post-referendum strategy in board and staff meetings. Women's organisations designated as strategic intermediaries by their funder Scottish Government also participated in the pre-referendum work of government, as it brought together civil society to discuss a future constitution and shape of a constitutional convention and to make plans for the commitments set out in the independence White Paper, *Scotland's Future*.

The white paper, which dropped in November 2013, was a hefty volume that attempted to combine a set of answers to the many detailed critical questions circulating about tax, citizenship, currency, pensions, social security, media, and defence with a somewhat visionary tone (Scottish Government 2013). Although it certainly had more readers than most 650-page policy tracts, Engender produced a 'gender edit' that pulled out all of the commitments and question responses that related to women or equality so that we could share this with those who did not want to trawl through the whole document. This ran to a mere 11 pages, which was perhaps an indicator of the extent to which this vision of an independent Scotland was adequately gendered. The most eye-catching of the gendered offers was the commitment to provide free-at-the-point-of-use childcare to all children between the age of one and school age. The white paper noted that 'with independence the benefits of [women's] work—in economic growth and tax revenues—will stay in Scotland, contributing to meeting the cost of this childcare provision' (ibid.). Interestingly, press coverage of this commitment quickly bounced from a consideration of the policy itself—and mostly framed that as about children's wellbeing, rather than being about women and paid work—into the political space of a lengthy row between the SNP and Labour Party about costs, benefits and the quality of economic modelling that evidenced the policy. Those commentators who stuck with the content of the policy were concerned about its normative quality: was the only specific proposal targeted at women really about having children? What if women didn't want to have any? Notwithstanding some excellent female journalists who write with mastery of the details and rigour around gender (Zero Tolerance 2018) this exposed the broad lack of capacity among political journalists in Scotland to comfortably apply a gender lens.

There was a cogent gendered point within some of the political coverage of the childcare offer: it was read as an effort to narrow the gender gap in voting intentions. Since polling began, women have always expressed less enthusiasm for Scottish independence. This gender difference garnered headlines in 2013 as a Panelbase survey found that the gap was widening and that men were almost twice as likely to support independence as women (Riddoch 2014). Work by ScotCen and others has not quite put a finger on why this should be (Ormston 2013) although hypotheses advanced include women's slightly different political priorities, women's propensity to be interested in gender parity, and women's scepticism about the extent to which any promises made about future benefits would be realised in their interests. A recurring theme throughout the referendum was a sense of disconnect between women and the messages being targeted at them. Although gender advocates, including WfI, repeatedly made the point that women were not a homogenous group, the attempts to engage with women en masse repeatedly misfired even with regards to the modal white non-disabled, heterosexual woman. The most egregious example of this was the Better Together spot in which a cereal-eating woman shared that she didn't really understand politics and intended to leave it to her husband (Huffington Post UK 2014). The notion that it had been produced and signed-off by a contemporary political campaign seemed extraordinary, but some of the post hoc accounts of the independence campaigns suggested a possible explanation.

Scotland-based journalists and political commentators hurried books into print before and after the referendum vote, including David Torrance (2013), Iain Macwhirter (2014) and Peter Geoghegan (2015). Joe Pike, whose husband Gordon Aikman was Director of Policy for Better Together, wrote an insider-y book based on his interviews with staffers from that campaign (Pike 2015). One of their common features—which does not distinguish them from books written about most elections or key political figures of recent decades—was the relative dearth of women as both actors in events and as the focus of policy considerations. Of course, there are women inside the Holyrood bubble of political staff, journalists and commentators, but they are a numerical minority. Engender's 2017 survey of women in positions of power in Scotland identified that only 33% of special advisors are women and only 8% of political editors of Scottish newspapers (Wood 2017). Mainstream lines, messages, and frames seem to be developed— whether consciously or unconsciously—for an audience that is modally male, even if numerically female-dominated. There appears to be far less capacity and competence to target groups of women, or women's concerns. The frustration felt by women from Better Together after 'eat your cereal' became a meme suggests that campaigners had trouble ensuring their advice on gender reached decision-makers within the campaigns (Kirkaldy 2014).

Nonetheless, despite the regrets from women within both campaigns about the extent to which they had spoken to women, Lesley Riddoch's post-referendum update to her independence apologetic *Blossom* described women as 'the real indyref winners' (Riddoch 2014). Citing the women in party leadership and the first female First Minister in Nicola Sturgeon, Riddoch hoped for a more gender-sensitive kind of politics. It is interesting to look back on her predictions: she worried that gender quotas for public boards might be too tough a fight even given the First Minister's determination to see them brought about. In fact, the Gender Representation on Public Boards (Scotland) Act passed without much fuss, perhaps because of its relative gentleness with malefactors. Riddoch was right to highlight the challenge of creating a care economy that was truly cognisant of the needs and aspirations of women. The rollout of increased childcare provision has been beset with challenge, including the sufficiency of facilities and the expansion of the childcare workforce in a way that does not increase the gender pay gap by widening the pool of low-paid women.

After the independence referendum, it *was* possible to reflect and see that a great many women were galvanised by participation in one or other of the campaigns and by the breaking out of a grand public political discussion. WfI, which launched and furthered numerous political careers, credits enabling women's talk at dinners and community halls and coffee shops as a way of 'doing politics differently'. As WfI staffer Kathleen Caskie notes in an unpublished memoir of the referendum, 'What was happening was that women were having conversations with each other. They weren't leafletting or canvassing or writing 400-word opinion pieces at each other; they were talking to each other.' Famously, 1000 women turned up to the first post-referendum meeting of WfI in Perth, and the organisation is still going strong some two and a half years after the vote. Having been politically engaged by the referendum many women who had previously not been involved in organised politics averred that they were 'not going back to the sofa' and started to look for new avenues to pursue women's equality and rights. WfI members began mass observations of Scottish courts in order to analyse women's experience of the justice system; gathered and distributed school uniforms to families who could not afford them; and campaigned to end period poverty in Scotland and against the building of a replacement for the notorious Cornton Vale prison (BBC 2012).

Paul Cairney and others have described the anticipation that animated the period before devolution that a 'new politics' of "consensus, participation, and deliberation"' would take hold (Cairney et al. 2009). A similar hope suffused civil society in late 2014 and early 2015, and Scottish Government certainly acquired and deployed some of the tools of engagement and deliberative democracy in areas of its policymaking. Its Fairer Scotland action plan, intended to tackle some of the results of poverty and disadvantage, was the product of hundreds of discussion and deliberation events across Scotland. The new social security powers are being developed and delivered with the benefit of experience panels composed of over a thousand people who rely on social security payments. In the immediate period post-referendum this renewed commitment to the benefits of devolution expressed itself in civil society's enthusiastic engagement with the Smith Commission. This was a product of 'The Vow', made by the Liberal Democrat, Labour and Conservative parties that if Scotland voted 'no' to independence that there would be a transfer of additional powers to the Scottish Parliament. The Smith Commission, announced by Prime Minister David Cameron on the day after the referendum, brought together two representatives from each political party with elected members within the Scottish Parliament[2] and was convened by Lord Smith of Kelvin. The pace of its deliberations was intense, with a mere month given for organisations and individuals to develop proposals for the devolution of additional powers. Early meetings between the women's sector and the secretariat were not encouraging about the extent to which its heads of agreement or recommendations would be gendered. Engender convened a meeting of the women's sector and Commission secretariat, and our own written submission broadly reflected the view of feminist organisations that a wide range of additional powers, including over social security, anti-discrimination law and equality, and employment law should be devolved (Wood 2014b). An optimism about newness had persisted through the referendum and its aftermath.

EU Referendum

One of the few precise parallels between the independence referendum and the EU referendum is that both were called with the political calculation that they couldn't possibly be lost. That commonality aside, they have been experienced very differently by individual feminists and feminist civil society organisations in Scotland.

The EU referendum campaign period was breathtakingly short, relatively, with its date announced only four months before the vote. Although some of the arguments for and against leaving the EU had been extensively rehearsed in Conservative circles, there was less familiarity with the complexity of the arguments across the wider public. A deficit of European correspondents at major news publications, and a steady drip of misleading stories about curved bananas and the European Court of Human Rights, had induced a staggering lack of familiarity with the institutions and purposes of the EU.

In Scotland, the campaign period overlapped with that of the Holyrood 2016 elections. The Scottish parliamentary elections took place

---

[2]Scottish Labour Party were represented by Greg McClymont MP and Iain Gray MSP; Scottish Green Party were represented by Maggie Chapman and Patrick Harvie MSP; Scottish National Party were represented by Linda Fabiani MSP and John Swinney MSP; Scottish Conservatives were represented by Adam Tomkins and Annabel Goldie MSP; and Scottish Liberal Democrats were represented by Michael Moore MP and Tavish Scott MSP.

on 5 May and the EU vote on 23 June. With new Ministers to seek meetings with and a programme for government to influence, there was a distinct lack of capacity for civil society to turn its attention completely to Brexit until the last few weeks of the campaign. Polling figures also suggested that engaging with the EU referendum would be relatively pointless, with all available data confirming that Scotland was markedly less Eurosceptic than England and likely to vote to remain by some fifteen points (Eardley 2016). To add the final note of futility to the thought of spending resources weighing into the Brexit debate, all of the major political parties in Scotland—including the Scottish Conservatives—backed Remain (McCall 2016).

Engender committed a small amount of resources to working with local women's centres to hold conversations about Brexit; learning from some of the methodologies that had been refined during the independence referendum. We also developed a briefing that set out the ways in which Scotland and the UK's anti-discrimination law was underpinned by EU law and regulation, gender equality approaches that were enabled by EU policies and programmes—including gender mainstreaming—and the way that the EU was driving forward ratification of Council of Europe instruments like the Istanbul Convention on domestic abuse and other forms of violence against women (Wood 2016b). Despite these clear benefits to EU membership, Engender could not take a formal position on the outcome of the referendum. Although a significant risk, it is not a given that women's equality would necessarily be undermined by leaving the EU. It is possible, for example, that the UK Government could elect to increase its use of temporary special measures such as quotas without worrying about the threat it frequently cites of being in breach of EU law (Clayton 2014).

The Brexit campaigns did not set the heather alight in Scotland, and the lack of gender content made them unengaging to gender advocates. The media focused on repatriation of funds for the NHS (in England, although with consequences for Scotland as a result of the Barnett formula [Lawrence 2015]), a series of internecine campaign stories, the arrangements for and personnel at televised debates, trade and the single market, and the customs union. The majority of discussion appeared to be squarely on business and economics terrain, with a sprinkling of conversation about 'taking back control' from an activist Court of Justice of the European Union in Strasbourg. Although all of these issues have a gender dimension, this formed no part of the messaging or framing coming from either campaign.

Tim Shipman offers us an explanation for this curious omission: 'At one of the Remain cabinets Andrew Cooper gave a presentation pointing out that a typical Leave voter believed "gender equality has gone too far". [...] The education secretary had asked other female ministers to contribute essays to a booklet on the importance of the EU, under the title "Women for Remain"' (Shipman 2016). According to a 'source close to [Nicky] Morgan' space could not be found for it on the campaign communications grid (ibid.). Shipman notes that it was finally slated for release some three hours before the murder of Jo Cox MP. The impression is given of either a piece of political calculus that talking about women's equality was likely to be unpersuasive to Leave-leaning voters who felt the whole thing was silly or harmful, or of a lack of gender competence within the male-dominated campaign team. If the former, one might have expected to see the institutional feminism of the EU invoked more frequently as a reason to vote Leave by that campaign, but perhaps this was folded into their broadsides against human rights.

The post-referendum engagement by gender advocates in Scotland suggests that the failure to engage with the referendum campaign was also a product of the certainty that the vote would be for Remain. With polls, media reporting, and Number 10 all exuding confidence in victory the result was a shock to feminist civil society. But there are other explanations for the failure of a coherent women's sector response. These include the atomisation of the women's sectors; the dismantling of gender architecture by UK Government; a reduction in leadership capacity in the women's sector in England; and a lack of co-ordinating four-nations mechanisms.

Taking these points in turn, the women's sectors in the four nations of the UK are principally focused on their own concerns, with the detail of their work and engagement driven by what is happening in their own national context. For organisations in Scotland, Wales, and Northern Ireland these are increasingly targeted at the devolved administrations—even though there is no Government in Northern Ireland at the time of writing civil society organisations continue to work with civil servants at Stormont. Women organised in their own nations before devolution, but the transfer of power from Westminster to devolved parliaments and assemblies has exacerbated the extent to which feminist organisations agree on broad analysis, but differ considerably on tactics, strategy, workplans, and priorities.

When the 2010 UK Coalition Government elected to scrap the Women's National Commission it removed a statutory engagement mechanism that had worked across the four nations since its establishment in 1969. Although there were pertinent questions about the extent to which it represented the interests of women in Scotland, Northern Ireland, and Wales, it was a conduit between the women's sector and UK Government, and—when it worked well—a mechanism for accountability as well as the sharing of ideas and perspectives. Since 2010, UK Government has consulted with the women's sector in an ad hoc, divisive, and increasingly superficial way. Sensing decreasing interest and political commitment, women's organisations in Scotland, Wales, and Northern Ireland have consequently rebalanced their efforts away from Westminster and towards more fertile or urgent discussions with their national governments.

The women's sector in England, which as a result of its proximity to the UK Parliament frequently provides leadership on pan-UK work, has been beleaguered by funding cuts as well as political inhospitality to its ideas and priorities. This has placed those national organisations that depend on UK Government funding or gatekeeping in a position of great challenge. An example of the different tone taken by some England-based organisations could be seen around 2017 campaigning on the 'rape clause' and 'family cap', as two statutory instruments were passed by negative procedure to enable Universal Credit to be denied to all third and subsequent children apart from those conceived as a result of rape (Mumford 2017). Violence against women national bodies in Scotland, Wales, and Northern Ireland said that they would not collude with the implementation of the policy that UK Government developed to record the details of children conceived as a result of rape (Ritch 2017). Rape Crisis England and Wales and Women's Aid Federation England took a different view, and agreed with UK Government that they would be 'third-party referrers' as set out in the policy.

There are no pan-UK women's organisations operating around a feminist agenda, and only one four-nations mechanism. This is the UK Joint Committee on Women, of which Engender is the Scotland representative, which exists in order to act as the UK's national co-ordination of the EWL. At the moment this body is entirely resourced by its members, and there is not consensus on how it could develop to facilitate the types of cooperation and collaboration that would extend its role beyond engagement with the Lobby. The question of how to improve and enhance the capacity of the women's sector across the UK may be urgent but it is yet to be answered.

5   So What Happens Now with Brexit?

Brexit, because of the political context in which it is being delivered, is being read almost entirely as a threat by gender advocates in Scotland to women's equality and rights. The hasty general election of 2017 appears to have shifted the political consensus towards a 'hard' Brexit, although notions of 'hard' and 'soft' are perilously ill-defined. With statements emerging daily that appear to shun the possibility of post-Brexit cooperation on trade or customs, the economic future of the UK appears gloomy, with concomitant risks to women's economic and social rights. Even if anti-discrimination protections remain untouched, a further period of austerity will widen gaps between men and women and immiserate and impoverish families across Scotland (Wood 2016a).

Engender joined a number of women's, equalities, and human rights organisations in writing to then Brexit secretary, David Davis MP (Trottier 2017) to express concern at the invisibility of women's equality and rights in what we can discern to be the UK Government's negotiating agenda. The response (DExEU Correspondence Unit 2017)—from the Correspondence Unit and not from either the Minister or an identifiable civil servant—was not reassuring.

The general sense of confusion about what has to happen, and how Brexit will be worked out is giving rise to a demand for information by feminist activists and gender advocates that is not readily available. Engender is working with the Human Rights Consortium Scotland, Scottish Universities Legal Network on Europe, and other stakeholders to provide contributions to written briefings, and inputs to events, but the lack of clarity is coming from UK Government and not at any significant point downstream.

The UK Government's already tepid enthusiasm for human rights appears to be waning, and the current version of the enormous European Union Withdrawal Bill contains a clause to remove the protections of the Charter of Fundamental Rights from UK citizens (EHRC 2018). Despite the hopes of activists, this weeks' news headlines indicate that this is unlikely to be ameliorated by the House of Lords. The Prime Minister's public statements suggest that the non-EU European Convention on Human Rights may be on a shaky nail, and the spectre of the British Bill of Rights that would replace the Human Rights Act has not gone away (Stone 2017). With recent cases in which the Human Rights Act has been used to impeach the Metropolitan Police's investigation of rape complaints[3] and to require Scottish Ministers to ensure that legal aid is available for rape complainers wishing to object to the production of their medical records,[4] there are clear reasons for feminist organisations to be concerned at this possible loss in protection. Engender and other women's organisations in Scotland joined the Scottish Human Rights Commission, Equality and Human Rights Commission, Human Rights Consortium Scotland and a range of other civil society actors in signing the Scotland Declaration on Human Rights (*New Scotland Declaration on Human Rights Calls for Leadership in Face of Brexit Risks, as New Research Shows Considerable Public Support for Human Rights* 2018) which calls for progression instead of regression on human rights, transparency of process, and participation.

Amid the many losses that Brexit is likely to present, the loss of engagement with the EWL is small but significant to feminist organisations in Scotland. This internationalist network has been a source of ideas and solidarity to Scottish feminism, and a way in which we can share some of our learning and success. The pan-European feminist collaboration on the development of the Council of Europe's Istanbul Convention has resulted in a regional violence against women instrument of huge significance and value. EWL campaigning sat behind the efforts of Scottish and other feminists that led to Dr. Eilidh Whiteford MP pushing forward successfully with a private members' bill that will compel the UK Government to ratify the Convention (Logan 2017). The European Commission's funding of the EWL is intended for member states and EU-wide organisations, but we are working creatively to find a way to maintain these links.

6   Conclusion

Constitutional politics continues to flavour the Scottish political context. The outcome of the Brexit referendum has placed Scottish independence on the news agenda, even as the Scottish Government—with one eye on the polling data—tries to downplay the likelihood of a further independence referendum in the near future.

The new women's organisations and networks that were created to counterbalance a marginalisation of women's concerns in the official

---

[3] *DSD & Anor v The Commissioner of Police for the Metropolis* [2014], EWHC 436 (QB).
[4] WF, Re Judicial Review [2016] ScotCS CSOH_27 (12 February 2016).

independence campaigns continue to work on gender justice, and have adopted a wide range of concerns and campaigns. The independence referendum also leaves a legacy within the women's sector of capacity and competence to think about the constitutional future of Scotland, and institutional facility with a new range of tools with which to engage women.

Reflecting on the outcomes of the work to gender the devolution, independence, and Brexit campaigns raises the possibility that the length of time a political process takes may have a connection with the extent to which gender advocates can influence it. Certainly, the abbreviated Brexit campaign was over almost before gender advocates had found a way into the discussion.

Although feminists and gender advocates are still largely working in national silos around Brexit, the relative organisational confidence of women's organisations in Scotland, Wales, and Northern Ireland has been burnished by several years' worth of advocacy and campaigning successes and by the links forged during the independence referendum. Scottish feminist policy organisations are contemplating the opportunities and threats of further devolution occasioned by Brexit, and considering the impact on women's equality of new powers coming to Holyrood, having already chewed over the possibilities offered by the newness of maximalist devolution. With decades of experience behind us, women and women's organisations are also considering how we can work across national boundaries to continue to engage post-Brexit with pan-European feminist structures and feminists. The work goes on.

BIBLIOGRAPHY

Barnes, E. 2012. Scottish Independence: Campaign to Convince Women to Vote 'Yes'. *Scotsman*, August 12. https://www.scotsman.com/news/politics/scottish-independence-campaign-to-convince-women-to-vote-yes-1-2463196. Accessed 22 June 2018.

BBC. 2012. Angiolino Commission to Call for Cornton Vale to Be Demolished. *BBC News*, April 17. https://www.bbc.co.uk/news/uk-scotland-tayside-central-17735991. Accessed 22 June 2018.

Boyd, C., and J. Morrison. 2014. *Scottish Independence: A Feminist Response*. Rotherham: Word Power Books.

Brown, A. 1999. Taking Their Place in the New House? Women and the Scottish Parliament. *Scottish Affairs* 28 (First Series) (1): 44–50. Retrieved from: https://www.euppublishing.com/doi/abs/10.3366/scot.1999.0035?journalCode=scot.

Brown, A., et al. 1998. *Shaping's Scotland's Parliament.* Consultative Steering Group on the Scottish Parliament. Retrieved from: http://www.parliament.scot/PublicInformationdocuments/Report_of_the_Consultative_Steering_Group.pdf.

Cairney, P., et al. 2009. New Scottish Parliament, Same Old Interest Group Politics? In *The Scottish Parliament 1999–2009: The First Decade,* ed. C. Jeffery and J. Mitchell, 105–112. Edinburgh: Luath Press.

Cavaghan, R. 2017. *Making Gender Equality Happen: Knowledge Change and Resistance in EU Gender Mainstreaming.* New York: Routledge.

Clayton, E. 2014. EHRC Says No to Women only Shortlists. *Economia,* July 24. https://economia.icaew.com/news/july-2014/ehrc-says-no-to-women-only-shortlists. Accessed 22 June 2018.

Close the Gap. 2014. *Women and Work: What Comes Next in a Post-referendum Scotland?* Glasgow: Close the Gap. Retrieved from: https://www.close-thegap.org.uk/content/resources/CTG-Working-Paper-13—Women-and-work-what-comes-next-in-a-post-referendum-Scotland.pdf.

Dalzell, C. 2017. *Social Security for All of Us—An Independent Scotland as a Modern Welfare State.* Glasgow: Common Weal. Retrieved from: http://allofusfirst.org/tasks/render/file/?fileID=070095CB-9D41-6067-5DEA03BDB005D078.

DExEU Correspondence Unit. 2017. *Letter to Engender.* DExEU Correspondence Unit, November 2017.

Eardley, N. 2016. Is Scotland the Most Pro-UK Part of the UK? *BBC News,* February 18. https://www.bbc.co.uk/news/uk-politics-35602861. Accessed 22 June.

EHRC. 2018. *Brexit and the EU Charter of Fundamental Rights: Our Concerns.* Equality and Human Rights Commission. https://www.equalityhumanrights.com/en/what-are-human-rights/how-are-your-rights-protected/what-charter-fundamental-rights-european-union-0. Accessed 22 June 2018.

Equality Network. 2014. *Equal Marriage Now Legal in Scotland.* https://www.equality-network.org/equal-marriage-legal-in-scotland/. Accessed 22 June 2018.

Gani, A. 2014. Scottish Blogs: What Next for Alternative Media Post-Referendum? *Guardian,* December 1. https://www.theguardian.com/media/media-blog/2014/dec/01/scottish-blogs-so-what-next-for-scottish-media. Accessed 22 June 2018.

Geoghegan, P. 2015. *The People's Referendum: Why Scotland Will Never Be the Same Again.* Edinburgh: Luath Press.

Grierson, J. 2017. Survey Reveals Impact of Proposed Funding Cuts on Women Fleeing Abuse. *Guardian,* November 29. https://www.theguardian.com/society/2017/nov/29/survey-reveals-impact-of-proposed-funding-cuts-on-women-fleeing-abuse. Accessed 22 June 2018.

Huffington Post UK. 2014. Scottish Independence No Campaign Given Savage Mauling on Twitter, The Best of #PatronisingBTLady. *Huffington Post,* August 27.

https://www.huffingtonpost.co.uk/2014/08/27/patronisingbtlady-scottish-independence_n_5721048.html?guccounter=1. Accessed 22 June 2018.

Khaleeli, H. 2014. Is Post-referendum Scotland a Feminist Paradise? *Guardian*, September 30. https://www.theguardian.com/politics/2014/sep/30/post-referendum-scotland-feminist-paradise. Accessed 22 June 2018.

Kirkaldy, L. 2014. Eat Your Cereal. *Holyrood Magazine*, August 27. http://referendum.holyrood.com/blog/eat-your-cereal. Accessed 22 June 2018.

Lawrence, T. 2015. *Funding the UK Nations: The Barnett Formula and Devolved Governments*. Local Government Information Unit. Retrieved from: https://www.lgiu.org.uk/wp-content/uploads/2015/11/Funding-the-UK-nations-%E2%80%93-the-Barnett-formula-and-devolved-governments.pdf.

Logan, C. 2017. UK Government Under Pressure to Ratify Violence Against Women Convention as Deadline Looms. *CommonSpace*, October 19. https://www.commonspace.scot/articles/11883/uk-government-under-pressure-ratify-violence-against-women-convention-deadline-looms. Accessed 22 June 2018.

Mackay, F. 2006. *The Impact of Devolution on Women's Citizenship in Scotland*. Fukuoaka: Fiona Mackay. Retrieved from: https://www.researchgate.net/publication/251780619_The_Impact_of_Devolution_on_Women's_Citizenship_in_Scotland.

Mackay, F. 2009. Travelling the Distance? Equal Opportunities and the Scottish Parliament. In *The Scottish Parliament 1999–2009: The First Decade*, ed. C. Jeffery and J. Mitchell, 49–55. Edinburgh: Luath Press.

Mackay, F. 2014. Nested Newness, Institutional Innovation and the Gendered Limits of Changes. *Politics & Gender* 10 (4): 549–571. https://doi.org/10.1017/S1743923X14000415.

Macwhirter, I. 2014. *Disunited Kingdom: How Westminster Won a Referendum but Lost*. Scotland: Cargo Publishing.

Mair, V. 2013. OSCR: Scottish Charities Can Campaign for Yes or No Vote. *Civil Society*, July 23. https://www.civilsociety.co.uk/news/oscr–scottish-charities-can-campaign-for-yes-or-no-vote.html. Accessed 22 June 2018.

McCall, C. 2016. EU Referendum: Where Do Scotland's Political Parties Stand? *Scotsman*, February 26. https://www.scotsman.com/news/politics/general-election/eu-referendum-where-do-scotland-s-political-parties-stand-1-4038649. Accessed 22 June 2018.

Morrison, J. 2015. *Feminist Radicalism? Feminism and the Radical Independence Campaign*. Presentation. http://www.academia.edu/11847336/Feminist_Radicalism_Feminism_and_the_Radical_Independence_Campaign. Accessed 28 February 2018.

Mumford, A. 2017. 5 Things You Need to Know About the 'Family Cap' and 'Rape Clause'. *Engender Blog*. https://www.engender.org.uk/news/blog/-5-things-you-need-to-know-about-the-family-cap-and-rape-clause1/. Accessed 22 June 2018.

National Collective. 2011. National Collective—About Us. http://www.nationalcollective.com/about-us/. Accessed 22 June 2018.

New Scotland Declaration on Human Rights Calls for Leadership in Face of Brexit Risks, as New Research Shows Considerable Public Support for Human Rights. 2018. http://www.scottishhumanrights.com/news/new-scotland-declaration-on-human-rights-calls-for-leadership-in-face-of-brexit-risks-as-new-research-shows-considerable-public-support-for-human-rights/. Accessed 22 June 2018.

O'Hagan, A. 2014. *Women of Independent Mind: Women's Equality in a Future Scotland.* Glasgow: Common Weal. Retrieved from: http://www.allofusfirst.org/tasks/render/file/?fileID=4EA329A1-9D57-44BE-B2112C2F43354934.

O'Hagan, A. 2015. *Gender Budgeting in Scotland: Towards Feminist Policy Change.* Glasgow: Women in Scotland's Economic Research Centre. Retrieved from: https://www.gcu.ac.uk/wise/media/gcalwebv2/theuniversity/centresprojects/wise/93248_WiSEBriefingSheet_Dec2015_05.pdf.

Ormston, R. 2013. *Why Don't More Women Support Independence? Findings from the Scottish Social Attitudes Survey.* Edinburgh: ScotCen Social Research. Retrieved from: http://www.scotcen.org.uk/media/270731/ssa-2012-gender-and-independence.pdf.

Planning Group. 2010. 'Something Understood'? A Perspective on the Turn of the Century. *The Maidie Hart Lectures 1999–2005.*

Pike, J. 2015. *Project Fear: How an Unlikely Alliance Left a Kingdom United but a Country Divided.* London: Biteback Publishing.

Pudelek, J. 2013. Scottish Charity Workers Sign up to a Pro-independence Campaign. *Third Sector,* December 16. https://www.thirdsector.co.uk/scottish-charity-workers-sign-pro-independence-campaign/communications/article/1224915. Accessed 22 June 2018.

Red Tape Challenge. 2011. https://www.gov.uk/government/news/red-tape-challenge–7. Accessed on 22 June 2018.

Riddoch, L. 2014. *Wee White Blossom.* Edinburgh: Luath Press.

Ritch, E. 2017. The 'Family Cap' and 'Rape Clause': Where Do We Go from Here? *Engender Blog.* https://www.engender.org.uk/news/blog/the-family-cap-and-rape-clause-where-do-we-go-from-here-/. Accessed 22 June 2018.

Ritch, E. 2017. Seven Principles for a Gender-Competent Scottish National Investment Bank. *Engender Blog.* https://www.engender.org.uk/news/blog/seven-principles-for-a-gender-competent-scottish-national-investment-bank/. Accessed 22 June 2018.

Scottish Government. 2013. *Scotland's Future: Your Guide to an Independent Scotland.* Scottish Government. Retrieved from: http://www.gov.scot/Resource/0043/00439021.pdf.

Scottish Government. 2014. *Equally Safe: Scotland's Strategy for Eradicating Violence Against Women and Girls.* Scottish Government. Retrieved from: http://www.gov.scot/Resource/0045/00454152.pdf.

Scottish Government. 2017. *Scottish National Investment Bank Consultation.* Scottish Government. Retrieved from: http://www.gov.scot/Resource/0052/00526276.pdf.

Scottish Parliament. 2018. Creche. http://www.parliament.scot/visitandlearn/12522.aspx. Accessed 5 January 2018.

Shipman, T. 2016. *All Out War: The Full Story of How Brexit Sank Britain's Political Class*. London: William Collins.

SPICe. 2003. *Summaries of Bills Passed by the Scottish Parliament in the First Session*. Scottish Parliament Information Centre. Retrieved from: http://www.parliament.scot/S1_Bills/Summaries_of_Bills_Passed_by_the_Scottish_Parliament_in_the_First_Session_Introduction.pdf.

Stone, J. 2017. British Bill of Rights Plan Shelved Again for Several More Years, Justice Secretary Confirms. *Independent*, February 23. https://www.independent.co.uk/news/uk/politics/scrap-human-rights-act-british-bill-of-rights-brexit-liz-truss-theresa-may-a7595336.html. Accessed 22 June 2018.

Strickland, K. 2017. Political Parties, You Have a Role to Play in Fixing Media Gender Imblanance. *CommonSpace*, May 22. https://www.commonspace.scot/articles/11015/kirsty-strickland-political-parties-you-have-role-play-fixing-media-gender-imbalance. Accessed 22 June 2018.

Sweeney, M. 2014. Pro-independence Daily Paper the National to Launch in Scotland. *Guardian*, November 21. https://www.theguardian.com/media/2014/nov/21/the-national-pro-independence-newspaper-launch-scotland?view=classic. Accessed 22 June 2018.

Torrance, D. 2013. *The Battle for Britain: Scotland and the Independence Referendum*. London: Biteback Publishing.

Trottier, T. 2017. *Letter to Rt Hon David Davis MP, Secretary of State for Leaving the European Union*, September. Edinburgh: Engender.

UN CEDAW Committee. 2013. *Concluding Observations on the Seventh Periodic Report of the United Kingdom of Great Britain and Northern Ireland*. Geneva: United Nations Convention on the Elimination of all forms of Discrimination Against Women Committee. Retrieved from: http://tbinternet.ohchr.org/_layouts/treatybodyexternal/Download.aspx?symbolno=CEDAW/C/GBR/CO/7&Lang=En.

Wood, J. 2014a. *Gender Equality and Scotland's Constitutional Futures*. Edinburgh: Engender. Retrieved from: https://www.engender.org.uk/content/publications/Gender-equality-and–Scotlands-constitutional-futures.pdf.

Wood, J. 2014b. *Engender Submission to the Smith Commission on Devolution*. Edinburgh: Engender. Retrieved from: https://www.engender.org.uk/content/publications/Engender-Smith-Commission-submission-October-2014.pdf.

Wood, J. 2015. *A Widening Gap: Women and Welfare Reform*. Edinburgh: Engender. Retrieved from: https://www.engender.org.uk/content/publications/A-Widening-Gap---Women-and-Welfare-Reform.pdf.

Wood, J. 2016a. *Securing Women's Futures: Using Scotland's New Social Security Powers to Close the Gender Equality Gap*. Edinburgh: Engender. Retrieved from: https://www.engender.org.uk/content/publications/Securing-Womens-

Futures---using-Scotlands-new-social-security-powers-to-close-the-gender-equality-gap.pdf.

Wood, J. 2016b. *The EU Referendum and Gender Equality*. Edinburgh: Engender. Retrieved from: https://www.engender.org.uk/content/publications/The-EU-referendum-and-gender-equality.pdf.

Wood, J. 2017. *Sex & Power in Scotland 2017*. Edinburgh: Engender. Retrieved from: https://www.engender.org.uk/content/publications/SEX-AND-POWER-IN-SCOTLAND-2017.pdf.

Zero Tolerance. 2018. Write to End Violence Against Women Awards—About. https://writetoendvaw.com/. Accessed 22 June 2018.

CHAPTER 14

Brexit, Gender and Northern Ireland

Yvonne Galligan

1 INTRODUCTION

The negotiations on Britain's exiting the European Union (EU) identified a number of priorities in relation to Northern Ireland, and are specified in the December 2017 UK/EU joint report. One was the avoidance
of a hard border between the UK and the EU on the island of Ireland.[1]
The second was a commitment to uphold the 1998 Belfast/Good Friday
Agreement (henceforth referred to as 'the 1998 Agreement') facilitating
continued North-South co-operation on the island and development of
an all-island economy.[2] The latter provision has become known as the

[1] Joint report from the negotiators of the European Union and the United Kingdom
Government on progress during phase 1 of negotiations under Article 50 TEU on the
United Kingdom's orderly withdrawal from the European Union; para. 43 'The United
Kingdom also recalls its commitment to the avoidance of a hard border, including any
physical infrastructure or related checks and controls'.

[2] Joint report from the negotiators of the European Union and the United Kingdom
Government on progress during phase 1 of negotiations under Article 50 TEU on the
United Kingdom's orderly withdrawal from the European Union; para. 49 'The United
Kingdom remains committed to protecting North-South cooperation and to its guarantee

Y. Galligan (✉)
Technological University Dublin, Grangegorman, Dublin 7, Ireland
e-mail: yvonne.galligan@dit.ie

© The Author(s) 2019   363
M. Dustin et al. (eds.), *Gender and Queer Perspectives on Brexit*,
Gender and Politics, https://doi.org/10.1007/978-3-030-03122-0_14

'backstop' guarantee. Two further provisions, less highlighted, but no less important, are contained in the report. One is a recognition of Irish citizens' right to continue to hold and access their European citizenship and its related benefits, rights and opportunities.[3] The other is a commitment to uphold and maintain human rights and equality standards, and the bodies charged with implementing these standards set up under the 1998 Agreement.[4]

First, this chapter will outline the constitutional and policy challenges of Brexit for Northern Ireland, Ireland north and south, and the UK-Ireland relationship. This will include a discussion on the relevance of the 1998 Agreement in the Brexit context. It then considers the Brexit referendum and evidence of gender differences in the vote. This is followed by a detailed discussion on citizenship and rights, paying attention to gender equality issues. This theme is expanded on in a section considering the substantive issues in relation to gender equality that are affected by Brexit, and by the absence of functioning political institutions. Before concluding, the chapter turns to the effect of Brexit on the fragile peace and reconciliation efforts in which local women's groups are deeply involved. Finally, the chapter suggests a differentiated Brexit for Northern Ireland that offers some resolution to the difficult high politics issues and provides gender equality advocates with a forum supportive of the value—regional membership of the European Economic Area (EEA).

---

of avoiding a hard border.' ... 'In the absence of agreed solutions, the United Kingdom will maintain full alignment with those rules of the Internal Market and the Customs Union which, now or in the future, support North-South cooperation, the all-island economy and the protection of the 1998 Agreement.'

[3] Joint report from the negotiators of the European Union and the United Kingdom Government on progress during phase 1 of negotiations under Article 50 TEU on the United Kingdom's orderly withdrawal from the European Union; para. 52 'The people of Northern Ireland who are Irish citizens will continue to enjoy rights as EU citizens, including where they reside in Northern Ireland. Both Parties therefore agree that the Withdrawal Agreement should respect and be without prejudice to the rights, opportunities and identity that come with European Union citizenship for such people.'

[4] Joint report from the negotiators of the European Union and the United Kingdom Government on progress during phase 1 of negotiations under Article 50 TEU on the United Kingdom's orderly withdrawal from the European Union; para. 53 'The United Kingdom commits to facilitating the related work of the institutions and bodies, established by the 1998 Agreement, in upholding human rights and equality standards.'

2   Constitutional Issues

Brexit presents constitutional and policy challenges that are unique to Northern Ireland. The country voted to remain in the EU by a modest margin of 11% (440, 707 voted to remain, 55.7%; 349,442 voted to leave, 44.3%). Shortly thereafter, two challenges to the UK government's intention to use the Royal Prerogative to invoke Article 50 of the Treaty on the European Union (TEU) (the withdrawal notice procedure) were brought before the Northern Ireland High Court in August 2016. The Court focused on the impact of Northern Ireland's constitutional provisions in relation to triggering Article 50(2) TEU that would initiate the UK withdrawal from the EU.[5] This brought attention to the constitutional and legal framework flowing from the 1998 Agreement and the Northern Ireland Act 1998. In October 2016, the Northern Ireland High Court dismissed both challenges. The applicants (McCord; Agnew and others) then appealed to the UK Supreme Court, along with Miller.[6] The Court dismissed the McCord and Agnew (and others) cases in respect of the devolved aspects, but granted the wider case on requiring the UK Parliament rather than the UK government to invoke Article 50(2) TEU.

This brief overview of the constitutional issues relating to Brexit in the case of Northern Ireland shows the extent to which implementation of the 1998 Agreement is intrinsically affected by the intention of the UK to leave the EU.[7] The 1998 Agreement had two parts: one was a multi-party agreement between most of Northern Ireland's political parties (the main exception being the Democratic Unionist Party [DUP]), the second was a 1998 bilateral international agreement between the

---

[5] McCord's (Raymond) Application; Agnew (and others) v HMG, Secretary of State for Northern Ireland and Secretary of State for Exiting the European Union [2016] NIQB 85, at: https://www.judiciary-ni.gov.uk/judicial-decisions/2016-niqb-85, accessed 20 June 2018.

[6] R (Miller) v Secretary of State for Exiting the European Union [2017] UKSC5, at: http://www.bailii.org/uk/cases/UKSC/2017/5.html, accessed 21 June 2018; Tughans Legal Insights: *Brexit: The Supreme Court Decision—Only Parliament Can Pull the Brexit Trigger*, at: https://www.tughans.com/wp-content/uploads/2017/01/Only-Parliament-can-pull-Brexit-trigger-AMENDED-DRAFT.pdf, accessed 21 June 2018.

[7] The British Irish Council was created in 1999 to "to promote the harmonious and mutually beneficial development of the totality of relationships among the peoples of these islands."

British and Irish governments ratified as the British Irish Agreement.[8] The 1998 Agreement as a whole made complex provision for political relationships in three strands: Strand 1 provided for the system of government in Northern Ireland, and in relation to its devolved status within the UK system; Strand 2 provided for the relationship between Northern Ireland and the Republic of Ireland (formally by means of the North/South Ministerial Council and Bodies); Strand 3 structured the relationship between the UK and Republic of Ireland, with the British-Irish Intergovernmental Conference as an institutional component of that relationship.

The effect of the 1998 Agreement has been to bring peace and political stability to Northern Ireland; improve North-South relations on the island of Ireland (manifest in a 'soft' or negligible border between the jurisdictions, development of an 'all island' economy and increased security co-operation); and enhance friendly relations between the two sovereign governments as instanced by the visit of HM Queen Elizabeth II to the Republic of Ireland in 2011. Furthermore, the 1998 Agreement was formulated while both governments were full members of the EU. Accordingly, the document is infused with references to the EU, including the UK and Ireland self-describing as 'friendly neighbours and as partners in the EU' and coordination on EU issues and EU funding programmes.[9] As a consequence, the peace accord attracted considerable political and financial support from the European institutions, including a dedicated programme to fund peace and reconciliation activities in Northern Ireland and in the border region between Northern Ireland and Ireland.[10] Thus, their joint membership of the EU was an important context in bringing the 1998 Agreement into being (Hayward and Murphy 2018: 291–292).

The UK intention to leave the EU, then, was bound to destabilise the hard-won gains of the peace process, with potentially negative consequences for political and diplomatic relationships across and between the two states (Doyle and Connolly 2017, 156). For women on the island of

[8]http://www.irishstatutebook.ie/eli/1999/act/1/enacted/en/pdf, accessed 20 June 2018.

[9]https://www.gov.uk/government/publications/the-belfast-agreement, accessed 10 August 2018.

[10]Northern Ireland PEACE programme, at: http://www.europarl.europa.eu/atyourservice/en/displayFtu.html?ftuId=FTU_3.1.9.html, accessed 20 June 2018.

Ireland, and particularly in Northern Ireland, Brexit heralded the prospect of unwanted change in the materiality of their lives and in future opportunities for equality.

3   THE BREXIT REFERENDUM

The campaign to determine citizens' views on the proposal to leave the EU mirrored the polarisation of the rest of the UK: nationalist parties Sinn Féin (SF) and the Social Democratic and Labour Party (SDLP) along with the Greens and centrist Alliance Party supported a Remain vote. The DUP advocated for Leave, and Nigel Dodds MP, leader of the party's Westminster contingent, was a director of Vote Leave in Northern Ireland. The Ulster Unionist Party (UUP) campaigned to Remain, but quickly changed its stance to a Brexit-supporting one after the overall result to Leave was declared (Berberi 2017). The lead-up to the Brexit referendum gave little space for civil society perspectives, though business interests—mindful of the all-Ireland economy and the negative impact on business—articulated a Remain position.[11] Northern Ireland's Secretary of State Theresa Villiers MP openly aligned with the Leave side which had no position on the peace process and dismissed warnings of instability as Remain-side 'scaremongering'.[12] Her position on one side of the referendum raised doubts as to her ability to represent Northern Ireland's interests at cabinet. During the campaign, female politicians challenged one another corresponding to their party positions on the Brexit question. Margaret Ritchie MP (SDLP former leader), Alliance leader Naomi Long (former MP), and Martina Anderson (SF Member of European Parliament) strongly disagreed with Arlene Foster (DUP leader) on the implications of Brexit for Northern Ireland. Subsequent to the referendum, the pro- and anti-Brexit positions have hardened, with unionists led by Foster enthusiastically endorsing the 'take back our borders' political vision, seeing Brexit as a way of strengthening Northern Ireland's constitutional position in the UK.

---

[11] http://www.bdoni.com/en-gb/news/2016/cbi-bdo-northern-ireland-the-big-brexit, accessed 19 August 2018.

[12] https://www.irishtimes.com/opinion/ireland-an-afterthought-during-brexit-campaign-when-i-was-cameron-adviser-1.3242732, accessed 10 August 2018; https://www.belfasttelegraph.co.uk/news/northern-ireland/dup-confirms-it-will-campaign-for-brexit-in-leaveremain-referendum-34470806.html, accessed 10 August 2018.

SF and the nationalist community more generally view the Brexit result as offering the prospect of Irish unity. SF leaders MaryLou McDonald (all-Ireland leader) and Michelle O'Neill (Northern Ireland leader) have been frequent visitors to Brussels and to the European Commission chief negotiator Michel Barnier, lobbying for special status for Northern Ireland in the event of UK departure from the EU. They have also called for a Border poll, under the terms of the 1998 Agreement, to gauge the appetite for Irish unification.[13] Thus, the female leaders of the main parties in Northern Ireland were in the spotlight during the referendum. McDonald in particular has continued to dominate in public, setting a unification agenda that seeks to accommodate unionism. Arlene Foster (DUP) continues to favour a 'soft' border between Northern Ireland and the Irish Republic though opposes any special status for the region. Foster's profile and position as spokesperson on Brexit has been eclipsed by that of her party's Westminster MPs who have issued support for the Chequers agreement, but have not recognised the need for a 'soft' border on the island of Ireland.[14]

The views of party leaders distill the preferences of their supports. Thus it is no surprise that voter choice to support or oppose the Brexit question was driven by the underlying ethno-national divisions that configure constitutional questions in the region. In effect, 85% of voters from a Catholic background and 88% of those identifying as nationalist voted to remain in the EU. Conversely, 60% of voters brought up in the Protestant tradition, and 65% holding unionist political views expressed a wish to exit the EU (Garry et al. 2017).

However, this polarisation is nuanced by a recent study of voters in the Northern Ireland side of the border region where the UK and Ireland share contiguous territory. Of the voters supporting a Leave position, a small majority (58%) identified as British citizens, with others holding either Irish (26%) or dual (16%) citizenship. Of these border-region Leave voters, only 28% were female. Of the Remain voters, a significant majority (72%) identified as Irish citizens, 20% held dual citizenship and 7% British citizenship only. Of the Remain voters in this region, 50% were female. Thus, although there is evidence of polarisation

[13] http://www.thejournal.ie/ireland-rejoining-the-commonwealth-4174082-Aug2018/, accessed 10 August 2018.

[14] https://inews.co.uk/news/brexit/does-dup-support-theresa-may-chequers-brexit-plan/, accessed 10 August 2018.

of the vote along ethno-national lines, views on Brexit are not wholly aligned with civic and political identities. It is also interesting to note that female voters in the border region were significantly less in favour of Brexit than their male counterparts (Hayward and Irish Central Border Area Network 2018, 69).

Irrespective of the voting pattern, there continues to be one over-arching consensus among the general electorate and parties—that there be no hard border between Northern Ireland and the Republic of Ireland. For the majority (70%) of women and men in the border region, maintaining the border status quo (no hard border, and no change in cross-border movement) is a priority (Hayward and Irish Central Border Area Network 2018, 63). Views of those living in this part of Northern Ireland suggest that they expect a hard border as a result of Brexit, with remain voters (65% say it is likely or very likely) being more pessimistic on the topic than leave supporters (35% say it is likely or very likely) (Hayward and Irish Central Border Area Network 2018, 71). Resistance to North/South border checks is pronounced among Catholic-identifying respondents, with 80% saying that they would find it 'almost impossible to accept' having to apply in advance for documentation permitting travel across the border. This reluctance is also shared by a majority (60%) of Protestant identifiers (Garry et al. 2018, 19).

One can see why the disappearance of the current 'soft' border is a problem. Cross-border living and working is a regular feature of life—up to 30,000 people traverse the 300 mile border on a daily or weekly basis to work, avail of services, attend educational facilities and for cultural, recreational and family purposes. The impact of cross-border restrictions on the free movement of goods and people, cross-border employment, food prices and cross-border cooperation in health, education and other services were identified as having negative consequences for the daily lives of women and men living in border regions (Walsh and Women's Regional Consortium 2017, 30). Cross-border travel to access health-care during and after pregnancy is a common occurrence. The police services on both sides of the border co-operate closely on crime and security issues, including enforcing European Protection Orders where an abusing partner flees to the other jurisdiction in domestic violence cases (Patterson-Bennett 2018).

One young woman captured the challenge to everyday life a hard border would bring: 'What about normal day-to-day stuff? Say I want to walk the dog. I'm literally 10 minutes across the border. It would be a nightmare'. A hindrance to regular family routine was also the concern of a young man: 'half my family is from the South and half my family is from the North, and the last thing that I bloody want is to go across the border with my passport to visit my granny' (quoted in Garry et al. 2018, 7).

They are not alone in that view. In August 2017, the head of the Northern Ireland civil service David Sterling described the reality of the border economy in a letter to the UK chief Brexit negotiator Olly Robbins in the following terms: 'For example, bulk tankers owned or contracted by Irish milk processing firms collect raw milk from multiple farms in Northern Ireland before returning to Irish processing facilities'.[15]

However, there is a minority who are indifferent to border checks, with this view mainly held by Leave voters. One older woman drew a parallel with the Gibraltar border: 'It wouldn't annoy me at all. We had it years ago. And also too, I go to Spain and Gibraltar; its exactly the same' (quoted in Garry et al. 2018, 25).

There is also strong resistance to border checks between Ireland and Britain. Among political spokespersons, this view is strongly articulated by the DUP, including Foster and her Westminster team, as already noted. More interesting, though, is the ethno-national profile, as it is shared almost equally by Catholics and Protestants. For instance, 60% of Catholics and about 55% of Protestants would find it 'almost impossible to accept' having to secure advance travel documents for the East-West border (Garry et al. 2018, 26). These views had different motivations— for Protestants it was about undermining their British identity; for Catholics the economic implications were uppermost. As a Leave-voting male Protestant in middle age remarked 'We're still part of the UK. Why should there be a border'?, A female counterpart who voted Remain was of the view that 'We'd feel alienated in a way I think'. A younger Catholic woman saw the issue as an economic one: 'But I do think economically we need these connections with England and Wales for business' (Garry et al. 2018, 29–30).

---

[15] Jon Stone, 'Downing Street Was Warned About Brexit Border Plan by Head of Northern Ireland Civil Service,' *Independent*, 25 April 2018, https://www.independent.co.uk/news/uk/politics/brexit-irish-border-northern-ireland-uk-letter-eu-a8322611.html, accessed 10 August 2018.

In sum both quantitative and qualitative data show the inhibition of daily life, employment and access to services that a hard border on the island of Ireland could bring. Not surprisingly, women and men are in equal measure opposed to the reintroduction of a hard border, and a majority in both communities also resist this potential development. Politically, too, the possibility of a hard border worries government officials in terms of cross-border trade flows, diverging tariffs or regulatory standards, and policing and security matters. Thus, high policy and everyday living concerns are infused in all border-related discussions, particularly when focused on the land border on the island.

4   Citizenship and Rights

Citizenship claims are more complex in Northern Ireland than in Britain. This is because the 1998 Agreement provides for the right of Northern Ireland's citizens to hold British and Irish citizenship. Paragraph 52 of the December 2017 Joint Report[16] between the UK and the EU recognises that there is a choice of citizenship in Northern Ireland, and recognises that the EU-related rights of Irish citizens needs to be provided for in the Withdrawal Agreement:

> Both Parties acknowledge that the 1998 Agreement recognises the birth right of all the people of Northern Ireland to choose to be Irish or British or both and be accepted as such. The people of Northern Ireland who are Irish citizens will continue to enjoy rights as EU citizens, including where they reside in Northern Ireland. Both Parties therefore agree that the Withdrawal Agreement should respect and be without prejudice to the rights, opportunities and identity that come with European Union citizenship for such people and, in the next phase of negotiations, will examine arrangements required to give effect to the ongoing exercise of, and access to, their EU rights, opportunities and benefits.

These 'rights, opportunities and identity' include free movement and residency within the EU, the right to stand as a candidate for European Parliament elections, the right to access health care, and the right to complain to the European Ombudsman.

---

[16] https://assets.publishing.service.gov.uk/government/uploads/system/uploads/attachment_data/file/136652/agreement.pdf, accessed 21 June 2018.

This straightforward binary allocation of citizenship as British or Irish as applied to EU citizenship is problematized by Brexit. Recent research identified nine forms of residency and citizenship status in Ireland and Northern Ireland with entitlement to different combinations of rights (fn. 23 in IHREC-NIHRC 2018, 9). In this regard, the Equality Commission of Northern Ireland (ECNI) has highlighted the need to address the particular inequalities faced by women of multiple identities (ECNI 2018, 8).

Considering these rights and opportunities in a Brexit context, the issues of free movement and residency, access to goods and services (including health and education) in another member state, and the right of political representation are important matters to be teased out. Thus, if a person claiming Irish citizenship and living in Northern Ireland wishes to stand for election to the European Parliament, then that right will be respected, according to the Joint Report. Yet the practicalities are in doubt. While Britain remains a member of the EU, the constituency for which that EU citizen can stand is Northern Ireland, which has three seats in the European Parliament. The question as to whether Northern Ireland remains a regional constituency for the purpose of European Parliament elections is a matter of clarification (IHREC-NIHRC 2018, 9). The issue of representation matters, not least because two of the three MEPs from Northern Ireland elected in 2009 and again in 2014 from Northern Ireland are female.[17] Yet, in other spheres women's unequal representation in politics and civil society affects political debate on the matter. In 2017 women comprised only 25% of local councillors, 22% of MPs and 30% of Assembly members. On public boards, women held 41% of board positions, but held only 24% of chair positions (NISRA 2017, 27–29). Obstacles to the advancement of women's political and public office-holding comprise a combination of a conservative political culture, resistance from unionist parties (primarily) to recognising the democratic problem of the male dominance of political life, and an electoral system that facilitates conservative selection decisions (Galligan 2017; Matthews 2014). This triage of forces have successfully resisted a gender equality agenda, including temporary special measures such as all-women shortlists as permitted by the Sex Discrimination (Election Candidates) Act 2002.

The Brexit effect is not solely a domestic one in Northern Ireland. The 1998 Agreement created a joint human rights committee as an

[17]Martina Anderson (Sinn Féin); Diane Dodds (Democratic Unionist Party); Jim Nicholson (Ulster Unionist Party).

institutional forum for considering rights on an all-island basis. The intention was to ensure an equivalence of rights in both jurisdictions on the island. The mandate of the Joint Committee is potentially undermined by Brexit, and specifically since the Westminster vote on 21 November 2017 against retaining the EU Charter of Fundamental Rights (ECFR) in the Withdrawal Bill. While the exclusion of the ECFR has wide ramifications for the equality and human rights agenda in Great Britain, the decision has even more particular and significant implications for equality and human rights on the island of Ireland (LSE European Institute 2016; IHREC-NIHRC 2018). An example is the impending introduction of legislation in the Dáil (Irish parliament) requiring gender pay reporting for companies with 50 employees or more.[18] A similar (if less extensive) law cannot be put into effect in Northern Ireland due to the absence of regulations enacting gender pay reporting already provided for in the Employment (NI) Act 2016. Yet, if that law were in effect, the equivalence of rights on both sides of the border could be questioned, as there is as yet no Irish legislation on this issue.

Mindful of the strong possibility of divergence in equality and human rights in a post-Brexit scenario, the Joint Committee has called for

> ...the Withdrawal Agreement to provide for the continuing North-South equivalence of rights, post-Brexit, as established under the 1998 Agreement.
> ... recommends that at least Northern Ireland remains within the EU human rights and equality legislative framework, continues to incorporate key EU instruments, and remains within the jurisdiction of EU institutions or maintains an equivalence, at least, with EU human rights and equality instruments and jurisprudence on an evolving basis. (IHREC-NIHRC 2018, 7)

5 Women's Voices and Views

Complicating the Brexit context is the collapse of the Northern Ireland Assembly and Executive in January 2017 relating to the mishandling of renewable heating incentive scheme by the DUP.[19] The Secretary of

---

[18] https://www.irishtimes.com/business/legislation-to-reduce-gender-pay-gap-set-for-this-year-1.3451849.

[19] https://www.bbc.com/news/live/uk-northern-ireland-politics-38635708, accessed 19 August 2018.

State, James Brokenshire MP, called an election for 2nd March, the outcome of which was an almost equal share of seats for the DUP (28 seats) and SF (27 seats). For the first time in the history of Northern Ireland's parliaments, the unionist share of politics—39 seats in all—fell below a majority (46 seats) in the local parliament. The result made a negotiated return to devolved governance more problematic as the two main protagonists, SF and the DUP, clashed on cultural and language issues.[20] In the absence of functioning political institutions, and the high politics national focus on Brexit, important policy areas related to women's rights languish. There is no formal channel for organised women's views to be heard, especially their concerns about a risk to rights delivered by the EU being diminished or removed in the Brexit aftermath (NIRWN 2018, 31–32). These rights include equality in the workplace, protection of pregnant women and new mothers, flexible working, part-time workers rights (such as paid holidays), to name but a few.

Other outstanding unresolved policy issues of concern to women include the introduction of new legislation on domestic abuse to bring the region into line with provisions in England and Wales that requires ministerial attention to progress (House of Commons Northern Ireland Affairs Committee 2018). The Abortion (Fatal Fetal Abnormality) Bill, introduced into the Assembly on 6 December 2016 by the Minister for Justice, was a modest attempt to make provision for tragic in utero circumstances. The Bill fell when the Assembly collapsed some weeks later, as detailed above. The introduction of the Universal Credit 'rape clause' is more complicated in Northern Ireland than elsewhere in the UK as it is an offence, punishable by two years in prison, to fail to report a crime in Northern Ireland. This measure could result in women being criminalised, and their children stigmatised. Both the DUP and SF have resisted enacting this measure, but in the absence of a functioning Executive, there is no mechanism for moderating this provision.[21]

Although these are domestic policy matters, they draw attention to the lower standards of gender equality experienced by women in Northern Ireland as compared with the rest of the UK. Taken together with the rejection by the government of inclusion of the European

[20] http://www.irishnews.com/news/2017/10/19/news/new-deadline-set-in-power-sharing-talks-after-negotiations-stall-1166109/, accessed 19 August 20118.

[21] https://www.theguardian.com/uk-news/2017/jul/23/labour-sounds-alarm-universal-credit-rape-clause-northern-ireland.

Charter on Fundamental Rights in the Withdrawal Bill, women in Northern Ireland are fearful of a two-tier equality system emerging, with the region consolidating its already conservative gender regime. One woman expressed her concern that women's rights will be diminished post-Brexit in the following manner: 'We are supposed to be improving things, leaving a better legacy for our daughters and granddaughters; they will be so much worse off after Brexit' (quoted in NIRWN 2018, 31).

The issue of abortion starkly highlights the complexity of women's rights in the post-Brexit context. The region's restrictive abortion laws remain unchanged despite the Supreme Court finding in June 2018 that these laws contravene private and family life as guaranteed by the European convention on human rights. Women seeking abortions must travel to Britain, and in the coming years may choose to travel to the Republic of Ireland once legislation providing for the service is enacted and implemented (Potter 2014; Pierson 2018). The new provision of abortion services in the Irish Republic, following repeal of the constitutional ban in a referendum on 25 May 2018, will mark out a stark a difference in the rights of women in both jurisdictions. On 7 August 2018, the Irish Minister for Health, Simon Harris TD, declared that this service will be available to women from Northern Ireland.[22] This assurance was welcomed as an interim option by one of the main abortion advocacy groups, Alliance for Choice (AfC). However, AfC pointed out that this offer, the latest in a series by governments on these islands, is not an adequate alternative to policy and law reform on abortion in Northern Ireland.

An additional complication is presented by the differential travel rights that are likely to be accorded to UK, Irish and other nationalities following Brexit. Although it is expected that freedom of movement between UK and Irish citizens will continue under the Common Travel Area provisions, this will not necessarily apply to female citizens of other states and different citizenship entitlements, who seek to access reproductive health care services, including pregnancy terminations, in the Irish Republic. A hard post-Brexit border on the island will inevitably

---

[22] https://www.independent.ie/irish-news/abortions-will-not-stop-at-the-border-simon-harris-makes-assurances-to-women-in-northern-ireland-37194375.html, accessed 10 August 2018.

deny some non-Irish/non-UK women with crisis pregnancies access to this health care. In the meantime, despite calls from women's groups in Northern Ireland and supporters in Westminster for repeal of sections 57 and 58 of the 1861 Offences Against the Person Act, the Secretary of State for Northern Ireland, Karen Bradley MP, insisted that it was an issue for Northern Ireland's devolved (and non-functioning) institutions to resolve.

However, even with a functioning Assembly and Executive, there exists a major political obstacle to reform on abortion arising from the consociational settlement on which Northern Ireland's government rests. This obstacle is the veto, built into the 1998 Agreement and often found in consociational architecture, known in the Northern Ireland context as the petition of concern. Through this mechanism, the elected representatives of one community (nationalist or unionist) can veto any legislation it sees as injurious to the rights of the community it represents. The petition of concern has been repeatedly used to prevent progress on other socially liberal issues such as marriage equality. The mechanism is likely to be deployed to resist abortion reform against the wishes of over 70% of the population.[23]

Women's empowerment to speak on Brexit is further constrained by the absence of an updated gender equality strategy and action plan. This policy agenda has suffered from the instability of Northern Ireland's politics, the preference of the civil service for 'gender neutral' policies that do not address gender inequalities, and the effects of public spending cutbacks on service delivery (Patterson-Bennett 2018, 4–5). Qualitative research with women's organisations reveals a fear that a Brexit-associated economic downturn would exacerbate existing economic vulnerability, and intensify a feminised poverty in the region. As one woman expressed it: 'Brexit means less money all round, and therefore less money for the community and voluntary sector, which will not only mean job losses but it will also mean that the people that the sector support are also going to lose out' (quoted in Walsh and Women's Regional Consortium 2017, 30).

These are genuinely-held fears in a region where there is a heightened awareness of the contribution made by the EU regional fund to economic and social development and peace-building.

---

[23] https://www.amnesty.org.uk/press-releases/northern-ireland-nearly-34-public-support-abortion-law-change-new-poll-0, accessed 7 August 2018.

The European projects focus on enhancing women's employment opportunities in areas of high deprivation, rural communities and among marginalised women. Successful applications to the European Structural Funds (ESF) from women's organisations amounted to €1.7 million in the period 2014–2017, and €2 million in 2018–2020. Women's rate of economic inactivity in Northern Ireland is consistently higher than in the rest of the UK (in 2017 34% in NI, 26% in GB) with family responsibilities identified as the main inhibitor to taking up employment (NISRA 2017, 14–15). Although it is difficult to unravel the impact of EU membership for women in Northern Ireland from the more general gains of membership for women across the UK, there are some heightened benefits for women in this devolved region. The Equality Commission for Northern Ireland notes that EU directives have 'strengthened gender equality legislation in Northern Ireland, and enhanced rights for pregnant workers, part-time workers, agency workers, and in employment areas such as parental leave' (ECNI 2018, 3). In addition, European law has ensured that people from Northern Ireland who live in, or travel to, other parts of the EU enjoy legal privileges and protections commensurate to those they hold in Northern Ireland (ECNI 2017, 3). There is a real anxiety that the legal, legislative and institutional gains fostering equality will diminish as a consequence of Brexit, and a worry that the principles of equality and non-discrimination embedded in EU law will not be maintained after the Brexit process.

These concerns are all the more urgent given the gaps in equality protections between Northern Ireland and other parts of the UK following the introduction of the Equality Act 2010. For example, in Northern Ireland there is no protection against pay secrecy clauses designed to prevent employees disclosing their salaries. Nor is there protection against sex discrimination by public bodies or private clubs and associations. Furthermore, there is less scope for public bodies and employers in Northern Ireland to take positive measures to redress disadvantage suffered by under-represented groups (ECNI 2014, 4). These restrictions (among others) impact particularly on women in employment and public life—proactive measures to redress systemic inequality in pay and public office are rendered difficult under the existing devolved legislation. In the post-Brexit context, with the removal of the overarching EU rights and equalities framework, the gaps between Northern Ireland and UK law will be intensified.

6   PEACE IN TIMES OF AUSTERITY

The Northern Ireland peace process has had extensive support from the EU through funding for grass-roots peace and reconciliation projects along the border. This region has benefited from EUR1.5 billion courtesy of European tax-payers since 1995. The funding is managed by the Special European Union Programmes Body (SEUPB), created under Strand 2 of the 1998 Agreement. The content of the PEACE IV funding programme was agreed prior to the referendum vote by the Northern Ireland Executive and the Irish government as a means to 'address a number of key issues in order to support the overall peace process. These include more efforts to develop and deepen reconciliation between divided communities; increase tolerance and respect to reduce the levels of sectarianism and racism; promote increased community cohesion; and address the legacy of the past.'[24] The programme had a particular focus on children and young people, shared education, and shared spaces. In the aftermath of the UK referendum vote, the European Parliament voted to continue PEACE IV funding in recognition of the important peace-building role of this programme. The UK government has guaranteed remaining EU PEACE IV and INTERREG programme funding for strategic cross-border cooperation up to 2020, particularly important in the event of a non-transition Brexit when the EU could withdraw funding from the region (Tonge and European Parliament 2017, 7).

An independent evaluation of the Department for Communities regional infrastructure support programme for women in disadvantaged and rural areas recommended that the Northern Ireland Rural Women's Network be allocated more resources 'to animate and build critical mass' (quoted in NIRWN 2018, 7). Previously, a review of women's sector funding was critical of the historic funding deficit for rural women: 'There are also stark inequities between Government funding for service delivery to women's groups between rural and urban areas (1.3% v 98.7%)' (quoted in NIRWN 2018, 5). Meanwhile, 35% of the Northern Ireland population live in a rural area.[25] Furthermore, building

---

[24] http://www.seupb.eu/Libraries/PEACE_IV_Programme_Guidance/PIV_AdoptionByEC_30-11-2015.sflb.ashx, accessed 2 August 2016.

[25] https://wewillthrive.co.uk/audience-insights/reports/nisra-report-on-northern-irish-population-trends, accessed 21 June 2018.

peace in rural areas is a differently-nuanced process than found in urban areas. Breaking the tacit culture of silence, learning to share space, and the development of women's civic leadership are essential components to this task. Changing complex human micro-level interactions takes trust and time, for which funding is necessary. Yet, the role of women in rural peacebuilding has not been formally recognised, or adequately resourced, as a contribution to ongoing reconciliation and the building of a peaceful, secure society.

The Brexit decision came on the heels of a 2015 decision by Northern Ireland Executive to change the rules for allocating European Social Funds (ESF) following a reduction of about £600 million in the block grant to Northern Ireland from the Treasury. The women's and community sector were hit hardest in these changes through Executive decisions that prioritised investment in the private sector. The Department for Employment and Learning (DEL) took a decision to 'severely limit the training qualifications that a women's organisation could offer' in order to 'reroute' funding to colleges in the Further and Higher Education sector (WRDA 2016, 20, 23). The consequences were that many women's groups were forced to make redundant valuable education and training workers. For example, one long-standing service delivery and advocacy organisation lost its ESF allocation for the back to work training it provided for lone parents, and was forced to reduce its workforce from 15 to 7. A woman's centre, founded in 1987, lost 5 staff due to ESF funding restrictions, yet despite the cuts in their services the Jobs and Benefits Office continues to direct unemployed women to the centre for training (WRDA 2016, 28–29).

The Northern Ireland Council for Voluntary Agencies (NICVA) has added its voice as a representative of the community and voluntary sector to calls for a 'soft' Brexit deal on customs and trade, protection of citizenship, social and economic rights, and maintaining access to cross-border services on the island. Spokespersons have indicated an urgent need for agreement on post-Brexit social and economic strategies, including funding arrangements to provide for

> ...integrating vulnerable groups into employment, peace and reconciliation building, cross-border co-operation, and rural development. This discussion needs to include consideration of how to maximise retained access

to EU support; how the removal of the above subsidies and programmes will be factored into overall public funding for Northern Ireland; and also how additional funding from the UK Shared Prosperity Fund proposed to replace EU funding will be targeted to meet the current and future needs of NI society.[26]

The problem of coming to agreement on these issues is compounded through women being largely excluded from discussions on contentious issues such as the legacy of the past, revealing the male-gendered bias of post-conflict peace-building (Byrne and McCullough 2012; Pierson and Radford 2016; Hinds and Donnelly 2014; Pierson 2018). In a region where women's political and public representation lags persistently behind that of other countries in the UK, the gender aspects of democracy in a post-conflict country is a neglected casualty of Brexit.

7   Conclusion

Brexit intersects with gender in Northern Ireland in a multi-layered and multi-dimensional manner. While this dynamic is equally applicable in the other countries of the UK, the unique and particular circumstances of Northern Ireland—as a post-conflict society, an under-developed economy, and bordering a country remaining in the EU—lead to a gender-specific context not found in other parts of the UK. As a consequence, one can identify three broad dimensions in which Brexit will have implications for Northern Ireland, each containing a gendered aspect.

First, Brexit will lead to the return of at least 140 policy areas from the EU that intersect with the devolution settlement in Northern Ireland. Among them are significant areas relevant to gender equality such as private cross-border pensions; civil judicial co-operation (including family law); and reciprocal health care arrangements.[27] Second, Brexit will also require negotiation for Northern Ireland on the

[26] http://www.nicva.org/resource/nicva-position-paper-and-recommendations-for-the-brexit-negotiations, accessed 24 June 2018.

[27] http://www.niassembly.gov.uk/globalassets/documents/brexit-brief/brexit-and-devolution/powers-returning-from-eu-that-intersect-with-the-devolution-settlement-in-scotland.pdf, accessed 21 June 2018.

continuation of the all-island economy strategy adopted in the wake of the 1998 Agreement, in services such as tourism, health, energy, and more recently education. This negotiation includes the nature of the border ('hard' or 'soft'), and has significant implications for Strand 2 of the 1998 Agreement (the island's North-South aspect) and the retention of an equivalence of rights—including gender equality—between the two jurisdictions. Third, Brexit will require an internal domestic UK reallocation of EU funds, of particular importance in Northern Ireland due to the under-developed economy and the ongoing peace process. In the working through of these aspects, women's interests and concerns, along with the principles of equality and non-discrimination, risk being marginalised in a political tussle determined by economic priorities.

In the task of making sense of the ramifications of Brexit for gender equality, scare attention has been paid to creative solutions to the complexity introduced to relationships on the island of Ireland. Indeed, Harvey and Skoutaris (2018) make the case for a differentiated approach for Northern Ireland with regard to Brexit in a manner of 'carefully crafted formulas that facilitate honourable compromises' (Harvey 2018). One possible scenario that could preserve the equivalence of rights— especially women's rights—required by the 1998 Agreement is that Northern Ireland become a member of the EEA along with Iceland, Lichtenstein and Norway. The EEA solution for the UK has been extensively canvassed,[28] but its application to Northern Ireland has been given scarce consideration (an exception is found in McGowan 2017, 104–105). The scenario is that the UK leaves the EU, following which Northern Ireland will apply for special admission to the EEA as a region. Although this outcome would require negotiated amendments to treaty provisions, these would not be insurmountable. In a slightly different context there is already the example of Greenland, a regional part of the Danish state, which opted out of EU membership and now has 'associated territory' status with special arrangements with the EU.

There are particular benefits for the region to follow this course of action: Northern Ireland would remain in the single market, with its concomitant free movement of goods, services, capital and labour—resolving

---

[28] https://www.chathamhouse.org/expert/comment/eea-safe-harbour-brexit-storm; https://www.theguardian.com/politics/2016/dec/01/can-the-uk-adopt-the-norway-model-as-its-brexit-solution; and https://www.slaughterandmay.com/media/2535258/brexit-essentials-alternatives-to-eu-membership.pdf.

in considerable measure the thorny issue of the island border. The arrangement could facilitate maintenance of the spirit and practice of the 1998 Agreement, especially its Strand 2 North-South element which is essential to the provision of rights equivalence and problem-free access to services, including health services. Northern Ireland's constitutional position in the UK would be maintained. The EEA region is one that places particular focus on gender equality, funding activities that support and advance this value. Thus, advocates for gender equality would have a receptive context in which to pursue their objectives. In addition, as an EEA regional member/associate, the EU could find a mechanism to continue the PEACE funding and other programmes that have been so vital to the empowerment of grassroots women's groups in their pursuit of a reconciled and peaceful society. An essential condition of this differentiated approach is the restoration of governance mechanisms in Northern Ireland. As Harvey (2018) points out, the 1998 Agreement can provide a solution here, through the British-Irish Intergovernmental Conference. In the absence of a timely return to operation of the devolved institutions, and given that direct rule requires a law to be passed in Westminster, this mechanism offers an accountable governing process. On both points, admission to the EEA and the restoration of meaningful governance in Northern Ireland, the combined efforts of the UK and Irish governments, with support from the other EU member states, is required.

For Northern Ireland, Brexit sharpens and complicates the existing vacuum in democratic politics due to the absence of functioning devolved political institutions. While this state of affairs persists, opportunities to tackle the under-representation of women in formal politics and public life are few and far between. Urgent policy issues remain unaddressed. Policy monitoring and advising carried out by equality and human rights bodies is constrained. Studies of Brexit emanating from Northern Ireland call for a solution that does not exacerbate community divisions in the context of a fragile political and post-conflict settlement. This concern is reflected among women's groups, who also fear a reinforcement of conservative social and economic policies in the aftermath of Brexit. These fears are expressed most acutely by women living in the border region, where the economy is fragile, reconciliation with neighbours is slowly finding a foothold, and their lived reality is shaped by border crossings on a daily basis. For the gender pact between Northern Ireland and women, then, Brexit marks a defining moment whose ramifications will be felt for decades to come.

REFERENCES

Berberi, Carine. 2017. Northern Ireland: Is Brexit a Threat to the Peace Process and the 'Soft' Irish Border? *Revue Française de Civilisation Britannique* [online], XXII–2. http://rfcb.revues.org/1370; https://doi.org/10.4000/rfcb.1370.

Byrne, Siobhan, and Allison McCullogh. 2012. Gender, Representation and Power-Sharing in Post-conflict Institutions. *International Peacekeeping* 19 (5): 565–580.

Doyle, John, and Eileen Connolly. 2017. Brexit and the Northern Ireland Question. In *The Law and Politics of Brexit*, ed. Federico Fabbrini, 140–162. Oxford: Oxford University Press.

Equality Commission for Northern Ireland (ECNI). 2014. *Gaps in Equality Law Between Great Britain and Northern Ireland*. Belfast: ECNI.

Equality Commission for Northern Ireland (ECNI). 2017. *Protecting and Advancing Equality and Good Relations as the UK Exits from the European Union*. Belfast: ECNI.

Equality Commission for Northern Ireland (ECNI). 2018. *Women in Northern Ireland: UN CEDAW Submission to Inform 'List of Issues' Consideration (Examination of United Kingdom, 2019)*. Belfast: ECNI.

Galligan, Yvonne. 2017. Persistent Gender Inequality in Political Representation, North and South. In *Dynamics of Political Change in Ireland: Making and Breaking a Divided Island*, ed. Niall Ó Dochartaigh, Katy Hayward, and Elizabeth Meehan, 159–177. London: Routledge.

Garry, John, Brendan O'Leary, and John Coakley. 2017. How Northern Ireland Voted in the EU Referendum—And What It Means for Border Talks. http://theconversation.com/how-northern-ireland-voted-in-the-eu-referendum-and-what-it-means-for-border-talks-76677. Accessed 24 June 2018.

Garry, John, Kevin McNicholl, Brendan O'Leary, and James Pow. 2018. Northern Ireland and the UK's Exit from the EU: What Do People Think? http://ukandeu.ac.uk/research-papers/northern-ireland-and-the-uks-exit-from-the-eu-what-do-people-think/. Accessed 24 June 2018.

Harvey, Colin. 2018. Brexit, the Island of Ireland and the Good Friday Agreement. *The UK in a Changing Europe Blog*. http://ukandeu.ac.uk/brexit-the-island-of-ireland-and-the-good-friday-agreement/. Accessed 10 August 2018.

Harvey, Colin, and Nikos Skoutaris. 2018. A Special Arrangement for Northern Ireland? *QPol Blog*. http://qpol.qub.ac.uk/special-arrangement-northern-ireland/. Accessed 10 August 2018.

Hayward, Katy, and Irish Central Border Area Network. 2018. Bordering on Brexit: Views from Local Communities in the Central Border Region of Ireland/Northern Ireland. https://www.qub.ac.uk/brexit/Brexitfilestore/Filetoupload,780606,en.pdf. Accessed 24 June 2018.

Hayward, Katy, and Mary C. Murphy. 2018. The EU's Influence on the Peace Process and Agreement in Northern Ireland in the Light of Brexit. *Ethnopolitics* 17 (3): 276–291.

Hinds, Bronagh, and Deborah Donnelly. 2014. Women, Peace and Security: Women's Rights and Gender Equality—Strategic Guide and Toolkit. http://review.table59.co.uk/wrda/wp-content/uploads/2017/05/Toolkit_Booklet.pdf. Accessed 24 June 2018.

House of Commons Northern Ireland Affairs Committee. 2018. *Devolution and Democracy in Northern Ireland: Dealing with the Deficit, Third Report of Session 2017–19.* London: House of Commons.

IHREC-NIHRC. 2018. Joint Committee of the Irish Human Rights and Equality Commission and the Northern Irish Human Rights Commission: *Policy Statement on the UK Withdrawal from the European Union.* Dublin and Belfast: IHREC and NIHRC.

LSE European Institute. 2016. *The Implications of Brexit for Fundamental Rights Protections in the UK: Report.* London: LSE.

Matthews, Neil. 2014. Gendered Candidate Selection and the Representation of Women in Northern Ireland. *Parliamentary Affairs* 67 (3): 617–646.

McGowan, Lee. 2017. *Preparing for Brexit: Actors, Negotiations and Consequences* [online]. Palgrave Studies in European Union Politics. https://doi.org/10.1007/978-3-319-64260-4_6.

Northern Ireland Rural Women's Network. 2018. Rural Voices: Action Research and Policy Priorities for Rural Women. http://www.nirwn.org/wp-content/uploads/2018/03/NIRWN-Rural-Voices-Research-Report-March-2018.pdf. Accessed 24 June 2018.

Northern Ireland Statistical Research Agency (NISRA). 2017. *Women in Northern Ireland 2017.* Belfast: NISRA.

Patterson-Bennett, Emma. 2018. Women's Rights and Brexit. https://brexit-lawni.org/blog/womens-rights-brexit/. Accessed 24 June 2018.

Pierson, Claire. 2018. One Step Forwards, Two Steps Back: Women's Rights 20 Years After the Good Friday Agreement. *Parliamentary Affairs* 71: 461–481.

Pierson, Claire, and Katy Radford. 2016. *Peacebuilding and the Women's Sector in Northern Ireland.* Belfast: Institute for Conflict Research, Community Relations Council.

Potter, Michael. 2014. Review of Gender Issues in Northern Ireland, NI Assembly Research and Information Service Research Paper [NIAR-510-13]. http://www.niassembly.gov.uk/globalassets/Documents/RaISe/Publications/2014/ofmdfm/1514.pdf. Accessed 24 June 2018.

Tonge, Jonathan, and European Parliament. 2017. The Impact and Consequences of Brexit for Northern Ireland: Briefing. Policy Department C: Citizens' Rights and Constitutional Affairs. http://www.europarl.europa.eu/RegData/etudes/BRIE/2017/583116/IPOL_BRI(2017)583116_EN.pdf.   Accessed 24 June 2018.

Walsh, Caroline, and Women's Regional Consortium. 2017. Brexit: Women's Perspectives. https://www.nwci.ie/images/uploads/Brexit%2Bwomen_final_ii.pdf. Accessed 24 June 2018.

Women's Resource and Development Agency. 2016. Women at the Cutting Edge: The Impact of Spending Cuts on Women's Community and Voluntary Organisations in Northern Ireland. http://www.nirwn.org/wp-content/uploads/2016/12/WRDA_CuttingEdgeA4_v4_spreads.pdf.   Accessed   24 June 2018.

PART IV

Looking Beyond the UK, Beyond the EU

CHAPTER 15

Through the Looking Glass: Brexit, Defence and Security Through the Lens of Gender

Amy Barrow

1   INTRODUCTION

As Britain navigates its departure from the European Union (EU), commentators have embarked on scrutinising the withdrawal process and its implications across various legislative and policy arenas (Chalmers 2017; Henokl 2018; Whitman 2016). Although some scholars have also started to apply a gender lens to the implications of Brexit on UK laws and policies on gender equality (Guerrina and Masselot 2018), to date there has been limited analysis of how Brexit may affect women's involvement in security and defence policymaking, peace and conflict processes. Since the UK joined the European Economic Community in 1973, there has been significant integration of economic, social, foreign and security policies. The Common Foreign and Security Policy (CFSP) entered into force with the adoption of the Maastricht Treaty in 1993 (Treaty on European Union), which introduced the three-pillar structure of the EU. The European Security and Defence Policy (ESDP) was originally situated under the second 'intergovernmental' pillar of

A. Barrow (✉)
Macquarie Law School, Macquarie University, NSW, Sydney, Australia
e-mail: amy.barrow@mq.edu.au

© The Author(s) 2019   389
M. Dustin et al. (eds.), *Gender and Queer Perspectives on Brexit*,
Gender and Politics, https://doi.org/10.1007/978-3-030-03122-0_15

the EU, the CFSP. Initiated by France and the UK (Bailes 2008, 115), the policy was aimed at the improved coordination of member states' responses to civil and military crisis management and conflict prevention. In 2009, the Lisbon Treaty abolished the three-pillar structure of the EU, giving legal personality to a new Union and, as a result, the ESDP was reframed as the Common Security and Defence Policy (CSDP). The Lisbon Treaty also created the European External Action Service (EEAS)—the European diplomatic service, which is responsible for supporting the delivery of the CFSP. As an organisation, the EU has echoed international law and policy developments at the UN level in the area of women, peace and security.

On 31 October 2000, the UN Security Council unanimously adopted Security Council Resolution 1325 on women, peace and security (UNSCR 1325),[1] a civil society driven soft-law instrument framed around the three pillars of prevention, protection and participation. UNSCR 1325 aimed to mainstream gender at the Security Council and in peace and security processes. The Security Council has historically prioritized military actions and economic sanctions (Charlesworth 1994, 446), making the adoption of UNSCR 1325, which focuses on conflict prevention, a significant landmark. Parallel to this development, the European Parliament, a supranational body within the EU, adopted its own resolution on the participation of women in peaceful conflict resolution on 30 November 2000.[2] Subsequently, the EU has taken steps to mainstream gender in CSDP missions and operations with the Council of the EU adopting a policy on the *Implementation of UNSCR 1325 in the Context of ESDP* in 2005.[3] Following the adoption of a second state-sponsored resolution at the UN in 2008 which focuses on sexual violence in armed conflict, Security Council Resolution 1820, the EU adopted the *Comprehensive Approach to the EU Implementation of Security Council Resolutions 1325 and 1820,*[4] as well as a set of indicators

---

[1] UNSC Res 1325 (31 October 2000) UN Doc S/RES/1325.

[2] European Parliament Resolution on Participation of Women in Peaceful Conflict Resolution (2000/2025(INI)).

[3] Council of the European Union, 'Implementation of UNSCR 1325 as Reinforced by UNSCR 1820 in the Context of ESDP' (3 December 2008) 157282/3/08.

[4] Council of the European Union, 'Comprehensive Approach to the EU Implementation of the United Nations Security Council Resolutions 1325 and 1820 on Women, Peace and Security' (1 December 2008) 15671/1/08 REV 1.

to monitor and evaluate the *EU Comprehensive Approach*. Although promising, these policy developments at the EU level have delivered modest results. Compared with other EU policy domains, the institutionalization of UNSCR 1325 and UNSCR 1820 in the 'gender-neutral' security domain has proved challenging (Guerrina and Wright 2016). Women's participation in peace and security processes remains limited and has been criticized for perpetuating gender stereotypes (Valenius 2007; Deiana and McDonagh 2018, 40).

Although the CSDP and CFSP are the 'least integrated areas of policy' across the EU's 28 member states, meaning that there is less to untangle in terms of shared policies, legislation and resources (Hadfield 2018, 174; Whitman 2016, R44), the way in which the UK renegotiates its relationship with the EU in relation to both the CSDP and CFSP is not without its own complexities. Beyond Brexit, it is unclear what type of role the UK will play in relation to the EU's security and defence. The UK will no longer be a member of CSDP policy, though it may contribute to missions on an ad hoc basis (Chalmers 2017, 6). What implications this may have for domestic policymaking around women, peace and security and women's engagement in conflict and peace processes remains unclear.

This chapter seeks to explore what Brexit means in practice for women's involvement in defence and security policymaking, peace and conflict processes. The chapter will first explore how the UN agenda on women, peace and security has been institutionalized at the EU level, drawing on feminist institutionalism and mainstreaming theory. Two principal policy documents have been adopted, the *Implementation of UNSCR 1325 in the Context of CSDP* and the *Comprehensive Approach to the EU Implementation of Security Council's Resolution 1325 and 1820*, but how these policies have shaped CSDP missions and operations is open to debate. While there has been some integration of a gender perspective at a normative level in EU policy, the chapter will also explore how, if at all, gender has been mainstreamed into CSDP missions and operations on the ground, including the promise and limitations of this process. Drawing on this analysis, the chapter will then turn to consider the implications of Brexit for women's involvement in security and defence policymaking, peace and conflict processes. The chapter will argue that the UK's departure from the EU will not only weaken the UK's influence in European policymaking on defence and security, but that international peer pressure from states within the EU bloc will be diminished. As a result, some of the external drivers for proactive policymaking around women, peace and security that have influenced British policy on UNSCR 1325 and 1820 to date, may be undermined. The UK's withdrawal from the EU also has implications for civil society actors' access to transnational networks within and beyond the EU and may impact on civil society activism and organizing around UNSCR 1325.

2   Institutionalizing Women, Peace and Security in the EU

UNSCR 1325 is a soft law instrument centred on women's experiences of armed conflict and its aftermath. A coalition of women's organizations, which formed the NGO Working Group on Women, Peace and Security, played a pivotal role in tabling the resolution at the UN with the support of the then Namibian presidency at the Security Council. Framed around the three pillars of prevention protection and participation, the resolution includes a preamble and eighteen operative paragraphs engaging with: peacekeeping operations; disarmament, demobilization and reintegration (DDR); sexual violence in armed conflict; and women's role in conflict prevention and resolution. The transformative potential of UNSCR 1325 has been critiqued extensively (Kirby and Shepherd 2016; Otto 2009; Shepherd 2008). Implementation of the resolution by the UN, UN Member States as well as civil society actors has also been scrutinized (Barrow 2009, 2016; Basu 2016; True 2016).

Initially, the resolution did not gain much traction. As a soft law instrument, with indeterminate language and a lack of monitoring and evaluation mechanisms built into the resolution, it proved difficult to foster accountability for UNSCR 1325's implementation among UN Member States. Although the resolution notes the importance of existing international obligations relevant to women, peace and security, including the Geneva Conventions and the Convention on the Elimination of All Forms of Discrimination Against Women (CEDAW) (UNSCR 1325, operative paragraph 9), the resolution is an indicative rather than a formally binding resolution, as it does not invoke Chapter VII of the UN Charter, which gives authority to the Security Council to determine any threat to peace and maintain international peace and security. Despite these limitations, civil society organizations (CSO) have used the resolution to lobby governments (Barrow 2013) and UNSCR 1325's influence is growing amongst elite policy circles (Miller et al. 2014, 51).

While UNSCR 1325's framework may be flawed, it provides the foundation for a series of subsequent resolutions (UNSCR 1820 (2008) and UNSCR 1888 (2009) on sexual violence against civilians in armed conflict; and UNSCRs 1889 (2009), 1960 (2010), 2016 (2013) and 2122 (2013) on women, peace and security), which form the women, peace and security agenda at the UN (WPS agenda). The WPS agenda is invariably shaped by the nature of the institutional setting in which UNSCR 1325 and subsequent resolutions are diffused globally; the EU's experience of implementing UNSCR 1325 and UNSCR 1820 gives insight into how this process shapes norms on women, peace and security within the EU (Guerrina and Wright 2016, 293).

Gender has typically been incorporated into EU policies through equal treatment, affirmative action and latterly gender mainstreaming (Hafner Burton and Pollack 2002, 342), respectively referred to by Rees as 'tinkering,' 'tailoring' and 'transforming' (2005, 557). This has resulted in a hybrid of non-discrimination laws and various equality strategies (Beveridge and Shaw 2002, 2010). The Amsterdam Treaty of 1997 formalised the EU's commitment to the promotion of equality between men and women and modified Article 3 of the Treaty on European Union to include the principle of gender mainstreaming.[5] Affirmative action requires the use of targeted policies such as quotas, which are aimed at improving the gender balance between men and women in decision-making (Rees 2005, 566). In sharp contrast, gender mainstreaming, which was first formally articulated in the *Beijing Declaration and Platform for Action* 1995, requires policymakers to evaluate the implications of laws, policies and programmes on men and women, at all stages of their design, implementation and evaluation. Mainstreaming has been distinguished as a transformative strategy on the basis that it incorporates a cultural shift in attitudes and organizational practices (Moser and Moser 2005, 12). This transformative dimension suggests that

[5] IRS-Istituto per la Ricerca Sociale-Italy (2014), 'Evaluation of the Strategy for Equality Between Women and Men 2010–2015 as a Contribution to Achieve the Goals of the Beijing Platform for Action', Study for the Committee on Women's Rights and Gender Equality, PE 509.996 at 16, http://www.europarl.europa.eu/RegData/etudes/STUD/2014/509996/IPOL_STU(2014)509996_EN.pdf, last accessed 18 May 2018.

gender mainstreaming is dependent on a social and cultural acceptance of mainstreaming, which goes beyond a legislative or policy framework. Mainstreaming is seen as 'extraordinarily demanding' and given that the application of gender mainstreaming is multi-layered, some actors in the process may have little interest in applying a gender perspective or insufficient knowledge of gender issues (Walby 2005, 324).

Several scholars have theorized how mainstreaming operates in practice, including in institutions such as the EU and across different policy fields (see Beveridge and Shaw 2002; Walby 2005), although analysis of gender mainstreaming in the EU's security and defence policy remains limited (D'Almeida et al. 2017; Deiana and McDonagh 2018; Gya 2011; Guerrina and Wright 2016). Squires initially identified two models of mainstreaming: first, an integrationist model characterized by an 'add women and stir approach,' which incorporates women without addressing how existing institutional structures and decision-making mechanisms often fail to incorporate a gender perspective; second, the agenda-setting model of mainstreaming, which incorporates a range of actors, including civil society, to reorient existing policy paradigms in order to reflect a gender perspective—a model that is particularly complex to implement in practice (Squires 2005, 374–375).

The success of gender mainstreaming appears to be dependent on a number of factors, including the engagement of civil society actors, whether there is already a prior awareness of gender and whether there is a 'political opportunity structure' (Joachim et al. 2017, 106). Reinforcing Squire's agenda-setting model of mainstreaming, the role of CSO is critical in reorienting existing policy paradigms. In the EU, the transformative potential of gender mainstreaming has yet to be fully realized. The implementation of mainstreaming as an equality strategy has been challenged by masculine power and interests, which are institutionally embedded (Joachim et al. 2017, 109).

Intergovernmental in nature, the CSDP brings together both civilian crisis management as well as military operations, including the development of EU Battlegroups—armed forces on standby with the capacity to intervene in conflicts at short notice in order to restore stability. The CSDP's focus on both civilian and military crisis management may exacerbate the complexity of efforts to mainstream gender. Kronsell argues that, even if historically male only organizations such as the military alter their practices and integrate women, masculine norms remain embedded (2016, 315).

Feminist institutionalist theorists have questioned why gender has been successfully mainstreamed in some policy areas, but contested in others (Guerrina and Wright 2016, 296). Drawing on Woodward's work on 'velvet triangles' which identifies three determinants—the role of femocrats (essentially a feminist bureaucrat), CSO and epistemic communities—required for effective gender mainstreaming in policy-making (Woodward 2004), Guerrina and Wright analyse the diffusion of the WPS agenda in the EU (2016, 296–297). They argue that the complex institutional architecture of the EU has proved particularly challenging for the integration of a gender perspective in some policy areas (Guerrina and Wright 2016, 297). Compared with other policy fields, the area of security has been particularly resistant to the integration of gender mainstreaming (Joachim et al. 2017, 107). Although feminist actors have played a prominent role in relation to strengthening social policies on employment equality such as equal pay, in contrast security and defence policy is depicted as 'gender-neutral,' premised on 'traditional conceptions of security,' and there is a notable absence of feminist actors with the capacity to influence policymaking at the EEAS (Guerrina and Wright 2016, 298).

Since 2014, Federica Mogherini, an Italian politician, has served as the High Representative of the EU for Foreign Affairs and Security Policy. Mogherini was responsible for the EU's Global Strategy[6] in 2016, a major policy document that situates the EU in its global context. In December 2017, Mogherini announced the EU established Permanent Structured Cooperation on Defence (PESCO), which is central to the EU's goal of 'strategic autonomy' under the 2016 Global Strategy (Nováky 2018, 98). However, it is not clear that Mogherini is a femocrat as such. On International Women's Day (IWD) 2018, Mogherini voiced her support of women's equality with men as outlined in the Rome Treaty,[7] and the Global Strategy does refer to UNSCR 1325,

---

[6] European External Action Service, 'European Union Shared Vision, Common Action: A Stronger Europe: A Global Strategy for the European Union's Foreign and Security Policy' (June 2016), http://eeas.europa.eu/archives/docs/top_stories/pdf/eugs_review_web.pdf, last accessed 18 May 2018.

[7] European Union External Action 08/03/2018 'Mogherini Pledges Strong Support to Women Around the World on International Women's Day', https://eeas.europa.eu/headquarters/headquarters-homepage/22322/mogherini-pledges-strong-support-women-around-world-international-womens-day_en, last accessed 18 May 2018.

albeit superficially.[8] Particularly given that only a minority of women are appointed to elite policy positions, it is difficult to measure the impact of women's leadership on policymaking, and whether women's equality and empowerment are advanced as a result (Williams 2017). If anything, Mogherini's statements on women's rights do not 'push the envelope,' that is they do not appear to pioneer a new vision, the statements coincide with IWD and the release of major EU policy initiatives, and repeat familiar rhetoric.

In relation to the role of 'epistemic communities,' the intergovernmental nature of the CSDP has made it largely impenetrable to civil society actors (Guerrina and Wright 2016, 298). Guerrina and Wright note the absence of the European Women's Lobby (EWL), the largest umbrella organization of women's CSO in the EU (supported by the European Commission), in actively monitoring the implementation of the WPS agenda at the EU level (2016, 299). Instead, the European Peacebuilding and Liaison Office (EPLO) has played a prominent role in tracking UNSCR 1325's implementation by the EU and its Member States (Barrow 2016). Guerrina and Wright suggest that EPLO is not a feminist organization (2016, 299) and distinguish this lack of feminist scrutiny at the EEAS from civil society's pivotal role in domestic policymaking within individual EU Member States (2016, 301).

Several national-level NGO coalitions that include feminist organizations do exist across Europe, including GAPS-UK, 1325 Forum Norway, and the 1325 Network Finland.[9] Some civil society actors have also attempted to influence EU policy on defence and security or at least filled the gender-deficit gap with their expertise on gender equality. Kvinna til Kvinna, meaning 'woman to woman', is a prominent Swedish non-governmental organization that promotes women's rights

[8] For example, the *Global Strategy* states that the human rights and gender issues will be systematically mainstreamed across policy sectors and institutions, but beyond this statement, there is no further indication of how this will be done in practice. Above Footnote 6, at 51.

[9] For further information see respectively Gender Action for Peace and Security (GAPS-UK), http://gaps-uk.org/; 1325 Network Finland, http://www.1325.fi/in-english/; Forum Norway 1325, a network of 21 civil society organisations working on the Norwegian implementation of UNSCR 1325, is coordinated by the Forum for Women and Development, https://www.fokuskvinner.no/en/.

and peace.[10] Woman to Woman is a member of EPLO and has succeeded in securing funding from the EU to conduct research on women's participation in peace negotiations, which in turn has influenced the EU's monitoring of UNSCRs 1325 and 1820, as evidenced by references to Kvinna til Kvinna's research findings in EU reports.[11] Further, European national sections of the Women's International League for Peace and Freedom (WILPF), a transnational NGO and one of the founding coalition members of the NGO Working Group on Women, Peace and Security, have collaborated on projects to monitor the implementation of the WPS agenda in Europe. However, finding an entry point to influence policymaking has proved challenging and this may be due to the 'complex institutional architecture' of the EU. In 2007, the Swedish section of WILPF created a detailed guide on European security politics (WILPF 2007) that members of the Swedish section, as well as the general public, could use as a lobbying tool to influence members of the European Parliament. It is not possible to fully evaluate the impact of this lobbying, but given that the European Parliament only acts in an advisory capacity on matters of defence and security (Guerrina and Wright 2016) and does not have the authority to finance or shape CSDP missions and operations (Bailes 2008, 129), these campaign strategies may have had limited impact. As an institution, the European Parliament is more accessible to CSO than the EEAS. National CSO are able to consult with their respective members of the European Parliament and raise points of debate. The lack of transparency surrounding the EEAS, ESDP policy, missions and operations effectively closes down entry points for civil society engagement. In comparison, the European Parliament has been proactive in EU policymaking on WPS, as will now be discussed.

3   Mainstreaming the WPS Agenda at the EU

The European Parliament has taken steps to promote the implementation of UNSCR 1325 and 1820. Shortly before the adoption of UNSCR 1325 at the UN on October 31 2000, in a report, the European

---

[10] For more information about Woman to Woman, see http://thekvinnatillkvinnafoundation.org/

[11] The Council of the European Union, *Second Report on the EU Indicators for the Comprehensive Approach to the EU Implementation of UNSCR 1325 & 1820 on Women, Peace and Security* (6 February 2014) 6219/14 at 36.

Parliament called for the adoption of a resolution on the participation of women in peaceful conflict resolution. The EU Parliament recognized that the military is an inherently male institution, both culturally and in the number of military personnel (European Parliament 2000, 13). As discussed, the EU adopted a resolution on the participation of women in peaceful conflict resolution in November 2000.[12] While echoing UNSCR 1325, the resolution is substantively stronger and outlines actions to be taken by EU Member States to promote the equal participation of women in diplomatic conflict resolution and reconstruction initiatives at all levels (operative paragraph 13). The resolution also emphasizes the increased use of non-military crisis-management, requiring non-military peacekeeping skills, 'resulting in enhanced opportunities for women' (operative paragraph 15).

The EU has also taken steps to mainstream gender in its peace and security operations. It adopted a policy on *Implementing UNSCR 1325 in CSDP* [then ESDP] *operations*[13] as well as a *Check list to ensure on gender mainstreaming and implementation in the planning and conduct of ESDP [now CSDP] operations*[14] (2006), which focus on the planning, deployment and interaction of CSDP operations and missions with the host societies. However, these policy documents are quite vague and indeterminate and have been criticized for their almost exclusive framing of gender with vulnerable groups, specifically women and children (Deiana and McDonagh 2018, 40). Following the adoption of state-driven United Nations Security Council Resolution 1820,[15] which focuses on sexual violence in armed conflict, the EU took steps to integrate gender into peace and security policymaking.

In 2008, the EU adopted its *Comprehensive Approach to the EU Implementation of Security Council Resolutions 1325 and 1820*. The document outlines a three-pronged approach. First, in its engagement with partner governments, issues relating to women, peace and security will be integrated into the EU's dialogue, particularly conflict-affected states.

---

[12] Above, Footnote 2.

[13] Council of the European Union, 'Implementing UNSCR 1325 in ESDP Operations' (7 November 2005) 11932/2/05.

[14] Council of the European Union, 'Check list to ensure on gender mainstreaming and implementation in the planning and conduct of ESDP operations' (27 July 2006) 12068/06.

[15] UNSC Res 1820 (19 June 2008) UN Doc S/RES/1820.

Second, a 'gender equality approach' will be mainstreamed in EU's policies and activities in both crisis management and development cooperation. Third, the EU will support strategic actions that aim to protect and empower women. The EU also acknowledges that in its efforts to promote gender equality, a deeper understanding of men's involvement in the process is required (para. 18). Calling for greater cooperation with civil society and non-state actors in the planning, implementation and evaluation of EU activities (para. 19), the EU also encourages Member States to engage in an annual open exchange on lessons learnt, including both difficulties and positive examples of implementing UNSCR 1325 and UNSCR 1820 (para. 29).

Reinforcing the Global Indicators on UNSCR 1325, the EU developed a set of seventeen EU indicators[16] to support the *EU Comprehensive Approach*. The indicators cover a broad range of policy issues, including the development of National Action Plans (NAPs) or other national level initiatives by EU Member States (Indicator 6). Several indicators are specific to CSDP. Indicator 10 evaluates the interaction between EU actors and civil society organisations working on women's rights and gender equality, by measuring the number of meetings between EU Delegations, Member States embassies and CSDP missions with ngo's working on women, peace and security. Indicator 11 reviews the proportion of women and men at all levels of CSDP missions. Similarly, indicator 12 monitors the proportion of women and men staff in UN peacekeeping operations and CSDP missions that have received specific training on gender equality by EU Member States. Indicator 13 reviews the clear references made to gender or women, peace and security issues in CSDP missions and operations planning documents. Reports provide a summary of data and responses collected under each indicator.

While the EU indicators allow for increased scrutiny of how the *EU Comprehensive Approach* is being implemented, the reporting process relies on a biennial survey of EU Member States, Missions, EU Delegations and the information received is not always consistent, making it difficult to evaluate.[17] The nature of the EU indicators is based

---

[16] Council of the European Union, 'Indicators for the Comprehensive Approach to the EU Implementation of United Nations Security Council Resolutions 1325 and 1820' (14 July 2010) 11948/10.

[17] The Council of the European Union, *Report on the EU-indicators for the Comprehensive Approach to the EU implementation of the UN Security Council UNSCRs 1325 & 1820 on Women, Peace and Security* (11 May 2011) 9990/11 at 2.

on quantitative measures largely related to internal staffing and planning documents of UN Peacekeeping Operations and CSDP Missions and Operations. Although these indicators allow some insight into how gender is mainstreamed in CSDP missions and operations, the quantitative nature of these measures fails to give a clear evaluation of what difference these practices have made to women personnel and their experiences in missions and operations, as well as women civilians on the ground in their interaction with CSDP missions.

In the first EU indicators report (Council of the EU 2011), regarding the proportion of men and women at all levels in CSDP missions and operations (Indicator 11), among EU Member States women headed 18% of missions on average. Sweden had the highest percentage of women heads (34%), with almost a third of its diplomatic missions headed by women (32 women to 62 men). Women made up 26% of all Swedish staff participating in CSDP missions (18 women to 68 men). In comparison, women headed 14% of the UK's diplomatic missions (32 women to 189 men). The UK's representation of women in UN peacekeeping operations was at a similar level—women made up 13% of UN peacekeeping operations and 12% of staff participated in CSDP missions at all levels, including military and police staff. These statistics should be read cautiously, given that proportionately Sweden contributes a relatively small number of personnel to UN Peacekeeping Operations and CSDP missions compared with other EU Member States such as Poland, which has 815 women staff to 43,651 men in CSDP missions (2% of women).

This pan-European reporting on the EU indicators exerts diplomatic pressure on EU Member States to fulfil commitments made under the *Comprehensive Approach to the EU Implementation of UNSCR 1325 and 1820*, though the nature of reporting itself could be more transparent. In the Second EU indicators Report, the proportion of women who are heads of diplomatic missions among EU Member States has increased from 18 to 21%.[18] However, no figures are provided on EU Member States' staffing in UN Peacekeeping operations and CSDP missions, making it difficult to measure whether there has been any substantive improvement, or indeed reduction, in the proportion of men and women staff. Post-Brexit, the UK will not necessarily continue to engage

---

[18]According to the report, only 12 EU Member States provided information regarding Heads of Diplomatic Missions, therefore this figure may not accurately reflect levels of female leadership across EU Member States' diplomatic missions. Above Footnote 11, at 45.

in this type of intergovernmental exchange with other EU Member States on training and staffing in the military and civilian forces, meaning that critical information on best practices of integrating the WPS agenda into peacekeeping operations and civilian crisis management will potentially be lost.

Alongside these institutional policy developments, several EU Member States have also adopted NAPs—'living' policy tools aimed at supporting the implementation of UNSCR 1325 and subsequent Security Council resolutions on women, peace and security in domestic law and policymaking. The adoption of NAPs is dependent on a number of drivers, such as international peer pressure, political will, resources, accountability and the relationship of states with civil society (Miller et al. 2014, 17). Compared with other regional institutions such as ASEAN, which to date has not proactively engaged with UNSCR 1325, the EU has, at least at a normative level, appeared to support the UN's WPS agenda by adopting a series of policy documents on UNSCRs 1325 and 1820 (Barrow 2016, 8). This political will, together with international peer pressure from individual EU Member States and accountability, are drivers for individual EU Member States' adoption of NAPs. Indicator 6 relating to the *EU Comprehensive Approach* aims to monitor the commitments made by EU Member States including NAPs and other comprehensive policies on women, peace and security.[19] Seventeen EU Member States have adopted NAPs to date. Denmark was the first EU State to adopt a NAP in 2005 and the UK adopted a similar tool in 2006 (Barrow 2016, 3).

The UK's first-generation NAP was framed around twelve action areas including DDR, gender-based violence, civil society engagement, and the UK's support of the UN and training and policy (Barrow 2016, 19). However, the NAP does not clearly envisage what mainstreaming a gender perspective in peacekeeping operations would entail in practice (Barrow 2016, 20). The UK's second-generation NAP (2010–2013) included consultation with Gender Action for Peace and Security (GAPS UK), a coalition of domestic NGOs with expertise on gender, armed conflict and its aftermath that promotes the incorporation of a gender perspective in domestic policymaking on peace and security

---

[19] Above Footnote 16, at 12.

(Barrow 2016, 20). Primarily 'outward-looking' in nature to peace and security operations beyond the UK's borders, the NAP is more closely aligned to UNSCR 1325's pillars of prevention, protection and participation. A principal objective is the creation of Female Engagement Teams as a means of strengthening engagement with civilians in post-conflict situations.[20] Significantly, this provision reinforces the UK's role under the CSDP, pointing to the influence of the EU as an external driver in shaping the UK's implementation of UNSCR 1325 (Barrow 2016, 22).

The UK's third-generation NAP[21] is quite distinct from earlier incarnations, as it also includes 'inward-looking' priorities based on domestic policymaking, including violence against women more broadly, forced marriage, human trafficking and female genital mutilation (Barrow 2016, 23). Despite the third-generation NAP's greater focus on domestic policies, there is no consideration of how UNSCR 1325 is implemented in the context of Northern Ireland and the repercussions of the decades-long 'Troubles' (Barrow 2016, 23). Significantly, the UK acknowledges the importance of its multilateral relationships:

> The UK cannot realise its goals on women, peace and security alone. We have privileged positions in major multilateral organizations including the UN, NATO and the EU (...) Through our multilateral engagement we want to ensure that the work of the UN, NATO, EU and AU and other regional and sub-regional organizations uphold the principle that women must have an equal voice in addressing challenges in peace and security.[22]

Specifically, the NAP includes an overview of the UK's engagement with these multilateral organizations. With regard to the EU, the UK outlined its role in strongly advocating for a sustained focus on gender issues in the *EU Instrument contributing to Stability and Peace*, a policy tool designed to support 'security initiatives and peacebuilding activities

---

[20] Foreign and Commonwealth Office, United Kingdom of Great Britain and Northern Ireland (2012) United Kingdom National Action Plan on UNSCR 1325 Women, Peace and Security at 22.

[21] Foreign and Commonwealth Office, United Kingdom National Action Plan on Women, Peace and Security 2014–2017, https://www.gov.uk/government/publications/uk-national-action-plan-on-women-peace-and-security, last accessed 18 May 2018.

[22] Ibid., at 26.

in partner countries.'[23] Significantly, the UK stated that it was considering how gender could be effectively mainstreamed in CSDP missions, noting that gender-awareness training for CSDP staff was a 'key priority' of the UK Summit on Ending Sexual Violence in Conflict. Echoing the *Comprehensive Approach to the EU Implementation of UNSCR 1325 and UNSCR 1820*, which called for open exchange between EU Member States on their implementation of the WPS agenda, a key output of the NAP is to engage annually with multilateral organizations, including the EU, to report on the implementation of the NAP. As previously discussed, the UK's withdrawal from the EU will fundamentally alter how the UK engages with other EU Member States, in effect removing an external check and balance on the UK's policymaking on WPS and reducing political peer pressure from the EU bloc.

The UK's fourth generation NAP,[24] released in January 2018, sets out a five-year plan for implementation of the UN's women, peace and security agenda. No reference is made to the EU, the CFSP or CSDP, suggesting that the UK, at least in its own domestic policies, is already starting to withdraw from its obligations under the CSDP. The NAP's focus on other multilateral partnerships, including NATO and the OSCE, provides a clear indication of the UK's aim to reorient itself away from the EU.

While the EU and EU Member States, including the UK, appear, at least at a normative level, to have taken steps to integrate the UN's women, peace and security agenda, progress to date suggests that policymakers do not take gender seriously (Deiana and McDonagh 2018). Although the EU's policy on Implementing UNSCR 1325 was updated to respond to the adoption of UNSCR 1820 on sexual violence against civilians in conflict, and is described as a 'living document', neither this policy, the *EU Comprehensive Approach* nor the EU indicators have been updated to reflect more recent developments in the WPS agenda.

---

[23] European Commission, Service for Foreign Policy Instruments (2014), 'Instrument Contributing to Stability and Peace, Preventing Conflict Around the World', http://ec.europa.eu/dgs/fpi/what-we-do/instrument_contributing_to_stability_and_peace_en.htm, last accessed 18 May 2018.

[24] Department for International Development, Foreign and Commonwealth Office, Ministry of Defence and Stabilisation Unit, 'UK National Action Plan on Women, Peace and Security 2018–2022' (January 16, 2018), https://www.gov.uk/government/publications/uk-national-action-plan-on-women-peace-and-security-2018-to-2022, last accessed 18 May 2018.

CSDP missions and operations on the ground give insight into the operational implementation of UNSCRs 1325 and 1820.

4   Mainstreaming Gender in Common Security and Defence Policy Missions and Operations

Prior to the Lisbon Treaty, which restructured the EU and reframed ESDP as CSDP, Valenius undertook a detailed study of early efforts to mainstream gender in ESDP missions (2007). When initially introduced as a policy, gender entry points for mainstreaming in ESDP missions reinforced an overly bureaucratic approach, which did not extend to a clear evaluation of the impact of policies on gender relations on the ground (Valenius 2007, 24–25). Some women's organizations reported to Valenius that they had interacted with ESDP missions positively, but there was limited engagement with the local population (Valenius 2007, 51). ESDP missions appeared to view women as victims or 'passive recipients of abuse' (Valenius 2007, 51), assumptions that could potentially be detrimental to women's empowerment. Instead, the application of a gender perspective in ESDP focused largely on internal behavior within peacekeeping operations, including sexual harassment towards female peacekeepers (Valenius 2007, 44). A justification for the integration of gender mainstreaming in CSDP missions and operations is the positive impact women's involvement has on operational effectiveness.

Female peacekeepers are perceived to have greater knowledge of the 'host' society, as they are more likely to socialize with local women in their operations (Valenius 2007, 30), particularly in some cultures that prohibit women from engaging with men outside of the family unit (D'Almeida et al. 2017, 315). However, Valenius evaluated the UN mission in Eritrea and Ethiopia (UNMEE) and found that, in comparison with peacekeepers of an ethnic European background (who were considered as outsiders), Ghanaian and Kenyan female peacekeepers experienced greater interaction with the local population (2007, 38). Race, ethnicity and culture all intersect with gender, but the implications of identity and wider diversity considerations do not appear to inform the EU's evaluations of how women's inclusion in ESDP missions helps to ensure that a gender perspective is mainstreamed in peace and security operations. It has also been suggested that female peacekeepers act as 'civilizers', serving to monitor excessive behaviour among male soldiers (Valenius 2007, 40). Again contradicting this assertion, Valenius' engagement with female personnel suggested that, if anything, female peacekeepers withdrew from their counterpart's behaviour (2007, 129). Valenius' early observations indicate that gender stereotyping of female roles in CSDP initially shaped and moulded how gender mainstreaming policies operated in practice.

More recent studies suggest that women leaders have a stronger understanding of sex discrimination and harassment and are able to foster a safer working environment, whereby women are able to disclose incidents of sexual harassment more easily (D'Almeida et al. 2017, 316). Although this may suggest that gender mainstreaming in CSDP has had a modest impact, it also points to the ongoing challenges posed by sexual harassment. Further, women continue to face prejudice in the field from their own male counterparts (D'Almeida et al. 2017, 317). D'Almeida et al. point to the importance of gender balance in CSDP missions, including in leadership posts, which is a useful exercise for demonstrating women's professional capacity not only in host societies, but also to male colleagues (2017, 316). There are notable examples of female only teams in UN peacekeeping missions, such as an Indian all female police team that contributed to stabilizing Liberia. However, if female only teams are used in perceived 'soft' civilian crisis management only, it may continue to perpetuate gender stereotypes regarding women's capacity to lead military operations.

Since Valenius' early research on gender mainstreaming in ESDP missions in 2007, the number of women in civilan CSDP missions has increased from 240 to 869 (Meiske 2015, 1). There is no official gender-disaggregated data on CSDP military operations, but female personnel are estimated to comprise 3–8% of deployed personnel (Meiske 2015, 1). The limited number of women in CSDP military operations is in part due to the domestic policies of individual EU Member States and the disproportionate number of men in the military (D'Almeida et al. 2017, 317) and foreign and security institutions (Kronsell 2016, 317). D'Almeida et al. suggest that CSDP missions can learn from the experiences of Member States such as Sweden, which is reintroducing conscription (2017, 318). Although operational effectiveness may be a strategic method of encouraging female representation in CSDP missions and operations, thus enhancing gender balance, this discursive context undermines the principal objective of gender mainstreaming, which is to evaluate the design, implementation and monitoring of any adopted policy initiative or legislation on men and women. The rationale for integrating gender mainstreaming in CSDP missions was initially based on the right of equality, however, increasingly there has been a shift in rhetoric to 'functionalist arguments' based on operational effectiveness (Meiske 2015, 1).

The need to frame women's participation in terms of value added to CSDP missions, while reflective of the entrenched dominant masculinity and male power that continues to shape CSDP policy, is also due to the 'narrowing down' of the WPS agenda more broadly (Deiana and McDonagh 2018, 37). UNSCR 1325's pillars of prevention and participation have not been given the same weight as the protection pillar and states have prioritized sexual violence in armed conflict and gender balancing in peacekeeping operations (Deiana and McDonagh 2018, 37). In part, this is reflective of a shift in the WPS agenda away from UNSCR 1325's civil society roots to 'state-centric' priorities (Kirby and Shepherd 2016). Current efforts to translate the women, peace and security agenda into EU policymaking in the field of CSDP appear to be premised on an integrationist model of mainstreaming. Gender is not seen as a core strategic priority, but an afterthought (Deiana and McDonagh 2018, 45). Deiana and McDonagh's interview with a gender advisor reveals that unless gender mainstreaming is framed in terms of its 'operational effectiveness', it will not resonate with 'the more operationally-focused security and defence actors' who focus on 'what does this bring me as a commander…in my daily work?' (2018, 45).

The inclusion of a gender perspective within the EU, CSDP and among EU Member States has achieved modest results at best. The diffusion of the women, peace and security agenda in EU defence and security policy has not been discussed by mainstream security analysts and may not be considered to be significant to discourses on the post-Brexit landscape with regard to the future of European defence and security. However, it is important that a gender lens be applied to this domain of EU policymaking in the light of Brexit including how the UK's withdrawal from the EU will impact upon the inclusion of a gender perspective in defence and security policymaking both in the UK and in the EU.

5   Brexit and Its Implications for Gender, Defence and Security Policymaking

How Brexit might affect women's involvement in defence and security policymaking, peace and security peace processes is currently unclear and may be dependent on whether Britain negotiates a 'hard' or 'soft' Brexit. Although the UK has a prominent role and capacity in NATO and will retain some influence on EU security, it will be a challenge for the UK to hold the same political leverage (Chalmers 2017). Effectively, the UK will lose its seat at the table in decision-making over the EU's responses to international issues (Chalmers 2017, 2). Several scholars have speculated how the UK will position itself in any future engagement with the EU on defence and security. Whitman speculates that the UK's role in EU defence, security and external affairs will either be as an 'integrated player', 'associated partner' or 'detached observer' (2016, R48–49). Henokl points to the many 'unknowns' in the Brexit process and posits three potential Brexit scenarios—'scenario 1: total rupture and no involvement at all (disintegration); scenario 2: selective involvement in some initiatives and arrangements...(muddling-through); and scenario 3: continuing a strong UK engagement via existing EU DC [Development Cooperation] instruments (reformed partnership)' (2018, 3). Henokl suggests that the current state of Brexit negotiations have 'ruled out' a reformed partnership, with 'muddling-through' being a stronger possibility. The UK will most certainly increasingly focus on the protection of its own national interests (Chalmers 2017, 2), but what will this mean for women's participation in defence and security policymaking, peace and conflict processes? In its preliminary negotiations, the UK has prioritized issues of trade, immigration and sovereignty, and has only recently turned to issues of defence and security.

In December 2017, the UK Government released a paper on *Foreign Policy, Defence and Development: A Future Partnership*.[25] The paper outlines the UK's commitment to fostering a special relationship with the EU that goes deeper than that of EU-third party relationships. The UK Government points to the shared values, challenges and priorities as indicated in the UK's 2015 Strategic Defence and Security Review[26]

---

[25] HM Government, Department for Exiting the European Union, *Foreign Policy, Defence and Development: A Future Partnership Paper* (12 September 2017), https://assets.publishing.service.gov.uk/government/uploads/system/uploads/attachment_data/file/643924/Foreign_policy__defence_and_development_paper.pdf, last accessed 18 May 2018.

[26] HM Government Prime Ministers Office, 10 Downing Street, Cabinet Office, Department for International Development, Foreign and Commonwealth Office, Home Office and Ministry of Defence, 'National Security Strategy and Strategic Defence and Security Review 2015: A Secure and Prosperous United Kingdom' (23 November 2015), https://assets.publishing.service.gov.uk/government/uploads/system/uploads/attachment_data/file/478933/52309_Cm_9161_NSS_SD_Review_web_only.pdf, last accessed 18 May 2018.

(SDSR) and EU's 2016 Global Strategy. A number of areas are identified in the paper including defence and security, international development, foreign policy and cyber security. Though the SDSR explores the UK's continued commitment to the CSDP, Whitman suggests that the EU is framed in a 'minor supporting role' (2016, R44). The UK, together with France, played a pivotal role in developing the CSDP, but several policy analysts suggest that over the course of the past decade the UK has gradually reduced its engagement in CSDP missions and operations (Whitman 2016, R45; Black et al. 2017, 21). The SDSR does not frame the CSDP as a strategic priority in national security (Whitman 2016, R45), nor does it explicitly engage with gender mainstreaming or the integration of UNSCR 1325 into CSDP missions. The report briefly touches on sexual violence in conflict and modern day slavery. Beyond these references to gender-based security concerns, the SDSR also points to the UK's role in supporting family planning, presenting a limited and paternalistic understanding of how a gender perspective should be applied within the policy domain of defence and security.

No indication is given in the *Future Partnership* paper that a gender perspective is critical to the UK's post-Brexit plans for defence and security. Further, the UK's fourth-generation NAP on WPS (published only one month after the *Future Partnership* paper) emphasizes the UK's multilateral partnerships with the UN and NATO and fails to explore the type of relationship the UK hopes to foster with the EU in the future. No reference is made to the EU, to CFSP or to CSDP within the NAP. The UK is withdrawing from the EU at a period in history when security threats within the EU are more significant than the end of the Cold War (Chalmers 2017, 8). The EU is strengthening its status in foreign security and defence globally (D'Almeida et al. 2017, 313), aspiring to create an EU military headquarters (Black et al. 2017, 12). To neglect consideration of the EU within the revised NAP is not only contradictory to the *Future Partnership* paper's call for a special relationship that goes deeper than those with third parties, but also suggests that the WPS agenda has been overlooked by policymakers in their evaluation of how the UK may foster such a special relationship with the EU. In renegotiating its relationship with the EU, a strong signal is sent that the WPS agenda is not a core priority in the equation.

Even if the UK is formally withdrawing from the EU, it is critical that the UK broach how it will interact with the EU on WPS going forwards. Although the UK is currently navigating its departure from the EU, it is premature and unwise for the UK to neglect its existing commitments under the CFSP, which continues to apply. To exclude the EU, the second largest economy globally and an aspiring global actor in defence and security, from consideration within the NAP, gives a clear indication that the UK is prioritizing its own national interests. Civil society coalitions that have provided expertise to meet the gender deficit in the UK's policymaking on WPS (such as GAPS UK) are charged with reviewing the UK NAP, including compiling a shadow report. It is imperative that GAPS UK question how the UK will engage with the EU on WPS in the longer term, particularly given increasing insecurity within the European region as a result of forced displacement due to instability and conflict in the Middle East and the rise of violent extremism.

The exclusion of the EU from the updated NAP also raises questions about how CSO will influence policymaking on women, peace and security beyond the UK, in Europe and internationally. While the largest umbrella organization of women's CSO in the EU, the EWL, has not proactively engaged with UNSCR 1325 this does not mean that informally there is not pan-European organizing and activism around women, peace and security. WILPF is one such organization, with national sections throughout Europe that undertake collective campaigns and have attempted to find entry points to influence policymaking on CSDP. Whether the UK's pivot away from the EU will result in the reorientation of domestic NGOs' own campaign priorities remains to be seen, and will be dependent on the direction of the UK Government's implementation of the WPS agenda including which external actors and multilateral organizations the UK prioritizes. Domestically, the spaces for women's civic engagement on gender equality have already diminished within the UK context. The Women's National Commission, founded in 1969, was closed in 2010 as part of the Conservative Government's austerity drive. The Women's National Commission provided a channel for many smaller women's organizations to table their concerns within the British Parliament. Over the years, and particularly since the UN Decade on Women (1976–1985), women's organizing and activism within broader transnational networks has opened up the possibility of influencing policymaking within Europe and internationally at the UN, particularly during events such as the Commission on the Status of Women held at UN Headquarters in New York annually. Fortunately, GAPS-UK, have established a strong working relationship with the UK Government, which relies on its expertise, but GAPS-UK may still have to evaluate its working practices and priorities in relation to UK policymaking on WPS. It is likely that British CSO networks will also alter as a result of the UK's pivot away from Europe, but what shape and form these networks will take remains to be seen.

6   CONCLUSION

While the EU Parliament has promoted the WPS agenda within the EU, the institutionalization of the WPS agenda in the EU policy domain of security has proved particularly challenging. Given the complex institutional architecture of the EU and the intergovernmental nature of the CSDP, together with a lack of transparency at the EEAS, civil society actors have struggled to find an entry point to influence policymaking. However, several EU Member States have adopted NAPs in response to the *EU Comprehensive Agreement on the Implementation of UNSCR 1325 and 1820*. The EU indicators have also increased monitoring and evaluation of individual EU Member States' national efforts to implement the WPS agenda, including issues such as the proportion of men and women in the military and civilian staffing, as well as how regularly states interact with civil society actors. Although the integration of a gender perspective in CSDP has proved to be modest both in terms of institutionalization and in CSDP missions and operations on the ground, Brexit will potentially have detrimental consequences for UK policymaking in the area of gender, defence and security.

Following the UK's withdrawal from the EU, the CSDP will no longer apply to the UK. The imperative to mainstream gender in peace and security operations, including international peer pressure from other EU member states, will likely diminish. There will be no oversight of the UK's national level implementation of the WPS agenda by the EU, effectively removing an important external check and balance on the UK's progress in implementing UNSCRs 1325 and 1820. Further, international peer pressure from EU bloc states, an important driver in the development, monitoring and evaluation of NAPs, will be diminished. The effects of Brexit will not only impact on the UK's multilateral relationships, but also on civil society organizing and activism around UNSCR 1325, which may fundamentally alter. British CSO, which already have limited entry points to influence the 'gender neutral' (gender blind) policy domain of security, will no longer make their views heard through members of the European Parliament, yet EU policies and actions may continue to have implications for the UK even after its withdrawal, particularly given rising levels of insecurity across Europe and the threat of violent extremism. While the UK Government may be pivoting away from the EU to renew focus on other multilateral organisations, including NATO and the UN, it is short-sighted to exclude consideration of how the UK may work with EU Member States to implement the WPS agenda. Although the CSDP may be less entrenched in UK law and policy compared with other policy domains and it may therefore be less complex to disentangle from it, current analyses of the UK's future relationship with the EU overlook gender, reinforcing the worrying and erroneous perception that gender is irrelevant to future defence and security concerns.

BIBLIOGRAPHY

Bailes, A.J.K. 2008. The EU and a 'Better World': What Role for the European Security and Defence Policy? *International Affairs* 84 (1): 115–130.

Barrow, A. 2009. '[It's] like a Rubber Band'. Assessing UNSCR 1325 as a Gender Mainstreaming Process. *International Journal of Law in Context* 5 (1): 51–68.

Barrow, A. 2013. Mainstreaming Gender in Transitional Justice Processes. In *The Experiences of Women as Protagonists in Transitional Justice*, ed. L. Yarwood, 34–53. Abingdon, Oxon; New York: Routledge.

Barrow, A. 2016. Operationalizing Security Council Resolution 1325: The Role of National Action Plans. *Journal of Conflict and Security Law* 21 (2): 1–29.

Basu, S. 2016. The Global South Writes 1325 (Too). *International Political Science Review* 37 (3): 362–374.

Beveridge, Fiona, and Jo Shaw. 2002. Introduction: Mainstreaming Gender in European Public Policy. *Feminist Legal Studies* 10 (3–4): 313–328.

Black, J., A. Hall, K. Cox, M. Kepe, and E. Silfversten. 2017. *Defence and Security After Brexit: Understanding the Possible Implications of the UK's Decision to Leave Europe*. RAND Corporation.

Chalmers, Malcolm. 2017. UK Foreign and Security Policy After Brexit. Briefing Paper, RUSI Royal United Services Institute.

Charlesworth, Hilary. 1994. Transforming the United Men's Club: Feminist Futures for the UN. *Transnational Law & Contemporary Problems* 4: 421.

D'Almeida, Irina Bratosin, Rebecca Haffner, and Corinna Horst. 2017. Women in the CSDP: Strengthening the EU's Effectiveness as an International Player. *European View* 16: 313–324.

Deiana, Maria-Adriana, and Kenneth McDonagh. 2018. 'It Is Important, but...' Translating the Women, Peace and Security (WPS) Agenda into the Planning of EU Peacekeeping Missions. *Peacebuilding* 6 (1): 34–48.

European Parliament Report on Participation of Women in Peaceful Conflict Resolution (2000) A5-0308/2000.

Guerrina, Roberta, and Annick Masselot. 2018. Walking into the Footprint of EU Law: Unpacking the Gendered Consequences of Brexit. *Social Policy & Society* 17 (2): 319–330.

Guerrina, R., and K.A.M. Wright. 2016. Gendering Normative Power Europe: Lessons of the Women, Peace and Security Agenda. *International Affairs* 92 (2): 293–312.

Gya, Giji. 2011. Women, Peace and Security in EU Common Security and Defence Policy. Background Paper, CSDN Policy Meeting on EU-CSO Expert Meeting on Women, Peace and Security (WPS) in EU Common Security and Defence Policy Missions and Operations, June 21, Brussels, Belgium. http://eplo.org/wp-content/uploads/2017/02/CSDN_Policy-Meeting_WPS-in-CSDP_Background-paper.pdf. Last accessed 18 May 2018.

Hadfield, Amelia. 2018. Britain Against the World? Foreign and Security Policy in the 'Age of Brexit'. In *Beyond Brexit*. London: UCL Press.

Hafner Burton, Emilie, and Mark A. Pollack. 2002. Mainstreaming Gender in Global Governance. *European Journal of International Relations* 8 (3): 339–373.

Henokl, Thomas. 2018. How Brexit Affects EU External Action: The UK's Legacy in European International Cooperation. *Futures* 97: 63–72.

Joachim, Jutta, Andrea Schneiker, and Anne Jenichen. 2017. External Networks and Institutional Idiosyncransies: The Common Security and Defence Policy and UNSCR 1325 on Women, Peace and Security. *Cambridge Review of International Affairs* 30 (1): 105–124.

Kirby, P., and L.J. Shepherd. 2016. The Futures Past of the Women, Peace and Security Agenda. *International Affairs* 92 (2): 373–392.

Kronsell, Annica. 2016. Sexed Bodies and Military Masculinities: Gender Path Dependence in EU's Common Security and Defence Policy. *Men and Masculinities* 19 (3): 311–336.

Meiske, Maline. 2015. Gender Balancing in CSDP Missions. *European Union for Security Studies* (51): 1–2.

Miller, B., M. Pournik, and A. Swaine. 2014. Women in Peace and Security Through United National Security Council Resolution 1325: Literature Review, Content Analysis of National Action Plans, and Implementation. Global Gender Program Working Paper No. 09. Washington, DC, USA: George Washington Elliott School of International Affairs.

Moser, Caroline, and Annalise Moser. 2005. Gender Mainstreaming Since Beijing: A Review of the Success and Limitations in International Institutions. *Gender and Development* 13 (2): 11–22.

Nováky, Niklas. 2018. The EU's Permanent Structured Cooperation in Defence: Keeping Sleeping Beauty from Snoozing. *European View* 17 (1): 97–104.

Otto, Diane. 2009. The Exile of Exclusion: Reflections on Gender Issues in International Law Over the Last Decade. *Melbourne Journal of International Law* 10 (1): 11–26.

Rees, Teresa. 2005. Reflections on the Uneven Development of Gender Mainstreaming in Europe. *International Feminist Journal of Politics* 7 (4): 555–574.

Shepherd, Laura J. 2008. Power and Authority in the Production of United Nations Security Council Resolution 1325. *International Studies Quarterly* 52 (2): 383–404.

Squires, Judith. 2005. Is Mainstreaming Transformative? Theorizing Mainstreaming in the Context of Diversity and Deliberation. *Social Politics* 12 (3): 366–388.

True, Jacqui. 2016. Explaining the Global Diffusion of the Women, Peace and Security Agenda. *International Political Science Review* 37 (3): 307–323.

Valenius, Johanna. 2007. Gender Mainstreaming in ESDP Missions. Chaillot Paper No. 101. Paris: European Union Institute for Security Studies.

Walby, Sylvia. 2005. Gender Mainstreaming: Productive Tensions in Theory and Practice. *Social Politics* 12 (3): 321–343.

Whitman, Richard G. 2016. The UK and EU Foreign, Security and Defence Policy After Brexit: Integrated, Associated or Detached? *National Institute Economic Review* 238 (1): R43–R50.

Williams, Kristin P. 2017. Feminism in Foreign Policy. In *Oxford Research Encyclopedia of Politics*. USA: Oxford University Press.

WILPF. 2007. *European Security Politics – Peace, Security and Cooperation*. Stockholm: Women's International League for Peace and Freedom—Swedish section.

Woodward, Alison E. 2004. Building Velvet Triangles: Gender and Informal Governance. In *Informal Governance in the European Union*, ed. Thomas Christiansen and Simona Piattoni, 76–93. Cheltenham: Edward Elgar.

CHAPTER 16

The Likely Economic Impact of Brexit on Women: Lessons from Gender and Trade Research

Mary-Ann Stephenson and Marzia Fontana

1   INTRODUCTION

Brexit will mean new trading arrangements for the UK, not just with the EU but with the rest of the world. It is well established that trade agreements can have significantly different impacts on different groups of women and men, as a result of differences in economic position, caring responsibilities and political power. However, there has been little work to date on the potential gender impacts of the UK's post Brexit trade deals. With continued uncertainty about what trade agreement the UK will reach with the EU, and therefore what trade agreements with the rest of the world will be possible and/or necessary, it is difficult to predict with certainty what these gendered impacts might be.

M.-A. Stephenson (✉)
London, UK
e-mail: maryann.stephenson@wbg.org.uk

M. Fontana
Institute of Development Studies at Sussex, Brighton, UK
e-mail: M.Fontana@ids.ac.uk

© The Author(s) 2019   415
M. Dustin et al. (eds.), *Gender and Queer Perspectives on Brexit*,
Gender and Politics, https://doi.org/10.1007/978-3-030-03122-0_16

Since the early 2000s, a number of analytical frameworks have been developed to assess the gendered impacts of international trade expansion and liberalisation. One commonly used framework links the distributional implications of trade to effects on employment, consumption and public provision of services (Gammage et al. 2002; Fontana 2003). Using this model, this chapter will explore the key issues to consider when analysing the eventual trade agreements made by the UK. Section 2 draws on a few examples from the gender and trade literature to illustrate ways in which trade affects women and men differently with regard to employment, consumption and the provision of public services. Section 3 sets out the possible forms a post Brexit trade deal with the EU might take, while Section 4 summarises existing research on the impact that these are likely to have on UK GDP. Sections 5, 6 and 7 draw on selective evidence on the structure of the UK economy and its gendered features to suggest likely effects of Brexit on women as workers, consumers and users of public services respectively. Section 8 briefly highlights some of the implications of Brexit for victims and survivors of male violence. Section 9 concludes with a series of recommendations to avoid adverse effects on gender equality from new trade agreements in the post-Brexit era.

2   INSIGHTS FROM THE LITERATURE ON GENDER AND TRADE

The trade and inequality literature usually distinguishes three main channels through which changes in the composition and level of exports and imports affect individuals in a country: the employment channel, the consumption channel and the public provision channel (Gammage et al. 2002; Fontana 2003). Different groups of women and men are thus going to be affected by trade policies and agreements not only as workers and producers, but also as consumers and citizens/residents entitled to public services.

As for the employment effect, trade policies and agreements are likely to result in changes in the structure of production of a country, with some sectors expanding and other contracting. This, in turn, causes changes in the level and distribution of employment of different categories of workers employed with different intensities by different sectors. It is not only the quantity of employment which can be affected, but also its quality. The economic volatility frequently associated with production for world markets, as well as possible trade-related changes in the regulatory environment, are also likely to affect the quality and security of employment differently for various groups of workers and producers. Small-scale producers and low-skill workers, many of which are women, often bear the brunt of trade changes (Fontana 2016). In other words, gendered employment effects from trade changes are to be expected because of the different distribution of women and men across tradable and non-tradable sectors and employment statuses, combined with limited substitutability between female and male labour due to rigid gender roles in the labour market.

In manufacturing, for example, women all over the world tend to cluster in only a few sectors such as textiles and footwear, while men are more equally distributed across sectors and occupations (ILO 2017). In the 1980s and the 1990s, women benefitted from export-led industrialization in developing countries that specialised in labour-intensive exports (Pearson 1999; Berik 2011). But this resulted also at the same time in disproportionate job losses for women through import competition in high-income developed economies, such as the United States, Australia, Canada and Japan (Kucera and Milberg 2007). Moreover, regarding employment status, women tend to be over-represented in the category of micro-entrepreneurs, with restricted access to productive resources and networks, and hence often unable to take advantage of potential opportunities created by new trade agreements (OECD 2017).

As for the consumption effect, trade can bring about changes in the relative prices of goods and services, in their overall availability and quality. Gendered effects may result because of prevailing norms assigning women primary responsibility for food preparation and basic health care for their children and families. One of the effects of the North American Free Trade Agreement (NAFTA), for instance, has been an increase in the consumer price of food staples locally produced in Mexico, but a decline in the consumer price of junk food imported from the United States. This has had significant negative consequences for the diet and health of many Mexicans, including an increase in child obesity (Serdan-Rosales and Salas 2011).

As for the public provision effect, a concern frequently raised in the context of current trade agreements such as the Comprehensive Economic and Trade Agreement (CETA) (which liberalizes not only goods, but also investment as well as some services) relates to possible implications for the quality of social services and for equity in their access. For example, in high and middle-income countries, privatised and liberalised health services for the elderly are likely to affect women more than men, both because women tend to live longer but be poorer than men, and because they play a greater role as care providers for other family members even in their old age (Williams 2007; Eilis et al. 2016).

3   POSSIBLE MODELS FOR BREXIT

Predicting the possible gender impacts of post-Brexit trade deals is complicated by the lack of clarity about what form these deals will take. Theresa May came to power promising that 'Brexit means Brexit', later expanded to a call for a 'red, white and blue Brexit', but gave no real detail about what either phrase meant (*Guardian* 2016). May's speech to Conservative Party Conference in the autumn of 2016 seemed to establish a number of 'red lines' for any UK trade deal with the EU, specifically an end to free movement of people, an independent trade policy, no compulsory budget contribution and an end to the oversight of the Court of Justice of the European Union (CJEU) (May 2016).

Abiding by these red lines would involve rejecting membership of the customs union or single market access (Gasiorek et al. 2016). The Government's stated aim is for a 'bespoke' trade deal and the UK and EU have agreed an extended 'transition period' to allow for negotiations. This transition period involves the UK accepting EU rules which would appear to breach many of the 'red lines' set out in May's 2016 speech. The free trade deal between the EU and Canada (CETA) took seven years to negotiate, suggesting that uncertainty about the UK's post-Brexit trading arrangements will continue for some time. This uncertainty will apply not only to arrangements with the EU, but to trade agreements with other countries, which will be affected by the eventual deal reached with the EU. The likely length of the negotiations and the weak position of the current government, without an overall majority in parliament, makes it highly likely that there will be a general election before any deal is finally concluded. This creates still further uncertainty, as a change of government might lead to a change in UK negotiating priorities. With this uncertainty in mind, this section sets out the widest range of possible post-Brexit trade deals with the EU.

The 'softest' Brexit deal available would be for the UK to become a member of the European Economic Area (EEA) and remain in the Single Market like Iceland, Norway and Liechtenstein (O'Grady 2018). Remaining in the Single Market would have the economic benefit that the UK would avoid tariffs, quotas and non-tariff barriers on trade with the EU. However, Single Market membership would breach many of the promises made by the Leave campaign since the UK would be required to accept free movement of labour, make payments to the EU budget and accept the jurisdiction of the CJEU. The UK would also be bound to follow EU rules, but would have no say in the way these rules are created. Before the referendum, several prominent Leave campaigners argued that the UK could stay in the Single Market once it left the EU (Allegretti 2016). However, post-referendum, Leave campaigners have consistently argued that staying in the Single Market would be a betrayal of the referendum result. and Government has ruled out Single Market membership. Labour's position is unclear; Shadow Brexit Secretary Keir Starmer has called for a transition period that should be 'as short as possible and as long as necessary' and for a deal which retains the benefits of the Single Market in the longer term (Starmer 2017), while Jeremy Corbyn was reported as insisting that the UK cannot stay in the single market at a meeting of the Parliamentary Labour Party in early 2018 (Mason 2018). However, at the time of writing Jeremy Corbyn is coming under increased pressure from backbench MPs to commit to a clear policy of remaining in the Single Market (Labour List 2018).

The UK could leave the Single Market but remain in the Customs Union, which would mean that there would be no tariffs or quotas on most of goods traded with the EU, although services and agricultural goods would be excluded. However, if UK consumer, environmental and other regulatory standards started to diverge from those of the EU, UK manufacturers would face non-tariff barriers. Remaining part of the customs union would prevent the UK from negotiating separate trade deals with non-EU countries, as the UK would have to accept common tariffs set by the EU on goods from outside the customs union. In addition, trade in services, which account for £120 billion of UK exports (Eurostat 2017), would face significant barriers.

The stated aim of the UK Government is to negotiate a bespoke trade deal with the EU, described by David Davis as 'Canada plus plus plus', referring to the trade deal agreed between the EU and Canada (BBC 2017). The CETA between the EU and Canada, which took seven years to negotiate, removes most tariffs on goods and liberalises investment and only some services. A review of impact assessments and reports leading up to CETA, commissioned by the FEMM Committee of the European Parliament, suggests very little consideration has been given to gender equality objectives in the negotiation process

(Fontana 2016). David Davis has said the UK will 'start with the best of Canada, and the best of Japan and the best of South Korea and then add to that the bits that are missing which is the services' (BBC 2017), suggesting that the UK's aim is for a deal that goes beyond CETA to include trade in services, particularly financial services. This was rejected by the EU's chief negotiator, Michel Barnier, who argued in a press conference that the UK's 'red lines' on leaving the Single Market ruled out a free trade deal that would include financial services (Buchan 2017). This is likely to result in very high losses to the UK, as shown by an analysis by the Centre for Economics and Business Research, which has predicted a decline of 9.5–14% in UK service exports, representing a loss of £21–£30.5 billion in export revenue (CEBR 2017).

Barnier's comments highlight the tension that the UK faces between the Government's red lines on free movement, budget contributions, ability to set tariffs with other countries and the powers of the CJEU and the aim of maintaining access to EU markets for UK companies. The process of negotiating a deal that will balance these tensions is complicated by divisions within the Government and the need for any deal to be agreed by all EU member states. If a deal between the UK and the EU cannot be negotiated, then trade would take place on terms set by the World Trade Organisation (WTO). This would lead to average tariffs of 5.3%, but tariffs of up to 10% on some goods (UKTPO 2017). In addition, there would be very high losses for the service sector, including a decline of 18–25% representing £8.8–10.1 billion in UK financial services exports alone (CEBR 2017).

In addition to negotiating a deal with the EU, the UK will have to re-negotiate trade deals with the 65 countries with which the EU currently has trade agreements. It will also be looking to negotiate trade deals with other countries. Leave campaigners have argued that leaving the EU will free up the UK to negotiate better trade deals with other countries. However, the UK represents a far smaller market alone than as part of the EU, making its bargaining position weaker. In addition, a poor trade deal with the EU will make the UK more dependent on trade deals with other countries, which will make it harder for the UK to resist pressure to reduce environmental or consumer standards or open access to public services as part of a trade deal. Trade campaigners have raised concerns that trade deals with non-EU countries could include provisions that would give overseas companies the power to sue the UK government if it took action that would damage the profitability of these companies, such as increasing the national minimum wage or bringing services that have been privatised back 'in house' (see, for example, Johnston 2016). Such provisions, known as Investor-State Dispute Settlement mechanisms (ISDS), are a common feature of bilateral investment treaties and increasingly included in trade agreements (Fritz 2015). This, as discussed, could disproportionately impact women, particularly if health and/or social care sectors were to be affected.

4   Impact of Brexit on UK's GDP

There have been a series of attempts to model the impact of Brexit on UK's GDP (see, for example, Begg and Mushovel 2016). The vast majority have concluded that GDP will be smaller compared to what would have happened had the UK remained in the EU,[1] but estimates vary significantly depending on the possible post-Brexit trade arrangements modelled. In these studies, the lowest decline in projected GDP is based on a scenario where the UK stays within the Single Market. For example, prior to the referendum the UK Treasury projected that GDP would be 3.8% lower by 2030 than it otherwise would have been if the UK left the EU but remained in the Single Market (HM Treasury 2016). Dhingra et al. for the Centre for Economic Performance at the LSE (2016a, b) concluded that this estimate was 'too cautious by half' and estimated that GDP would be 6.3% lower in this scenario. Ebell and Warren (2016) were more optimistic, predicting a reduction in GDP of 1.5% by 2030 if the UK remained in the Single Market after leaving the EU.

The most damaging predicted outcomes are associated with a 'no deal' option, based on the UK trading with the EU under WTO rules. Projections range from 7.5% lower GDP (HM Treasury 2016) to 9.5% (Dhingra et al. 2016a, b). Ebell and Warren, although more optimistic than other analysts of the outcome if the UK remained in the Single Market, project that GDP would be 7.8% lower than it otherwise would have been if no deal is agreed with the EU post Brexit.

Post referendum the UK Government has shown itself unwilling to publish any meaningful assessment of the economic impact of Brexit. The Office for Budget Responsibility made it clear in their November

---

[1] The main exception has been work by Patrick Minford for Economists for Brexit/Economists for Free Trade, whose work has been widely critiqued (see, for example, Sampson et al. 2016).

2017 report to accompany the Budget that their ability to model the potential impact of Brexit was constrained by lack of information about the Government's intentions:

> Given the uncertainty regarding how the Government will respond to the choices and trade-offs it faces during the negotiations, we still have no meaningful basis on which to form a judgement as to their final outcome and upon which we can then condition our forecast. (OBR 2017, 38)

Although projections vary, there is a broad consensus that the overall impact of Brexit on the UK economy will be negative and that a no-deal 'Hard Brexit' would be the most damaging. The next section assesses the possible implications for women as workers, consumers and users of public services.

5   What Will Brexit Mean for Women as Workers?

Employment Opportunities and Threats

The uncertainty around what form Brexit will take makes it impossible to predict accurately the impact on women's jobs. The situation is further complicated since some sectors which rely heavily on EU exports may face a relatively small increase in tariffs even if the UK leaves the EU with no deal, while other sectors are likely to face a more significant increase in tariffs (see Sect. 3, above).

In the short term, predictions that increased uncertainty as a result of Brexit would lead to slower growth and a squeeze on wages (TUC 2016) appear to have been born out. In November 2017 the Office for Budget Responsibility projected that GDP would grow by only 1.4% annually over the next five years and would be 2% lower by 2022, in part as a result of Brexit. Low wage growth and increased inflation led to a real terms fall in average full-time wages of 0.4% in 2017 (ONS 2017a).

If there are increased costs from trade with the EU, the sectors initially hit hardest will be those that rely heavily on export to the EU and the industries that supply them, as well as those sectors that rely on the EU for their inputs (raw materials or products they need to operate). The three sectors most reliant on exports to the EU for revenues are mining and quarrying (43% of whose revenues come from EU exports), manufacturing (21%) and financial services (10%). The sectors most dependent on the EU for inputs are manufacturing (20% of non-staff costs), health (mainly the NHS) and social care (18%) and accommodation and food (15%) (House of Commons Library 2017a). These sectors are likely to see increased costs.

While mining and quarrying is among the sectors most reliant on EU exports, it is unlikely to face high tariffs even if the UK ends up trading with the EU on WTO terms since average EU tariffs for minerals and metals are 2% and for petroleum are 2.5%. In contrast, the textiles and clothing sectors, which employ a higher proportion of women, would face tariffs of 6.5 and 11.5% respectively, if the UK were to trade on WTO terms. However, both sectors may face significant non-tariff barriers.

Impact will also vary across different parts of the country. While 49% of UK exports go to the EU, some regions and nations rely more heavily on exports to the EU than others. 61% of exports from the north of England and Wales, for example, go to the EU, compared to 43% from London and the West Midlands (House of Commons Library 2017a). The TUC estimates that about one in ten jobs in the English regions and Scotland and one in twenty jobs in Wales and Northern Ireland are linked to EU exports (TUC 2016).

The gender impact of contractions in these sectors will vary. Mining and quarrying is a male dominated sector (84% of workers are men) (ONS 2017b). Many manufacturing jobs are male dominated as well, such as motor vehicles (80% of workers are men), but others such as textiles, leather and related goods, employ a majority of women (55% of the total workforce in these sectors is female) (ONS 2017b). Financial services employs 56% men and 44% women. Health and social care are heavily female dominated sectors (77% of workers in the health sector and 80% in social care are women) (ONS 2017b). These sectors have already been impacted by loss of EU staff, a trend which may increase post Brexit (Fahy et al. 2017). Increased cost of inputs may put further pressure on budgets, leading to further job losses (WBG 2018).

Contraction of these sectors is likely to have a knock-on impact on employment in other sectors as demand for goods and services from sectors that are directly impacted falls. In addition, job losses in male dominated sectors will impact women members of the households of the men concerned, either by reduction of consumption or by being forced to take paid work in addition to domestic commitments.

Moreover, evidence from other countries (reviewed in Fontana 2003, 2016) suggests that when women lose their jobs as a result of trade changes, they find it more difficult to get re-employed and obtain new comparable jobs (see, for instance, Balakrishnan and Elson 2011 in relation to NAFTA). This means that the UK Government should be planning for the needs of different groups of workers who will be affected by Brexit in a gender-sensitive manner, when considering potential trade deals. The Government should also take mitigating action in the form of compensation and/or re-training. It should invest especially in programmes aimed at vulnerable female workers, particularly in parts of the country likely to be hit hardest from Brexit and among low skilled workers who may find it harder to find alternative jobs.

Meanwhile, if the price of imports from the EU increases, this may create new opportunities in the UK for entrepreneurs producing import-competing goods and services and generate new forms of employment. Those with the most resources (wealth, transferable labour market skills, mobility) are more likely to be able to respond/adapt to and benefit from such opportunities (Fontana 2016). Men as a group tend to have more of these resources than women. In the UK, for example, women tend to have lower total wealth in the form of savings and investments than men (Kan and Laurie 2010). A 2016 study concluded that lack of access to start up funding was a greater barrier to women entrepreneurs than their male counterparts (RBS 2016). Therefore, gendered employment effects of new trading arrangements are likely, including women entrepreneurs gaining less than men entrepreneurs unless the government takes adequate measures to address these gaps.

Alongside manufacturing, Brexit will have a significant impact on workers in the service sector. The sectors most likely to be impacted include both those that rely on trade with the EU, such as finance or telecoms (see Sect. 3, above), and those which employ large numbers of EU workers. One example is health and social care which is heavily dominated by women (ONS 2017b). Over 60,000 NHS workers and 90,000 social care workers are from non-UK EU countries (Fahy et al. 2017). The majority of NHS workers are women (ONS 2017b). Even if these people are able to continue to work in the UK post-Brexit, it is likely that the UK will become less attractive to healthcare workers from the EU as a result of their changed legal status, the changed legal status of their families and uncertainty around recognition of professional qualifications (Fahy et al. 2017). While this may mean increased employment opportunities for UK women, in the context of a pre-existing staffing deficit and continued under investment in training, this has serious implications for the effectiveness of the NHS and social care, as well as for EU women whose talents the UK will lose. Furthermore, these increased employment opportunities for UK women may be short lived if the projected negative impact of Brexit on the economy leads to reduced spending on public services (see Sect. 7).

Any analysis of proposed post-Brexit trade deals should include gender-aware in-depth studies of the sectors likely to expand and contract as a result of a proposed deal, indicating the proportion of women and men working in these sectors, the quality of their jobs and working conditions. It should also include an assessment of net gendered employment effects and any other gendered effects due to possible changes in standards and regulations.

Employment Rights and Protections for Women

There is considerable concern that employment rights and protections for women are at risk after Brexit, creating a more hostile and less supportive working environment for many, both women and men. Much of the legislation protecting women's employment rights in the UK has its origins in the European Union or was strengthened by judgements made by the CJEU (O'Brien 2016).

The UK Government has committed to convert current EU legislation into domestic law in the first instance, meaning that there is no immediate threat that these rights will be lost. However, there is a real risk that the hard-won labour market rights of women, such as rights to unpaid parental leave, equal treatment and paid annual leave rights for part-time workers, could be rolled back under future plans for a 'competitive', highly deregulated 'flexible' labour market post-Brexit (Ford 2016). At particular risk is the Agency Workers Directive, which will disproportionately affect women. In October 2017, the Prime Minister appointed a new Brexit Minister, Martin Callanan, who made a speech to the European Parliament in 2012 in which he named the Agency Workers Directive and the Pregnant Workers Directive as "barriers to actually employing people" which "we could scrap" (Callanan 2012). This scenario is particularly likely under a reversion to WTO rules. This might encourage a 'race to the bottom', where competing for foreign direct investment (FDI) of the kind that is dependent on cheap labour could incentivise a roll-back on workers' rights (Andriescu and Giles 2017). Indeed, in the UK, workers in sectors that already have high FDI are more likely to report greater economic insecurity (Fontana 2016).

In addition, women workers in the UK will no longer benefit from ongoing developments in legislation and case law relating to women's rights. The UK does not have influential institutions comparable to those working in the EU to further gender equality, and at home, grassroots gender equality movements have been weakened by austerity (Bunyan et al. 2017) and are likely to be further weakened by the loss of EU funding, which makes up nearly a third of funding for women's organisations (Chilcott 2018). Inside the EU, the UK government has had a history of blocking progressive legislation, such as a proposal under the Pregnant Workers Directive for 20 weeks paid maternity and 2 weeks paid paternity leave (Plomien 2016), which does not bode well for progressive legislation once outside the EU. At the same time, the rights of workers within the EU may continue to be enhanced under new EU directives in the future. There is no guarantee that UK workers would benefit from these enhanced rights unless the UK remains within the Single Market and is therefore bound by EU rules.

6   What Will Brexit Mean for Women as Consumers?

Potential consumer impacts of Brexit include both loss of legal protections and changes to the price of consumer goods.

Consumer rights in the UK such as food and product safety, unfair commercial practices, rules about product labelling and packaging, and consumer redress, are underpinned by EU law and could be reduced by a future Government (Lipman 2016). These rights may be particularly vulnerable to erosion as a result of trade deals with non-EU countries such as the US, which allows for the chlorination of chicken and hormones in beef and would be likely to want to ensure access to UK markets for these products (Holmes 2017). A poor trade deal with the EU would leave the UK more reliant on trade with non-EU countries, which may result in the rolling back of consumer rights and the erosion of consumer protections including health and safety protections (Lipman 2016) and food standards (Peck 2017).

In the pre-Brexit period, UK food production has suffered from a lack of manual labour to harvest food and this situation is forecast to worsen after Brexit (Danesckhu 2017). Post-Brexit, different trading models would have different implications for food costs. Around 30% of the value of food purchased in the UK is imported; 70% of gross food imports are from the EU (Levell et al. 2017). In the case of a no deal 'hard Brexit', under WTO rules the UK would have to apply the same tariffs to food from the EU as from the rest of the world. This, combined with a falling value of the pound, has potential to have a substantial impact on the prices households pay for food. Poorest households would be hardest hit by rising food prices: the poorest household income decile spends 23% of their spending on food, compared to the richest decile that spends 10% (Levell et al. 2017).

Calculations of the actual impact of rising prices vary. Research by the trade union USDAW concluded that the average household would lose £580 a year as a result of increased tariffs and a fall in the value of the pound if the UK left the EU without a trade deal (USDAW 2016). Dhingra et al. calculated a decline in household income of between £850 and £6400 a year depending on the post-Brexit trade deal reached (Dhingra et al. 2016a, b).

These impacts will disproportionately affect women, who are more likely than men to be poor and who tend to have main responsibility for the purchase and preparation of food for their children and families (Food Standards Agency 2017). They manage the budgets of poor households and act as the 'shock absorbers of poverty', working to shield their families from the impact of stretched budgets (WBG 2005). Simultaneously to rising costs of food, the risks of cuts to welfare and public services (see Sect. 7) will affect women disproportionately. Some in the Conservative Party have supported the call by Economists for Free Trade for the UK to lift all tariff barriers, including for food (Rees-Mogg 2017). This would reduce food costs, but have a severe impact on UK agriculture (as well as large parts of the UK economy vulnerable to imported goods).

7   What Will Brexit Mean for Women as Users of Public Services?

It is widely accepted that good quality and inclusive public services have the potential to foster gender equality by enabling a more equal distribution of caring responsibilities and the development of human capabilities for all (UN Women 2015). Access to adequate education and health services of girls, boys, women and men from disadvantaged backgrounds, in particular, can significantly improve their opportunities in life. The arguments for providing easily accessible social services can also come from a women's rights perspective, emphasising the opportunity costs of caring for family members. Good quality and inclusive social services can leave women and girls more time to spend on other activities of their choice, including, but not only, education and paid employment. Public funding for health and care services in itself creates jobs for women, who are the vast majority of the paid workforce in these sectors (77% of the health workforce and 80% of the care workforce [ONS 2017b]). A 2016 study found that an investment of 2% of the GDP in the care sector would create twice as many jobs in the UK as the equivalent amount invested in construction (1.5 million compared to 750,000), raising women's employment rate by 5% (De Henau et al. 2016).

Funding for Public Services

A major plank of the Leave campaign during the referendum was a promise of additional money for the NHS if the UK no longer had to make financial contributions to the EU (BBC 2016a). However, the UK's net contribution to the EU is around £8 billion a year, approximately 0.4% of GDP (Emmerson et al. 2016), meaning even a small fall in GDP would wipe out any savings as a result of Brexit. The Institute for Fiscal Studies (IFS) forecasts that the projected budget deficit in 2019–20 as a result of the economic impacts of Brexit will be an additional £20–40 billion (Emmerson et al. 2016). By 2030, assuming tax and spending remain constant as a proportion of GDP, the IFS projects public spending will be between £7 and £48 billion lower than otherwise. If the Government decides to cut public spending in response to a fall in GDP, in the way that Governments since 2010 have done in response to the 2008 economic crisis (WBG 2017), this will have clear implications for widening inequality between women and men. As the UK Womens' Budget Group and others have repeatedly shown, public services and associated social infrastructure are relied upon more by women than by men (WBG 2017). Reductions in public spending have a disproportionate negative impact on women as the primary users of public services, majority of workers in the public sector and main providers of unpaid work when public services are cut (WBG 2017). The impact is likely to be particularly severe for the poorest and black and minority ethnic (BME) women. Austerity policies since 2010 have hit the poorest households hardest and among the poorest 20% of households, Black and Asian households are projected to see a fall in living standards of 11.6 and 11.2% by 2020, while the living standards of white households in this group are set to fall by 8.9% (WBG 2017). In cash terms, this represents a cut of £5090 for Black households, £6526 for Asian households and £3316 for white households (WBG 2017).

Entitlement to Quality Public Services

A number of services traditionally provided by the public sector are now at risk of being subject to competition from foreign companies, as trade agreements have included provisions to liberalise public services (Sinclair 2015). Recent trade agreements have included chapters on investment that have allowed businesses to take legal action against governments if regulation threatens profits, restricting the ability of governments to regulate in the public interest (Fontana 2016; Sinclair 2015). Concerns about the impact of the services and investment chapters in the EU–Canada trade agreement (CETA), led to a widespread campaign by trade unions and trade justice campaigners across Europe (TUC 2015). During the ratification process, the Belgian region of Wallonia voted against ratification of CETA, blocking the deal, although it voted in favour following further negotiations (BBC 2016b).

In response, the EU and Canada announced that they had agreed a new Investment Court System to increase transparency and preserve the rights of governments to regulate in the public interest (Malmstrom and Freeland 2016). The EU has also argued that CETA includes exemptions for public services from the services chapter. However, critics still argue that the investment provisions are still unduly favourable to multinational companies and, in particular, that the investment chapter does not include an exemption for public services (House of Commons Library 2017b).

David Davis's enthusiasm for CETA as a model for future trade deals raises concerns about the public service and investment provisions that these might contain. A weakened negotiating hand for the UK as a result of Brexit might result in trade agreements with third countries which do not contain the limited protections in CETA. These could allow a foreign service supplier to challenge regulations designed to protect the quality of public services, on the basis that they may constitute a trade barrier. Meanwhile the quality of public services, particularly the NHS, is additionally under threat from the potential loss of EU workers who may decide, or be forced to, leave the UK post-Brexit. Furthermore, the NHS is set to lose money through the loss of capital financing from the European Investment Bank, the rising cost of recruitment, and higher costs of pharmaceuticals and other medical products as a result of Brexit (Fahy et al. 2017).

8   Violence Against Women and Girls (VAWG)

Legislation on VAWG has outcomes for women in the economy, as users of public services as well as from the perspective of women's access to justice more widely, and for the realisation of women's human rights. Many of the advances made in respect of VAWG originated in the EU, including the Victims Directive.[2] While some progressive legislation has originated in the UK, such as the Violence against Women, Domestic Abuse and Sexual Violence (Wales) Act 2015,[3] there are concerns that Brexit may signal a departure for the UK from the progressive standards being promoted across the EU. It is relatedly of concern that many research projects of influence in the UK concerned with VAWG have been funded through the European Union such as the DAPHNE Programme (DAPHNE 2014) and there is as of yet no indication of whether, or how, such funding streams may be replaced. Similarly, EU social funds support large numbers of voluntary organisations providing support to women and there is no clear information about whether these will be replaced.

If a lower GDP leads to public spending cuts, this is also likely to exacerbate the impact of cuts to women's voluntary organisations that have had a devastating impact since 2010 (WRC 2015). The lifting of ring-fenced funding and introduction of competitive tendering procedures have had a disproportionate effect on women's voluntary and community organisations, particularly those supporting Black, Asian and Minority Ethnic women, which are losing out to larger generic providers (Agenda 2017).

---

[2] Directive 2012/29/EU of the European Parliament and of the Council of 25 October 2012 establishing minimum standards on the rights, support and protection of victims of crime, and replacing Council Framework Decision 2001/220/JHA.

[3] Text available at http://www.legislation.gov.uk/anaw/2015/3/contents/enacted.

9   KEY QUESTIONS TO ANSWER

To avoid adverse effects on gender equality from new trade agreements in the post-Brexit era, the Government should:

- Ensure that current legal rights and protections for people in the UK cannot be changed without appropriate parliamentary scrutiny and involvement of citizens and civil society.
- Ensure that independent equality impact assessments of different possible trade agreements with the EU and non-EU countries are carried out and used to inform decisions on which trade deals to pursue. These assessments should include careful modelling of the gender impact in every sector of the economy, including goods, services, public services provision and consumer effects. A sample of questions to consider has been developed by WBG (2018).
- Ensure that the findings of these impact assessments are reflected in negotiations and the substantive obligations in trade deals.
- Ensure that mitigating action is taken to address adverse impacts.
- Use sex-disaggregated statistics as standard and analyse for distributional effects across a variety of groups, workers and households.
- Ensure that gender experts (including gender-aware economists) are appointed to work on technical teams.
- Encourage more regular training for government officials and negotiators on gender and trade, and the systematic use of relevant analytical frameworks and tools.
- Consult widely with women's organizations and similar civil society organizations.

This article has briefly sketched out some of the main potential economic impacts of Brexit on women. As the Brexit negotiations continue, any proposed trade deal, whether with the EU or with other countries, should be subject to a full equality impact assessment, including a gender impact assessment.

At the time of writing the prospects for a meaningful gender and broader equality analysis of proposed Brexit trade deals appear unlikely. The UK Government has historically failed to carry out this type of analysis of economic or other policy (Mott 2016). The UK Government's failings in this regard have been documented extensively, for example in the Shadow CEDAW report of 2013 (WRC 2013). Women's and girls' rights and needs remain marginalised and conditional in the business of Government, with Westminster failing to meet many of the standards for the Inter-Parliamentary Union's evidence-based framework for gender-sensitive parliaments (Mott 2016). Gender impact assessments and gender-responsive budgeting and planning have not been mainstreamed, and a discussion of the gender impact of Brexit was largely absent from pre-referendum.

In addition, negotiating trade deals is highly complex and time-consuming. The UK is starting from a position of disadvantage, because it lacks experienced trade negotiators (since our trade negotiations have been carried out through the EU). Ensuring that, during negotiation, trade agreements and policies reflect gender equality objectives and do not undermine the realization of women's economic rights is known to be a highly complex process requiring specialist knowledge. This process is not universally embedded even in the practice of experienced trade negotiators (Fontana 2016). The UK will need to build from scratch the skills required to undertake impact assessments of potential trade deals and to conduct trade negotiations informed by complex technical analyses.

Acknowledgements This article draws on the findings of the WBG report Exploring the Economic Impact of Brexit on Women, Women's Budget Group, by Helen Mott with Mary-Ann Stephenson and Marzia Fontana, available online at: https://wbg.org.uk/wp-content/uploads/2018/03/Economic-Impact-of-Brexit-on-women-briefing-FINAL.pdf.

BIBLIOGRAPHY

Agenda and AVA. 2017. Mapping the Maze. https://weareagenda.org/wp-content/uploads/2015/11/Mapping-the-Maze-Literature-Review-Full-updated.pdf.

Allegretti, A. 2016. Open Britain Exposes All the Times Brexiteers Promised We Wouldn't Leave the Single Market. *Huffington Post*, November 17. Available online at: http://www.huffingtonpost.co.uk/entry/open-britain-video-single-market-nigel-farage-anna-soubry_uk_582ce0a0e4b09025ba310fce.

Andriescu, M., and L. Giles. 2017. Could a Bad Brexit Deal Reduce Workers' Rights Across Europe? Work Foundation. https://www.tuc.org.uk/sites/default/files/TUC_BrexitWorkersRights.pdf.

Balakrishnan, R., and D. Elson. 2011. *Economic Policy and Human Rights: Holding Governments to Account*. London: Zed Books.

BBC News Website. 2016a. Reality Check: Would Brexit Mean Extra £350m a Week for NHS? April 15. http://www.bbc.co.uk/news/uk-politics-eu-referendum-36040060.

BBC News Website. 2016b. Belgium Split Over EU-Canada Trade Deal Ceta, October 18. http://www.bbc.co.uk/news/world-europe-37688942.

BBC News Website. 2017. Brexit: David Davis Wants 'Canada Plus Plus Plus' Trade Deal, December 10. http://www.bbc.co.uk/news/uk-politics-42298971.

Begg, I., and F. Mushovel. 2016. The Economic Impact of Brexit: Jobs, Growth and the Public Finances. Briefing Paper, LSE. Available online at: http://eprints.lse.ac.uk/67008/1/Hearing-11—The-impact-of-Brexit-on-jobs-and-economic-growth-sumary.pdf.

Berik, G. 2011. Gender Aspects of Trade. In *Trade and Employment: From Myths to Facts*, ed. M. Jansen. Geneva: ILO.

Buchan, L. 2017. Theresa May Hits Back at EU Over Bespoke Brexit Deal. *Independent*, December 19. Available online at: http://www.independent.co.uk/news/uk/politics/theresa-may-eu-talks-michel-barnier-brexit-deal-city-london-bespoke-trade-a8118511.html.

Bunyan, D., J. Longworth, and M. Page. 2017. The Making of Feminist Democracy in a Brexit Environment. Symposium: Strengthening Gender Equality in Post-Brexit Britain, June 20. University of Bristol.

Callanan, M. 2012. Speech in a Debate on the Outcome of the February 2012 EU Summit, February 14. Available online at: http://ecrgroup.eu/martin-callanan-mep-speech-in-a-debate-on-the-outcome-of-the-february-2012-eu-summit/.

CEBR. 2017. The Economic Impact on Services from the UK Losing Single Market Access a Cebr Report for Open Britain. Available online at: https://www.cebr.com/wp/wp-content/uploads/2017/05/Open-Britain_services-report.pdf.

Chilcott, A. 2018. Gendering Brexit: The Role and Concerns of Feminists and Women's Rights Organisations in the UK, Gender 5+, Brussels. Available online at: https://docs.wixstatic.com/ugd/530efa_daf3572829014d2c81997f735f79a0b3.pdf.

Danesckhu, S. 2017. Migrant Labour Shortage Leaves Fruit Rotting on UK Farms. *Financial Times*, November 3. https://www.ft.com/content/13e183ee-c099-11e7-b8a3-38a6e068f464.

DAPHNE. 2014. Justice Programmes (2007–2013). Available online at: http://ec.europa.eu/justice/grants1/programmes-2007-2013/index_en.htm.

De Henau, J., S. Himmelweit, Z. Łapniewska, and D. Perrons. 2016. Investing in the Care Economy: A Gender Analysis of Employment Stimulus in Seven OECD Countries. Report by the UK Women's Budget Group for the International Trade Union Confederation, Brussels. Available online at: https://www.ituc-csi.org/IMG/pdf/care_economy_en.pdf.

Dhingra, S., G. Ottaviano, T. Sampson, and J. Van Reenen. 2016a. The UK Treasury Analysis of 'The Long-Term Economic Impact of EU Membership and the Alternatives'. *CEP Commentary*. Available online at: http://cep.lse. ac.uk/pubs/download/brexit04.pdf.

Dhingra, S., and G. Ottaviano, et al. 2016b. The Consequences of Brexit for UK Trade and Living Standards. LSE Centre for Economic Performance. http:// cep.lse.ac.uk/pubs/download/brexit02.pdf.

Ebell, M., and J. Warren. 2016. The Long Term Economic Impact of Leaving the EU. *National Institute Economic Review* 236 (1): 121–138.

Eilis, J., R. Pearson, B. Phipps, S. Rai, S. Smethers, and D. Tepe-Belfrag. 2016. Towards a New Deal For Care and Carers Report of the PSA Commission on Care, PSA. Available online at: http://www.commissiononcare.org/wp-content/ uploads/2016/10/Web-Care-Comission-Towards-a-new-deal-for-care-and-carers-v1.0.pdf.

Emmerson, C., and P. Johnson, et al. 2016. Brexit and the UK's Public Finances. IFS Report 116. https://www.ifs.org.uk/uploads/publications/comms/ r116.pdf.

Eurostat. 2017. International Trade in Services, June. Available online at: http://ec.europa.eu/eurostat/statistics-explained/index.php/International_ trade_in_services.

Fahy, N., T. Hervey, S. Greer, H. Jarman, D. Stuckler, M. Glasworthy, and M. McKee. 2017. How Will Brexit Affect Health and Health Services in the UK? Evaluating Three Possible Scenarios. *The Lancet* 390 (10107): 2110–2118. http://www.thelancet.com/journals/lancet/article/PIIS0140-6736(17)31926-8/fulltext.

Fontana, M. 2003. The Gender Effects of Trade Liberalization in Developing Countries: A Review of the Literature. Sussex Discussion Paper in Economics DP101, republished in Bussolo, M., and de Hoyos, R.E. 2009. *Gender Aspects of the Trade and Poverty Nexus: A Macro-Micro Approach*. Washington, DC: Palgrave and McMillan for the World Bank.

Fontana, M. 2016. Gender Equality in Trade Agreements. European Parliament. http://www.europarl.europa.eu/RegData/etudes/STUD/2016/571388/ IPOL_STU(2016)571388_EN.pdf.

Food Standards Agency. 2017. The Food and You Survey. https://www.food. gov.uk/sites/default/files/food-and-you-w4-exec-summary.pdf.

Ford, M. 2016. Workers' Rights from Europe: The Impact of Brexit. Legal Opinion, TUC. https://www.tuc.org.uk/sites/default/files/Brexit%20 Legal%20Opinion.pdf.

Fritz, T. 2015. Public Services Under Attack: TTIP, CETA, and the Secretive Collusion Between Business Lobbyists and Trade Negotiators, AITEC. Available online at: https://www.tni.org/en/publication/public-services-under-attack-0.

Gammage, S., H. Jorgensen, E. McGill, and M. White. 2002. *Trade Impact Review*. Washington, DC: Women's Edge Coalition.

Gasiorek, M., P. Holmes, and J. Rollo. 2016. UK-EU Trade Relations Post Brexit: Too Many Red Lines? UK Trade Policy Observatory, Briefing Paper 5, University of Sussex. Available online at: http://blogs.sussex.ac.uk/uktpo/files/2017/01/Briefing-paper-5-Final.pdf.

Guardian. 2016. Theresa May Calls for 'Red, White and Blue Brexit', December 6. Available online at: https://www.theguardian.com/politics/2016/dec/06/theresa-may-calls-for-red-white-and-blue-brexit.

HM Treasury. 2016. HM Treasury Analysis: The Long-Term Economic Impact of EU Membership and the Alternatives. Available online at: https://www.gov.uk/government/uploads/system/uploads/attachment_data/file/517415/treasury_analysis_economic_impact_of_eu_membership_web.pdf.

Holmes, P. 2017. Trade and Consumers After Brexit. UK Trade Policy Briefing Paper 12. Available online at: http://blogs.sussex.ac.uk/uktpo/publications/trade-and-consumers-after-brexit/.

House of Commons Library. 2017a. Importance of Trade with the EU for UK Industries, House of Commons Library Research Publications. Available online at: http://researchbriefings.parliament.uk/ResearchBriefing/Summary/CBP-8065#fullreport.

House of Commons Library. 2017b. CETA: The EU-Canada Free Trade Agreement, House of Commons Library Research Publications. Available online at: http://researchbriefings.files.parliament.uk/documents/CBP-7492/CBP-7492.pdf.

ILO. 2016. *Women at Work 2016.* Geneva: ILO. Available online at: http://www.ilo.org/wcmsp5/groups/public/---dgreports/---dcomm/---publ/documents/publication/wcms_457086.pdf.

ILO. 2017. *World Economic and Social Outlook.* Geneva: ILO.

Johnston, I. 2016. 'TTIP on Steroids': Campaigners Warn Post-Brexit UK Faces 'Disastrous' Trade Deal with US. *Independent,* June 24. Available online at: http://www.independent.co.uk/news/uk/politics/ttip-brexit-uk-steroids-disastrous-global-justice-now-war-on-want-a7099986.html.

Kan, M., and H. Laurie. 2010. Savings, Investments, Debts and Psychological Well-Being in Married and Cohabiting Couples. Institute for Social and Economic Research. Available online at: https://www.iser.essex.ac.uk/files/iser_working_papers/2010-42.pdf.

Kucera, D., and W. Milberg. 2007. Gender Segregation and Gender Bias in Manufacturing Trade Expansion: Revising the "Wood Asymmetry". In *The Feminist Economics of Trade,* ed. I. van Steveren, D. Elson, C. Grown, and N. Cagatay. London: Routledge.

Labour List. 2018. Backbenchers Hope New Poll Will Trigger Corbyn Shift on Single Market, January 22. Available online at: https://labourlist.org/2018/01/backbenchers-hope-new-poll-will-trigger-corbyn-shift-on-single-market/.

Levell, P., M. O'Connell, and K. Smith. 2017. How Might Brexit Affect Food Prices? IFS. Available online at: https://www.ifs.org.uk/publications/9562.

Lipman, M. 2016. Brexit and Consumer Rights: What Will Life Be Like for Consumers After Brexit? Citizens Advice Blog. https://blogs.citizensadvice.org.uk/blog/brexit-and-consumer-rights-what-will-life-be-like-for-consumers-after-brexit/.

Malmstrom and Freeland. 2016. Joint Statement Canada-EU Comprehensive Economic and Trade Agreement (CETA), bu EU Commissioner for Trade Cecilia Malmström and the Honourable Chrystia Freeland, Minister of International Trade of Canada, February 29. Available online at: http://trade.ec.europa.eu/doclib/docs/2016/february/tradoc_154330.pdf.

Mason, R. 2018. Jeremy Corbyn Insists UK Cannot Remain in Single Market After Brexit. *Guardian*, January 8. Available online at: https://www.theguardian.com/politics/2018/jan/08/jeremy-corbyn-eu-single-market-after-brexit.

May, T. 2016. Speech to Conservative Party Conference, October 5. Available online at: http://www.telegraph.co.uk/news/2016/10/05/theresa-mays-conference-speech-in-full/.

Mott, H. 2016. The Economy. In the British Council Report: Gender Equality and Empowerment of Women and Girls in the UK. Available online at: https://www.britishcouncil.org/sites/default/files/gender_equality_and_empowerment_in_the_uk.pdf.

OBR. 2017. Office for Budget Responsibility: Economic and Fiscal Outlook, HM Treasury. Available online at: http://cdn.budgetresponsibility.org.uk/Nov2017EFOwebversion-2.pdf.

O'Brien, C. 2016. Bonfires and Brexterity: What's Next for Women? http://www.referendumanalysis.eu/eu-referendum-analysis-2016/section-8-voters/bonfires-and-brexterity-whats-next-for-women/.

O'Grady, S. 2018. Brexicon: A Full Dictionary of Brexit-Related Jargon. *Independent*, February 21. Available online at: https://www.independent.co.uk/voices/brexit-hard-soft-boris-johnson-theresa-may-article-50-brexchosis-a8221566.html.

OECD. 2017. *The Missing Entrepreneurs 2017: Policies for Inclusive Entrepreneurship*. Paris: OECD Publishing. http://dx.doi.org/10.1787/9789264283602-en.

ONS. 2017a. Annual Survey of Hours and Earnings: 2017 Provisional and 2016 Revised Results. Available online at: http://bit.ly/2zGaZrV.

ONS. 2017b. Labour Force Survey, Employment by Industry. Available online at: https://www.ons.gov.uk/employmentandlabourmarket/peopleinwork/employmentandemployeetypes/datasets/employmentbyindustryemp13.

Pearson, R. 1999. 'Nimble Fingers' Revisited: Reflections on Women and Third World Industrialisation in the Late Twentieth Century. In *Feminist Visions of Development*, ed. C. Jackson and R. Pearson. London: Routledge.

Peck, T. 2017. Brexit: Food Standards Agency Should Be Able to Say No to Chlorinated Chicken. *The Independent*, July 31. http://www.independent. co.uk/news/uk/politics/brexit-chlorinated-chicken-food-standards-agency-no-ban-imports-food-us-fsa-a7869561.html.

Plomien, A. 2016. The EU and Gender Equality. http://blogs.lse.ac.uk/ gender/2016/06/29/the-eu-and-gender-equality-better-off-in-or-out/.

Rees-Mogg, J. 2017. Speech at the Launch of Economists for Free Trade's Budget for Brexit Report, November 14. Available online at: https://www. economistsforfreetrade.com/wp-content/uploads/2017/11/EFT-Budget-for-Brexit-Jacob-Rees-Mogg-speech.pdf.

RBS website. (2016), NatWest Research Finds Women See More Barriers to Entrepreneurship, September 14. https://www.rbs.com/rbs/news/ 2016/09/natwest-research-finds-women-see-more-barriers-to-entrepreneursh.html.

Sampson, T., D. Swati, G. Ottaviano, and J. Van Reene. 2016. Economists for Brexit: A Critique, LSE Centre for Economic Performance. Available online at: http://cep.lse.ac.uk/pubs/download/brexit06.pdf.

Serdan-Rosales, A., and C. Salas. 2011. Trade Policy and Human Rights: Mexico. In *Economic Policy and Human Rights: Holding Governments to Account*, ed. R. Balakrishnan and D. Elson. London: Zed Books.

Sinclair, S. 2015. Trade Agreements and Progressive Governance. In *Critical Perspectives on the Crisis of Global Governance*, ed. S. Gill. London: Palgrave Macmillan.

Starmer, K. 2017. No 'Constructive Ambiguity'. Labour Will Avoid Brexit Cliff Edge for UK Economy. *The Observer*, August 26. Available online at: https://www.theguardian.com/commentisfree/2017/aug/26/keir-starmer-no-constructive-ambiguity-brexit-cliff-edge-labour-will-avoid-transitional-deal.

Statistica. 2018. Motor Vehicle Ownership in the United Kingdom (UK) 2017, by Gender, Survey Data. Available online at: https://www.statista.com/statistics/682605/consumers-who-own-a-motor-vehicle-in-the-united-kingdom-uk-by-gender/.

TUC. 2015. Stop CETA, TTIP's Dangerous Cousin, TUC Campaigns. Available at: https://campaign.goingtowork.org.uk/petitions/stop-ceta-ttip-s-dangerous-cousin.

TUC. 2016. *Taking the Temperature of the Post-Brexit Economy: Britain's Economic Prospects After Leaving the EU*. Trades Union Congress. Available online at: https://www.tuc.org.uk/sites/default/files/Post-BrexitEconomy.pdf.

UKTPO. 2017. 'With or Without EU'—Priorities for the UK's Four Trading Nations Post Brexit, UK Trade Policy Observatory, University of Sussex. Available online at: https://blogs.sussex.ac.uk/uktpo/2017/03/29/with-or-without-eu-priorities-for-the-uks-four-trading-nations-post-brexit/.

UN Women. 2015. *Progress of the World's Women 2015–2016.* New York: United Nations. Available online at: http://progress.unwomen.org/en/2015/pdf/UNW_progressreport.pdf.

USDAW. 2016. The Impact of Brexit on Consumers. https://www.usdaw.org.uk/CMSPages/GetFile.aspx?guid=54a96cbd-1357-40aa-a16b-59f056455ac4.

WBG. 2005. Women's and Children's Poverty: Making the Links. http://oxfamilibrary.openrepository.com/oxfam/bitstream/10546/112550/1/women%27s-children%27s-poverty-010305-en.pdf.

WBG. 2017. Intersecting Inequalities: The Impact of Austerity on BME Women, Women's Budget Group and Runnymede Trust. Available online at: https://www.intersecting-inequalities.com/.

WBG. 2018. Exploring the Economic Impact of Brexit on Women, Women's Budget Group. Available online at: https://wbg.org.uk/wp-content/uploads/2018/03/Economic-Impact-of-Brexit-on-women-briefing-FINAL.pdf.

Williams, M. 2007. Gender Issues in the Multilateral Trading System. In *The Feminist Economics of Trade*, ed. I. van Staveren, D. Elson, C. Grown, and N. Cagatay. London: Routledge.

WRC. 2013. Shadow CEDAW Report, Appendix 1. https://thewomensresourcecentre.org.uk/wp-content/uploads/Appendix-1_Impact-of-the-economic-crisis-on-womens-equality_FINAL2.pdf.

WRC. 2015. The Net Beneath the Net. https://thewomensresourcecentre.org.uk/wp-content/uploads/Net-Beneath-the-Net_Role-of-the-Women-Apr-2015.pdf.

CHAPTER 17

Splendid Isolation? On How a Non-member Is Affected by—And Affects—EU Gender Equality Policy

Hege Skjeie, Cathrine Holst and Mari Teigen

1 Introduction: Europeanisation Through EEA Affiliation

Historically, the Nordic region has been viewed as both a strong and a unified agent of gender equality advocacy. Nordic countries have comparatively strong equality records and Nordic policy innovations travel the world. Different Nordic polities have, through their own initiative, produced innovations such as low threshold monitoring of equality legislation (1970s), gender mainstreaming of public policies (1980s), bans

H. Skjeie
University of Oslo, Oslo, Norway
e-mail: hege.skjeie@stv.uio.no

C. Holst
University of Oslo, Oslo, Norway
e-mail: cathrine.holst@sosgeo.uio.no

M. Teigen (✉)
CORE—Centre for Research on Gender Equality, Institute for Social
Research, Oslo, Norway
e-mail: mari.teigen@samfunnsforskning.no

© The Author(s) 2019   439
M. Dustin et al. (eds.), *Gender and Queer Perspectives on Brexit*,
Gender and Politics, https://doi.org/10.1007/978-3-030-03122-0_17

on the purchase of sex (1990s), and corporate board quotas (2000s) (Skjeie et al. 2017). The 'Nordicness' of gender equality policy is still most famously recognised in the welfare state policies to promote work–family balance through extensive parental leave and public child care schemes (Esping-Andersen 2009; Leira 2012; Walby 2009).The different Nordic countries have however chosen quite different European Union tracks. Denmark has been a member of the EUfor 45 years, since 1973, and Danish gender equality policy was thus Europeanised much earlier than their Nordic neighbours' (Borchorst and Agustin 2019). In popular referendums both Sweden and Finland chose to join the EU in 1994, while a majority in Norway and Iceland voted to remain outside. But Iceland and Norway have both participated, since 1994, in the European Economic Area (EEA) Agreement which makes the countries full participants in the EU's internal market.

The EU affects Norwegian hard law through the EEA and also through the 73—as of 2017—additional agreements between the EU and Norway (see Eriksen and Fossum 2015; Holst and Stie 2016). Furthermore, policies and governance have been Europeanised more softly through the increased coordination among the different levels of public administration in Europe, including the Norwegian ministries, agencies, and offices; transnational social movements and civil society actors; and through Norwegian participation in border-crossing knowledge-sharing communities, such as the European Commission's expert groups, or when national inquiry commissions are influenced by Europeanised value sets, problem definitions, and conceptions of best practices (Skjeie et al. 2017, see also Egeberg and Trondal 2015).

The commitments as part to the EEA apply directly to the area of gender equality policy (NOU 2012: 2, in particular 17.5). Yet, as we know, gender equality policy varies considerably in the EU area, including among member states. Unsurprisingly, in Norway there has been substantive hard law harmonisation as a result of EU regulations and court decisions and most of the central EU anti-discrimination directives have been transposed into Norwegian legislation as part of the EEA Agreement, but also as a result of voluntary adoption. Changes in Norwegian equality policy due to EEA commitments are, however, not fully visible in public gender equality debate. Instead, they appear mainly as important reform themes within bureaucratic and epistemic communities (see for instance Kraglund 2019), but even here the attention given EU integration processes and adaptations vary (Holst 2019).

In this chapter we address EU influence on changes in Norwegian gender equality policy since the mid 1990s. Our discussion is inspired by approaches in Europeanisation theory that emphasise the filtering role of nation-specific meaning frames (Börzel and Risse 2003), but also how European norms may constitute important resources for national agenda-setting (Jacquot and Woll 2003). In particular, we pay attention to the notion of discursive uses of the EU, i.e. the situations where national policy actors frame agendas with reference to EU standards and norms. Finally, we look not only at how EU laws and policies have been incorporated into the Norwegian political system—the 'import side', but also at how Norwegian or Nordic arrangements affect the EU area and EU initiatives—the 'export' side. We thus strive to combine top-down and bottom-up perspectives on EU influence. To illustrate how discursive uses of EU may play out in actual policy formation processes we rely on recent studies, but also use our own experience as members of a governmental appointed expert commission—The Gender + Equality Commission—which in 2010–2012 was mandated to investigate Norwegian gender equality policies, paying particular attention to the intersection of gender, ethnicity, and class.[1] Four specific areas of equality policy are discussed. We first address EU influence on Norwegian policy traditions with regard to equality legislation, work-life balance and gender mainstreaming, before we turn to the question of Norwegian influence on EU attempts to regulate the gender composition of corporate boards. This choice of themes obviously leaves other core gender equality areas unexamined, such as violence against women, gender perspectives on health, or broad equal pay policies—policy areas which all are important in the public debate on gender equality.

In 2012, a comprehensive public inquiry report (NOU 2012: 2) on the consequences of Norway's affiliation status concluded that EEA commitments and other EU agreements had had limited impact on the scope and content of actual policy making in the gender area, not least because Norwegian regulatory schemes were assessed to easily meet EU "minimum standards". As our discussion shows this is an overly superficial notion of EU influence on Norwegian gender equality policy.

---

[1] "Gender + equality" is a term borrowed from political science's gender equality research: see summary and sources for the European research project QUING, led by Mieke Verloo, http://www.quing.eu/index.php?option=com_content&task=view&id=17&Itemid=34, visited 10-28-14.

It treats "minimum standards" as standards that are easily achieved when in reality, as we argue EU regulatory standards present quite profound challenges to dominant, mainly social democratic, convictions about how gender equality should be sought.

2   EQUALITY LEGISLATION—EUROPEAN JUDICIALISATION

The dominant gender equality policy tradition in Norway prioritises, first, building family-oriented welfare state policies through publically financed childcare facilities and generous parental leave schemes, and second, promoting gender balance norms through quotas and various forms of preferential treatment (Skjeie and Teigen 2012; NOU 2012: 15, Chapter 2). This priority is largely built on the country's social democratic heritage: The Labour Party's main gender equality policy has been building and expanding gender equality-friendly welfare state arrangements aimed at improving the balance of work and family life and thus helping to secure women's economic independence through labour market integration (NOU 2012: 15; cf. Borchorst et al. 2012). Norway was however an "early achiever" in terms of legislating against gender based discrimination: As early as 1978 a comprehensive law on gender equality was passed by parliament. The law covered "all areas of society" although with a series of limitations to this general scope, in particular related to the competencies of the low threshold system set up to monitor the law. The legislative initiative established the world's first Gender Equality Ombud and Gender Equality Tribunal as a low threshold mechanism. The low threshold system was however only able to rule on discrimination complaints, deciding whether or not discrimination occurred. The parties to the complaint were then expected to acknowledge the ruling and agree among themselves on what, if any, form of compensation was appropriate. While individual discrimination cases also could be brought before the courts, the low threshold instantly became the regular route. In spite of severe limitations to the low threshold competencies, very few discrimination cases have thus been decided by regular courts in Norway (cf. NOU 2011: 18).

From the outset, the Norwegian gender equality legislation combined bans on direct and indirect discrimination with regulations that relate to proactive advancement of gender equality (cf. later section on gender mainstreaming). Proactive duties for state agencies and public and private employers form a central part of current equality legislation. However, due to a lack of proper enforcement, the proactive duties mainly function as symbolic legal statements. In comparison to broad welfare state initiatives on public childcare and parental leave schemes, individual and systemic discrimination have received scant attention within the social democratic gender equality order. It is mainly processes of Europeanisation in the Norwegian context that has contributed to widening protection against discrimination (NOU 2012: 2; NOU 2011: 18; Skjeie et al. 2017).

The EEA agreement covers all EU gender equality directives. Norwegian gender equality law has most notably been changed to incorporate more efficient legal remedies to address discrimination, such as the principles of strict liability and shared burden of proof. Limitations put on wage comparisons in the equal pay regulation have also been modified to comply with EU law. Moreover, important new rules on protection against harassment and sexual harassment and against retribution are directly tied to national implementation of EU regulations (Skjeie and Teigen 2003; Hedlund 2008; Kraglund 2019). However, there is still much leeway in adoption at national level. For instance, while low threshold monitoring applies to the general ban on harassment, the sexual harassment ban is not enforced through the low threshold system but only by the regular courts.

It is only on the issue of preferential treatment that interpretation of Norwegian gender equality law has been limited, rather than extended as a consequence of interpretation of EU law. The institutionalisation of quota arrangements is a hallmark of Norwegian gender equality policy. Quotas applying to the nomination procedures of political parties have been sequentially adopted since the late 1970s; to the appointment of public boards and commissions since the 1980s and 1990s, and—most famously—to the boards of private and public corporations since the early 2000s (for an overview see Skjeie and Teigen 2012). Various forms of preferential treatment policies have long been applied in both admission to higher education and in hiring within such institutions, as well as within public administration in general. Yet, in 2003, a case before the EFTA court decided against the University of Oslo's targeted earmarking of specific postdoctoral positions. The earmarking arrangement was found to violate the EEA agreement as it reserved the positions exclusively for women (NOU 2012: 2, 498)[2] and the further interpretation of

---

[2] http://www.eftacourt.int/uploads/tx_nvcases/1_02_RH_EN.pdf.

this decision by Norwegian authorities put new limitations on a hitherto favoured preferential treatment tool of Norwegian gender equality policy (NOU 2012: 2).

Over the past two decades, there has been a significant broadening of legal protection against discrimination in Europe. This development has also contributed to profound change in Norwegian equality legislation. Implementing new EU directives, member states' equality legislation has expanded to cover not only gender, but also racial or ethnic origin, religion or belief, disability, age and sexual orientation—the EU "six strands" policy base (Krizsan et al. 2012). This has been accompanied by an increasingly complex set of institutional arrangements to address inequalities[3] and new politics of equality have emerged within a multiple discrimination framework. However, EU directives on non-discrimination take a 'ground-by-ground' approach; the need to protect against multiple discrimination has mainly been addressed in recitals and soft law supplements to formal legal texts. In contrast to, for instance, CEDAW-based approaches, the specificities of intersectional discrimination are rarely noted and multiple equality initiatives are still largely contained within a strict non-discrimination framework, with positive duty programs or gender mainstreaming policies tending to remain one-dimensional (Skjeie 2015).

The first Norwegian moves to legislate against discrimination on the basis of race, ethnicity and religion were made in the late 1990s through amendments to the Work Environment Act; this, however, was foremost as a domestic follow up of the ILO convention 111. International pressures in particular contributed to the establishment of a Centre for Combatting Ethnic Discrimination (Borchorst et al. 2012, 66), an agency which however, had no legal enforcement competencies. Comprehensive equality laws aiming to cover all of the EU directives' protected strands were enacted from 2005 onward, mainly modelled on the Gender Equality Act and this law's general scope ("all areas of society", cf. above). For sexual orientation, gender identity and gender expression comprehensive legislation was not passed until 2013. Age received similar broad protection only when this ground was included in a new unified equality and antidiscrimination law in 2017

---

[3]For a comprehensive mapping of equality institutions in Europe, see for instance Andrea Krizsan, Hege Skjeie, and Judith Squires (eds). *Institutionalising Intersectionality: The Changing Nature of European Equality Regimes.* Basingstoke: Palgrave, 2012

(Lovvedtak 118 (2016–2017)). The new equality legislation also contains a clause which prohibits multiple discrimination ("combinations of grounds" in §6).When trying to pinpoint the most important consequences of EU law for protection against discrimination, the public inquiry report analysing Norway's affiliation status concluded that "age" had benefited the most. Discrimination on the basis of age is also the strand which is most frequently tried in court (NOU 2012: 2, 498–499).

The comprehensive set of EU antidiscrimination directives has clearly led to improved protection for vulnerable groups in Norway. Their transposition in member states has meant a spread in the number of low threshold anti-discrimination bodies, previously found in just a few countries (Krizsan et al. 2012, 211). Norway has, however, maintained a low threshold monitoring system in the form of Ombud and Tribunal since the enactment of the Gender Equality Law in the late 1970s. With the adoption of the new equality laws this arrangement was simply extended to cover the newly protected strands. This meant that the significant limitations built into the low threshold enforcement and monitoring system also applied to the new equality legislation. In general terms, these limitations, in combination with the lack of public legal aid in discrimination cases before the courts, bring the whole issue of access to justice to the fore, as explored in the following paragraphs. It was only in 2017 changes were made to contain competence for the Equality Tribunal to grant compensation to victims of employment related discrimination. The authors of this chapter all partook in the initiative which finally secured this reform, which we will explain more closely. From 2010 to 2012 we were part of a government-appointed expert commission mandated to investigate gender equality status and policies, paying particular attention to the intersection of gender, ethnicity, and class.[4] The efforts of the Norwegian Gender + Equality Commission to draw attention to the lack of effective sanctions within the Norwegian system strategically tapped into European Union developments to strengthen protection against discrimination, in what is conceptually characterised as "discursive use of EU" (see Kraglund 2019; cf. Lombardo and Forest 2012). As outlined, the Norwegian low threshold system was only able to rule on discrimination complaints, deciding whether or not discrimination occurred.

---

[4]The Commission delivered two reports: NOU 2011: 18, *Struktur for likestilling* (Structure for equality) and NOU 2012:15 *Politikk for likestilling* (Policy for equality).

The parties to the complaint were then expected to acknowledge the ruling and agree among themselves on what, if any, form of compensation was appropriate. If they could not agree, the only option for victims of discrimination was bringing the case before the regular courts. No public legal aid is available for bringing discrimination cases to court. The Commission described the entire development of anti-discrimination legislation in Norway in the early 2000s as mainly EU-inspired and the issue of 'effective sanctions' was then placed within this context, motivationally combining references to EU requirements on "efficient" and "proportional" sanctions with CEDAW obligations and the Paris principles on access to justice (NOU 2011: 18, particularly 10.3–10.4).

The Commission thus pointed to the obvious political inconsistency of combining strong substantive legislation with weak enforcement mechanisms and lack of legal aid, and deplored the lack of reform in this respect—that is, the blatant neglect of legal efficiency during nearly 40 years of expanding equality legislation. In terms of remedies there was, however, no common EU model available, simply because none exists (Kraglund 2019; Wladasch 2015). The Commission chose a Nordic path and borrowed a relevant model from Denmark and the competencies of the Danish equality tribunal to rule on compensation; an alternative model was borrowed from the competencies of the Swedish Equality Ombud to try discrimination cases in court. The Commission also stressed that the ban on sexual harassment should be included within the scope of low threshold competencies (NOU 2011: 18).

The centre-left cabinet then in office were, however, not interested in legal reform. It was not until a governmental change of guard to a predominantly rightist cabinet in 2013 that reform of the low threshold sanction system was finally carried through—however, leaving sexual harassment to be handled in its old and obviously ineffective way whereby few cases are tried in the regular courts.[5] Reflecting on the reasons why judicial efficiency has been neglected in the Norwegian context, we point mainly to a strong policy tradition which tends to treat gender equality as an "evolving process" rather than a judicially enforceable right

---

[5] It is only the global #metoo movement, and a consequent series of harassment scandals within the major Norwegian political parties, that has moved establishment thinking towards a new solution in this respect.

(Skjeie et al. 2017). The general lack of concern expressed about access to justice in the Norwegian context is clearly due to embedded views on the inappropriateness of judicialisation of gender equality policy (for Danish parallels see Borchorst and Agustin 2019). Thus judicialisation is probably the key benefit that gender equality agency in Norway has received from EU affiliation.

3 WORK-LIFE BALANCE: FAMILY POLICY WITH A NORDIC SIGNATURE

Work-life balance has long been flagged as a central goal in EU's gender equality strategies. Yet, social policies are the responsibility of member states, putting strains on EU policy-making in this area (Kantola 2010). The European Commission's 2015 withdrawal of the proposed maternity leave directive illustrates how current procedures allow unfriendly member states to block progressive initiatives, but the EU's limited engagement also reflects a lack of prioritisation, and, recently, austerity pressures (Kantola and Lombardo 2017). Nevertheless, over time, the EU's equal treatment requirements have facilitated women's inclusion and equal standing in the labour market, and the EU's equal pay legislation in particular has contributed massively to increasing women's wages (van der Vleuten 2007). The Union has moreover stimulated the diffusion of norms and best practice, soft policy coordination and the development of common benchmark mechanisms in the area of work-life balance (see, for example, Hubert et al. 2011).

Nordic family policy has been perceived as an essential Nordic model trademark and as looming far above EU standards (for overviews, see Leira 2002, 2012; Ellingsæter 2014; Skevik 2003). Hence, one might expect to see Norwegian policies in this area exported to both member states and EU initiatives, rather than seeing EU approaches and measures imported to Norway. And indeed, manifest traces of Europeanisation in Norway are few. Over time, a range of family- and parent-friendly services and benefits have been institutionalised in Norway, but the EU seems to have played a rather marginal role. The development of publicly subsidised kindergartens, day-care centres and out-of-school care had been a priority from the 1990s onwards if not earlier, and Norway is currently regarded as having full kindergarten coverage. Paid parental leave has been gradually extended and is now 49 weeks at 100% coverage (or 59 weeks with 80% coverage). Ten weeks are reserved for the mother, 10 weeks for the father, while the remaining weeks are a shared period.[6] In addition, there are rights for parents to unpaid long-term leave to care for new-borns and small children, the right to paid leave of absence for nursing mothers, and the right to paid leave to care for sick children. A set of special benefits for single parents are in place. Finally, there is universal child benefit for anyone supporting children under the age of 18, and also tax benefits for families, and a cash-for-care benefit for parents with children that do not attend state-sponsored nurseries. However, studies of the history of Norwegian family policy show few, if any of these inspirations coming from the EU, or indeed EU set limitations (Vollset 2011).

Norwegian fertility rates are relatively high and commonly regarded as an outcome of this package of work-life policies. Worries about decreasing fertility are thus not pronounced. Norway has also no explicit fertility policy, which contrasts with the increased focus on fertility in many European countries, but also at EU-level (Neyer 2017). Reproductive rights are firmly protected, and The Norwegian Abortion Act (1978) is relatively liberal: abortion is available on demand until the end of the 12th week of pregnancy. Norway was also a pioneer when it comes to codifying children's rights, with its early progressive Children Act (1915) that obliged both parents to provide for extra-marital children, and entitled single mothers with financial support. An Ombud for Children, the first of its kind, was established in 1981 (Skevik 2003).

This policy field then is generally and quite reasonably conceived of as largely homegrown; it bears the signature of Nordic social democracy and was first and foremost developed here. However, policies and approaches have not been controversy-free and contemporary debates on family policy in Norway, although grounded in the national context, cover concerns and issues familiar from elsewhere that is also on the EU agenda (European Commission 2016). One such issue is how to strike the right balance between ensuring universal welfare rights and providing incentives to increase employment rates for all groups of women. In Norway, a concrete expression of this concern is the vivid debate over the cash-for-care scheme and its implications for women's inclusion in the labour market and integration of minority women in particular

---

[6]However, in accordance with proposal from the Gender + Equality Commission, from 2018 on the parental leave will be split in three equal shares, 1/3 reserved for the mother, 1/3 for the father, and 1/3 as a shared period.

(Ellingsæter 2014). Another controversy occurred around paternity leave, which proponents see as a decisive step towards reduced gender gaps in the work-family area, whereas critics worry about families' freedom of choice. A third debate concerns the relationship between services and benefits in the family policy infrastructure, where a 2017 proposal from a public commission on family policy (NOU 2017: 6) to replace the universal child benefit with a means-tested benefit in combination with free kindergarten for all children, received much attention, including during that year's election campaign (Holst 2019).

Moreover, there is a trend towards greater Europeanisation even in the area of family policy (Holst 2019). Yet, typically for this policy domain, European integration is primarily regarded as creating new difficulties and policy challenges. Illustratively, the mandate of the above mentioned family policy commission, asks for a review of existing policies in light of the problem of so-called "benefit export" said to arise from the free movement and equal treatment principles of the EEA agreement. The commission focuses in its response on the child benefit and the cash-for-care benefit—to what extent do working parents in Norway send off these benefits to children residing in other EEA area countries? It concludes, however, that public spending on such "export" of benefits is still very limited.

Furthermore, the European Court of Justice's 2015 decision in the Maistrellis case has raised the question of whether equal treatment requirements are properly ensured in cases of parental leave schemes where fathers' leave rights are conditional upon mothers' employment. As the Norwegian scheme includes such a clause, the Maistrellis case has triggered an exchange between the EFTA Surveillance Authority (ESA) and the Norwegian government about whether Norwegian parental leave arrangements are in accordance with EU law. The Norwegian government claims that it is, while ESA has remained skeptic over this interpretation. Some feminist law scholars have supported ESA's approach (see, for example, Ketscher 2019). Yet, the family policy commission, while recognising the disagreement, decided in the end to be loyal to the government's interpretation on this point, stating that it is "outside its mandate" to position itself in legal disagreements in absence of a court decision on the Norwegian scheme specifically (NOU 2017: 6, 10.1.1).

This is a reminder of how the strength and shape of Europeanisation depends on actors' interpretations and strategies (Radaelli and Pasquier 2006; Kraglund 2016), and that the judicialisation of Norwegian gender equality policy triggered by the EU is not an automatic, top-down process. Interestingly, the approach of the family policy commission differs from that of another commission close to the work-life area, namely the equal pay commission (NOU 2008: 6). In accordance with the strategies of previous commissions on the issue of equal pay, the 2008 report made reference to EU gender equality directives, court decisions and supportive legal scholarship to question limitations put on wage comparisons by Norwegian equal pay legislation (Holst 2019).

4   GENDER MAINSTREAMING—A WIDESPREAD POLICY FAILURE

Gender mainstreaming has been the official strategy of gender equality policy in Norway for forty years, that is to say, since the adoption of the Gender Equality Act in 1978. The mission statement of the Act was "to promote equality and in particular the position of women" (§1a). To fulfill this aim it was stated that "all public authorities shall facilitate for gender equality on all areas of responsibility" (§1b). Since the late 1990s, gender mainstreaming strategy also corresponded with change in EU's approach to equal opportunities from a narrow focus on equal treatment in the workplace to an acceptance of positive action and institutionalisation of gender sensitive norms and practices in public policy more broadly (Hafner-Burton and Pollack 2002; Rees 2005). Gender mainstreaming simply implies that all policies should address relevant gender issues and through this promote gender equality. In the Nordic context, mainstreaming has had a particularly high standing in Swedish gender equality policy, and it has been argued that Scandinavian impulses were important for the EUs adoption of the gender mainstreaming approach (Pollack and Hafner-Burton 2000), in particular tied to Sweden and Finland's entrance to the European Union in 1995.

The development of Swedish gender equality policy undoubtedly shows a particular strong tradition of institutionalisation of equality policies, and through this a structure for the implementation of gender mainstreaming (Daly 2005; Sainsbury and Bergquist 2009; Freidenvall 2019). However, implementation studies tend to show varied degrees of success (Callerstig 2014; Ahrens and Callerstig 2017; Freidenvall 2019). Freidenvall, for instance, finds that processes of Europeanisation and national knowledge production have dynamically developed Swedish gender equality policies but that European influences have been stronger in the development and expansion of discrimination policies than for gender mainstreaming policy (Freidenvall 2019). It seems fair to state that in terms of policy traditions, Swedish gender mainstreaming is "exported", not "imported", and in this sense it tends to remain a nationally instigated policy endeavor.

EU-based implementation of gender mainstreaming is still far from being a strategic success in Norway. In their analysis of the implementation of both gender mainstreaming and environmental policy integration in the European Commission, Hafner-Burton and Pollack (2009) conclude that such soft policies fail in changing the behavior of European Commission officials. Hence they argue that hard incentive policies are needed to give such gender perspectives any chance of competing with concerns about economic competitiveness that enjoy "principle priority" in contemporary EU policymaking (Hafner-Burton and Pollack 2009).

Nevertheless, the EU formal prioritization of gender mainstreaming resonates in Norwegian law. As far back as the preparatory work for the Gender Equality Act in 1978, integration of a gender equality perspective across all policy fields was argued as necessary for effective gender equality policy, and was consequently anchored within the activity duty in the mission statement of the Gender Equality Act.[7] The activity duty was strengthened as part of a comprehensive revision of the Gender Equality Act in 2002, where the duty to make active, targeted and systematic efforts to promote gender equality was extended to all employers (including in the private sector) and to social partners in the labour market, who then became obliged to improve gender equality in their businesses and in their field of responsibility.[8] In its reasoning for the revision, the Government drew a connection between the activity duty in the Gender Equality Act and the EU's gender mainstreaming policy. The strengthening of the EU's gender equality policy, and the introduction of gender mainstreaming following the Amsterdam treaty entering into force in 1997 was explicitly linked with the proposal to strengthen the activity duty. EU developments were discursively used to underpin new national legislation in this respect: While the government

---

[7] The Activity Duty in the Gender Equality Act was included in 1978 obliging all public authorities to make active, targeted and systematic efforts to promote gender equality. In 2008 the Activity Duty was extended to include ethnicity, religion and disability.

[8] Ot. prp. nr. 77 (2000–2001), s. 25–33, https://www.regjeringen.no/contentassets/d495493b08ef4fdc9f46412c524f2466/no/pdfa/otp200020010077000dddpdfa.pdf.

argued that EU mainstreaming initiatives did not directly affect the EEA agreement at this point in time, they added that this might be the case later.[9] Otherwise, the government was vague about the relevance of EU/EEA concerns in relation to Norway's gender mainstreaming policy.

Gender mainstreaming is, of course, a particularly demanding approach because of its requirement that all central actors analyse the gender aspects of any policy process (cf. Pollack and Hafner-Burton 2000). Gender mainstreaming in Norway presupposes that equality efforts should be integrated into the daily work of all authorities, in all decision-making processes, and by all relevant actors. However, the Gender + Equality Commission's investigation into the implementation of mainstreaming activities in national, regional and local public administration made it abundantly clear that such activities were scarce (NOU 2011: 18). Although gender mainstreaming is anchored in the activity duty of the Gender Equality Act and in government instructions for policy preparation, where an obligation to conduct gender-sensitive consequence analysis has existed since the mid-2000s, there has been no monitoring of such written obligations. No comprehensive gender budgeting is in place; no systematic assessment of equality consequences in legislation and policy formulation has been carried out; equality work has mainly been geared towards temporality in the form of various "action plans" on different areas; and there has been little equality expertise available to guide equality eager authorities etc. (NOU 2011: 18).

The overall lack of good practices with regard to mainstreaming is clearly related to the lack of proper enforcement mechanisms in Norwegian equality legislation. The Commission consequently argued for the importance of anchoring oversight authority and building an institutional structure to secure the implementation of gender equality policy. To further this cause, it first explained the overarching relevance of the Beijing Platform of Action to equality mainstreaming efforts, and then extensively outlined the Swedish governments' large-scale investment in mainstreaming activities over the past decade. No mention was made of the Amsterdam Treaty's mainstreaming obligations, and EU-based mainstreaming efforts were generally not discussed. The Commission needed to show best practices and the EU level had little to offer in this respect. However, this effort to increase the institutional

---

[9] Ot. prp. nr. 77 (2000–2001), s. 25–33, https://www.regjeringen.no/contentassets/d495493b08ef4fdc9f46412c524f2466/no/pdfa/otp200020010077000dddpdfa.pdf.

capabilities of gender + equality promotion in the Norwegian context did not succeed as the political will to anchor authority over legal obligations to do gender mainstreaming was not present.

5 GENDER QUOTAS FOR CORPORATE BOARDS—A NORWEGIAN INNOVATION WITH EUROPEAN REPERCUSSIONS

Promoting gender balance norms through quotas and various forms for preferential treatment is a dominant tradition in Norwegian gender equality policy (Skjeie and Teigen 2012; Teigen 2015). Since 1981, as part of a revision of the Gender Equality Act, the Act has stated that both genders should be represented on state appointed commissions, councils and boards, and since 1988 the Act specified the demand for gender parity to at least 40% of each gender in state appointed commissions, etc.; the same regulation was applied to municipal commissions etc. in the Municipal Act since 1992.[10] Other Nordic countries have passed similar legislation, yet in line with its comparatively strong quota tradition, Norway was also the first country to propose (1999), adopt (2003), and implement (2008) corporate board gender quotas (CBQ).[11] The formulation of this regulation was modelled on the regulation covering the gender composition of public commissions in the Gender Equality Act. However, it was not made a part of the equality legislation. Instead, CBQ became part of Companies legislation. Interestingly, a main reason for situating CBQ in Companies legislation was to ensure strict enforcement of the regulation, so that similarly strict sanctions would apply to this regulation as to other company regulations. The sanction system specifies that a company that does not have a legal board, despite several warnings (followed by fines) allowing it to correct the matter, will be subject to forced dissolution. The Norwegian Business register is designed to ensure compliance with the law. CBQ thus forms a clear exception to the general trend for weak enforcement mechanisms in equality legislation that we have identified in this chapter.

---

[10]The gender composition of commissions etc. appointed by the government has been regulated since 1970s, and finally included in legislation in 1981, as part of the Gender Equality Act (Solhøy 1999).

[11]However with the exception that Israel from 1999 the statuary requirement that all publicly traded companies should have at least one woman on the company board (Hughes et al. 2017).

The CBQ reform was a highly controversial legal regulation. The "women in management" debate, particularly high on the public agenda in the 1990's Norway, as well as in most of the industrialised world, is an important part of the context explaining Norway's introduction of CBQ. This debate hit Norway particularly hard because it interfered with the country's national self-image of itself as particularly successful on issues of gender equality. In Norway, as in the other Nordic countries, a discrepancy exists between a relatively balanced representation of men and women in political decision-making on the one hand, and strong vertical gender segregation in the labour market, and especially in the business sector (Teigen and Wängnerud 2009; Niskanen 2011).

Through the introduction of corporate board quotas, Norway became an initiator of the wave of corporate board quota requirements that have since swept across Europe and other parts of the world (Fagan et al. 2012; Teigen 2012; Terjesen et al. 2015; Hughes et al. 2017). Since the early 2000s, the issue of gender quotas on corporate boards has been much discussed by governments, parties and parliaments in a wide range of countries. In an impressive burst of policy diffusion, parliaments in Spain (2007), Iceland (2009), France (2011), Belgium (2011), the Netherlands (2011), Italy (2011) and Germany (2016), have introduced gender quotas for corporate boards. Other countries have introduced voluntary measures, such as Austria, Denmark, Finland, and United Kingdom (Mensi-Klarback 2017). Gender balance on corporate boards is generally progressing in Europe, although significant progress is restricted to countries that have introduced legislative measures.[12]

In tandem with the policy diffusion of CBQ in several European countries, regulation of gender balance on corporate boards was placed on the agenda of the European Commission after a new commission entered into power in 2010 (Barosso II), and with Viviane Reding as Vice-President and Commissioner of Justice, Fundamental Rights and Citizenship. A lengthy policy process in the European Commission finally resulted in the proposal for a directive on the regulation of the gender balance of boards of large corporations: Proposal for a Directive of the European Parliament and of the Council on improving the gender balance among non-executive directors of companies listed on stock exchanges and related measures. The proposition was considered

---

[12]http://www.womenlobby.org/Cracks-in-the-glass-ceiling-or-just-a-trick-of-the-light.

controversial by some key actors, but was passed by the European Parliament, however, a blocking minority in the Council of Ministers have prevented the proposition to be passed (Seierstad et al. 2017; Lépinard and Rubio Marin 2018; Inderhaug 2019).

Inderhaug (2019) shows how Norwegian experiences played a central role in the directive process in EU. Norwegian politicians, bureaucrats and experts were invited to share their experiences and analysis in meetings, hearings and conferences. The case of Norway was central in the reasoning leading to the European Commission directive proposal, and in the debate leading to the vote in favour of the proposal in the European parliament. In the European Council of Ministers debate, however, where the proposal was turned down, the Norwegian example was less central. In the Council, representation reflects the size of the population of each member country, hence Germany's opposition to the directive and the strong voice of Germany Chancellor Angela Merkel on this matter became weighty factors explaining why the directive was not adopted (Inderhaug 2019).[13]

Norwegian experiences have clearly played a significant role in placing the CBQ issue on the European agenda, both in individual European countries and at the supranational level in the EU. However, as pointed out by Inderhaug (2019), Norwegian experiences played a less prominent role in the European Council of Ministers than in other parts of the EU system. While Norwegian policy influence managed to change the EU agenda, the directive process in EU is still pending. In this respect it is tempting to suggest that absence from the table matters, and as a result, Norwegian influence on EU policymaking will be modest at best.

6   CONCLUSION: JUDICIALISATION WITH LEEWAY

Broadly speaking, Norway has adopted the European Union's increasingly ambitious equality agenda from the early 2000s, when this agenda was significantly broadened through the Amsterdam Treaty. The Nordic countries are commonly portrayed as in the vanguard of gender equality policy innovation, and, as shown in this chapter, Norway can also boast a comparatively long tradition of gender equality advocacy.

---

[13] Article from the European Women's Lobby on the European Commission's Directive on Women on Boards, https://www.womenlobby.org/The-European-Commission-s-Directive-on-Women-on-Boards.

However, it seems clear that EU regulatory standards have presented a profound challenge to the dominant, mainly social democratic, legacy of policy convictions about how gender equality should be pursued. Bluntly stated, this legacy prioritises the development of a welfare state ensuring public childcare and parental leave to promote women's labour market participation, rather than seeking effective remedies to discrimination, or promoting educational and workplace equality. Instead of treating such policies as complementary the first have been prioritised over the latter in the social democratic order, so that judicialisation of gender equality claims has been minimised and welfare state infrastructure maximised. The comprehensive set of antidiscrimination directives has led to improved protection for vulnerable groups in Norway while generous arrangements to promote work-family balance have, so far, remained largely immune to EU influence. Gender mainstreaming policy is still as inefficient in Norway as it is in EU at large, and the exceptional Norwegian board quota model has not yet succeeded in making a distinct mark at European level.

While present day Norwegian equality law owes much to the strict standards of EU law, this development has not been uncontroversial as it challenges a systemic unwillingness to ensure the effectiveness of gender equality legislation. Anxiety about judicialisation in the Norwegian context is primarily expressed as a domestic concern driven by the increasing influence of supranational law on domestic law and policymaking. It resonates across Europe not least as a result of the enforcement of the European Convention on Human Rights by the European Court of Human Rights and through EU member states' obligations to comply with the rulings of the Court of Justice of the EU. In Norway, attempts to broaden the scope of directly enforceable human rights through 'full text' incorporation of international conventions have for example been met with hesitance and avoidance strategies by every government since the early 2000s. The dynamic interpretive style of international human rights bodies is argued in particular to skew the balance (cf. Skjeie et al. 2017).

Interestingly, "judicialisation" is sometimes fiercely contested, while on other occasions it goes almost unnoticed, despite significant implications. Controversy has for instance been harsh over several rulings of the European Court of Human Rights. EEA obligations have also spurred controversy, recently among unions who worry over deregulation, increased competition and lowered social standards (Holst and Stie 2016). However, in the gender equality area the EU and EU agreements are still regarded as having limited impact. As this chapter has shown, this is somewhat of a misconception, even if this view is supported by the 2012 official report on the relationship between EU and Norway.

The European Court of Justice's 2015 decision in the Maistrellis case, however, holds the potential to change this state of affairs, as the case has direct relevance for present-day Norwegian parental leave regulations. How this EU challenge will evolve is still unclear. It could represent a blow to the very heart of national self-determination over what is commonly regarded as core gender equality policy; the welfare state infrastructure which primarily aims to promote women's labour market participation. Fathers' independent rights to parental leave have in this context—so far—clearly been subordinated.

Generally, the judicialisation of Norwegian gender equality policy triggered by the EU is still not an automatic, top-down process. There is much leeway for national initiative in the development of policy and a large scope for strategic uses of EU. Our discussion has shown how EU is discursively used—or strategically non-used—to promote the views already held by national constituencies of gender equality-friendly actors. In this sense, in this policy area Norway's ties to EU has so far mainly constituted a win-win situation: EU influence has unequivocally contributed to judicialisation many would regard as progressive, but arguably not at the expense of the women- and family-friendly welfare state.

BIBLIOGRAPHY

Ahrens, Petra, and Anne-Charlott Callerstig. 2017. The European Social Fund and the Institutionalisation of Gender Mainstreaming in Sweden and Germany. In *Towards Gendering Institutionalism*, ed. Heather Mc Rae and Elaine Weiner, 69–100. Rowman & Littlefield International, ISBN 9781783489961.

Borchorst, Anette, Lenita Freidenvall, Johanna Kantola, Liza Reisel, and Mari Teigen. 2012. Institutionalizing Intersectionality in the Nordic Countries? Anti-Discrimination and Equality in Denmark, Finland, Norway, and Sweden. In *Institutionalizing Intersectionality? The Changing Nature of European Equality Regimes*, ed. Andrea Kriszan, Hege Skjeie, and Judith Squires, 59–88. Basingstoke: Palgrave Macmillan.

Borchorst, Anette, and Lise Rolandsen Agustin. 2019. Køn, ligestilling og retliggjørelse: Europeiseringen av dansk likgestillingspolitik. In *Europeisering av nordisk likestillingspolitikk*, ed. Cathrine Holst, Hege Skjeie, and Mari Teigen. Oslo: Gyldendal Akademisk.

Börzel, Tanja, and Thomas Risse. 2003. Conceptualizing the Domestic Impact of Europe. In *The Politics of Europeanization*, ed. Kevin Featherstone and Claudio M. Radaelli, 57–80. Oxford: Oxford University Press.

Callerstig, Anne-Charlott. 2014. Making Equality Work: Ambiguities, Conflict and Change Agents in the Implementation of Equality Policies in Public Sector Organizations. PhD thesis, Linköping University.

Daly, Mary. 2005. Gender Mainstreaming in Theory and Practice. *Social Politics* 12 (3): 433–450. https://doi.org/10.1093/sp/jxi023.

Egeberg, Morten, and Jarle Trondal. 2015. National Administrative Sovereignty: Under Pressure. In *The European Union's Non-Members*, ed. Erik Oddvar Eriksen and John Erik Fossum, 173–188. London: Routledge.

Ellingsæter, Anne-Lise. 2014. Nordic Earner-Carer Models—Why Stability and Instability? *Journal of Social Policy* 43 (3): 555–574.

Eriksen, Erik Oddvar, and John Erik, Fossum (eds.). 2015. *The European Union's Non-Members*. London: Routledge.

Esping-Andersen, Gösta. 2009. *The Incomplete Revolution*. Cambridge: Polity Press.

European Commission. 2016. *Strategic Engagement for Gender Equality 2016–2019*. Brussels: Justice, Consumers and Gender Equality, European Commission.

Fagan, Colette, Maria C. Gonzalez Menendez, and Silvia Gomez Ansón. 2012. *Women on Corporate Boards and in Top Management: European Trends and Policy*. London: Palgrave.

Freidenvall, Lenita. 2019. Institutionaliseringen av svensk jämställdhet: lager-på-lager-processer och fokusförflyttning. I: *Europeisering av nordisk likestillingspolitikk*, ed. Cathrine Holst, Hege Skjeie og Mari Teigen. Oslo: Gyldendal Akademisk.

Hafner-Burton, Emilie M., and Mark A. Pollack. 2002. Mainstreaming Gender in Global Governance. *European Journal of International Relations* 8 (3): 339–373.

Hafner-Burton, Emilie M., and Mark A. Pollack. 2009. Mainstreaming Gender in the European Union: Getting the Incentives Right. *Comparative European Politics* 7 (1): 114–138.

Hedlund, Mary-Ann. 2008. Bevisbyrde. I: *Diskriminerings- og likestillingsrett*, red. Anne Hellum og Kirsten Ketscher. Oslo: Universitetsforlaget.

Holst, Cathrine. 2019. Ekspertifisering og europeisering i norske likestillingsutredninger. In *Europeisering av nordisk likestillingspolitikk*, ed. Cathrine Holst, Hege Skjeie and Mari Teigen. Oslo: Gyldendal Akademisk.

Holst, Cathrine, and Anne Elizabeth Stie. 2016. I takt eller utakt? Europeiseringen av Norge. In *Det norske samfunn*, ed. Ivar Frønes and Lise Kjølsrød, 270–290. Oslo: Gyldendal Akademisk.

Hubert, Agnes, et al. 2011. The European Institute for Gender Equality: A Window of Oppurtunity for Gender Equality Policies. *The European Journal of Women's Studies* 18 (2): 169–181.

Hughes, Melanie M., Pamela Paxton, and Mona Lena Krook. 2017. Gender Quotas for Legislatures and Corporate Boards. *Annual Review of Sociology* 43: 331–352. https://doi.org/10.1146/annurev-soc-060116-053324.

Inderhaug, Erle. 2019. En norsk likestillingsreform I EU. I: *Europeisering av nordisk likestillingspolitikk*, ed. Cathrine Holst, Hege Skjeie og Mari Teigen. Oslo: Gyldendal Akademisk.

Jacquot, Sophie, and Cornelia Woll. 2003. Usage of European Integration-Europeanisation from a Sociological Perspective. *European Integration Online Papers (EIoP)* 7 (12): 1–14.

Kantola, Johanna. 2010. *Gender and the European Union*. New York: Palgrave Macmillan.

Kantola, Johanna, and Emmanuela Lombardo. 2017. *Gender and the Economic Crisis in Europe*. New York: Palgrave Macmillan.

Ketscher, Kirsten. 2019. Uden titel. Diskriminering? Nej Tak! I: *Europeisering av nordisk likestillingspolitikk*, ed. Cathrine Holst, Hege Skjeie og Mari Teigen. Oslo: Gyldendal Akademisk.

Kraglund, Karin O. 2016. Nødvendig, ønskelig – eller verken eller? En analyse av norske aktørers diskursive bruk av EU i reformprosesser på likestillingsfeltet. Masteroppgave. Institutt for statsvitenskap. Universitetet i Oslo.

Kraglund, Karin O. 2019. Diskursiv Europeisering. En analyse av fire likestilling-spolitiske reformprosesser. I: *Europeisering av nordisk likestillingspolitikk*, ed. Cathrine Holst, Hege Skjeie og Mari Teigen. Oslo: Gyldendal Akademisk.

Krizsan, Andrea, Hege Skjeie, and Judith Squires (eds.). 2012. *Institutionalizing Intersectionality? The Changing Nature of European Equality Regimes*. Basingstoke: Palgrave Macmillan.

Leira, Arnlaug. 2002. *Working Parents and the Welfare State: Family Change and Policy Reform in Scandinavia*. Cambridge: Cambridge University Press.

Leira, Arnlaug. 2012. Omsorgens institusjoner, Omsorgens kjønn. In *Velferdsstatens familier – Nye sosiologiske perspektiver*, ed. A.L. Ellingsæter and K. Widerberg, 76–93. Oslo: Gyldendal Akademisk.

Lépinard, Eléonore, and Ruth Rubio Marin. 2018. *Transforming Gender Citizenship: The Irresistible Rise of Gender Quotas in Europe*. Cambridge: Cambridge University Press.

Lombardo, Emanuela, and Maxime Forest. 2012. *The Europeanization of Gender Equality Policies: A Discursive Sociological Approach*. Basingstoke: Palgrave Macmillan.

Mensi-Klarback, Cathrine Seierstad, and Patricia Gabaldon. 2017. Setting the Scene: Women on Boards: The Multiple Approaches Beyond Quotas. In *Gender Diversity in the Boardroom: Multiple Approaches Beyond Quotas*, vol. 2, ed. Cathrine Seierstad, Patricia Gabaldon and Heike Mensi-Klarbach. London: Palgrave Macmillan.

Neyer, Gerda, et al. 2017. EU-Policies and Fertility: The Emergence of Fertility-Related Family Policies at the Supra-National Level, Families & Societies.

Niskanen, Kirsti. 2011. *Gender and Power in the Nordic Countries—With Focus on Politics and Business,* vol. 1. Oslo: NIKK-Publication.

NOU. 2008: 6. Kjønn og lønn. Fakta, analyser og virkemidler for likelønn. Oslo: Departementenes servicesenter, Informasjonsforvaltningen.

NOU. 2011: 18. Struktur for likestilling. Oslo: Departementenes servicesenter, Informasjonsforvaltningen.

NOU. 2012: 2. Innenfor og utenfor. Norges avtaler med EU. Oslo: Departementenes servicesenter, Informasjonsforvaltningen.

NOU. 2017: 6. Offentlig støtte til barnefamiliene. Oslo: Departementenes servicesenter, Informasjonsforvaltningen.

Pollack, Mark A., and Emilie Hafner-Burton. 2000. Mainstreaming Gender in the European Union. *Journal of European Public Policy* 7 (3): 432–456. https://doi.org/10.1080/13501760050086116.

Radaelli, Claudio M., and Romain Pasquier. 2006. Encounters with Europe: Concepts, Definitions, and Research Design. *Politik* 3 (9): 6–14.

Rees, Teresa. 2005. Reflections on the Uneven Development of Gender Mainstreaming in the European Union. *International Feminist Journal of Politics* 7 (4): 555–574. https://doi.org/10.1080/14616740500284532.

Sainsbury, Diane, and Christina Bergquist. 2009. The Promise and Pitfalls of Gender Mainstreaming. *International Journal of Feminist Politics* 1 (2): 216–234.

Seierstad, Cathrine, Patricia Gabaldon, and Heike Mensi-Klarbach (eds.). 2017. *Gender Diversity in the Boardroom: Multiple Approaches Beyond.* London: Palgrave Macmillan.

Skevik, Anne. 2003. Family Policies in Norway. NOVA—Norwegian Social Research.

Skjeie, Hege, and Mari Teigen. 2003. *Menn i mellom. Mannsdominans og likestillingspolitikk.* Oslo: Gyldendal Akademisk.

Skjeie, Hege. 2015. Gender Equality and Nondiscrimination: How to Tackle Multiple Discrimination Effectively? In *Visions for Gender Equality,* 79–82. European Commission 2015, ISBN 978-92-79-47777-5.

Skjeie, Hege, and Mari Teigen. 2012. Duties to Promote Equality. In *Comparisons, Quotas and Critical Change,* ed. Lenita Freidenvall and Michelle Micheletti, 51–61. Stockholm: Stockholm University.

Skjeie, Hege, Cathrine Holst, and Mari Teigen. 2017. Benevolent Contestations: Mainstreaming, Judicialization, and Europeanisation in Norwegian Gender + Equality Debate. In *Towards Gendering Institutionalism,* ed. Heather Mc Rae and Elaine Weiner, 121–144. Rowman & Littlefield International, ISBN 9781783489961.

Solhøy, Stina Hansteen. 1999. *Politisk vilje møter institusjonell autonomi. Hovedoppgave i statsvitenskap.* Oslo: Universitetet i Oslo.

Teigen, Mari. 2012. Gender Quotas in Corporate Boards—On the Diffusion of a Distinct National Policy Reform. In *Firms, Boards and Gender Quotas:*

Comparative Perspectives: Comparative Social Research, vol. 29, ed. Fredrik Engelstad and Mari Teigen, 115–146. Bingley: Emerald.

Teigen, Mari. 2015. The Making of Gender Quotas for Corporate Boards in Norway. In *Cooperation and Conflict the Nordic Way: Work, Welfare and Institutional Change in Scandinavia*, ed. Engelstad, Fredrik and Anniken Hagelund. Berlin: De Gruyter Open. ISBN 978-3-11-044428-5. 6. s 96–117.

Teigen, Mari, and Lena Wängnerud. 2009. Tracing Gender Equality Cultures: Elite Perceptions of Gender Equality in Norway and Sweden. *Politics & Gender* 5: 21–44.

Terjesen, Siri, Ruth Aguilera, and Ruth Lorenz. 2015. Legislating a Woman's Seat on the Board: Institutional Factors Driving Gender Quotas for Boards of Directors. *Journal of Business Ethics* 128 (2): 233–251.

van der Vleuten, Anna. 2007. *The Price of Gender Equality: Member States and Governance in the European Union*. Aldershot: Asgate.

Vollset, Gerd. 2011. *Familiepolitikkens historie – fra 1970 til 2000*. Oslo: Nova.

Walby, Sylvia. 2009. *Globalisation and Inequalities*. London: Sage.

Wladasch, Katrin. 2015. *The Sanctions Regime in Discrimination Cases and Its Effects*. Brussels: Equinet, the European Network of Equality Bodies.

CHAPTER 18

Conclusion: Brexit, Gender Justice and the Overton Window

Moira Dustin, Nuno Ferreira and Susan Millns

1 INTRODUCTION

It is tempting to talk about Brexit, and in the context of this book, gender and Brexit, in clichés, analogies and metaphors: is gender 'the elephant in the Brexit room'? Is gender a 'known unknown' or an 'unknown unknown' in the Brexit discourse? The framing device we have chosen is the Overton window or window of discourse[1]; that is to say, the metaphor for describing the parameters of public debate at any one moment—a concept we will return to.

When we first had the idea for this collection, our concern was that we saw little recognition of the importance of gender, sexual orientation

---

[1] John Lanchester, 'Brexit Blues', *London Review of Books* 38 (28 July 2016), 3.

M. Dustin · N. Ferreira (✉) · S. Millns
School of Law, University of Sussex, Brighton, UK
e-mail: N.Ferreira@sussex.ac.uk

M. Dustin
e-mail: M.Dustin@sussex.ac.uk

S. Millns
e-mail: S.Millns@sussex.ac.uk

and gender identity (SOGI) to Brexit discourse, either in political, public or academic discourse, in the run-up to the referendum, the psephology of the vote itself or the post-referendum negotiations. We started from the premise that feminist and queer studies provide a lens to look through every area of public policy and legislation. Similarly, we recognised that Brexit is not a project or process that can be contained within a few or even many areas of public policy. Nevertheless, we did not anticipate how diverse a collection of chapters would result from our call for contributions when we brought together the two topics—gender and Brexit. In the opening chapter we highlight this diversity and here, in this final chapter, we try to bring together some overarching themes, while avoiding imposing commonalities where none exist.

We start by looking at the extent to which our authors take an optimistic or pessimistic view of future prospects for gender and LGBTQI+ rights. We then identify issues relating to globalisation, and specifically migration, as a recurring motif in many chapters. Finally, we note the extent to which the contributions to this book are underpinned by intersectional analysis. Before concluding, we highlight some of the considerations we were unable to explore, which in no way reflects their lack of importance. We hope that by flagging them, they will be addressed in future publications.

2   Horizon Scanning

Editors of an academic collection such as this generally attempt to bring together a balanced and nuanced set of contributions, reflecting different perspectives, and we were no different. The purpose of the publication was to provide thinking and analysis of how Brexit might affect women and sexual and gender minorities, and how a gendered and queer perspective shows aspects of the Brexit debate in a different light. Our starting point was not any judgement on the desirability of the UK leaving the EU and we did not prejudge the overall predictions of our authors as to whether Brexit would be 'good' or 'bad' for women and sexual and gender minorities.

Yet, it is fair to say that none of the contributors is looking forward with enthusiasm to a post-Brexit world in which women and sexual and gender minorities have greater rights and freedoms, and where they are freed from the constraints of bureaucrats in Brussels. Rather, our writers express a range of views. Gill and Ahmed bring to life the sense of shock felt by many women on hearing the referendum result. A number of contributors find cause for pessimism in the likelihood that leaving the EU will aggravate existing social or legal problems—see, for example, Solanke's analysis of the plight of the 'Zambrano' families. Yet others outline alternative scenarios in terms of future prospects: Caracciolo di Torella presents alternative paths that are positive, negative or that maintain the status quo. Walker identifies ways in which Brexit offers both opportunities and losses in relation to family law.

Nor is it the case that the UK was ever fully 'in' in the first place. To take the example of asylum, as Iusman points out, the UK opted out of the Family Reunification Directive[2] and only signed up to the 2004 incarnation of the EU Qualification Directive,[3] so is not signed up the 2011 recast Directive[4] with its extended recognition of both SOGI.[5] Additionally, as Querton argues, opting into the 2004 Directive did not lead to a more inclusive and gender-sensitive approach to asylum. Thus, the 'risks' are less concrete and it is rather a case that UK citizens and residents will not benefit from what are currently unknown future enhanced rights and protections.

A consistent undercurrent is that gender and LGBTQI+ rights are contingent and precarious, and that Brexit, as a political enterprise, will not stand or fall alone. The devolution agendas in Northern Ireland and Scotland are most obviously affected by the particular form that Brexit takes (see chapters by Galligan, Ritch and Weldon-Johns). The UK's human rights legislation and framework is also contingent on Brexit— not least in that, without a vote in favour of leaving the EU and the vast workload that it has created for civil servants and politicians, it is likely that there would have been greater headway on the Government's

---

[2] Family Reunification Directive 2003/86/EC.

[3] Council Directive 2004/83/EC.

[4] Council Directive 2011/95/EU.

[5] With regard to the right to asylum, the 2004 EU Qualification Directive referred explicitly to sexual orientation, and the amended version, adopted in 2011, marks further progress in ensuring LGBTQI+ applicants' rights by adding gender identity as a basis for identifying a Particular Social Group, http://www.europarl.europa.eu/RegData/etudes/BRIE/2016/582031/EPRS_BRI(2016)582031_EN.pdf.

manifesto commitment to replace the Human Rights Act 1998 with a 'British Bill of Rights'.[6]

Nevertheless, despite clear concerns on the part of many—indeed most—contributors that Brexit will threaten the legal, economic or social gains of women and sexual and gender minorities, there is also a strong sense of resistance and positivity about the potential for addressing some of these risks if only they are identified and publicly recognised. Solanke, for example, suggests an approach for ensuring that non-discrimination principles and policies apply equally to all children, whether or not they are migrants and regardless of their parents' nationality. Equally, Iusman argues that the UK could adopt the measures in the reformed Common European Asylum System to act in 'the best interests of the child'. Stephenson and Fontana highlight the specific recommendations of the Women's Budget Group for avoiding regression in economic areas affecting women.

The less than positive assessment of the potential results of leaving the EU for the UK's women and sexual and gender minorities raises some larger questions for the editors. Are women and sexual and gender minorities likely to be *more* disadvantaged by Brexit than other citizens and residents in the UK? One of the common perceptions of the EU and arguments in the taking-back-control camp, is that the EU is heavily bureaucratic and imposes a high regulatory burden on its Member States.[7] Outside the EU, UK citizens will be free from the shackles of Brussels' red tape. The argument of many Remainers is that EU regulation is not unnecessary bureaucracy, but very necessary protection for marginalised and disadvantaged individuals—including, disproportionately, women and sexual and gender minorities.[8] So far, the UK Government has not suggested that it will use exiting the EU as an opportunity for regression on rights, whether or not they

---

[6]The Conservative Party, 'The Conservative Party Manifesto 2017', https://www.conservatives.com/manifesto, accessed 26 June 2018.

[7]http://www.voteleavetakecontrol.org/briefing_control.html, accessed 30 June 2018.

[8]See, for example, submissions by Fawcett Society, Stonewall and other equality and human rights NGOs to the Women and Equalities Select Committee inquiry 'Ensuring strong equalities legislation after EU exit', https://www.parliament.uk/business/committees/committees-a-z/commons-select/women-and-equalities-committee/inquiries/parliament-2015/ensuring-strong-equalities-legislation-after-eu-exit-16-17/publications/, accessed 30 June 2018.

derive from Brussels. In this, the Government is perhaps responding to the many expressions of concern on this front from statutory and non-governmental bodies, such as the House of Commons Women and Equalities Committee, which recommended that '[t]he Government should include a clause in the Great Repeal Bill that explicitly commits to maintaining the current levels of equalities protection when EU law is transposed into UK law.'[9] Thanks to lobbying by equality campaigners, the Act as passed included an amendment requiring Ministers to make a statement to the House before any proposed changes to equality legislation.[10]

3   MIGRATION AND GLOBALISATION

In media and political discourse since the referendum, we have seen the many ways in which the UK is bound to the EU—ways that most people would previously not have thought about. Continuing involvement in the Galileo satellite project might be one example.[11] If the purpose of Brexit was demonstrating that 'no person is an island', then it succeeded. If the purpose of this collection is to demonstrate that no woman or LGBTQI+ person is an island, we feel that we have also succeeded in this. In part, this is because the movement of people has never been so visible as it is today,[12] alongside recognition of the need for protection that this generates in a world of extreme inequality. That is reflected in the preceding chapters, where we repeatedly see that the rights of migrant,

---

[9]'Ensuring Strong Equalities Legislation after EU Exit Inquiry—Publications—UK Parliament', 27, https://www.parliament.uk/business/committees/committees-a-z/commons-select/women-and-equalities-committee/inquiries/parliament-2015/ensuring-strong-equalities-legislation-after-eu-exit-16-17/publications/, accessed 30 June 2018. See also joint statement, Joint statement on Brexit from the UK's four statutory bodies for human rights and equality, 13 June 2018, https://www.equalityhumanrights.com/en/our-work/news/joint-statement-uks-human-rights-and-equality-bodies-brexit, accessed 30 June 2018.

[10]European Union (Withdrawal) Act, Schedule 7, Part 3, Para. 28.

[11]https://www.theguardian.com/technology/2018/jun/13/eu-member-states-block-uks-access-to-galileo-satellite-programme-after-brexit, accessed 30 June 2018.

[12]Martina Tazzioli and William Walters, 'The Sight of Migration: Governmentality, Visibility and Europe's Contested Borders' (2016) 30 Global Society 445; Stephen Castles, Dr. Hein de Haas, and Prof. Mark J. Miller, *The Age of Migration: International Population Movements in the Modern World* (5th ed., Basingstoke: Palgrave Macmillan, 2013).

refugee and asylum seeking women and LGBTQI+ individuals are at risk, perhaps most starkly in the case of the 'Zambrano families' (Solanke). Writing just before the outburst of anger at the separation of children from their parents under Trump's presidency,[13] Iusman's chapter is prophetic in highlighting growing recognition of the specific threat to children, specifically to male unaccompanied minors, created by apparently neutral or abstract decisions about borders and territorial lines.

Following on from this, leaving the EU will not only affect women and sexual and gender minorities in the UK, but should also be a priority for feminists and LGBTQI+ campaigners across Europe. The lack of a UK voice in negotiations may slow down progress on LGBTQI+ rights in other Member States (see Danisi, Dustin and Ferreira). The chapter by Holst, Skjeie and Teigen shows some of the possibilities, but also the complexities, of promoting gender equality for a state sitting alongside but not among EU Member States.

A circular process is at work: the EU has been a driver for policy and regulation, enhancing the rights of women and minorities of all kinds; the UK, as a long-standing EU Member State, has contributed to that process and in some cases been at the forefront of the drive for change. Without the UK as a cog in the larger wheel, change will be determined by a different set of relationships, not always likely to have a positive outcome for women and sexual and gender minorities living around the EU, if the concerns of our contributors materialise.

Recognition that individuals' ability to live fulfilling lives, protected from arbitrary injustice and abuse, is dependent at least in part on membership of an international community suggests that, in the absence of the EU, other supranational bodies will need to take their place—and that women and sexual and gender minorities experiencing discrimination or marginalisation will need to look to these bodies in the future. The Council of Europe and the United Nations are the obvious candidates, however, as a number of contributors point out (Danisi, Dustin and Ferreira), the legislation that gives further effect to the European Convention on Human Rights (ECHR) in UK law is also under threat, and most UN

---

[13] Stephen Castles, Dr. Hein de Haas, and Prof. Mark J. Miller, *The Age of Migration: International Population Movements in the Modern World* (5th ed., Basingstoke: Palgrave Macmillan, 2013); Martina Tazzioli and William Walters, 'The Sight of Migration: Governmentality, Visibility and Europe's Contested Borders' (2016) 30 Global Society 445, accessed 30 June 2018.

instruments lack the kinds of enforcement mechanisms that EU law has. The UK will then find itself in a situation where it is trying, as Iusman argues, 'to solve transnational problems with national means'.

4   INTERSECTIONALITY

Lastly, in our attempt to compare and draw together themes from this collection, we identify intersectionality as a theme that is sometimes explicit and sometimes implicit in many chapters. Perhaps what these contributions show most strongly is that there is no value in talking about women or sexual and gender minorities as homogenous groups. Aside from gender and sexuality identifiers, individuals need to be seen as workers, consumers, public service users, carers (Caracciolo di Torella, Walker, Stephenson and Fontana). They also need to be seen as people seeking asylum (Querton), people from minority ethnic communities (Solanke), people with disabilities (Dyi Huijg), young people (Iusmen, Walker). The part of the UK they come from makes a difference (Galligan, Ritch, Weldon-Johns).

To take one example, Dyi Huijg highlights the importance of considering the impact of leaving the EU for disabled EU citizens and carers—the majority of whom are likely to be women but who are disadvantaged in different ways, because of who they are and what they do. Yet, as she convincingly explains, no one is inherently vulnerable. Rather, disabled people are 'vulnerabilised' by the state. The concept of being made vulnerable—and perhaps more vulnerable—by the fallout of leaving the EU may usefully be applied beyond disability to people historically marginalised because of ethnicity, nationality, religion or age, as well as gender and sexuality.

We also feel that the collection benefits from the interface and juxtaposition of the authors' disciplines and sectors. The editors of the book are based at Sussex Law School, but we were keen that this should not be a legal text book, and we hope that the contributors' diversity of disciplines has enabled us to give a sense of the wide range of implications of Brexit—implications in the areas of legislation, policy and regulation; employment; economic and financial considerations; potential changes to social provision and protection, and more. Moreover, while this is essentially an academic collection, we knew that it would benefit from input from outside 'the academy' and that it should bridge academia, NGO and policy sectors. From the perspective of Engender, a Scottish women's organisation, Ritch shows the difference that including women's voices makes to political debates. Stephenson and Fontana end their contribution with specific recommendations for policy makers taken from their work with the Women's Budget Group.

5   WHAT DID WE MISS?

In producing this work, we are fully conscious that it is a patchwork quilt with some holes in it. We could not address all the ways in which Brexit will make a difference to women and sexual and gender minorities in the UK (and other EU countries) and, while many of these holes may not yet be visible, we are very conscious of some others. In particular, we have no contribution specifically addressing the concerns of and prospects for Welsh women and LGBTQI+people. Like England, but in contrast to Scotland and Northern Ireland, most voters in Wales favoured Brexit yet Welsh women are likely to be particularly vulnerable—according to the Director of the Women's Equality Network Wales, who pointed out the role that the European Social Fund has had in helping Welsh women out of poverty.[14]

Nor have we addressed regional and socio-economic differences within UK countries through a gendered or queer lens. The geographical boundaries of the UK featured strongly in post-Brexit analysis, with the assumption that the wealthier Southern electorate voted mainly to remain, while the poorer Northern regions favoured leaving. And the rural–urban divide is similarly important, given that one way of viewing the referendum outcome is that country dwellers voted for Brexit,[15] while cities—with their more heterogenous ethnic communities—voted to remain. As Galligan points out, the withdrawal of EU funding is a particular concern for women's rural networks in Northern Ireland.

Regional and country-specific perspectives are important because, as the contributions from Northern Ireland and Scotland clearly show, there is no single pan-UK response to Brexit by women and sexual and gender minorities. Moreover, one result of leaving the EU may be that differences between gender and queer politics across the four nations become more pronounced. Weldon-Johns, in her contribution, points to

[14] https://www.bbc.co.uk/news/uk-wales-politics-41528416, accessed 30 June 2018.

[15] Sascha O. Becker, Thiemo Fetzer, and Dennis Novy, 'Who Voted for Brexit? A Comprehensive District-Level Analysis' (2017) 32 Economic Policy 601.

the potential for Scotland to take a different path on family conflict resolution to the rest of the UK. Likewise, rights for women and sexual and gender minorities in Scotland may take a more distinct path, reflecting Scottish positions on issues such as integration and human rights.[16]

In line with our recognition of the importance of intersectionality, we also recognise the challenges that it imposes. While we have been able to highlight the issues for some groups—disabled women, LGBTQI+ people seeking asylum, black and Asian British families—we have not been able to drill down in all areas. Age, for example, is largely unaddressed, yet we know that older people have been 'blamed' for swinging the vote and 'selling out' the younger generation.[17] Inevitably, that age dimension also has a gender dimension. There are many other important dimensions we have not been able to address, such as the gendered dimensions of health, employment and education policies and disparities that might arise here.

6   NOT 'JUST' LAW

There seems to be general agreement that, as Dunne says in relation to sexual minorities, 'the de jure outcome of Brexit may be limited'. We are unlikely to see a bonfire of gender and LGBTQI+ equality protections. Yet, as Caracciolo di Torella points out in relation to promoting a work-life balance, it is not 'just' about legislation. It is also about principles, values, discourse and the parameters of possibility. This is where the Overton window is a useful descriptor. As Barrow suggests, while leaving the EU's Common Security and Defence Policy may not be as complex as withdrawal from other areas of EU policy, it may mean that momentum on mainstreaming gender in peace and security is lost and there is a return to the traditional assumption that gender is irrelevant to security matters. Combine this with recognition that the Brexit debate in the UK has been dominated by militaristic language and metaphors from the world of business (Achilleos-Sarll and Martill), and we see a narrow window of policy debate focussed on winners and losers. Thus, we suggest

---

[16] See, for example, Scotland's National Action Plan on Human Rights, http://www.snaprights.info, accessed 30 June 2018 or the New Scots Refugee Integration Strategy, http://www.gov.scot/Publications/2018/01/7281, accessed 30 June 2018.

[17] https://yougov.co.uk/news/2016/06/27/how-britain-voted/, accessed 30 June 2018.

that the Overton window is likely to shrink after Brexit. Outside the EU, the possibilities for solidarity between NGO activists and for participation in new rights measures will inevitably dwindle over time—Ritch, for example, highlights the concern that Scottish feminist organisations have about loss of engagement with the European Women's Lobby.

Our conclusion, based on these contributions, is that the immediate threat is not to the broad categories of 'gay' or 'female' UK citizens and residents, but rather to those sometimes termed 'minorities within minorities'[18]—BME families, disabled women, unaccompanied asylum-seeking boys, women living in border regions of Northern Ireland, to give just a few examples. We hope that highlighting such threats will be the first step in addressing them, not simply with the defensive demand for no regression on rights, but also the inclusive aspiration for an expanding rather than narrowing of horizons.

BIBLIOGRAPHY

Becker, S.O., T. Fetzer, and D. Novy. 2017. Who Voted for Brexit? A Comprehensive District-Level Analysis. 32 Economic Policy 601.

Castles, S., D.H. de Haas, and P.M.J. Miller. 2013. *The Age of Migration: International Population Movements in the Modern World*, 5th ed. Basingstoke: Palgrave Macmillan.

Eisenberg, A., and J. Spinner-Havel (eds.). 2009. *Minorities Within Minorities: Equality, Rights and Diversity*. Cambridge: Cambridge University Press.

Ensuring Strong Equalities Legislation After EU Exit Inquiry—Publications—UK Parliament. https://www.parliament.uk/business/committees/committees-a-z/commons-select/women-and-equalities-committee/inquiries/parliament-2015/ensuring-strong-equalities-legislation-after-eu-exit-16-17/publications/. Accessed 30 June 2018.

Lanchester, J. 2016. Brexit Blues. *London Review of Books* 38 (28 July): 3.

Tazzioli, M., and W. Walters. 2016. The Sight of Migration: Governmentality, Visibility and Europe's Contested Borders'. 30 Global Society 445.

The Conservative Party. The Conservative Party Manifesto 2017. https://www.conservatives.com/manifesto. Accessed 26 Jan 2018.

---

[18]Avigail Eisenberg and Jeff Spinner-Havel (eds.), *Minorities Within Minorities: Equality, Rights and Diversity* (Cambridge: Cambridge University Press, 2009).

INDEX

© The Editor(s) (if applicable) and The Author(s) 2019   473
M. Dustin et al. (eds.), *Gender and Queer Perspectives on Brexit*,
Gender and Politics, https://doi.org/10.1007/978-3-030-03122-0